Parallel and High Performance Programming with Python (2nd Edition)

Transform Your Python Code into a High-Performance Powerhouse Using Multithreading, CUDA, PyTorch, Spark, and Dask

Fabio Nelli

www.orangeava.com

First Published: February 2026

Published By: Orange Education Pvt Ltd, AVA®

Address: 9, Daryaganj, Delhi, 110002, India

275 New North Road Islington Suite 1314 London,
N1 7AA, United Kingdom

ISBN (PBK): 978-93-49887-14-5
ISBN (E-BOOK): 978-93-49887-00-8

Scan the QR code to explore our entire catalogue

www.orangeava.com

Dedicated To

My Wife, Pamela

And

My Son, Valerio.

About the Author

Fabio Nelli is a Data Analyst at a private research center, where he transforms complex datasets into actionable insights for R&D and product teams. He holds a bachelor's degree in Automation Engineering (computer science track) and a master's degree in Organic Chemistry—an uncommon combination that shapes his analytical mindset.

An accomplished author, Fabio has written several books on data science and Python programming. His works are known for being practical and example-driven, tailored for engineers and scientists who need to deliver real results. He also publishes technical articles regularly, drawing from his experience in building pipelines, optimizing training and inference, and benchmarking end-to-end performance.

Earlier in his career, Fabio worked as a consultant, automation specialist, and analyst-programmer for international organizations. This breadth of experience informs his pragmatic style: start simple, profile before optimizing, automate what matters, and design for maintainability. His current professional interests focus on high-performance computing, large-scale data processing, cloud architecture, and applied machine learning—particularly where these disciplines converge.

Through his books and articles, Fabio seeks to bridge the gap between theory and practice. He is passionate about crafting concise explanations, production-ready examples, and actionable checklists that readers can apply immediately to accelerate their projects.

About the Technical Reviewer

Kumar Kanishk is a seasoned developer and technical project engineer with demonstrated expertise in building and deploying scalable web applications using Python and Django. Known for his technical leadership and commitment to engineering excellence, Kanishk has guided teams through complex project cycles, methodically conducting code reviews and fostering a culture of quality and collaboration. His hands-on experience includes designing RESTful APIs and optimizing AWS cloud resources for performance and security, enabling robust, cost-efficient deployments in dynamic business environments.

As a dedicated corporate trainer, Kanishk has delivered impactful sessions across a wide range of technical fields, sharing industry-focused knowledge and fostering practical skill development. He has been recognized as an outstanding co-instructor for conducting over twenty workshops at various academic campuses, including Amity and Graphic Era Hill University. Additionally, he has contributed to over 10 well-received Udemy courses and played a pivotal technical role in reviewing a leading publication on cryptography, helping establish quality standards in technical literature.

Kumar's project portfolio is both broad and innovative, spanning over 25 projects in Artificial Intelligence and AIoT, along with five significant blockchain initiatives. His work includes the development of an AI-powered Kubernetes dashboard, certification and skill development portals, automated system vulnerability assessments, and AI-powered chatbots engineered for enhanced user engagement. Kanishk has earned accolades such as the Hall of Fame Award from Akeyless for software vulnerability discovery. His dynamic approach and multidisciplinary skills make him a respected figure in both corporate and community settings, balancing technical mastery with an advocacy for real-world applied learning.

Acknowledgments

This book came to life through the publisher's confidence and relentless support, complemented by the dedication, patience, and professionalism of the editorial team at Orange Education Pvt. Ltd. I am deeply grateful for this opportunity and for the meticulous editorial care that shaped this work. I also offer my heartfelt gratitude for the steady support from my peers, associates and family members who stood by me at every stage of the project—from planning to the final review of the book.

Preface

This second edition of *Parallel and High Performance Programming with Python* was created to reflect how parallel and high-performance computing is practiced today. It introduces updated approaches, real-world examples, and thoughtful comparisons to the original structure. Six new chapters address practical needs that emerged over time, including cloud and serverless computing for elastic scaling and cost-efficient execution.

The book presents reusable patterns such as fan-out/fan-in, strategic caching, and idempotency, alongside production-focused checklists covering observability, cost control, and data sensitivity. It also clearly explains real-world limitations, including the GIL, I/O-bound workloads, shuffle costs, cold starts, serialization overhead, and memory constraints.

Designed as a hands-on reference, the book provides concepts and practical pathways that readers can apply immediately, helping professionals prepare for a future where effectively combining software, data, cloud, and hardware is essential.

Chapter 1: Introduction to Parallel Programming

The chapter explains the difference between concurrency and parallelism, the role of CPUs, cores, threads, and processes, and the technological evolution that led to parallel architectures. Specific challenges in Python such as the Global Interpreter Lock (GIL) are addressed along with strategies to overcome them. Key programming models, synchronization issues, and the transition from shared memory to distributed systems are also covered, concluding with methods for evaluating performance and scalability.

Chapter 2: Parallel Programming with Threads

This chapter introduces multithreading in Python as a way to implement parallel execution. It explains how threads are created and managed, the mechanisms available for synchronization, and the challenges of resource sharing and race conditions. Both high-level tools such as concurrent.futures and low-level primitives like locks, semaphores, and events are discussed thoroughly. Practical approaches for customizing threads and coordinating tasks are also presented, highlighting Python's standard features for safe and efficient parallel execution.

Chapter 3: Parallel Programming with Processes

This chapter introduces the multiprocessing module, explaining how to create and manage processes, distribute workloads efficiently, and handle communication between them through queues and pipes. It also covers the mpi4py library for large-scale distributed computing, highlighting point-to-point and collective communication methods. Comparisons between threading and multiprocessing are made, and advanced optimization techniques, including job scheduling and resource management, are also explored to improve scalability and performance.

Chapter 4: Asynchronous Programming

This chapter explains the differences between synchronous and asynchronous models, showing the advantages and trade-offs of each approach. The asyncio library is presented as the core framework, with concepts such as coroutines, tasks, futures, and the event loop at its foundation. Advanced features such as asynchronous iterations, queues, and alternative libraries are introduced, along with limitations in I/O-intensive and CPU-bound contexts. The chapter concludes with error-handling strategies and design patterns for building scalable and resilient applications.

Chapter 5: Distributed Python

This chapter introduces the principles and trade-offs of distributed programming, and presents three key Python frameworks: Celery, a robust system for task queues with advanced features; Dramatiq, a simpler alternative designed for quick integration; and SCOOP, a lightweight library for distributed execution of parallel tasks. Practical examples such as the Monte Carlo method illustrate their use. The chapter concludes with a comparison of these frameworks in terms of architecture, performance and suitability for different applications.

Chapter 6: GPU Programming with Python

This chapter introduces the CUDA programming model, and the use of Python libraries such as Numba and PyOpenCL. It explains how to set up GPU development environments, write and run kernels, manage memory efficiently, and benchmark GPU-based applications. Practical examples, including matrix operations and MapReduce calculations, demonstrate how GPUs accelerate scientific and data-intensive workloads.

Chapter 7: Parallel Computing Applications

This chapter highlights the role of High-performance Computing (HPC) in solving complex problems, explains the benefits of distributing workloads across thousands of processors, and illustrates the efficiency and scalability achieved through parallel methods. Real-world applications are explored in domains such as meteorology, seismology, astrophysics, engineering, medicine, finance, and energy, as well as in the entertainment industry, where parallelism powers game engines, visual effects, and 3D animation.

Chapter 8: Parallel Computing for Data Science

This chapter introduces Pandas and its constraints, then presents Dask as a framework for scaling analysis on both single machines and distributed clusters. Practical platforms such as Kaggle and Saturn.io illustrate real-world workflows, while tools for monitoring, profiling, and optimizing performance are explored. Finally, GPU acceleration with Dask-CUDA and the RAPIDS ecosystem demonstrates how parallelism can further speed up machine learning and data processing tasks.

Chapter 9: Parallel Computing for Artificial Intelligence

Artificial intelligence (AI) depends on parallel computing to reach the scale required for training and deploying modern models. This chapter introduces the main branches of AI, including machine learning and deep learning, and shows how parallelism accelerates training, supports large datasets, and enables real-time inference. Libraries such as Scikit-learn with Dask-ML, as well as PyTorch and TensorFlow with GPU and distributed execution, are presented through practical examples, including dataset training and model visualization.

Chapter 10: Future of Parallel Programming

The future of parallel programming is shaped by emerging paradigms such as exascale and quantum computing, massively parallel AI, and distributed infrastructures. These advances are transforming both technology and professional opportunities, with direct implications for Python and modern AI frameworks. From edge computing and cyber-physical systems to breakthroughs in scientific simulations, parallelism is moving toward decentralized, scalable, and intelligent infrastructures. For Python to remain central, its ecosystem must evolve with stronger concurrency models, GPU integration, and scalable frameworks.

Chapter 11: Modern Frameworks for Parallelism and Distribution: Ray and Modin

Modern frameworks such as Ray and Modin extend Python's capabilities for distributed and parallel computing. Ray provides a general-purpose system for scaling tasks and actors across clusters, supporting both traditional workloads and AI/ML applications. Modin builds on Ray to deliver a parallel alternative to Pandas, enabling large-scale data analysis with minimal code changes. The chapter also compares these frameworks with alternatives such as Dask and Celery, highlighting their strengths, trade-offs, and best-fit use cases.

Chapter 12: PySpark

The chapter introduces Spark's execution model, and how PySpark allows parallel operations through a Pythonic interface. It covers MLlib for large-scale machine learning, optimization strategies, and monitoring with the Spark UI. Real-time data pipelines are addressed with Spark Streaming and integrations with Kafka, HDFS, and cloud storage. Finally, GraphFrame is presented as a tool for graph analytics, supporting advanced applications like network analysis and recommendations.

Chapter 13: Joblib

This chapter explores how Joblib streamlines process-based parallelism for tasks that can be split into independent units, and how it integrates seamlessly with NumPy through memory mapping and serialization. Its caching mechanisms are highlighted as a way to optimize repetitive computations, making it valuable in data processing and machine learning workflows. Finally, the chapter examines Joblib's limitations, particularly its narrower scope and lack of scalability compared to more advanced distributed frameworks.

Chapter 14: Parallelization on Cloud and Serverless Systems

This chapter introduces cloud-native tools that provide elastic scaling and distributed execution, with a focus on AWS Lambda, Google Cloud Functions, and Azure Functions. Practical examples include parallel file processing and data pipelines, while Kubernetes is presented as a key orchestration tool for containerized workloads. The discussion highlights cost, scalability, and complexity trade-offs between serverless and traditional approaches, concluding with real-world use cases where cloud-based parallelism improves efficiency, and reduces operational overhead.

Chapter 15: Parallel Programming with FPGAs

This chapter introduces their architecture and programming approaches in Python through tools such as PyOpenCL, PyCUDA, PYNQ, and AMD Vitis. Simulation frameworks such as MyHDL are discussed with examples like vector addition and FPGA-based parallel tasks. A comparison with GPUs highlights the trade-off between efficiency, flexibility, and development complexity. The chapter concludes with advanced applications of FPGAs in domains such as artificial intelligence, cryptography, and physical simulations.

Chapter 16: Introduction to Quantum Computing and Quantum Architectures

This chapter introduces the foundations of quantum gates and circuits, explains how Qiskit enables simulation and experimentation in Python, and presents visualization tools like Bloch's Sphere for understanding qubit states. Core concepts such as quantum parallelism are illustrated through algorithms like Deutsch–Jozsa and Grover's search. The chapter concludes with applications in quantum machine learning, including Quantum Neural Networks and hybrid quantum–classical approaches.

Get a Free eBook

We hope you are enjoying your recently purchased book! Your feedback is incredibly valuable to us, and to all other readers looking for great books.

If you found this book helpful or enjoyable, we would truly appreciate it, if you could take a moment to leave a short review with a 5 star rating on Amazon. It helps us grow, and lets other readers discover our books.

As a thank you, we would love to send you a free digital copy of this book, and a **30%** discount code on your next cart value on our official websites:

www.orangeava.com

www.orangeava.in (For Indian Subcontinent)

☑ **Here's how:**

Leave a review for the book on Amazon.

Take a screenshot of your review, and send an email to **info@orangeava.com** (it can be just the confirmation screen).

Once, we receive your screenshot, we will send you the digital file, within 24 hours.

Thank you so much for your support – it means a lot to us!

Downloading the code bundles and colored images

Please follow the links or scan the QR codes to download the
Code Bundles and Images of the book:

https://github.com/OrangeAVA/Parallel-and-High-Performance-Programming-with-Python---2nd-Edition

The code bundles and images of the book are also hosted on
https://rebrand.ly/612059

In case there's an update to the code, it will be updated on the existing GitHub repository.

Errata

We take immense pride in our work at **Orange Education Pvt Ltd,** and follow best practices to ensure the accuracy of our content to provide an indulging reading experience to our subscribers. Our readers are our mirrors, and we use their inputs to reflect and improve upon human errors, if any, that may have occurred during the publishing processes involved. To let us maintain the quality and help us reach out to any readers who might be having difficulties due to any unforeseen errors, please write to us at :

errata@orangeava.com

Your support, suggestions, and feedback are highly appreciated.

DID YOU KNOW

Did you know that Orange Education Pvt Ltd offers eBook versions of every book published, with PDF and ePub files available? You can upgrade to the eBook version at **www.orangeava.com** and as a print book customer, you are entitled to a discount on the eBook copy. Get in touch with us at: **info@orangeava.com** for more details.

At **www.orangeava.com**, you can also read a collection of free technical articles, sign up for a range of free newsletters, and receive exclusive discounts and offers on Print Books and eBooks.

PIRACY

If you come across any illegal copies of our works in any form on the internet, we would be grateful if you would provide us with the location address or website name. Please contact us at **info@orangeava.com** with a link to the material.

ARE YOU INTERESTED IN AUTHORING WITH US?

If there is a topic that you have expertise in, and you are interested in either writing or contributing to a book, please write to us at **business@orangeava.com**. We are on a journey to help developers and tech professionals to gain insights on the present technological advancements and innovations happening across the globe and build a community that believes Knowledge is best acquired by sharing and learning with others. Please reach out to us to learn what our audience demands and how you can be part of this educational reform. We also welcome ideas from tech experts and help them build learning and development content for their domains.

REVIEWS

Please leave a review. Once you have read and used this book, why not leave a review on the site that you purchased it from? Potential readers can then see and use your unbiased opinion to make purchase decisions. We at Orange Education would love to know what you think about our products, and our authors can learn from your feedback. Thank you!

For more information about Orange Education, please visit **www.orangeava.com**.

Table of Contents

Chapter 1
Introduction to Parallel Programming

Introduction

In this chapter, we will introduce the concept of parallel programming and the fundamental principles that are required to understand its features and applications. We will begin with the hardware components that enable parallel execution on modern computers, such as CPUs and cores. We will then examine the operating system entities that implement parallelism in practice: processes and threads. Next, we will present the main programming models and introduce key concepts such as concurrency, synchronicity, and asynchronicity. We will also focus on Python, while discussing its peculiarities in this domain, with special reference to threads, the **Global Interpreter Lock (GIL)**, and the issues it introduces. We will also highlight standard Python library modules such as **threading** and **multiprocessing**, which will be explored in more depth in later chapters. Finally, we address methods for evaluating parallel programs including speedup and scalability, and discuss common issues such as race conditions and deadlocks.

Thus, by the end of this chapter, you will have a clear understanding of the fundamental concepts and terminology of parallel programming, and how the various components interact to achieve it. This foundation will prepare you for the practical programming techniques covered in the rest of the chapters.

Structure

This chapter will address the following topics:

- Parallel Programming
- Technical Evolution of Computers and Parallelism
- CPU and Cores
- Processes and Threads
- Concurrent Programming
- GIL and Threads with Python
- Cloud Basics: VMs, Instances and vCPUs
- Map and Reduce
- Memory Organization in Parallel Programming
- Speedup and Scaling

Parallel Programming

If you are reading this book, you must already understand the need to increase the potential of your code while discovering the limits of traditional models for historical reasons.

The advent of new hardware technologies has given us the opportunity to be able to run multiple programs simultaneously on our computers. In fact, our computers, even the simplest ones, have a *multi-core system* that allows programs to run in parallel. *Why not take advantage of this architecture then?*

You must have found yourself developing a Python program to perform a series of operations. In the scientific field, it is necessary to implement a series of algorithms to carry out laborious calculations. There might have been several times when you are disappointed with the speed and long execution times when you run the program at the end of your work. However, it is not just a speed issue. Today, as we have to deal with ever larger amounts of data and calculations, programs need greater memory resources. However, several computers cannot keep up with the demand.

This is where parallel programming comes in, as it allows you to execute parts of the code of one of our programs simultaneously, while significantly increasing performance. Programming in parallel, therefore, means reducing the execution time of a program by using resources more efficiently and performing more complex operations.

Technological Evolution of Computers and Parallelism

For many programmers, parallel programming is still an unfamiliar concept as it is fairly recent. In fact, only a few years ago, all computers available to developers were equipped with a single **Arithmetic Logic Unit (ALU)** which could only execute the instructions sequentially (see *Figure 1.1*).

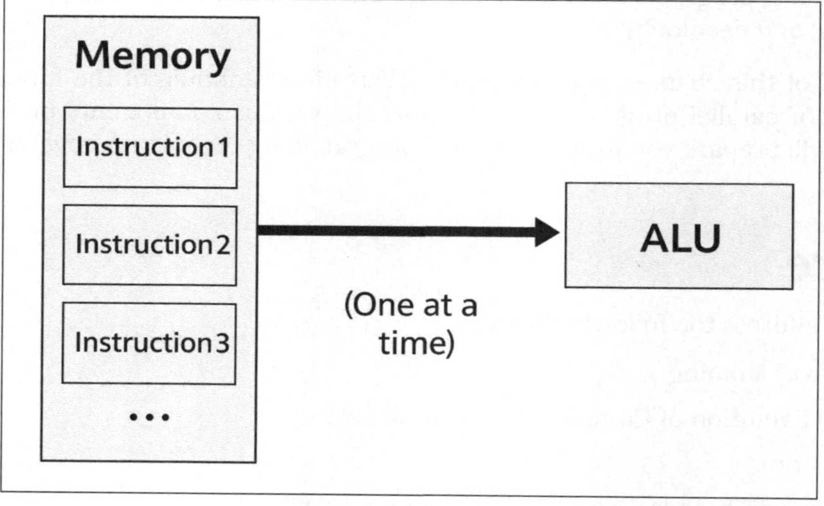

***Figure 1.1**: Serial Execution*

You might remember that the characteristics of the computer are generally indicated by the frequency of the processor in **Hz**, which further indicates the instructions that can be *executed per second*. The power of a computer/CPU is primarily measured by its computing frequency. In other words, the higher this value is, the faster the programs will run.

The concept of *parallelism* gradually emerged with the evolution of computer hardware. Until 1980s, computers were very limited in their capacity: they ran *one program at a time*, instruction after instruction, in a strictly *sequential manner*. It is thus clear that in such an environment, the concept of parallelism could not even be imagined in the slightest.

With the advent of the *Intel 80386 processor*, the possibility of parallelism was introduced for computers to interrupt the execution of one program to work on another. Consequently, concepts such as *pre-emptive programming* and *time-slicing* emerged in this light. These advances introduced a **pseudo-parallelism** effect, with the user seeing multiple programs working at the same time. With the subsequent *Intel 80486 processor*, the situation was further improved by introducing a pipeline system based on the subdivision of programs into subtasks. These were performed independently, while alternating between the various programs. Furthermore, the internal architecture made it possible to assemble several different instructions (even from different programs) and execute them altogether, but not simultaneously. This is where **concurrent programming** really developed. The instruction portions of the different subtasks are completed, so that they can be executed as soon as possible (see *Figure 1.2*):

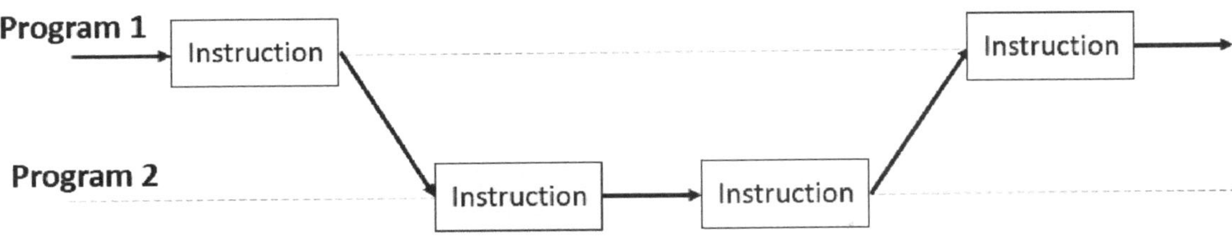

***Figure 1.2**: Concurrent Execution*

The situation went on for over a decade and witnessed the release of increasingly powerful processor models that were able to work at higher frequencies than the previous ones. However, this situation soon spiraled into a crisis due to several problems and physical limitations. Increasing the frequency of execution also led to a consequent increase in heat generation and energy consumption. It was clear that the frequency boost would soon reach its limits.

This is when processors took a leap of innovation, with the introduction of cores. These cores, also known as **logical processors**, could simulate the presence of multiple processors within a single CPU, which resulted in multi-core CPUs. In practice, one could have a multiprocessor computer capable of executing instructions from different programs simultaneously, in parallel. Therefore, **parallel programming** was developed in the *early* 2000s, giving developers the ability to simultaneously execute different parts of the same program.

CPU, Cores, Threads, and Processes

To understand the concepts that we will cover in this book, it is essential to know what **threads** and **processes** are, and how they are related to CPU as well as core execution modes.

These are not *abstract* concepts, but real entities that exist in our operating system. In order to be familiar with them, we can have a look at our operating system. For example, if you are working on *Windows*, open the **Task Manager** and click on the **Performance** tab.

A similar window is shown in *Figure 1.3*, where it is possible to monitor the *real-time* consumption of the various resources like the CPU, *memory*, and *Wi-Fi network*:

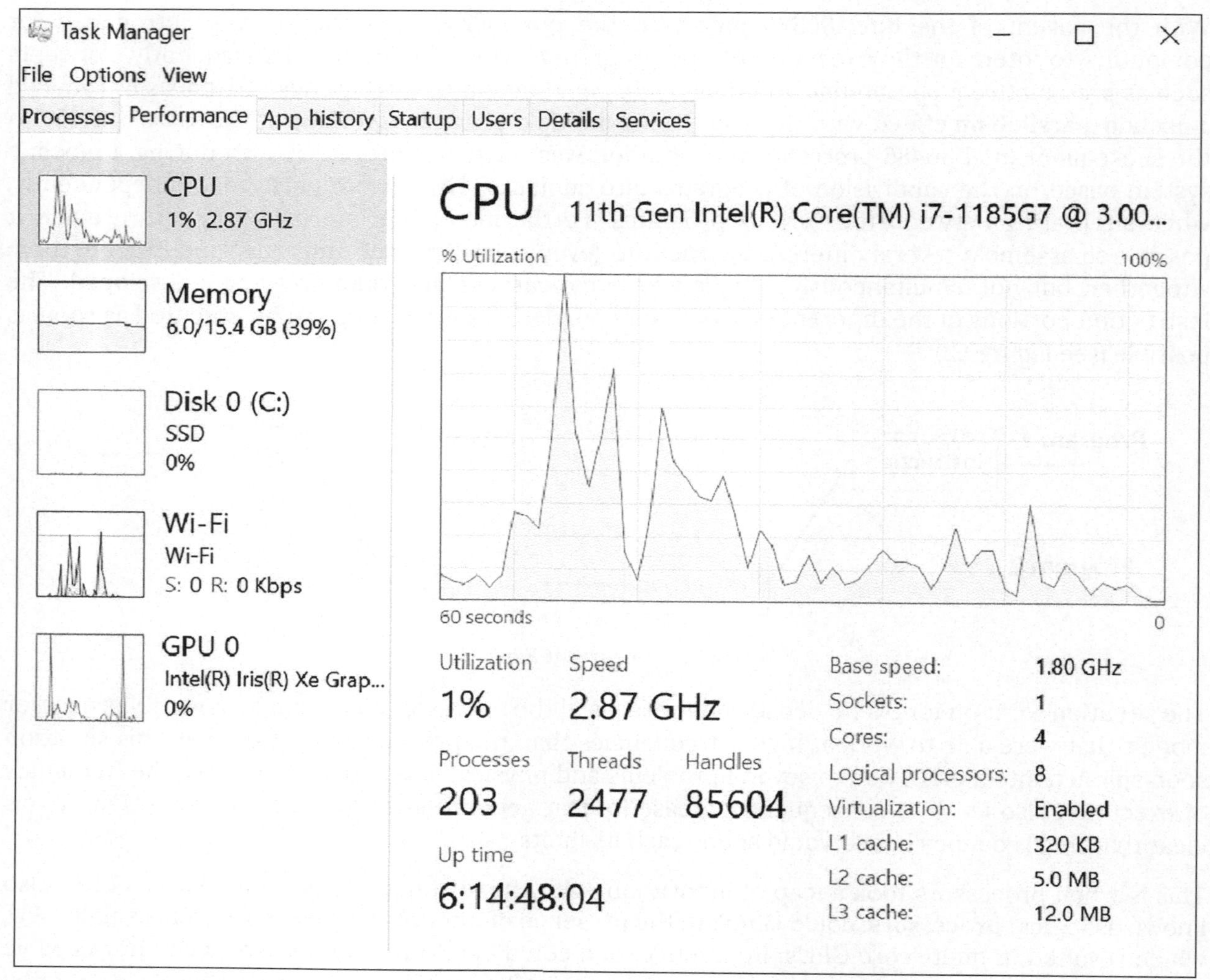

Figure 1.3: *Task Manager in Windows*

In addition to this, you can access more information, such as the number of processes and the threads that are currently running. On the right, are some characteristics of the system we are working on, such as the number of cores.

If, on the other hand, you work on Linux systems like Ubuntu, you can use the following command:

```
$ top
```

A screen very similar to the one shown in *Figure 1.4* will appear. Alternatively, you may use the more interactive **htop** command, which will provide the same information with improved navigation and visualization:

```
top - 11:02:51 up 2 days, 2 min,  1 user,  load average: 0,30, 0,12, 0,04
Tasks: 292 total,   2 running, 287 sleeping,   0 stopped,   3 zombie
%Cpu(s):  2,6 us,  1,2 sy,  0,0 ni, 96,2 id,  0,0 wa,  0,0 hi,  0,0 si,  0,0 st
MiB Mem :  11876,7 total,   5497,6 free,   2625,6 used,   3753,5 buff/cache
MiB Swap:  12188,0 total,  12188,0 free,      0,0 used.   8709,1 avail Mem

    PID USER      PR  NI    VIRT    RES    SHR S  %CPU  %MEM     TIME+ COMMAND
   2176 fabio     20   0 4872388 361280 120732 S   6,6   3,0  18:22.75 gnome-shell
   2024 fabio     20   0  641244 103316  62224 S   6,0   0,8  21:46.73 Xorg
  50377 fabio     20   0  817760  53964  39952 S   1,7   0,4   0:02.17 gnome-terminal-
     10 root      20   0       0      0      0 S   0,7   0,0   4:35.29 ksoftirqd/0
     18 root      20   0       0      0      0 R   0,3   0,0   3:19.68 ksoftirqd/1
     24 root      20   0       0      0      0 S   0,3   0,0   3:26.51 ksoftirqd/2
     30 root      20   0       0      0      0 S   0,3   0,0   3:00.53 ksoftirqd/3
    114 root     -86   0       0      0      0 S   0,3   0,0   0:32.64 irq/125-xhci_hc
    429 root     -51   0       0      0      0 S   0,3   0,0   1:08.64 irq/130-i915
   1399 mysql     20   0 2180360 391488  37004 S   0,3   3,2   8:13.47 mysqld
   2143 fabio     20   0    7588   4504   4016 S   0,3   0,0   0:01.20 dbus-daemon
  50225 root      20   0       0      0      0 I   0,3   0,0   0:00.25 kworker/0:2-events
  50323 root      20   0       0      0      0 I   0,3   0,0   0:00.09 kworker/u8:1-i915
  50403 fabio     20   0   12212   4276   3436 R   0,3   0,0   0:01.00 top
      1 root      20   0  171012  12892   8140 S   0,0   0,1   0:37.23 systemd
      2 root      20   0       0      0      0 S   0,0   0,0   0:00.04 kthreadd
      3 root       0 -20       0      0      0 I   0,0   0,0   0:00.00 rcu_gp
```

Figure 1.4: *Top on Ubuntu Terminal*

At the top of the screen, you can see system resources that are being used (such as CPU and memory) and are continuously updated in real time. The lower half shows a list of all active processes in the operating system. Each process is identified by a unique **Process Identification Number (PID)**.

Since Linux systems are much more *flexible* due to numerous shell commands, we can also monitor all the threads related to every single command. For this purpose, we will use a more specific command to monitor processes, which is: **ps**.

```
$ ps -T <PID>
```

The **-T** option indicates that the threads relevant to the process will be shown. The **pid** of the process is then passed to the **pid** command. Here, in the process with **pid 2176**, one will see the result in *Figure* 1.5. It shows the threads with their respective identification number, **SPID**:

```
(base) fabio@fabio-Lenovo-ideapad-310-15IKB:~$ ps -T 2176
    PID    SPID TTY      STAT   TIME COMMAND
   2176    2176 ?        Ssl   17:36 /usr/bin/gnome-shell
   2176    2185 ?        Ssl    0:04 /usr/bin/gnome-shell
   2176    2187 ?        Ssl    0:20 /usr/bin/gnome-shell
   2176    2188 ?        Ssl    0:00 /usr/bin/gnome-shell
   2176    2190 ?        SNsl   0:00 /usr/bin/gnome-shell
   2176    2192 ?        Ssl    0:00 /usr/bin/gnome-shell
   2176    2195 ?        Ssl    0:04 /usr/bin/gnome-shell
   2176    2196 ?        Ssl    0:04 /usr/bin/gnome-shell
   2176    2197 ?        Ssl    0:04 /usr/bin/gnome-shell
   2176    2198 ?        Ssl    0:04 /usr/bin/gnome-shell
   2176    2653 ?        Ssl    0:00 /usr/bin/gnome-shell
   2176    2654 ?        Ssl    0:00 /usr/bin/gnome-shell
   2176    2655 ?        Ssl    0:00 /usr/bin/gnome-shell
   2176    2656 ?        Ssl    0:00 /usr/bin/gnome-shell
   2176    7152 ?        Ssl    0:00 /usr/bin/gnome-shell
   2176   50433 ?        Ssl    0:00 /usr/bin/gnome-shell
```

Figure 1.5: *ps Command Results on Ubuntu Terminal*

Since the **Central Processing Unit** (**CPU**) is where our code is processed, it is characterized by cycles, which refer to the time units used to perform an operation on the processor. Often, we indicate the power of a CPU through the *frequency of cycles per second* (see the **2.87GHz** speed value in *Figure 1.3*).

A CPU may contain one core (*single-core* CPU) or multiple cores (*multi-core* CPU). Each core can run one instruction stream (**thread**) at a time, while the operating system schedules multiple processes across available cores, thereby creating the effect of **concurrent execution**. A process is essentially a program running on the machine, with its own reserved section of memory. Each process can start other processes (subprocesses), or run one or more threads. Every process always contains at least one thread, called the **`MainThread`**, and may create additional threads as needed. *Figure 1.6* illustrates this structure as follows:

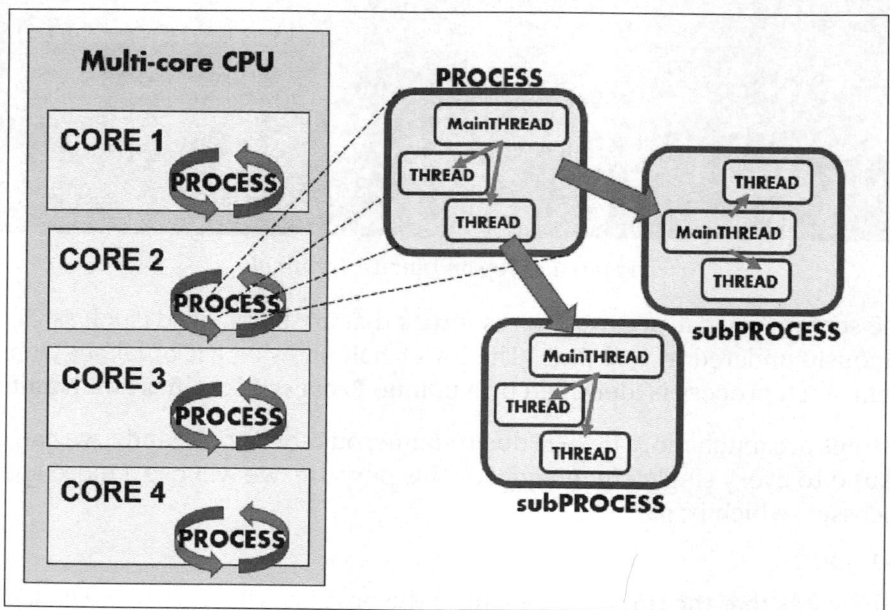

Figure 1.6: *CPU, Core, Process, and Threads*

Threads are the smaller units of execution that run inside a process. While a process is an independent program with its own memory space, threads share the memory and resources of the process that creates them.

Like processes, threads also require mechanisms to coordinate their execution. These include synchronization tools, methods for data exchange, and management of their states (such as *ready*, *running*, or *blocked*). *Figure 1.7* provides a visual overview of how processes and threads relate to each other and how threads transition between states during execution:

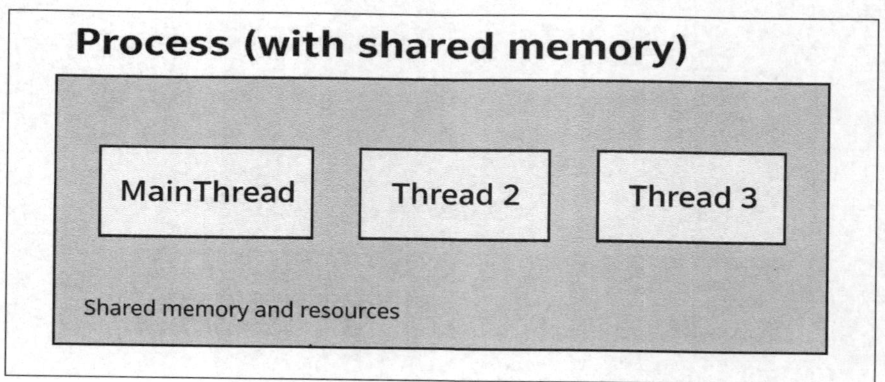

Figure 1.7: *Process and Threads*

Cloud Basics: VMs, Instances, and vCPUs

So far, we have focused on parallelism within a single physical machine, as well as reasoning in terms of CPUs, cores, processes, and threads. However, modern computing increasingly takes place in the cloud, where the same concepts reappear under slightly different names. Instead of buying one machine with a certain number of cores, we may request a virtual machine with a given number of vCPUs and memory. Understanding these terms is important as the programming models we use in Python, which includes threads for concurrency, processes for parallelism, and distributed frameworks for scaling, map directly to the resources exposed by cloud providers.

In cloud platforms, compute capacity is exposed through **Virtual Machines (VMs)**, that are often called *instances*. These run on shared physical hosts. Each VM is allocated a number of **vCPUs** and a certain amount of memory. A vCPU is the virtual processing unit presented by the hypervisor: in most cloud providers, **1 vCPU corresponds to one hardware thread** (hyper-thread) of a physical core. For example, a 16-vCPU instance usually maps to 8 physical cores with Hyper-Threading enabled. While we usually talk in terms of **cores** when it comes to local machines, we request **vCPUs** in the cloud. The tools and scaling models (like threads, processes, pools, MPI, and Dask) apply in the same way; however, it is important to remember that two vCPUs with the same physical core, can also compete for execution resources and cache.

As instance sizes grow larger, issues like **NUMA effects** and **memory bandwidth** become relevant; data placement and process affinity can significantly impact performance. Many cloud instance families also provide **accelerators** such as GPUs or TPUs. In these cases, the process still runs inside the VM, but the heavy numerical computation is offloaded to the device, often following a **data-parallel** pattern.

Concurrent and Parallel Programming

Many users and developers are often confused about the difference between *concurrency* and *parallelism*. While it is not uncommon for the two terms to be used interchangeably, it is still incorrect. The two concepts, although closely related, mean different things in the context of parallel programming.

Let us learn about the similarities between concurrency and parallelism: both arise when a program must perform multiple tasks.

Concurrency means managing multiple tasks at the same time, while not necessarily executing them simultaneously. On a single-core CPU, the processor can only run one instruction stream at a time, so the tasks are interleaved: the CPU executes a portion of one task (a subtask), then switches to another, and so on. Eventually, all tasks are completed, one piece at a time, which delivers the impression that they were being run simultaneously. You can think of tasks as competing for execution in *Figure 1.8*.

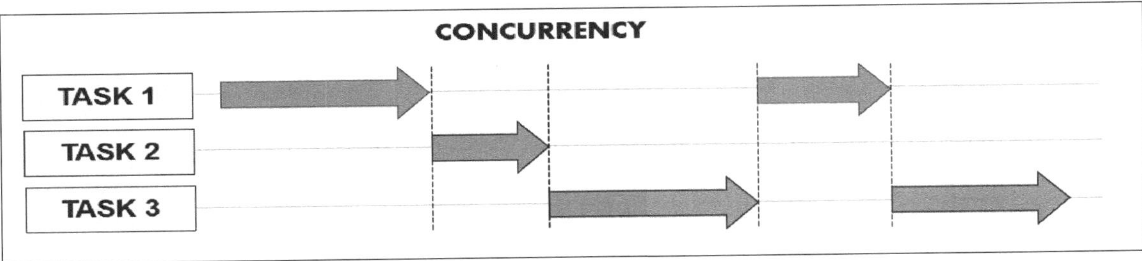

***Figure 1.8**: Concurrency in a Single-Core CPU*

Parallelism, on the other hand, means genuinely performing multiple tasks at the same time. This requires hardware with more than one processing unit, such as a multi-core CPU. In this case, different tasks (or subtasks) can be assigned to different cores and run simultaneously in parallel. Parallelism is therefore a special case of concurrency (see *Figure 1.9*).

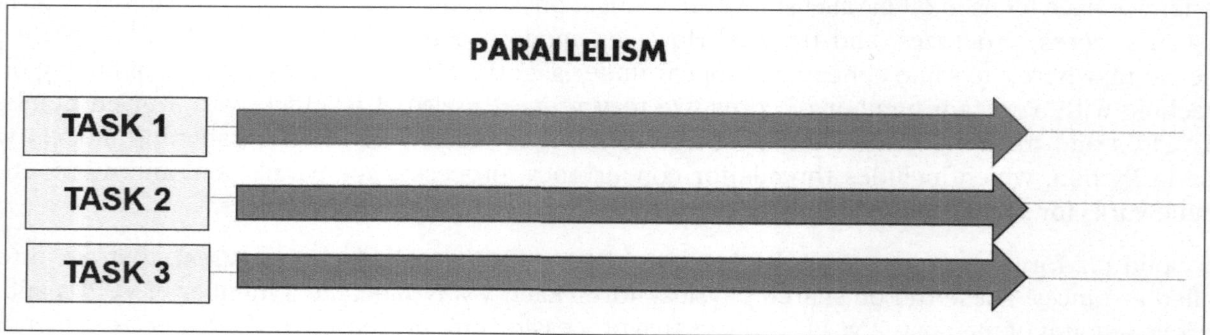

***Figure 1.9**: Parallelism in a Multi-Core CPU*

Concurrency and parallelism can also appear together on a multi-core system. Some tasks may run simultaneously on separate cores, while others share a core and alternate in time. This combination is referred to as *concurrency with parallelism*, and it is the model that is used in most modern systems (see *Figure 1.10*).

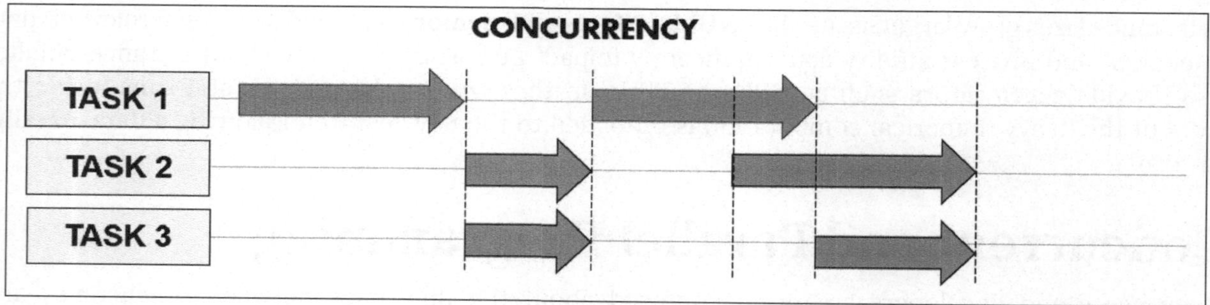

***Figure 1.10**: Concurrency with Parallelism in a Multi-Core CPU*

In summary, concurrency is a property of program design, whereas parallelism depends on hardware support. Together, they form the foundation of modern parallel programming.

Threads and Processes in Python for Concurrent and Parallel Models

Having now understood the difference between concurrent programming and parallel programming, let us take it a step further. In many programming languages, it is common practice to associate threads with concurrency and processes with parallelism. In fact, these two entities of the operating system will incorporate the two different functionalities of concurrency and parallelism.

As far as Python is concerned, it is good to divide these cases into two distinct programming models. In fact, threads in Python do not behave as perfectly as threads do in an operating system. Threads in Python provide concurrency (mainly for I/O-bound tasks), but CPU-bound workloads do not scale in parallel due to the Global Interpreter Lock (GIL); for that, you will require processes or hardware.

Python Thread Problem: The GIL

Threads in Python cannot be executed simultaneously on two different cores. The fact is closely linked to the Python interpreter itself. In fact, the interpreter on which Python code has always been running was originally implemented in **CPython**. During its implementation, it was realized that the interpreter was not fully thread-safe. That is, when more threads tried to access a certain object in common (the memory is shared between the threads), the interpreter often ran into a state of inconsistency due to the phenomenon of the *race condition*. To avoid this huge problem, the **Global Interpreter Lock** (**GIL**) has now been included within the interpreter. The Python designers therefore decided that within a process, only *one thread can be executed at a time*, eliminating the parallelism of this type of entity (no *multithreading*).

GIL is only acquired by one thread at a time while all the other threads wait. As soon as the thread has finished its task, the GIL is released and is acquired by the next thread. Therefore, a real concurrent execution takes place. **Concurrent programs** are generally less costly in terms of resources than parallel programs, as creating new processes is much more expensive than creating threads. It should be considered, however, that the operations of acquisition and release of the lock slow down the execution of the entire program.

However, things are not that bad. In fact, later we will learn about adapting this peculiarity in parallel programming models. Furthermore, many external libraries do not rely on the GIL, since they have been implemented with other languages such as **C** and **FORTRAN**. Thus, they take advantage of internal mechanisms that use multithreading. One of these libraries is `NumPy`, which is used for numerical computation in Python.

Elimination of GIL to Achieve Multithreading

The possibility of removing the GIL from the Python interpreter has always been a *hot topic*. However, this possibility has become increasingly difficult with time since it would be too difficult to remove the GIL without excluding many official, third-party packages and modules used in Python.

Another possibility could be to use other Python implementations other than CPython. The most widespread of these is **PyPy**, which is famous for its greater performance, but has unfortunately also implemented a GIL similar to that of CPython. Instead, **Jython**, a version of Python implemented in **Java** and **IronPython**, which is implemented with .NET, do not have GILs. They can use multithreading and therefore, take advantage of multiple cores or processors.

Threads versus Processes in Python

In summary, *threads* and *processes* are tools provided by Python to implement programs in concurrent and parallel forms, respectively.

In *Table 1.1*, you can see a comparison of the these, which must be taken into account during programming:

Feature	**Process (Heavyweight)**	**Thread (Lightweight)**
Memory	Separate memory space for each process	Shared memory space within the same process
Creation Time	Slower, higher overhead	Faster to create, low overhead
Context Switching	Expensive, requires saving full process state	Cheaper, only thread state needs to be saved
Communication	Uses Inter-Process Communication (IPC), slower	Easier through shared memory
Crash Impact	One process crashing doesn't affect others	A crashing thread can affect the entire process
Resource Usage	Heavier, requires more OS resources	Lighter, uses fewer resources

Isolation	Stronger isolation between processes	Weaker isolation, threads share address space
Use Cases	Running independent programs, high reliability	Concurrent tasks within the same application

Table 1.1: *Threads versus Processes in Python*

Concurrency and Parallelism in Python

Therefore, for concurrent programming in Python, we can correct the previous definition of concurrency, and eliminate the possibility of *parallelism* by factoring in the behavior of threads.

As we learned before, *concurrency* means managing multiple tasks at the same time, but not necessarily running them simultaneously.

Therefore, we can imagine that concurrent programming in Python involves threads that perform their tasks independently and also compete with each other for execution. They alternate with each other in the general flow of execution, until they are completed, as shown in *Figure 1.11*:

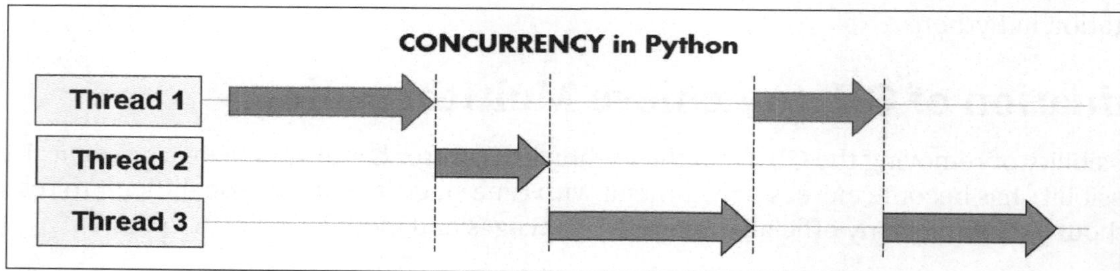

Figure 1.11: *Concurrency in Python*

Meanwhile, in parallel programming in Python, *processes* are perfect for executing tasks simultaneously. Each of them is assigned a task and all of them execute the instructions at the same time, until the program is completed. This is shown in *Figure 1.12*:

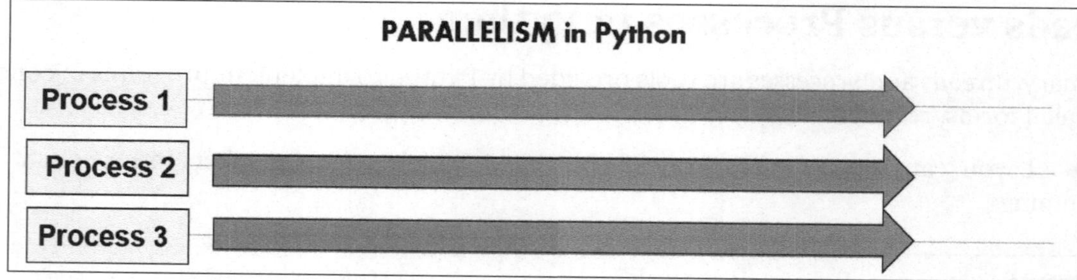

Figure 1.12: *Parallelism in Python*

It is clear that while for other programming languages the terms *concurrent* and *parallel* could lead to confusion; in Python, concurrency and parallelism do not share the same aspects of simultaneity, and are two completely different concepts.

The Light Weight Concurrency with Coroutines (Greenlets in Python)

As we have seen, threads provide a useful mechanism to implement concurrency models. However, Python also offers an alternative: **greenlets**, which is a form of coroutine. Using greenlets or threads is equivalent from the perspective of concurrency, since threads do not execute in true parallelism in Python. Both approaches work well for concurrent programming instead.

The key difference here is efficiency: creating and managing greenlets is less resource-intensive than working with threads. For this reason, they are often described as a *lightweight concurrency*. Greenlets are particularly useful when dealing with a large number of simple I/O-bound tasks, such as those commonly found in web servers. We will see how to create and manage greenlets with practical examples later in the book.

Parallel Programming with Python

In Python, parallel programming is expressed exclusively with respect to processes. A **program** is divided into *several* parallelizable subtasks, where each is assigned to a different process. Within each of them, we can therefore choose whether to perform the steps *synchronously* or *asynchronously*.

Synchronous and Asynchronous Programming

In this book as well as in much of the online documentation about parallel programming, the terms *synchronous* or *asynchronous* are often referred to as **sync** and **async**.

Unconsciously, whenever we implement a program in parallel or in competition between multiple processes or threads, it comes naturally to us that we should structure it synchronously. In the presence of two or more processes (but they could also be threads or even simple functions within a program), one process (PROCESS 1 in *Figure* 1.13) continues to execute until it makes an external call. At that point, it suspends and passes control to another process (PROCESS 2 in *Figure* 1.13), which provides a service, performs a calculation, or carries out any other operation. Once PROCESS 2 has completed its task, it delivers the result to PROCESS 1, which was waiting in the meantime. Thereafter, PROCESS 1 can resume execution.

A simple example of this concept is a program that needs to read data from a file or make a request to a web server. The main process starts the execution, but when it calls the file system or the network (PROCESS 2), it must wait until the requested data is returned. Only after the result is received can the main process continue.

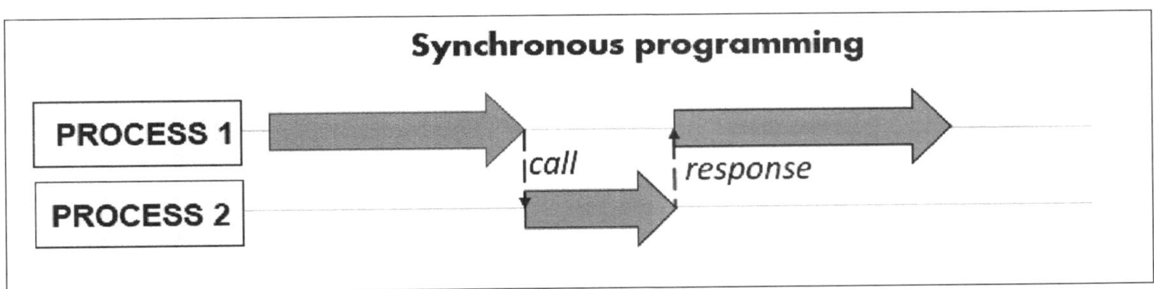

Figure 1.13: *Synchronous Programming*

This synchronous behavior is shown in *Figure* 1.13. For instance, imagine a web application (Process 1) that needs data from a database (Process 2). The application sends a query (call) and must wait until the database completes the operation and sends the result (response). Only then can the application resume its execution.

But in reality, *asynchronous programming* models are much more efficient than synchronous ones, both in the use of computing resources and the amount of time spent in running the program. Let us look at the previous case together, but this time perceive it asynchronously, as shown in *Figure* 1.14:

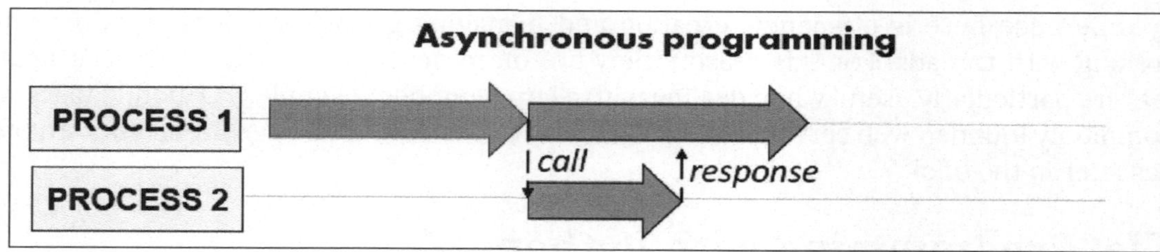

Figure 1.14: Asynchronous Programming

As in the *synchronous* case, the *initial* process (**PROCESS 1** in *Figure* 1.14) will continue its execution until the call that will initiate a *second* process (**PROCESS 2** in *Figure* 1.14). However, in this illustration, the initial trial will not interrupt its execution, while waiting for the second trial to be completed. It will continue the execution, regardless of when and how it will obtain the outcome of the second trial.

As we can guess, *asynchronous programming* allows us to deploy it in many cases, where we could have wasted time waiting for operations that require an external response or a long execution time. It is therefore important to know both models well if you want to make the most of parallel programming.

As for its practical applications, which are not yet completely intuitive for us, it is perfectly possible. All programming languages have internal mechanisms that allow for their implementation. We will cover asynchronous programming in depth in *Chapter* 6, *GPU Programming with Python.*

Map and Reduce

Map–Reduce is a general paradigm, which will be discussed later in the context of distributed systems. This scheme is mainly based on two phases:

- Mapping
- Reducing

The first phase of **mapping** is based on the subdivision of the *tasks* into parts that will be carried out by a program. The program then assigns these tasks to different processes that will execute them simultaneously, or in *parallel.* Often, executing each process generates a result. So, there will be a phase following the one strictly linked to parallel execution, in which all the results must be recombined together. This is also called the **reducing** phase. *Figure* 1.15 can help you better understand this process:

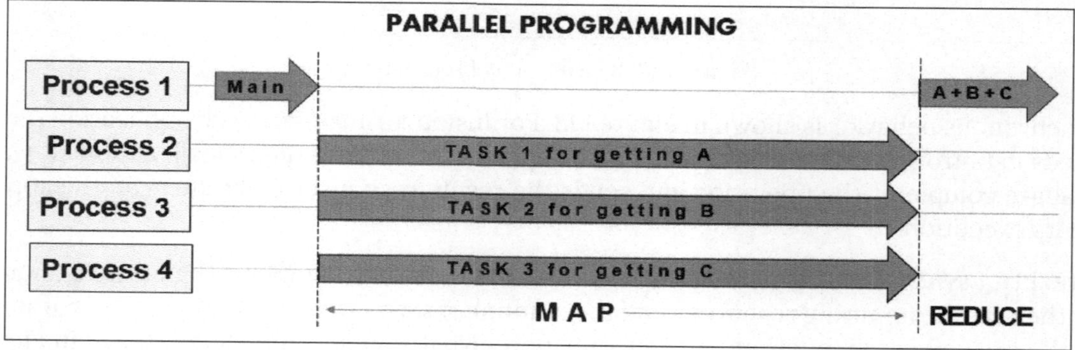

Figure 1.15: Map and Reduce Pattern in Parallel Programming

CPU-Bound and I/O-Bound Operations

When designing a parallel program, it is important to evaluate the type of work assigned to each task. If one task requires significantly more time than the others, the overall performance may degrade; the faster tasks will be forced to wait until the slowest one completes, before the program can move on to the next phase. *Figure 1.16* illustrates such a situation, where one parallel process takes longer than the others, THEREBY delaying the entire reduce phase.

This observation naturally leads us to distinguish between two categories of operations: **CPU-bound** and **I/O-bound**, which behave very differently in parallel and concurrent programming as shown in the following figure:

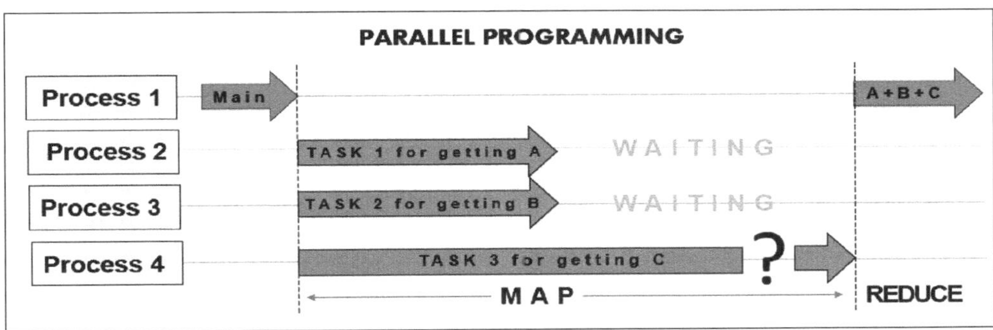

Figure 1.16: *Parallel Programming with Low Performance*

In situations like the one shown in *Figure* 1.16, it is important to analyze the type of operations performed within each task. Some operations involve waiting for external resources, such as reading a file or calling a web service. In these cases, the execution time depends on the response of external devices and can be unpredictable. Such operations are called **I/O-bound**. In contrast, operations that mainly involve internal calculations by the CPU are referred to as **CPU-bound**.

For CPU-bound tasks, parallel programming with multiple processes is effective, as each process can execute its portion of work on a different core, thus leading to real performance gains. However, when tasks are I/O-bound, simply adding more processes does not help because each process may still spend a significant amount of time waiting.

The most suitable approach in this case is **concurrent programming**. Within a process, we can create multiple threads: a thread can handle the CPU-bound part, while others can manage I/O-bound operations. If a thread is waiting for data from an external resource, the other threads can continue their work without being blocked. In this way, concurrency allows us to make better use of time that would otherwise be wasted while waiting. *Figure* 1.17 illustrates this model of parallel and concurrent programming as follows:

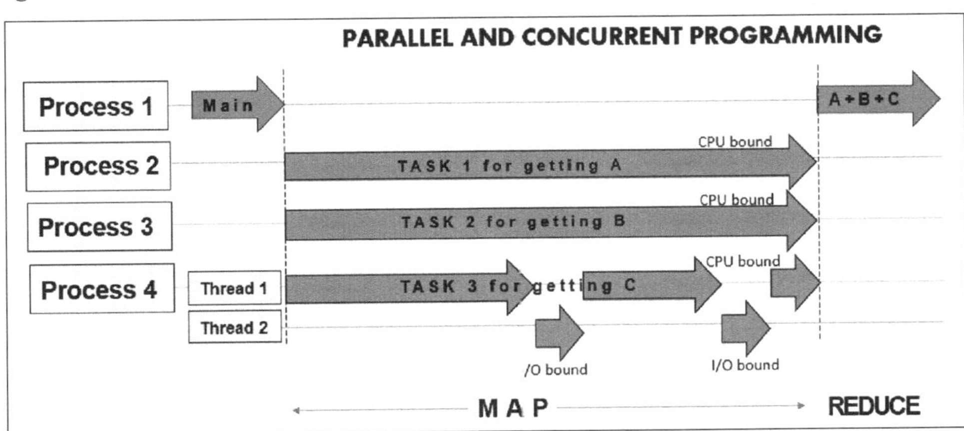

Figure 1.17: *Concurrency by Threads for I/O Bound Operations*

As shown in *Figure* 1.17, creating an additional thread besides the **MainThread** (which is always present in a process) makes it possible to handle I/O-bound operations independently. This allows the MainThread to continue processing data without waiting for external responses.

Additional Precautions in Parallel Programming

When dealing with concurrent programming, one must pay particular attention to when are the threads being used while managing shared data. As shown in *Figure 1.18*, the threads within a process possess their individual memory (which is not accessible to other threads) and occupy a shared memory space, where objects are accessible to all threads. This is demonstrated as follows:

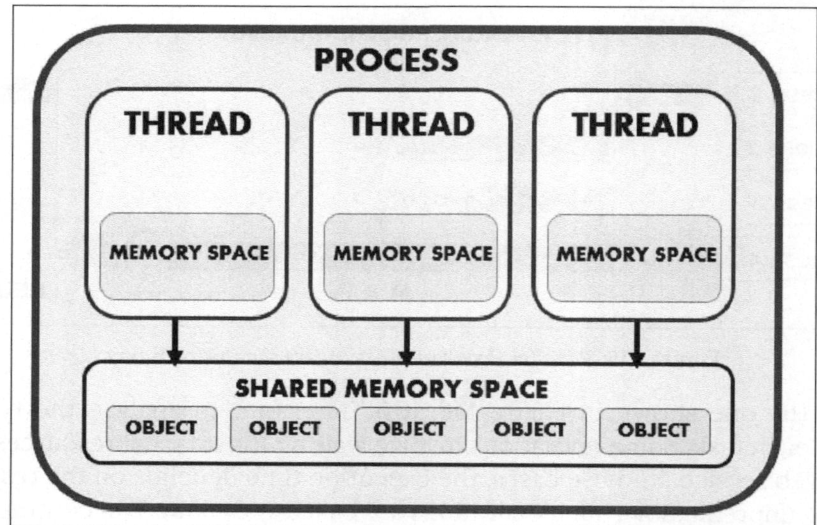

Figure 1.18*: Process with Its Threads*

Despite the presence of GIL in the Python interpreter working with multiple threads, it is still necessary to lock the global objects present in the shared memory space to avoid encountering *data inconsistency* problems. But how is this possible if the GIL guarantees that only one thread is executed at a time within a process?

The fact is that the interpreter will only take care of the internal objects of Python. However, when we consider the objects defined and created during the execution phase, there will be *no control* or *lock* that could be managed independently. It will be up to us to lock the global objects we create in order to prevent unexpected results.

In this regard, Python's standard library provides modules like threading and multiprocessing. In addition to creating and managing threads and processes, these modules will include synchronization primitives such as locks that allow us to safely coordinate access to shared objects.

Threading and Multiprocessing Modules

During the implementation phase, we can take advantage of both concurrency and parallelism with threads and processes, via two modules provided by the Python standard library: threading and multiprocessing. These modules can be integrated with the operating system to create, execute, and manage processes and threads.

Notice that the module for threads is called threading, and not multithreading. This is because, due to the Global Interpreter Lock (GIL), Python cannot execute multiple threads in true parallelism on CPU-bound tasks. Threads in Python are mainly useful for concurrent programming, especially when dealing with I/O-bound operations; while true parallel execution of CPU-bound tasks requires **processes.**

The **threading** module offers an abstraction layer to the `_thread` module, which is a low-level module that provides primitives for working with multiple threads. In addition, the threading module also provides several tools that help the programmer manage concurrent systems such as threads: **lock**,

condition, and **semaphores**. The module along with these tools will be addressed in depth in *Chapter 2, Parallel Programming with Threads*, along with a whole series of example codes.

The **multiprocessing** module, on the other hand, offers a valid API for the implementation of *process-based parallelism*. In addition to creating and managing processes, this module offers a large number of features to manage multiple processes within a program. For example, **Queue** and **Pipe** facilitate the exchange of information (objects) between the various processes, or the pools that simplify the management of multiple processes simultaneously. This module and its functionalities will be extensively discussed in *Chapter 3 - Parallel Programming with Processes*.

Memory Organization and Communication

So far, we have focused on how parallel execution is achieved through hardware such as multi-core CPUs. However, the performance of a parallel program does not depend only on the number of processing units; it is also influenced by how memory is organized and accessed.

Modern computers follow a **memory hierarchy**: the CPU registers and caches are extremely fast, while the main memory (RAM) is slower than cache access by 10 to 100 times. Accessing the disk is slower still. As a result, even with a powerful CPU, program performance can degrade due to inefficient access to memory, as the processor often ends up waiting for data.

Memory also plays a central role in **communicating** between processes and threads. When multiple execution units share data through memory, synchronization mechanisms (such as locks, semaphores, or message queues) are required to ensure consistency and prevent problems like race conditions or deadlocks.

Therefore, memory is not just a passive component but an active factor in determining the efficiency of parallel programming. Understanding how memory speed and organization affect execution, and how it facilitates communication between concurrent entities, is essential for designing correct and high-performance parallel programs.

Memory Models within a Single Process

For Python, there are essentially *three* different memory organization models that exist within a program:

- Embarrassingly Parallel
- Shared Memory
- Message Passing

These models are explained as follows:

- The first model, **embarrassingly parallel**, refers to the particular case in which the program entities, whether *threads* or *processes*, do not require any exchange of information and are able to carry their execution to the point where single results will be combined together. In fact, there are particular algorithms that respond to this behavior and are thus called **precisely embarrassingly parallel**.
- **Shared memory** is the model of memory organization typical of threads in Python. The threads within a process can communicate with each other through a shared memory in the process itself. There are several possible mechanisms that respond to this model, where some are valid and others are not.
- **Message passing**, on the other hand, is the memory organization model of processes. These in fact have no shared memory and therefore their only way of communicating is through

messages. There are several solutions to this, which are often offered in the form of *ready-made packages* called **Message Passing Interface** (**MPI**). In Python, MPI support is available through third-party packages such as **mpi4py**, but not in the standard library.

Memory Models across Multiple Processors

So far we have dealt with a single *multi-core* CPU *machine*. However, the reality of parallel programming naturally extends to the use of multiple CPUs. These may be present on a single machine or on different machines connected to each other.

It is clear that here too the organization of memory plays a role in determining the perfect functioning of parallel computing.

The two previous models of shared memory and message passing are also extended in this area as:

- Shared Memory
- Distributed Memory

In the systems that follow the *shared memory model*, all the processors can access a particular memory area to share data and pass information. Systems of this kind are normally based on a physical bus that facilitates the connection between a certain number of physically separate processors (but they can be on the same machine or on different machines) as shown in *Figure 1.19*:

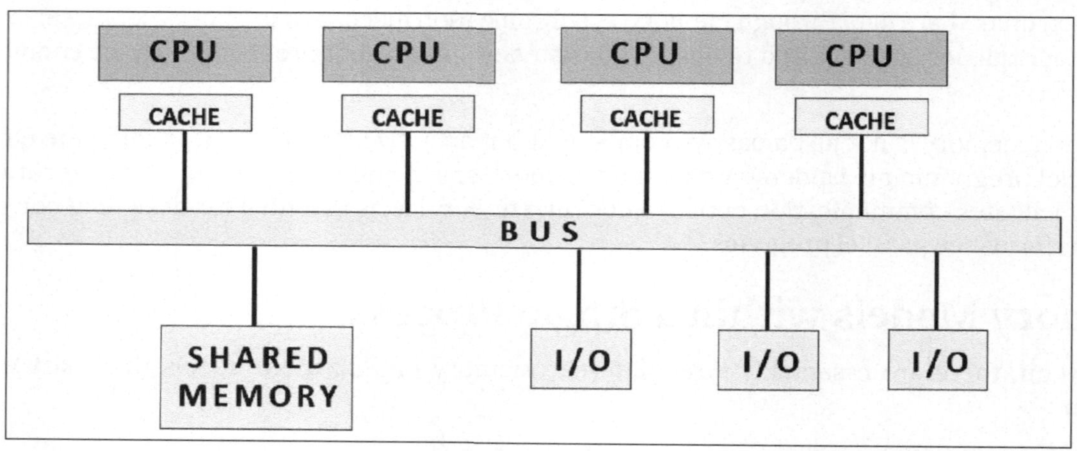

Figure 1.19: *Shared Memory Systems*

Each processor has its own local memory represented by a cache, generally with *high performance*, as the exchange of data between the CPU and this memory area is very frequent. But this area is limited as various processors will have to share data to work on. This can only be achieved via the shared memory connected to the bus.

This is also the point from where the situation starts becoming delicate. The programmer will have to carefully manage the synchronization of the data that is used simultaneously between the various processors.

One of the CPUs will take the value of data from shared memory and copy it to its cache to process it. In the meantime, another CPU that requires the same value will copy it from the shared memory to its cache. After some time, the first CPU will finish its processing and write the result in the shared memory, updating the value inside. In the meantime, the second CPU is processing a value that is no longer valid. As a result, the data coherency is lost. It is therefore clear that *concurrency management mechanisms* and *synchronization* must be implemented (via hardware or programmatically) in a way that is similar to how we dealt with threads in a single process.

The reason behind using this model is that shared memory systems are very fast, since they rely heavily on hardware rather than software. In fact, many synchronization and control mechanisms that regulate how CPUs access shared memory resources are implemented directly in hardware (for example, through cache coherence protocols and atomic instructions).

Distributed Memory is another model that is widely used today. Unlike the previous models, it functions with a network interconnection, instead of using a physical bus that connects various CPUs to each other. This is mainly used for CPUs that are located on physically separate machines and are located at a considerable distance from each other. This scheme is shown as follows in *Figure 1.20*:

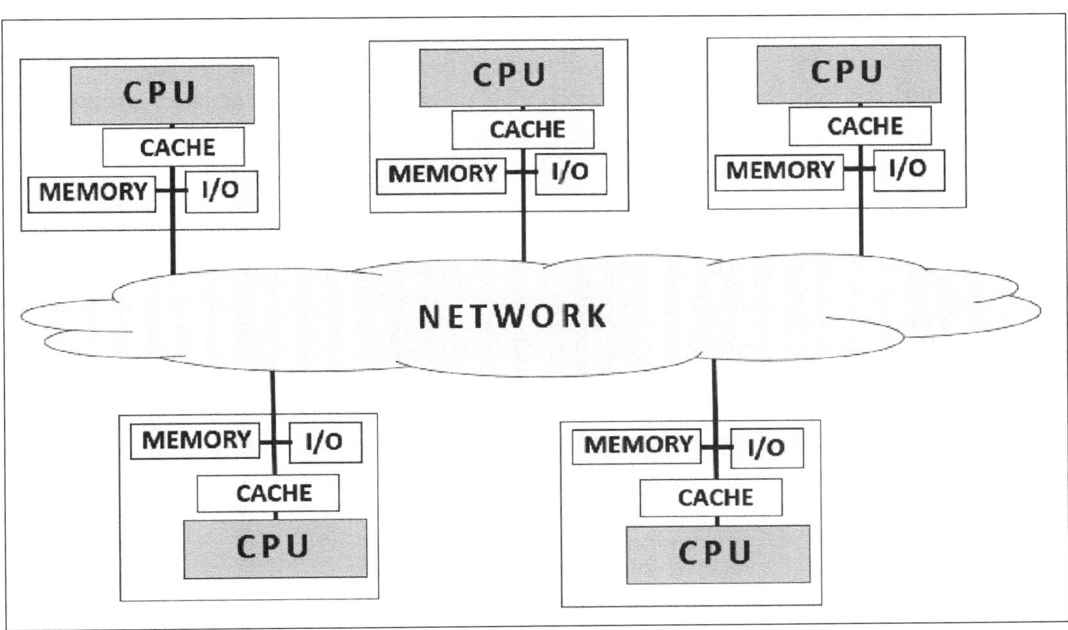

***Figure 1.20**: Distributed Memory System*

In this type of model, besides having its own dedicated cache, each CPU has a *local memory*, which it can use at full load. As a result, it can send data over the network whenever another CPU needs it. In this way, this mechanism eliminates data coherency problems, as each processor is responsible for its own data. Another advantage of a distributed model is that since it does not rely on a physical bus but uses a network connection instead, a user can add several CPUs to the system.

However, this system has a few disadvantages. One of them is that the network connection is not as fast as a physical bus. Moreover, we require a **message passing** mechanism to facilitate communication and data exchange between various CPUs. While the individual management of messages, along with their creation, sending eliminates coherency problems, but the attribute significantly slows down the overall execution of programs.

Distributed Programming

The existence of complex models such as distributed memory has prompted an intense evolution of parallel programming, so much so that it is defined as distributed programming. In fact, a program can be executed in parallel by different processes that run on different machines connected to the network. Today this system is widespread, and many Python packages provide libraries and abstractions to support parallel and distributed programming based on this model. We will deal with this extension of parallel programming later and use some packages freely available on the internet in *Chapter 5 - Distributed Python*.

Evaluation of Parallel Programming

An important aspect of parallel programming is the need to develop a series of methods to evaluate its performance. Doing so is essential in order to decide if the choices made are convenient and if it is necessary to devise another solution.

You might use parallelism to solve big problems in the shortest possible time. However, many factors come into play during the process, such as the degree of parallelism used, the hardware, and the choice of programming model. It is therefore necessary to carry out a *performance analysis* to evaluate the validity of our choices.

There are several series of performance indices that can be used for this purpose by evaluating their numerical value to measure a program's performance. These numerical values are obtained through appropriate calculations, which allow us to compare programs or algorithms in a systematic way. Among these indices, **speedup** is the best known, and is used widely.

Speedup

Speedup is a number expressing the difference between the performance of two systems that are running the same problem. In our case, the speedup S can be considered as the ratio between the time taken in the execution of a serial program t_s with the time t_p taken by our parallel program. The time taken (t) is a function of the number of processing units (referred to as N), which can include CPUs, cores or GPUs. Here, N is generally referred to as the number of processors. Therefore, the time taken in a parallel system can be expressed as *t*(N), while in a serial system it is taken as *t*(1) since it is equivalent to a system with a single processor. This equation is represented as follows:

$$S = \frac{t_s}{t_p} = \frac{t(1)}{t(N)}$$

In other words, *speedup* informs us about the performance benefits that have been witnessed after adopting the solution in parallel, as compared to the serial one. Furthermore, if we compare the number of N *processors* with the speedup index, we can further classify our algorithm or program as follows:

- If S = N, then the speedup is **linear** or **ideal.**
- If S <N, then the speedup is **sub-linear.**
- If S> N, then the speedup is **super-linear** (which is rare, often due to cache effects or algorithmic optimizations).

The speedup index is also linked to **Amdahl's law**, which is widely used in parallel computing. In fact, speedup is limited by the serial fraction of the code. Amdahl's law expresses this as:

$$S(N) = \frac{1}{(1 - \alpha) + \frac{\alpha}{N}}$$

Where α is the fraction of the program that can be parallelized. As N→∞, the maximum theoretical speedup will be:

$$S_{max} = \frac{1}{1 - \alpha}$$

Here, S is the speedup index and α is the portion of the time taken by the part of the program implemented in parallel.

If we assume that a program takes 100 minutes to execute, with 10 minutes being strictly serial, the remaining 90 minutes can be parallelized. In this case, the parallel fraction will be α = 0.9. Therefore, maximum obtainable speedup will be:

$$S_{max} = \frac{1}{1-0.9} = \frac{1}{0.1} = 10$$

The maximum *speedup* that can be obtained by our program will be 10. This means that even with many processors, the speedup cannot exceed 10. We can improve the program's performance by adding more processors. However, then the speedup will asymptotically approach this limit (see *Figure* 1.21).

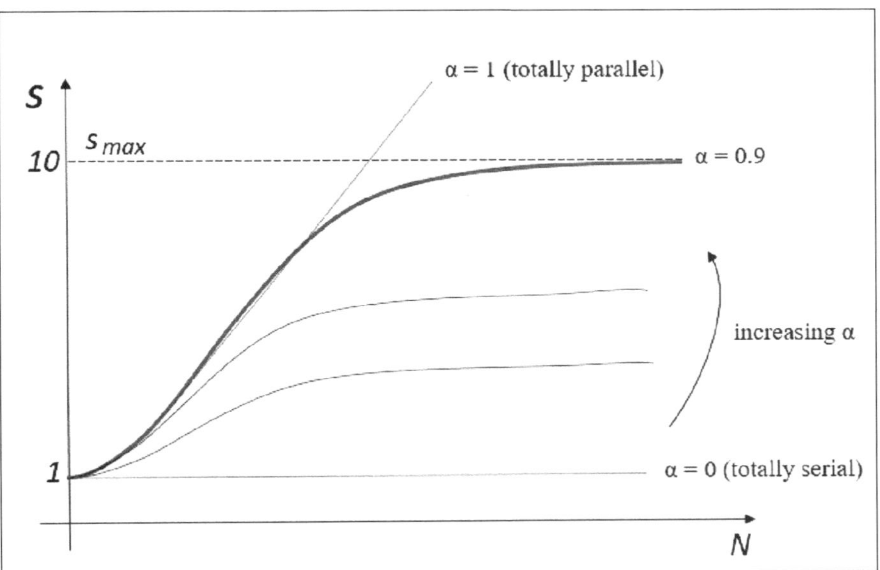

Figure 1.21: *Amdahl's Law*

Figure 1.21 illustrates Amdahl's law. The X-axis shows the number of processors N, and the Y-axis shows the speedup S(N).

- The diagonal line represents the **ideal linear speedup** (S=N).
- The red curve corresponds to α=0.9. This means that the program is 90% parallelizable and therefore its maximum speedup is limited to S_{max}=10.
- The other curves correspond to smaller values of α. As α decreases, the curves flatten sooner, which shows that the presence of serial code strongly limits scalability.
- At the extremes:
    - When α=0, the program is totally serial (S=1).
    - When α=1, the program is totally parallel and the speedup would scale linearly with N.

This shows that reducing the serial fraction is the only way to improve the potential speedup of a program. The smaller 1−α1 will be, the curve will be closer to the ideal case.

Therefore, if we want to improve the speedup of a program or an algorithm, it is necessary to reduce the serial code parts as much as possible. Only by increasing the number of processors (or cores) will we see an even more linear performance improvement.

Furthermore, once the parallelizable part of the code has been *maximized*, the next task is to find the right compromise. This means seeking a combination where the speedup is as high as possible along with using the correct *number of processors* (see *Figure 1.22*). This avoids unnecessary workloads with too much *parallelism* that might stem from adding too many processors:

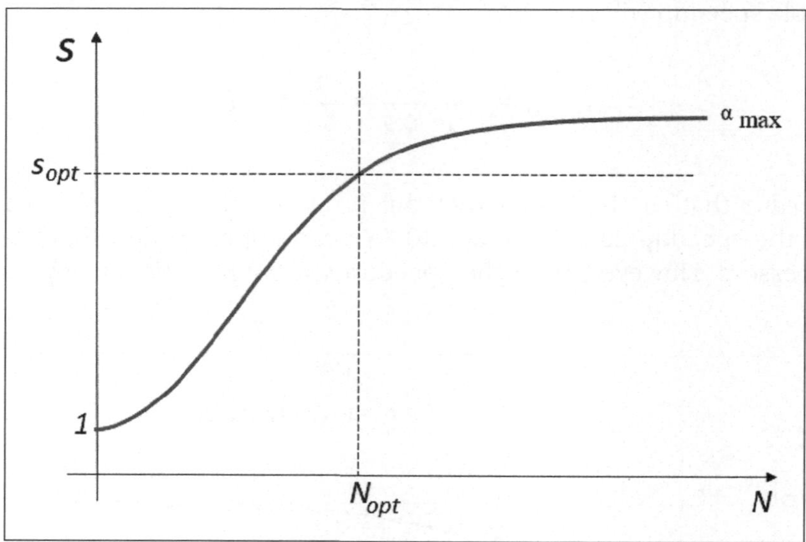

***Figure 1.22**: Optimizing the Number of Processors*

Scaling

Scaling refers to the efficiency of a parallel program in exploiting additional hardware resources (processors or cores). Scaling can be *strong* or *weak* and has two complementary ways of measuring system scalability with respect to workload size and processor count. These are mentioned in detail as follows:

- **Strong scaling** measures the decrease in execution time as the number of processors increases, while the problem size stays unchanged. Ideally, doubling the processors halves the runtime. This type of scaling is useful when the size of the problem is constant (for example, running a fixed-size simulation or processing a dataset of fixed dimensions).
- **Weak scaling** measures how the change in execution time when the number of processors increases, which in turn also increases the problem size proportionally in a way that the workload per processor remains constant. Ideally, the runtime stays the same as both workload and processors grow together. This type of scaling is more meaningful when problems grow larger with the addition of resources (for example, weather forecasting with finer resolution, or analyzing increasingly large datasets).

In practice, **strong scaling** is limited by Amdahl's law; even if the parallel portion is large, the serial fraction of the code eventually dominates, and the communication overhead between processors grows as their number increases. For example, a fluid dynamics simulation on a fixed grid will eventually stop benefiting from additional processors once communication outweighs computation.

Weak scaling, on the other hand, is often described by Gustafson's law, which shows that as we increase the problem size with more processors, the parallel fraction of work dominates, allowing for nearly linear speedup. This explains why large-scale applications like climate modeling or big data analytics are usually evaluated with weak scaling.

Unlike Amdahl's law, which assumes a fixed problem size (strong scaling), **Gustafson's law** considers cases where the problem size grows proportionally to the number of processors (weak scaling). In this scenario, the execution time remains nearly constant as both workload and processors increase. Moreover, the speedup does not have a strict upper bound.

Gustafson's law expresses speedup as:

$$S = (1 - \alpha) + \alpha * N$$

Where α is the fraction of the workload that can be parallelized. The serial fraction $(1-\alpha)$ stays constant, while the parallel part grows with N.

This means that as we increase the number of processors, the total parallelizable work dominates, which allows the speedup to grow almost linearly with N. *Figure 1.23* illustrates this behavior: the red line corresponds to α=0.9, showing that speedup keeps increasing as more processors are added, unlike in Amdahl's law where it saturates.

For example, in large-scale simulations (for example, climate modeling), doubling the number of processors allows the simulation to run with twice the resolution in approximately the same time. In this case, weak scaling and Gustafson's law provide us a more realistic picture of performance than Amdahl's law.

In fact, Gustafson's Law implies that despite increasing the size of the problem, only the speedup of the parallel part of the code α increases when more processors are added, while the serial one $(1-\alpha)$ does not. In fact, *Figure 1.23* shows the trends of the various speedups growing linearly with the addition of processors without ever reaching a *limit*:

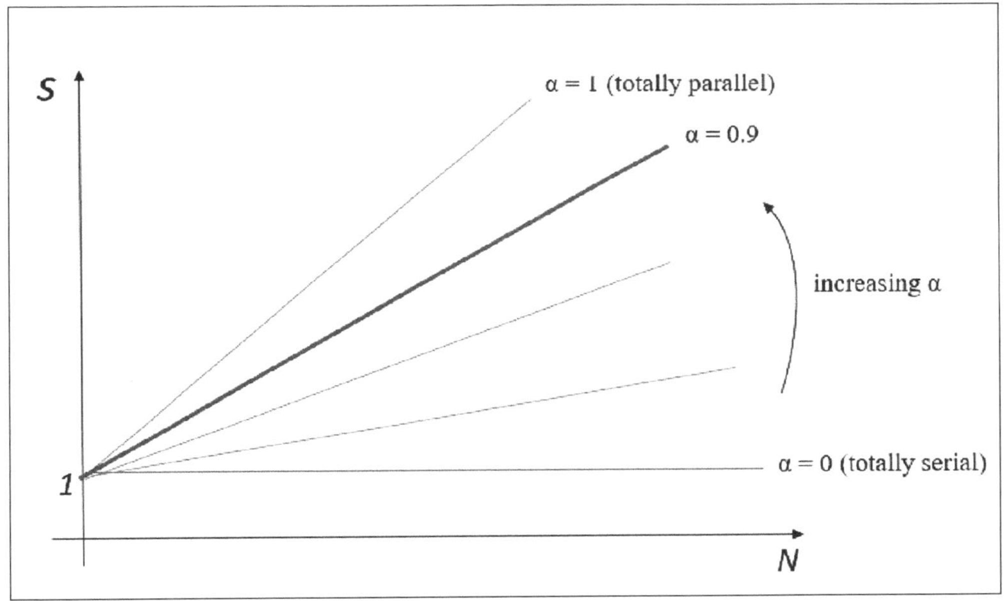

Figure 1.23: *Gustafson's Law*

In summary, strong and weak scaling, together with Amdahl's and Gustafson's laws, give us two complementary perspectives. For fixed-size problems, adding processors will eventually hit a performance ceiling (Amdahl's law). For workloads that grow with resources, the performance can improve almost linearly (Gustafson's law).

Benchmarking in Python

Systematically testing performance under different conditions is referred to as **benchmarking**. So far we have seen the evaluation of the performance of a program from a theoretical point of view. However, when we consider the practical aspect, Python offers a series of tools that can measure the performance of a program or a piece of code.

In the following chapters, we will explore some practical examples of creating these measurements. For instance, to calculate the time taken (which is also useful for calculating the speedup) for the execution of a portion of code, we will use the time module of the standard Python library. This module provides access to several types of clocks. By using the call to the **time()** method, we can obtain real stopwatch readings. Then, by making differences between the *times read*, we can obtain the time taken by the code included between the *two calls*. This is shown as follows:

```
started = time.time()

# Code here

elapsed = time.time()
print("Elapsed time=", elapsed - started)
```

Profiling

Profiling refers to the analysis of the parts of the program that contribute to performance and identify any bottlenecks during the process.

In Python, there are several tools that are useful in this regard. When it comes to consuming memory resources, it is possible to use the **package memory profiler,** which is a powerful tool that allows you to monitor the memory consumption of different processes/jobs in Python. It is also able to perform a *line-by-line analysis* of the code for the consumption of resources, and is therefore useful as a line profiler.

Conclusion

In this chapter, we have discussed how parallel programming has evolved over time. The processes and threads that run within the operating system are matched in parallel programming via process and thread objects implemented with the *threading* and *multiprocessing* modules of a standard Python library. In the following chapters, we will learn how to use these two modules for parallel programming, while leveraging their features.

Points to Remember

- **Concurrency**: Refers to managing multiple tasks at the same time, which might not run simultaneously
- **Parallelism**: Running multiple tasks simultaneously
- **Threads**: Threads in Python cannot run concurrently, and therefore cannot operate in parallel.

Questions

1. What is the difference between parallelism and concurrency?
2. What are the advantages and disadvantages of a distributed memory system?
3. When and how can you maintain weak scaling and strong scaling?

References

- https://wiki.python.org/moin/GlobalIntepreterLock
- https://www.udacity.com/blog/2020/04/what-is-python-parallelization.html
- https://www.infoworld.com/article/3542595/6-python-libraries-for-parallel-processing.html
- https://en.wikipedia.org/wiki/Monkey_patch
- https://greenlet.readthedocs.io
- https://www.koyeb.com/blog/introduction-to-synchronous-and-asynchronous-processing
- https://medium.com/fintechexplained/advanced-python-concurrency-and-parallelism-82e378f26ced
- https://sebastianraschka.com/Articles/2014_multiprocessing.html
- https://medium.com/fullstackai/concurrency-in-python-cooperative-vs-preemptive-scheduling-5feaed7f6e53
- https://carpentries-incubator.github.io/lesson-parallel-python/
- http://code.tutsplus.com/articles/introduction-to-parallel-and-concurrent-programming-in-python--cms-28612
- https://en.wikipedia.org/wiki/Speedup
- https://hpc-wiki.info/hpc/Scaling
- https://www.meccanismocomplesso.org/python/

CHAPTER 2
Parallel Programming with Threads

Introduction

In this chapter, we will cover the concepts of threads and concurrent programming. Python's standard library provides the **threading** module, which makes it easy to create and use threads. It also includes a wide range of tools for managing and synchronizing them. The entire chapter will illustrate this module, and introduce its main classes and their respective functionalities step by step.

Structure

This chapter will address the following topics:

- Threads
- ThreadPoolExecutor
- Synchronization Mechanisms

Threads

The main protagonists of concurrent programming are the threads, and in this regard, the **threading** module provides the **Thread** class in the following way:

```
class threading.Thread(group=None,
                       target=None,
                       name=None,
                       args=(),
                       kwargs={},
                       *,
                       daemon=None)
```

The **Thread()** constructor takes a number of arguments. Among the most important and commonly used are **target** and **args**. These respectively refer to the function that will be executed by the thread is passed to target, while the arguments to that function are passed through args.

Another useful parameter is **daemon**. A *daemon thread* runs in the background and does not block program termination; when all non-daemon threads have finished, the Python interpreter will exit, even if daemon threads are still running. By default, daemon inherits the value from the creating thread (usually False for the main thread). This makes daemon threads suitable for background tasks (such as monitoring), but not for critical work that must be completed before the program exits.

We can immediately see the functionality of this type of object with a practical example. In the program, we will define five threads that will act concurrently. All of them will target the same function, which we will call function() for convenience. This function will not perform tasks, but will only occupy a short period of time, just to simulate the time spent in executing a set of instructions:

```
import threading
import time

def function(i):
  print ("start Thread %i\n" %i)
  time.sleep(2)
  print ("end Thread %i\n" %i)
  return

t1 = threading.Thread(target=function , args=(1,))
t2 = threading.Thread(target=function , args=(2,))
t3 = threading.Thread(target=function , args=(3,))
t4 = threading.Thread(target=function , args=(4,))
t5 = threading.Thread(target=function , args=(5,))
t1.start()
t2.start()
t3.start()
t4.start()
t5.start()
print("END Program")
```

As we can see in the code, the five instances of the **Thread** class are defined and correspond to as many threads using the variables **t1**, **t2**, and so on. The execution of the threads will then be started later by invoking the `start()` method. On running the program, we may get the following output:

```
start Thread 1
start Thread 2
start Thread 3
start Thread 4
start Thread 5
END Program
$ end Thread 1
end Thread 2
end Thread 4
end Thread 3
end Thread 5
```

If we look at the result of the execution, we can see that the program starts all five threads at the same time and then closes without waiting for them to finish their execution. This causes the prompt to enter a new command to appear. Meanwhile, the five threads continue their execution in the background and will display their output on the command line.

Another interesting observation is that the closing order of execution differs from the initial one and can vary from execution to execution. This is normal behavior with threads, since they are running concurrently. Their duration of execution and their order is seldom predictable. Therefore, it is important to use synchronization methods that we will explore later in the chapter.

If you run the code on your machine, the output can be very different on each execution from what we have above. It could even look like this:

```
start Thread 1
start Thread 2
start Thread 3
END Program
start Thread 5
```

```
start Thread 4

end Thread 1
end Thread 2
end Thread 3
end Thread 5
end Thread 4
```

join() method

In the previous case, we saw that the program could finish before its threads complete. This can be solved by using the **join()** method. Calling **join()** on a thread blocks the caller until that thread finishes execution. By applying **join()** to all threads in our example, we ensure that the program terminates only after all threads have completed.

Apply it to the previous case as follows:

```
import threading
import time

def function(i):
  print ("start Thread %i" %i)
  time.sleep(2)
  print ("end Thread %i" %i)
  return

t1 = threading.Thread(target=function , args=(1,))
t2 = threading.Thread(target=function , args=(2,))
t3 = threading.Thread(target=function , args=(3,))
t4 = threading.Thread(target=function , args=(4,))
t5 = threading.Thread(target=function , args=(5,))
t1.start()
t2.start()
t3.start()
t4.start()
t5.start()
t1.join()
t2.join()
t3.join()
t4.join()
t5.join()
print("END Program")
```

In this case, we will get the following result:

```
start Thread 1
start Thread 2
start Thread 3
start Thread 4
start Thread 5
end Thread 3
end Thread 1
end Thread 2
end Thread 4
end Thread 5
END Program
```

As we can see, the program will now wait for all threads to finish their execution before closing.

However, let us think about it further. Calls to the **join()** method can be used at some point in the program, such as during a simple synchronization mechanism. For example, we want to execute a part of the main program code and then wait for the threads to execute to restart the process, perform other operations, or start other threads.

Let us now modify the previous example code:

```
...
t1.start()
t2.start()
t1.join()
t2.join()
print("First set of threads done")
print("The program can execute other code here")
t3.start()
t4.start()
t5.start()
t3.join()
t4.join()
t5.join()
print("Second set of threads done")
print("END Program")
```

By running the newly modified code, we will get the following result:

```
start Thread 1
start Thread 2
end Thread 2
end Thread 1
First set of threads done
The program can execute other code here
start Thread 3
start Thread 4
start Thread 5
end Thread 3
end Thread 5
end Thread 4
Second set of threads done
END Program
```

As we can see, via the **join()** methods, you can add a point in the program where you wait for the execution to begin, and then start again with the code.

Common Thread Synchronization Pattern

In the previous examples, you can see identical lines of code being used multiple times when you use multiple threads. We have defined for each thread a call for the **start()** and **join()** methods and have written numerous similar lines. The situation worsens as the number of threads increases. However, there are other convenient ways to write code.

In our example involving the 5 threads, we can write the code as follows:

```
import threading
import time

def function(i):
  print ("start Thread %i" %i)
  time.sleep(2)
  print ("end Thread %i" %i)
```

```
    return

n_threads = 5
threads = [ ]
for i in range(n_threads):
  t = threading.Thread(target=function , args=(i,))
  threads.append(t)
  t.start()

for i in range(n_threads):
  threads[i].join()
```

In this form, the code is much more *readable* and *simpler*. By using a for loop that iterates for as many threads as we want, we have avoided defining each thread individually (**t1**, **t2**, **t3**, ...), and calling the **start()** and **join()** methods for each of them.

By executing we will obtain a result identical to the previous examples:

```
start Thread 0
start Thread 1
start Thread 2
start Thread 3
start Thread 4
end Thread 0
end Thread 1
end Thread 2
end Thread 3
end Thread 4
```

Note: *Be careful not to write this, unless intentional:*

```
for i in range(n_threads):
  t = threading.Thread(target=function , args=(i,))
  threads.append(t)
  t.start()
  t.join()
```

Placing the call to **join()** *immediately after* **start()** *in the same loop causes the main thread to wait for each new thread to finish before launching the next one. This results in serial execution; the first thread is started, then the main thread blocks until it completes; the second thread is started, and so on. This defeats the purpose of parallel programming, since the threads are no longer running concurrently.*

The concurrent.futures Module and the ThreadPoolExecutor

In addition to the threading module, Python's standard library provides the **concurrent.futures** module, which offers a high-level interface for asynchronously executing callables. One of its most useful classes is **ThreadPoolExecutor**, which is designed to manage a pool of worker threads. This allows you to submit tasks without manually creating and starting individual Thread objects: the executor handles thread creation, scheduling, and reuses them automatically.

The real benefit becomes clear when you have **more tasks than available threads**. The executor keeps a fixed number of workers active; the next waiting task is picked up automatically by the freed thread as soon as a task concludes. This avoids the complexity of managing **start()** and **join()** calls manually, and makes it easy to scale to dozens or hundreds of tasks.

To illustrate this behavior, let us create a pool with three workers, but submit ten tasks of varying duration. You will see that at most three tasks run in parallel, and another queued task immediately starts on the same thread as soon as one ends.

```
import concurrent.futures:
import time
import random
import threading

def task(i, sleep_s):
    tname = threading.current_thread().name
    print(f"[{time.strftime('%H:%M:%S')}] START task={i:02d}
sleep={sleep_s:.1f}s  on {tname}")
    time.sleep(sleep_s)  # simulate I/O wait
    print(f"[{time.strftime('%H:%M:%S')}] END task={i:02d} on {tname}")
    return i, sleep_s

durations = [1.5, 0.8, 2.2, 0.5, 1.0, 1.7, 0.6, 2.0, 0.9, 1.3]  # 10 tasks

with concurrent.futures.ThreadPoolExecutor(max_workers=3) as executor:
    # Submit more tasks than workers (10 >> 3)
    futures = [executor.submit(task, i, d) for i, d in enumerate(durations,
start=1)]

    # Option A: handle results as each task finishes (completion order)
    for fut in concurrent.futures.as_completed(futures):
        i, d = fut.result()  # propagate exceptions if any
        # (Optional) print or collect results here

print("Program ended")
```

While running the code, you will notice that only three tasks start immediately, because we have set **`max_workers = 3`**. The remaining tasks will wait in a queue. As soon as a thread completes its assigned task (for example, task 2), the executor automatically reuses the same thread to pick up the next one (task 4 in this case).

The following sample output illustrates this behavior:

```
[18:39:35] START  task=01  sleep=1.5s  on ThreadPoolExecutor-0_0
[18:39:35] START  task=02  sleep=0.8s  on ThreadPoolExecutor-0_1
[18:39:35] START  task=03  sleep=2.2s  on ThreadPoolExecutor-0_2
[18:39:35] END    task=02  on ThreadPoolExecutor-0_1
[18:39:35] START  task=04  sleep=0.5s  on ThreadPoolExecutor-0_1
[18:39:36] END    task=04  on ThreadPoolExecutor-0_1
[18:39:36] START  task=05  sleep=1.0s  on ThreadPoolExecutor-0_1
[18:39:36] END    task=01  on ThreadPoolExecutor-0_0
[18:39:36] START  task=06  sleep=1.7s  on ThreadPoolExecutor-0_0
[18:39:37] END    task=03  on ThreadPoolExecutor-0_2
[18:39:37] START  task=07  sleep=0.6s  on ThreadPoolExecutor-0_2
[18:39:37] END    task=05  on ThreadPoolExecutor-0_1
[18:39:37] START  task=08  sleep=2.0s  on ThreadPoolExecutor-0_1
[18:39:37] END    task=07  on ThreadPoolExecutor-0_2
[18:39:37] START  task=09  sleep=0.9s  on ThreadPoolExecutor-0_2
[18:39:38] END    task=06  on ThreadPoolExecutor-0_0
[18:39:38] START  task=10  sleep=1.3s  on ThreadPoolExecutor-0_0
[18:39:38] END    task=09  on ThreadPoolExecutor-0_2
[18:39:39] END    task=08  on ThreadPoolExecutor-0_1
[18:39:39] END    task=10  on ThreadPoolExecutor-0_0
Program ended
```

Here we can clearly see that **threads are reused**: the worker ThreadPoolExecutor-0_1 first runs task 2, then immediately takes task 4, then task 5, and so on. This confirms that the executor maintains a fixed pool of workers and keeps them busy until all tasks in the queue are completed.

The output may look somewhat ordered, but this is only due to the relative sleep times of the tasks. In reality, the threads are running concurrently, and the executor internally manages scheduling as well as synchronization to ensure that each task is executed once, and that workers are properly reused.

If we had written the same program without a **`ThreadPoolExecutor`**, we would need to manually create, start, and join each thread. This quickly becomes cumbersome as the number of tasks grows, while rendering resource management error-prone. The executor model avoids this complexity by abstracting thread lifecycle management and providing a clean, scalable way to run many tasks with a limited number of worker threads.

Thread Competition

A simple example to observe how two competing threads behave in concurrent programming is shown in this section. Each thread is assigned a different function, **`addA()`** and **`addB()`**, which simulate operations performed cyclically with a short, random delay at each iteration. The two threads are launched together and compete for execution: due to Python's Global Interpreter Lock (GIL), only one thread runs Python bytecode at a time, but the operating system switches between them, while creating interleaved and non-deterministic results.

To monitor the execution sequence, each function appends the letters A and B to a shared string. By running the code multiple times, you will notice that the order of letters changes across runs, illustrating the unpredictable scheduling of concurrent threads.

```
import threading
import time
import random

sequence = ""
COUNT = 10

def addA():
    global sequence
    for _ in range(COUNT):
        time.sleep(random.uniform(0.1, 0.3))
        sequence = f"{sequence}A"
        print("Sequence:", sequence)

def addB():
    global sequence
    for _ in range(COUNT):
        time.sleep(random.uniform(0.1, 0.3))
        sequence = f"{sequence}B"
        print("Sequence:", sequence)

# Main program
t1 = threading.Thread(target=addA)
t2 = threading.Thread(target=addB)
t1.start()
t2.start()
t1.join()
t2.join()
```

During the program, you will be able to see the sequence of execution. So, if you run the code you just wrote, you will get a sequence like this:

```
Sequence: A
 Sequence: AB
Sequence: ABA
Sequence: ABAB
Sequence: ABABA
Sequence: ABABAB
Sequence: ABABABB
Sequence: ABABABBA
Sequence: ABABABBAB
Sequence: ABABABBABA
Sequence: ABABABBABAB
Sequence: ABABABBABABA
Sequence: ABABABBABABAB
Sequence: ABABABBABABABA
Sequence: ABABABBABABABAB
Sequence: ABABABBABABABABA
Sequence: ABABABBABABABABAB
Sequence: ABABABBABABABABABA
Sequence: ABABABBABABABABABAB
Sequence: ABABABBABABABABABABA
```

As we can see from the result, the two threads alternate in execution in a non-deterministic way. Running the program multiple times produces different sequences, since the operating system schedules the threads differently at each run. By adjusting the delay values (for example, changing the random range), you can influence the frequency of alternation between the two threads, but the sequence will always remain unpredictable due to the nature of concurrent execution.

Using Thread Subclasses

In the previous example, we created threads by instantiating the Thread class and passing a function via the target parameter:

```
t = threading.Thread(target = function_name)
```

This approach separates the **thread object** (created with Thread) from the **task code** (written as an external function)..

Another way is to **subclass the `Thread` class**. In this case, the thread logic is placed directly inside the class by overriding its **`run()`** method. This is useful when you want the thread to have its own state or additional methods, which makes it a self-contained object consistent with object-oriented programming.

```
from threading import Thread

class MyThread(Thread):
    def __init__(self, *args, **kwargs):
        super().__init__(*args, **kwargs)  # call parent constructor
        # add custom initialization here

    def run(self):
        # this method is executed when .start() is called
        # place the thread's logic here
        pass
```

```
# create and start a thread
t = MyThread()
t.start()
t.join()
```

In the following code, we will rewrite the previous example (where two functions were passed to different threads) using subclasses. Each subclass overrides **run()** with its own implementation, which can be seen as follows:

```
from threading import Thread
import time

sequence = ""
COUNT = 5
timeA = 1
timeB = 2

class ThreadA(Thread):
    def run(self):
        global sequence
        for _ in range(COUNT):
            time.sleep(timeA)
            sequence += "A"
            print("Sequence:", sequence)

class ThreadB(Thread):
    def run(self):
        global sequence
        for _ in range(COUNT):
            time.sleep(timeB)
            sequence += "B"
            print("Sequence:", sequence)

# Main program
t1 = ThreadA()
t2 = ThreadB()
t1.start()
t2.start()
t1.join()
t2.join()
```

The output of the previous code looks like the following:

```
Sequence: A
Sequence: AB
Sequence: ABA
Sequence: ABAA
Sequence: ABAAB
Sequence: ABAABA
Sequence: ABAABAA
Sequence: ABAABAAB
Sequence: ABAABAABB
Sequence: ABAABAABBB
```

Here, each thread is represented by a dedicated class (**ThreadA** and **ThreadB**), and the code that was previously in external functions (**addA** and **addB**) now resides inside the run() methods of the subclasses.

Synchronization Mechanisms

As we saw in the previous section, threads are executed concurrently, meaning they operate simultaneously (though not truly in parallel, due to Python's GIL). This often leads to unpredictable behavior which, if not controlled, can cause **race condition**–situations where two or more threads access and modify a shared resource at the same time, while the final result depends on the unpredictable order of execution. To prevent such issues, the threading module provides several classes and primitives that implement synchronization mechanisms (for example, Lock, RLock, Semaphore, Event, and Condition).

In this regard, the **`threading`** module provides a whole series of classes useful for implementing *thread synchronization* mechanisms. There are various types with their respective peculiarities. In the course of this chapter, we will see how each will be implemented in a simple example, which is useful to understand how they function.

The synchronization objects provided by the **`threading`** module are:

- Lock
- RLock
- Semaphore
- Condition
- Event
- Queue

Lock

The **Lock** is the object with the lowest synchronization level among all the classes provided by the **`threading`** module. Lock can essentially assume *two* states:

- Locked
- Unlocked

It also has two methods that are:

- **`acquire()`**
- **`release()`**

These can modify the status of the lock between *locked* and *unlocked*. When we define a lock using the **`Lock()`** constructor, it is in the *unlocked* state. When a thread invokes the **`lock.acquire()`** method, the lock switches to the *locked* state and blocks the execution of the thread, which is put *on hold*. When another thread invokes the **`lock.release()`** method, the lock will return to the *unlocked* state, and the *waiting* thread will resume its execution (see *Figure 2.1*):

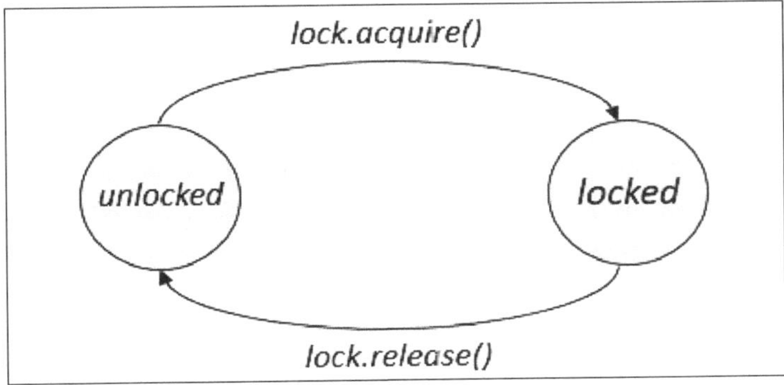

Figure 2.1: The States of the Lock Class

If this *synchronization mechanism* is not well managed, it can lead to even more confusion in synchronization than not using it at all. In fact, there may be multiple threads that have invoked the **lock.acquire()** method, with all of them waiting for at least one other thread to call **lock.release()** and change the status to *unlocked*. In this case, the *waiting* thread that will restart with the execution is unpredictable, and can vary across implementations.

To illustrate how locks work, let us take an example with two threads, where each performs a different function. We will call the two functions **funcA()** and **funcB()**. From the first chapter, we know that competing threads share process memory. In our example, we will use a shared variable, which is an integer accessible to both threads.

The first thread, connected to **funcA()**, will repeatedly increase this value by 10, while the other thread, connected to **funcB()**, will decrease it by 10. Each function will perform this operation **10,000 times**, which is large enough to expose the effects of concurrent access.

To maximize the chance of interleaving between the two threads, we insert a **time.sleep(0)** call in the critical gap between reading and writing the shared variable. This forces the thread to yield control, thus making race conditions more likely and easier to observe.

So, let us write the following code:

```
import threading, time

shared_data = 0

def funcA():
    global shared_data
    for i in range(10_000):
        v = shared_data
        time.sleep(0)            # yield in the non-atomic gap
        shared_data = v + 10
        if i % 2000 == 0:
            print(f"A i={i:5d} -> {shared_data}")

def funcB():
    global shared_data
    for i in range(10_000):
        v = shared_data
        time.sleep(0)            # yield in the non-atomic gap
        shared_data = v - 10
        if i % 2000 == 0:
            print(f"B i={i:5d} -> {shared_data}")

t1 = threading.Thread(target=funcA)
t2 = threading.Thread(target=funcB)
t1.start(); t2.start()
t1.join(); t2.join()

print("Final (unsynchronized):", shared_data)

:
```

This example is designed to highlight inter-thread concurrency and the problems that can arise without synchronization. Each thread updates the same shared variable 10,000 times, with **funcA()** incrementing and **funcB()** decrementing. The **time.sleep(0)** call deliberately increases the chance of context switches, so that the two threads interleave frequently.

When we run the program, we get an output like this:

```
A i=    0 -> 10
B i=    0 -> 1490
A i= 2000 -> 20010
B i= 2000 -> -16590
A i= 4000 -> 10980
B i= 4000 -> -22720
A i= 6000 -> 10
B i= 6000 -> -37950
A i= 8000 -> -12560
B i= 8000 -> -45910
Final (unsynchronized): -45140
```

Here, we can see that both threads interleave frequently, but the final value of the shared variable is not consistent. In principle, since one thread increments by 10 and the other decrements by 10 the same number of times, the result **should always be 0**. Instead, the final value fluctuates widely across runs, depending on the timing of context switches: in one execution it may be –45140, while in another it could be positive or closer to zero.

This phenomenon is a classic **race condition**. Both threads read and modify the shared variable without coordination, so their operations overlap in unpredictable ways. Even with only two threads and a simple update, the result is nondeterministic.

To fix this, we need a synchronization mechanism that ensures only one thread at a time can read and update the shared variable. The Global Interpreter Lock (GIL) does not help here, because it does not make this sequence atomic. The simplest synchronization tool in Python is the Lock class from the threading module.

We can create a Lock at the beginning of the program and use its **`acquire()`** and **`release()`** methods around the critical section in both threads, as shown in the following code:

```
import threading, time

shared_data = 0
lock = threading.Lock()

def funcA():
    global shared_data
    for i in range(10_000):
        with lock:
            shared_data += 10
            if i % 2000 == 0:
                print(f"A i={i:5d} -> {shared_data}")
        time.sleep(0)  # yield fuori dal lock

def funcB():
    global shared_data
    for i in range(10_000):
        with lock:
            shared_data -= 10
            if i % 2000 == 0:
                print(f"B i={i:5d} -> {shared_data}")
        time.sleep(0)  # yield fuori dal lock

t1 = threading.Thread(target=funcA)
t2 = threading.Thread(target=funcB)
t1.start(); t2.start()
```

```
t1.join(); t2.join()

print("Final (synchronized):", shared_data)
```

If we run the code this time, we get a very different result. Thanks to the synchronization provided by the lock, the two threads can no longer interleave in the middle of the update, therefore, the shared variable is updated in a consistent way. The outcome is now reproducible: the final value is always exactly **0**, as expected, regardless of how many times the program is executed. This is one of the possible results of running the previous code:

```
 A i=    0 -> 10
B i=    0 -> 1170
A i= 2000 -> 11020
B i= 2000 -> 12210
A i= 4000 -> 12480
B i= 4000 -> 13180
A i= 6000 -> 13910
B i= 6000 -> 14150
A i= 8000 -> 12690
B i= 8000 -> 15130
Final (synchronized): 0
```

As we can see, there are no more race condition problems. The shared variable is now read and modified by only one thread at a time due to synchronization, which prevents inconsistent values from appearing. Moreover, unlike in the unsynchronized case where the final result was unpredictable, here the outcome is always reproducible and exactly **0** as expected.

However, it should be noted that introducing this synchronization mechanism also has an impact on execution timing. In the unsynchronized version, the two threads interleaved their operations in an unpredictable way, so increments and decrements appeared mixed together and the program sometimes finished faster. In the synchronized version, the threads do not interleave within the protected code. As a result, a thread may complete its entire loop before the other even starts updating the shared variable, which conveys the reduction in concurrency.

This contrast highlights a trade-off: synchronization ensures correctness and determinism, but it can also reduce concurrency, and slightly increase execution time compared to the unsynchronized case.

Context Management Protocol with `Lock`

All objects within the **`threading`** module that use the **`acquire()`** and **`release()`** methods, such as the **`Lock`** objects, can be used in a context manager through the **`with`** statement (see **Note** as follows).

Note: *In Python, the* `with` *statement creates a runtime context that allows you to execute a block of statements under the control of a context manager.*

```
with expression:
      #code
```

The context manager evaluates the expression relative to the block of code related to with (context). Therefore, the expression must return an object that implements a context management protocol which essentially consists of two methods:

- `__enter__()`*, which is called when entering the context.*
- `__exit__()`*, which is called when exiting the context.*

In addition to this, the `with` *statement has the advantage of incorporating the functionality of the* `try ... finally` *construct.*

You thus get a more readable and easily reusable code. Precisely for these numerous advantages, many classes of the standard library support the use of ***with*** *statements as an alternative to traditional constructs.*

In the case of locks, the **acquire()** method will be called when entering the block and the **release()** method will be called when *exiting*.

Hence, the form looks like:

```
lock.acquire()
try:
#code
finally:
      lock.release()

can be written in the following way:
with lock:
      #code
```

We then rewrite the previous code using the supported context manager protocol:

```
import threading
import time

shared_data = 0
lock = threading.Lock()

def funcA():
  global shared_data
  for i in range(10):
    with lock:
      local = shared_data
      local += 10
      time.sleep(1)
      shared_data = local
      print("Thread A wrote: %s" %shared_data)


def funcB():
  global shared_data
  for i in range(10):
    with lock:
      local = shared_data
      local -= 10
      time.sleep(1)
      shared_data = local
      print("Thread B wrote: %s" %shared_data)

t1 = threading.Thread(target = funcA)
t2 = threading.Thread(target = funcB)
t1.start()
t2.start()
t1.join()
t2.join()
```

As we can see, the code is much more *readable*. Functionally, it behaves the same as the previous version, but the with statement has an important **advantage**: it guarantees that the lock is always released, even if an exception occurs inside the block. This prevents subtle bugs that might arise if a programmer forgets to call **lock.release()** or accidentally removes it.

The *Context Manager protocol* using the with statement is also supported by other objects in the **threading** module that we will see later in the chapter:

- RLock
- Condition
- Semaphore

These are objects that use the **acquire()** and **release()** methods in their synchronization mechanism.

Another Possible Synchronization Solution with Locks

As we have seen, the simplest and most effective way to use locks is to enclose the critical section within a balanced pair of **acquire()** and **release()** calls, or more idiomatically, to use the with lock: context manager.

Technically, nothing prevents a programmer from invoking **acquire()** and **release()** in an **asymmetric** way; for example calling **acquire()** in one thread and **release()** in another, or placing them in different parts of the code. This approach, however, leads to programs that are **difficult to read, fragile, and prone to errors**. In particular, it increases the risk of race conditions and deadlocks, and the behavior is no longer deterministic.

For this reason, we will not show concrete code examples of such usage. The recommendation is to **always use balanced acquire/release pairs inside the same block of code**, or preferably the with lock: statement. This ensures clarity, maintainability, and correctness of concurrent programs.

If we are not sure that the two threads are progressing alternately, but suspect that one of them might remain blocked while the other continues execution, we can check this during the debugging phase by printing additional information.

For example, by including the current iteration index in the output of each thread, we make it possible to **trace their progress side by side**. This way, we can directly verify whether both threads are running and alternating as expected.

```
import threading
import time

shared = 0
lock = threading.Lock()

def funcA():
  global shared
  for i in range(10):
    time.sleep(1)
    shared += 10
    print("Thread A wrote: %s, %i" %(shared,i))
    lock.acquire()

def funcB():
  global shared
  lock.acquire()
  for i in range(10):
    time.sleep(1)
    shared -= 10
    print("Thread B wrote: %s, %i" %(shared,i))
    lock.release()
```

```
t1 = threading.Thread(target = funcA)
t2 = threading.Thread(target = funcB)
t1.start()
t2.start()
t1.join()
t2.join()
```

After running the modified code, we will notice that both threads complete their execution by alternating between them, as shown here:

```
Thread A wrote: 10, 0
Thread B wrote: 0, 0
Thread B wrote: -10, 1
Thread A wrote: 0, 1
Thread B wrote: -10, 2
Thread A wrote: 0, 2
Thread B wrote: -10, 3
Thread A wrote: 0, 3
Thread B wrote: -10, 4
Thread A wrote: 0, 4
Thread B wrote: -10, 5
Thread A wrote: 0, 5
Thread B wrote: -10, 6
Thread A wrote: 0, 6
Thread B wrote: -10, 7
Thread A wrote: 0, 7
Thread B wrote: -10, 8
Thread A wrote: 0, 8
Thread B wrote: -10, 9
Thread A wrote: 0, 9
```

The **Lock** mechanism in this case continues to work, even if it is executed in the code *asymmetrically*, and does not conclude with certainty that all executions will run exactly this way.

RLock

Another class used for thread synchronization is **RLock**, also known as the **reentrant lock**. This class is very similar to the Lock class, but it can be acquired multiple times by the same thread. Inside it, in addition to the *locked-unlocked state*, there exists information on the owner thread and on the recursion level.

Like a *Lock*, an *RLock* can be acquired from a thread using the **`acquire()`** method. At this point RLock becomes *locked*, and the calling thread becomes one of the owners. Similarly, an RLock can be unlocked by calling the **`release()`** method. This time, however, unlike the Lock synchronization mechanism, the calls to the acquire() and release() methods can be nested. This means that the same thread may acquire the RLock several times before releasing it. However, the number of release() calls must exactly match the number of acquire() calls made by that thread. If a thread acquires an RLock three times, it must also release it three times. Otherwise, the lock will never be fully released and will result in a deadlock. Other threads that will invoke the **`acquire()`** method will be added to the list of owners. Only the last matching release() call from the owning thread will fully unlock the RLock, while allowing another thread that is waiting on acquire() to proceed. Intermediate release() calls just decrease the recursion depth, but they keep the lock reserved for the same thread. Importantly, only the thread that acquired the lock can release it—other threads cannot call release() on its behalf.

In the following example, each thread executes a function that runs three outer iterations. In each iteration, the thread acquires the lock once at the outer level, and two times more inside a nested loop. At each inner loop step, it increments the shared variable by 1. After completing the nested loop, it increments the shared variable one more time before releasing the lock. As a result, each outer iteration increases the shared value by **(2 from the inner loop + 1 from the outer loop) = 3 increments**. Since there are three outer iterations, each thread contributes a total of **9 increments**. With three threads running, the expected final value of the shared variable is 27. This expected outcome helps the reader understand how the RLock ensures consistent, and predictable updates despite concurrent execution.

```
import threading
import time

shared = 0
rlock = threading.RLock()

def func(name, t):
  global shared
  for i in range(3):
    rlock.acquire()
    local = shared
    time.sleep(t)
    for j in range(2):
      rlock.acquire()
      local += 1
      time.sleep(2)
      shared = local
      print("Thread %s-%s wrote: %s" %(name, j, shared))
      rlock.release()
    shared = local + 1
    print("Thread %s wrote: %s" %(name, shared))
    rlock.release()

t1 = threading.Thread(target = func,args=('A',2,))
t2 = threading.Thread(target = func,args=('B',10,))
t3 = threading.Thread(target = func,args=('C',1,))
t1.start()
t2.start()
t3.start()
t1.join()
t2.join()
t3.join()
```

By running the previous code, we will get a result like the following:

```
Thread A-0 wrote: 1
Thread A-1 wrote: 2
Thread A wrote: 3
Thread A-0 wrote: 4
Thread A-1 wrote: 5
Thread A wrote: 6
Thread A-0 wrote: 7
Thread A-1 wrote: 8
Thread A wrote: 9
Thread B-0 wrote: 10
Thread B-1 wrote: 11
Thread B wrote: 12
Thread B-0 wrote: 13
Thread B-1 wrote: 14
Thread B wrote: 15
```

```
Thread B-0 wrote: 16
Thread B-1 wrote: 17
Thread B wrote: 18
Thread C-0 wrote: 19
Thread C-1 wrote: 20
Thread C wrote: 21
Thread C-0 wrote: 22
Thread C-1 wrote: 23
Thread C wrote: 24
Thread C-0 wrote: 25
Thread C-1 wrote: 26
Thread C wrote: 27
```

Also, in this case, the synchronization has led to perfect management of the **shared** variable, but at a loss of the concurrent behavior of the threads. Without the use of the *RLock synchronization mechanism*, (that is, eliminating the calls to the **acquire()** and **release()** methods), the program will give a result similar to the following:

```
Thread C-0 wrote: 1
Thread A-0 wrote: 1
Thread C-1 wrote: 2
Thread C wrote: 3
Thread A-1 wrote: 2
Thread A wrote: 3
Thread C-0 wrote: 4
Thread C-1 wrote: 5
Thread C wrote: 6
Thread A-0 wrote: 4
Thread B-0 wrote: 1
Thread A-1 wrote: 5
Thread A wrote: 6
Thread C-0 wrote: 7
Thread B-1 wrote: 2
Thread B wrote: 3
Thread C-1 wrote: 8
Thread C wrote: 9
Thread A-0 wrote: 7
Thread A-1 wrote: 8
Thread A wrote: 9
Thread B-0 wrote: 4
Thread B-1 wrote: 5
Thread B wrote: 6
Thread B-0 wrote: 7
Thread B-1 wrote: 8
Thread B wrote: 9
```

As you can see from the result, we have race condition phenomena that has caused the **shared** variable to be valued with incorrect values.

Semaphore

Another synchronization mechanism available in the threading module is the **semaphore**, one of the oldest primitives in the history of computer science, which was introduced by Edsger W. Dijkstra in the 1960s. The main purpose of a semaphore is to regulate concurrent access to a finite set of resources. Conceptually, a semaphore behaves like a counter: each call to acquire() decreases its value by one, while each call to release() increases it again. As long as the counter remains greater than or equal to zero, a thread that calls acquire() is allowed to proceed. If, however, the counter has reached zero, the thread is blocked and must wait until another thread releases the semaphore, thus freeing up one "*slot*" for access.

It is important to distinguish the semaphore from the simpler lock. A lock can be seen as a particular case of semaphore, which is initialized with a counter equal to one. In this situation, only a single thread at a time can enter the protected section, while enforcing strict mutual exclusion. A semaphore, on the other hand, can be initialized with any integer value, allowing up to that number of threads to simultaneously access the resource. This makes it more flexible and suitable in scenarios where resources are limited but can be shared by more than one thread at once–for example, a pool of database connections, a set of network sockets, or even a limited number of printers in a system.

When a thread calls acquire() it must eventually call release() once it has finished with the shared resource; otherwise other threads will remain blocked and the program may encounter a deadlock. *Figure* 2.2 sketches the classic **producer–consumer** pattern: a producer thread generates data and places it into shared memory, while a consumer thread removes and processes that data. The two run at different and variable speeds, and there may be multiple producers or consumers. This makes the pattern a natural fit for concurrency.

***Figure 2.2**: The Producer-Consumer Model*

To coordinate the handoff correctly with semaphores we will model a **single-slot buffer**. We use two counting semaphores: one (slots) tracks whether the slot is available, and the other (items) tracks whether a produced item is ready to be consumed. The producer waits on slots, writes the value, and then signals items; the consumer waits on items, reads the value, and then signals slots. This scheme guarantees that the consumer never reads before the producer has written, and that the producer never overwrites an unread value. With this in mind, let us implement the example in the following code:

```
import threading
import time
import random

# --- Single-slot producer-consumer using two semaphores ---

N_ITEMS = 5                          # how many values to produce/consume
slots = threading.Semaphore(1)       # counts free slots (1 slot available at
start)
items = threading.Semaphore(0)       # counts ready items (none at start)

buffer = {"value": None}            # single-slot shared buffer
print_lock = threading.Lock()        # only for tidy printing (not required for
                                     correctness)

def producer():
    for i in range(1, N_ITEMS + 1):
        slots.acquire()                              # wait until the slot is
                                                     free
        v = random.randint(0, 100)                   # "produce" a value
```

```
        time.sleep(random.uniform(0.2, 0.6))      # simulate variable
                                                  production time
        buffer["value"] = v
        with print_lock:
            print(f"producer -> put {v:3d} (item {i})")
        items.release()                           # signal that an item is
                                                  available

def consumer():
    for i in range(1, N_ITEMS + 1):
        items.acquire()                           # wait until an item is
                                                  available
        v = buffer["value"]
        time.sleep(random.uniform(0.1, 0.5))      # simulate variable
                                                  consumption time
        with print_lock:
            print(f"consumer <- got {v:3d} (item {i})")
        buffer["value"] = None
        slots.release()                           # signal that the slot is
                                                  free again

tp = threading.Thread(target=producer, name="Producer")
tc = threading.Thread(target=consumer, name="Consumer")

tp.start(); tc.start()
tp.join();  tc.join()

print("Done.")
```

This implementation uses two semaphores—slots (initialized to 1) and items (initialized to 0)—to enforce correct handoff on a single-slot buffer. The producer must acquire a free slot before writing and then releases an available item; the consumer waits for an available item, reads it, and then releases the slot. The **print_lock** exists only to keep the output lines neat. By executing the code just written, we will get the following:

```
producer -> put   4 (item 1)
consumer <- got   4 (item 1)
producer -> put  65 (item 2)
consumer <- got  65 (item 2)
producer -> put  92 (item 3)
consumer <- got  92 (item 3)
producer -> put  39 (item 4)
consumer <- got  39 (item 4)
producer -> put   5 (item 5)
consumer <- got   5 (item 5)
Done.
```

As we can see, the producer and consumer are alternating perfectly. Each value produced is immediately consumed, and no items are skipped or overwritten. This happens because we are now using two semaphores to model the two aspects of the problem: the number of free slots in the buffer and the number of available items. The slots semaphore ensures that the producer cannot add more items than the buffer can hold, while the items semaphore guarantees that the consumer waits until there is something to consume. In this way, production and consumption remain synchronized, avoiding the race conditions and data losses we observed in the earlier examples.

This pattern is a canonical use of semaphores: they are not only used for mutual exclusion like locks, but also for coordinating access to limited resources between multiple threads.

In conclusion, semaphores are a powerful tool but require careful design. They are not a universal replacement for locks in critical sections—instead, they provide more flexible control over how many threads can simultaneously access a resource. In our single-buffer example, the combined use of semaphores for "*free slots*" and "ready items" ensures that the producer does not overwrite data that has not yet been consumed and that the consumer does not wait unnecessarily. This scheme eliminates the race conditions we observed in the less protected versions.

However, it is important to be aware of their limitations: semaphores can introduce overhead (in terms of acquire/release operations), they may lead to starvation of certain threads if not managed fairly, and they can complicate program logic when many resources or many threads are involved. Moreover, because semaphores allow multiple threads to enter simultaneously (up to the configured limit), they do not enforce the total exclusion that a Lock provides. This can be perfectly acceptable when the resource allows concurrent use, but insufficient when strict consistency is required, especially with complex shared data structures.

Finally, when designing concurrent programs, it is always essential to define clearly what the "*atomic unit*" of work should be, to check whether the resource is truly shared, whether the number of accessing threads needs to be limited, and that every **`acquire()`** is always paired with a **`release()`**, even in the case of exceptions. Using semaphores within a **`with`** statement (when supported as a context manager) or by placing the corresponding **`release()`** call in a **`finally`** block ensures that the semaphore is always released, even if an exception occurs, thereby improving both reliability and code readability.

With these precautions in mind, semaphores can become a valuable synchronization tool that strike a balance between performance, safety, and controlled parallelism.

Condition

An alternative synchronization primitive provided by the threading module is the Condition class. Unlike a simple Lock or Semaphore, which only regulates access to resources, a Condition is designed for situations where threads must wait for a **particular state** of shared data before continuing.

A Condition is always associated with a lock to ensure that checks and updates to the shared state happen atomically. Beyond the usual acquire() and release() operations, it provides three key methods:

- **`wait()`**, which releases the lock and suspends the thread until it is notified.
- **`notify()`**, which wakes up one waiting thread.
- **`notify_all()`**, which wakes up all waiting threads.

This makes conditions especially useful for coordination patterns like the producer–consumer model, where a consumer should not proceed until data has been produced and a producer should wait until the previous data has been consumed. In such cases, Condition allows threads to signal each other explicitly, which ensures that work is carried out in the right order without busy waiting or resource overwriting.

To illustrate, we can rewrite our earlier producer–consumer example so that the producer signals the consumer when new data is available and the consumer signals the producer when it has finished using the data. The result is a clean alternation between the two threads as is shown here:

```
from threading import Thread, Condition
import time, random

condition = Condition()
shared = None   # buffer starts empty
count = 5       # number of items to produce/consume
```

```
class Consumer(Thread):
    def __init__(self, count):
        super().__init__()
        self.count = count

    def run(self):
        global shared
        for _ in range(self.count):
            with condition:
                while shared is None:
                    condition.wait()  # wait until producer provides data
                print(f"consumer <- got {shared}")
                shared = None
                condition.notify()    # signal producer to produce next item

class Producer(Thread):
    def __init__(self, count):
        super().__init__()
        self.count = count

    def run(self):
        global shared
        for i in range(self.count):
            time.sleep(1)
            item = random.randint(0, 100)
            with condition:
                while shared is not None:
                    condition.wait()  # wait until consumer has used the item
                shared = item
                print(f"producer -> put {item}")
                condition.notify()    # signal consumer that data is ready

t1 = Producer(count)
t2 = Consumer(count)
t1.start(); t2.start()
t1.join(); t2.join()
```

In this code, both the producer and the consumer coordinate through the same Condition object. The producer acquires the condition lock, generates a new value, and then calls **`notify()`** to signal the consumer that fresh data is available. The consumer, on the other hand, waits on the condition whenever the shared resource is not ready. When it is awakened by the producer's signal, it consumes the value, resets the shared variable, and notifies the producer that it can generate the next item.

This back-and-forth mechanism ensures that the two threads alternate their work, without interfering with each other. Unlike the semaphore-based solution, which only controlled how many threads could enter a critical section, the condition variable explicitly models the **state of the shared resource**, and allows threads to wait until that state changes.

When we run the program, the result shows the producer and consumer operating in strict alternation like this:

```
producer -> put 46
consumer <- got 46
producer -> put 71
consumer <- got 71
producer -> put 65
consumer <- got 65
producer -> put 65
```

```
consumer <- got 65
producer -> put 53
consumer <- got 53
```

As we can see, the output confirms that the producer and consumer alternate correctly without missing or overwriting values. The important difference from the semaphore-based solution is that the Condition is not just controlling access, but also **encoding the protocol of interaction** between the two threads: the producer waits until the consumer has consumed the last value and the consumer waits until the producer has generated a new one. This makes conditions particularly useful when threads must coordinate on an occasion something happens, and not just on *how many* threads can enter a critical section.

Event

In addition to the **Semaphore** and the **Condition**, there is another synchronization mechanism. It is called **Event**, which can be understood as a basic mechanism of communication between threads in which a thread signals a certain event to another thread waiting for it to happen.

An **Event** object manages an internal *Boolean* flag. There are also two methods that determine its value. The **set()** method sets the flag value to *True*, while the **clear()** method to *False*. *False* is the default value of the **Event** object when it is created. There is also a third method, **wait()**, which blocks the calling thread until the flag becomes True. If multiple threads are waiting on the same Event, they will all be released as soon as another thread calls **set()**.

In other words, a thread, during its execution, freezes by calling the **wait()** method, while waiting for an event to continue. In another thread, when this event occurs, the **set()** method *unlocks* the previous thread, which performs its operations, and then calls **clear()** to reset everything.

In our example of the two threads **Producer** and **Consumer**, we can replace the previous mechanisms with the *Event-based synchronization* mechanism.

Let us modify the code as follows:

```
from threading import Thread, Event
import time
import random

event = Event()
shared = 1
count = 5

class Consumer(Thread):
  def __init__(self, count):
    Thread.__init__(self)
    global event
    self.count = count

  def run(self):
    global shared
    for i in range(self.count):
      event.wait()
      print("consumer has used this: %s" %shared)
      shared = 0
      event.clear()

class Producer(Thread):
  def __init__(self, count):
    Thread.__init__(self)
```

```
        self.count = count
        global event

      def request(self):
        time.sleep(1)
        return random.randint(0,100)

      def run(self):
        global shared
        for i in range(self.count):
          shared = self.request()
          print("producer has loaded this: %s" %shared)
          event.set()

t1 = Producer(count)
t2 = Consumer(count)
t1.start()
t2.start()
t1.join()
t2.join()
```

After running the code, we will get a result like this:

```
producer has loaded this: 40
consumer has used this: 40
producer has loaded this: 100
consumer has used this: 100
producer has loaded this: 15
consumer has used this: 15
producer has loaded this: 27
consumer has used this: 27
producer has loaded this: 94
consumer has used this: 94
```

We can see here that the synchronization between the two threads is *perfect*.

Queue

We will continue to develop the previous example. So far, we have only used one **Producer** thread and one **Consumer** thread. But *what happens if we increase the number*?

We modify the previous program, this time making four threads work at the same time: two **Producer** and two **Consumer**:

```
from threading import Thread, Event
import time
import random

event = Event()
shared = 1
count = 5

class Consumer(Thread):
  def __init__(self, count):
    Thread.__init__(self)
    global event
    self.count = count

  def run(self):
```

```
    global shared
    for i in range(self.count):
      event.wait()
      print("consumer has used this: %s" %shared)
      shared = 0
      event.clear()

class Producer(Thread):
  def __init__(self, count):
    Thread.__init__(self)
    self.count = count
    global event

  def request(self):
    time.sleep(1)
    return random.randint(0,100)

  def run(self):
    global shared
    for i in range(self.count):
      shared = self.request()
      print("producer has loaded this: %s" %shared)
      event.set()

t1 = Producer(count)
t2 = Producer(count)
t3 = Consumer(count)
t4 = Consumer(count)
t1.start()
t2.start()
t3.start()
t4.start()
t1.join()
t2.join()
t3.join()
t4.join()
```

If we run the code, we will get a result like this:

```
producer has loaded this: 92
consumer has used this: 92
consumer has used this: 0
producer has loaded this: 53
consumer has used this: 53
consumer has used this: 0
producer has loaded this: 62
consumer has used this: 62
producer has loaded this: 70
consumer has used this: 70
consumer has used this: 0
producer has loaded this: 7
consumer has used this: 7
producer has loaded this: 46
consumer has used this: 46
producer has loaded this: 30
producer has loaded this: 43
```

```
consumer has used this: 43
producer has loaded this: 36
producer has loaded this: 59
```

As we can see here, the behavior of the four threads is incorrect. It no longer has a synchronization in the use of the **shared** variable, with the loss of many values produced by the two **Producer** threads, and with the **Consumers** that are sometimes read as **0**, without waiting for a new value.

How to then solve this problem?

In these cases, the **Queue** comes to our aid.

By modifying the previous code, we remove the **shared** variable and replace it with a **Queue** that will be able to correctly manage the distribution between concurrent threads, whether it is a **Producer** or a **Consumer**.

```
from threading import Thread
from queue import Queue
import time
import random

queue = Queue()
shared = 1
count = 5

class Consumer(Thread):
  def __init__(self, count):
    Thread.__init__(self)
    self.count = count

  def run(self):
    global queue
    for i in range(self.count):
      local = queue.get()
      print("consumer has used this: %s" %local)
      queue.task_done()

class Producer(Thread):
  def __init__(self, count):
    Thread.__init__(self)
    self.count = count

  def request(self):
    time.sleep(1)
    return random.randint(0,100)

  def run(self):
    global queue
    for i in range(self.count):
      local = self.request()
      queue.put(local)
      print("producer has loaded this: %s" %local)

t1 = Producer(count)
t2 = Producer(count)
t3 = Consumer(count)
t4 = Consumer(count)
t1.start()
t2.start()
```

```
    t3.start()
    t4.start()
    t1.join()
    t2.join()
    t3.join()
    t4.join()
```

Running the code will give you the following result:

```
producer has loaded this: 31
producer has loaded this: 33
consumer has used this: 31
consumer has used this: 33
producer has loaded this: 11
consumer has used this: 11
producer has loaded this: 2
consumer has used this: 2
producer has loaded this: 27
consumer has used this: 27
producer has loaded this: 68
consumer has used this: 68
producer has loaded this: 92
consumer has used this: 92
producer has loaded this: 19
consumer has used this: 19
producer has loaded this: 87
consumer has used this: 87
producer has loaded this: 91
consumer has used this: 91
```

Now, the behavior is *correct*.

Conclusion

In this chapter, we have given a comprehensive overview of everything there is to learn about the tools provided by the **threading** module. We have seen how to define a set of threads within a program in different ways, either by calling functions, using subclasses, or inserting them into a **ThreadPoolExecutor**. We also investigated the different possible thread synchronization mechanisms and how they differ from each other. In any case, we have seen the unpredictable nature of thread behavior, and how easy it is to run into race condition problems.

In the next chapter, we will explore real parallel programming, which is expressed exclusively with processes in Python. We will also talk about the multiprocessing module provided by the standard Python library.

Points to Remember

- **Synchronization Methods**: These are indispensable when you want to use memory shared between multiple threads.
- **Over-Synchronization**: This suppresses the concurrent behavior of threads, executing them serially.

References

- https://realpython.com/python-with-statement/
- https://peps.python.org/pep-0343/
- https://en.wikipedia.org/wiki/Semaphore_(programming)
- https://www.meccanismocomplesso.org/i-thread-in-python-threading-parte-1/
- https://www.meccanismocomplesso.org/thread-in-python-lock-e-deadlock-parte-4/
- https://www.meccanismocomplesso.org/thread-in-python-il-modello-producer-consumer-parte-5/

CHAPTER 3
Parallel Programming with Processes

Introduction

In this chapter, we will work with parallel programming. In fact, it is only the processes that can run simultaneously in Python and brings the real benefits of parallel computing. In Python, there are *two* main approaches through which processes can be implemented in parallel programming: the multiprocessing module of the standard library and the **`mpi4py`** library, which extends the MPI *protocol* for Python. Multiprocessing implements the shared memory programming paradigm, where processes within the program can access a common memory area. As with threads, this approach would create race conditions and synchronization problems. To tackle this, we will introduce two communication channels between processes that are provided by the same multiprocessing module: **Queue** and **Pipe**. These will allow parallel processes to exchange data in perfect synchronization without encountering the problems associated with shared memory. The **`mpi4py`** library, on the other hand, is based on the message passing paradigm. In this model, there are no shared resources and all communication between processes takes place via the exchange of processes.

Structure

In this chapter, we will cover the following topics:

- Multiprocessing Module
- Process ID (PID)
- Process as Subclass
- Channels of Communication: Queue and Pipe
- Process Pool
- `ProcessPoolExecutor`
- Mpi4py Library
- Point-to-point Communication
- Collective Communication
- Topologies

Processes and the Multiprocessing Module

In Python, the real protagonists of parallel programming are processes. This is because are the only way to achieve true parallel execution of CPU-bound code. This limitation is due to the Global Interpreter Lock (GIL) in CPython, which prevents multiple threads from executing Python bytecode simultaneously. However, it is important to note that threads are very effective for I/O-bound tasks (such as file operations or network communication), since in these cases the GIL is released during I/O operations, which allows concurrent and even parallel progress for multiple threads.

Programming processes in Python is very important, so much so that we have a module completely dedicated to them in the standard library, which is known as **multiprocessing**.

This module offers all the possible operations for creating and managing processes within a program. It is akin to what the threading module does with threads. The instructions and constructs used in the implementation are almost identical:

- The **`Process()`** constructor allows the creation of a process.
- Calling the **`start()`** method starts the process activity.
- Calling the **`join()`** method causes the main process to wait until the specific process on which it is invoked has completed its execution. Therefore, if multiple processes have been launched in parallel, **`join()`** must be called individually on each of them (as shown in the exemplar code in this section) to ensure that all processes are completed before the program continues.

The process life cycle is based on three states:

- Ready
- Running
- Waiting

It is only then that the multiprocessing module structures parallel programming. The main process starts with the execution of the program. Within it, a number of processes are defined using the **`Process()`** constructor. At this point the processes just defined are in the *Ready* state. Then at a certain point, the part of the program is started for execution in parallel. All defined processes (children processes) will be activated together by calling the **`start()`** method for each of them. The **`main`** process, in this case also the parent process, will continue its execution asynchronously, and will not wait for the execution of the child processes (see *Figure* 3.1):

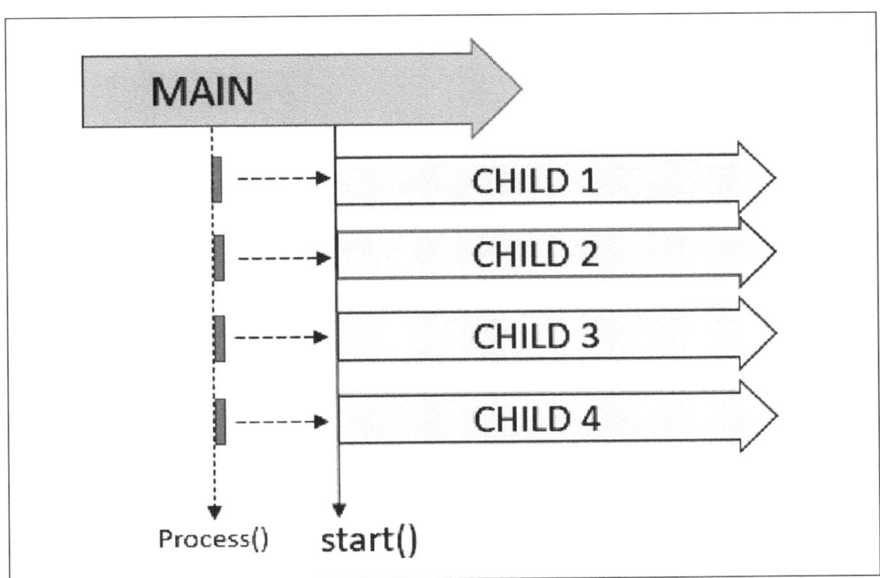

***Figure* 3.1**: *Asynchronous Mode Without Join()*

If instead, we want a synchronization mechanism, and would like the main process to wait for the result of the child processes, we will call the **`join()`** method for each process as shown in *Figure* 3.2:

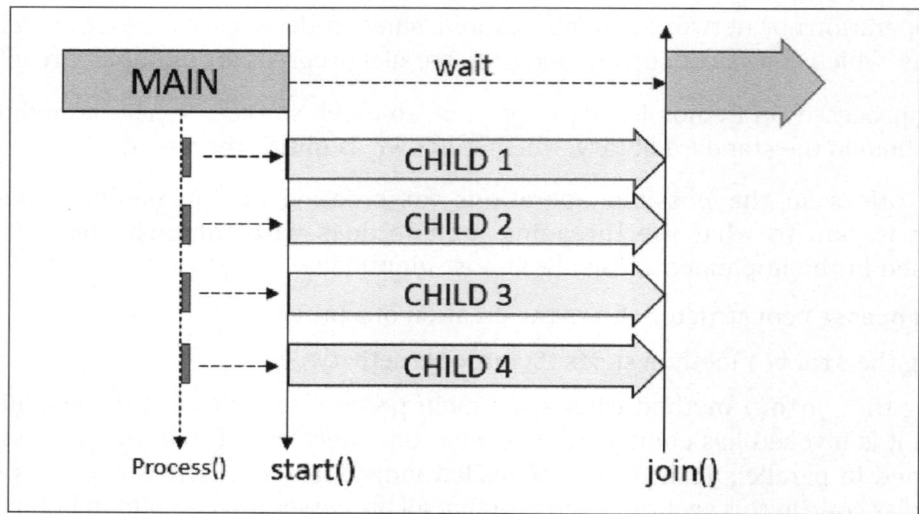

***Figure 3.2**: Synchronous Mode With Join()*

Like how we dealt with the threads of the threading module, we write the code with the processes. As you can see, the API design between threads and processes is consistent.

Each process that is activated in parallel will perform certain operations specified by the *target* function. The processes may all perform the same operation or each of the different operations. In fact, the **target** function is specified for every single process by passing its name as the target argument in the constructor.

To better understand these concepts, let us consider following code:

```
import multiprocessing
import time

def function(i):
  print ("start Process %i" %i)
  time.sleep(2)
  print ("end Process %i" %i)
  return

if __name__ == '__main__':
  p1 = multiprocessing.Process(target=function, args=(1,))
  p2 = multiprocessing.Process(target=function, args=(2,))
  p3 = multiprocessing.Process(target=function, args=(3,))
  p4 = multiprocessing.Process(target=function, args=(4,))
  p5 = multiprocessing.Process(target=function, args=(5,))
  p1.start()
  p2.start()
  p3.start()
  p4.start()
  p5.start()
  p1.join()
  p2.join()
  p3.join()
  p4.join()
  p5.join()
  print("END Program")
```

As we can see in the code, five processes are defined in parallel through the **Process()** constructor. They will all perform the same target function. If the function needs some arguments here, you can also pass them to the **Process()** constructor as a tuple to the **args** argument. In the code, we will pass a number that we need to identify the process running within the function. All these processes will be activated with the **start()** method and then synchronized with the main processes through the **join()** method.

After running the code, we will get the following:

```
start Process 1
start Process 2
start Process 3
start Process 4
start Process 5
end Process 1
end Process 2
end Process 4
end Process 3
end Process 5
END Program
```

The result is very similar to those obtained with threads and the threading module. However, in this case, the five processes have worked in parallel.

The way to implement the code in parallel as we did in the previous case is very *readable* as all the instructions are expressed individually and explicitly. Since we have to use five processes in parallel, we have defined five lines for the constructors, five lines to activate them with the start method, and five lines to synchronize them with the main process with the **join()** method. However, if the number of processes was more than in this code, implementing them could have been very problematic.

There are many more efficient constructs that take advantage of iterations and other mechanisms to generalize all the previous steps. An example of modifying the preceding code could be as follows:

```
import multiprocessing
import time

def function(i):
  print ("start Process %i" %i)
  time.sleep(2)
  print ("end Process %i" %i)
  return

if __name__ == '__main__':
  processes = []
  n_procs = 5

  for i in range(n_procs):
    p = multiprocessing.Process(target=function, args=(i,))
    processes.append(p)
    p.start()

  for i in range(n_procs):
    processes[i].join()

  print("END Program")
```

If you run the modified code, you will see that the result obtained remains unchanged.

Using Process IDs

In the previous case, we used the passage of the arguments within the **Process()** constructor to communicate the process number through the iterator **i**. There is another way to identify running processes among themselves, by means of their **Process ID** (**PID**). It is a very simple operation, we import the **os** module of the standard library that provides us with the **getpid()** function. The latter allows us to obtain the PID of each running process.

We apply the following changes to the previous code, replacing the numbers with the process ID, as follows:

```
import multiprocessing
import os
import time

def function():
  pid = os.getpid()
  print ("start Process %s" %pid)
  time.sleep(2)
  print ("end Process %s" %pid)
  return

if __name__ == '__main__':
  processes = []
  n_procs = 5

  for I in range(n_procs):
    p = multiprocessing.Process(target=function)
    processes.append(p)
    p.start()

  for i in range(n_procs):
    processes[i].join()

  print("END Program")
```

You can see that the **Process()** constructor no longer needs to use **args** as an argument, as the function itself will handle it. Inside it, there is the call to the **getpid()** function that will return the PID of the process in which it will be executed. We will get five different PIDs from the same function, without having to use arguments passed from the main process.

If we run the code, we will obtain the following result:

```
start Process 20644
start Process 20000
start Process 16240
start Process 1988
start Process 24388
end Process 20644
end Process 20000
end Process 16240
end Process 1988
end Process 24388
END Program
```

As we can see from the result, instead of progressive numbers, we have the PIDs that allow us to identify different processes running in parallel. These PIDs are the same as those recognized by the operating system. It will therefore be possible to monitor their progress from other tools or applications that monitor the consumption of resources or manage active processes, which is outside the scope of the Python interpreter.

Process Pool

A further evolution of the programming pattern to manage multiple processes together is to use a **process pool**, which is expressed in Python by **multiprocessing.Pool** class.

A **pool** is that object responsible for a certain number of processes. Through it you will have control of their status, from creation to use, and whether or not some of them should be paused to save computational resources. **multiprocessing.Pool** is an interface for the ad hoc execution of a specific task, while making use of a set of processes, without having to specify how many and which processes will have to perform this task. This allows us to simplify the code and make it more readable.

Let us take the previous code, and convert it this time using **multiprocessing.Pool**:

```
import multiprocessing
import time

def function(i):
  process = multiprocessing.current_process()
  print ("start Process %i(pid:%s)" %(i,process.pid))
  time.sleep(2)
  print ("end Process %i(pid:%s)" %(i,process.pid))
  return

if __name__ == '__main__':
  pool = multiprocessing.Pool()
  print("Processes started: %s" %pool._processes)
  for i in range(pool._processes):
    results = pool.apply(function, args=(i,))
  pool.close()

  print("END Program")
```

There are many changes within the code that we need to account for. First, we used the constructor of the class to define a process pool:

```
pool = multiprocessing.pool.Pool()
```

This will create a process pool that will use a number of worker processes that match the number of logical CPU cores in your system. This number is accessible in code via **pool._processes**. Then **pool.apply()** is used to make the pool execute a given task represented by the **function()** function, while passing it the number of the process generated via **args** as an argument. Once all the tasks required in the code have been performed, the pool will be closed using the **pool.close()** function.

As for the **function()** function, we have added the PID of the process, so that it can be recognized unambiguously. To obtain this value, first, the running process is obtained with **current_process()** and then the **pid** attribute is invoked on this.

After running the code, we will get this result:

```
Processes started: 12
start Process 0(pid:18196)
end Process 0(pid:18196)
start Process 1(pid:5300)
end Process 1(pid:5300)
```

```
start Process 2(pid:11984)
end Process 2(pid:11984)
start Process 3(pid:23436)
end Process 3(pid:23436)
start Process 4(pid:16224)
end Process 4(pid:16224)
start Process 5(pid:3784)
end Process 5(pid:3784)
start Process 6(pid:9196)
end Process 6(pid:9196)
start Process 7(pid:6248)
end Process 7(pid:6248)
start Process 8(pid:9272)
end Process 8(pid:9272)
start Process 9(pid:4168)
end Process 9(pid:4168)
start Process 10(pid:22676)
end Process 10(pid:22676)
start Process 11(pid:16500)
end Process 11(pid:16500)
END Program
```

As we can see from the result, the *first twelve workers* are created corresponding to the number of cores present on the computer from which the code is executed (this value can change from *computer* to *computer*). Each of them executes the called function, following the steps dictated by **for** iteration. As is evident from the result, the execution of each task takes place sequentially. We will see later how to make the most of the process pools by running them in parallel using the **map()** function.

Let us make a small change to better understand how the process pool works. During the invocation of **Pool()**, it is possible to determine a fixed number of processes inside the pool regardless of the cores present in the CPU. In the constructor, the number of processes that will become part of the pool is defined, using the **processes** parameter, as shown here:

```
pool = multiprocessing.Pool(processes=4)
```

We will make the appropriate changes to the previous code, replacing the definition of **Pool()** and leaving the **for** loop with twelve calls to the function. Within **function()**, we replace the term Process with the more correct term **Task**:

```
import multiprocessing
import time

def function(i):
  process = multiprocessing.current_process()
  print ("start Task %i(pid:%s)" %(i,process.pid))
  time.sleep(2)
  print ("end Task %i(pid:%s)" %(i,process.pid))
  return

if __name__ == '__main__':
  pool = multiprocessing.Pool(processes=4)
  print("Processes started: %s" %pool._processes)
  for i in range(12):
    results = pool.apply(function, args=(i,))
  pool.close()

  print("END Program")
```

So, in this case, we will have twelve tasks to be performed by only **4** processes. By executing the newly modified code, we will have a result similar to the following:

```
Processes started: 4
start Task 0(pid:5284)
end Task 0(pid:5284)
start Task 1(pid:2220)
end Task 1(pid:2220)
start Task 2(pid:15236)
end Task 2(pid:15236)
start Task 3(pid:4692)
end Task 3(pid:4692)
start Task 4(pid:5284)
end Task 4(pid:5284)
start Task 5(pid:2220)
end Task 5(pid:2220)
start Task 6(pid:15236)
end Task 6(pid:15236)
start Task 7(pid:4692)
end Task 7(pid:4692)
start Task 8(pid:5284)
end Task 8(pid:5284)
start Task 9(pid:2220)
end Task 9(pid:2220)
start Task 10(pid:15236)
end Task 10(pid:15236)
start Task 11(pid:4692)
end Task 11(pid:4692)
END Program
```

As we can see from the result, all twelve tasks are executed *sequentially* as in the previous case, but this time the four processes (workers) will take turns activating, and deactivating themselves to execute all the tasks.

Define Processes as Subclasses

So far, we have seen how to define in code the processes that will work in parallel via the **`Process()`** constructor. This was then assigned a target function containing the code to execute in *parallel*. Another way to implement the scheme of processes in parallel is to define the latter as subclasses of **`Process()`**. Within these, their functionality will then be specified by overriding the **`__init __()`** and **`run()`** methods. In this case, the code to run in parallel will be inserted into the **`run()`** method of the class.

Let us get a better understanding of this concept in a practical way, taking the following code as an example:

```
from multiprocessing import Process
import time
import random

class ChildProcess(Process):
  def __init__(self, count):
    Process.__init__(self)
    self.count = count

  def run(self):
    print ("start Process %s" %self.count)
    time.sleep(2)
```

```
        print ("end Process %s" %self.count)

if __name__ == '__main__':
    processes = []
    n_procs = 5

    for i in range(n_procs):
        p = ChildProcess(i)
        processes.append(p)
        p.start()

    for i in range(n_procs):
        processes[i].join()
```

As we can see from the code, we define a subclass of **Process()** which we have called **ChildProcess()**. Within the class, we have *two* overridden methods. In **__init __()**, we will define the attributes of the subclass to be added, as in this case, the **count** argument is passed to the constructor. While in the **run()** method, we will insert the code that was present in the target function.

Running the code, we will get the following result:

```
start Process 0
start Process 1
start Process 2
start Process 3
start Process 4
end Process 0
end Process 1
end Process 2
end Process 4
end Process 3
```

Channels of Communication between Processes

Processes, unlike *threads*, generally do not share a memory space, and therefore need a different mechanism to be able to communicate with each other and exchange data. The multiprocessing module, however, is based on a *shared memory paradigm*, and allows users to share resources between processes. Since this practice leads to the same problems we encountered, while dealing with threads with race condition phenomena and lack of synchronization between processes, it is not recommended to use it. The multiprocessing module provides like the *threading* module the same tools for process synchronization, such as **semaphores**, **locks**, **events**, and so on, but it is not recommended to follow this approach. Unlike threads, to work with a set of processes in parallel, the multiprocessing module provides communication channels to be used as secure and synchronized data exchange mechanisms. There are two different modes of communication channels:

- Queues
- Pipes

These channels are defined within the code through the **Queue** and **Pipe** classes provided by the multiprocessing module. Both are equipped with **Queue()** and **Pipe()** constructors, and a whole series of methods that manage the exchange of data between processes and their internal synchronization mechanisms. These communication channels, once defined at the main process level, are excellent tools for exchanging data in a perfectly synchronized manner. In fact, thanks to them, the processes will be able to send and receive data in a *safe* and *synchronized* way, without the risk of race conditions. Furthermore, if the data sent is more than requested, these will not be overwritten, but accumulated within these objects, and provide for the buffering of data.

The Queues

The **Queues** that we will use as a communication channel between the processes are implemented by the *multiprocessing* module. In Python, there are queues belonging to the queue module (which we have already used with threads). But in reality, the internal implementations are different and **multiprocessing.Queue** uses a different data transfer mechanism which is specific to working with processes. In other words, they use the *message passing paradigm* exclusively for processes, and avoid using synchronization mechanisms to add to the queues.

Queue is a data structure that implements a **First IN-First OUT** (**FIFO**) queue. Processes will be able to add data to the queue through the **put()** method or receive data from it through the **get()** method. The order of the data entered is maintained within the queue and the data sent to the processes that request them will then follow the order of entry.

The data can be accumulated within the queue, which can store both simple numerical values and complex objects. By default, the **Queue()** constructor sets **maxsize=0**, which means the queue has no logical size limit. However, the actual capacity is still constrained by the system's available memory. If you wish, you can specify a capacity limit by passing a positive integer to the **maxsize** parameter, which represents the maximum number of objects the queue can contain.

```
queue = multiprocessing.Queue(maxsize=100)
```

In the context of the capacity of a queue, it is important to know the current number of objects contained within it during execution. For this purpose, there is a **qsize()** method which returns this number:

```
size = queue.qsize()
```

Still, in the context of managing a queue when you want to affix conditions to the program flow, it might be useful to know if a queue is empty or full. The **empty()** method returns a Boolean that has the value *True* when the queue is *empty*, while the **full()** method returns *True* if the queue is *full*. This is demonstrated as follows:

```
if queue.empty():
    ...

if queue.full():
    ...
```

In order to better understand how a queue works, we can use the *consumer-producer paradigm*, which is useful while sending and receiving data. The *producer* can be any process that will provide data after its execution and the consumer can be any process that will need that data in order to complete its execution. To make this mechanism work, which is created by at least two processes, an exchange of data will be necessary. Since the processes do not have a common memory area, they will exchange their data through the queue. The *consumer* will send the produced data to the queue, while the *consumer* will request them from the *producer*. *Consumers* and *producers* are always *asynchronous* as they usually do not depend except for the data flow that happens via the queue. Since the times of the consumer and producer rarely coincide, there may be cases in which the *producer* produces *consumer* data faster, and these can be accumulated in an orderly manner within the queue, without being overwritten. The *consumer* will thus have plenty of time to use this produced data in an orderly manner.

The following code implements a simple *producer-consumer paradigm* which is based on two parallel processes that use a queue to exchange data:

```
from multiprocessing import Process, Queue
import time
import random
```

```
class Consumer(Process):
  def __init__(self, count, queue):
    Process.__init__(self)
    self.count = count
    self.queue = queue

  def run(self):
    for i in range(self.count):
      local = self.queue.get()
      time.sleep(2)
      print("consumer has used this: %s" %local)

class Producer(Process):
  def __init__(self, count, queue):
    Process.__init__(self)
    self.count = count
    self.queue = queue

  def request(self):
    time.sleep(1)
    return random.randint(0,100)

  def run(self):
    for i in range(self.count):
      local = self.request()
      self.queue.put(local)
      print("producer has loaded this: %s" %local)

if __name__ == '__main__':
  queue = Queue()
  count = 5
  p1 = Producer(count, queue)
  p2 = Consumer(count, queue)
  p1.start()
  p2.start()
  p1.join()
  p2.join()
```

Running the code will produce the following result:

```
producer has loaded this: 55
producer has loaded this: 30
consumer has used this: 55
producer has loaded this: 60
producer has loaded this: 14
consumer has used this: 30
producer has loaded this: 97
consumer has used this: 60
consumer has used this: 14
consumer has used this: 97
```

As we can see, the values generated by the producer process are accumulated within the queue and subsequently used by the consumer process in perfect synchrony, without losing or overwriting of values.

Pipes

The other class that performs the functions of the communication channel between processes is the **Pipe**. The pipe implements *two-way communication* between the two processes and is designed to send and receive data between them. Like the queue class, it has its own **Pipe()** constructor which will create two different **multiprocessing.connection.Connection** objects when it is declared. So, when you declare the **Pipe()** constructor, you put the two instances of the connections separately:

```
conn1, conn2 = multiprocessing.Pipe()
```

With **duplex=True** (the default), both ends of the pipe are full-duplex; each connection can be used to both send and receive data. In practice, it is often convenient to adopt a convention (for example, using one end primarily for sending and the other for receiving), but this is not enforced by Python.

In addition to the *bidirectional mode*, a pipe can also be created in *duplex mode*, in which each of the two connections can be used to both send and receive data. In this case, we will have to set the duplex argument passed in the constructor to **True**:

```
conn1, conn2 = multiprocessing.Pipe(duplex=True)
```

In both modes, the processes, through the two generated *Connection* objects, will be able to send data through the **send()** method and receive them through the **recv()** method:

```
conn2.send(object)
object = conn1.recv()
```

As for the queues, there is no limit to the size of the objects to be sent; the only condition is that they are *pickable*. When sent, they will be picked, and then upon being received, they will automatically be unpicked.

As with the Queue, the **Pipe** class also provides a set of methods that manage the connections that were created for their use. For example, the state of the pipe can be controlled by the **poll()** function. This function returns a *Boolean*: *True* if there is data in the connection waiting to be received by a process. This method is very useful in conditions to manage the flow of execution of a program and is shown as follows:

```
if conn1.poll():
```

Let us see the concepts just exposed through an example code, like the following one:

```
from multiprocessing import Process, Pipe
import time
import random

class Consumer(Process):
  def __init__(self, count, conn):
    Process.__init__(self)
    self.count = count
    self.conn = conn

  def run(self):
    for i in range(self.count):
      local = self.conn.recv()
      time.sleep(2)
      print("consumer has used this: %s" %local)

class Producer(Process):
  def __init__(self, count, conn):
    Process.__init__(self)
    self.count = count
    self.conn = conn
```

```
    def request(self):
      time.sleep(1)
      return random.randint(0,100)

    def run(self):
      for i in range(self.count):
        local = self.request()
        self.conn.send(local)
        print("producer has loaded this: %s" %local)

if __name__ == '__main__':
    recver, sender = Pipe()
    count = 5
    p1 = Producer(count, sender)
    p2 = Consumer(count, recver)
    p1.start()
    p2.start()
    p1.join()
    p2.join()
    recver.close()
    sender.close()
```

Also, in this case, we used the *producer-consumer paradigm*, and retained the code used with the queue previously. This is to help the reader make appropriate comparisons between the two modes. After running the code, you will get the following result:

```
producer has loaded this: 0
producer has loaded this: 76
consumer has used this: 0
producer has loaded this: 28
producer has loaded this: 90
consumer has used this: 76
producer has loaded this: 75
consumer has used this: 28
consumer has used this: 90
consumer has used this: 75
```

At the end of using the pipe, we called the **close()** method for each of the two connections. This operation is important to release all the resources used by the pipe.

The most important, and perhaps, the most limiting aspect of pipes is that they work exclusively between two endpoints, and therefore between only two processes. If you have to work with several processes at the same time, you will need to establish a pipe for each pair. It is clear that when there are several processes that work in parallel, managing pipes will become *problematic*.

Pipe versus Queue

We have just seen that as communication channels, the multiprocessing module provides both *pipes* and *queues* as a solution. So, *which of the two should we choose to exchange data between processes in parallel?*

At the first glance, given the limited use of Pipes between only two processes, it would seem that a queue is always the best solution. But that is not necessarily *true*.

Pipe is a much simpler class than a queue. They are implemented at a low level and it is this feature that makes them more efficient and potentially faster for exchanging data between two processes. Therefore, if this type of connection can be used between pairs of processes, it is preferable to a queue. If, on the other hand, the data exchange is consistent and the number of processes involved in this exchange is large, queue is the more appropriate option.

Mapping of a Function through a Process Pool

Another important aspect of parallel programming is the mapping of a function. In fact, it is possible to extend the functionality of **map()** in Python between multiple processes in parallel. This function is useful when you want to apply a function on an **iterable** object. The **map()** function applies the function to each element of the object and returns an array of elements of *equal size*, where each bears the result of the function.

To better understand how the **map()** function works, consider the following code:

```
import time
import math
import numpy as np

def func(value):
    result = math.sqrt(value)
    print("The value %s and the elaboration is %s" %(value, result) )
    return result

if __name__ == '__main__':
   data = np.array([10,3,6,1])
   results = map(func, data)
   for result in results:
      print("This is the result: %s" %result)
```

In the code, we have chosen a **NumPy** array of four elements on which we will apply the function **func()**. As a result, we will get an array of four elements, each with the return value of the function applied to the corresponding element.

After running the code, we will obtain the following:

```
The value 10 and the elaboration is 3.1622776601683795
This is the result: 3.1622776601683795
The value 3 and the elaboration is 1.7320508075688772
This is the result: 1.7320508075688772
The value 6 and the elaboration is 2.449489742783178
This is the result: 2.449489742783178
The value 1 and the elaboration is 1.0
This is the result: 1.0
```

This **iterable** object mapping mechanism can be extended in parallel programming. The efficiency can grow enormously if the calculation of the function on each element takes place in parallel. For example, each element can be assigned to a process whose target is just the function passed in **map()**. In this case, all elements would be calculated at the same time. For an array of n elements, a normal program would take $n * t$ time, where t is the execution time of the function. In the parallel case, the same array of n elements would be passed to n processes, and the execution time would be limited to t (if there are n cores or n processors in the system). Therefore, the increase in efficiency is clear.

For parallel mapping of a function, the multiprocessing module provides the **multiprocessing.pool.Pool** class. This class provides two methods for this:

- **map()**
- **map_async()**

In the case of parallel programming, there are *two* methods that exist because of the different synchronizations that are possible. They both work similarly, except that the **map()** function should be used when we need to block program execution until all target functions in *parallel* have completed their work. The **map_async()** function should be used when it does not block the entire execution of the program.

The **map()** method receives two arguments, the **target** function, and the **iterable** object, which is as follows:

```
results = pool.map(target, iterable):
```

As the name implies, the **pool** class will create a pool of processes equal to the number of elements of the **iterable** and will pass the **target** function to these processes.

However, to better understand these concepts and how they work, it is necessary to move on to practical examples like this code here:

```
import time
import math
import numpy as np
from multiprocessing.pool import Pool

def func(value):
    result = math.sqrt(value)
    print("The value %s and the elaboration is %s" %(value, result) )
    time.sleep(value)
    return result

if __name__ == '__main__':
    with Pool() as pool:
        data = np.array([10,3,6,1])
        results = pool.map(func, data)
        print("The main process is going on...")
        for result in results:
            print("This is the result: %s" %result)
    print("END Program")
```

This program will generate the following result:

```
The value 10 and the elaboration is 3.1622776601683795
The value 3 and the elaboration is 1.7320508075688772
The value 6 and the elaboration is 2.449489742783178
The value 1 and the elaboration is 1.0
The main process is going on...
This is the result: 3.1622776601683795
This is the result: 1.7320508075688772
This is the result: 2.449489742783178
This is the result: 1.0
END Program
```

As for the **map_async()** function, we can modify the previous code by making the appropriate substitutions as in the following code:

```
import time
import math
import numpy as np
from multiprocessing.pool import Pool

def func(value):
    result = math.sqrt(value)
    print("The value %s and the elaboration is %s" %(value, result) )
    time.sleep(value)
```

```
    return result

if __name__ == '__main__':
    with Pool() as pool:
        data = np.array([10,3,6,1])
        results = pool.map_async(func, data)
        print("Main Process is going on...")
        for result in results.get():
            print("This is the result: %s" %result)
    print("END Program")
```

This program will generate the following result:

```
Main Process is going on...
The value 10 and the elaboration is 3.1622776601683795
The value 3 and the elaboration is 1.7320508075688772
The value 6 and the elaboration is 2.449489742783178
The value 1 and the elaboration is 1.0
This is the result: 3.1622776601683795
This is the result: 1.7320508075688772
This is the result: 2.449489742783178
This is the result: 1.0
END Program
```

As we can see from the two different results, we got the behavior we expected. Using the **map()** method, you have a synchronization mechanism that interrupts the flow of execution of the **main** process. This does not restart until all parallel processes launched by **map()** finish their execution. In fact, the text **Main process is going on...** appears only after all *child* processes have finished their task and returned their results. While using **map_async()**, the execution of the **main** process goes on and does not wait for the complete evaluation of results. The text **Main process is going on...** appears at the beginning of the text.

Mapping in Parallel with Chunksize

The **map()** function will apply a function to each element in an **iterable**. If the **iterable** has a large number of elements, it may be very inefficient to call as many processes to execute them.

A more efficient approach is to divide the elements of the **iterable** into portions of a certain number of elements, where each is assigned to a process. This can be achieved by passing the **chunksize** argument to the **map()** function.

Let us modify the example code we used earlier for the **map()** method, while increasing the number of elements in the **np.array()**. We will then set portions of four elements of the array for each process, passing the **chunksize** argument equal to **4** to the **map()** method.

```
import time
import math
import numpy as np
from multiprocessing.pool import Pool

def func(value):
    result = math.sqrt(value)
    print("The value %s and the elaboration is %s" %(value, result) )
    time.sleep(value)
    return result

if __name__ == '__main__':
    with Pool() as pool:
```

```
        data = np.array([10,3,6,1,4,5,2,9,7,3,4,6])
        results = pool.map(func, data, chunksize=4)
        print("The main process is going on...")
        for result in results:
            print("This is the result: %s" %result)
    print("END Program")
```

This code will generate the following result:

```
The value 10 and the elaboration is 3.1622776601683795
The value 4 and the elaboration is 2.0
The value 7 and the elaboration is 2.6457513110645907
The value 5 and the elaboration is 2.23606797749979
The value 3 and the elaboration is 1.7320508075688772
The value 2 and the elaboration is 1.4142135623730951
The value 3 and the elaboration is 1.7320508075688772
The value 4 and the elaboration is 2.0
The value 9 and the elaboration is 3.0
The value 6 and the elaboration is 2.449489742783178
The value 6 and the elaboration is 2.449489742783178
The value 1 and the elaboration is 1.0
The main process is going on...
This is the result: 3.1622776601683795
This is the result: 1.7320508075688772
This is the result: 2.449489742783178
This is the result: 1.0
This is the result: 2.0
This is the result: 2.23606797749979
This is the result: 1.4142135623730951
This is the result: 3.0
This is the result: 2.6457513110645907
This is the result: 1.7320508075688772
This is the result: 2.0
This is the result: 2.449489742783178
END Program
```

In addition to the **map()** function, the **Pool** class provides a whole series of methods with similar behavior, such as **imap()** and **apply()**, which will also be seen in the asynchronous versions.

The ProcessPoolExecutor

We have a similar mechanism to that of process pools with another class, the **ProcessPoolExecutor,** which is distributed by the **concurrent.future** module. This class also provides a pool of reusable processes to perform specific operations, including **map()**.

Also, in this case, you will specify the name of the **target** function to execute and the **iterable** on which the function will be applied. Once all the assigned tasks have been completed, the **ProcessPoolExecutor** must be closed in order to release all the resources used. The **shutdown()** function is used for closing.

But even in this case, there are simpler and more efficient constructs that can be used. In fact, the **ProcessPoolExecutor** is compatible with the context manager and the **with** declaration as shown here:

```
with ProcessPoolExecutor() as executor:
```

In this case, when execution exits the context manager block, the **shutdown()** function is called automatically. The context manager is equivalent to the following:

```
try:
   executor = ProcessPoolExecutor()
finally:
   executor.shutdown()
```

It is therefore clear that the use of a context manager is very convenient in these cases. The **ProcessPoolExecutor** is thus useful for running the **map()** function in *parallel*. We can see it in the following code:

```
import time
import math
import numpy as np
from concurrent.futures import ProcessPoolExecutor

def func(value):
    result = math.sqrt(value)
    print("The value %s and the elaboration is %s" %(value, result) )
    time.sleep(value)
    return result

if __name__ == '__main__':
    with ProcessPoolExecutor(10) as executor:
        data = np.array([10,3,6,1])
        for result in executor.map(func, data):
           print("This is the result: %s" %result)
    print("END Program")
```

This code will generate the following result:

```
The value 10 and the elaboration is 3.1622776601683795
The value 3 and the elaboration is 1.7320508075688772
The value 6 and the elaboration is 2.449489742783178
The value 1 and the elaboration is 1.0
This is the result: 3.1622776601683795
This is the result: 1.7320508075688772
This is the result: 2.449489742783178
This is the result: 1.0
END Program
```

Previously, we saw the **map()** method of **Pool(),** which offered the possibility of using portions of multiple elements to be assigned to each process due to the **chunksize** argument. However, the **map()** method takes the same argument in the case of the **ProcessPoolExecutor**.

We then modify the previous code by extending the number of elements in the **np.array()** and adding the **chunksize** argument equal to **4**. To recognize which process treats the different elements of the **np.array,** we will import the **os** module, which uses the **getpid()** to get the ID of the various processes, as shown here:

```
import time
import math
import os
import numpy as np
from concurrent.futures import ProcessPoolExecutor

def func(value):
    result = math.sqrt(value)
```

```
    pid = os.getpid()
    print("[Pid:%s] The value %s and the elaboration is %s" %(pid, value,
result) )
    time.sleep(value)
    return result

if __name__ == '__main__':
    with ProcessPoolExecutor(10) as executor:
        data = np.array([10,3,6,1,4,5,2,9,7,3,4,6])
        for result in executor.map(func, data, chunksize=4):
           print("This is the result: %s" %result)
    print("END Program")
```

This code will generate the following result:

```
[Pid:14716] The value 10 and the elaboration is 3.1622776601683795
[Pid:22496] The value 4 and the elaboration is 2.0
[Pid:6508] The value 7 and the elaboration is 2.6457513110645907
[Pid:22496] The value 5 and the elaboration is 2.23606797749979
[Pid:6508] The value 3 and the elaboration is 1.7320508075688772
[Pid:22496] The value 2 and the elaboration is 1.4142135623730951
[Pid:14716] The value 3 and the elaboration is 1.7320508075688772
[Pid:6508] The value 4 and the elaboration is 2.0
[Pid:22496] The value 9 and the elaboration is 3.0
[Pid:14716] The value 6 and the elaboration is 2.449489742783178
[Pid:6508] The value 6 and the elaboration is 2.449489742783178
[Pid:14716] The value 1 and the elaboration is 1.0
This is the result: 3.1622776601683795
This is the result: 1.7320508075688772
This is the result: 2.449489742783178
This is the result: 1.0
This is the result: 2.0
This is the result: 2.23606797749979
This is the result: 1.4142135623730951
This is the result: 3.0
This is the result: 2.6457513110645907
This is the result: 1.7320508075688772
This is the result: 2.0
This is the result: 2.449489742783178
END Program
```

The `mpi4py` Library

A completely different approach to parallel programming in Python using processes is using the **Message Passage Interface (MPI)**. This is a *communication protocol* which is standard for parallel programming and is particularly useful in systems with multiple nodes (multiple processors). This protocol has been implemented in many programming languages such as Fortran and C.

Python also has a number of MPI modules useful for parallel programming. The most interesting of these is the **mpi4py** library. This was developed based on the MPI-1/2 *specification* and provides an object-oriented interface based on MPI-2 C ++ *bindings*.

This library is based on general concepts that are very different from those used in the multiprocessing module and with the standard Python library. These concepts are based on standards developed specifically for multiprocessor and distributed architectures, as well as clusters. It is therefore clear that the execution methods and the code constructs are very different from those seen in the first part of the chapter.

But, *why should one use MPI modules instead of the multiprocessing module?* This is due to many factors. The first is because MPI has practically become a standard of parallel programming for many programming languages, including Python, and is adaptable to the most varied architectures. At the same time, it can also be used on simple systems with a single multi-core computer, where the efficiency of the calculation is not so evident. However, it is useful for practicing and developing programs in parallel and can be adapted to very complex architectures.

First, you need to install the **mpi4py** library. For Anaconda, run the command:

```
conda install mpi4py
```

If you are using Python, you will use **pip**:

```
pip install mpi4py
```

Installing the Python module alone is not enough to work with this library. In order to work, it requires an MPI implementation such as MPICH, Open MPI, or Microsoft-MPI. So, you will need to download one of these implementations and then install it on your system.

For Windows: Download and Install Microsoft MPI (MS-MPI).

For Linux and MacOS: Download MPICH or OpenMPI.

On Ubuntu:

```
sudo apt update
sudo apt install mpich
```

On MacOS:

```
brew install mpich
```

For the execution of programs in Python, instead of the classic **python** command, you will have to use the following wording from the shell:

```
mpiexec -n x python mpi4py _name.py
```

Add **mpiexec** to your PATH if it is not already there to run it directly from your current working directory. The **mpiexec** command is typically used to directly start multiple processes in parallel, where **x** is the number of processes running in parallel.

To see how the library works, let us start with the simplest program you can run with **mpiexec**:

```
from mpi4py import MPI
comm = MPI.COMM_WORLD
rank = comm.rank
print("The process %d is started" %rank)
```

To execute the code, we will have to use the **mpiexec** command. If you want to start **2** processes in parallel, use this:

```
$ mpiexec -n 2 python mpi01.py
```

We will get the output of the two processes that looks like:

```
The process 0 is started
The process 1 is started
```

If, on the other hand, we want to start **6** in parallel, it will be sufficient to modify the value of the parameter **n** passed on the command line, as demonstrated here:

```
$ mpiexec -n 6 python mpi01a.py
```

This will generate the following:

```
The process 2 is started
The process 5 is started
The process 1 is started
```

```
The process 4 is started
The process 3 is started
The process 0 is started
```

As we can see from the outputs, the rank order of the processes is not *ordered* but is a random result that varies from execution to execution. While analyzing the code, the **comm** parameter expresses the communicator, and defines the group of processes that can communicate through the *message passing mechanism*:

```
comm = MPI.COMM_WORLD
```

Here, the rank is the identification number of the process within a group of communicating processes. That is, all the processes launched by the **mpiexec** command become part of this communication group, and each of them is identified by a *rank*.

Parallelism of the Processes

As we have seen for the *multiprocessing* module, the processes allow the execution of the code in parallel. We can perform the same tests with the **mpi4py** library. This time, we will perform benchmarking by measuring the execution times. For this purpose, we launch a program:

```
import time
from mpi4py import MPI
comm = MPI.COMM_WORLD
rank = comm.rank
print("The process %d is started" %rank)
time.sleep(10)
print("The process %d is ended" %rank)
```

To measure the time taken with the **mpiexec** command, we cannot use the **time** module, but we can use the **time** command on Linux as follows:

```
time mpiexec -n 4 python3 mpi01b.py
```

Instead on Windows PowerShell, you can do the same thing by running the following command:

```
> Measure-Command { mpiexec -n 4 python mpi01b.py | Out-Host }
```

In both cases, we will get the following result:

```
The process 2 is started
The process 2 is ended
The process 3 is started
The process 3 is ended
The process 1 is started
The process 1 is ended
The process 0 is started
The process 0 is ended

Days              : 0
Hours             : 0
Minutes           : 0
Seconds           : 10
Milliseconds      : 298
Ticks             : 102985516
TotalDays         : 0,000119196199074074
TotalHours        : 0,00286070877777778
TotalMinutes      : 0,171642526666667
TotalSeconds      : 10,2985516
TotalMilliseconds : 10298,5516
```

As we can see, the execution takes about **10** seconds, which is the expected time for the execution of each process. The sequential version of the previous program results in the following code:

```
import time

for i in range(4):
      print("The process %d is started" %i)
      time.sleep(10)
      print("The process %d is ended" %i)
```

We measure the time taken to run the previous program again via PowerShell with the **Measure-Command** command (although we could have used the **time** module):

```
> Measure-Command { python mpi01c.py }

Days              : 0
Hours             : 0
Minutes           : 0
Seconds           : 40
Milliseconds      : 99
Ticks             : 400994538
TotalDays         : 0,000464114048611111
TotalHours        : 0,0111387371666667
TotalMinutes      : 0,66832423
TotalSeconds      : 40,0994538
TotalMilliseconds : 40099,4538
```

As we can see, it takes **40** seconds from a sequential execution (four executions of **10** seconds each), compared to about **10** seconds for four executions (four processes) in parallel. We observe a significant increase in efficiency here.

Efficiency of Parallelism Based on the Number of processors/cores

As for the efficiency of *parallelism* based on the number of processors or cores, different time measurements can be made by varying the number of parallel processes. We will use the following code:

```
import time
from mpi4py import MPI
comm = MPI.COMM_WORLD
rank = comm.rank
print("The process %d is started" %rank)
n = 0
for i in range(100000000):
   n += i
print("The process %d is ended" %rank)
```

We will execute the code with **mpiexec** by varying the number of processors. Measurements are obtained as shown in *Table 3.1*. In the first column, we have the number of processes launched in parallel. In the second column, we have the measured times related to the number of processes.

N	**t**	**s**
1	10,7	10,7
2	13,8	6,9
4	16,0	4

6	19,9	3,317
8	27,6	3,45
12	39,6	3,3

Table 3.1: *Execution Times Depending on the Number of Processes*

However, what interests us is the ratio s = t / N, that is, the execution time for the task to be performed for each process. As you can see, this value progressively decreases as the number of processes increases. However, the value leans towards a threshold beyond which it does not drop further, of about 3.3s. This is much more visible in the following figure (see *Figure* 3.3):

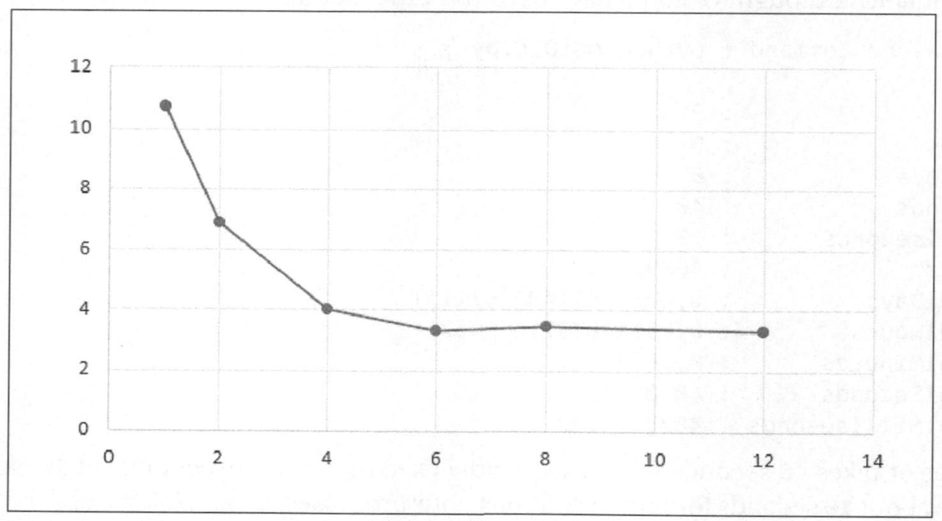

Figure 3.3: *Time Taken Based on the Number of Processes*

From *Figure* 3.3, it can be seen that over six processes, the time taken for each task remains almost the same. This happens because this system has six cores and it is not possible to work in parallel beyond the capacity.

Main Applications of mpi4py

The **mpi4py** library is based on the message passing according to MPI standards. Its applications in the world of parallel programming can be divided into three different groups:

- Point-to-Point Communication
- Collective Communication
- Topologies

In the second half of the chapter, we will look at these applications through a series of examples.

Point-to-Point Communication Implementation

Point-to-point operations consist of an exchange of messages between two processes. In a perfect world, each sending operation should be perfectly synchronized with the respective receiving operation. Obviously, this is not the case, and the MPI implementation must be able to preserve the data sent even when the sending process and the receiving process are not synchronized. Typically, a buffer is used, which is transparent to the developer and entirely managed by the **mpi4py** library.

The **mpi4py** module enables point-to-point communication through *two* functions:

- **`comm.send(data, receiver_process)`**

- **`comm.recv(sender_process)`**

The **`send()`** function sends data to the receiving process through its rank in the communication group. The **`recv()`** function receives data from the sending process, which is also identified by its communication group rank number as demonstrated here:

```
from mpi4py import MPI
comm = MPI.COMM_WORLD
rank = comm.rank
print("Process %s started" %rank)
if rank==0:
    msg = "This is the message"
    receiver = 1
    comm.send(msg, dest=receiver)
    print("Process 0 sent a message to %d" %receiver + ": %s" %msg)
elif rank==1:
    source = 0
    msg = comm.recv(source=source)
    print("Process 1 received a message from %d" %source + ": %s" %msg)
```

You will run the preceding code in parallel by running the following shell command:

```
$ mpiexec -n 9 python programma01.py
```

This will generate a result, where the **`send()`** and **`recv()`** methods are blocking, that is, they block the calling process until the buffered data can be used safely.

Collective Communications

The most commonly used collective communications include the following:

- Barrier Synchronization
- Broadcasting Data
- Gathering Data
- Scattering Data
- Reduction Operation

Collective Communication Using Data Broadcast

During parallel programming, we might find ourselves in a situation where it is necessary to share the value of a certain variable at runtime among several processes or to distribute different operations on variables, to which each process provides a partial solution. To solve this kind of situation, tree communication groups are used (for example, *process* 0 sends data to *processes* 1 and 2, which in turn will send it to *processes* 3,4,5,6...*and so on*).

A method of communication that involves all the processes that belong to a communicator is called **collective communication**. Consequently, collective communication is based on more than two processes. In this case, we can call it *broadcast*, where a single process sends the same data to the processes (see *Figure* 3.4).

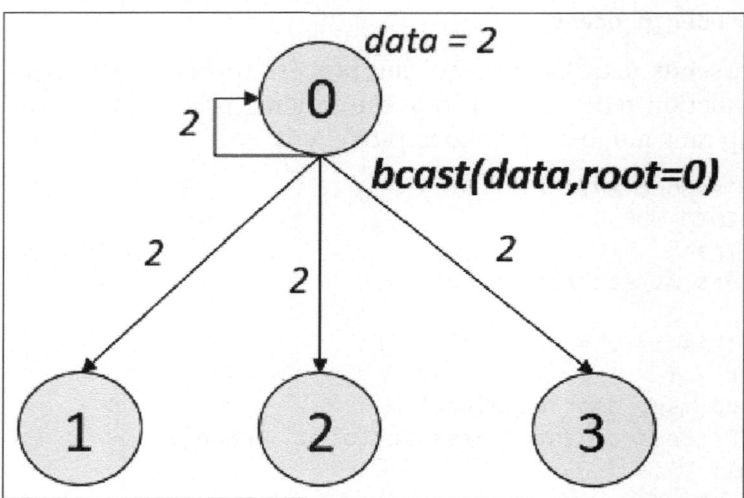

Figure 3.4: *Broadcasting*

This will read the data defined in *process* 0 defined as *root* and then it will distribute it among all processes, including the *root* process itself:

```
from mpi4py import MPI
from mpi4py import MPI
import random
comm = MPI.COMM_WORLD
rank = comm.rank
if rank == 0:
    data = random.randint(1, 10)
else:
    data=None
data = comm.bcast(data, root=0)
if rank == 1:
    print("The square of %d is %d" %(data, data*data))
elif rank == 2:
    print("Half of %d is %d" %(data, data/2))
elif rank == 3:
    print("Double of %d is %d" %(data, data*2))
```

This code will generate the following result:

```
$mpiexec -n 4 python mpi04a.py
The square of 6 is 36
Half of 6 is 3
Double of 6 is 12
```

Collective Communication Using Data Scattering

The scattering functionality is very similar to that of broadcast, but is slightly different. While **`comm.bcast()`** sends the same type of data to all listening processes, **`comm.scatter()`** sends portions of data in an array to different processes (see *Figure* 3.5).

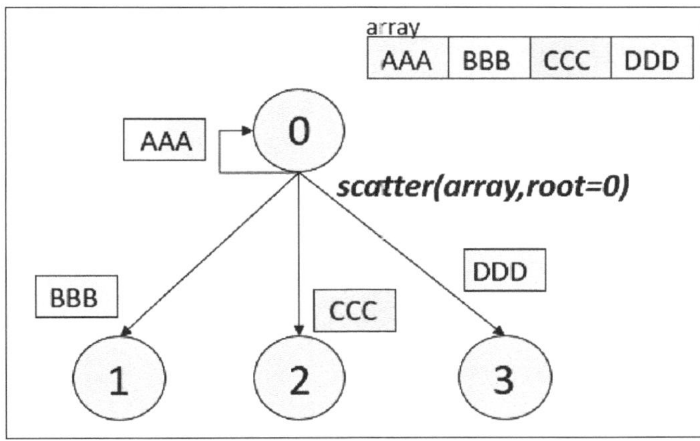

Figure 3.5: *Scattering*

The **`comm.scatter()`** function takes the elements of the array and distributes them among the processes based on their rank; so, the first element will be sent to *process* 0, the second element to *process* 1, and so on:

```
from mpi4py import MPI
comm = MPI.COMM_WORLD
rank = comm.rank
if rank == 0:
   array = ['AAA','BBB','CCC','DDD']
else:
   array = None
data = comm.scatter(array,root=0)
print("Process %d is working on %s element" %(rank,data))
```

This code will generate the following result:

```
$mpiexec -n 4 python mpi05a.py
Process 0 is working on AAA element
Process 1 is working on BBB element
Process 2 is working on CCC element
Process 3 is working on DDD element
```

Collective Communication Using Data Gathering

The gathering function performs the inverse operation of scattering. In this case, all the processes involved in the calculation send their portions of data to a receiving *root* process that collects them at once (see *Figure* 3.6).

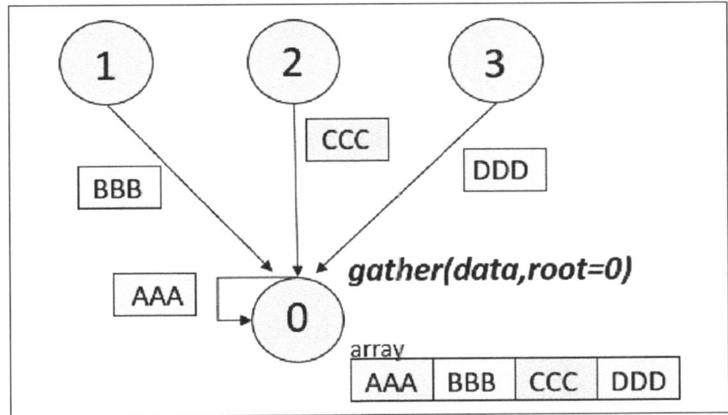

Figure 3.6: *Gathering*

```
from mpi4py import MPI
comm = MPI.COMM_WORLD
rank = comm.rank
if rank == 0:
    data = 'AAA'
elif rank == 1:
    data = 'BBB'
elif rank == 2:
    data = 'CCC'
elif rank == 3:
    data = 'DDD'
array = comm.gather(data, root=0)
if rank == 0:
    print("The new array is %s " %array)
```

This code will generate the following result:

```
$mpiexec -n 4 python mpi06a.py
The new array is ['AAA', 'BBB', 'CCC', 'DDD']
```

This method of passing messages can be useful for parallel computing. Many algorithms rely on calculations that can be broken down into *smaller identical chunks*. By assigning each of them to a parallel process, you can effectively reduce execution times. At the end of the calculation, many partial results will be obtained which will all be added together to give a final result.

Let us take a simple example to see how this concept fits well with collective communication with gathering:

```
from mpi4py import MPI
comm = MPI.COMM_WORLD
rank = comm.rank
size = comm.size
data = 2*rank + 1
print("Process %d calculated this value: %d" %(rank,data))
array = comm.gather(data, root=0)
if rank == 0:
   result = 0
   for i in range(0, size):
      result += array[i]
   print("The result of the parallel computation is %d" %result)
```

This code will generate the following result after it is run on four processes:

```
$mpiexec -n 4 python mpi06b.py
Process 3 calculated this value: 7
Process 1 calculated this value: 3
Process 2 calculated this value: 5
Process 0 calculated this value: 1
The result of the parallel computation is 16
```

As can be seen from the result, we have divided the calculation into four equal portions. In these cases, the calculation present in the code exploits the number of ranks of every single process for iterations and indexes the computation portions. The individual results are then added together to produce the final result. By varying the number of parallel processes, it is possible to extend the iteration of the calculation to extended values.

For example, by extending the parallel computation to eight processes we will obtain the following result:

```
$mpiexec -n 8 python mpi06b.py
Process 5 calculated this value: 11
```

```
Process 7 calculated this value: 15
Process 3 calculated this value: 7
Process 6 calculated this value: 13
Process 1 calculated this value: 3
Process 2 calculated this value: 5
Process 4 calculated this value: 9
Process 0 calculated this value: 1
The result of the parallel computation is 64
```

Collective Communication Using the `AlltoAll` Mode

Another way of collective communication is using the **`AlltoAll` mode**. In this case, there is behavior by the processes similar to gathering and scattering at the same time. In this communication group, each process sends and receives portions of an array of data from other processes belonging to the group (see *Figure 3.7*).

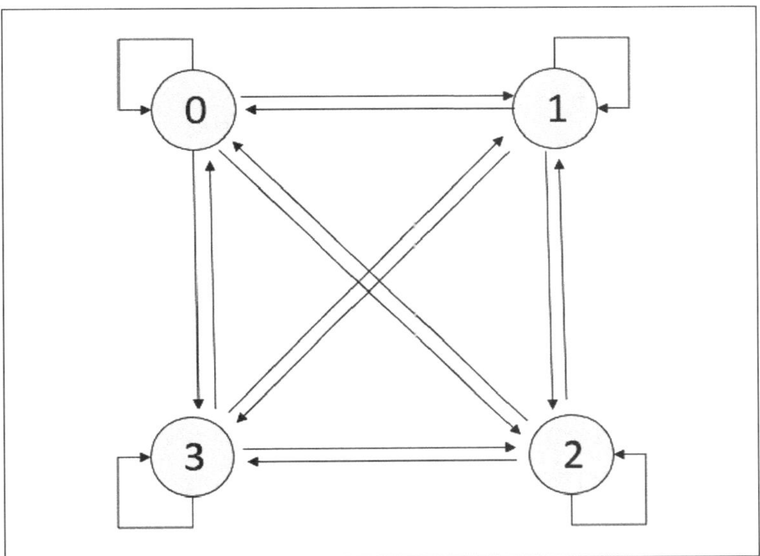

***Figure 3.7**: AllToAll*

```
from mpi4py import MPI
comm = MPI.COMM_WORLD
rank = comm.rank
if rank == 0:
    output = ['0A','0B','0C','0D']
elif rank == 1:
    output = ['1A','1B','1C','1D']
elif rank == 2:
    output = ['2A','2B','2C','2D']
elif rank == 3:
    output = ['3A','3B','3C','3D']
input = comm.alltoall(output)
print("Process %s recived %s" %(rank, input))
```

This code will generate the following result:

```
$mpiexec -n 4 python mpi07a.py
Process 0 received ['0A', '1A', '2A', '3A']
Process 2 received ['0C', '1C', '2C', '3C']
Process 3 received ['0D', '1D', '2D', '3D']
Process 1 received ['0B', '1B', '2B', '3B']
```

As we can see from the result:

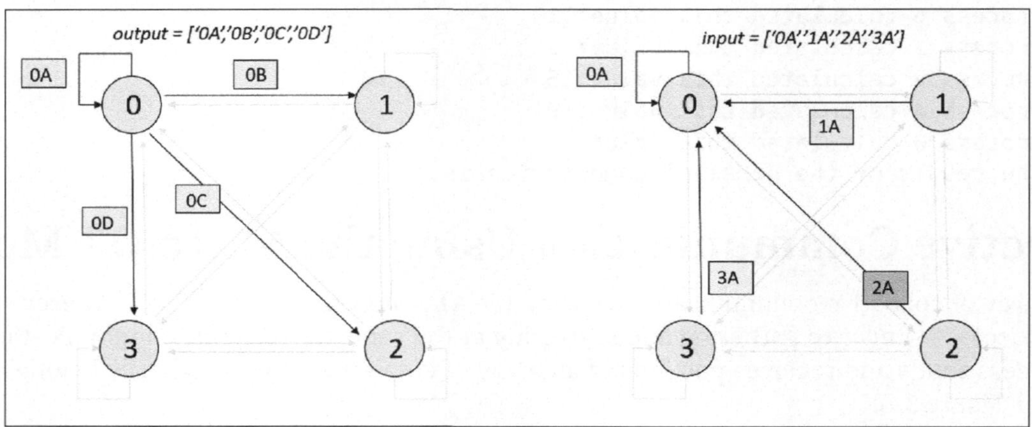

***Figure 3.8**: AllToAll for Process 0*

Reduction Operation

The reduction operation performed by **comm.reduce()** takes an array of input elements from each process and returns an array of output elements to the root process. The output items contain the reduced result:

```
from mpi4py import MPI
import numpy as np

comm = MPI.COMM_WORLD
rank = comm.rank

if rank == 0:
    output = np.array([0,0,0,0])
elif rank == 1:
    output = np.array([1,1,1,1])
elif rank == 2:
    output = np.array([2,2,2,2])
elif rank == 3:
    output = np.array([3,3,3,3])
print("Process %d. Sending %s" %(rank, output))
input = comm.reduce(output, root=0, op=MPI.SUM)
if rank == 0:
    print("The result of the parallel computation is %s" %input)
```

This code will generate the following result:

```
$mpiexec -n 4 python mpi08a.py
Process 3. Sending [3 3 3 3]
Process 2. Sending [2 2 2 2]
Process 1. Sending [1 1 1 1]
Process 0. Sending [0 0 0 0]
The result of the parallel computation is [6 6 6 6]
```

The operations available in the reduction are different, as shown in *Table 3.2*:

SUM	Sum of the elements
PROD	Multiplication of the elements
MAX	The maximum value of the elements

MAXLOC	The maximum value and the rank of the related process.
MIN	The minimum value of the elements
MINLOC	The minimum value and rank of the related process
LAND	Logical AND across the elements
LOR	Logical OR across the elements
BAND	Bitwise AND across the elements
BOR	Bitwise OR across the elements

Table 3.2: *List of Reduction Operations*

Optimization of Communications through Topologies

An interesting feature provided by MPI is the possibility to intervene in virtual topologies. All communication between processes occurs through communication groups. So far, by using **`MPI_COMM_WORLD`**, all processes are assigned to a group and each of them is assigned a rank number starting from 0 up to n-1, where n is the number of processes launched in parallel execution.

The **`mpi4py`** library allows us to define a virtual topology for this communicator, or the way in which ranks assigned can be redefined. By defining a virtual topology, each node (process) will only be able to communicate with neighboring nodes in the virtual topology. In this way, we can improve the performance given the reduction in execution times. In fact, in complex cases, as the ranks are randomly assigned to the various processes, the messages could pass through many of them before reaching the correct destination, that is the process for which this message was intended.

MPI provides two ways of building a topology:

- Cartesian
- Adjacency matrix

The first creates a **Cartesian** topology, while the second requires an adjacency matrix of the graph we want to create.

In this example, we will use only the Cartesian topologies, through which it is possible to build many topologies that are widely used as *rings* and *toroids*:

```
from mpi4py import MPI
comm = MPI.COMM_WORLD
rank = comm.rank

comm_3D = comm.Create_cart(dims = [3,3,3],
                            periods=[False,False,False],
                            reorder=False)
xyz = comm_3D.Get_coords(rank)
print ("In this 3D topology, process %s has coordinates %s " %(rank,xyz))
```

This code will generate the following result:

```
$mpiexec -n 27 python mpi09.py
In this 3D topology, process 0 has coordinates [0, 0, 0]
In this 3D topology, process 1 has coordinates [0, 0, 1]
In this 3D topology, process 4 has coordinates [0, 1, 1]
In this 3D topology, process 6 has coordinates [0, 2, 0]
In this 3D topology, process 7 has coordinates [0, 2, 1]
In this 3D topology, process 8 has coordinates [0, 2, 2]
In this 3D topology, process 12 has coordinates [1, 1, 0]
```

```
In this 3D topology, process 10 has coordinates [1, 0, 1]
In this 3D topology, process 9 has coordinates [1, 0, 0]
In this 3D topology, process 11 has coordinates [1, 0, 2]
In this 3D topology, process 13 has coordinates [1, 1, 1]
In this 3D topology, process 14 has coordinates [1, 1, 2]
In this 3D topology, process 15 has coordinates [1, 2, 0]
In this 3D topology, process 16 has coordinates [1, 2, 1]
In this 3D topology, process 17 has coordinates [1, 2, 2]
In this 3D topology, process 20 has coordinates [2, 0, 2]
In this 3D topology, process 5 has coordinates [0, 1, 2]
In this 3D topology, process 2 has coordinates [0, 0, 2]
In this 3D topology, process 18 has coordinates [2, 0, 0]
In this 3D topology, process 24 has coordinates [2, 2, 0]
In this 3D topology, process 26 has coordinates [2, 2,2]
In this 3D topology, process 21 has coordinates [2, 1, 0]
In this 3D topology, process 3 has coordinates [0, 1, 0]
In this 3D topology, process 22 has coordinates [2, 1, 1]
In this 3D topology, process 19 has coordinates [2, 0, 1]
In this 3D topology, process 25 has coordinates [2, 2, 1]
In this 3D topology, process 23 has coordinates [2, 1, 2]
```

This result allows us to graphically place the typology, as shown in the following figure (see *Figure* 3.9):

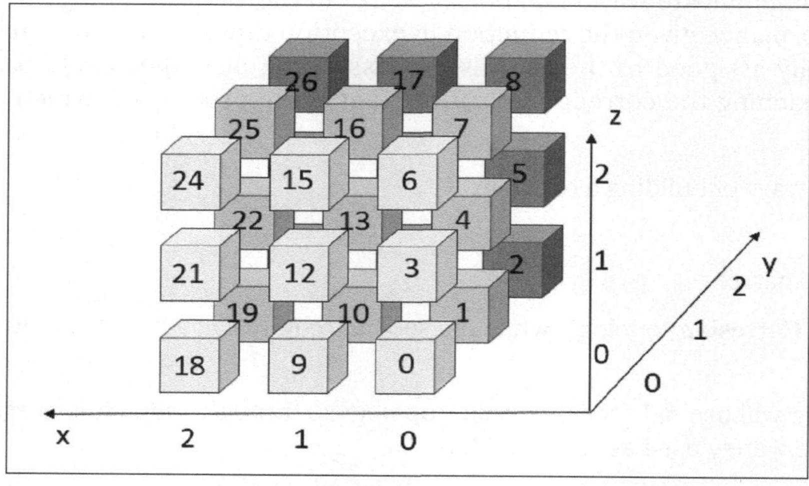

***Figure* 3.9**: *Cartesian Ranking on 3D Topology*

As one of the processes is given, it is possible to know which processes are adjacent to it via the following function:

```
shift(direction,displacement)
```

This function returns *two* integers, which correspond to the ranks of two adjacent processes on one of the Cartesian axes. The direction argument indicates in which direction we want to know the neighbors, corresponding to the Cartesian axes. The direction range is *[0, n-1]*, where *n* is the size of the Cartesian mesh. So, in our case **0** will be **Z**, **1** will be **X**, and **2** will be **Y** (based on the previous figure). The other argument indicates when we need to move.

```
displacement (> 0: upwards shift, < 0: downwards shift) (integer)
```

However, in our case, since we want to know the adjacent processes, this value will always be **1**. Continuing with our example, if we want to know the neighbors of *process* 12, we can add new lines to the code:

```
from mpi4py import MPI
comm = MPI.COMM_WORLD
```

```
rank = comm.rank

comm_3D = comm.Create_cart(dims = [3,3,3],
                       periods =[False,False,False],
                       reorder=False)
xyz = comm_3D.Get_coords(rank)

if rank==12:
  print ("In this 3D topology, process %s has coordinates %s " %(rank,xyz))
  right,left = comm_3D.Shift(0,1)
  up,down = comm_3D.Shift(1,1)
  forward,backward = comm_3D.Shift(2,1)
  print("Neighbors (left-right): %s %s" %(left,right))
  print("Neighbors (up-down): %s %s" %(up,down))
  print("Neighbors (forward-backward): %s %s" %(forward,backward))
```

This code will generate the following result:

```
$mpiexec -n 27 python mpi09b.py
In this 3D topology, process 12 has coordinates [1, 1, 0]
Neighbors (left-right): 21 3
Neighbors (up-down): 9 15
Neighbors (forward-backward): -1 13
```

So, if during our parallel calculations, we need to exchange information only between topologically adjacent processes, we can directly insert their rank into the code, with nested ifs to make selections between the various processes without using collective forms of communication, to select only the ones you want.

So, we can use the methods directly:

- **comm.send(data, neighbor)**
- **comm.recv(neighbor)**

These can be used to send and receive messages between adjacent processes directly and efficiently.

Comparison of Threading and Multiprocessing in Python: Advantages and Disadvantages

By now, you should have gained a good understanding of threading and multiprocessing techniques. Choosing which one to apply is fundamental in Python in order to develop efficient applications and make the most of system resources, especially in multi-core environments. It is therefore important to analyze the differences between the two different approaches, while highlighting the most suitable use cases and the practical implications for optimizing performance. Before going into the heart of the matte, let us get an overview of the fundamental characteristics that distinguish the two different approaches:

- **Threading**: Threading creates threads, which refer to the execution units that operate within the same process. Threads share the same memory space and can communicate with each other easily as they are part of the same process. However, in Python, the Global Interpreter Lock (GIL) limits the concurrent execution of threads in CPU-bound applications (that require a lot of processing power), causing a serialized execution. Despite this limitation, threading is beneficial for I/O-bound applications that frequently interact with external resources such as files, databases, or networks.
- **Multiprocessing**: Unlike threading, multiprocessing creates separate processes, each with its own memory space and an independent instance of the Python interpreter. This approach

bypasses the GIL, while allowing CPU-bound operations to be executed in parallel on multiple cores. However, since they are separate processes, data is not directly shared between processes. This levels an additional cost on the communication between processes.

It is evident that the **Global Interpreter Lock (GIL)** is intrinsic to the structure of Python, while playing a key role. This synchronization mechanism limits the execution of concurrent threads to a single thread at a time, even on multi-core processors. This means that while one thread executes Python code, the other threads must wait for the GIL to be released, even if CPU resources are available. This limits the effectiveness of threading in CPU-bound Python applications. However, the GIL does not have a significant impact on I/O-bound applications, since during input/output operations, the GIL is released, while allowing other threads to advance. Therefore, the choice of threading or multiprocessing often depends on the nature of the application:

- **I/O-Bound Applications**: For example, web servers or web scrapers benefit from threading, since many I/O operations can be handled simultaneously.
- **CPU-Bound Applications**: Data-intensive applications such as scientific calculations or image transformations require multiprocessing to take advantage of parallelism across multiple cores.

Advantages of Threading

- **Memory Sharing**: Since threads share the same memory space, they can directly access the same variables and data. This makes it easy for them to communicate with each other without having to implement complex communication mechanisms.
- **Lightweight:** Creating threads is less expensive in terms of system resources than creating processes, so that it can be a more efficient option when working on I/O-bound tasks.
- **Suitable for I/O-Bound Tasks:** Threading is particularly advantageous for tasks such as network operations or disk reads/writes, where the CPU is often waiting (blocked) for input/output.

Disadvantages of Threading

- **Global Interpreter Lock (GIL)**: In Python, the GIL prevents threads from executing code on multiple CPU cores at the same time. As a result, threading cannot take advantage of the CPU's parallelism.
- **Data safety**: Since threads share the same memory, there is a risk of race conditions and other synchronization problems, which make it more difficult to manage concurrency.

Advantages of Multiprocessing

- **Full CPU Usage**: Multiprocessing allows you to bypass the GIL as each process has its own Python interpreter, which allows you to use the various CPU cores.
- **Process Isolation:** Since each process has its own memory space, data is isolated and there is no risk of direct interference between processes. This simplifies the management of concurrency.

Disadvantages of Multiprocessing

- **Higher Resource Consumption:** Creating processes is more expensive than creating threads, since each process has its own memory and context. This can result in a higher consumption of RAM and system resources.
- **More Complex Communication:** Communication between processes requires inter-process (IPC) mechanisms such as pipes or queues, which can be complex and add latency.
- **Not Suitable for I/O-Bound Tasks:** When compared to threads, multiprocessing is less efficient for I/O operations as processes commonly occupy resources while waiting for their completion.

Now we will show two examples of Python code where we will compare threading and multiprocessing modules on two different types of tasks:

- I/O bound, where threading is more efficient
- CPU bound, where multiprocessing is more advantageous

In the first example, we simulate an I/O-bound task using **time.sleep** to mimic a network or disk read/write operation. Here, the CPU does not play a fundamental role.

We will define two different functions for this purpose. In the **threading_example()** function, we create 5 threads that execute **io_bound_task** where each thread waits for 1 second for the I/O task to be executed. In the **multiprocessing_example()** function, we will create 5 separate processes to execute the same operation. Since the task is I/O bound and does not require much CPU, threading should be faster and lighter than multiprocessing, since the threads can perform the wait without interference from the GIL.

```
import threading
import multiprocessing
import time

def io_bound_task():
    print(f"{threading.current_thread().name} is working...")
    time.sleep(i)
    print(f"{threading.current_thread().name} ended its work.")

# Threading
def threading_example():
    start_time = time.time()
    threads = []
    for _ in range(5):
        thread = threading.Thread(target=io_bound_task)
        threads.append(thread)
        thread.start()
    for thread in threads:
        thread.join()
    end_time = time.time()
    print(f"Time with threading: {end_time - start_time:.2f} seconds")

# Multiprocessing
def multiprocessing_example():
    start_time = time.time()
    processes = []
    for _ in range(5):
        process = multiprocessing.Process(target=io_bound_task)
        processes.append(process)
        process.start()
    for process in processes:
        process.join()
    end_time = time.time()
    print(f"Time with multiprocessing: {end_time - start_time:.2f} seconds")

if __name__ == '__main__':
    print("Execution of I/O-bound task:")
    print("Using threading...")
    threading_example()
    print("Using multiprocessing...")
    multiprocessing_example()
```

This will generate the following result:

```
Execution of I/O-bound task:
Using threading...
Thread-1 (io_bound_task) is working...
Thread-2 (io_bound_task) is working...
Thread-3 (io_bound_task) is working...
Thread-4 (io_bound_task) is working...
Thread-5 (io_bound_task) is working...
Thread-5 (io_bound_task) ended its work.
Thread-2 (io_bound_task) ended its work.
Thread-3 (io_bound_task) ended its work.
Thread-4 (io_bound_task) ended its work.
Thread-1 (io_bound_task) ended its work.
Time with threading: 1.00 seconds
Using multiprocessing...
MainThread is working...
MainThread is working...
MainThread is working...
MainThread is working...
MainThread is working...
MainThread ended its work.
MainThread ended its work.
MainThread ended its work.
MainThread ended its work.
MainThread ended its work.
Time with multiprocessing: 1.22 seconds
```

In the second example, we will define a CPU-bound task this time, where each worker has to compute prime numbers in a specific range. Here, multiprocessing will be more advantageous as it bypasses the GIL by exploiting the multiple cores available in the CPU in a parallel manner. Again, we will use two different functions to differentiate between the two different approaches. In the **threading_example_cpu()** function, we create 4 threads to compute prime numbers up to 10000, while in the **multiprocessing_example_cpu()** function, we create 4 separate processes to perform the same operation. In this case, multiprocessing should be faster since each process can execute the code on one CPU core without interference from the GIL, which makes the processing of a CPU-bound task like a mathematical calculation more efficient.

```
import threading
import multiprocessing
import time

def cpu_bound_task(n):
    count = 0
    for i in range(2, n):
        for j in range(2, i):
            if 1 % j == 0:
                break
            else:
                count += 1
    print(f"Prime numbers found: {count}")

# Threading
def threading_example_cpu():
    start_time = time.time()
    threads = []
    for _ in range(4):
        thread = threading.Thread(target=cpu_bound_task, args=(10000,))
```

```
        threads.append(thread)
        thread.start()
    for thread in threads:
        thread.join()
    end_time = time.time()
    print(f"Time with threading: {end_time - start_time:.2f} seconds")

# Multiprocessing
def multiprocessing_example_cpu:
    start_time = time.time()
    processes = []
    for _ in range(4):
        process = multiprocessing.Process(target=cpu_bound_task,
args=(10000,))
        processes.append(process)
        process.start()
    for process in processes:
        process.join()
    end_time = time.time()

if __name__ == '__main__':
    print("Execution of CPU-bound task:")
    print("Using threading...")
    threading_example_cpu()
    print("Using multiprocessing...")
    multiprocessing_example_cpu()
```

This code will generate the following result:

```
Execution of CPU-bound task:
Using threading...
Prime numbers found: 49975003
Prime numbers found: 49975003
Prime numbers found: 49975003
Prime numbers found: 49975003
Time with threading: 7.99 seconds
Using multiprocessing...
Prime numbers found: 49975003
Prime numbers found: 49975003
Prime numbers found: 49975003
Prime numbers found: 49975003
Time with threading: 3.36 seconds
```

From this example, we can deduce that threading is generally the best choice for applications that frequently wait for responses from external resources (such as networks or files).

Multiprocessing is better suited to tasks that require a high computational load, while exploiting parallelism on multi-core CPUs. Another thing to consider is that using one approach does not exclude the other. When a combination of CPU-bound and I/O-bound tasks is needed, it is possible to use both the models, with threads to handle I/O operations, and processes to process complex calculations via the CPU.

Improving Performance with Advanced Multiprocessing

Returning to the multiprocessing technique, we will now expand the general framework by adding more advanced concepts such as CPU affinity. When implementing high-performance CPU-bound applications, simple parallelization via multiprocessing may not be enough to optimize the use of system resources. In these situations, advanced techniques such as configuring CPU affinity allow you to further improve performance by distributing the workload more efficiently.

To fully understand the importance of CPU affinity, it is useful to consider how processes are normally managed by the operating system (OS). The operating system assigns available processes to CPUs based on the availability of cores by default to redistribute the load as needed. While this approach is effective, in CPU-bound intensive applications where processes perform complex calculations, moving a process from one CPU to another can incur overhead due to the need to reload the CPU caches. Setting CPU affinity for each process can reduce this overhead, and improve execution speed and efficiency.

CPU affinity is a configuration that assigns one or more specific CPU cores to a given process. When a process is limited to certain cores, it reduces the risk of migration to other CPUs, thus minimizing context and cache management costs. This advanced technique offers several advantages in computationally intensive applications such as:

- Minimization of Context Costs: By keeping a process on the same core, the cost of context switching between different CPUs is avoided, which improves cache coherence.
- Reduction of Latency Times: Computationally intensive processes benefit from reduced execution times, since they avoid interruptions caused by dynamic CPU reassignment.
- Optimization of Multi-Core Resource Use: Explicitly assigning cores to different processes can help balance the load between CPU cores, thereby improving the overall efficiency of the system.

In Python, configuring CPU affinity is not natively supported by the multiprocessing library, but can be handled via modules such as os for Unix-based systems or third-party libraries on Windows. The following is an example of CPU affinity configuration on a Linux system.

Note: *On Linux, the `os.sched_setaffinity` command allows you to specify which cores can run a process.*

Let us write an example for CPU affinity configuration. In this code, each process is created and executed separately using **`multiprocessing.Process`**. The **`os.sched_setaffinity`** function assigns each process to a specific CPU core, while alternating between available cores to distribute the load.

```
import os
import multiprocessing
import time

def cpu_bound_task(task_id):
    """Simulation of an intensive operation that requires a lot of CPU
resources."""
    print(f"Process {task_id} assigned to CPU {os.sched_getaffinity(0)}")
    # CPU-bound Task (e.g.,calculating a sum for large numbers)
    result = sum(i * i for i in range(10**6))
    print(f"Process {task_id} finished, result: {result}")

if __name__ == '__main__':
    processes = []

    # Configure processes with different CPU affinity
    for i in range(4):
        process = multiprocessing.Process(target=cpu_bound_task, args=(i,))
        process.start()

        # Assign each process to a specific CPU
        cpu_core = i % os.cpu_count()
```

```
        os.sched_setaffinity(process.pid, {cpu_core})  # Assign the process to a
specific CPU
        processes.append(process)

    for process in processes:
        process.join()

    print("All processes are completed.")
```

Running the code will give the following result:

```
Process 0 assigned to CPU {0}
Process 1 assigned to CPU {1}
Process 2 assigned to CPU {2}
Process 3 assigned to CPI {3}
Process 0 finished, result: 333332833333500000
Process 1 finished, result: 333332833333500000
Process 2 finished, result: 333332833333500000
Process 3 finished, result: 333332833333500000
All processes are completedic CPU
```

Other Advanced Multiprocessing Optimization Methods

In addition to CPU affinity configuration, there are other advanced techniques that can improve the performance of CPU-bound applications. Here, we will discuss these two techniques in this section:

- Balancing Process Priority
- Sharing Data Between Processes with Shared Objects

In Python, you can use the **os** module to change the execution priority of processes, while assigning higher priorities to critical processes and lower priorities to less important processes. Changing the priority can reduce the execution time for critical tasks in multi-process environments. It is worth remembering that access to priority levels may be limited on some operating systems, and would require administrator permissions.

For example, on Linux, we can develop an example on how to change the priority of processes, thanks to the **os.setpriority()** function. To run it, run it as administrator using:

```
sudo python3 Ch03_30.py
```

```
import os
import multiprocessing

def intensive_task():
    print(f"Process ID: {os.getpid()} with Priority: {os.getpriority(os.PRIO_
PROCESS, 0)}")
    # Computationally intensive simulation
    result = sum(i * i for i in range(10**6))
    print(f"Result: {result}")

if __name__ == "__main__":
    process = multiprocessing.Process(target=intensive_task)
    process.start()
```

```
    # Set high priority for the process (on Linux: -20 to 19, -20 is highest)
    os.setpriority(os.PRIO_PROCESS, process.pid, -10)

    process.join()
    print("Process completed.")
```

Running the code will give the following result:

```
Process ID: 17987 with Priority: -10 Result: 333332833333500000 Process
completed.
```

In scenarios where it is necessary to reduce the load of data transfer between processes, Python offers shared data structures such as **multiprocessing.Value** and **multiprocessing.Array** that allow multiple processes to access the same data, without having to continuously pass information through queues.

Here is an example (valid on all operating environments) using this technique for sharing data. In this example, **multiprocessing.Value** is used to share a single value between different processes, while a lock guarantees that only one process at a time can increment the counter to avoid race conditions.

```
import multiprocessing
import time

def increment(shared_counter, lock):
    """Increment a shared counter by protecting it with a lock."""
    with lock:  # Use a lock to avoid race conditions
        shared_counter.value += 1
        print(f"Counter incremented to {shared_counter.value}")

if __name__ == "__main__":
    counter = multiprocessing.Value('i', 0)  # 'i' indicates a shared integer
    lock = multiprocessing.Lock()  # Lock protection

    processes = [multiprocessing.Process(target=increment, args=(counter,
lock)) for _ in range(10)]

    for process in processes:
        process.start()

    for process in processes:
        process.join()

    print(f"Final counter value: {counter.value}")
```

Running the code will give the following result:

```
Counter incremented to 1
Counter incremented to 2
Counter incremented to 3
Counter incremented to 4
Counter incremented to 5
Counter incremented to 6
Counter incremented to 7
Counter incremented to 8
Counter incremented to 9
Counter incremented to 10
Final counter value: 10
```

Implementing Job Scheduling with Multiprocessing

Another advanced method to improve the efficiency of parallel execution is job scheduling. In contexts like those discussed in this book, where tasks are numerous and require an optimized use of available resources, it is essential to coordinate the execution of tasks efficiently.

Job scheduling consists of planning and distributing the execution of tasks so that system resources are used at their best, maintaining optimal execution times and balancing the load among the available cores. Python offers several scheduling features through multiprocessing such as Pool for process management, asynchronous functions (**apply_async**. **map_async**) and queue mechanisms. In Python, job scheduling through multiprocessing can be divided into some key operations:

Creating and Managing Processes: Through **multiprocessing.Process**, it is possible to start single independent processes, but in environments with many tasks, a pool of processes is more efficient.

Dynamic Scheduling: Asynchronous functions like **apply_async** allow you to schedule tasks and distribute them dynamically to available processes.

Queue and Load Balancing: Queues and data structures like Queue allow you to manage a large number of tasks, while distributing them gradually and in a balanced way.

Let us start with a basic approach to see how Pool facilitates job scheduling. In the previous sections, we have already introduced **multiprocessing.Pool** in an introductory context on its use. Now let us see how to use it in a more advanced context. This module provides an interface to create and manage a pool of processes, which will allow you to automatically distribute tasks to available processes. Using this, you can easily scale an application on multi-core systems without having to manually manage each process. In particular, we will use it through asynchronous functions like **Pool.apply_async** to distribute tasks asynchronously. Let us see an example where we will use this method to schedule tasks that will be executed as soon as a process in the pool becomes available:

```
import multiprocessing
import time

def process_task(task_id):
    """Simulation of a task that takes time to complete."""
    print(f"Starting the task {task_id} in the process {multiprocessing.
current_process().name}")
    time.sleep(2)  # Simulate a long task
    print(f"Task {task_id} completed")
    return f"Task result{task_id}"

if __name__ == "__main__":
    # Creating a pool of 4 processes
    with multiprocessing.Pool(processes=4) as pool:
        tasks = [pool.apply_async(process_task, args=(i,)) for i in range(10)]

        # Collects results at the end of each task
        results = [task.get() for task in tasks]

    print("Results:", results)
```

Running the code will give the following result:

```
Starting the task 0 in the process SpawnPoolWorker-1
Starting the task 1 in the process SpawnPoolWorker-2
Starting the task 2 in the process SpawnPoolWorker-3
```

```
Starting the task 3 in the process SpawnPoolWorker-4
Task 0 completed
Starting the task 4 in the process SpawnPoolWorker-1
Task 1 completed
Starting the task 5 in the process SpawnPoolWorker-2
Task 2 completed
Starting the task 6 in the process SpawnPoolWorker-3
Task 3 completed
Starting the task 7 in the process SpawnPoolWorker-4
Task 4 completed
Task 5 completed
Starting the task 9 in the process SpawnPoolWorker-2
Task 7 completed
Starting the task 8 in the process SpawnPoolWorker-1
Task 6 completed
Task 9 completed
Task 8 completed
Results: ['Task result0', 'Task result1', 'Task result2', 'Task result3',
'Task result4', 'Task result5', 'Task result6', 'Task result7', 'Task
 result8', 'Task result9']
```

In this example, each task is started as soon as a process in the pool becomes available, while using **apply_async** for asynchronous execution. Then, the results are collected using **task.get()**, which blocks the execution until the specific task completes. This scheduling method is ideal for distributing tasks that can be executed in parallel, and require load balancing to optimize resource usage.

In addition to **Pool.apply_async()**, the module provides additional job scheduling tools. **Pool.map** and **Pool.map_async** are particularly useful methods for managing a series of homogeneous tasks, such as repetitive operations on a dataset. map executes tasks in parallel and waits for all processes to complete, while **map_async** allows you to schedule tasks asynchronously. Let us develop some sample code where map executes tasks simultaneously and waits for all of them to complete before continuing, while blocking the program execution. **map_async** starts tasks, and allows the program to continue execution until the results are requested with **.get()**.

```
import multiprocessing
import time

def square(number):
    """Simulates a long calculation operation to square a number."""
    time.sleep(1)
    return number * number

if __name__ == "__main__":
    numbers = [1, 2, 3, 4, 5, 6, 7, 8]

    # Synchronous execution with map (all tasks run in parallel and awaited)
    with multiprocessing.Pool(processes=4) as pool:
        results_sync = pool.map(square, numbers)

    print("Synchronous results:", results_sync)

    # Asynchronous execution with map_async
    with multiprocessing.Pool(processes=4) as pool:
        result_async = pool.map_async(square, numbers)
```

```
        # .get() blocks until all asynchronous tasks are completed
        results_async = result_async.get()

    print("Asynchronous results:", results_async)
```

Running the code will give the following result:

```
Synchronous results: [1, 4, 9, 16, 25, 36, 49, 64]
Asynchronous results: [1, 4, 9, 16, 25, 36, 49, 64]
```

The **map_async** method is useful where the execution time of tasks is variable and you want to manage the results as soon as they are available, while keeping the program reactive. In addition to what we have seen so far, there may be contexts where the number of tasks is high or unknown. In these cases, using a **multiprocessing.Queue** allows you to add tasks dynamically, while adapting the management of processes to variable needs. Processes can take tasks from the queue as they become available, facilitating dynamic scheduling. Let us also make a practical example here to see how queues in the context of multiprocessing can be used for job scheduling. In this example, tasks are inserted into the queue, and each process takes a task from the queue until it is emptied. This approach allows for dynamic scheduling, which distributes the load flexibly among processes.

```
import multiprocessing
import time

def dynamic_task(queue):
    """Executes tasks dynamically fetched from the queue."""
    while not queue.empty():
        task_id = queue.get()  # Gets the next task from the queue
        print(f"Task execution {task_id} in the process {multiprocessing.
current_process().name}")
        time.sleep(2)  # Simulates a long run
        print(f"Task {task_id} completed")

if __name__ == "__main__":
    task_queue = multiprocessing.Queue()

    # Inserts tasks into the queue
    for i in range(10):
        task_queue.put(i)

    # Start 4 processes to perform tasks
    processes = [multiprocessing.Process(target=dynamic_task, args=(task_
queue,)) for _ in range(4)]

    for process in processes:
        process.start()

    for process in processes:
        process.join()

    print("All tasks have been completed.")
```

Running the code will give the following result:

```
Task execution 0 in the process Process-1
Task execution 1 in the process Process-2
Task execution 2 in the process Process-3
Task execution 3 in the process Process-4
Task 0 completed
Task execution 4 in the process Process-1
```

```
Task 2 completed
Task execution 5 in the process Process-3
Task 1 completed
Task 3 completed
Task execution 6 in the process Process-2
Task execution 7 in the process Process-4
Task 4 completed
Task execution 8 in the process Process-1
Task 5 completed
Task execution 9 in the process Process-3
Task 6 completed
Task 7 completed
Task 8 completed
Task 9 completed
All tasks have been completed.
```

In some cases, it may be necessary to assign a priority to the most urgent tasks. An advanced scheduler with prioritized tasks should be implemented through a **multiprocess.PriorityQueue** that allows us to order tasks based on their priority. Again, we will show an example where tasks are inserted into the **PriorityQueue** with priority (numeric values: lower values = higher priority). The different processes take the tasks from the queue following the priority order, allowing for optimized scheduling of critical tasks.

```
import multiprocessing
import time
from queue import PriorityQueue

def prioritized_task(priority_queue):
    """Executes tasks fetched from a PriorityQueue with priority."""
    while not priority_queue.empty():
        priority, task_id = priority_queue.get()  # Get the task with the
highest priority
        print(f"Task execution {task_id} (Priority {priority}) in the process
{multiprocessing.current_process().name}")
        time.sleep(1)  # Simulate task completion
        print(f"Task {task_id} completed")

if __name__ == "__main__":
    priority_queue = PriorityQueue()

    # Puts tasks with priority into the queue (lowest priority executed first)
    tasks = [(3, "Low"), (2, "High"), (4, "Very Low"), (1, "Very High")]
    for priority, task_id in tasks:
        priority_queue.put((priority, task_id))

    # Start processes to execute tasks with priority
    processes = [multiprocessing.Process(target=prioritized_task,
args=(priority_queue,)) for _ in range(2)]

    for process in processes:
        process.start()

    for process in processes:
        process.join()

    print("All priority tasks have been completed.")
```

Running the code will give the following result:

```
Task execution Very High (Priority 1) in the process Process-1
Task execution Very High (Priority 1) in the process Process-2
Task Very High completed
Task execution High (Priority 1) in the process Process-1
Task Very High completed
Task execution High (Priority 2) in the process Process-2
Task High completed
Task execution Low (Priority 3) in the process Process-1
Task High completed
Task execution Low (Priority 3) in the process Process-2
Task Low completed
Task execution Very Low (Priority 4) in the process Process-1
Task Low completed
Task execution Very Low (Priority 4) in the process Process-2
Task Very Low completed
Task Very Low completed
All priority tasks have been completed.
```

Thus, job scheduling with multiprocessing allows you to optimize the use of system resources, balance the workload, and organize the execution of tasks in an efficient way. The techniques illustrated here provide a complete framework for implementing flexible, scalable scheduling systems that can handle different types of tasks and priorities. In production environments, these approaches are particularly advantageous for complex and distributed applications.

Conclusion

In this chapter, you have learned about all the basic tools to carry out programming in parallel. The concepts are related to the *parent-children process mechanisms*, on which the multiprocessing module works have been highlighted and treated with a series of examples. You have also acquired the ability to extend the powerful features of the **map()** function to parallel systems, while significantly increasing the efficiency of your programs. At the same time, we have seen the **mpi4py** library which is based on the MPI standard and allows you to launch a certain set of parent processes in parallel. This uses the message passing paradigm for data exchange. In the next chapters, we will go into detail on more advanced concepts of parallel programming with a series of libraries that further extend its potential.

References

- https://mpi4py.readthedocs.io/en/stable/
- https://docs.python.org/3/library/multiprocessing.html
- https://github.com/PowerShell/PowerShell/releases/tag/v7.2.6
- https://superfastpython.com/multiprocessing-pipe-in-python/

CHAPTER 4
Asynchronous Programming

Introduction

Previously, we have looked at concurrent programming based on threads and the threading module in particular. The limitations imposed by the GIL pose major problems which will have to be resolved if we want to work with threads in Python. This feature of Python, therefore, imposes thread concurrency, which is an inevitable limitation compared to parallel programming. Thus, in Python, a concurrent programming approach becomes indispensable for managing tasks involving I/O communications where unpredictable waiting times have to be managed in conjunction with other tasks. In this chapter, we return to this type of programming through alternative approaches like the **asynchronous model** and the AsyncIO **library**.

Structure

This chapter will address the following topics:

- Asynchronous and Synchronous Programming
- AsyncIO Library
- Async/Await Syntax
- Coroutines
- Tasks
- Future
- Event Loop
- `async for`
- Queues

Asynchronous and Synchronous Programming

In the world of programming, there are *two* opposing models:

- Synchronous Model (also referred to as **sync**)
- Asynchronous Model (also referred to as **async**)

Asynchronous programming is based on a model with multiple entities acting concurrently. These entities may be threads, processes, or anything else, which can act simultaneously and be executed in any order, independently of each other. The asynchronous model is a *non-blocking* architecture. This means that there are no execution interruptions in the programs created with this, even if one or more operations within it are waiting for some event and service.

In asynchronous programming, it is possible to manage multiple operations at the same time independently from the other. Their execution does not depend on others and they all simultaneously try to complete their task (competition). In addition, the execution of each component of the program can be controlled and can be activated when it is convenient or when it is possible to do so. This allows you to manage multiple requests at the same time, while making the most of both resources and execution times. As an example, this is the behavior required by server applications referenced by multiple clients. Each of them will request the server for a service through a message and the server will manage which message to process and when to send the responses to the client. This behavior might not be required, but is preferred owing to the waiting times for data on the network.

On the other hand, **synchronous programming** is based on a model with a single executing entity (single thread in a single process), where the code is the sequence of operations to be performed. In fact, *synchronous server-side applications* usually use one thread per request. The execution of these operations is mutually dependent. Only when an operation is completed, the execution will go to the next operation. The synchronous model is a blocking architecture; programs created with this model have a rigid flow of execution, and if an operation is blocked waiting for a response, the entire program will crash.

Pros and Cons of Asynchronous and Synchronous Programming

Asynchronous programming, if well designed for correct and consistent execution, is more *fluid* and more responsive to external events like a user or an external service that provides data. This type of programming is mainly based on the exploitation of competition (even if they are not the same thing), and therefore, the programs that use them can be *quick*, *high performing*, and more *powerful*. Asynchronous programming eliminates waiting times within code execution, while waiting for responses from external services.

The most obvious example of this programming is the one used to create **Graphical User Interfaces (GUI)**. Here the user sees fluid behavior with no waiting times between button presses, text interaction, and drop-down menus that appear and disappear, thanks to the different event handlers that seem to work simultaneously (but often *do not*).

Synchronous programming, on the other hand, follows a predetermined execution, where the tasks are often sequential and never concurrent. Here, each task waits for the previous one to be executed. Even if there are running tasks in parallel, they all perform the same function and are expected to execute the program. This programming is used when a task requires the result of the previous task to be executed.

The advantage of *synchronous programming* is that it rarely causes problems in *run-time*. The behavior of the program is easily predictable and its implementation generates codes that are easy to create and read. On the contrary, *asynchronous programming* can be very *complex*, both in the implementation of the code and in its correct reading. Such a program can give rise to unpredictable and anomalous behaviors that are difficult to predict in the development phase, and even more difficult to fix. Asynchronous programming has therefore very high maintenance.

Concurrent Programming and Asynchronous Model

The concepts underlying concurrent programming have already been covered in depth. Unlike parallel programming, this mode is capable of working on both *single-processor* and *multi-processor systems*. As we compared asynchronous to synchronous models, now let us compare it to concurrent programming.

The *asynchronous model* in Python, as implemented by **`asyncio`**, typically runs all user coroutines within a single thread managed by the event loop. This design means that tasks share the same execution flow and must cooperatively alternate it. However, **asyncio** is not restricted to a single core or incapable of using threads; the underlying process can run on a multi-core CPU and functions such as **loop.run_in_executor()** allow tasks to be offloaded to worker threads or processes when needed. Most asynchronous models use background worker threads for operations which are not published in most documents. In the thread model, different tasks are distributed among the various threads that simultaneously (but not in parallel) compete for the execution timeline and the same shared resources. In an asynchronous model, the tasks all belong to the same thread and must alternate in the single flow of execution asynchronously. The execution of each task can be suspended at any time to make room for other pending tasks, which can then be resumed when others are pending until all operations are completed (as it is shown in *Figure 4.1*).

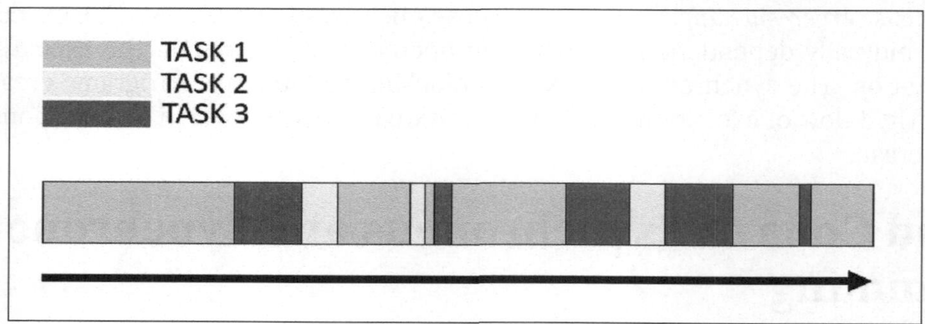

***Figure 4.1**: Asynchronous Execution*

The asynchronous model, in Python, has proved to be much more *efficient* and secure than the one used with threads and has been more dominant in programming, so much so that it completely replaces the threading module in concurrent programming whenever it is necessary to manage *IO-bound tasks*. Furthermore, it is perfect for working in complete synergy with parallel programming as the latter responds efficiently to the management of *CPU-bound tasks*. The complementarity of the two programs often makes it necessary to use both programs.

AsyncIO library

In Python, the asynchronous model is implementable with the **AsyncIO** library. Although other alternatives are currently being developed, the **AsyncIO** library still remains the reference for concurrent programming asynchronously.

In this chapter, we will introduce the concepts behind the asynchronous model, using the **AsyncIO** library where we find these concepts in the form of components. In this way, you will be able to become familiar with the asynchronous model through direct examples.

The main components of the module are:

- **Coroutine**
- **Task**
- **Future**
- **Event loop**

async/await Syntax

The **AsyncIO** library has undergone many changes in recent years and many programming patterns have been used. It is often possible to find on the internet code with obsolete structures linked to old words and patterns (decorators such as **@asyncio.coroutine**, and so on). The current syntax is one based on the **async-await** keywords.

Let us take a very simple example of how to implement code with the **asyncio** library following this syntax:

```
import asyncio

async def main():
    print('Awaiting for ...')
    await asyncio.sleep(1)
    print('... AsyncIO!')

asyncio.run(main())
```

As we can see, the code presents the definition of a function we called **main()** with the **async** keyword. Well, in this case, we have not defined a function but a coroutine, which is a specific entity of the asynchronous programming model.

Inside the code, we find a call to **asyncio.sleep()** (this is not a function either, but a co-routine) preceded by the **await** keyword. This indicates that the called *object* will be included in the scheduling for concurrent execution. Its execution, therefore, will be subject to interruptions, pending the execution of other similar objects. It will then resume its execution once the latter have finished their task.

The **asyncio.sleep()** co-routine works in the same way as the **time.sleep()** function, while delaying the execution of a certain number of seconds passed as a parameter. Being a coroutine, it operates correctly in an asynchronous execution context.

In the AsyncIO library, objects such as co-routines, tasks, and futures are classified as *awaitable* objects. All these objects, once defined and created within the code, can later be scheduled for concurrent execution using the await prefix.

The reason why the **async-await** syntax was added in Python was to eliminate any form of ambiguity in the code. As we have seen, **async** allows us to quickly distinguish co-routines from functions and await allows us to quickly recognize calls that must be scheduled asynchronously.

Coroutines

The heart of the asynchronous model is the coroutines. A **coroutine** is a specialized version of a generator function in Python.

Generator Functions:

In Python, a generator function is a function that returns an iterator.

```
def generator():
 yield "A"
 yield "B"
 yield "C"
```

Instead of return, the generators use the yield statement. In this way, the generator returns one element at a time of the iteration if it is called with the **next()** *function.*

```
iterator = generator()
print("First call: %s" %next(iterator))
print("Second call: %s" %next(iterator))
print("Third call: %s" %next(iterator))
```

By running the code, you get the following result:

```
First call: A
Second call: B
Third call: C
```

As can be seen from the result, each call has a different result; that is, the corresponding value in the iteration sequence is defined by yield in the generator function.

A coroutine is a function that can suspend its execution before reaching a return and passes control to another coroutine for some time.

In AsyncIO, we can define a function as a coroutine through the **async** keyword. In the previous example, the coroutine is the **main()** function, whose definition is anticipated by **async**:

```
async def main():
    print('Awaiting for ...')
    await asyncio.sleep(1)
    print('... AsyncIO!')
```

If you try to make a call to the coroutine by itself, like any other function, it will show the following:

```
>>> main()
```

You will see that you will not get any results: in fact, it has not been performed.

In fact, coroutines are not simple functions. To perform them, the AsyncIO library provides three different ways:

- The first is shown in the preceding example. The **asyncio.run()** function accepts as an argument a coroutine that will be considered the entry point of program execution. To execute the previous coroutine, we can run the following instruction:
  ```
  >>> asyncio.run(main())
  ```
- Another way in which a coroutine can be performed is through another coroutine. For example, let us define a second coroutine always with **async** as a prefix:
  ```
  async def other():
    print("I am a coroutine")
  ```
  In the **main()** coroutine, the call to the new coroutine to execute is placed after await, which is shown here:
  ```
  import asyncio

  async def other():
    print("I am a coroutine")

  async def main():
      print('Awaiting for ...')
      await asyncio.sleep(1)
      await other()
      print('... AsyncIO!')

  asyncio.run(main())
  ```
  Executing the code gives the following result:
  ```
  Awaiting for ...
  I am a coroutine
  ... AsyncIO!
  ```

- There is also a third method that uses AsyncIO's **task** class. By calling the **asyncio.create_task()** function, we create a new object of the **Task** class that executes the coroutine concurrently:

```
import asyncio

async def other():
  print("I am a coroutine")

async def main():
    task = asyncio.create_task(other())
    print('Awaiting for ...')
    await asyncio.sleep(1)
    await task
    print('... AsyncIO!')

asyncio.run(main())
```

If we execute the code, we will get the same result as we did in the previous code. The latter case anticipates the tasks, which we will explore in the next section.

Task

The **tasks** in AsyncIO allow you to schedule the coroutines to work in a competitive way. Coroutines can be wrapped in objects of the **task** class through the **asyncio.create_task()** function as we saw in the previous code. The tasks thus created are then called with **await** in the **main()** coroutine and executed in a competitive manner. Let us look at this via a practical example. We will modify the previous code in order to create a coroutine that accepts *two* parameters: **id** is an integer value that we will use as the identifier of the coroutine, and another integer that will indicate the *execution time* of the coroutine simulated using the function **asyncio.sleep()**.

```
import asyncio

async def other(id,t):
  await asyncio.sleep(t)
  print("I am a coroutine %s" %id)

async def main():
    task1 = asyncio.create_task(other(1,10))
    task2 = asyncio.create_task(other(2,4))
    task3 = asyncio.create_task(other(3,1))
    await task1
    await task2
    await task3

asyncio.run(main())
```

Executing the code gives the following result:

```
I am a coroutine 3
I am a coroutine 2
I am a coroutine 1
```

As we can see from the result, the three coroutines were performed concurrently and since **coroutine 3** is the one that takes the least time, it is also the one that finishes execution first without waiting for the results of the others.

If we had used the coroutines without the tasks, we would not have achieved any concurrent behavior. We will write the previous code version using coroutines as follows:

```
import asyncio

async def other(id,t):
  await asyncio.sleep(t)
  print("I am a coroutine %s" %id)

async def main():
    t1 = time.perf_counter()
    await other(10,1)
    await other(4,2)
    await other(3,3)
    t2 = time.perf_counter()
    elapsed_time = t2 - t1
    print("Elapsed time %s" %elapsed_time)

asyncio.run(main())
```

Executing the code gives the following result:

```
I am a coroutine 1
I am a coroutine 2
I am a coroutine 3
Elapsed time 17.021660084999894
```

As we can see from the result, the behavior is not *concurrent*, since the coroutines finish their task in the same sequence in which they were launched. This happens even if the first coroutine takes much longer than the others. The *total time taken* is the sum of the execution time of the *three coroutines* (10 + 4 + 3 = 17).

If we measure the execution time of the code version with the tasks, we get:

```
I am a coroutine 3
I am a coroutine 2
I am a coroutine 1
Elapsed time 10.006599820999327
```

As we can see, the execution time is almost that used by the slowest coroutine. In fact, the advantage of concurrent programming is to take advantage of the *dead times of execution*, putting the slow coroutines on hold, and in the meantime letting the faster ones run. This code is a splendid example of this behavior.

We will continue with the tasks by making changes to the previous code. Tasks created within the program can have an identifying name. This can be assigned at the time of their creation, through the *optional* **name** parameter:

```
asyncio.create_task(coroutine,name="..")
```

Or later, through the **set_name()** method:

```
task.set_name('...')
```

In the coroutine, **other()** we used an input parameter to identify the task in which it is wrapped. This can be avoided since it is possible to trace the current task within the coroutine without having to pass external parameters. The **asyncio.current_task()** function returns the current task. Since, we only need the task name, we can call the **get_name()** method. Then the previous code can be modified in the following way:

```
import asyncio

async def other(t):
  await asyncio.sleep(t)
  id =  asyncio.current_task().get_name()
  print("I am a coroutine %s" %id)

async def main():
    task1 = asyncio.create_task(other(10),name="1")
    task2 = asyncio.create_task(other(4),name="2")
    task3 = asyncio.create_task(other(3),name="3")
    await task1
    await task2
    await task3

asyncio.run(main())
```

Executing the code gives the following result:

```
I am a coroutine 3
I am a coroutine 2
I am a coroutine 1
```

As can be seen from the result, using tasks instead of coroutines is evidence of concurrent behavior. In fact, the first to be performed will be the *third coroutine* which takes only 2 *seconds* to run. The first coroutine, taking more time (10 *seconds*), will finish at the last.

Gathering of the Awaitables for Concurrent Execution

A more explicit way to launch a set of *awaitable* objects such as coroutine, task, and future concurrently is with the **asyncio.gather()** function. This function accepts a sequence of awaitables as parameters. If there are coroutines in the sequence, they will be automatically scheduled as tasks. The order of execution, even if concurrent, follows the order of the sequence. When all the *awaitable* objects are completed, the **asyncio.gather()** function will return an aggregated list of values, whose order follows that of the sequence of awaitable passed as a parameter:

```
import asyncio
async def coroutine(t,id):
   await asyncio.sleep(t)
   print("I am the coroutine %s" %id)
   return t+2

async def main():
    results = await asyncio.gather(
        coroutine(10,"A"),
        coroutine(4,"B"),
        coroutine(2,"C"),
    )
    print("The results are: %s" %results)

asyncio.run(main())
```

Executing the code gives the following result:

```
I am the coroutine C
I am the coroutine B
I am the coroutine A
The results are: [12, 6, 4]
```

As we can see from the result, we have obtained concurrent behavior while using the coroutines instead of the tasks. In reality, these passed to the **asyncio.gather()** function converted them implicitly, making the code much more *readable* and *intuitive*. Here is what the corresponding code would have looked like if we had used tasks:

```
async def main():
    task1 = asyncio.create_task(coroutine(10,"A"))
    task2 = asyncio.create_task(coroutine(4,"B"))
    task3 = asyncio.create_task(coroutine(2,"C"))
    r1 = await task1
    r2 = await task2
    r3 = await task3
    results = [ r1, r2, r3]
    print("The results are: %s" %results)

asyncio.run(main())
```

Future

Another concept related to asynchronous programming is the use of futures that are implemented in the **asyncio** module by the **Future** class. A **future** conceptually represents a result (including an exception) that is not yet available at the time of processing.

Let us consider the following code:

```
import asyncio

async def get_result(result):
    await asyncio.sleep(5)
    result = '...an awaited result'

async def main():
    my_result = ' '
    task1 = asyncio.create_task(get_result(my_result))
    await task1

    print("I'm waiting for ...")
    print(my_result)

asyncio.run(main())
```

Executing the code gives the following result:

```
I'm waiting for ...
```

As we can see, no result was printed out; *the program finished its execution without waiting for the result.*

A **Future** is used in similar cases. After making the appropriate substitutions in the previous code, we will obtain a code like this:

```
import asyncio

async def get_result(future):
```

```
        await asyncio.sleep(5)
        future.set_result('...a future result')

    async def main():
        my_future = asyncio.Future()
        task1 = asyncio.create_task(get_result(my_future))
        await task1

        print("I'm waiting for ...")
        print(await my_future)
        print('Before continuing with my execution')

    asyncio.run(main())
```

Executing the code gives the following result:

```
I'm waiting for ...
...a future result
Before continuing with my execution
```

As we can see, this time the program waited for the result (5 *seconds*) and then printed all the outputs.

By introducing a **future** with **await**, the program will have to wait for the **get_result()** coroutine to produce the result (the **future** itself) and to continue with its execution.

The mechanism of a **Future** is therefore based on callback functions, (such as **get_result()** in the previous example) whose task is to process any result and assign it to the instance of the **Future()** class using the **set_result()** method.

Callback Functions

A callback is a function that is passed as an argument to another function.

```
def callbackFunc():
    #It Does something

def mainFunc(callbackFunc):
    ...
    callbackFunc()
    ...
```

The instance of the **Future** class is generated through its constructor.

```
future = asyncio.Future()
```

The new instance is thus passed as an argument in the callback function which must value it. When the result contained in the future is to be used, it will be inserted into the code with the await prefix, so that it can enter the **AsyncIO** scheduling mechanism. In this way, all program execution will be adjusted according to the *awaitable* objects. which will all be taken into account according to their execution times, asynchronously. The program, therefore, will wait for the valorization of the future, while executing everything possible in a *concurrent* manner, and then continue the *flow of execution.*

A **Future** is therefore also an *awaitable* object. A **future** is a result of a process (the callback function) whose execution status is *unknown*, but requires attention until its completion (in the future). So, when calling a **future** with **await**, it is already assumed that the result is not yet available. In this case, the following cases may occur:

- The process that **future** represents has finished and a result has already been entered for future. In this case, the **await** statement immediately returns that value.

- The process that **future** represents has *failed*, returning an *exception*. In this case, the **await** statement immediately throws the exception.
- The process that **future** represents is still running and the **future** is not valued. In this case, all the other tasks await the end of the process and the valorization of the **future**. As soon as the status of the **future** is completed, then the **await** statement will return the result or raise an exception depending on the case, and the execution of the program will go on.

The distinction between a **coroutine** and a **future** is very important. A **coroutine** code will *not* execute while it is waiting. A **future** represents something that is running anyway, and it simply allows your code to wait for it to finish, check if it is done, and then deliver the result.

`Asyncio.futures` and `concurrent.futures`: Despite the similarity between the two, one must be very careful not to confuse these future classes. The futures of the concurrent module are based on a multi-threaded construct, while those of asyncio are strongly single-threaded. Although they perform the same tasks semantically, they work in different ways, and cannot be interchanged with each other.

Event Loop

From the point of view of programming models, as far as events are concerned, we have *three* entities at play:

- Event Source
- Event Handler
- Event Loop

In a calculation system, an **event source** is defined as the entity that generates events. The latter is managed by another entity, defined as an **event handler**. The **event loop** acts as a link between the *event sources* and the *event handler* (refer to *Figure* 4.2).

Figure 4.2: *The EventL*

In fact, **events** are generated *randomly* and *asynchronously*. Therefore, there is a rare direct correspondence between event generation and event management. There is always a *period of time* (*asynchronicity*) between the *two* operations when events are generated to be managed later.

The AsyncIO library implements the *event loop* through the **`Loop`** class with the following methods:

- **`asyncio.new_event_loop()`**: Creates and returns a new event loop
- **`asyncio.get_event_loop()`**: Returns the event loop of the current context
- **`asyncio.set_event_loop()`**: Sets the event loop for the current context
- **`Loop.call_later()`**: Schedules a callback to be called after the given delay number of seconds
- **`Loop.call_soon()`**: Schedules a callback to be called at the next iteration of the event loop
- **`Loop.run_until_complete()`**: Runs until the coroutine (passed as argument) has been completed

- **Loop.run_forever()**: Runs the event loop until **stop()** is called
- **Loop.stop()**: Stops the event loop
- **Loop.close()**: Closes the event loop

The event loop is an *intrinsic object* in the asynchronous execution mechanism of **asyncio** and is implicitly activated when this command is launched:

```
asyncio.run(main())
```

Event loop can be understood as a **while True** loop created to monitor the execution status of the coroutines involved in asynchronous scheduling through **async / await** construct. The event loop will thus know which coroutines are in an *idle* state and which tasks must be executed in the meantime. So, it will be the event loop that wakes a coroutine from its *idle* state and makes it perform its operations. When each of the coroutines is finished, the event loop will mark the related task as *complete*. Finally, when all the tasks are finished, then the event loop will close.

Therefore, the event loop can be considered the great director of asynchronous operation of the **AsyncIO** library. Normally, the event loop starts, carries out its operations, and closes implicitly. In fact, we have not seen any reference to it in the previous examples with coroutines, tasks, and futures.

However, it is also possible to manage the event loop in the code explicitly. The typical pattern is:

```
loop = asyncio.new_event_loop()
asyncio.set_event_loop(loop)
try:
    loop.run_until_complete(main())
finally:
    loop.close()
```

This is perfectly equivalent to just the **asyncio.run(main())** command, as you can see in the following code:

```
import asyncio

async def main():
    print('Starting...')
    await asyncio.sleep(10)
    print('...Ending')

loop = asyncio.new_event_loop()
asyncio.set_event_loop(loop)
try:
    loop.run_until_complete(main())
finally:
    loop.close()
```

In the code, we see how the **asyncio.get_event_loop()** function is used to assign the current event loop to a loop reference variable. In this way, it will be possible to explicitly control the workflow of the event loop. Within a **try-finally** construct, we then launch the scheduling and execution of the **main()** coroutine and at the same time, all the *awaitables* called within it. Upon the completion of all scheduled asynchronous operations, or in the eventual launch of exceptions, the event loop must be closed to release the resources via the **loop.close()** method.

This is the simplest case, but many more complex cases can be implemented where greater control is required over its operation. There is a whole series of methods that regulate its flow and allow its monitoring. For example, the methods **loop.is_running()** and **loop.is_closed()** allow you to check the execution status of the event loop.

It must be said that in many cases, it is never necessary to make the event loop explicit in our code.

Asynchronous Iterations With and Without `async for`

`async for` allows you to iterate over an asynchronous iterator. It is able to make asynchronous calls at each step of the iteration. An extension of this concept is the asynchronous generator, which is a coroutine where you can use **`await`** and **`yield`** together, as demonstrated here:

```
async def gen(n):
  for i in range(n):
    await asyncio.sleep(1)
    yield i
```

This asynchronous generator can be used as an asynchronous iterator in an **`async for`**, as in the case of the following code:

```
import asyncio

async def gen(n):
  for i in range(n):
    await asyncio.sleep(1)
    yield i
async def main():
    async for i in gen(10):
      print(i)

asyncio.run(main())
```

Running the code gives the following result:

```
0
1
2
3
4
5
6
7
8
9
```

However, as we can see, asynchronous generators fail to make the iteration concurrent. The results of the various steps are shown in the same iteration order. **`Async for`** therefore does not allow the implementation of concurrent execution. All it provides is the ability to leave the event loop in control for some other running coroutine.

If, on the other hand, we want to obtain an iteration in which the various steps compete with each other, we will use another way. The **`asyncio.as_completed()`** function accepts a sequence of *awaitable*, similar to **`asyncio.gather()`**. This function returns an iterator of coroutines that act in competition with each other.

We can see this with a simple example implemented through the following code:

```
import asyncio

async def f(i):
    print('start iteration step %s' %i)
    await asyncio.sleep(1)
    print('end iteration step %s' %i)
```

```
        return i

async def main():
    for j in asyncio.as_completed([f(i) for i in range(10)]):
        result = await j
        print('result received: %s' %result)

asyncio.run(main())
```

As we can see, we have passed a sequence of ten coroutines **f(i)** ranging from **f(0)** to **f(9)** to the **asyncio.as_completed()** function. This will return an iterator whose steps will represent the coroutines in the order they are completed (not of the incoming sequence). The coroutine of the sequence that ends *first* will be the first iteration step and its result will be also collected first and printed in the output. Then it will end immediately after and so on, until the last one.

By executing the preceding code, you get a result that perfectly reflects the behavior just described:

```
start iteration step 2
start iteration step 0
start iteration step 6
start iteration step 9
start iteration step 3
start iteration step 7
start iteration step 4
start iteration step 8
start iteration step 5
start iteration step 1
end iteration step 2
end iteration step 0
end iteration step 6
end iteration step 9
end iteration step 3
end iteration step 7
end iteration step 4
end iteration step 8
end iteration step 5
end iteration step 1
result received: 2
result received: 0
result received: 6
result received: 9
result received: 3
result received: 7
result received: 4
result received: 8
```

As we can see, the execution of the various steps of the iteration no longer follows the *sequential* order of the iteration. However, each step competes in its execution, trying to finish its task as soon as possible.

Queue in the Asynchronous Model

The **AsyncIO** library provides many tools to implement the asynchronous model. Like the *threading* and *multiprocessing* module, it can use **queues** to manage shared memory. In this case, threads will not compete for this resource, but coroutines will. In fact, the **asyncio.Queue** class allows you to implement the *producer-consumer* model in asynchronous programming akin to the queue seen in the previous two chapters.

Creating a shared space organized as regards asynchronous programming is no longer linked to a race condition problem as was the case with threads. Let us remember once again that AsyncIO works on a *single thread* and therefore, you should not have to deal with the thread-safety problems of the Python language.

In the case of **asyncio**, a queue carries out the task of connecting between *coroutine producer* and *coroutine consumer* which may not know of their reciprocal existence and may not be included in the same scheduling scheme. As a result, there will be a group of coroutine producers who add items to a queue one at a time, *asynchronously*. The *consumer coroutine* group will not have to wait for the completion of all the *producer coroutines*, but will receive a *signal* that they can in turn operate and take the items already processed within the queue.

So, let us create an example code in which we establish the number of *producers* and *consumers* through *two* variables that will be passed as arguments to the **main()** coroutine:

```
import asyncio
import random

async def producer(name, queue):
    n = random.randint(0, 10)
    await asyncio.sleep(n)
    await queue.put(n)
    print("Producer %s adds %s to the queue" %(name,n))

async def consumer(name, queue):
    while True:
        n = await queue.get()
        await asyncio.sleep(n)
        print("Consumer %s receives %s from the queue" %(name,n))
        queue.task_done()

async def main(nproducers, nconsumers):
    q = asyncio.Queue()
    producers = [asyncio.create_task(producer(n, q)) for n in range(nproducers)]
    consumers = [asyncio.create_task(consumer(n, q)) for n in range(nconsumers)]

    await asyncio.gather(*producers)
    await q.join()
    for c in consumers:
        c.cancel()

asyncio.run(main(4,2))
```

We have chosen *four producers* and *two consumers* as an example. All coroutine producers will insert a random integer from 0 to 9 sec into the column, and in doing so they will take as many seconds as this random value, *thanks* to the **asyncio.sleep()** function. All coroutine producers will be launched in competition with each other using the **asyncio.gather()** function. A queue object will be instantiated and the values generated by the producers will be added to it according to the runtime via the **queue.put()** method. As you can see from the code, this method is also a coroutine anticipated by the **await** prefix. The *consumer coroutines* will then be created and scheduled separately for the producers. In fact, they are not present in the **asyncio.gather()** method, but are implicitly activated with the queue at each call **queue.get()** with which the coroutines obtain the values contained within it. This relationship between the *consumers* and the *queue* allows for the perfect functioning of the whole *producer-consumer system*. This is because the queue will take care of activating the consumers available when there are items inside.

If we execute the code, we will get a result like the following:

```
Producer 1 adds 0 to the queue
Consumer 0 receives 0 from the queue
Producer 2 adds 1 to the queue
Consumer 1 receives 1 from the queue
Producer 3 adds 8 to the queue
Producer 0 adds 9 to the queue
Consumer 0 receives 8 from the queue
Consumer 1 receives 9 from the queue
```

Alternatives to the `AsyncIO` library

In recent years, *thanks* also to the success of asynchronous programming that does not use threads, other interesting libraries have developed that are valid alternatives to the **`AsyncIO`** library. These are explained as follows:

- **Curio (https://curio.readthedocs.io/)** is a library that uses coroutines, tasks, and queues. It also has an **`async`** / **`await`** syntax. Those who already know **`asyncio`** and the concepts that structure the implementation of the asynchronous model are therefore recommended to use this.
- **Trio (https://trio.readthedocs.io/)** is an even more ambitious project since it is a direct alternative to the **`asyncio`** library. It is more simple and in step with the continuous innovations added to the Python language. This is a young, exciting project that deserves special attention.

Comparison of Competing Approaches

In the previous chapter, we have already seen the main differences between threading and multiprocessing and the advantages and disadvantages of applying one or the other of the two approaches. In this chapter, we have talked about AsyncIO. Before exploring the practical differences between this and the two previous techniques, it is useful to clarify the concepts of concurrency and parallelism.

- **Concurrency**: This refers to the interleaved execution of multiple tasks, apparently occurring at the same time. Concurrency can be implemented through threads, AsyncIO, or other asynchronous task management systems.
- **Parallelism**: It refers to the simultaneous execution of multiple tasks on different CPU cores. True parallelism requires multi-core hardware resources and can be achieved mainly through multiprocessing.

AsyncIO is Python's solution for non-blocking asynchronous programming, where tasks are managed through an event loop that schedules and coordinates operations. This allows for other activities to be performed during waits (for example, input/output, sleep, and so on). The AsyncIO approach is particularly effective for I/O-bound applications, such as web servers, scrapers, and networking tools, as it reduces processor idle time.

Advantages of AsyncIO

- **Non-Blocking**: Allows the process to advance without waiting for I/O tasks to complete
- **Memory Efficient**: Runs everything in a single process without creating new threads or processes, thus reducing memory consumption
- **Coroutine Support**: AsyncIO uses coroutines (**`async`** and **`await`**), which makes the code readable and maintainable even for complex operations

Limitations of AsyncIO

- **Limited to I/O-Bound Tasks**: AsyncIO is not ideal for CPU-bound (compute-intensive) applications, as each compute operation blocks the event loop.
- **Single-Threaded**: AsyncIO operates on a single thread and is limited to one CPU core.

Let us see an example of AsyncIO for I/O-bound tasks:

```
import asyncio

async def fetch_data(n):
    print(f"Start fetch_data {n}")
    await asyncio.sleep(2)  # Simulates an I/O wait
    print(f"fetch_data {n} completed")

async def main():
    tasks = [fetch_data(i) for i in range(3)]
    await asyncio.gather(*tasks)

asyncio.run(main())
```

Running the code will give you the following result:

```
Start fetch_data 0
Start fetch_data 1
Start fetch_data 2
fetch_data 0 completed
fetch_data 1 completed
fetch_data 2 completed
```

The following table (*Table 4.1*) presents a simple way to analyze the differences between these three approaches:

Technique	Ideal for	Advantages	Disadvantages
AsyncIO	I/O-bound tasks (network, file)	Lightweight, non-blocking, efficient memory usage	Limited to a single core, not suitable for CPU-bound tasks
Threading	I/O-bound tasks, lightweight parallel tasks	Memory sharing, good network operations management	Limited by GIL for CPU-bound tasks, concurrency issues
Multiprocessing	CPU-bound tasks (intensive calculations)	True parallelism across multiple cores, memory isolation	Higher memory consumption, complex communication between processes

***Table 4.1**: Overview of Python Concurrency Techniques and Their Main Advantages and Disadvantages*

At first glance, we can see that the main competitors (and this is not a joke) are threading and AsyncIO, which share common fields of use such as I/O-bound tasks (for example, web server, scraper, network operations). In fact, AsyncIO is generally the preferred solution to handle numerous I/O tasks without blocking the program, unless heavy computations are also needed. In the latter case, threading may be more suitable. As for multiprocessing, the conclusions from the previous chapter remain unchanged: it remains the most suitable method in CPU-bound tasks.

Limitations of AsyncIO in I/O-Intensive or CPU-Bound Applications

Despite the advantages of AsyncIO for handling I/O-bound tasks in a non-blocking and asynchronous manner, it has some limitations when it comes to handling highly I/O-intensive or CPU-bound applications. In this section, we will explore the constraints of AsyncIO in these scenarios, discussing the causes of the limitations and possible alternatives or workarounds. AsyncIO is designed to handle concurrent operations on a single thread using an event loop, which makes it well-suited for I/O-bound applications, such as those involving network operations or file access. However, because AsyncIO operates in a single-threaded manner, its use in applications that are I/O-intensive or require CPU-bound processing is limited. Let us review the main limitations of AsyncIO in these contexts.

In I/O-intensive applications, AsyncIO effectively handles tasks that asynchronously perform network operations, file reads and writes, or database interactions. However, when the I/O load is extremely high, the following disadvantages may arise:

Single-Threaded High-Load Handling: AsyncIO executes all coroutines in a single thread, which can be a bottleneck when there are too many I/O tasks to handle at the same time. Since operations are sequenced based on the order of the event loop, a large number of tasks can cause the event loop to become saturated and increase waiting times.

Limited Scalability across Multiple Cores: Since AsyncIO is single-threaded, it cannot leverage multiple CPU cores to handle parallel I/O requests. In scenarios with thousands of concurrent connections or extreme I/O loads, solutions like threading or the use of networking frameworks (for example, uvloop, Tornado, or multiprocessing-based libraries) may be more effective.

Let us consider a scenario where there are many concurrent network requests. Here, we will use the **aiohttp** module. If it is not present on your system, install it via:

```
pip install aiohttp
```

```
import asyncio
import aiohttp

async def fetch_url(url):
    async with aiohttp.ClientSession() as session:
        async with session.get(url) as response:
            await response.text()
            print(f"Completed: {url}")

async def main():
    urls = ["http://example.com" for _ in range(1000)]  # Simula molte
richieste
    tasks = [fetch_url(url) for url in urls]
    await asyncio.gather(*tasks)

asyncio.run(main())
```

Running the code will display the following repetition of the http calls:

```
Completed: http://example.com
Completed: http://example.com
Completed: http://example.com
...
```

In this example, the event loop attempts to handle 1000 HTTP requests in parallel. With a high load like this, sequentially handling the event loop can slow down significantly and result in slower response times.

Alternatives for I/O-Intensive Applications

- **Optimized Networking Libraries**: **uvloop** can replace the default AsyncIO event loop and improve performance on many I/O-intensive operations.

- **Multi-Process Architectures**: Using multiprocessing to distribute the load across multiple processes can help manage overhead and improve scalability.

As mentioned in the previous section, AsyncIO is not designed to run CPU-bound tasks. CPU-bound applications require intensive computations that consume a lot of resources, which is problematic for AsyncIO due to the following reasons:

- **Event Loop Blocking**: A CPU-bound task can block the event loop, preventing other tasks from progressing. Since AsyncIO operates in a single-threaded mode, a CPU-intensive task monopolizes the thread, while slowing down or blocking other coroutines.
- **Inability to Leverage Multiple CPU Cores**: Since AsyncIO is not multi-threaded or multi-processed by default, it cannot distribute the workload across multiple cores, thus dramatically reducing performance in CPU-bound applications, compared to solutions like multiprocessing.

Consider a task that performs an intensive computation like the one here:

```
import asyncio

import sys
# For increase the limit of digits for integer string conversion
sys.set_int_max_str_digits(0)

def compute_factorial(n):
    result = 1
    for i in range(1, n + 1):
        result *= i
    return result

async def main():
    loop = asyncio.get_running_loop()
    # Performs the calculation synchronously
    result = await loop.run_in_executor(None, compute_factorial, 10000)
    print("Calculated factorial:", result)

asyncio.run(main())
```

```
Calculated factorial: 51841810604808769398058197974277269856511005319368417706
723611545954294753166061875566435447626784821572166271778342402091402355456360
759666129510947303593450836804933452905378077728424422343094866850420754576162
984869739063028010804560477838079341985337337324170215687830760514651898649654
74928431081298506769884431393829005536805059336923233701577761195418139577992
7796928247982170444256906306429759566061528421738794329359339468...
```

In this example, **compute_factorial** performs a heavy computation. If it were executed inside the event loop, it would block other operations. Using **run_in_executor** allows you to delegate the computation to a separate thread or process, but it introduces overhead and requires careful resource management.

Alternatives for CPU-Bound Applications

- **Multiprocessing**: For intensive tasks that require parallel computations, multiprocessing allows you to distribute the load across multiple processes, effectively using all cores.
- **Delegation to Threads or Processes with run_in_executor**: If some parts of the application need to be CPU-bound, they can be delegated to separate threads or processes using **run_in_executor**, while avoiding blocking the event loop.

For this purpose, Python offers **run_in_executor** to run synchronous tasks in a separate thread or process. This can be useful when an asynchronous application has some CPU-bound tasks. However,

run_in_executor introduces management overhead and is not always as effective as a fully multi-process architecture for heavy loads. Let us see an example of how to apply it:

```
import asyncio
import time

def heavy_computation(n):
    start = time.time()
    sum = 0
    for i in range(n):
        sum += i * i
    end = time.time()
    print(f"Computation took {end - start:.2f} seconds")
    return sum

async def main():
    loop = asyncio.get_running_loop()
    result = await loop.run_in_executor(None, heavy_computation, 10**7)
    print("Result:", result)

asyncio.run(main())
Computation took 0.35 seconds
Risultato: 333333283333335000000
```

In this example, **heavy_computation** runs on a separate thread to avoid blocking the main event loop. This approach reduces the impact on the main asynchronous flow, but may be a less efficient tradeoff for high-performance CPU-bound tasks.

For applications that require handling large-scale I/O-intensive or CPU-bound tasks, there are several alternatives and approaches that can be combined with AsyncIO to improve scalability. These are mentioned as follows:

- **Threading and AsyncIO Combined**: AsyncIO can be used in conjunction with threads to handle I/O-bound and CPU-bound tasks separately, where AsyncIO handles the I/O and threading delegates the CPU-bound load.
- **Multiprocessing with AsyncIO**: In contexts where scalability and parallelism are critical, multiprocessing can be used to handle CPU-bound tasks, while AsyncIO coordinates the I/O tasks.
- **Distributed Computing Frameworks**: For compute-intensive applications, frameworks like Dask or Ray allow you to distribute the load across clusters of machines, while easily integrating with AsyncIO.

Advanced Error Handling in Asynchronous Applications

For asynchronous applications, error handling is critical, as non-sequential execution makes it more difficult to trace exceptions and identify the source of problems. In this section, we explore advanced techniques for error handling in asynchronous applications, while focusing on how to implement robust error handling with AsyncIO.

Asynchronous applications offer great benefits for I/O-bound tasks and reactive systems, but they present complexities in error handling. While in synchronous applications, an error can propagate sequentially through the call stack; in asynchronous applications with AsyncIO, errors can occur in multiple coroutines and require more advanced techniques to catch and handle exceptions correctly.

In this section, we cover the best practices for handling errors in AsyncIO, including techniques for catching exceptions, implementing automatic retries, using advanced timeouts, and logging. In AsyncIO, exceptions in coroutines can be caught as in synchronous code using try...except, but they must be implemented within individual coroutines. However, for asynchronous applications that call multiple coroutines in parallel, the traditional approach may not be sufficient, as exceptions may not propagate in a predictable manner.

Let us start with an example of how to handle exceptions inside a coroutine:

```
import asyncio

async def fetch_data(n):
    try:
        if n == 3:
            raise ValueError("Error in task 3")
        await asyncio.sleep(1)
        print(f"Task {n} completed successfully")
    except ValueError as e:
        print(f"Error caught: {e}")

async def main():
    tasks = [fetch_data(i) for i in range(5)]
    await asyncio.gather(*tasks)

asyncio.run(main())
```

Running the code will give you the following result:

```
Error caught: Error in task 3
Task 0 completed successfully
Task 2 completed successfully
Task 1 completed successfully
Task 4 completed successfully
```

In this example, the error thrown in task 3 is handled locally. However, when you are running many coroutines in parallel, it is useful to handle exceptions at a higher level as well. For this purpose, **asyncio.gather** allows you to gather multiple coroutines and wait for all of them to complete. By default, if any of the coroutines in the group throws an exception, gather stops the others and propagates the error to the higher level. However, we can handle exceptions individually by configuring gather with the **return_exceptions=True** option. This is shown as follows:

```
import asyncio

async def fetch_data(n):
    if n == 2:
        raise ValueError("Error in task 2")
    await asyncio.sleep(1)
    return f"Task {n} completed"

async def main():
    tasks = [fetch_data(i) for i in range(5)]
    results = await asyncio.gather(*tasks, return_exceptions=True)

    for i, result in enumerate(results):
        if isinstance(result, Exception):
            print(f"Task {i} generated an error: {result}")
        else:
            print(f"Task result {i}: {result}")

asyncio.run(main())
```

Running the code gives the following result:

```
Task result 0: Task 0 completed
Task result 1: Task 1 completed
Task 2 generated an error: Error in task 2
Task result 3: Task 3 completed
Task result 4: Task 4 completed
```

In this example, **`return_exceptions=True`** causes all tasks to complete, even if one or more of them raise exceptions. Errors are logged as part of the results list, that allow for centralized exception handling.

Automatic Retry, Timeout, and Logging in Asynchronous Operations

While learning about exception handling, let us also talk about other related concepts. In asynchronous applications, it is often useful to implement automatic retry for tasks that can fail due to temporary errors (for example, problems connecting to a network). Automatic retry can be implemented directly in the coroutine by adding a loop that manages the maximum number of retries and the time interval between each retry. This is shown as follows:

```
import asyncio
import random

async def fetch_data_with_retry(n, retries=3, delay=2):
    """Simulates an asynchronous task with automatic retry."""
    for attempt in range(retries):
        try:
            if random.random() < 0.5:  # Simulates a random error
                raise ValueError(f"Errore temporaneo nel task {n}")
            await asyncio.sleep(1)
            print(f"Task {n} successfully completed on attempt {attempt + 1}")
            return f"Risultato del task {n}"
        except ValueError as e:
            print(f"Attempt {attempt + 1} for the task {n} failed: {e}")
            await asyncio.sleep(delay)
    raise RuntimeError(f"Task {n} failed after {retries} attempts")

async def main():
    tasks = [fetch_data_with_retry(i) for i in range(5)]
    results = await asyncio.gather(*tasks, return_exceptions=True)
    print("Risults:", results)

asyncio.run(main())
```

Running the code gives the following result:

```
Attempt 1 for the task 0 failed: Errore temporaneo nel task 0
Attempt 1 for the task 3 failed: Errore temporaneo nel task 3
Attempt 1 for the task 4 failed: Errore temporaneo nel task 4
Task 1 successfully completed on attempt 1
Task 2 successfully completed on attempt 1
Attempt 2 for the task 3 failed: Errore temporaneo nel task 3
Task 4 successfully completed on attempt 2
Task 0 successfully completed on attempt 2
Attempt 3 for the task 3 failed: Errore temporaneo nel task 3
```

```
Risults: ['Risultato del task 0', 'Risultato del task 1', 'Risultato del task 2', RuntimeError('Task 3 failed after 3 attempts'), 'Risultato del task 4']
```

In this example, each task is retried up to a maximum of retries times, with a delay interval between retries. Transient errors are handled, and only if all retries fail will an exception be raised.

Another concept related to exceptions is timeout. In asynchronous applications, some operations may block or take too long to complete. To handle these cases, we can use **asyncio.wait_for**, which allows us to set a maximum timeout for each operation. If the operation does not finish within the specified time, a **TimeoutError** exception is raised, as is shown in the following code:

```
import asyncio

async def fetch_data(n):
    await asyncio.sleep(n)
    return f"Task {n} completed"

async def main():
    tasks = [asyncio.wait_for(fetch_data(i), timeout=2) for i in range(5)]

    results = await asyncio.gather(*tasks, return_exceptions=True)
    for i, result in enumerate(results):
        if isinstance(result, asyncio.TimeoutError):
            print(f"Task {i} is expired")
        else:
            print(f"Task result {i}: {result}")

asyncio.run(main())
```

Running the code gives the following result:

```
Task result 0: Task 0 completed
Task result 1: Task 1 completed
Task 2 is expired
Task 3 is expired
Task 4 is expired
```

In this example, **asyncio.wait_for** sets a time limit of 2 seconds for each task. If a task does not complete within the timeout, a **TimeoutError** exception is raised, and handled in the final loop.

Another great concept which is closely related to error handling, is error tracing. To detect and analyze errors in an asynchronous application, it is useful to set up an advanced logging system. Python's logging module can be configured to trace exceptions and record detailed information about each task, which allows for easier and more complete diagnosis.

```
import asyncio
import logging

# Configure logging
logging.basicConfig(level=logging.INFO, format='%(asctime)s - %(levelname)s - %(message)s')

async def fetch_data(n):
    try:
        if n % 2 == 0:
            raise ValueError("Errore simulato")
        await asyncio.sleep(1)
        logging.info(f"Task {n} completed successfully")
    except Exception as e:
        logging.error(f"Error in task {n}: {e}")
```

```
async def main():
    tasks = [fetch_data(i) for i in range(5)]
    await asyncio.gather(*tasks)

asyncio.run(main())
```

The executed code gives the following result:

```
2024-11-07 17:46:07,624 - ERROR - Error in task 0: Simulated error
2024-11-07 17:46:07,624 - ERROR - Error in task 2: Simulated error
2024-11-07 17:46:07,624 - ERROR - Error in task 4: Simulated error
2024-11-07 17:46:08,636 - INFO - Task 1 completed successfully
2024-11-07 17:46:08,636 - INFO - Task 3 completed successfully
```

In this example, errors and success messages are logged with the logging module. Exceptions are handled at the coroutine level, and each error is logged with a timestamp and severity level (ERROR).

Advanced errors handling in asynchronous applications is essential to ensure system stability and reliability. With techniques such as automatic retry, the use of timeouts, and logging, you can improve the resilience of asynchronous applications, while ensuring that errors are detected and handled effectively without compromising overall performance.

Design Patterns for Scalable Applications with AsyncIO

To design scalable applications with AsyncIO, using design patterns allows you to structure your code in a more organized way, manage complexity, and improve the application's ability to adapt to increased demand. In this section, we will explore some AsyncIO-specific design patterns, such as the Task Aggregation Pattern, the Rate Limiter Pattern, the Producer-Consumer Pattern, and other useful patterns that help create robust and scalable asynchronous applications.

As we have seen in this chapter, asynchronous applications, thanks to non-blocking task management, are particularly suited to handle high loads and adapt to different scalability needs. However, designing scalable applications with AsyncIO requires a clear organization of asynchronous logic to achieve optimized and easy-to-maintain execution flows. Let us see how common design patterns can be applied in AsyncIO to improve scalability.

The Task Aggregation Pattern is used to group multiple asynchronous tasks and manage them as a single unit. With **asyncio.gather** or **asyncio.wait**, you can launch multiple coroutines and handle them as a group, while improving your ability to scale your application, without having to coordinate tasks individually. Let us see an example of this pattern with **asyncio.gather**:

```
import asyncio

async def fetch_data(n):
    await asyncio.sleep(1)
    print(f"Task {n} completed")
    return n

async def main():
    # Runs multiple tasks in parallel and collects the results
    tasks = [fetch_data(i) for i in range(5)]
    results = await asyncio.gather(*tasks)
    print("Aggregate results:", results)

asyncio.run(main())
```

Running the code gives the following result:

```
Task 0 completed
Task 2 completed
Task 4 completed
Task 1 completed
Task 3 completed
Aggregate results: [0, 1, 2, 3, 4]
```

In this example, **asyncio.gather** runs the **fetch_data** coroutines in parallel, aggregating the results. This pattern is useful for executing batches of tasks that can be completed independently, and collected in a single data structure.

Another commonly used pattern that is useful in applications with high loads of requests to an external service is the Rate Limiting Pattern. As an API, it is important to manage the frequency of calls to avoid overloading the servers or exceeding the rate limits. This pattern uses a control on execution times to respect the imposed limits. Here, we can see an example of how this pattern is structured using **asyncio.Semaphore**:

```
import asyncio
import random

async def fetch_data(n, rate_limiter):
    async with rate_limiter:  # Restrict access to tasks
        await asyncio.sleep(random.uniform(0.5, 1.5))
        print(f"Task {n} completed")
        return n

async def main():
    rate_limiter = asyncio.Semaphore(3)  # Limit to 3 simultaneous requests
    tasks = [fetch_data(i, rate_limiter) for i in range(10)]
    results = await asyncio.gather(*tasks)
    print("Results with rate limiting:", results)

asyncio.run(main())
```

Running the code gives the following result:

```
Task 1 completed
Task 2 completed
Task 0 completed
Task 5 completed
Task 3 completed
Task 4 completed
Task 6 completed
Task 8 completed
Task 9 completed
Task 7 completed
Results with rate limiting: [0, 1, 2, 3, 4, 5, 6, 7, 8, 9]
```

In this example, **asyncio.Semaphore** controls the number of tasks running at the same time, while keeping the limit at 3 active tasks. This pattern allows you to control the flow of requests, and respect the limits without overloading the system.

Another very common pattern with AsyncIO is the Producer-Consumer Pattern that is used to manage data flows in which one or more producers generate data and one or more consumers process them. In AsyncIO, this pattern can be implemented with **asyncio.Queue** to dynamically manage the task queue and distribute the loads. Let us see an example of using this pattern:

```
import asyncio
import random
```

```
async def producer(queue, n):
    for i in range(n):
        item = random.randint(1, 100)
        await queue.put(item)  # Aggiunge un task alla coda
        print(f"Prodotto: {item}")
        await asyncio.sleep(1)

async def consumer(queue):
    while True:
        item = await queue.get()
        print(f"Consumato: {item}")
        await asyncio.sleep(2)
        queue.task_done()  # Segnala il completamento del task

async def main():
    queue = asyncio.Queue()
    num_items = 5

    # Avvia il produttore e il consumatore
    producer_task = asyncio.create_task(producer(queue, num_items))
    consumer_task = asyncio.create_task(consumer(queue))

    await producer_task  # Aspetta che il produttore termini
    await queue.join()  # Aspetta che tutti i task in coda siano processati
    consumer_task.cancel()  # Interrompe il consumatore una volta terminato

asyncio.run(main())
```

Running the code will give the following result:

```
Producted: 9
Consumed: 9
Producted: 27
Consumed: 27
Producted: 78
Producted: 7
Consumed: 78
Producted: 43
Consumed: 7
Consumed: 43
```

In this example, the producer generates items and adds them to the queue, while the consumer fetches and processes them. The **asyncio.Queue** automatically manages tasks between producer and consumer, while balancing the load in a scalable way.

Another pattern is the Circuit Breaker, which is commonly used to prevent repeated calls to a failed service from causing further overload. This pattern intervenes by temporarily disabling requests to an external service if too many errors occur and re-enabling it after a waiting period. Here is an example of this pattern:

```
import asyncio

class CircuitBreaker:
    def __init__(self, max_failures, reset_timeout):
        self.max_failures = max_failures
        self.reset_timeout = reset_timeout
        self.failures = 0
        self.open = False
```

```
    async def call(self, func, *args):
        if self.open:
            print("Open circuit, attempt refused.")
            return
        try:
            result = await func(*args)
            self.failures = 0
            return result
        except Exception as e:
            self.failures += 1
            print(f"Error: {e}, failed attempts: {self.failures}")
            if self.failures >= self.max_failures:
                self.open = True
                print("Open circuit, waiting for reset.")
                await asyncio.sleep(self.reset_timeout)
                self.failures = 0
                self.open = False

async def unstable_task(n):
    if n % 2 == 0:
        raise ValueError("Simulated Error")
    return f"Task {n} completed"

async def main():
    circuit_breaker = CircuitBreaker(max_failures=2, reset_timeout=5)
    tasks = [circuit_breaker.call(unstable_task, i) for i in range(5)]
    await asyncio.gather(*tasks)

asyncio.run(main())
```

Running the code will give the following result:

```
Error: Simulated Error, failed attempts: 1
Error: Simulated Error, failed attempts: 1
Error: Simulated Error, failed attempts: 1
```

In this example, **CircuitBreaker** counts the failures. Once the **max_failures** limit is reached, it blocks further attempts for a **reset_timeout** period. This pattern is useful to efficiently handle recurring errors and maintain system stability.

Last but not least, the Bulkhead Pattern segments resources so that a group of tasks or services do not overload the entire system. Through multiple **asyncio.Semaphores**, it is possible to separately limit different sections of tasks to prevent the overloading in one section from affecting other parts of the application. Let us see an example:

```
import asyncio

async def limited_task(n, limiter, section_name):
    async with limiter:
        await asyncio.sleep(1)
        print(f"Task {n} completed in section {section_name}")

async def main():
    limiter_a = asyncio.Semaphore(2)  # Limit for section A
    limiter_b = asyncio.Semaphore(3)  # Limit for section B

    tasks = [limited_task(i, limiter_a, 'A') for i in range(5)] + \
            [limited_task(i, limiter_b, 'B') for i in range(5, 10)]
```

```
        await asyncio.gather(*tasks)

    asyncio.run(main())
```

Running the code will give the following result:

```
Task 0 completed in section A
Task 5 completed in section B
Task 7 completed in section B
Task 1 completed in section A
Task 6 completed in section B
Task 2 completed in section A
Task 9 completed in section B
Task 8 completed in section B
Task 3 completed in section A
Task 4 completed in section A
```

In this example, two sections (A and B) each enforce a limit on the number of tasks that can execute concurrently, thereby isolating resources. This pattern helps protect critical sections of the application from potential overloads.

AsyncIO design patterns provide well-established structures for managing the complexity of large-scale asynchronous applications.

Conclusion

In this chapter, we have explored the concept of asynchronous programming and the different cases in which it becomes concurrent. You will be able to understand the subtle consequences of different types of execution and how these differ from the results of parallel programming. You have seen that parallel programming is most effective for CPU-bound workloads, and that its advantages diminish when dealing with I/O-bound tasks. In contrast, asynchronous programming–and, more generally, concurrent programming–excels in these scenarios by allowing I/O-bound operations to be managed efficiently. All these concepts can be implemented **witg** the AsyncIO library and its basic tools. In the next chapter, we will deal with distributed programming, where we will apply the concepts learned in systems that are no longer limited to a single machine, but in systems that involve multiple processors distributed on different machines that are located in different places.

References

- https://docs.python.org/3/library/asyncio.html
- https://realpython.com/async-io-python/
- https://trio.readthedocs.io/en/stable/
- https://curio.readthedocs.io/en/latest/

Chapter 5
Distributed Python

Introduction

Distributed systems fall within the scope of parallel and concurrent programming and can be a valid solution due to their performance levels. Therefore, it is important to be familiar with these types of systems, as well as the related solutions that Python offers in this regard. In this chapter, we will cover several possible solutions. We will first learn about **Celery,** which is the reference point in Python for the realization of distributed systems. This library is a valid tool to construct this type of system and will help us understand the possible architectures, the elements that compose it, and the various mechanisms underlying them. Through a series of examples, we will see how to use this library to perform multiple concurrent operations, called **tasks**. We will also learn how tasks are distributed and executed in parallel on a Celery-based system. In addition to this, we will consider alternative solutions such as **Dramatiq** and conceptually different ones like **SCOOP**.

Structure

This chapter will address the following topics:

- Distributed Systems
- Client-Server Model
- Celery Framework
- Dramatiq
- Docker
- SCOOP

Distributed Systems and Programming

In a **distributed system**, the component application elements run on different machines and work in synergy. Despite the fact that these elements are located on different machines that are possibly geographically distant, they can communicate with each other via messages passed through a connection network.

The presence of entities that perform their tasks independently and simultaneously is a further extension of the threads and processes we saw in previous chapters. Thus, distributed systems, besides carrying out their useful operations in the key of the *client-server model*, can also carry out a series of operations in concurrency or even in parallel. It is therefore clear that distributed systems can be perfectly inserted in the context of parallel programming. Furthermore, most of the concepts that are dealt with in this chapter are also perfectly valid for these systems.

Therefore, we can extend the parallel programming in the client-server model (*Figure 5.1*) where a *client* requests a series of tasks from the *server*, which searches for an equal series of computation entities, called workers, in a distributed system. Hence, it can perform these tasks in parallel, which is also shown in the following figure:

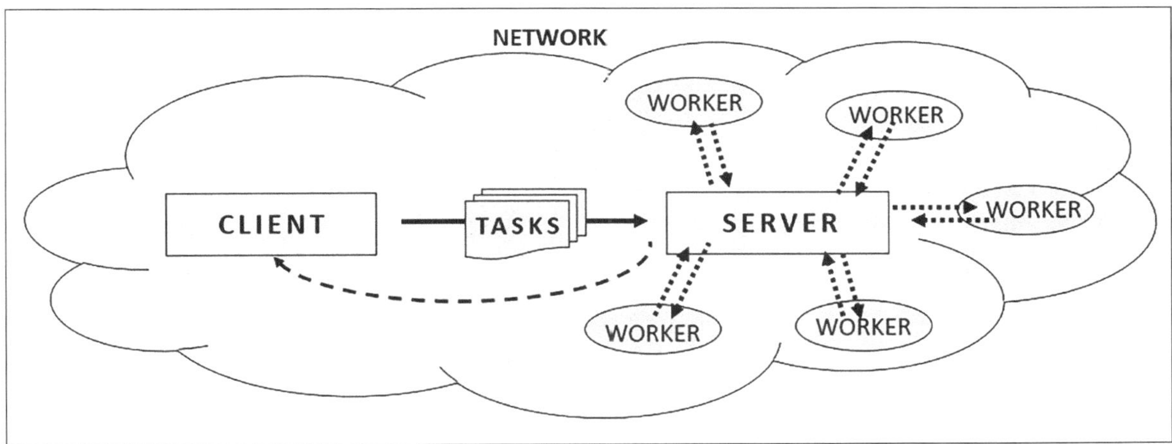

***Figure 5.1**: Distributed System in Parallel Programming*

The *server* will collect the results produced asynchronously and send them to the requesting client. This type of programming can be defined as distributed programming.

Pros and Cons of Distributed Systems

Distributed systems perform well due to the following factors:

- Scalability
- Concurrency
- Flexibility
- Robustness (Fault Tolerance)

All these factors are explained in considerable detail as follows:

- **Scalability**: It is achieved by increasing the number of elements in the system as the demand for resources grows. In theory, distributed systems allow for horizontal scaling by adding more machines or replicas of system components to share the workload. In practice, however, scalability is constrained by factors like network bandwidth, latency, consistency requirements, and the limits of the underlying software architecture. It is therefore more accurate to say that distributed systems are designed for horizontal scalability, despite limitations in achieving it.
- **Concurrency**: This is another feature implicit in the architecture of distributed systems. While carrying out a series of tasks, a distributed system assigns each of them to an independent processing unit, which acts simultaneously with the other units. All the tasks are subsequently carried out in competition as well as in parallel.
- **Flexibility**: The flexibility of a distributed system stems from the fact that each component plays a certain role and is distributed across machines connected to the system. These machines can be heterogeneous in nature. The components of the system can be viewed as independent applications that can be replaced by other compatible applications fulfilling the same role. When building a distributed system, this attribute opens up the possibility of choosing the application that will serve as a specific component, which is in turn motivated by factors like operating system, functionality, or special requirements. However, such flexibility is only achievable if the system is designed while factoring in strict interface contracts and backward compatibility; otherwise, replacing the components may obstruct functionality.
- **Robustness (Fault Tolerance)**: This is guaranteed by the redundancy of elements distributed in the system. Having copies of elements on different machines guarantees the possibility of continuing the work even if an application the entire machine fails. These systems manage

the movement of a task from an application in a transparent way. As a result, there will be no discontinuity in the execution of the requested services even after a failure at the customer's end.

Despite the merits of distributed systems, there also exist significant challenges.

As distributed systems are based on several elements that are possibly distributed on different machines, we might require robust communication mechanisms like **messaging**. The components of distributed systems message each other to exchange information. Therefore, it is necessary to create a message and send it over the network to the right recipient, who receives and unpacks it to search for information. It is clear that such distributed systems will also require sub-systems that manage it. This, in turn, results in a heavy consumption of resources.

Moreover, since distributed systems are composed of many different elements, maintaining them can be a major challenge. In fact, there are many applications that can perform these tasks. However, they should be implemented in a way that they are compatible with all the systems and are able to perform all possible functionalities. As it is nearly impossible, incompatibilities may arise, especially if you have updated versions of some elements compared to others.

Furthermore, as the elements grow, the complexity of operation also deepens. Thus, in the case of problems or management, it becomes increasingly difficult to ensure the perfect functioning of a system.

The last challenge is encountering the *dependence* of the network infrastructure of a distributed system. Maintaining such infrastructure is essential to ensure the efficiency of a distributed system. Network failures, bad configurations, or other problems are signs of imperfect network management. This task is often out of the developer's purview.

Celery Framework

Celery is a Python framework designed for distributed task processing. By relying on a message broker and a pool of workers, it executes tasks asynchronously and in parallel across multiple machines. This makes it possible to build scalable distributed systems of varying complexity, from relatively simple deployments with a broker and workers running on the same host, to large-scale clusters that span many machines and different technologies. It is important to note that when Celery is confined to a single machine, it provides for concurrent or parallel task execution, rather than providing for a truly distributed system. Given Python's ability to run across multiple architectures and operating systems, Celery is hence widely adaptable and portable.

The main characteristics of a Celery distributed system can be summarized in the following key points:

- Portability
- High Availability
- Scaling

In this system, even if the architecture is mainly controlled by Celery, its various components can be added, replaced, and modified without major problems (these are also referred to as *pluggable* components). This design makes the system highly adaptable to different needs and technologies. This approach is perfectly suited to distributed systems as each of these components generally reside in a different machine, are physically separated, and even geographically distant, while being connected to the system.

Another advantage of this architecture is that the components that perform services for clients (such as **brokers** and **workers**) can be present in a variable number and distributed on different machines. In this way, one might guarantee continuous operability, even if some machines encounter hardware or software problems. This makes the system highly available. Furthermore, the number of such components is variable depending on the request. From a theoretical point of view, this number has no upper limit. It is easy to add additional machines to the system via network connections and share the consumption of resources while keeping it unchanged for each component. Therefore, as the problem grows, it is possible to add additional components, distribute resources efficiently, and ensure horizontal scaling.

Architecture of Celery Systems

In a *Celery-based distributed system*, many different components come into play, each of which plays a specific role in the mechanism of distributed computing (see *Figure* 5.2). The main components are:

- Broker
- Task Queue
- Clients
- Workers
- Result Backend (*optional*)

These components exchange values and information with each other through a *message mechanism*. In order for this to work, it must be supported by a message transport application, which is referred to as a **Broker**. There are several message transport applications compatible with Celery systems, and each of them uses a different *communication protocol* as demonstrated in the following figure:

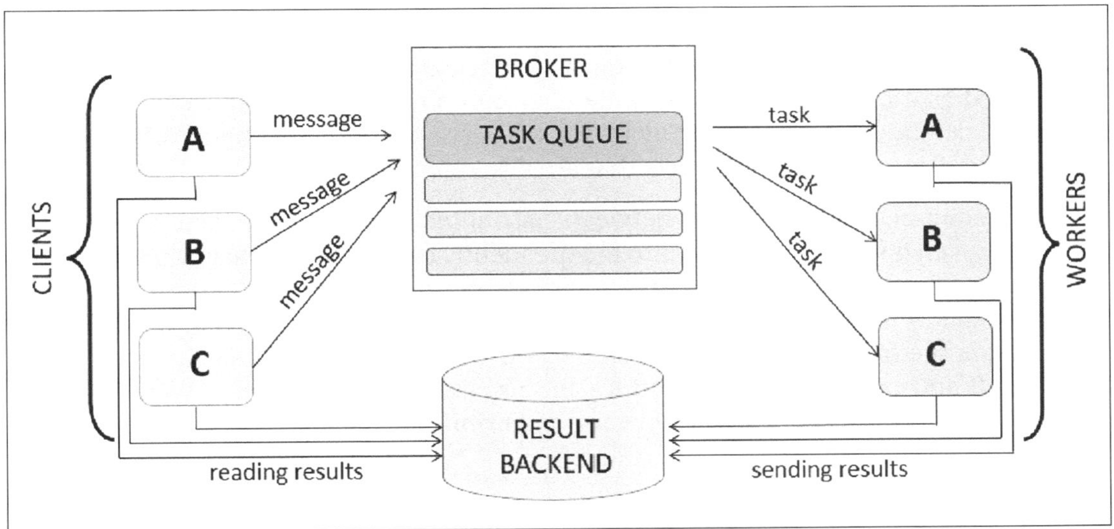

Figure 5.2: *Celery Architecture*

CLIENTS are processes that require certain services made available by the distributed system as they carry out their respective tasks. These requests are made through messages that indicate the task to be performed. These messages are then sent to the *broker* who will manage them. At the end of the processing phase, the *client* finds the result of the request in the result backend, which is usually a database. A schematic diagram of this architecture is shown in *Figure* 5.2.

WORKERS are the processes present either on the same machine or on other machines distributed on the network that are connected to the Celery system. These processes have been specifically designed to perform the tasks dispatched to them by the broker. The workers wait till they receive the tasks assigned to them. Then they execute it, and send the result to the result backend.

Generally, these workers can perform various tasks. This increases the efficiency of the system. If a worker does not receive a specific task, it can perform other tasks in the queue instead of waiting.

The broker and inherent task queues play a central role in Celery's distributed architecture. The broker performs *two* basic tasks that are mentioned as follows:

- It receives messages sent by various customers by entering the related tasks within the task queue.
- It then dispatches the various tasks queued to the corresponding waiting workers.

The queues accumulate the tasks requested by the various clients. In this way if a worker is not immediately available to entertain a client service request, the task will remain in the task queue and will wait to be processed. The broker will distribute the various tasks to the various waiting workers. Therefore, it will be possible to manage the execution of tasks in an *asynchronous* and *concurrent* manner.

The result backend collects the results produced by the different workers during the execution phase. These results will then be available to clients through reading. Here, the returned values enter an asynchronous mechanism, which allows the results to accumulate without managing a single result immediately after it returns. These mechanisms are necessary in a distributed system, where various components act independently from each other, while requesting, processing, and managing the result in unpredictable times. This makes wait times necessary.

Tasks

As we have seen previously, Celery systems (and distributed systems in general) are based on the distribution of tasks that have to be performed efficiently among the various components. Any task that needs to be distributed in the system must be encapsulated within another task. A **task** can also be identified as a unit of work that can be distributed in such a system. This last definition is very useful as it can be traced back to concurrent and parallel programming, in which any task can generally be divided into small *atomic* parts that are also referred to as a task.

It is here that a point of contact emerges between distributed systems and concurrent programming. Once we have broken down our problem into independently executable tasks; in a distributed system, these can be sent to a broker and executed concurrently by different workers distributed on the network. The results will then be collected in the result backend and will be recomposed by the client program to obtain the final output. We have already encountered similar behavior when dealing with *threading threads* and *asynchronous co-routines*. In this case, however, we have workers that identify different realities like **processes**, **threads**, **events**, and **eventlets**. All are managed transparently or via appropriate settings.

Setting Up the Celery System

Having defined the components of a system distributed on Celery, let us now move on to its practical implementation, and learn about installing and setting all the components.

Anaconda Installation

A *practical tip*: When you want to build test systems, like the ones in this book, it is good practice to create a virtual environment where you can install the different Python packages and modules. It can be removed without problems in case of errors and will not create any conflicts between the basic versions of Python already installed in our system and all the dependencies, deletions, and manual installations that were made during our test environment installations.

We can use the **Anaconda** development platform to manage virtual environments and package installations. For the unversed, this platform can be downloaded for *free* from the web (**https://www.**

anaconda.com/products/distribution). The web page will suggest to you the most updated and stable distribution for your operating system as shown in *Figure* 5.3:

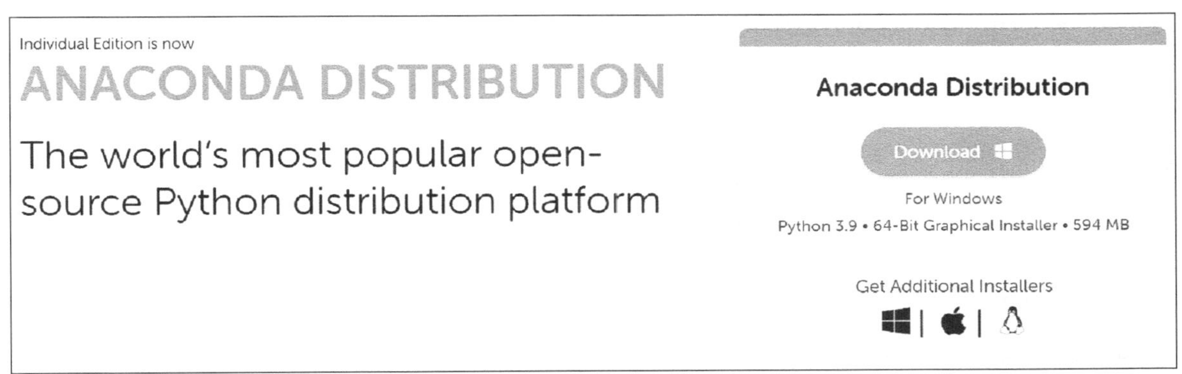

Figure 5.3: *Anaconda Distribution Web Page*

Once installed, you can create a virtual environment from the **Environments** panel (see *Figure* 5.4).

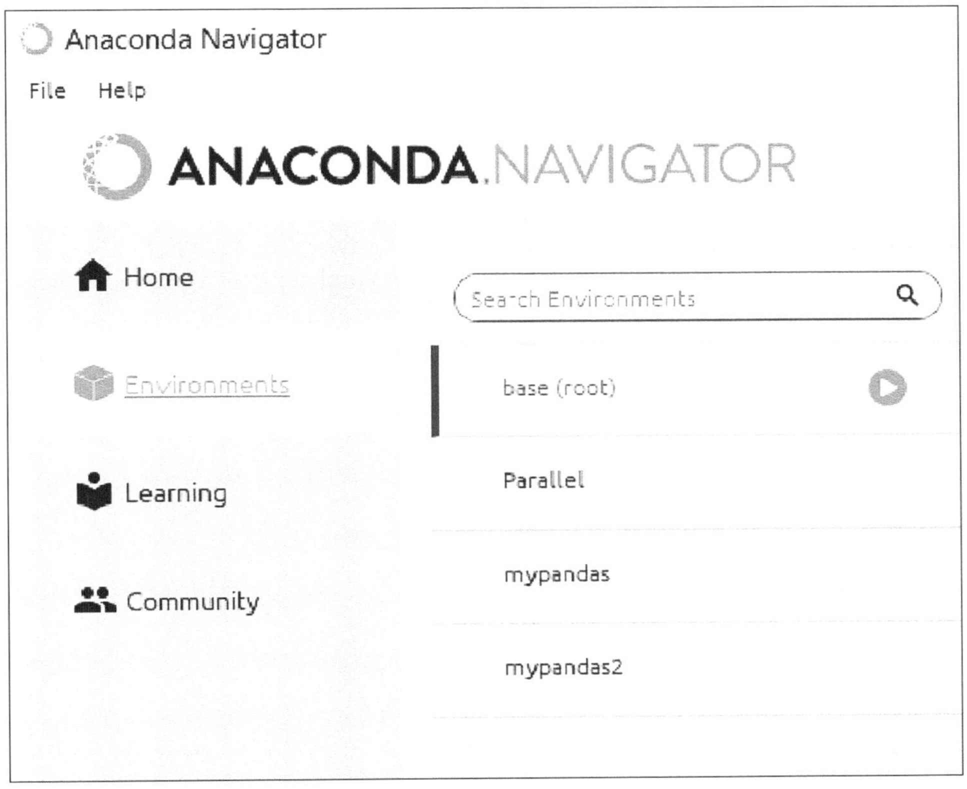

Figure 5.4: *Anaconda Navigator*

Then click on the **Create** button as shown in the following *Figure* 5.5:

Figure 5.5: *Create a Virtual Environment Button in Anaconda Navigator*

Pressing this button will open a dialog box where you can enter the name of the virtual environment you want to use. You can also choose the version of Python on which it will be based, as shown in *Figure* 5.6:

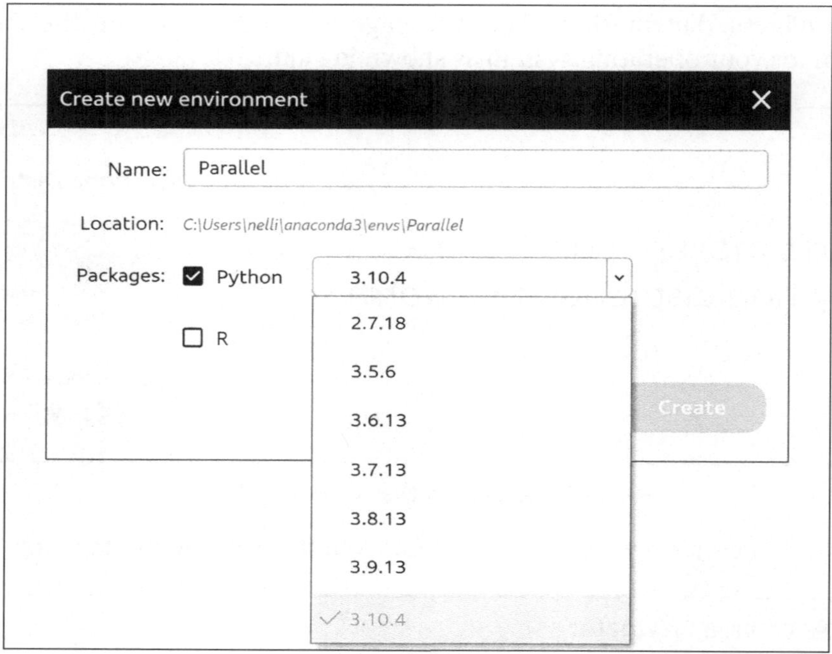

***Figure 5.6**: Dialog Box for Creating Virtual Environments on Anaconda*

Once you have set the Python name and version, simply press the **Create** button to create the virtual environment and find it on the **Anaconda Navigator** panel. At this point, you can activate the virtual environment by simply clicking on the name that appears in the list in the center. In my case, I chose to call the virtual environment **Parallel**. When the virtual environment is active, a *green icon* (PLAY) will appear, as shown in *Figure* 5.7. On the right side of the panel, a list of all Python packages installed in the virtual environment will appear. Those with the *Anaconda icon (green circle)* will be installed through the distribution itself, while those with the Python icon will have to be installed externally through the **pip** command:

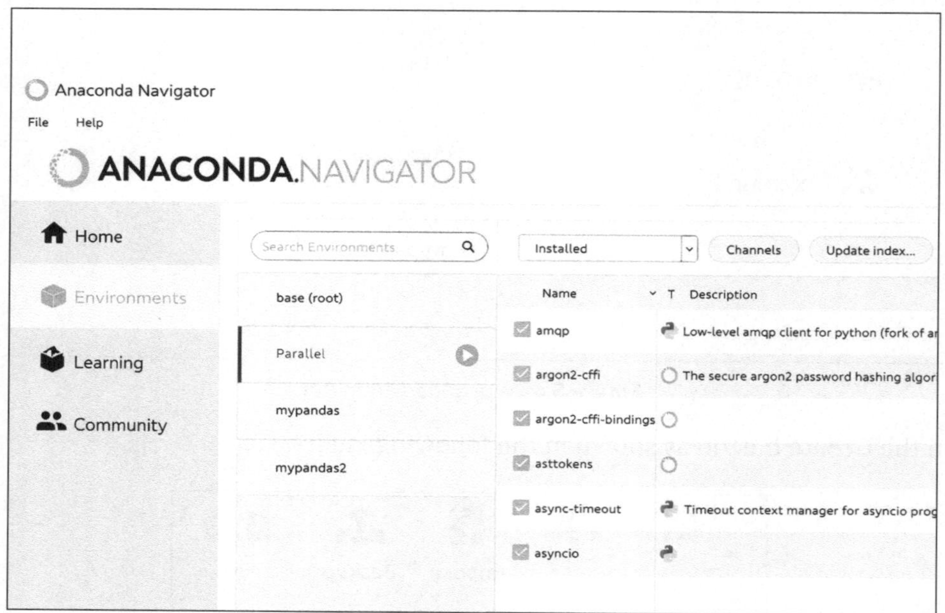

***Figure 5.7**: A Virtual Environment with Packages in Anaconda Navigator*

Anaconda is a very useful and flexible platform. It provides a whole series of development applications that allow you to work in many ways. The **Home** panel displays all the applications available for the virtual environment we have just created (see *Figure* 5.8):

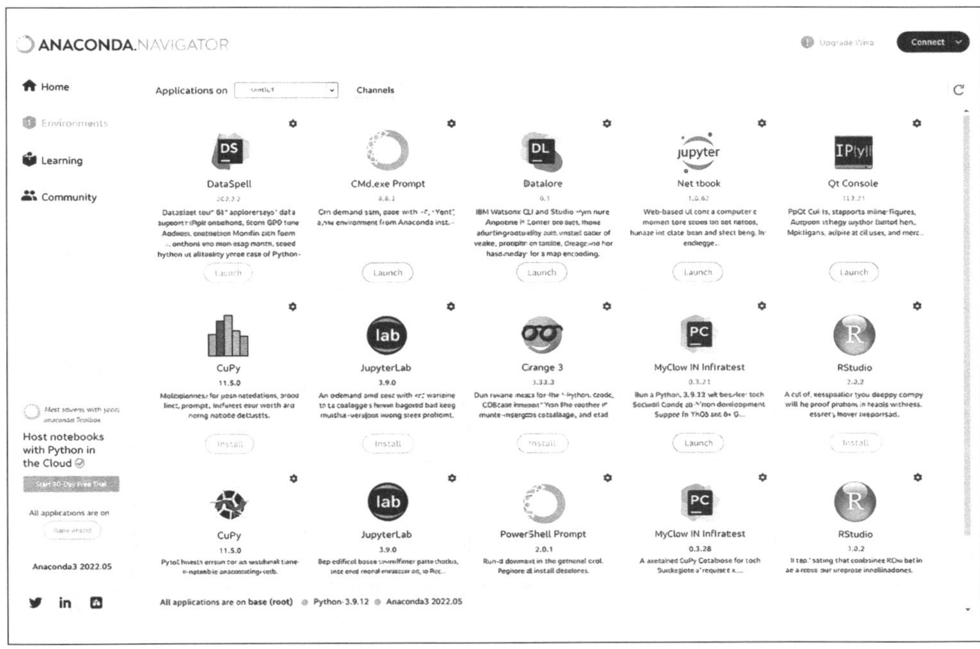

***Figure 5.8**: Anaconda Navigator Home Page*

As we can see, there are many applications here, including a **Jupyter Notebook** and the **`CMD.exe`** Prompt. For the latter, clicking on the **Launch** button will open a command console that is completely set up to work with the virtual environment, as shown in *Figure 5.9*:

```
C:\windows\system32\cmd.exe
Microsoft Windows [Versione 10.0.22000.978]
(c) Microsoft Corporation. Tutti i diritti riservati.

(Parallel) C:\Users\nelli>_
```

***Figure 5.9**: Virtual Environment Command Console*

Celery Installation

In the newly opened command console, we will install the Celery library using the following pip command:

```
pip install celery
```

While the `celery` package is present in the Anaconda distribution, it might not be complete. You can download Celery directly from the pip, which will also provide all the other related packages. In this way, you can access all the applications to work with the examples in this book.

Docker Installation

Another application highly recommended for getting test environments is **Docker Desktop**. It allows you to isolate through packages called **containers** and applications that offer services such as servers, databases, and so on. It is really useful in development environments as these applications that are enclosed in containers can be *activated*, *deactivated*, *deleted*, and *cloned* in a very simple way. It can work excellently if you want to test a distributed environment with many active *listening* services such as Celery. Given the complexity of Python versions and package dependencies, Docker allows you to change and test versions of various server applications without having to perform complicated installations and configurations. Furthermore, as in the case of Celery, there are different applications that play the same role and can be directly evaluated in *real-time* in the Celery distributed system. You can install them together as containers and activate and test them one after the other, while the rest of the system remains unchanged.

To install Docker Desktop, simply visit the official application page (**https://www.docker.com/**). You will then be prompted to download the latest stable version suitable for your operating system, as shown in *Figure* 5.10:

***Figure* 5.10**: *Docker Web Page*

Once Docker Desktop is installed, you can install a whole series of ready-made containers of the various applications in various distributed versions through the following command line:

```
docker run -d appname:version
```

Installing a Message Transport (Broker)

After installing Celery, you will also need to install **Broker**. Here, you will find several message transport applications compatible with Celery. However, not all of them will fully support all the mechanisms of Celery brokers. The most complete and compatible message transport applications in terms of functionality are:

- RabbitMQ
- Redis

Both applications can be easily installed on systems through the following systems:

1. Install the **Redis** application on a Linux machine through:
   ```
   $ sudo apt-get install redis-server
   ```
2. Then, you can start the server by entering this from the command line:
   ```
   $ redis-server
   ```
3. Since we will use a single machine in this case (*client-server*), you can install Docker and Redis to install and start all the services through:
   ```
   $ docker pull redis
   ```

This command will download the Redis server image into Docker. Once the image is installed, you can run it with the following command:

```
$ docker run -d -p 6379:6379 redis
```

4. Then you install both the specific Celery module to use Redis within it through:

```
pip install celery[redis]
```

5. If, you prefer to use the **RabbitMQ** application, it can be installed via:

```
$ sudo apt-get install rabbitmq-server
```

6. To install RabbitMQ image in Docker, use:

```
$ docker pull rabbitmq
```

Once it is installed, you can run it with the following command:

```
$ docker run -d -p 5672:5672
```

At the end of the Docker Desktop, we will have active services like **RabbitMQ** and **Redis**, which are shown in *Figure 5.11*:

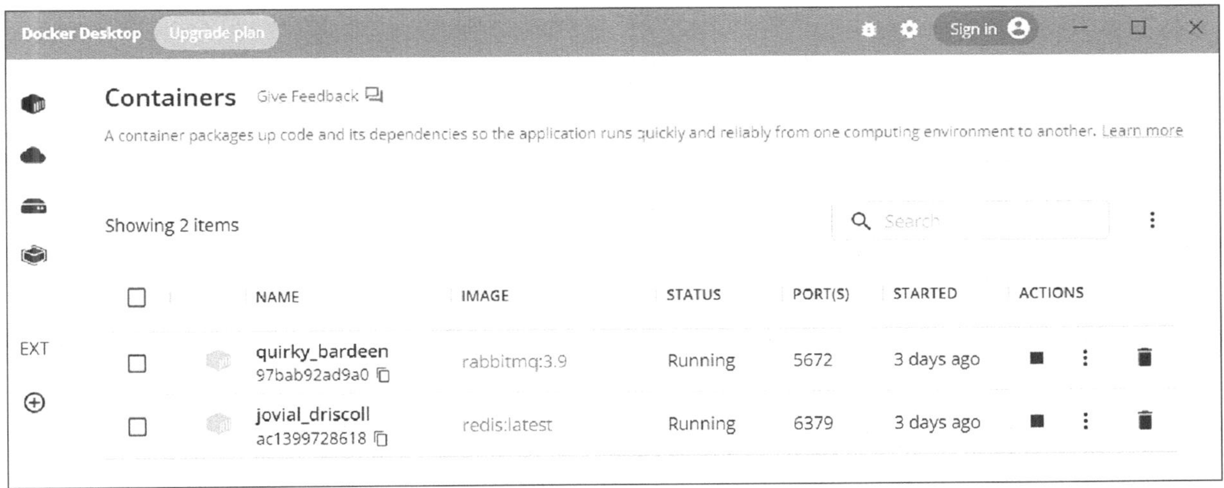

***Figure 5.11**: Docker Desktop*

Also, in this case, it is necessary to install the Celery module to use RabbitMQ inside it. This can be done via:

```
pip install celery[librabbitmq]
```

Installation of the Result Backend

There are many different applications available for a component such as a result backend. Among the result backends well supported by Celery, we can find:

- RabbitMQ
- Redis
- MongoDB
- Memcached

For simplicity's sake, we will use RabbitMQ and Redis as result backends. Therefore, it will not be necessary to make further installations.

Set Up a Celery System

Celery does not require *special configurations* to function, at least in the most general cases. You need to program only a few settings for it. In fact, you can define the components that will eventually become part of the Celery system, at the time of instantiation:

1. To create an instance of Celery, which we will call **app**, we will use the **Celery()** constructor. This accepts the module containing the tasks provided to the clients by the system (**tasks.py**), the various URLs, and the protocols of system components.

   For example, if we want to use the RabbitMQ server application as a Broker, we will write:

   ```
   from celery import Celery
   app = Celery('tasks', broker='pyamqp://guest@localhost//', backend='rpc://')
   # configuration from Celery 6.0 version
   app.conf.broker_connection_retry_on_startup = True
   ```

   As you can see, the RabbitMQ server works on the **pyamqp** protocol and is available at the local host address (that is, on the same machine as ours) as a *guest* user.

2. However, if we want to use the Redis application as a Broker, we will write:

   ```
   from celery import Celery
   app = Celery('tasks', broker='redis://localhost//', backend='redis://local-
   host')
   # configuration from Celery 6.0 version
   app.conf.broker_connection_retry_on_startup = True
   ```

   These code snippets will have to be inserted into the **tasks.py** file.

3. Now that the appropriate configurations have been made, we can start the Celery service through:

   $ celery -A tasks worker --loglevel=INFO

   By running this command, we will get an output like this:

   ```
    -------------- celery@LAPTOP-1STIRGLU v5.4.0 (opalescent)
   --- ***** -----
   -- ******* ---- Windows-11-10.0.22631-SP0 2024-12-01 10:06:28
   - *** --- * ---
   - ** ---------- [config]
   - ** ---------- .> app:         tasks:0x15e24e96b40
   - ** ---------- .> transport:   amqp://guest:**@localhost:5672//
   - ** ---------- .> results:     rpc://
   - *** --- * --- .> concurrency: 12 (prefork)
   -- ******* ---- .> task events: OFF (enable -E to monitor tasks in this worker)
   --- ***** -----
    -------------- [queues]
                   .> celery           exchange=celery(direct) key=celery


   [tasks]
     . tasks.add
     . tasks.my_task

   [2024-12-01 10:06:28,662: INFO/MainProcess] Connected to amqp://
   guest:**@127.0.0.1:5672//
   [2024-12-01 10:06:28,676: INFO/MainProcess] mingle: searching for neighbors
   [2024-12-01 10:06:29,690: INFO/SpawnPoolWorker-1] child process 15288 calling
   self.run()
   [2024-12-01 10:06:29,755: INFO/SpawnPoolWorker-4] child process 18824 calling
   self.run()
   [2024-12-01 10:06:29,765: INFO/MainProcess] mingle: all alone
   ```

```
[2024-12-01 10:06:29,787: INFO/SpawnPoolWorker-3] child process 23192 calling
self.run()
[2024-12-01 10:06:29,797: INFO/SpawnPoolWorker-7] child process 18348 calling
self.run()
[2024-12-01 10:06:29,804: INFO/SpawnPoolWorker-8] child process 10812 calling
self.run()
[2024-12-01 10:06:29,805: INFO/SpawnPoolWorker-5] child process 7772 calling
self.run()
[2024-12-01 10:06:29,805: INFO/SpawnPoolWorker-2] child process 21096 calling
self.run()
[2024-12-01 10:06:29,824: INFO/MainProcess] celery@LAPTOP-1STIRGLU ready.
[2024-12-01 10:06:29,830: INFO/SpawnPoolWorker-10] child process 1312 calling
self.run()
[2024-12-01 10:06:29,835: INFO/SpawnPoolWorker-6] child process 14808 calling
self.run()
[2024-12-01 10:06:29,835: INFO/SpawnPoolWorker-11] child process 20724 calling
self.run()
[2024-12-01 10:06:29,846: INFO/SpawnPoolWorker-12] child process 8008 calling
self.run()
[2024-12-01 10:06:29,846: INFO/SpawnPoolWorker-9] child process 23900 calling
self.run().
```

4. As you can see, the server generated twelve worker processes by default. This number depends on the characteristics of the machine you are running Celery on. Here, there are twelve cores and therefore twelve workers were created. The Broker will remain *active* waiting for the calls to the tasks to be assigned to the workers.

   Celery is optimized for Unix-like environments (such as Linux and macOS). However, some features might not be available. For example, Celery's default mode of operation is **`prefork`**:

   ```
   $ celery -A tasks worker –pool=prefork –loglevel=INFO
   ```

   This mode is not supported on Windows as it relies on process forks, which is not present on the OS. Therefore, it can lead to code execution errors. However, there are alternative pools compatible with this operating system. Two common options are:

   - **`--pool=threads`**
   - **`--pool=eventlet`**

   As you might have guessed from the names, the two cited options activate thread-based or **`eventlet`**-based pools. You can start Celery with the options as shown here:

   ```
   $ celery -A tasks worker --pool=threads --loglevel=INFO
   ```

   If you want to shut down Celery, press CTRL + C. The following messages will appear on the Celery console:

   ```
   worker: Hitting Ctrl+C again will terminate all running tasks!
   worker: Warm shutdown (MainProcess)
   ```

5. Once all the processes are finished, the prompt will be returned to you.

6. For a complete list of command line options, use:

   ```
   $ celery worker -help
   ```

   There might be other available commands. To explore them, you can write:

   ```
   $ celery -help
   ```

Define the Tasks

Now that we have a simple and sufficient *Celery-based distributed system* in place, we can start defining tasks and testing examples.

In Celery, the tasks.py module file is present on the server side. You can implement the tasks that the system will make available to clients. To identify a task in the code, the **@app.task** decorator is used; where app is the Celery instance, used within the **tasks.py** file. This is shown as follows:

```
@app.task
def my_task():
    return "This is a task"
```

Calling Tasks

Tasks are the services available from the distributed system that clients can request. Therefore, in the *customer code*, we can make the request for a service that is the call to a task, at any time. To do this, Celery provides us with two different methods:

- **delay()**
- **apply_async()**

Both methods send the task to the broker via a message, what changes between them is the type of passable arguments. The **delay()** method takes arguments placed separately, as shown in the following illustration:

```
task.delay(arg1, arg2, kwarg1='x', kwarg2='y')
```

while **apply_async()** wraps them in a list and a dictionary, shown as follows:

```
task.apply_async(args=[arg1, arg2], kwargs={'kwarg1': 'x', 'kwarg2': 'y'})
```

When we make a call to a task, we will have an **AsyncResult** value as a *return* value. This object will allow us to check the status of the task from the client side.

Example Task

In the module file on the server **tasks.py**, we define a task like we have here:

```
@app.task
def add(x, y):
   return x + y
```

On the client side, we will open a Python session at the level of the same directory where **tasks.py** is present. This simplifies things considerably. After opening the session, we will first import the task created within **tasks.py** and then call it via the **delay()** method. This is demonstrated in the code as follows:

```
>>> from tasks import add
>>> add.delay(4,4)
```

When the client code is executed, the task will be encapsulated in the message and sent to the *listening broker*. Once processed by a worker, you can see the output on the console of the machine where the worker is present, just like it is demonstrated here:

```
[2022-09-22 15:30:46,024: INFO/MainProcess] Task tasks.add[4966d730-5334-4089-8395-cb04f40de3c9] received
[2022-09-22 15:30:46,041: INFO/MainProcess] Task tasks.add[4966d730-5334-4089-8395-cb04f40de3c9] succeeded in 0.01600000000325963s: 8
```

As we can see, there are *two* lines in the output. The first shows that the broker has received the message and the second shows that the task has been successfully executed. The latter reports the execution time and the returned result.

If we wanted to use **apply_async()**, we would have had to pass the *two* arguments required by the task within a list, which might look like:

```
>>> add.apply_async([4,4])
```

If we set Celery that uses the result backend, we can also get this value on the client side in the following way:

```
>>> ares = add.delay(4,4)
>>> ares.get()
8
```

Calling the task returns an **AsyncResult** object. With the **get()** method, we will ask the object to read the result from the result backend. This value will only be available when the task has been processed. Therefore, it will take some time. Since the **get()** call must be *asynchronous*, it would be necessary to check the state of the called task *first*. For example, through the **ready()** method, it is possible to know if the task has been completed or not. This is shown as follows:

```
>>> ares.ready()
True
```

This will return a Boolean: **True** if the task has been completed, otherwise, it will return a **False**. Another fundamental piece of information will be knowing if the task was successful or if it failed by raising an exception with the methods **successful()** and **failed()**, respectively. These also return Boolean values. All these methods and other similar ones are useful for managing program execution control depending on the status of the task. One such example is shown as follows:

```
>>> ares.successful()
True
>>> ares.failed()
False
```

Signatures and Primitives

We have seen how to call tasks within a client program. However, the possibilities offered by Celery do not end here. In fact, the library also provides a series of tools that allow you to build complex workflows on a number of tasks at the same time in the code.

First of all, Celery makes use of a concept such as **signatures**, which allow you to simplify the call of a task such as:

```
>>> s1 = add.signature((2,2), countdown=10)
```

In this case, we have stored the call to the task in a signature, which will allow us to use it within the code without rewriting everything. Here, we will simply use the signature defined as:

```
>>> s1.delay()
```

There is also a default signature **s()**, which will replace the call to **delay()**:

```
>>> add.delay(4,5)
```

Therefore, you will see this signature:

```
>>> add.s(4,5)
```

The above example can make a programmer's job a lot easier. In fact, the following signatures can be used as essential arguments in a series of functions made available by the Celery library:

- **group()**
- **chain()**
- **chord()**

These functions are based on *primitives*, which are signatures with complex call structures that generate particular workflows within distributed systems because of their shape.

For example, the **group()** method takes as an argument a list of tasks that will be executed at the same time. The returned value allows it to be inspected as a group and obtains a list with the elements that follow the order of the called tasks as demonstrated in the code here:

```
>>> from celery import group
>>> g = group(add.s(i,i) for i in range(10))()
>>> g.get()
[0, 2, 4, 6, 8, 10, 12, 14, 16, 18]
```

From the server console, we will see the following output:

```
[2022-09-22 16:24:24,645: INFO/MainProcess] Task tasks.add[4dfadc20-7deb-459c-8dc5-9db5ea377263] succeeded in 0.031000000017229468s: 2
[2022-09-22 16:24:24,670: INFO/MainProcess] Task tasks.add[fb8fa5fc-7c9f-4659-8168-26133100f17b] succeeded in 0.01600000000325963s: 6
[2022-09-22 16:24:24,695: INFO/MainProcess] Task tasks.add[1b9b73e9-a8f4-43d5-aacc-791a19789a1c] succeeded in 0.030999999959021807s: 4
[2022-09-22 16:24:24,721: INFO/MainProcess] Task tasks.add[f2764fb6-ed38-4f8c-927a-0b4c4810a03f] succeeded in 0.031000000017229468s: 14
[2022-09-22 16:24:24,746: INFO/MainProcess] Task tasks.add[9e6d6b83-1b3f-4b9f-963f-2a94bea21b93] succeeded in 0.01600000000325963s: 18
[2022-09-22 16:24:24,771: INFO/MainProcess] Task tasks.add[c4b3b795-329b-4f88-8409-4f425ad986a7] succeeded in 0.031000000017229468s: 8
[2022-09-22 16:24:24,796: INFO/MainProcess] Task tasks.add[72bc-2b1c-189b-4d56-921d-decbc17cc29f] succeeded in 0.01600000000325963s: 16
[2022-09-22 16:24:24,825: INFO/MainProcess] Task tasks.add[30d86bf8-2f46-4e50-b2df-1a9b051c283a] succeeded in 0.01600000000325963s: 12
[2022-09-22 16:24:24,850: INFO/MainProcess] Task tasks.add[bdb-c022a-2e01-4cf9-870a-3ae0cf20ea9e] succeeded in 0.031000000017229468s: 10
```

As we can see, the **10** tasks sent were performed at different times, while not executing the order of the iteration used in the call. We can see that the execution times also differ between various tasks. However, the results of the individual operations were collected and sorted according to this order.

Now, let us add more tasks to tasks.py that can perform different operations besides simple addition:

```
@app.task
def mul(x, y):
    return x * y

@app.task
def xsum(numbers):
    return sum(numbers)
```

Another very useful method is **chain()**, which links several tasks together in a chain so that the result of *one task* can be used as the argument of the *second task*, and so on:

```
>>> from tasks import add, mul
>>> from celery import chain
>>> c = chain(add.s(4,4) | mul.s(8))()
>>> c.get()
```

While from the server console, we will get the following output:

```
[2022-09-22 16:41:52,501: INFO/MainProcess] Task tasks.add[9bad176a-937d-4742-8698-469b0918fe69] received
```

```
[2022-09-22 16:41:52,539: INFO/MainProcess] Task tasks.add[9bad176a-937d-4742-
8698-469b0918fe69] succeeded in 0.031000000017229468s: 8
[2022-09-22 16:41:52,540: INFO/MainProcess] Task tasks.mul[21339f93-56f3-45c1-
a09a-09b24b36999a] received
[2022-09-22 16:41:52,565: INFO/MainProcess] Task tasks.mul[21339f93-56f3-45c1-
a09a-09b24b36999a] succeeded in 0.030999999959021807s: 64
```

From here we can see that the message from the *first task* in the chain is received and executed immediately thereafter. Its result is then passed as an argument to the *second task* and is sent back as a message to the *broker*. The final result is then returned to the client.

Another method is **chord()** which uses a group of tasks in a callback as shown here:

```
>>> from tasks import add, mul, xsum
>>> from celery import chord
>>> c = chord((add.s(i,i) for i in range(10)), xsum.s())()
>>> c.get()
90
```

Note: *If you try getting a chord with RPC, you will get an error message as the feature is not implemented in this type of result backend.*

NotImplementedError: The **"rpc"** *result backend does not support chords.*

Note that a group chained with a task is also upgraded to be a chord, as this pattern requires synchronization.

Some result backends that support chords are Redis, Database, Memcached, *and more.*

In this case, you must use Redis as a result backend. Replace *the settings and restart the* Celery *server.*

In the Celery server console, you will get the following output:

```
[2022-09-22 16:59:09,209: INFO/MainProcess] Task tasks.add[c4a4c71c-3c4b-45ce-
aef2-842cfe024330] received
[2022-09-22 16:59:09,242: INFO/MainProcess] Task tasks.add[a03d2f04-347b-47da-
b052-087ef34f478f] received
[2022-09-22 16:59:09,279: INFO/MainProcess] Task tasks.add[e3af658d-d41f-4714-
87e1-1af6a63c2401] received
[2022-09-22 16:59:09,309: INFO/MainProcess] Task tasks.ad-
d[920cbf97-7a20-4c57-8024-22f69fbdccea] received
[2022-09-22 16:59:09,335: INFO/MainProcess] Task tasks.add[c4a4c71c-3c4b-45ce-
aef2-842cfe024330] succeeded in 0.125s: 0
[2022-09-22 16:59:09,344: INFO/MainProcess] Task tasks.add[a03d2f04-347b-47da-
b052-087ef34f478f] succeeded in 0.10899999999674037s: 2
[2022-09-22 16:59:09,349: INFO/MainProcess] Task tasks.add[2bc571ef-794a-4581-
8cbe-3a8cf6dea136] received
[2022-09-22 16:59:09,379: INFO/MainProcess] Task tasks.add[e3af658d-d41f-4714-
87e1-1af6a63c2401] succeeded in 0.09399999998277053s: 4
[2022-09-22 16:59:09,382: INFO/MainProcess] Task tasks.add[2e5bc833-b47e-40a7-
85e9-74fc152eeb16] received
[2022-09-22 16:59:09,398: INFO/MainProcess] Task tasks.ad-
d[920cbf97-7a20-4c57-8024-22f69fbdccea] succeeded in 0.0940000000409782s: 6
[2022-09-22 16:59:09,419: INFO/MainProcess] Task tasks.add[004d45e8-1b93-4377-
9695-fe000432be75] received
[2022-09-22 16:59:09,448: INFO/MainProcess] Task tasks.add[2bc571ef-794a-4581-
8cbe-3a8cf6dea136] succeeded in 0.09399999998277053s: 8
[2022-09-22 16:59:09,451: INFO/MainProcess] Task tasks.add[ff29e563-cc91-44f9-
a3cb-b2a1895444e3] received
[2022-09-22 16:59:09,484: INFO/MainProcess] Task tasks.add[2e5bc833-b47e-40a7-
85e9-74fc152eeb16] succeeded in 0.10899999999674037s: 10
```

```
[2022-09-22 16:59:09,488: INFO/MainProcess] Task tasks.add[760cf014-8613-44f5-bbc3-77abcf6a7901] received
[2022-09-22 16:59:09,507: INFO/MainProcess] Task tasks.add[004d45e8-1b93-4377-9695-fe000432be75] succeeded in 0.09399999998277053s: 12
[2022-09-22 16:59:09,521: INFO/MainProcess] Task tasks.add[2938bca7-6566-4c47-8d0d-c8e94045ea52] received
[2022-09-22 16:59:09,538: INFO/MainProcess] Task tasks.add[ff29e563-cc91-44f9-a3cb-b2a1895444e3] succeeded in 0.07800000003771856s: 14
[2022-09-22 16:59:09,560: INFO/MainProcess] Task tasks.add[760cf014-8613-44f5-bbc3-77abcf6a7901] succeeded in 0.06199999997625127 4s: 16
[2022-09-22 16:59:09,575: INFO/MainProcess] Task tasks.xsum[3329ba27-eb79-47b2-9618-7e71a8cad91e] received
[2022-09-22 16:59:09,616: INFO/MainProcess] Task tasks.add[2938bca7-6566-4c47-8d0d-c8e94045ea52] succeeded in 0.09399999998277053s: 18
[2022-09-22 16:59:09,622: INFO/MainProcess] Task tasks.xsum[3329ba27-eb79-47b2-9618-7e71a8cad91e] succeeded in 0.0470000000204891s: 90
```

The **chunks()** method allows us to split an *iterable* into *smaller chunks*. In this way, if we have 100 *objects*, these can be divided into 10 *tasks* of 10 *objects* each, which is shown here:

```
>>> from tasks import add
>>> from celery import chunks
>>> z = zip(range(10),range(10))
>>> list(z)
[(0, 0), (1, 1), (2, 2), (3, 3), (4, 4), (5, 5), (6, 6), (7, 7), (8, 8), (9, 9)]
>>> ch = add.chunks(z,10)()
>>> ch.get()
[[0, 2, 4, 6, 8, 10, 12, 14, 16, 18]]
```

An Application Example: Monte Carlo Method

The Monte Carlo method is a probabilistic technique used to solve numerical problems through random simulations, one of which is calculating the value of π.

To perform this operation, the Monte Carlo method is developed over several steps:

- First, a unit square is considered (side of length 1) which contains an inscribed circle of radius 1.
- Random points are generated inside the square.
- It is verified how many of these points fall inside the circle. A point (x,y) is inside the circle when it satisfies the equation x2 + y2 ≤ 1.
- The proportion between the points in the circle and the total points is multiplied by 4, which will approximate the value of π.

This method is particularly useful in scenarios where a direct analytical approach cannot be used, since it relies on easily scalable statistical techniques.

Why is it a good solution to apply Celery to solve the Monte Carlo method? Celery is a distributed system for asynchronously processing tasks and in this case, the simulation of random points is highly parallel; each group of points can be calculated independently. Celery allows you to exploit this property by dividing the work on multiple workers, which can be distributed on different machines or CPUs.

So let us start implementing the file that manages the tasks: **pi_calculator.py**.

```
from celery import Celery, group, chord

app = Celery('pi_calculator', broker='redis://localhost//', backend='redis://localhost')
```

```
app.conf.task_routes = {'tasks.*':{'queue': 'pi_queue'}}

import random
@app.task
def simulate_points(n_points):
    inside_circle = 0
    for _ in range(n_points):
        x,y = random.random(), random.random()
        if x**2 + y**2 <= 1:
            inside_circle += 1
    return {'inside_circle': inside_circle, 'total': n_points}

@app.task
def calculate_pi(results):
    total_points = sum(result['total'] for result in results)
    total_inside_circle = sum(result['inside_circle'] for result in results)
    pi_estimate = 4 * total_inside_circle / total_points
    return pi_estimate

@app.task
def run_simulation(n_points_per_task, n_tasks):
    simulation_group = group(simulate_points.s(n_points_per_task) for _ in
range(n_tasks))
    return chord(simulation_group, calculate_pi.s())()
```

We can see that three different tasks have been defined for our Monte Carlo calculation. The **simulate_points** task simulates the number of random points (x,y) and checks how many of them fall inside the circle. The function returns a dictionary containing the number of points inside the circle (**inside_circle**) and the total number of points generated (**n_points**). The **calculate_pi** task instead takes care of aggregating the partial results received from the different previous tasks (**results**) and calculates the total. Finally, it approximates the value of π (**pi_estimate**). The last task defined, **run_simulation**, divides the work into **n_tasks** and assigns **n_points_per_task** to each of them. This operation is performed using the Celery group function seen in the previous sections, which can create groups of independent tasks that can be executed in parallel. Finally, another important Celery function called chord is used. It passes the results to the final task **calculate_pi**.

For the client, we will implement the following code, saving it as **pi_calculation.py**:

```
if __name__ == "__main__":

    from pi_calculator import run_simulation, simulate_points, calculate_pi
    from time import sleep
    from celery import group

    n_points_per_task = 1000000
    n_tasks = 10
    group_result = group(simulate_poirts.s(n_points_per_task) for _ in
range(n_tasks))() #add
    results = group_result.get() # adc

    final_result = calculate_pi(results)

    print(f"Estimate of pi: {final_result}")
```

The client first imports all the task functions and sets some parameters needed for the calculation, such as **n_points_per_task**, which are the random points generated by each single task and **n_task**, which defines their number. The group command creates a group of asynchronous tasks where each task runs the **simulate_points** function. The for loop generates a total of 10 tasks, as specified by n_task. The **group_result.get()** method waits for all tasks to complete and collects the results. The **calculate_pi(results)** function takes the aggregated results from all tasks and calculates the estimate of the value of π.

To start Celery, enter the following command (for Windows use threads for pools. For other systems, you can omit the **--pool** option):

```
$ celery -A pi_calculator worker --loglevel=INFO --pool=threads
```

Once all services including workers are up and running, the client is run on Windows using:

```
$ python pi_calculation.py
```

This will generate the following result:

```
Estimate of pi: 3.1417132
```

As we can see, we have obtained a fairly accurate estimate of the value of π which is 3.14159 for the first few decimal places. We therefore observe a variation only in the fourth decimal place.

Queue Management with Celery

Queue management is one of the most important aspects of Celery, as it allows you to optimize your workload and organize the execution of tasks efficiently. Celery offers a flexible queue system that allows you to define priorities, balance the workload, and assign specific tasks to specific queues.

A queue in Celery is a container that collects tasks waiting to be processed by workers. Queues are managed by brokers (such as Redis or RabbitMQ) and are used to distribute tasks to workers. Queues can be defined using the **task_queues** setting, setting their priority.

```
from kombu import Queue
app.conf.task_queues = (
        Queue('default', routing_key='default'),
        Queue('hight_priority', routing_key='high.#'),
        Queue('low_priority', routing_key='low.#'),
)
```

The default queues for all tasks without routing specifications are defined as **default**, while **high_priority** and **low_priority** define queues with different priority levels assigned. Once the queues are defined, the tasks must be assigned. This is done through the **@app.task** decorator, in the following way:

```
@app.task(queue='high_priority')
def important_task():
        # Code here
        pass
@app.task(queue='low_priority')
def background_task():
        # Code here
        pass
```

Another feature of Celery related to queues is task routing, which allows you to determine in which queue a task should be inserted. You can define the routing rules using the **task_routes** setting as shown:

```
app.conf.task_routes = {
        'myapp.tasks.important_task': {'queue': 'high_priority'},
        'myapp.task.background_task': {'queue': 'low_priority'},
}
```

Therefore, working at different priority levels involves using different queues. You can tackle this by configuring a particular worker to listen only to certain queues. This is useful for assigning specific tasks to specialized workers. For example, if we wanted to start a worker that listens exclusively to the **high_priority** queue, we will use the following:

```
$ celery -A tasks worker --queues high_priority -loglevel=INFO
```

If we want a worker to listen to multiple queues, we will use:

```
$ celery -A tasks worker --queues high_priority, low_priority -loglevel=INFO
```

Given the complexity of such configurations, Celery also offers a way to monitor the status of queues through the **celery inspect** command. For example, to list the currently running tasks, use the following command:

```
$ celery -A myapp inspect active
```

However, if we are interested in tasks present in the queue:

```
$ celery -A tasks inspect reserved
```

Celery also offers Flower, a dashboard that allows you to monitor queues and workers in real time.

```
$ celery -A tasks flower
```

In addition to the options seen previously, there are many other features related to queue management that are beyond the scope of this book. Those who want to learn more about this topic can visit the official Celery documentation page at https://docs.celeryq.dev/en/stable/index.html .

After providing an overview of the features related to queues, let us create a Celery application that manages queues. Here, we will define three queues which we have seen previously: default, **high_priority** and **low_priority**. As for the tasks, we will define different types: a light task that sends emails that we will call **send_email**, a heavy data processing task, **process_data** and a backup task, **backup_database**. Finally, we will monitor the execution using different priority levels for the tasks.

The application will be based on 3 different files mentioned as follows:

- **celery_app.py**: the configuration file
- **tasks.py**: the task definition file
- **main.py**: the client file that runs the tasks

Let us implement the configuration file first (**celery_app.py**):

```
from celery import Celery
from kombu import Queue, Exchange

app = Celery('myapp', broker='redis://localhost//', backend='redis://localhost/')

# Queues definition
app.conf.task_queues = (
    Queue('default', Exchange('default'), routing_key='default'),
    Queue('high_priority', Exchange('priority'), routing_key='hihg.#'),
    Queue('low_priority', Exchange('priority'), routing_key='low.#'),
)

# Routing rules
app.conf.task_routes = {
    'tasks.send_email': {'queue': 'high_priority'},
    'tasks.process_data': {'queue': 'low_priority'},
    'tasks.backup_database': {'queue': 'default'},
}

# Other configurations
app.conf.imports = ('tasks',)
```

```
app.conf.task_default_queue = 'default'
app.conf.task_default_exchange = 'default'
app.conf.task_default_routing_key = 'default'
app.conf.result_expires = 3600
```

Let us now implement the **tasks.py** file containing the different tasks to be used:

```
from celery_app import app
import time

@app.task(queue='high_priority', priority=0) # Maximum priority
def send_email(recipient, subject, body):
    print(f"Sent email to {recipient} with subject '{subject}'")
    time.sleep(2)
    return f"Email sent to {recipient}"

@app.task(queue='low_priority', priority=9) # Minimum priority
def process_data(data):
    print(f"Start processing data: {data}")
    time.sleep(10)
    return f"Processed Data: {data}"

@app.task(queue='default')
def backup_database():
    print("Backup of database is running...")
    time.sleep(5)
    return "Backup completed"
```

Finally, we will implement the **main.py** client file as follows:

```
from tasks import send_email, process_data, backup_database

if __name__ == "__main__":
    print("Starting tasks...")
    send_email.delay("user@example.com", "Welcome!", "Thanks for registration")
    send_email.delay("admin@example.com", "Alarm", "Critic problem found")
    process_data.delay("dataset_1")
    process_data.delay("dataset_2")
    backup_database.delay()
    print("Task sent")
```

To activate and test the code, we will need to open 4 command consoles. Remember, while working with Windows, you must add the option **--pool=threads**. However, this is omitted by Linux or MacOs environments.

Then launch this series of commands, one for each console. It is shown as follows:

```
$ celery -A tasks worker --queues high_priority --pool=threads --loglevel=INFO
$ celery -A tasks worker --queues low_priority --pool=threads --loglevel=INFO
$ celery -A tasks worker --queues default --pool=threads --loglevel=info
$ python main.py
```

Once all of them have started, you will see the series of results in the different consoles.

In the console dedicated to the high priority queue, you will see:

```
[2024-12-02 22:10:25,831: INFO/MainProcess] Task tasks.send_email[135a16f1-59
ca-445a-bb81-7495111837ab] received
[2024-12-02 22:10:25,831: WARNING/MainProcess] Sent email to user@example.com
with subject 'Welcome!'
```

```
[2024-12-02 22:10:25,831: INFO/MainProcess] Task tasks.send_email[6aeb8969-78
54-4252-9c87-7a8778925c3a] received
[2024-12-02 22:10:25,831: WARNING/MainProcess] Sent email to admin@example.com
with subject 'Alarm'
[2024-12-02 22:10:27,892: INFO/MainProcess] Task tasks.send_email[135a16f1-59
ca-445a-bb81-7495111837ab] succeeded in 2.062000000005355s: 'Email sent to
user@example.com'
[2024-12-02 22:10:27,908: INFO/MainProcess] Task tasks.send_email[6aeb8969-78
54-4252-9c87-7a8778925c3a] succeeded in 2.077999999994063s: 'Email sent to
admin@example.com'
```

In the console dedicated to the low priority queue:

```
[2024-12-02 22:10:25,831: INFO/MainProcess] Task tasks.process_data[6d3dab81-
291f-4978-815b-18e627718153] received
[2024-12-02 22:10:25,831: WARNING/MainProcess] Start processing data: data-
set_1
[2024-12-02 22:10:25,847: INFO/MainProcess] Task tasks.process_data[a61656f8-
3261-41e6-928c-921e8639804e] received
[2024-12-02 22:10:25,847: WARNING/MainProcess] Start processing data: data-
set_2
[2024-12-02 22:10:35,902: INFO/MainProcess] Task tasks.process_data[6d3dab81-
291f-4978-815b-18e627718153] succeeded in 10.062000000005355s: 'Processed
Data: dataset_1'
[2024-12-02 22:10:35,910: INFO/MainProcess] Task tasks.process_data[a61656f8-
3261-41e6-928c-921e8639804e] succeeded in 10.062999999994645s: 'Processed
Data: dataset_2'
```

In the default queue console, you will see:

```
[2024-12-02 22:10:25,847: INFO/MainProcess] Task tasks.backup_database
[b246df86-eac4-4c5d-bcec-34ae15129e3c] received
[2024-12-02 22:10:25,855: WARNING/MainProcess] Backup of database is
running...
[2024-12-02 22:10:30,941: INFO/MainProcess] Task tasks.backup_data-
base[b246df86-eac4-4c5d-bcec-34ae15129e3c] succeeded in 5.0939999999973224s:
'Backup completed'
```

While in the last console where the client runs `main.py,` the results look like:

```
Starting tasks...
Task sent
```

As we can see from the results, the tasks have correctly performed their allocated functions, with each using the specific queue to which it was assigned.

This is a good example to understand how distributed environments are managed by the Celery framework. However, this framework is not the only choice for those who want to work with distributed systems in the Python language.

Dramatiq Library as an Alternative to Celery

Although Celery is currently the main reference library for those who want to set up distributed systems in Python, other valid alternatives are gradually gaining momentum. An alternative that functions similar to Celery is the **Dramatiq** library. It shares many similarities with Celery as both are based on *asynchronous tasks* and rely on applications like **Redis** or **RabbitMQ**

One of Celery's flaws is its complexity. On the other hand, Dramatiq offers a much simpler and more intuitive interface.

Installing Dramatiq

Before starting with some examples, let us install the latest release of **Dramatiq** (currently *version* 1.13) on our virtual environment. We will open the command console and insert:

```
pip install dramatiq
```

For our examples, we will use the Redis application with **Dramatiq**; therefore, we need to install the necessary dependencies to be able to use it. To do this, we will write the following command:

```
pip install dramatiq[redis]
```

However, if you want to use RabbitMQ you can write:

```
pip install dramatiq[rabbitmq]
```

At this point, you only need to *activate* the Redis (or RabbitMQ) container that we had loaded into Docker Desktop, as shown in *Figure* 5.12:

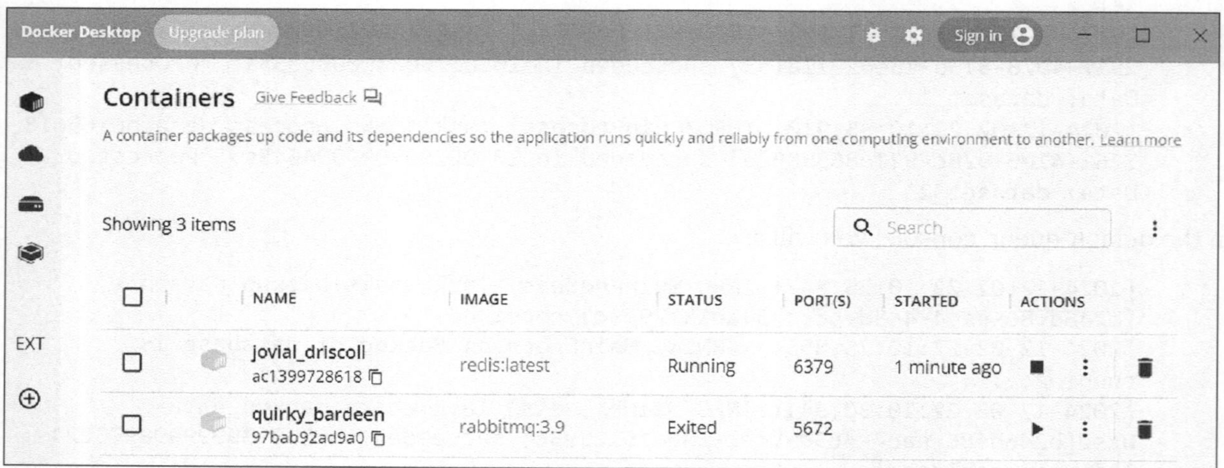

Figure 5.12: *Redis Container Activated in Docker Desktop*

Getting Started with Dramatiq

Now that we have installed Dramatiq and all other necessary dependencies, we can start working with this library.

In Dramatiq, the tasks are replaced by the actors, that are functions containing the code which will be executed by the workers and created by Redis. The latter's architecture will work similar to Celery. Redis will encapsulate the activity of the *actors (task)* in messages dispatched to various waiting workers (see *Figure* 5.13).

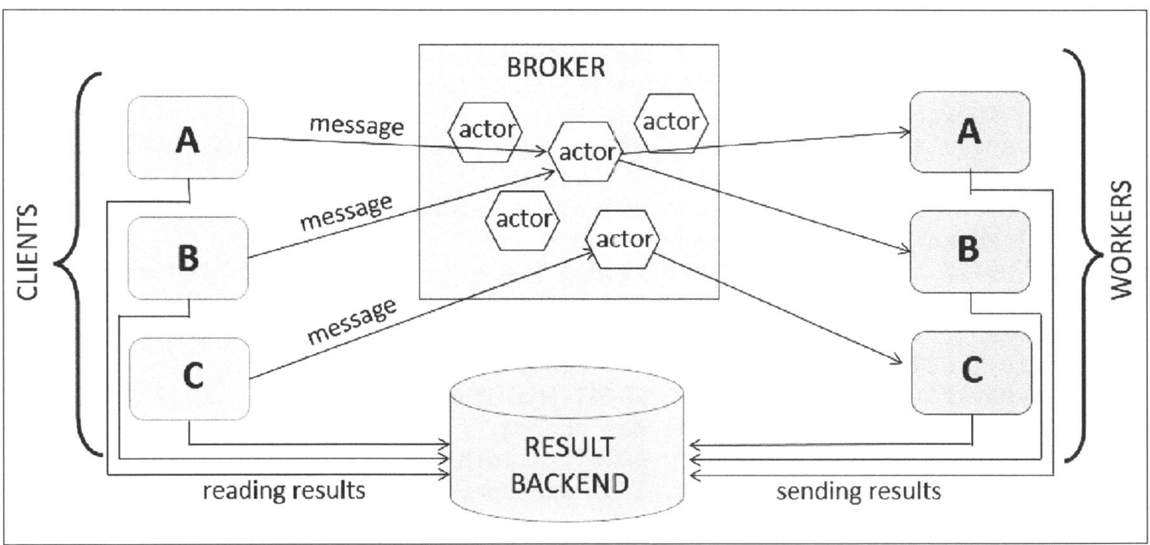

***Figure 5.13**: The Dramatiq Architecture*

Follow these steps:

1. First, we will implement the code that will act as a server. We will save it as **dramaserver.py**. This is shown as follows:

```
import dramatiq
import time

@dramatiq.actor
def wait(t,n):
   time.sleep(t)
   print("I am the actor %s and I will wait for %s secs" %(n,t))
```

   As we can see from the code, we first import the necessary libraries like **dramatiq**. Then we will define the functions that perform the activities of the workers, which is recognized in the code through the **@dramatiq.actor** decorator. In our example, we will define actor as a **wait()** function that waits for a few seconds and then print a message about the expected seconds in output.

2. Now that we have defined a file server which describes the services *performed (actors)* by the distributed Dramatiq system, we can activate the latter through the following command from the virtual environment console:

   dramatiq dramaserver

   As you can see, you enter the name of the file server to activate the actors defined in it. Once the command has been launched, the following text will appear in the output:

```
[2022-09-27 16:46:00,775] [PID 18332] [MainThread] [dramatiq.MainProcess]
[INFO] Dramatiq '1.13.0' is booting up.
[2022-09-27 16:46:00,685] [PID 7452] [MainThread] [dramatiq.WorkerProcess(0)]
[INFO] Worker process is ready for action.
[2022-09-27 16:46:00,580] [PID 25400] [MainThread] [dramatiq.WorkerProcess(1)]
[INFO] Worker process is ready for action.
[2022-09-27 16:46:00,685] [PID 25192] [MainThread] [dramatiq.WorkerProcess(2)]
[INFO] Worker process is ready for action.
[2022-09-27 16:46:00,705] [PID 6828] [MainThread] [dramatiq.WorkerProcess(3)]
[INFO] Worker process is ready for action.
[2022-09-27 16:46:00,705] [PID 17300] [MainThread] [dramatiq.WorkerProcess(4)]
[INFO] Worker process is ready for action.
```

```
[2022-09-27 16:46:00,700] [PID 18248] [MainThread] [dramatiq.WorkerProcess(5)]
[INFO] Worker process is ready for action.
[2022-09-27 16:46:00,666] [PID 10216] [MainThread] [dramatiq.WorkerProcess(6)]
[INFO] Worker process is ready for action.
[2022-09-27 16:46:00,661] [PID 9372] [MainThread] [dramatiq.WorkerProcess(7)]
[INFO] Worker process is ready for action.
[2022-09-27 16:46:00,736] [PID 25952] [MainThread] [dramatiq.WorkerProcess(8)]
[INFO] Worker process is ready for action.
[2022-09-27 16:46:00,705] [PID 20300] [MainThread] [dramatiq.WorkerProcess(9)]
[INFO] Worker process is ready for action.
[2022-09-27 16:46:00,721] [PID 15876] [MainThread] [dramatiq.WorkerPro-
cess(10)] [INFO] Worker process is ready for action.
[2022-09-27 16:46:00,770] [PID 6644] [MainThread] [dramatiq.WorkerProcess(11)]
[INFO] Worker process is ready for action.
[2022-09-27 16:46:01,270] [PID 6640] [MainThread] [dramatiq.ForkProcess(0)]
[INFO] Fork process 'dramatiq.middleware.prometheus:_run_exposition_server' is
ready for action.
```

As we can see, twelve workers have been created in Dramatiq that correspond to 12 different processes (the PIDs are indicated in the text). These will wait to receive messages from Redis that contain the actors to be executed.

Note: *To shut down the server on Windows, press the X button at the top right. The window will not close, but all active services on Dramatiq will shut down promptly.*

3. At this point, we will implement the client of the client side, which we will save as **dramaclient.py** as shown here:

```
import dramatiq
import time
from dramaserver import wait

[wait.send(10,i) for i in range(10)]
print("End Program")
```

4. We now have to open another virtual environment console and run the following customer code:

   python dramaclient.py

5. After executing the code, you will immediately see the text signifying the end of the program:

   End Program

   After a few seconds, we will obtain an output similar to the following:

```
I am the actor 10 and I will wait for 0 secs
I am the actor 10 and I will wait for 7 secs
I am the actor 10 and I will wait for 3 secs
I am the actor 10 and I will wait for 9 secs
I am the actor 10 and I will wait for 1 secs
I am the actor 10 and I will wait for 6 secs
I am the actor 10 and I will wait for 4 secs
I am the actor 10 and I will wait for 2 secs
I am the actor 10 and I will wait for 5 secs
I am the actor 10 and I will wait for 8 secs
```

In the previous code, we used an inline command to launch multiple actors at the same time. But it can only be used in limited cases, where the actors are all the same and one of the parameters is the value of the iterator itself. A more generic way to launch multiple actors in parallel together is through **grouping**.

6. Let us rewrite the previous client code as follows:

```
import dramatiq
import time
from dramaserver import wait
from dramatiq import group

g = group([
    wait.message(10,'A'),
    wait.message(5,'B'),
    wait.message(4,'C'),
    wait.message(7,'D'),
]).run()

print("End Program")
```

7. As we can see, a **group()** function is used which accepts a list of calls to *actors*, which can also be different from each other. But this time the actors will call the **message()** method to send the parameters to use them.

   After execution, a result similar to the following is obtained as the output:

```
I am the actor C and I will wait for 4 secs
I am the actor B and I will wait for 5 secs
I am the actor D and I will wait for 7 secs
I am the actor A and I will wait for 10 secs
```

Here, the execution times are different and the lines will appear in the chronological order of execution.

Management of Results

So far, we have managed actors who did not produce results (*return values*). These actually require special management with Dramatiq. These too will have to be enclosed in messages and collected in a result backend similar to what we had seen with Celery. Here, you can choose whether to use Redis or RabbitMQ for the result backend.

To add all the necessary settings and activate the broker and result backend services, we will have to make changes and additions to the previous codes via an implementation distributed through Dramatiq.

As for the code that manages the server side, we will apply the following changes:

```
import dramatiq
import time

from dramatiq.brokers.redis import RedisBroker
#from dramatiq.brokers.rabbitmq import RabbitmqBroker
from dramatiq.results import Results
from dramatiq.results.backends import RedisBackend

broker = RedisBroker(host="localhost")
#broker = RabbitmqBroker(host="localhost")
dramatiq.set_broker(broker)
result_backend = RedisBackend(host="localhost")
broker.add_middleware(Results(backend=result_backend))

@dramatiq.actor(store_results=True)
```

```
def wait(t,n):
   time.sleep(t)
   print("I am the actor %s and I will wait for %s secs" %(n,t))
   return "I waited for {0} secs".format(t)
```

As we can see, all the classes responsible for the *Broker* and *Result Backend* services will have to be imported. In our example, we have decided to use Redis for both features. However, you will see the author's comments on the classes corresponding to RabbitMQ. Since the example takes place locally on the same computer, we have used a local host for both services. If you were to operate on the network, replace these values with the corresponding IP address. As for the actor, we have added a return value which is still a string. In this case, our purpose will be to display this string from the *client side* on the console.

The *client-side code* also needs some modifications, which are shown as follows:

```
import dramatiq
import time
from dramaserver import wait
from dramatiq import group

from dramatiq.brokers.redis import RedisBroker
from dramatiq.results import Results
from dramatiq.results.backends import RedisBackend

broker = RedisBroker(host="localhost")
dramatiq.set_broker(broker)
result_backend = RedisBackend(host="localhost")
broker.add_middleware(Results(backend=result_backend))

g = group([
    wait.message(10,'A'),
    wait.message(5,'B'),
    wait.message(4,'C'),
    wait.message(7,'D'),
]).run()

for res in g.get_results(block=True, timeout=12000):
   print(res)

print("End Program")
```

As we can see, it will be necessary to import the same classes of the Broker and Result Backend services that we used for the client side. This also helps the client understand the location of various component services of Dramatiq by specifying the different IPs.

As for the actors, gathering them in a group will keep their results in memory in the result backend for a certain period of time. With the **get_results()** method, you can retrieve them from the group. The dwell time of the results in the result backend by default is **10** seconds. Since we have worked with this time in our example, we can extend the timeout to **12** seconds (12,000 *ms*).

By running the two codes in the Dramatiq system, we will obtain the following result on the client-side console:

```
I waited for 10 secs
I waited for 5 secs
I waited for 4 secs
I waited for 7 secs
End Program
```

The following will be visible on the server-side console:

```
I am the actor C and I will wait for 4 secs
I am the actor B and I will wait for 5 secs
I am the actor D and I will wait for 7 secs
I am the actor A and I will wait for 10 secs
```

SCOOP Library

Another library available online for distributed computing using Python is **Scalable Concurrent Operation in Python** (**SCOOP**). This project is still in beta (currently in version 0.7) and consists of a single module called **scoop**, whose task is to distribute concurrent tasks called **Futures** to worker processes distributed on different machines in a network:

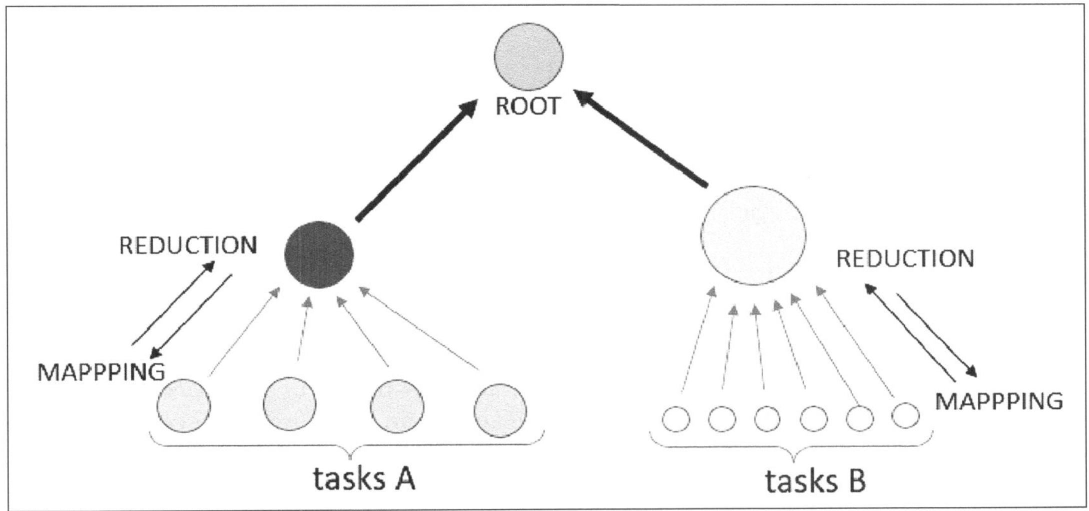

Figure 5.14: *The SCOOP Multi-Layer Mechanism*

Here, the SCOOP developers have set the main purpose of keeping the management of *distributed* and *parallel* programming as simple and transparent as possible. SCOOP is able to manage different tasks at multiple processing levels, while passing through mapping and reduction mechanisms (see *Figure* 5.14). The module will then deal with the physical considerations regarding how to distribute the tasks based on the physical potential of the constituent machines and the parallelization methods that can be applied in the various cases.

As for the elements that make up the architecture, SCOOP is much simpler than distributed systems like Celery. This is because it only includes **WORKERS** and a **BROKER**, as shown in *Figure* 5.15:

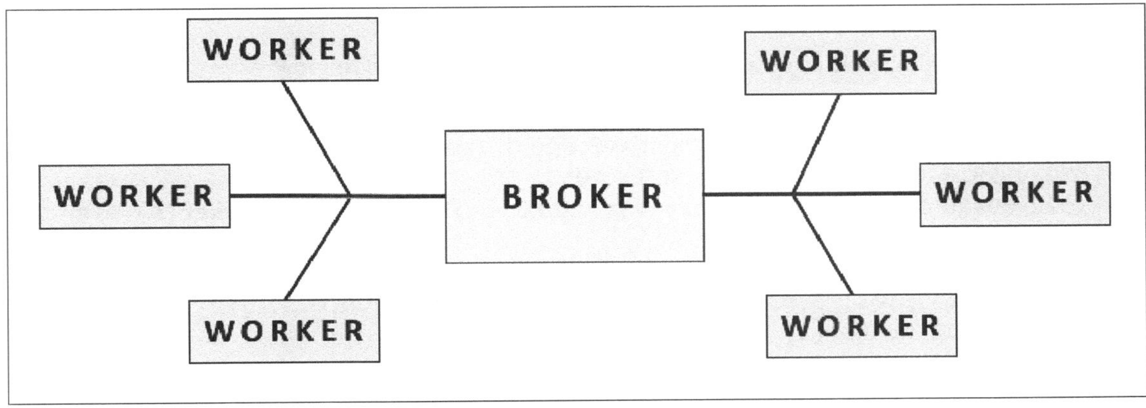

Figure 5.15: *SCOOP Architecture*

The central element of the communication system is the **broker** who interacts with all the independent workers to dispatch messages between them. **Futures** are then created in worker elements instead of the broker with a centralized serialization procedure. This makes the architecture more *reliable* and *improves performance*. In fact, the broker's main workload consists of networking and I / O exchange between the various processes present in the workers with a relatively low response time.

Installing SCOOP

To install SCOOP, we can use the same virtual environment created previously or create a new one. Once the virtual environment is activated, we can open the command line console, and install SCOOP using **pip**:

```
pip install SCOOP
```

To test SCOOP directly, we will write the following code in a text editor and then save it as **scoopy.py** in the workspace directory of the virtual environment, as shown here:

```
from scoop import futures
def worker(value):
    print("I am the Worker %s" %value)

if __name__ == "__main__":
    list(futures.map(worker, range(4)))
```

Before running the code, let us take a quick look. From the **scoop** module, we will import futures, which refers to the pool of tasks that will be assigned to the workers by the broker. The broker then builds the tasks through the **map()** method which will accept an *iterable* as a second argument, which in this case is **range(4).** The said iterable is a sequence of four elements with the following integers in ascending order: **(0,1,2,3)**. The **map()** function must in turn be passed as an argument to a **list()** function, to synchronize all the workers at the end of the execution phase. Thereafter, the program will wait for the outcome of all workers before stopping.

Every single element of the iterable is passed to the first argument of **map()**, that is worker. This is the name of the **worker()** function as defined in the code. This function incorporates the operations that will be assigned to each individual worker. Therefore, in our example, we will have four tasks (number of elements of the *iterable*) that will be assigned to the available workers. Each worker will then print a string where it will add its identification number that corresponds precisely to the value of the iterable.

To run the code that uses SCOOP, you need to specify the **-m** scoop option in the Python code execution command. So, let us write:

```
python -m scoop scoopy.py
```

Executing the code will result in console output will look like the following:

```
[2022-09-26 15:01:08,933] launcher  INFO    SCOOP 0.7 2.0 on win32 using
Python 3.10.4 | packaged by conda-forge | (main, Mar 30 2022, 08:38:02)
[MSC v.1916 64 bit (AMD64)], API: 1013
[2022-09-26 15:01:08,933] launcher  INFO    Deploying 12 worker(s) over 1
host(s).
[2022-09-26 15:01:08,933] launcher  INFO    Worker distribution:
[2022-09-26 15:01:08,933] launcher  INFO       127.0.0.1:       11 + origin
Launching 12 worker(s) using an unknown shell.
I am the Worker 0
I am the Worker 1
I am the Worker 3
I am the Worker 2
[2022-09-26 15:01:09,934] launcher  (127.0.0.1:64064) INFO    Root process is
```

```
done.
[2022-09-26 15:01:09,934] launcher  (127.0.0.1:64064) INFO    Finished
cleaning spawned subprocesses.
```

As we can see from the execution result, SCOOP automatically created twelve workers on the computer (11 + *origin*). This value is automatically set by SCOOP as per the characteristics of the machine where the program is being executed. The four tasks are performed concurrently, which is apparent from the output printed by the individual **worker()** functions that highlight a random order of execution.

Let us make the previous example more complex by adding a mathematical calculation with a result to the function, which is called **func()**:

```
from scoop import futures
import math
import numpy as np

def func(value):
    result = math.sqrt(value)
    print("The value %s and the elaboration is %s" %(value, result))
    return result

if __name__ == "__main__":
    data = np.array([10,3,6,1,4,8,25,9])
    results = list(futures.map(func, data))
    for result in results:
      print("This is the result: %s" %result)
```

As we can see from the code, the **func()** function is processed by the workers, besides writing a string as output. It will return the result to the broker, which will then be passed to the return value of the **map()** function. The result will be saved in a **results** variable via **list()**. We also replaced the ordered sequence, **range(4),** with a NumPy array of eight elements. At the end of the program, the results will be printed in the output.

Let us save the code in a file and call it **scoopy2.py**. In the previous example, we had seen that SCOOP had created twelve workers automatically. This number can be set per command line by adding the **-n** option to the **python** command. For example, if we wanted to use **4** workers, we would have to run the following command from the virtual environment console:

```
python -m scoop -n 4 scoopy2.py
```

Running the code will produce a result like:

```
[2022-09-26 15:12:25,473] launcher  INFO    SCOOP 0.7 2.0 on win32 using
Python 3.10.4 | packaged by conda-forge | (main, Mar 30 2022, 08:38:02)
[MSC v.1916 64 bit (AMD64)], API: 1013
[2022-09-26 15:12:25,473] launcher  INFO    Deploying 4 worker(s) over 1
host(s).
[2022-09-26 15:12:25,489] launcher  INFO    Worker distribution:
[2022-09-26 15:12:25,489] launcher  INFO       127.0.0.1:       3 + origin
Launching 4 worker(s) using an unknown shell.
The value 10 and the elaboration is 3.1622776601683795
The value 3 and the elaboration is 1.7320508075688772
The value 6 and the elaboration is 2.449489742783178
The value 1 and the elaboration is 1.0
The value 4 and the elaboration is 2.0
The value 8 and the elaboration is 2.8284271247461903
The value 25 and the elaboration is 5.0
The value 9 and the elaboration is 3.0
This is the result: 3.1622776601683795
```

```
This is the result: 1.7320508075688772
This is the result: 2.449489742783178
This is the result: 1.0
This is the result: 2.0
This is the result: 2.8284271247461903
This is the result: 5.0
This is the result: 3.0
[2022-09-26 15:12:26,474] launcher  (127.0.0.1:64354) INFO   Root process is
done.
[2022-09-26 15:12:26,474] launcher  (127.0.0.1:64354) INFO    Finished
cleaning spawned subprocesses.
```

As we can see, we still have a random order of execution of the various tasks. However, in the results output, it should be noted that **list(map())** will return all the results in the same order in which they were defined in the **NumPy** array. A *synchronization phase* can be thus observed. It waits for the outcome of all the results to value the **returned** variable.

Now that we have seen how the SCOOP architecture manages tasks via mapping, let us add the reduction step. In the previous example we have seen how by passing an *iterable of n* elements, we obtain an *iterable of n* results. Now it is possible to add a reduction phase, which will further add an *aggregation-reduction function* of the result. For example, we can replace the function **list()** which synchronizes all the results of the different workers and sorts them in a list with a reduction function such as **sum()**. This function will sum up all the results of the various workers, regardless of their execution times. It will gradually add up all the results and will then return the cumulative result. Therefore, we will again witness of a *synchronization mechanism.*

Let us modify the previous code as follows:

```
if __name__ == "__main__":
    data = np.array([10,3,6,1,4,8,25,9])
    result = sum(futures.map(func, data))
    print("This is the reduction result: %s" %result)
```

After executing this, you will get the result of the reduction, which is the sum of all the results of the workers. This is shown as follows:

```
…
This is the reduction result: 21.172245335266624
…
```

In SCOOP, there is another method that incorporates both mapping and reduction. It is called **mapReduce()**. We will keep modifying the previous code by importing the operator module, which will allow us to call operators as methods. In our example, we will use **add()** to add up. Finally, we will replace **map()** with **mapReduce()** and add the aggregating method **operator.add** as a second function to apply the following:

```
from scoop import futures
import math
import numpy as np
import random
import operator

def func(value):
    result = math.sqrt(value)
    print("The value %s and the elaboration is %s" %(value, result))
    return result

if __name__ == "__main__":
```

```
        data = np.array([10,3,6,1,4,8,25,9])
        result = futures.mapReduce(func, operator.add, data)
        print("This is the reduction result: %s" %result)
```

By running the preceding code, you will get the same result as in the previous case. The matter can be further complicated by concatenating the *mapping* and *reduction* functions.

For example, after calculating the square roots of the entered data, we can convert them to *integer values*. We will then calculate the *average* by making the following modifications to the code:

```
    if __name__ == "__main__":
        data = np.array([10,3,6,1,4,8,25,9])
        result = np.mean(list(futures.map(int, futures.map( func, data))))
        print("This is the reduction result: %s" %result)
```

Executing the code will give the following result:

```
[2022-09-26 16:09:50,661] launcher  INFO    SCOOP 0.7 2.0 on win32 using
Python 3.10.4 | packaged by conda-forge | (main, Mar 30 2022, 08:38:02)
[MSC v.1916 64 bit (AMD64)], API: 1013
[2022-09-26 16:09:50,661] launcher  INFO    Deploying 4 worker(s) over 1
host(s).
[2022-09-26 16:09:50,661] launcher  INFO    Worker distribution:
[2022-09-26 16:09:50,661] launcher  INFO       127.0.0.1:       3 + origin
Launching 4 worker(s) using an unknown shell.
The value 10 and the elaboration is 3.1622776601683795
The value 3 and the elaboration is 1.7320508075688772
The value 6 and the elaboration is 2.449489742783178
The value 1 and the elaboration is 1.0
The value 4 and the elaboration is 2.0
The value 8 and the elaboration is 2.8284271247461903
The value 25 and the elaboration is 5.0
The value 9 and the elaboration is 3.0
This is the reduction result: 2.375
[2022-09-26 16:09:52,039] launcher  (127.0.0.1:65396) INFO    Root process is
done.
[2022-09-26 16:09:52,054] launcher  (127.0.0.1:65396) INFO    Finished
cleaning spawned subprocesses.
```

As we can see, things can gradually get complicated. This makes distributed computing even more powerful.

Monte Carlo Method with SCOOP

As we did with Celery, we will apply the Monte Carlo method for calculating π via the SCOOP framework. Unlike Celery, SCOOP does not require a messaging system like Redis or RabbitMQ to distribute tasks. This results in less overhead while communicating and aggregating results, which makes it faster, albeit only in local contexts. This feature makes the code simpler and is therefore more practical as an approach for scientific calculations when you want to work on a single machine, while exploiting multi-thread or multi-process parallelism automatically. Furthermore, methods like Monte Carlo are embarrassingly parallel (that is, each task is independent from the others). This makes them ideal for the said context, where SCOOP has a good scope to perform. Therefore, SCOOP is much more efficient than Celery in cases where the machine has several cores and does not require a high degree of scalability (that is, adding workers that can dynamically operate on remote machines).

SCOOP's relative simplicity can be immediately seen in the code that performs the same operations we have performed previously:

```
from scoop import futures
import random

def simulate_points(n_points):
    inside_circle = 0
    for _ in range(n_points):
        x, y = random.random(), random.random()
        if x**2 + y**2 <= 1:
            inside_circle += 1
    return inside_circle

def main():
    n_points_total = 10000000
    n_workers = 4
    n_points_per_worker = n_points_total // n_workers
    results = futures.map(simulate_points, [n_points_per_worker] * n_workers)
    total_inside_circle = sum(results)
    pi_estimate = 4 * total_inside_circle / n_points_total
    print(f"Estimate value of pi: {pi_estimate}")

if __name__ == "__main__":
    main()
```

The code is contained in a single file and does not require any configuration file. SCOOP is able to exploit aspects of parallelism and concurrency, while distributing the different tasks among the workers in a completely automatic and transparent way. To run the program, you will enter the following:

```
$ python -m scoop scoopy5.py
```

Which will provide you the following result:

```
a[2024-12-02 19:51:13,467] launcher  INFO    SCOOP 0.7 2.0 on win32 using
Python 3.12.7 | packaged by Anaconda, Inc. | (main, Oct  4 2024, 13:17:27)
[MSC v.1929 64 bit (AMD64)], API: 1013
[2024-12-02 19:51:13,467] launcher  INFO    Deploying 12 worker(s) over 1
host(s).
[2024-12-02 19:51:13,467] launcher  INFO    Worker distribution:
[2024-12-02 19:51:13,467] launcher  INFO       127.0.0.1:       11 + origin
Launching 12 worker(s) using an unknown shell.
Estimate value of pi: 3.1423436
[2024-12-02 19:51:18,086] launcher  (127.0.0.1:59363) INFO    Root process is
done.
[2024-12-02 19:51:18,086] launcher  (127.0.0.1:59363) INFO    Finished
cleaning spawned subprocesses.
```

As we can see, we have an estimate of π as 3.1423436. This displays a deviation from the third decimal place when compared to the real value of 3.14159.

A Comparison between Celery, Dramatiq and SCOOP

In this chapter, we have seen three different possible solutions to distributed applications where they can be managed asynchronously and in parallel. Celery, Dramatiq, and SCOOP seemingly offer the same functionality, but each of them represents a "*good*" solution for particular contexts. The choice of framework will thus depend on its specific strengths and limitations, the nature of the project, its technical needs, and the level of complexity required.

Celery is undoubtedly the most well-known and consolidated among these solutions for managing asynchronous tasks in Python. Its strength lies in its ability to manage large-scale distributed systems, which makes it ideal for complex applications that require high scalability and robustness. However, Celery requires a complex initial configuration and its learning curve can be steep. Despite inherent challenges, its large ecosystem makes it the most popular choice amongst developers.

Dramatiq is quite recent when compared to Celery. Its lighter nature makes it a simpler and a more immediate modern alternative. Its configuration is minimal; while Celery requires setting up every component, Dramatiq is ready to use. It supports popular brokers such as RabbitMQ and Redis, but its ecosystem is much smaller than Celery. However, it is more efficient, quick, less resource intensive, and is easy to learn and integrate into existing systems. Its drawback is that it does not have all the features of Celery.

Scoop represents an approach to distributed programming which is completely different from the two previous frameworks; it is not designed to manage distributed systems, but to execute parallel tasks on a single machine. It uses an architecture based on futures and threads, which makes it ideal for scientific or computational applications that require maximum exploitation of the resources that a local machine has. This feature makes it extremely simple as it does not require any configuration. However, its scalability is limited to the number of cores available on the local system, which makes it unsuitable for tasks distributed across multiple servers or for applications that require managing complex and distributed workloads.

Conclusion

This chapter introduced the concept of distributed systems and explained how they can enter the context of parallel programming. We also discussed the **Celery** framework, which acts as the main reference point for the implementation of distributed systems in Python. Furthermore, we have seen the most useful features of concurrent task computation. Later, we also considered two possible alternatives to this framework that offer similar solutions to our context: **Dramatiq** and **SCOOP**.

In the next chapter, we will explore the possibility of using parallel programming, that is, the use of GPU graphics processors and their libraries. We will also delve into how to exploit the computing power of such processors.

References

- https://www.capitalone.com/tech/software-engineering/distributed-systems-using-python-ray/
- https://scoop.readthedocs.io/en/0.7/
- https://pypi.org/project/scoop/
- https://www.pedaldrivenprogramming.com/2018/07/dramatiq-celery-alternative/
- https://dramatiq.io/

CHAPTER 6
GPU Programming with Python

Introduction

So far, we learned about the kinds of CPUs in the context of parallel programming. But CPUs are not the only processors capable of doing parallel calculations; another alternative is through **Graphics Processing Units** (**GPUs**). GPUs process vector data extremely quickly and efficiently for image rendering, 3D engines, and manipulate polygonal primitives. Their development is mainly due to evolutions and new trends in the gaming market, which have led to exceptional results over the years. Thanks to gaming technology, GPUs now have a moment to shine as powerful tools instrumental for scientific computing.

Structure

This chapter addresses the following topics:

- GPU Architecture
- GPU Programming
- Numba for CUDA
- OpenCL

GPU Architecture

GPUs are made up of millions of light cores in parallel, each of which is able to carry out calculations independently. This highly parallel structure is able to perform calculations on very large vectors and matrices rapidly, which is a feat that is yet to achieve by CPUs. These characteristics have therefore captured the attention of the scientific world and have led to the development of models, tools, and highly specialized libraries in this area.

Let us see in detail how a GPU is structured inside. These concepts will then come in handy to develop a better understanding of GPU programming models. Inside, GPUs are divided into *two* levels of parallelism. The first level consists of several processing units that make up the GPU and is called **Streaming Multiprocessor** (**SM**). Each of these units works *independently* of the others and performs tasks *simultaneously*. The second level of parallelism occurs within the **SM itself**. Each SM is subdivided into further computing units called **Stream Processor** (**SP**). Each SP has a core capable of executing a *thread*, which works independently and simultaneously with the other SPs. The schematic of this structure is shown in *Figure 6.1*:

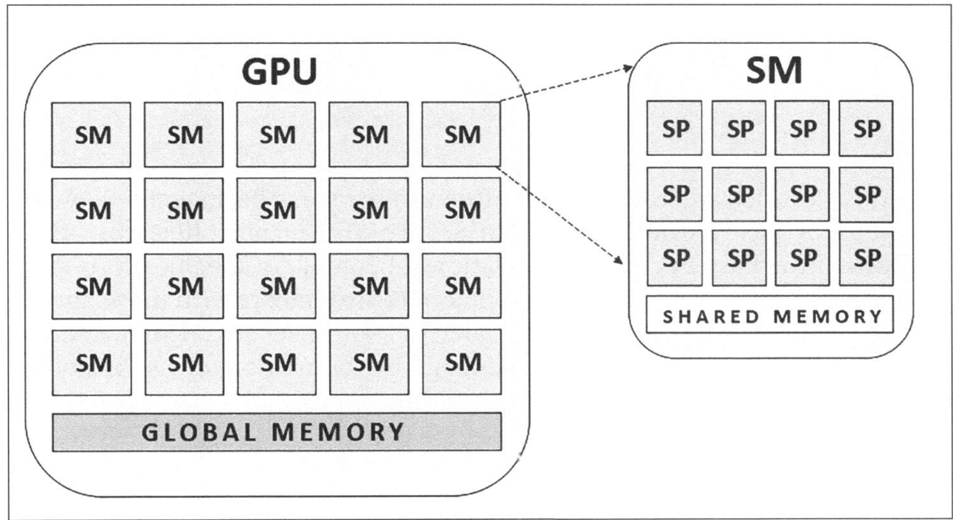

***Figure 6.1**: Internal Structure of a GPU*

The subdivision into **SM** and **SP** is structural. We can create a logical organization based on it which we will use for the GPU programming model. The SPs which are the basic unit of calculation of the GPUs can be grouped into blocks. These logic blocks will be used to execute a specific execution mode. In other words, all the cores within them will execute the same instruction simultaneously and point to different memory areas, while each processes a particular portion of data assigned to it. The memory they will access will be inside the GPU itself to help users access the values inside it as quickly as possible. This data will then be transferred and reloaded by the CPU again for further processing.

The highly parallel nature with thousands or millions of *processing units* (or *threads*) that are capable of doing many calculations makes GPUs extremely powerful, yet completely different from CPU. It is therefore necessary to develop specific programming methods different from conventional ones. You must take advantage of different drivers and compilers capable of compiling portions of code for the specific language that can be processed by the GPUs, which in turn are produced by different manufacturers and therefore require a specific approach.

At present, efficient solutions allow us to take advantage of the computing power of GPUs and integrate it with the classic and sequential execution of CPUs. Among the various manufacturers of graphics cards, **NVIDIA** is perhaps the most popular, both in terms of computing power and diffusion on PCs. To work with such cards, a specific development environment, the **Compute Unified Device Architecture (CUDA)** has been created specifically. This development environment is mainly based on the C language which uses particular extensions that allow developers to use specific features of GPUs, as well as other programming languages like Fortran, Java, and Python.

Another technology that allows us to program the GPUs together with the CPU to exploit its parallel computing potential is the **OpenCL framework**. It is based on the C and C ++ languages, but can also be integrated with other programming languages such as Python. This technology is more general than CUDA which is created specifically for NVIDIA cards. In fact, OpenCL is able to use GPU cards from other manufacturers (Intel, AMD, and so on) as well as NVIDIA cards, thanks to the release of SDK *toolkits* and specific drivers for the integration of OpenCL. As for NVIDIA GPU cards, OpenCL will still rely on CUDA technology as it is fully compatible and can be integrated with it.

GPU Programming in Python

GPU programming in Python is possible, thanks to a series of Python libraries that act as wrappers of corresponding C libraries. After years of rapid development, these libraries have been successful and have evolved continuously with these technologies. Currently, *two* libraries are particularly suitable for programming GPUs in parallel:

- Numba
- pyOpenCL

However, many other libraries are available and often use the same basic technologies such as **CUDA** and **OpenCL**, but some of these are quite difficult to use, are often *incompatible* with other libraries, and require compilations of the base in C (with installations of compilers specifications that must comply with particular versions). Often, setting up development environments with these libraries takes days, with little updated documentation, and does not always lead to success. **Numba** and **pyOpenCL** are perfectly integrated with Python package management environments such as **Pip** and **Anaconda**, and therefore their *installation* is *quick* and *easy*, which allows you to start working immediately.

Numba

Numba is an open-source library that includes a *JIT compiler* capable of translating portions of Python code and NumPy objects directly into specific machine code, using *LLVM technology*. This technology, provided by the **`llvmilite`** package, is integrated within **Numba**. Thanks to this integrated compilation system, Numba allows us to create code that uses the characteristics of the CPU and GPU in an easy way without making too many changes to the Python language.

Therefore, Numba allows us to write classic codes in Python to which we can add particular notations (appropriate Python decorators) that will identify portions of code to be compiled specifically for the different GPU cards.

Numba for CUDA

In this book, we will be using Numba to work specifically with NVIDIA GPUs and will therefore be relying on CUDA. In order to work with this technology, it is necessary to take a look at its programming model and understand its basic concepts. Only then will we be able to understand well the various steps that should be implemented if we want to make the most out of GPU.

Firstly, you need to identify the CPU on which the program written in Python will run, as well as the GPUs connected to it. The CPU will be identified as the *host* since it will host the mainstream program execution, often sequentially. GPUs will instead be identified as devices since they can be heterogeneous and require different drivers and compilers to function. Python code written specifically to work on CPU and GPUs at the same time will be coded and executed in the traditional way on the host. When portions of code intended to run on GPUs are found, they will be compiled based on the technology they will address. Since we are considering NVIDIA GPU cards, Numba will use CUDA *technology* and the compiler inside it to create particular compiled packages called **kernels**. It will send the kernels to the cards on which they will run. As we will see, these kernels are easily *identifiable* within the code and assume the form of functions that can be identified by particular decorators.

In addition to kernels, there are other functions intended for GPUs which are called **device functions**. These are compiled specifically to be run on different devices, but are called by the kernels while they are running on the GPU.

With respect to *memory*, it is necessary to make some clarifications. The portions of the program executed on the CPU have access to the system memory, which is called the **host memory**. As for the kernels, these will be executed on GPUs and will have to access the specific **device memory** on the cards.

In the GPU programming model, you will have to explicitly allocate the memory (host memory and device memory) and manage the transfer between them. Since GPUs work optimally with vectors, they will be used in the CUDA-based model of **NumPy** arrays, that are specifically optimized for these transfer and allocation operations on the GPUs.

By re-listing the protagonists of the GPU programming model with CUDA, we will obtain the following list:

- **Host** (CPU)
- **Device** (GPU)
- **Kernel** (a GPU function launched by the host and executed on the device)
- **Device Function** (a GPU function launched on the device and executed on the device)
- **Host Memory** (the main memory of the system)
- **Device Memory** (the memory on the GPU card)

Logical Hierarchy of the GPU Programming Model

As we have seen, CUDA responds to a different execution model than the traditional sequential model used for CPU programming. With CUDA, the code will be executed by *multiple threads at a time*. In addition to a multi-level physical structure that includes the SM and SP units, the CUDA programming model provides for a logical subdivision organized through a hierarchy of *threads*, which is further grouped into *grids* and *blocks*. A representative diagram of the logical hierarchy is shown in *Figure* 6.2:

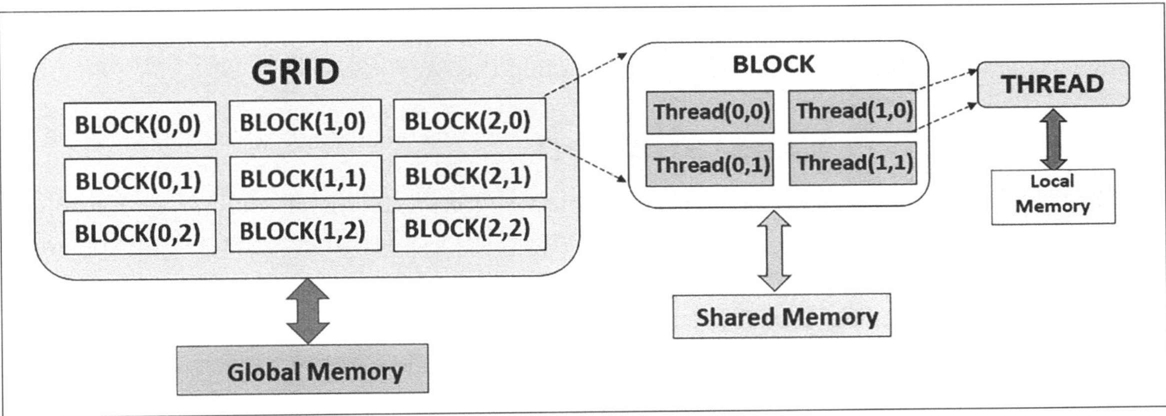

Figure 6.2: *Logical Hierarchy of Threads in GPU*

Numba provides a whole series of functions, classes and attributes that allow you to manage this hierarchy and the elements that compose it. As shown in *Figure* 6.2, it can be seen that every hierarchical level corresponds to a specific type of memory present in the GPU:

- Global Memory
- Shared Memory
- Local Memory

When implementing a program with Numba (but also with other libraries that make use of CUDA) you must always consider these types of memory. The creation of efficient algorithms necessarily requires their optimized use, minimizing access and data exchange, and operations that require time resources.

Installation of CUDA

The first thing to do is to install the **CUDA toolkit** from the internet. It can be downloaded for free on the NVIDIA developer site at the dedicated page (**https://developer.nvidia.com/cuda-downloads**).

Once the page is loaded, you will be shown a window where you can choose between different options to select your development environment, as shown in *Figure 6.3*:

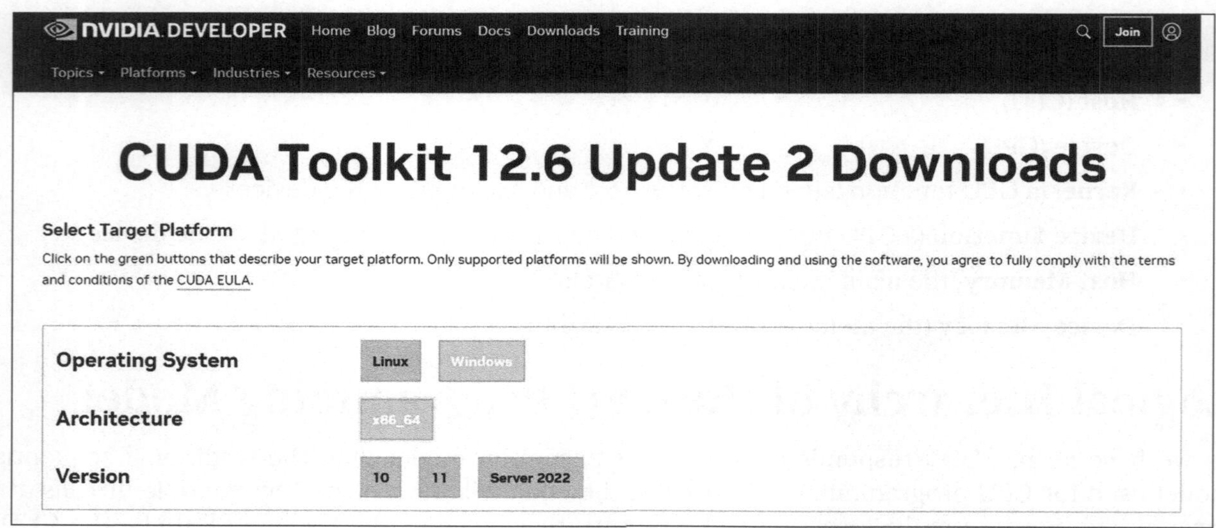

Figure 6.3*: Development System Options Window*

In our case, after selecting the characteristics of the system (*Windows* 11, *x86_64*), the following version has been automatically downloaded:

```
cuda_12.6.2_560.94_windows.exe
```

Make sure to install the latest version after downloading the executable.

Numba for CUDA Installation

Numba installation is very simple with the *Anaconda platform*. To install Numba, simply open the console of the virtual environment that you have prepared to work with GPUs and enter the following command:

```
conda install numba cudatoolkit
```

As you can see, the **`cudatoolkit`** package must also be installed. Many libraries that use NVIDIA GPUs already have the dependencies for this package, but Numba has many uses and does not always have to be used to work with this type of GPU. So, it is necessary to install **`cudatoolkit`** separately as well.

Declaration and Invocation of Kernel

Before starting the program, we saw that the portions of code intended for execution on GPUs are defined as kernel functions. This type of function has *two* fundamental characteristics that differentiate them from normal functions in Python. First, kernels are functions that *cannot* return a value explicitly; in other words, they cannot return a value outside the function. These functions work exclusively on the data contained in arrays that are passed as arguments to the function; therefore, one of these arrays must be destined to contain the results of the calculation. In the kernel declaration, you have to take into account the *thread hierarchy* that will be set when invoked. It is thus necessary to specify the number of thread blocks involved in calculation, and the number of threads present in each block.

Within the Python code, you can easily identify the portion of code that implements a *kernel* function, through the use of a particular decoder: **@cuda.jit**, as indicated here:

```
@cuda.jit
def kernel_func(array):
    """
    Code here
    """
```

Once you define a kernel, you will have to invoke it in your code. Before doing this, remember to express the thread hierarchy that must be set up and used for its execution. We will then set the number of threads for each block and then the *number of blocks per grid*, which is indicated here:

```
threadsperblock = 32
blockspergrid = (array.size // threadsperblock) + 1
```

By defining these two parameters in this way, the *size* of the array used will be taken into account each time and a corresponding number of threads will be arranged in a hierarchy suitable for calculating them in the most optimal way.

Then we will invoke the **kernel** function, specifying these parameters as indexes of the function. The product of these two values will actually match the threads used in the computation:

```
kernel_func[blockspergrid, threadsperblock](array)
```

Once invoked, the **kernel** function will be compiled and sent as a kernel to the corresponding device which will be executed by all the invoked threads. All kernels will run parallel *asynchronously*, each running the kernel *independently*. It is possible to synchronize their calculations by adding **cuda.synchronize()**. In this case, the code will wait for all kernels to finish their execution before continuing with the code.

As we will see in the following examples, choosing the correct thread hierarchy is essential for optimal computing performance on the GPU. The *block size* determines how many threads will share a certain memory area (shared memory) and also must be large enough to be able to take care of the calculation of the input data in a single step.

Furthermore, within the kernel function declaration, we will have to optimally manage the indexes of the threads involved and of the blocks to ensure that each thread knows exactly which element of the input array to deal with. There are special objects supplied by CUDA in this regard. For example, **threadIdx**, **threadIdy**, and **threadIdz** specify the indices of the various threads used within a block along the three dimensions. While **blockIdx**, **blockIdy**, and **blockIdz** specify the indices of the various blocks enclosed within the grid. The size of the blocks can instead be specified through **blockDim.x**, **blockDim.y**, and **blocDim.z**.

For example, if you want to implement a kernel that only puts the increment of **1** for all the elements present within an array, we will have to use the previous index objects as follows:

```
@cuda.jit
def add_one(array):
    tx = cuda.threadIdx.x
    ty = cuda.blockIdx.x
    dim = cuda.blockDim.x

    pos = tx + ty * dim
    if pos < array.size:
        array[pos] += 1
```

Since the array we are considering is *one-dimensional*, we can consider a 1D geometry inside the kernel where only **x** is present. So, the iteration between all the indices involved in the calculation can be related to the position of the array elements with the expression:

```
pos = tx + ty* dim
```

Furthermore, during the calculation, it is useful to set a condition to ensure that the index obtained is contained in the dimensions of the array. We then add the condition:

```
if pos < array.size:
```

Eventually, all kernels indexed with *pos* with each element of the array will increase their value by one unit simultaneously in a *parallel* and *asynchronous* manner.

Device Functions

As for the device functions, they differ slightly from the declaration, when compared to the kernel functions. Just add **device = True** to the decorator:

```
@cuda.jit(device=True)
def device_func(a, b):
    return a + b
```

Unlike **kernel** functions, a **device** function can return a value like all normal functions.

Programming Example with Numba

The notions we have learnt so far about Numba are enough for us to put them into practice and compile a small sample code. We will use the kernel seen before to increase the values of the elements of an array by one unit.

Let us write the following code:

```
import numpy as np
from numba import cuda
@cuda.jit
def add_one(a):
    tx = cuda.threadIdx.x
    ty = cuda.blockIdx.x
    dim = cuda.blockDim.x

    pos = tx + ty * dim
    if pos < a.size:
        a[pos] += 1

n = 10
a_host = np.random.random(n)
print("Vector a: %s" %a_host)
a_dev = cuda.to_device(a_host)

threadsperblock = 128
blockspergrid = (a_host.size // threadsperblock) + 1
add_one[blockspergrid, threadsperblock](a_dev)

a_host = a_dev.copy_to_host()
print("New Vector a: %s" %a_host)
```

As we can see, we first imported the necessary modules to integrate the kernels into the code. In particular, for those who want to work with NVIDIA GPUs, we will import the part related to CUDA:

```
from numba import cuda
```

The **numpy** library is also essential since the preferred data for this technology (both for memory allocation and for transfer) are the NumPy arrays. Therefore, we also imported this module:

```
import numpy as np
```

We then copied the kernel we had defined for the example previously:

```
@cuda.jit
def add_one(a):
    tx = cuda.threadIdx.x
    ty = cuda.blockIdx.x
    dim = cuda.blockDim.x

    pos = tx + ty * dim
    if pos < a.size:
        a[pos] += 1
```

Then we defined a simple array **a_host** (because it is on the host memory) of **10** elements, where the values are randomly generated (floating numbers):

```
n = 10
a_host = np.random.random(n)
print("Vector a: %s" %a_host)
```

At this point we have transferred this array to the device memory through the function **cuda.to_device()**, which allocates a memory space identical to the vector **a_host** on the device memory and then copies the content, which is identified with the array **a_dev** (because it is located on the device memory).

The next step is to define the hierarchy of threads that run the kernel. Here too, we have copied the definitions seen previously:

```
threadsperblock = 128
blockspergrid = (a_host.size // threadsperblock) + 1
```

We have inserted a large number of threads (**n = 128**) to prevent getting a warning message in the output:

```
NumbaPerformanceWarning: Grid size 10 will likely result in GPU
under-utilization due to low occupancy.
```

This error message appears because the program recommends using grids of a size that is comparable to the number of SPs present in the GPU and not too small that is not able to sufficiently leverage the potential of this hardware.

After defining an appropriate hierarchy for the threads, the **kernel** function is invoked on the **a_dev** array with the parameters just defined:

```
add_one[threadsperblock, blockspergrid](a_dev)
```

Once the kernel has been invoked, you will then have to manage the result of the calculation, that is, the vector **a_dev** whose elements have been increased by *one unit*. However, this vector is on the GPU, so you will need to transfer it back to the host memory. To do this, use the **copy_to_host()** function which copies a memory area from the GPU (device) to the host:

```
a_host = a_dev.copy_to_host()
```

The variable **a_host** will now contain the updated values. We can print it in the output and compare the results with the values prior to the *calculation*:

```
print("New Vector a: %s" %a_host)
```

By running the code in its entirety, we will get a result like this:

```
Vector a: [0.41384874 0.45213153 0.65042446 0.08814434 0.1537844  0.1184357
 0.61263638 0.86474909 0.91423873 0.34284854]
New Vector a: [1.41384874 1.45213153 1.65042446 1.08814434 1.1537844
1.1184357
 1.61263638 1.86474909 1.91423873 1.34284854]
```

As we can see, the calculations were done correctly.

Further Changes

Let us continue modifying the previous code while illustrating some other useful concepts. Let us consider the definition of *thread geometry* now. We have seen that its management can be complicated and difficult to understand at a simple level. In our favor, there is another alternative method that facilitates things: the definition of the absolute position.

In fact, simple algorithms such as the one examined in our example, tend to use all thread indexes in the same way. Numba provides us with functions that facilitate defining the positions of the thread indexes within the kernel.

The **cuda.grid(ndim)** function allows us to know the absolute position of the current thread in the current hierarchy. With **ndim**, we can define the number of dimensions the kernel is based on. Thanks to this function, the **kernel** function code is greatly simplified, as shown here:

```
@cuda.jit
def add_one(a):
    pos = cuda.grid(1)
    if pos < a.size:
        a[pos] += 1
```

Replacing it in the previous code will not change the results.

Extension to Matrices (2D array)

Another change we can make is to extend the previous example to 2D arrays; therefore, we will talk about *matrices* instead of vectors.

To perform this extension, you will have to make some changes to the code. First, we can define a matrix **A** instead of the vector **a**. We then make the appropriate changes and reduce the number of elements to **4** for better readability of the result, it will look like:

```
n = 4
A_host = np.random.random(n*n).reshape(n,n)
print("Matrix A: \n %s" %A_host)
A_dev = cuda.to_device(A_host)
```

We have therefore replaced the previous vector with a *4x4 matrix* both on the host, **A_host**, and on the device, **A_dev**. We then modify the **kernel** function to increase all the elements within a matrix by *one unit*, as shown here:

```
@cuda.jit
def add_one_2D(A):
    x, y = cuda.grid(2)
    if x < A.shape[0] and y < A.shape[1]:
        A[x, y] += 1
```

Thanks to absolute position, it is very easy to define a *two-dimensional kernel function*. As for the thread hierarchy, these will need to have a new geometry capable of responding optimally to working with two-dimensional vectors. To assign a thread for each element of the matrix, you will have to define the new hierarchy as follows:

```
import math
threadsperblock = (128,128)
blockspergrid_x = math.ceil(A_host.shape[0] / threadsperblock[0])
blockspergrid_y = math.ceil(A_host.shape[1] / threadsperblock[1])
blockspergrid = (blockspergrid_x, blockspergrid_y)
add_one_2D[threadsperblock, blockspergrid](A_dev)
```

Finally, we will retransfer the result obtained from the device to the host and display it in the output:

```
A_host = A_dev.copy_to_host()
print("New Matrix A: \n %s" %A_host)
```

Let's review the modified code in its entirety:

```
import numpy as np
from numba import cuda
import math

@cuda.jit
def add_one_2D(A):
    x, y = cuda.grid(2)
    if x < A.shape[0] and y < A.shape[1]:
       A[x, y] += 1

n = 4
A_host = np.random.random(n*n).reshape(n,n)
print("Matrix A: \n %s" %A_host)
A_dev = cuda.to_device(A_host)

threadsperblock = (128,128)
blockspergrid_x = math.ceil(A_host.shape[0] / threadsperblock[0])
blockspergrid_y = math.ceil(A_host.shape[1] / threadsperblock[1])
blockspergrid = (blockspergrid_x, blockspergrid_y)
add_one_2D[threadsperblock, blockspergrid](A_dev)

A_host = A_dev.copy_to_host()
print("New Matrix A: \n %s" %A_host)
```

Running the code will give us the following result:

```
Matrix A:
 [[0.00993464 0.99662295 0.6271492  0.39916735]
 [0.81896746 0.9282727  0.74802307 0.06418345]
 [0.54618904 0.92098866 0.13560085 0.41312367]
 [0.34544717 0.90828693 0.8784179  0.96724232]]
New Matrix A:
 [[1.00993464 1.99662295 1.6271492  1.39916735]
 [1.81896746 1.9282727  1.74802307 1.06418345]
 [1.54618904 1.92098866 1.13560085 1.41312367]
 [1.34544717 1.90828693 1.8784179  1.96724232]]
```

Transfer of Data through the Queue

Another change that applies to all examples (both for **vectors** and **matrices**) here is to use a *queue* for transferring data to and from the GPU. Editing is very simple, just create a CUDA stream as indicated:

```
stream = cuda.stream()
```

Then, add it to the two functions that manage data transfer in the following manner:

```
A_dev = cuda.to_device(A_host, stream=stream)
A_host = A_dev.copy_to_host(stream=stream)
```

In this way, you can transfer data more efficiently and manage it via a specific queue to streamline the passage of data correctly and efficiently between host and device.

Sum between Two Matrices

We will further extend the case of matrices by introducing an operation between multiple 2D vectors. In this case, we will add the elements of *two matrices* **A** and **B** to obtain the third matrix. This example shows how to introduce multiple input vectors to the kernel and how to manage them in the rest of the code.

Now, we no longer have a single vector (matrix) but three to define, one of which will be empty because it will host the results of the calculation. This is indicated as follows:

```
n = 4
A_host = np.random.random(n*n).reshape(n,n)
B_host = np.random.random(n*n).reshape(n,n)
C_host = np.zeros((n,n))
print("Matrix A: \n %s" %A_host)
print("Matrix B: \n %s" %B_host)
```

Transferring the data from the *host to the device* and *vice versa* must be done individually, as shown here:

```
stream = cuda.stream()
A_dev = cuda.to_device(A_host, stream=stream)
B_dev = cuda.to_device(B_host, stream=stream)
C_dev = cuda.to_device(C_host, stream=stream)
```

As for the data transferred from the *device to the host*, we will need to transfer only **C_dev**, since it is the only one that contains the results of the kernel calculation. While **A_dev** and **B_dev** are used for *read-only* and are identical to those on the host, **A_dev** and **B_dev** do not need to be copied again, as indicated here:

```
C_host = C_dev.copy_to_host(stream=stream)
print("Matrix C: \n %s" %C_host)
```

Now that we have managed the 2D vectors, let us move on to the kernel which will require some changes, even if everything remains simple.

```
@cuda.jit
def add_one_2D(A,B,C):
    x, y = cuda.grid(2)
    if x < A.shape[0] and y < A.shape[1]:
       C[x,y] = A[x, y] + B[x, y]
```

The position of the threads remains *unchanged* in this example, as the correspondence of the calculation between the elements of *two matrices* **A** and **B** remains. Only the corresponding elements of **A** and **B** will be added and the result will be the element of **C**. In this case, it was sufficient to add the sum of the elements between the various matrices, as shown here:

```
C[x,y] = A[x, y] + B[x, y]
```

As far as the thread hierarchy is concerned, things remain the same.

What should be changed is the *invocation* of the **kernel** function, which this time requires three arguments–the three matrices **A**, **B**, and **C**:

```
add_one_2D[threadsperblock, blockspergrid](A_dev, B_dev, C_dev)
```

Let us now rewrite the modified code in its entirety:

```
import numpy as np
from numba import cuda
import math

@cuda.jit
def add_one_2D(A,B,C):
    x, y = cuda.grid(2)
    if x < A.shape[0] and y < A.shape[1]:
       C[x,y] = A[x, y] + B[x, y]

n = 4
A_host = np.random.random(n*n).reshape(n,n)
B_host = np.random.random(n*n).reshape(n,n)
C_host = np.zeros((n,n))
print("Matrix A: \n %s" %A_host)
print("Matrix B: \n %s" %B_host)

stream = cuda.stream()
A_dev = cuda.to_device(A_host, stream=stream)
B_dev = cuda.to_device(B_host, stream=stream)
C_dev = cuda.to_device(C_host, stream=stream)

threadsperblock = (16,16)
blockspergrid_x = math.ceil(A_host.shape[0] / threadsperblock[0])
blockspergrid_y = math.ceil(A_host.shape[1] / threadsperblock[1])
blockspergrid = (blockspergrid_x, blockspergrid_y)
add_one_2D[threadsperblock, blockspergrid](A_dev, B_dev, C_dev)

C_host = C_dev.copy_to_host(stream=stream)
print("Matrix C: \n %s" %C_host)
```

Running the code will produce the following result:

```
Matrix A:
 [[0.82645664 0.14077644 0.36426624 0.65039297]
 [0.10257125 0.30826244 0.82165832 0.90301203]
 [0.19817223 0.95656813 0.61620533 0.1200333 ]
 [0.8798604  0.11889796 0.31937825 0.0725755 ]]
Matrix B:
 [[0.83451822 0.37569725 0.91302873 0.061711  ]
 [0.04279979 0.13255439 0.96567441 0.51154525]
 [0.8677725  0.34670277 0.2593976  0.50304275]
 [0.91463535 0.96564344 0.91629866 0.17960097]]
Matrix C:
 [[1.66097486 0.51647368 1.27729497 0.71210397]
 [0.14537104 0.44081682 1.78733273 1.41455728]
```

```
[1.06594473 1.3032709  0.87560292 0.62307604]
[1.79449575 1.0845414  1.23567691 0.25217646]]
```

Multiplication between Matrices

The last modification of the previous code is to consider multiplication between matrices like A * B = C. This is quite expensive for a sequential program running on the CPU. Instead, we will discover that this operation lends itself perfectly to being processed on GPUs, that perform much better than a CPU. The example is indicated here:

```
import numpy as np
from numba import cuda
import math

@cuda.jit
def matmul(A, B, C):

    i, j = cuda.grid(2)
    if i < C.shape[0] and j < C.shape[1]:
        tmp = 0.
        for k in range(A.shape[1]):
            tmp += A[i, k] * B[k, j]
        C[i, j] = tmp

n = 4
A_host = np.random.random(n*n).reshape(n,n)
B_host = np.random.random(n*n).reshape(n,n)
C_host = np.zeros((n,n))
print("Matrix A: \n %s" %A_host)
print("Matrix B: \n %s" %B_host)

stream = cuda.stream()
A_dev = cuda.to_device(A_host, stream=stream)
B_dev = cuda.to_device(B_host, stream=stream)
C_dev = cuda.to_device(C_host, stream=stream)

threadsperblock = (128,128)
blockspergrid_x = math.ceil(A_host.shape[0] / threadsperblock[0])
blockspergrid_y = math.ceil(A_host.shape[1] / threadsperblock[1])
blockspergrid = (blockspergrid_x, blockspergrid_y)
matmul[threadsperblock, blockspergrid](A_dev, B_dev, C_dev)

C_host = C_dev.copy_to_host(stream=stream)
print("Matrix C: \n %s" %C_host)
```

As we can see, the differences after excluding the **kernel** are very minimal. By running the preceding code, we will get a result like this:

```
Matrix A:
 [[0.75926968 0.92657886 0.68471105 0.17324253]
 [0.40790221 0.45988319 0.39122078 0.6198121 ]
 [0.10698571 0.43140089 0.58631454 0.38644777]
 [0.17504734 0.76003441 0.68634873 0.94149139]]
Matrix B:
 [[0.79381329 0.96132662 0.16316954 0.5995909 ]
 [0.74119391 0.85658564 0.85753895 0.65944347]
 [0.98787907 0.04619411 0.70690497 0.51689578]
 [0.85581547 0.67852783 0.84931887 0.30510469]]
```

```
Matrix C:
 [[2.11416833 1.6727798  1.54963095 1.47305894]
 [1.58158443 1.22468845 1.263899   0.93916938]
 [1.31461425 0.76167987 1.13008593 0.76960271]
 [2.18606024 1.48984562 1.96513125 1.24818073]]
```

The example we have chosen requires *less execution time* since we used small matrices. As the size grows, the situation becomes different. We will now add **`time`** meters via the **`time`** module. We will see how the execution times vary with this kind of operation, as the number of threads per block varies. Let us now modify the code to record the execution times:

```
import numpy as np
from numba import cuda
import time
import math

@cuda.jit
def matmul(A, B, C):

    i, j = cuda.grid(2)
    if i < C.shape[0] and j < C.shape[1]:
        tmp = 0.
        for k in range(A.shape[1]):
            tmp += A[i, k] * B[k, j]
        C[i, j] = tmp

print("Matrix Size: ")
n = input()
print("\n")
A_host = np.random.random(n*n).reshape(n,n)
B_host = np.random.random(n*n).reshape(n,n)
C_host = np.zeros((n,n))

stream = cuda.stream()
A_dev = cuda.to_device(A_host, stream=stream)
B_dev = cuda.to_device(B_host, stream=stream)
C_dev = cuda.to_device(C_host, stream=stream)

threadsperblock = (128,128)
blockspergrid_x = math.ceil(A_host.shape[0] / threadsperblock[0])
blockspergrid_y = math.ceil(A_host.shape[1] / threadsperblock[1])
blockspergrid = (blockspergrid_x, blockspergrid_y)
matmul[threadsperblock, blockspergrid](A_dev, B_dev, C_dev)

t1 = time.perf_counter()
C_host = C_dev.copy_to_host(stream=stream)
t2 = time.perf_counter()
elapsed_time = t2 - t1
print("Elapsed time %s" %elapsed_time)
```

As we can see from the code, we have eliminated the printing of the values of the matrices and inserted the size of the matrices from the console during execution. This is done so **`tgat`** one does not have to modify the code every time. Another solution could be using input parameters during the *program launch*.

If we measure the time taken as the *size of the matrices varies* and the *size of the blocks* (number of threads per block) varies, we obtain a table like this (see *Table* 6.1):

Matrix size	**threads in block**			
	n=128	n=256	n=512	n=1024
1024	0,06	0,06	0,22	0,71
2048	0,68	0,42	0,42	1,36
3072	2,14	1,78	1,28	2,26
4092	7,24	4,87	2,04	3,28
5120	N/A	12,32	7,22	5,29
6144	N/A	17,08	14,79	10,37
7168	N/A	40,73	25,6	17,51
8192	N/A	67,36	40,24	23,36
9216	N/A	N/A	63,97	46,58
10240	N/A	N/A	121,47	60,23

Table 6.1: *Elapsed Times for Matrices Multiplication*

If plot the values shown in *Table* 6.1 on a graph, we will obtain an interesting result (see *Figure* 6.4):

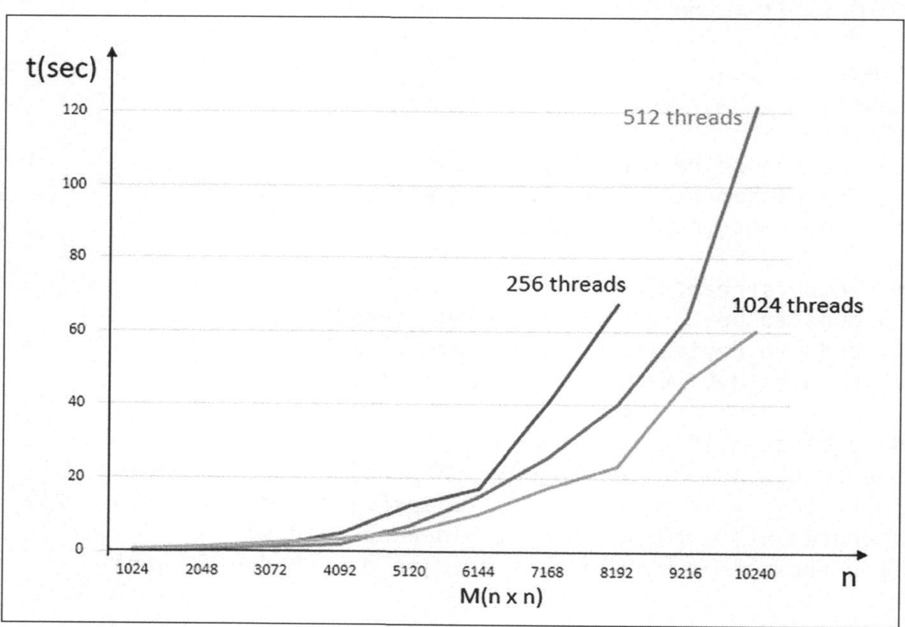

Figure 6.4: *Elapsed Time for Matrices Multiplication with Numba for CUDA, Varying Threads for Block*

You can see the *trend of the times* used in calculating the multiplication of the matrices as their size increases. *Three* trends are reported, each with a different number of threads per block. As you can see, the higher this number, the better the GPU performance will be.

Improving Performance with Advanced Memory Management Techniques in CUDA

To achieve maximum performance in GPU applications, it is essential to manage memory efficiently with CUDA. Memory is one of the main limitations for high-performance computing on GPUs. Advanced memory management techniques in CUDA can reduce data access times, and improve parallelism, while optimizing kernel execution. In this section, we will explore advanced memory management techniques in CUDA, such as the use of shared memory, coalescing global memory access, unified memory, and optimizations to reduce memory latency. In CUDA, different types of memory can be used to optimize kernel execution. We have already seen a schema of these memories in *Figure 6.2* that depicted the logical structure of a GPU with the following levels of memory:

- Global Memory
- Shared Memory
- Local Memory

In fact, the basis of advanced techniques is the efficient use of these types of memory by leveraging their characteristics in the best possible way. It will therefore be important to understand all these memory characterizations available within the GPU.

Coalescing Access in Global Memory

Global memory is the main memory area that is accessible to all GPU threads. It is a large memory, but relatively slow compared to other memories that are closer to the GPU core. Unified Memory is also based on global memory, but is managed automatically between the CPU and GPU, which makes it easier to transfer data without the need for explicit transfers.

Coalescing access is a fundamental technique for optimizing the performance of CUDA kernels. The main idea is to make consecutive threads access consecutive memory locations. This minimizes the number of memory transactions and fully utilizes the GPU bandwidth. To demonstrate coalescent access, we implement a simple vector sum where each element of an array a is added to each element of an array b and the result is saved in an array c. If threads access consecutive locations in the arrays, the global memory access will be coalescent. This is demonstrated here:

```
import numpy as np
from numba import cuda
import time

@cuda.jit
def vector_add_coalesced(a, b, c):
    idx = cuda.grid(1)
    if idx < a.size:
        c[idx] = a[idx] + b[idx]

n = 10**7  # Very great array for avoiding cache compensation
a = np.random.rand(n).astype(np.float32)
b = np.random.rand(n).astype(np.float32)
c = np.zeros_like(a)

# Transfer data to GPU
a_device = cuda.to_device(a)
b_device = cuda.to_device(b)
c_device = cuda.to_device(c)

# Threads and block configuration
threadsperblock = 256
blockspergrid = (n + threadsperblock - 1) // threadsperblock

# Coalesced Kernel
start_time = time.time()
vector_add_coalesced[blockspergrid, threadsperblock](a_device, b_device,
c_device)
```

```
cuda.synchronize()
coalesced_time = time.time() - start_time
c_device.copy_to_host(c)
print("Array A (coalesced, first 10 elements):", a[:10])
print("Array B (coalesced, first 10 elements):", b[:10])
print("Array C (coalesced, first 10 elements):", c[:10])

print("Coalesced access time: {:.6f} sec".format(coalesced_time))
```

First, we defined the kernel function **vector_add_coalesced**, which is recognizable by the **@cuda.jit** decoration. This indicates that the function must be compiled and executed by the GPU. Inside it, the global index idx is calculated and then checked to ensure that it is less than the size of the array a to avoid out-of-bounds accesses. Each thread reads **a[idx]** and **b[idx]** and saves the sum in **c[idx]**. Since these positions are consecutive like the threads that perform the calculation, the access is said to be coalesced. Moving on to the execution code, we first initialize the arrays and convert them to the CUDA-compatible **np.float32** format. We copy these arrays to the global memory of the CPU. Then we configure the blocks and the number of threads per block (256). Finally, we launch the kernel **vector_add_coalesced** that were defined previously based on the grid configuration we have considered here. The computation time is measured via the time module. The results of the calculation present in the global memory in **c_device** are copied to the host memory (CPU). The results and the starting arrays are printed. Running the code gives the following result:

```
Array A (coalesced, first 10 elements): [0.51330817 0.65680534 0.5620223
0.16023143 0.7678593  0.60751337
 0.2930813  0.05836558 0.3252436  0.527797  ]
Array B (coalesced, first 10 elements): [0.8741073  0.61918634 0.40172398
0.06008506 0.12828662 0.13789588
 0.01910437 0.9049279  0.74846655 0.21055742]
Array C (coalesced, first 10 elements): [1.3874154  1.2759917  0.9637463
0.22031648 0.8961459  0.74540925
 0.31218567 0.9632935  1.0737102  0.7383544 ]
Coalesced access time: 0.978873 sec
```

Let us now compare this to an identical case that does not have coalescence: that is, the case in which consecutive threads perform operations on elements that are not elements.

For example, let us define this kernel function:

```
@cuda.jit
def vector_add_non_coalesced(a, b, c):
    idx = cuda.grid(1)
    if idx < a.size:
        c[idx] = a[(idx * 512) % a.size] + b[(idx * 512) % b.size]
```

This is a CUDA kernel designed to simulate non-coalescing memory access where consecutive threads access elements 512 locations apart. We can make the necessary substitutions in the execution-related code as follows:

```
start_time = time.time()
vector_add_non_coalesced[blockspergrid, threadsperblock](a_device, b_device,
c_device)
cuda.synchronize()
non_coalesced_time = time.time() - start_time
c_device.copy_to_host(c)
print("Array C (non-coalesced, first 10 elements):", c[:10])

# Performance comparison
print("Non-coalesced access time: {:.6f} sec".format(non_coalesced_time))
```

Running the code gives the following result:

```
Array A (coalesced, first 10 elements): [0.17582351 0.05370485 0.560497
0.5976044  0.1812575  0.22156523
 0.16826814 0.20292132 0.23948562 0.26082572]
Array B (coalesced, first 10 elements): [0.77052814 0.73420006 0.3231831
0.7828882  0.10432568 0.36891106
 0.15359579 0.35808575 0.7570364  0.33711216]
Array C (coalesced, first 10 elements): [0.94635165 1.4685063  1.0711944
0.6870343  1.1184626  1.2444644
 1.0322264  1.4413192  0.9999696  0.48229057]
Non-coalesced access time: 1.312598 sec
```

As we can see, we observe higher efficiency while coalescing global memory access operations. However, in some situations this efficiency may not be so evident, thanks to the technological compensation of many modern GPUs. These use advanced caches to hide the global memory latency, which make the difference between coalescing and non-coalescing less relevant for small datasets or repetitive accesses. The cache can temporarily store the requested data, while also optimizing non-coalescing access patterns. In this case, a factor not to be overlooked is the size of the data. If the data fits entirely in the GPU cache, global memory access becomes less frequent, thereby reducing the impact of non-coalescing access. Only with large datasets that cannot be entirely cached, does coalescence show its advantage. In the previous example, we used a large array. Other situations are Occupancy and Latency Masking: the GPU uses occupancy, that is, the ability to execute a large number of threads in parallel, to mask the memory latency. If there are enough threads to occupy the GPU, the waiting time for global memory accesses can be covered by the execution of other threads, while partially hiding the inefficiencies of non-coalesced access. GPUs are also designed for high-speed memory transfers. Even non-coalesced access can be relatively fast if there are enough blocks and threads to ensure a balanced load, thus reducing the impact of access inefficiencies.

Using Shared Memory

Shared memory is a low-latency memory accessible to all threads in a block, which makes it ideal for storing temporary data and optimizing intra-block computations. Since it is much faster than global memory, reducing global memory accesses using shared memory can result in significant performance improvements.

To highlight the effectiveness of shared memory, we can use matrix multiplication as an example. Matrix multiplication is an operation that benefits from shared memory as each element of the output requires repeated access to the elements of rows and columns of the input matrices. Again, we will compare two approaches: the use of shared memory and the exclusive use of global memory. In the case of shared memory, we can load the rows and columns in each block into the shared memory. This allows all threads in the block to quickly access the same data without having to repeatedly reload it from global memory, while significantly reducing latency. To do this, we will define the kernel **matrix_mult_shared**.

```
import numpy as np
from numba import cuda, float32
import time

@cuda.jit
def matrix_mult_shared(A, B, C, N):
    sA = cuda.shared.array((32, 32), dtype=float32)
    sB = cuda.shared.array((32, 32), dtype=float32)

    tx = cuda.threadIdx.x
    ty = cuda.threadIdx.y
```

```
    bx = cuda.blockIdx.x
    by = cuda.blockIdx.y

    row = by * 32 + ty
    col = bx * 32 + tx

    temp = 0.0

    for i in range((N + 32 - 1) // 32):
        if row < N and i * 32 + tx < N:
            sA[ty, tx] = A[row, i * 32 + tx]
        else:
            sA[ty, tx] = 0.0

        if col < N and i * 32 + ty < N:
            sB[ty, tx] = B[i * 32 + ty, col]
        else:
            sB[ty, tx] = 0.0

        cuda.syncthreads()

        for j in range(32):
            temp += sA[ty, j] * sB[j, tx]

        cuda.syncthreads()

    if row < N and col < N:
        C[row, col] = temp


def run_matrix_multiplication(N):
    A = np.random.rand(N, N).astype(np.float32)
    B = np.random.rand(N, N).astype(np.float32)
    C = np.zeros((N, N), dtype=np.float32)

    A_device = cuda.to_device(A)
    B_device = cuda.to_device(B)
    C_device = cuda.to_device(C)

    threads_per_block = (32, 32)
    blocks_per_grid = ((N + 32 - 1) // 32, (N + 32 - 1) // 32)

    start_time = time.time()
    matrix_mult_shared[blocks_per_grid, threads_per_block](A_device, B_device,
C_device, N)
    cuda.synchronize()
    shared_time = time.time() - start_time
    C_device.copy_to_host(C)
    print("Time with shared memory: {:.6f} sec".format(shared_time))

# Matrices size
un_matrix_multiplication(1024)
```

By running the above code we will get the following result:

```
Time with shared memory: 0.491227 sec
```

For the approach that makes exclusive use of global memory, we will define the kernel **matrix_mult_global** as follows:

```
@cuda.jit
def matrix_mult_global(A, B, C, N):
    row, col = cuda.grid(2)
    if row < N and col < N:
        temp = 0.0
        for k in range(N):
            temp += A[row, k] * B[k, col]
        C[row, col] = temp
```

By substituting in the code wherever appropriate, this second version is also executed, which gives us the following result:

```
Time without shared memory: 0.381844 sec
```

This result is certainly unexpected, given that not using shared memory would be faster. However, let us not let mere appearances deceive us. To perform the calculation, we used a matrix of size 1024×1024. However, as the matrix size increases, results are immediately inverted, and increasingly discriminate against the choice of using global memory exclusively. See the table below with the relative graph:

N	Shared Memory Time(s)	Global Memory Time(s)
1024	0.49	0.38
2048	0.89	0.93
4096	3.16	5.15
6144	9.38	17.18
8192	21.73	46.48
10240	42.03	93.55
15360	140.31	613.61

***Table 6.2**: Comparison of Execution Times with and without Shared Memory (Only Global memory)*

As we can see from the data, matrices larger than 4096 use shared memory with significant performance improvements.

Buffer Reuse and Memory Pooling

Buffer reuse and **memory pooling** reduce frequent allocations and deallocations, while avoiding memory management overhead. Allocating memory buffers once and reusing them for multiple subsequent tasks can improve kernel efficiency, as shown in the code here:

```
import numpy as np
from numba import cuda
import time

# Example kernel using a temporary buffer for intermediate calculations
@cuda.jit
def example_kernel(data, temp_buffer, factor):
    idx = cuda.grid(1)
    if idx < data.size:
        # an intermediate calculation using the temporary buffer
        temp_buffer[idx] = data[idx] * factor
        # use the result in the temporary buffer to update the output
        data[idx] = temp_buffer[idx] + data[idx]
```

```
# Repeated calculations with buffer reuse
def run_reused_buffer_example(n, iterations, factor):
    # GPU Memory Buffer and Data Array Allocation
    data = cuda.to_device(np.random.rand(n).astype(np.float32))
    temp_buffer = cuda.device_array(n, dtype=np.float32)  # Reusable temporary
buffer
    threads_per_block = 256
    blocks_per_grid = (n + threads_per_block - 1) // threads_per_block

    start_time = time.time()
    for i in range(iterations):
        # Use the temporary buffer to perform intermediate calculations
        example_kernel[blocks_per_grid, threads_per_block](data, temp_buffer,
factor)
        cuda.synchronize()

    total_time = time.time() - start_time
    print(f" Total time with buffer reuse: {total_time:.6f} sec")
    return total_time

# Function without buffer reuse (with allocations in each iteration)
def run_no_reuse_example(n, iterations, factor):
    data = cuda.to_device(np.random.rand(n).astype(np.float32))

    threads_per_block = 256
    blocks_per_grid = (n + threads_per_block - 1) // threads_per_block

    start_time = time.time()
    for i in range(iterations):
        # Allocate a new temporary buffer in each iteration
        temp_buffer = cuda.device_array(n, dtype=np.float32)
        example_kernel[blocks_per_grid, threads_per_block](data, temp_buffer,
factor)
        cuda.synchronize()

    total_time = time.time() - start_time
    print(f" Total time without buffer reuse: {total_time:.6f} sec")
    return total_time
```

Now, let us compare the two approaches:

```
def compare_reuse(n=10**8, iterations=100, factor=1.1):
    time_with_reuse = run_reused_buffer_example(n, iterations, factor)

compare_reuse()
```

The result obtained is:

```
Total time with buffer reuse: 0.884191 sec
```

Now, let us try the other approach:

```
def compare_no_reuse(n=10**8, iterations=100, factor=1.1):
    time_without_reuse = run_no_reuse_example(n, iterations, factor)

compare_no_reuse()
```

The result obtained is:

```
Total time without buffer reuse: 2.202776 sec
```

These results clearly show how buffer reuse significantly improves efficiency for large datasets and numerous iterations. This is mainly due to the reduced memory overhead, when the buffer is reused compared to continuous allocation and deallocation.

Let us look at some important points in the code. The kernel **example_kernel** performs a simple operation: it uses a temporary buffer **temp_buffer** to store an intermediate result (product of **data[idx]** and **factor**). It then updates the value of **data[idx]** by adding the intermediate result. The function **run_reused_buffer_example** pre-allocates the buffer **temp_buffer** only once during the entire iteration cycle. In each iteration, the kernel uses **temp_buffer** as temporary storage for computations, without reallocating it. This approach minimizes the number of allocations and deallocations, while reducing the overhead. In the function **run_no_reuse_example**, the buffer **temp_buffer** is allocated each time the kernel is launched. After each iteration, the temporary memory is automatically deallocated. This introduces a significant overhead for allocation and deallocation, which becomes particularly evident with large array sizes (**n=10**8**).

Remember, when testing these functions, high efficiency is evident only in the case of large arrays and a high number of iterations (iterations=100) and when the cost of allocation and deallocation becomes more proportional.

Benchmarking and Profiling GPU Applications

Optimizing GPU applications requires carefully evaluating their performance and identifying bottlenecks through benchmarking and profiling. These techniques are key steps to maximize the efficiency of GPU applications. Benchmarks measure the total execution time to assess overall performance, while profiling provides a detailed analysis and identifies specific areas for improvement such as memory latency, thread occupancy, and parallelism efficiency. Through tools such as NVIDIA Nsight, CUDA Profiler Tools Interface (CUPTI), and CUDA timing functions, developers can get a comprehensive view of application performance.

Benchmarking measures the execution time of key sections of the application, especially the CUDA kernels, which are the most computationally intensive parts. CUDA provides a series of events to accurately measure execution times. Events allow you to record the start and end time of a GPU operation, along with millisecond resolution, as shown here:

```
import numpy as np
from numba import cuda
import time

@cuda.jit
def vector_add_kernel(a, b, c):
    idx = cuda.grid(1)
    if idx < a.size:
        c[idx] = a[idx] + b[idx]

def benchmark_vector_add(n=10**7):
    # Allocazione dei dati
    a = np.random.rand(n).astype(np.float32)
    b = np.random.rand(n).astype(np.float32)
    c = np.zeros_like(a)

    # Transferring data to the GPU
    a_device = cuda.to_device(a)
    b_device = cuda.to_device(b)
    c_device = cuda.to_device(c)
```

```
    threads_per_block = 256
    blocks_per_grid = (n + threads_per_block - 1) // threads_per_block

    # Creating CUDA events
    start_event = cuda.event()
    end_event = cuda.event()

    # Start measurement
    start_event.record()

    # Run the kernel
    vector_add_kernel[blocks_per_grid, threads_per_block](a_device, b_device,
c_device)

    # End of measurement
    end_event.record()
    end_event.synchronize()  # Ensures the kernel is completed

    # Calculate the elapsed time
    elapsed_time = cuda.event_elapsed_time(start_event, end_event)
    print(f" Kernel execution time: {elapsed_time:.3f} ms")

benchmark_vector_add()
```

By executing the code, you get the execution time as:

```
Kernel execution time: 134.820 ms
```

Here, you can see that the **cuda.event()** function creates events to record the start (**start_event**) and end (**end_event**) times. These events are useful for recording and measuring these times. For instance, functions such as **record()** record the current time on the event, while **event_elapsed_time()** calculates the time elapsed between the two events. Finally the synchronization is done by **end_event.synchronize()** which makes sure that the kernel is completed before measuring the time.

Profiling is an in-depth performance analysis technique that identifies bottlenecks at GPU level by analyzing:

- **Thread Occupancy**: Number of active threads compared to the maximum supported
- **Memory Utilization**: Efficiency of accesses to global, shared, and constant memory
- **Parallelism Efficiency**: The degree of utilization of streaming multiprocessors (SMs)

There are several profiling tools for this purpose. NVIDIA Nsight Systems is a graphical tool that allows you to analyze in detail execution times, CPU and GPU concurrency, and memory usage. CUDA Profiler Tools Interface (CUPTI) is an advanced interface for obtaining detailed performance metrics. There are also profiling functions provided by the Numba library. These are indicated here:

```
from numba import cuda
import numpy as np

@cuda.jit
def example_kernel(a, b, c):
    idx = cuda.grid(1)
    if idx < a.size:
        c[idx] = a[idx] + b[idx]

def run_with_profiling():
    # Initialize data
    n = 10**7
```

```
    a = np.random.rand(n).astype(np.float32)
    b = np.random.rand(n).astype(np.float32)
    c = np.zeros_like(a)

    # Copy data to GPU
    a_device = cuda.to_device(a)
    b_device = cuda.to_device(b)
    c_device = cuda.to_device(c)

    threads_per_block = 256
    blocks_per_grid = (n + threads_per_block - 1) // threads_per_block

    # Start profiling
    cuda.profile_start()

    # Kernel execution
    example_kernel[blocks_per_grid, threads_per_block](a_device, b_device, c_
device)
    cuda.synchronize()

    # Stop profiling
    cuda.profile_stop()

    # Copy results from GPU to CPU
    c_device.copy_to_host(c)

    print("Profiling completed!")

run_with_profiling()
```

To perform profiling, it is necessary to use the tools provided by the NVIDIA development kit. To profile the execution of the previous code (for example, by saving it as *Ch06_11.py*), the `nsys` executable is used. On Windows, it can be found in a directory under NVIDIA *Corporation* named *Nsight Systems*, with the version number appended. Profiling is performed by adding the `profile` option followed by the command to be recorded, which in our case is the execution of the code using Python.

```
 C:\Program Files\NVIDIA Corporation\Nsight Systems 2024.5.1\target-windows
-x64>nsys profile python C:\Users\nelli\Downloads\code\Ch06_11.py
WARNING: CPU context switches trace requires administrative privileges,
disabling.
WARNING: CPU sampling requires administrative privileges, disabling.
Collecting data...
Generating 'C:\Users\nelli\AppData\Local\Temp\nsys-report-be1f.qdstrm'
[1/1] [========================100%] nsys-report-9173.nsys-rep
```

A report file like this will be generated:

```
report1.nsys-rep
```

To study the profiling of the execution here, we can use a graphical interface called **`nsys-ui`**, which allows us to analyze the execution in a visually.

```
C:\Program Files\NVIDIA Corporation\Nsight Systems 2024.5.1\host-windows-
x64>nsys-ui
```

The graphical interface will look like the one in *Figure 6.5*:

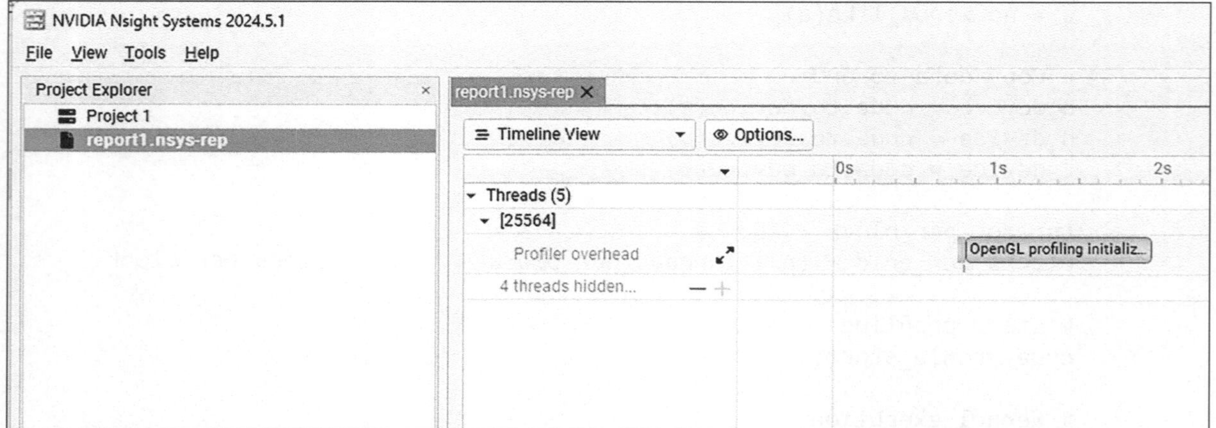

Figure 6.5: *The Graphic Interface of NSYS Nvidia*

PyOpenCL

Another library that allows us to leverage the potential of GPUs through Python is **pyOpenCL**. This package is a Python wrapper of **Open Computing Language** (**OpenCL**). This framework, based on the use of the C99 *language*, allows you to work on different and heterogeneous platforms that include both CPU and GPU. The programs implemented with OpenCL will then be compiled by appropriate drivers in different languages specific to each technology. Therefore, its use is not limited exclusively to NVIDIA cards and CUDA. OpenCL is an excellent solution for extending programming to many other different environments that use GPU cards made by different manufacturers such as IBM, AMD, and Intel.

OpenCL was initially created by *Apple*, but it was later passed to *Khronos Group*, a non-profit consortium, which keeps the project active to this day with new releases. Since OpenCL is not based exclusively on CUDA, it is an excellent alternative for anyone who does not have NVIDIA graphics cards but wants to use other GPUs from different manufacturers for parallel computing.

Installation of pyOpenCL

Getting your *Windows* machine ready to work with OpenCL is quite simple. The latest drivers must be installed for all *OpenCL-compatible devices.*

You can simply install **pyOpenCL** through a common **conda** installation:

```
conda install -c conda-forge pyopencl
```

To take advantage of Intel's CPU, the following drivers can also be added:

```
conda install intel-opencl-rt
```

For other platforms, you will need to look up specific packages on the web. It is clear that if we want to use NVIDIA GPUs, the CUDA toolkit will have to be installed on the system. However, if you have used Numba in the first part of this chapter, you will not need to install more toolkits.

After completing the installation of these packages, you can check everything via the following example. A very useful function that allows us to investigate the system we are working on is **get_platforms()**. This function gives us the list of platforms on our system that work with OpenCL. From this, it is possible to obtain further information on the devices inside them (the GPUs) using the **get_**

devices() function. We then use these *two* functions to get a general picture of the system we are working on by writing the following code:

```
import pyopencl as cl

for platform in cl.get_platforms():
   print("Platform %s " %platform.name)
   print("  Vendor: %s " %platform.vendor)
   print("  Version: %s " %platform.version)
   for device in platform.get_devices():
      print("     Device %s " %device.name)
      print("       Max Clock Speed: %s MHz " %device.max_clock_frequency)
      print("       Compute Units: %s " %device.max_compute_units)
      print("       Local Memory: %s Kb" %(device.local_mem_size/1024.0))
      print("       Global Memory: %s Gb " %(round(device.global_mem_
size/1073741824.0,2)))
```

Running the code will deliver the following result:

```
Platform NVIDIA CUDA
  Vendor: NVIDIA Corporation
  Version: OpenCL 3.0 CUDA 11.7.101
     Device NVIDIA GeForce GTX 1650 Ti
       Max Clock Speed: 1485 MHz
       Compute Units: 16
       Local Memory: 48.0 Kb
       Global Memory: 4.0 Gb
Platform Intel(R) OpenCL HD Graphics
  Vendor: Intel(R) Corporation
  Version: OpenCL 2.1
     Device Intel(R) UHD Graphics
       Max Clock Speed: 1150 MHz
       Compute Units: 24
       Local Memory: 64.0 Kb
       Global Memory: 6.31 Gb
```

As we can see, we get the list of platforms in our system that are compatible with OpenCL and the devices that can be used within them. In the previous case, we have *two* graphics cards, that of NVIDIA and that of Intel integrated into the motherboard.

PyOpenCL Programming Model

The programs created with **PyOpenCL** must be structured in such a way that they take into account the particular architecture of the systems on which you are working, such as GPUs, and the underlying concepts. Within the code, we will always have to refer to the **host** (CPU) and **devices** (GPUs).

First, the program must be developed so that it can be run on the *host*. It will then be coded and compiled, while identifying the different portions that can be assigned for the devices. This will generate several executable packages, each compiled according to the rules of the device they are intended for (models from different manufacturers have different drivers). These will then be dispatched at runtime for execution. These particular packages are identified by the *kernels*, which are the parts of the code that will be executed on devices.

The systems managed by the *OpenGL framework* can be seen as distributed systems (we saw them in the previous chapter), in which heterogeneous processors are connected to each other by exchanging *kernels* (instead of messages). So, like distributed systems, there will be a need to manage the exchange and dispatching of these kernels. In OpenCL, we will have the presence of a **Command Queue**, which is a data structure containing different kernels that a device receives. This structure manages the order of execution of various kernels. In addition, a **Context** is also defined as part of the OpenCL programming model, which identifies a particular group of devices. It facilitates the transfer of kernels and data within the *host-device system* (see *Figure* 6.6).

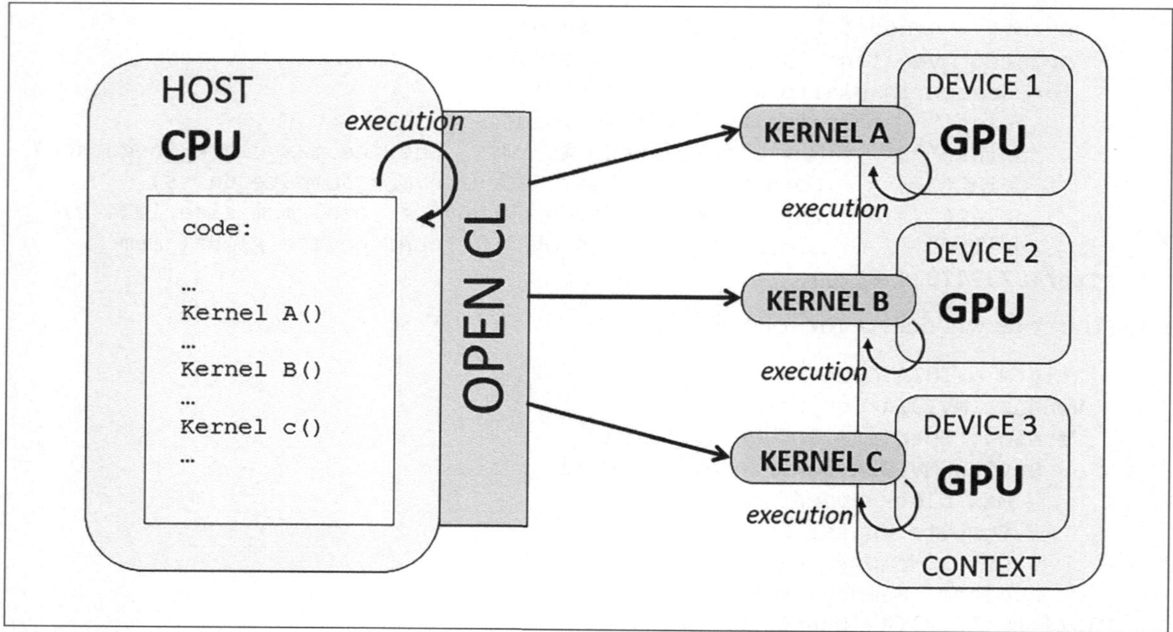

Figure 6.6: *OpenCL Programming Model*

Developing a Program with pyOpenCL

The implementation of a program that uses **pyOpenCL** must follow the guidelines of the OpenCL programming model. Since OpenCL is mainly based on operations with NumPy arrays, we can start with a simple example where the elements of one of these vectors will be doubled. This operation will be implemented within a *kernel* and will then be compiled to run on a GPU (device).

First, you will have to import the basic modules needed to implement a program with pyOpenCL:

```
import numpy as np
import pyopencl as cl
```

At this point, the next step will be to define the memory area in the *host* and the *data* contained within the GPU programming model. This is simple in OpenCL, as we will use NumPy arrays. In this example, we can define a couple of vectors: **`a_host, which`** is a vector of **4** elements containing the values to be subjected to the *calculation*, and **`res_host`** which will be the vector of **4** elements which contain the results of the calculation. The following code indicates these:

```
a_host = np.array([0.1 , 1.4, 2.3, 1.7])
a_host = a_host.astype(np.float32)
res_host = np.zeros((4), dtype=np.float32)
```

The next step will be to define the kernel dispatch management objects. In our example, the context is created using the **`cl.create_some_context()`** helper and its queue with the **`cl.CommandQueue()`** constructor, as shown here:

```
ctx = cl.create_some_context()
queue = cl.CommandQueue(ctx)
```

This approach is convenient for quick testing, since it automatically selects a platform and device. However, in production code, it is a better practice to explicitly create the context with **cl.Context()**, while specifying the exact platform and device to avoid ambiguity when multiple OpenCL devices are available.

```
# Get all available platforms
platforms = cl.get_platforms()
# Select a platform (e.g., the first one)
platform = platforms[0]
# Select a device from that platform (e.g., the first GPU)
device = platform.get_devices(device_type=cl.device_type.GPU)[0]
# Create context with the chosen device
ctx = cl.Context([device])
```

Since we are dealing with GPUs, we also need to explicitly manage memory allocation on the device and transfer data between host memory and device memory. OpenCL provides the Buffer class for this purpose. In the following example, we define a buffer that transfers the values contained in **a_host** into a memory area of the GPU device, identified by the variable **a_dev**. As this memory area will only be read from, it is defined as **READ_ONLY**.

The same will be done with the vector that will contain the results. A **res_dev** vector of the same size as **a_dev** is created, but this will contain the results that will be a **WRITE_ONLY** memory. This is shown as follows:

```
mf = cl.mem_flags
a_dev = cl.Buffer(ctx, mf.READ_ONLY | mf.COPY_HOST_PTR, hostbuf=a_host)
res_dev = cl.Buffer(ctx, mf.WRITE_ONLY, a_host.nbytes)
```

Now, having completed the memory allocation in the device and the ensuing data transfer, we can implement the kernel. In pyOpenCL, the **kernel** code is inserted as an argument of the **Program()** class constructor, as shown here:

```
prg = cl.Program(ctx, """
__kernel void doubled(
    __global const float *a_dev, __global float *res_dev)
{
  int gid = get_global_id(0);
  res_dev[gid] = a_dev[gid]*2;
}
""").build()
```

As we can see, the kernel has the structure of a *classic function*, where the arguments represent both the input and the returned values. In fact, kernels cannot have return values, but operate on vectors passed as arguments. Once the kernel has been defined, it must be invoked to be executed. Once the kernel has been declared and invoked, it is assigned to a *queue*, which will dispatch it to the device but also transfer the memory area containing the result from the device to the host via the **enqueue_copy()** method. This is shown in the following code:

```
knl = prg.doubled
knl(queue, a_host.shape, None, a_dev, res_dev)
cl.enqueue_copy(queue, res_host, res_dev)
```

Now that the results have been copied to the host in the **res_host** array, the results obtained will be:

```
print("Vector a: %s" %a_host)
print("Result: %s" %res_host)
```

Let us review the code now:

```
import numpy as np
import pyopencl as cl
```

```
a_host = np.array([0.1 , 1.4, 2.3, 1.7])
a_host = a_host.astype(np.float32)
res_host = np.zeros((4), dtype=np.float32)

ctx = cl.create_some_context()
queue = cl.CommandQueue(ctx)

mf = cl.mem_flags
a_dev = cl.Buffer(ctx, mf.READ_ONLY | mf.COPY_HOST_PTR, hostbuf=a_host)
res_dev = cl.Buffer(ctx, mf.WRITE_ONLY, a_host.nbytes)

prg = cl.Program(ctx, """
__kernel void doubled(
    __global const float *a_dev, __global float *res_dev)
{
  int gid = get_global_id(0);
  res_dev[gid] = a_dev[gid]*2;
}
""").build()


knl = prg.doubled
knl(queue, a_host.shape, None, a_dev, res_dev)
cl.enqueue_copy(queue, res_host, res_dev)

print("Vector a: %s" %a_host)
print("Result: %s" %res_host)
```

Running the code will give the following result:

```
Choose platform:
[0] <pyopencl.Platform 'NVIDIA CUDA' at 0x1612071dd60>
[1] <pyopencl.Platform 'Intel(R) OpenCL HD Graphics' at 0x1611ff6cb80>
Choice [0]:0
Set the environment variable PYOPENCL_CTX='0' to avoid being asked again.
Vector a: [0.1 1.4 2.3 1.7]
Result: [0.2 2.8 4.6 3.4]
```

As you can see, you will be asked which environment to work in (this happens if your system has multiple platforms that use OpenCL technology). Enter the desired value. If you press *Enter*, the program will perform the calculation on the default platform (value **0**). To correct this choice later, you can insert the environment variable in the code. We, therefore, insert the following instructions in the initial part of the previous code:

```
import os
os.environ['PYOPENCL_CTX'] = '0'
```

This way we will already tell the compiler that we want to work on the NVIDIA platform. Rerunning the program after the modification, we will get this result:

```
Vector a: [0.1 1.4 2.3 1.7]
Result: [0.2 2.8 4.6 3.4]
```

Multiplication between Matrices: An Example

Matrix multiplication is a great example of measuring GPU power in the Numba library. Let us implement it this time using **pyOpenCL**. For instance, we can use the following code to *multiply two matrices* **A * B** of dimension **8** and obtain a third matrix **C** containing the result of this operation.

```
import pyopencl as cl
import numpy as np

import os
os.environ['PYOPENCL_CTX'] = '0'

n = 8

a = np.random.randint(10, size=(n*n))
b = np.random.randint(10, size=(n*n))
c = np.zeros((n*n), dtype=np.float32)

a = a.astype(np.float32)
b = b.astype(np.float32)

ctx = cl.create_some_context()
queue = cl.CommandQueue(ctx)

mf = cl.mem_flags
a_buf = cl.Buffer(ctx, mf.READ_ONLY | mf.COPY_HOST_PTR, hostbuf=a)
b_buf = cl.Buffer(ctx, mf.READ_ONLY | mf.COPY_HOST_PTR, hostbuf=b)
c_buf = cl.Buffer(ctx, mf.WRITE_ONLY, c.nbytes)

prg = cl.Program(ctx, """
    __kernel void multiply(ushort n,
    ushort m, ushort p, __global float *a,
    __global float *b, __global float *c)
    {
      int gid = get_global_id(0);
      c[gid] = 0.0f;
      int rowC = gid/p;
      int colC = gid%p;
      __global float *pA = &a[rowC*m];
      __global float *pB = &b[colC];
      for(int k=0; k<m; k++)
      {
         pB = &b[colC+k*p];
         c[gid] += (*(pA++))*(*pB);
      }
    }
    """).build()

prg.multiply(queue, c.shape, None,
             np.uint16(n), np.uint16(n), np.uint16(n),
             a_buf, b_buf, c_buf)

cl.enqueue_copy(queue, c, c_buf)

print("Matrix A")
print(a.reshape(n,n))
print("Matrix B")
print(b.reshape(n,n))
print("Matrix A*B")
print(c.reshape(n, n))
```

Running this code will give you the following result:

```
Matrix A
[[6. 4. 2. 5. 3. 7. 4. 7.]
 [3. 0. 2. 0. 8. 5. 4. 4.]
 [4. 6. 3. 3. 3. 8. 7. 2.]
 [7. 4. 7. 6. 0. 3. 3. 2.]
 [8. 1. 6. 1. 5. 9. 4. 4.]
 [9. 9. 6. 4. 4. 3. 5. 3.]
 [9. 4. 9. 0. 1. 8. 7. 4.]
 [7. 7. 8. 0. 8. 9. 2. 5.]]
Matrix B
[[6. 3. 1. 0. 0. 6. 8. 7.]
 [3. 0. 1. 0. 9. 3. 3. 4.]
 [2. 4. 7. 1. 5. 1. 8. 1.]
 [3. 3. 4. 8. 1. 4. 6. 3.]
 [7. 3. 3. 8. 4. 0. 8. 9.]
 [6. 3. 0. 6. 0. 8. 8. 4.]
 [3. 0. 8. 9. 2. 6. 3. 4.]
 [2. 0. 2. 7. 8. 6. 5. 3.]]
Matrix A*B
[[156.  71.  99. 193. 127. 192. 233. 167.]
 [128.  56.  81. 160.  82. 108. 176. 143.]
 [151.  66. 112. 176. 114. 175. 211. 157.]
 [117.  76. 112. 114.  99. 139. 203. 120.]
 [175.  93. 110. 172. 100. 181. 265. 178.]
 [172.  84. 134. 154. 165. 175. 257. 194.]
 [168.  90. 143. 156. 131. 205. 269. 169.]
 [205. 104. 120. 179. 179. 185. 308. 216.]]
```

Now, let us make some changes to the previous program to introduce the measurement of the times used for the calculation of the product between matrices:

```
import pyopencl as cl
import numpy as np
import time

import os
os.environ['PYOPENCL_CTX'] = '0'

n = 8

a = np.random.randint(10, size=(n*n))
b = np.random.randint(10, size=(n*n))
c = np.zeros((n*n), dtype=np.float32)

a = a.astype(np.float32)
b = b.astype(np.float32)

ctx = cl.create_some_context()
queue = cl.CommandQueue(ctx)

mf = cl.mem_flags
a_buf = cl.Buffer(ctx, mf.READ_ONLY | mf.COPY_HOST_PTR, hostbuf=a)
b_buf = cl.Buffer(ctx, mf.READ_ONLY | mf.COPY_HOST_PTR, hostbuf=b)
c_buf = cl.Buffer(ctx, mf.WRITE_ONLY, c.nbytes)

prg = cl.Program(ctx, """
    __kernel void multiply(ushort n,
```

```
        ushort m, ushort p, __global float *a,
        __global float *b, __global float *c)
        {
          int gid = get_global_id(0);
          c[gid] = 0.0f;
          int rowC = gid/p;
          int colC = gid%p;
          __global float *pA = &a[rowC*m];
          __global float *pB = &b[colC];
          for(int k=0; k<m; k++)
          {
             pB = &b[colC+k*p];
             c[gid] += (*(pA++))*(*pB);
          }
        }
        """).build()

t1 = time.perf_counter()
prg.multiply(queue, c.shape, None,
             np.uint16(n), np.uint16(n), np.uint16(n),
             a_buf, b_buf, c_buf)
t2 = time.perf_counter()

cl.enqueue_copy(queue, c, c_buf)
elapsed_time = t2 - t1
print("Elapsed time %s" %elapsed_time)
```

We have removed the printing of the output results of the matrices involved in the calculation, and instead have inserted the **perf_counter()** functions of the time module to calculate the times used in the product between matrices.

By running the previous code, we will get the result:

```
Elapsed time 0.007469899996067397
```

Here, we obtained the *time taken in seconds* as output. This information will be useful to make decisions on the time taken for multiplying the matrices as their size increases, which in our code is expressed by the variable **n**. We perform a series of measurements on our computer, modifying the value of **n** for each execution, and assigning it the powers of 2 (4, 8, 16, 32, 64, *and so on*). We will get *Table 6.2*:

n	t(GPU)
4	0,0063
8	0,0056
16	0,0066
32	0,0058
64	0,0058
128	0,0065
256	0,0076
512	0,0082
1024	0,0086
2048	0,0164
4096	0,0484

Table 6.3: *Elapsed Time for Matrices Multiplication*

As we can see from the result, the times used are almost the same up to 1024 and then they increase for *powers of 2 and onwards*. This indicates that this timing is related to the number of threads available in my GPU. Up to a certain value, we will have *n* threads in parallel, which will take the same time to calculate the product between matrices (*n x n*). So, according to this mechanism the multiplication between two matrices (4 × 4) will take the same time as the multiplication of the other two matrices (512 × 512).

To understand the potential offered by GPU programming and computing, let us consider the multiplication between two matrices carried out *sequentially*. An example of how to implement the product between *two matrices* **A** and **B** on a classic Python program that does not use GPU could be the following code:

```
import numpy as np

n = 8
a = np.random.randint(10, size=(n*n))
b = np.random.randint(10, size=(n*n))
c = np.zeros((n*n), dtype=np.float32)

a = a.astype(np.float32)
b = b.astype(np.float32)

def matmul(n, A, B, C):
    # Iterate over the rows of A.
    for i in range(n):
        # Iterate over the columns of B
        for j in range(n):
            tmp = 0.0
            # Iterate over the rows of B.
            for k in range(n):
                tmp += A[i * n + k] * B[k * n + j]
            C[i * n + j] = tmp

matmul(n, a, b, c)
print("Matrix A")
print(a.reshape(n,n))
print("Matrix B")
print(b.reshape(n,n))
print("Matrix A*B")
print(c.reshape(n,n))
```

By executing the code we will obtain a result identical to the one obtained in the previous example with pyOpenCL. The values are randomly generated, so the results will vary for *each run*, but the calculation and the results are practically the same.

```
Matrix A
[[9. 6. 2. 0. 1. 5. 4. 2.]
 [4. 6. 1. 2. 1. 3. 0. 2.]
 [8. 9. 3. 3. 4. 3. 3. 0.]
 [5. 2. 0. 1. 4. 7. 6. 6.]
 [3. 5. 2. 6. 7. 6. 1. 8.]
 [0. 2. 2. 4. 0. 2. 5. 6.]
 [9. 9. 0. 2. 6. 7. 7. 3.]
 [8. 1. 4. 5. 8. 7. 7. 2.]]
Matrix B
[[6. 6. 8. 3. 0. 6. 6. 8.]
 [9. 8. 5. 9. 3. 9. 4. 4.]
 [9. 9. 6. 1. 9. 9. 0. 5.]
```

```
 [2. 6. 0. 7. 0. 7. 5. 2.]
 [2. 9. 9. 4. 9. 5. 1. 9.]
 [2. 4. 6. 3. 8. 0. 1. 7.]
 [5. 3. 3. 6. 0. 8. 8. 8.]
 [8. 4. 4. 7. 0. 5. 4. 3.]]
Matrix A*B
[[174. 169. 173. 140.  85. 173. 124. 188.]
 [115. 122. 103. 108.  60. 116.  70. 101.]
 [191. 222. 190. 172. 114. 221. 130. 202.]
 [150. 158. 170. 155.  98. 153. 126. 201.]
 [188. 234. 195. 206. 144. 206. 121. 203.]
 [121. 105.  73. 126.  40. 134.  94.  98.]
 [224. 253. 246. 230. 137. 250. 181. 280.]
 [184. 251. 236. 181. 167. 234. 156. 281.]]
```

At this point, we will also modify this code to carry out measurements on the time taken by the multiplication between matrices as their *size varies* and also for varying values of **n**:

```
import numpy as np
import time

n = 8
a = np.random.randint(10, size=(n*n))
b = np.random.randint(10, size=(n*n))
c = np.zeros((n*n), dtype=np.float32)

a = a.astype(np.float32)
b = b.astype(np.float32)

def matmul(n, A, B, C):
    # Iterate over the rows of A.
    for i in range(n):
        # Iterate over the columns of B
        for j in range(n):
            tmp = 0.0
            # Iterate over the rows of B.
            for k in range(n):
                tmp += A[i * n + k] * B[k * n + j]
            C[i * n + j] = tmp

t1 = time.perf_counter()
matmul(n, a, b, c)
t2 = time.perf_counter()
elapsed_time = t2 - t1
print("Elapsed time %s" %elapsed_time)
```

By executing a series of executions for the values of *n* used with the code in **pyOpenCL**, we will get a series of times, as shown in *Table 6.3*:

n	t(CPU)	t(GPU)
4	0,000074	0,0063
8	0,00035	0,0056
16	0,0034	0,0066
32	0,014	0,0058
64	0,12	0,0058

128	0,8	0,0065
256	6,77	0,0076
512	61,5	0,0082
1024		0,0086
2048		0,0164
4096		0,0484

Table 6.4: *Elapsed Times Compared between CPU e GPU*

As we can see, the trend of the times is completely different from the previous case. We SEE an exponential increase as the size of the matrices used increases, so much so that the times become prohibitive after a certain point. Interestingly, sequential computation for small arrays (<32) is much more efficient than the one obtained from GPUs via pyOpenCL. *Figure* 6.7 clearly shows the time trends in the two types of programming:

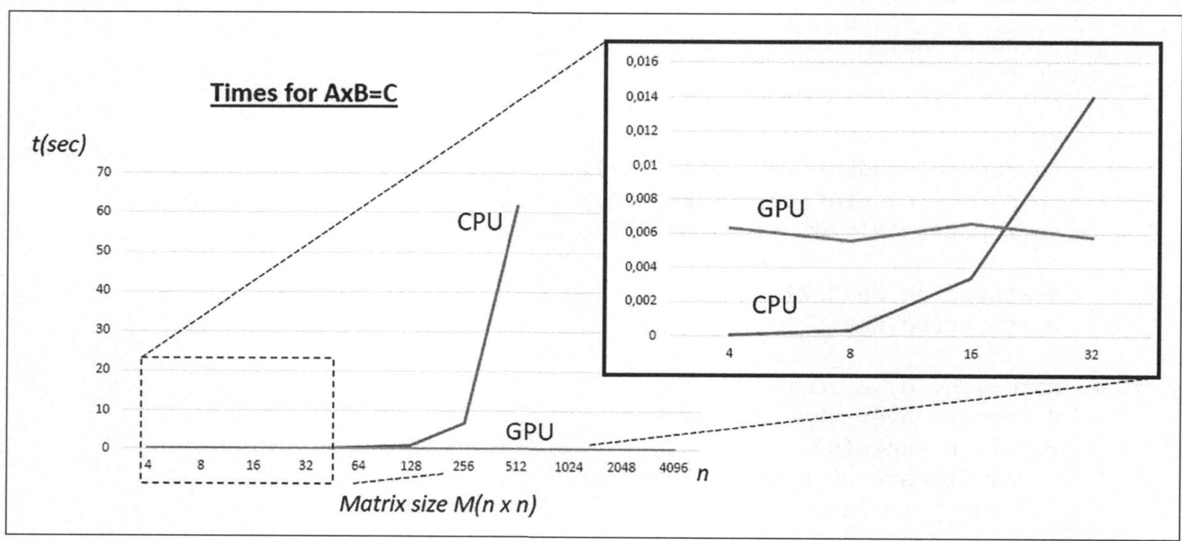

Figure 6.7: *Times Used to Calculate A * B on CPU (Sequential Program) and on GPU (with OpenCL)*

For small matrices (up to order 16), the sequential calculation performed on the CPU to calculate the *product between matrices* is more efficient than the one on the GPU that uses threads in parallel. However, the trend of times is exponential on the CPU. For larger matrices, the calculation is prohibitive and requires longer calculation times. Instead, we observe a completely different behavior with the GPU that keeps the time taken *constant*, despite the growth in the size of the matrices used in multiplication. This is largely due to the large amount of threads on the GPU that can handle the parallel computing of thousands of threads at the same time.

Element-Wise Calculation with PyOpenCL

PyOpenCL has the possibility to perform *element-wise calculations* in an implicit way and uses complex expressions in a single computational step. The function that is used here is **`ElementwiseKernel()`**.

Let us see an example:

```
import numpy as np
import pyopencl as cl
import pyopencl.array
from pyopencl.elementwise import ElementwiseKernel
```

```
import os
os.environ['PYOPENCL_CTX'] = '0'

a_host = np.array([0.1 , 1.4, 2.3, 1.7])
a_host = a_host.astype(np.float32)
b_host = np.array([0.2 , 0.3, 1.0, 0.5])
b_host = b_host.astype(np.float32)

ctx = cl.create_some_context()
queue = cl.CommandQueue(ctx)

a_dev = cl.array.to_device(queue, a_host)
b_dev = cl.array.to_device(queue, b_host)

sum = ElementwiseKernel(ctx,
    "float *a_dev, float *b_dev, float *res_dev",
    "res_dev[i] = a_dev[i] + b_dev[i]",
    "sum")

res_dev = cl.array.empty_like(a_dev)
sum(a_dev, b_dev, res_dev)

print("Vector A: %s" %a_host)
print("Vector B: %s" %b_host)
print("Vector Result: %s" %res_dev)
```

Running the code will produce the following result:

```
Vector A: [0.1 1.4 2.3 1.7]
Vector B: [0.2 0.3 1.  0.5]
Vector Result: [0.3 1.7 3.3 2.2]
```

MapReduce Calculation with pyOpenCL

Like the previous example, there is another construct that allows the implicit use of complex expressions, such as those aimed at **MapReduce**. PyOpenCL provides **ReductionKernel()** for this purpose:

```
import numpy as np
import pyopencl as cl
import pyopencl.array
import pyopencl.reduction

import os
os.environ['PYOPENCL_CTX'] = '0'

ctx = cl.create_some_context()
queue = cl.CommandQueue(ctx)

ah = np.array([0.1 , 1.4, 2.3, 1.7])
ah = ah.astype(np.float32)
bh = np.array([0.2 , 0.3, 1.0, 0.5])
bh = bh.astype(np.float32)

a = cl.array.to_device(queue, ah)
b = cl.array.to_device(queue, bh)

krnl = pyopencl.reduction.ReductionKernel(ctx, np.float32, neutral="0",
```

```
            reduce_expr="a+b", map_expr="x[i]*y[i]",
            arguments="__global float *x, __global float *y")

    res = krnl(a, b).get()

    print("Vector A: %s" %a)
    print("Vector B: %s" %b)
    print("Vector Result: %s" %res)
```

Running the code produces the following result:

```
Vector A: [0.1 1.4 2.3 1.7]
Vector B: [0.2 0.3 1.  0.5]
Vector Result: 3.59
```

This program will first perform the product between the corresponding elements of the two vectors **a** and **b**. The mapping process is expressed by the expression **x [i] * y [i], which is** assigned to the **map_expr** parameter. The vectors **x** and **y** passed as **kernel** arguments must be indexed with the index **i**, as indicated here:

0.1 x 0.2 = 0.02

1.4 x 0.3 = 0.42

2.3 x 1.0 = 2.3

1.7 x 0.5 = 0.85

All the results will be added together as a reducing operation, expressed by **a + b, which is** assigned to the **reduce_expr** parameter. In this case, the formal values **a** and **b** are used to indicate the operands of a *binary reduction operation*:

0.02 + 0.42 + 2.3 + 0.85 = 3.59

If we want to see another example, we can replace the previous **mapreduce** kernel with this one:

```
krnl = pyopencl.reduction.ReductionKernel(ctx, np.float32, neutral="0",
        reduce_expr='max(a,b)', map_expr="x[i]+y[i]",
        arguments="__global float *x, __global float *y")
```

Running the code generates the following result:

```
Vector A: [0.1 1.4 2.3 1.7]
Vector B: [0.2 0.3 1.  0.5]
Vector Result: 3.3
```

In this operation, the corresponding elements of the two vectors are added together and the expression **x [i] + y [i]** is assigned to the **map_expr** parameter, shown here:

0.1 + 0.2 = 0.3

1.4 + 0.3 = 1.7

2.3 + 1.0 = 3.3

1.7 + 0.5 = 2.2

From these results, the greater value will be chosen through the binary expression expressed as **max (a, b)**, which is assigned to the **reduce_expr** parameter.

Conclusion

In this chapter, we have seen how GPU programming is used to enhance parallel computing. Thanks to libraries such as **Numba** and **pyOpenCL**, we can leverage the computing potential of GPUs, as well as their particular internal architecture that performs complex calculations in parallel. These libraries are based on CUDA technology which specializes in NVIDIA graphics cards. We then explored the programming models that form the basis of CUDA and allow us to insert kernels into the code in Python. With this chapter, we conclude learning about all the parallel programming models and their related libraries. In the next chapter, we will analyze all the possible fields of application of these technologies and the models covered in the previous chapters.

References

https://www.tutorialspoint.com/cuda/cuda_introduction_to_the_gpu.htm

CHAPTER 7
Parallel Computing Applications

Introduction

In this chapter, we will introduce the practical aspects of parallel programming seen in the previous chapters. Here, we will go beyond mere introductions of parallel programming and its associated aspects and explore specifically designed infrastructures capable of managing the former two. Supercomputers are often defined as high-performance systems composed of many CPUs and GPUs that are interconnected by high-bandwidth networks, supported by large shared storage, and equipped with specialized cooling systems. In such environments, parallel computing and **High-Performance Computing (HPC)** methodologies are applied. This chapter, therefore, provides an overview of the sectors and disciplines that use parallel computing for research and innovation.

Structure

This chapter addresses the following topics:

- High-Performance Computing (HPC)
- Parallel Computing
- Meteorology
- Oceanography
- Seismology
- Astrophysics
- Oil and Energy Industry
- Finance
- Engineering
- Medicine and Drug Discovery
- Genomics
- Game Engines

High-Performance Computing (HPC)

High-Performance Computing (HPC) is not new to scientific research as supercomputers have played a vital role in the domain for decades.

The amount of data has increased rapidly in recent years, and there are many application areas that benefit from HPC systems. These systems perform computationally intensive operations through shared resources in order to obtain results in less time.

HPC techniques may work on a single computer or node, but its true power lies in the creation of clusters where many computers are linked together to form a supercomputer.

Supercomputers are mainly used for *simulation*, *artificial intelligence*, and *analysis of large amounts of data*. These operations underlie many applications in scientific and industrial sectors.

While supercomputers are not new, the technologies they use have developed tremendously over the past 20 years. The exponential growth of computing speeds and data-carrying networks make parallel architecture a necessary idea. New technologies such as **BigData** and **Internet of Things (IoT)** are producing streams of trillions of data that need to be analyzed in *real-time* and *simultaneously*. It is clear that parallel computing applied to powerful machines will be able to process a copious amount of data.

Parallel Computing

Parallel computing is a broader concept that includes parallel programming. In fact, it is the simultaneous execution of one or more programs on architectures that offer multiple processors simultaneously, whether they are CPUs, cores, or GPUs.

You can encounter parallel computing in a single-core machine, multi-core ones (for example, *Intel Xeon W has 28 cores*), as well as supercomputers or clusters of computers with thousands of microprocessors. In the lattermost case, we speak of massively parallel computing.

Therefore, we are using parallel computing even if we might not be aware of it. Our smartphones also use this technology. For example, if our iPhone could perform only one operation at a time, all operations would be much slower. Opening an email could take more than a few seconds and switching between the different applications would not be so seamless. The latest serial smartphones in the market date back to 2010 (*iPhone4*), which is prehistory if we think about the abilities of current smartphones. For instance, *iPhone* 5 has a 1.5GHz *dual-core processor*, while *iPhone* 11 has 6 *cores*. The *Samsung Galaxy Note* 10 has 8 *cores*. These smartphones are examples of parallel computing in compact settings.

Benefits of Parallel Computing

Program performance can improve thanks to higher clock speeds, that benefit single-thread execution. However, true scalability comes from parallelism, which allows different parts of the same program to run simultaneously. Parallel computing reduces execution time and increases the volume of data that can be processed at once. The more powerful the parallel computing infrastructure is, the more complex the problems it will be able to solve. Saving time often means saving money, which explains why parallel computing is becoming a mandatory option in many industrial and engineering sectors. In the scientific world, the main objective is not just reducing time, but also solving increasingly complex problems. In both cases, one of the primary use cases of parallel computing is *simulation*.

Parallel computing has proven to be ideal for modeling the real world around us. In fact, the real world is not serial and the things that surround us unfold simultaneously. Increasingly complex mathematical models are thus elaborated in parallel to reconstruct portions of the real world, that comprises macroscopic entities such as *stars* or *black holes*, and microscopic ones like *molecules* and *enzymes*. With the growth of parallel computing, it is possible to use increasingly complex mathematical models with fewer approximations that generate increasingly accurate simulations. The study of the behavior and properties of the systems reconstructed in the simulations is the basis of innovation and research in many scientific and industrial sectors.

Another application window that demonstrates the need for parallel computing is that of monitoring several data signals simultaneously. You often have to work in real-time with several independent data streams with massive amounts of data that need to be processed as a whole. Computing must not only process these data streams, but also extract real-time information useful for any action. This problem can be solved with parallel signal processing algorithms, which are extensions of classical methods of signal processing that contribute to parallel computing. We find its use in medicine with *bio signals*, in finance while controlling stock market trends, in seismology, and many other applications.

Projects and Examples of Parallel Computing

Having understood the importance of parallel processing for scientific and industrial sectors, let us now see some examples in greater detail:

Meteorology

Meteorology is based on extraordinarily complex mathematical models that take into account numerous climatic and environmental factors. These changes are observed over time to make forecasts on the weather as correctly as possible.

It is therefore clear that in this domain, it is necessary to use extraordinarily powerful computers based on parallel computing and employ **Numeric Weather Prediction** (**NWP**).

NWP is a weather forecasting method based on a series of dynamic equations describing the flow of fluids. This system is very mathematically complex and it is tedious devise solutions on the basis of mere equations. In order to be submitted to computers, these equations must first be converted into numerical methods through a series of processes. *Parameterizations* are made and initial and boundary conditions are imposed. Unfortunately, these steps introduce approximations, along with omissions, parameter estimates, and other factors that simplify the calculation, but also introduce numerous inaccuracies at the same time.

The purpose of NWP is to simulate the atmosphere of a geographical area in its temporal evolution to predict climatic trends. The volume occupied by the atmosphere covering the geographical area is divided into a grid of *three-dimensional points* that define its resolution. Advances in parallel computational processing increase the resolution of the model and the computation speed, which generates results. The higher the *resolution* of the model, the more accurate predictions will be. However, manipulating models of this level is highly challenging. Despite the increase in resolution and simulation speed, current algorithms can reach their limits due to the communication requirements of the algorithms used to solve the equations that predict how the weather evolves over time.

At present, these algorithms combine computational parallelism with geographic parallelism. The geographical area under analysis is divided into overlapping parts and each part is assigned to a different processor. During the forecast calculation, each processor will have to exchange data that concerns the overlapping area with other processors involved in the calculation to account for the climatic effects on neighboring areas.

The increase in resolution and speed has led to the analysis of ever smaller geographical areas. However, expanding the area of overlap between various processors also increases the exchange of information and reduces the model's performance.

Another critical point of the NWP model is the parameterized part. There are many physical processes in meteorology that cannot be predicted directly (see *Figure 7.1*). These are brief, complex, or still poorly understood and are therefore introduced into the model via appropriate parameters based on empirical or statistical considerations. Also, in this case, the development of new algorithms that best utilize parallel computing responds well to these additional factors, thereby increasing the effectiveness and accuracy of the forecasts. This is shown in the following figure:

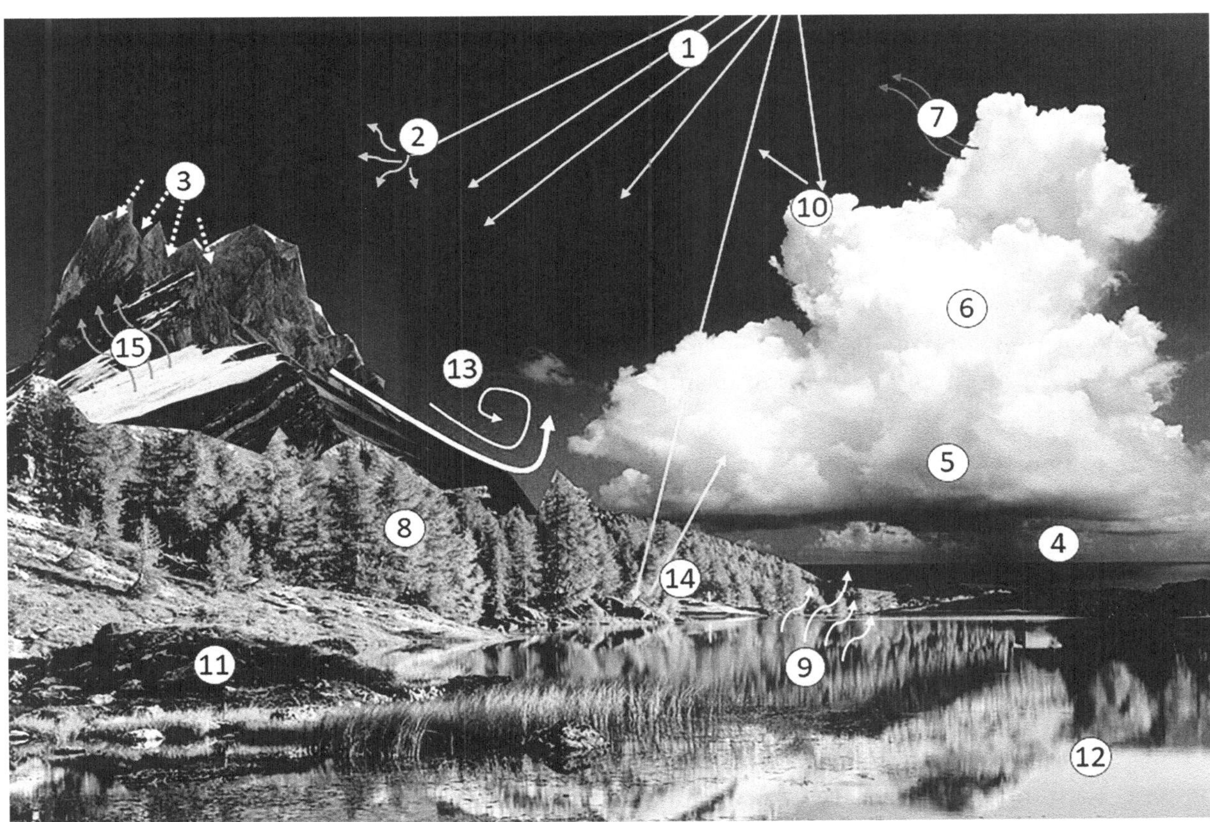

Figure 7.1: *Factors to Detect Weather Patterns: 1. Incoming Solar Radiation, 2. Scattering by Aerosols and Molecules, 3. Snow, 4. Rain, 5. Condensation, 6. Deep Convection, 7. Emission of Longwave Radiation from Clouds, 8. Vegetation, 9. Evaporation, 10. Reflection/Absorption by Clouds, 11. Topography, 12. Water Coverage, 13. Turbulence, 14. Reflection/Absorption at Earth's Surface, 15. Emission of Longwave Radiation from Earth's Surface*

MetView can be reported for Python. This platform provides a useful meteorological workstation which is designed to provide a comprehensive meteorological data research and analysis environment (see *Figure* 7.2). It includes many tools that facilitate analysis at all stages. One can access multiple data sources and converters of different formats. Furthermore, there are many tools to process and display them. All these operations are managed through scripting commands via Python:

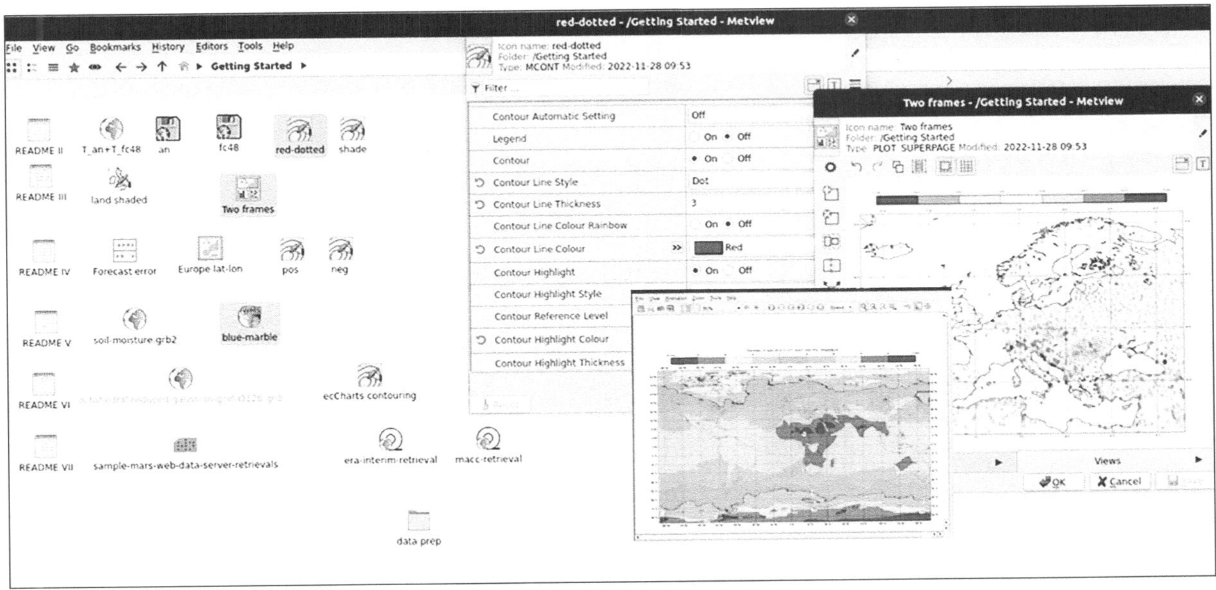

Figure 7.2: *MetView Platform*

The **MetView** platform is available on *Anaconda* for *Linux* and *macOS* only. To install it, simply enter the following:

```
$ conda install -c conda-forge metview
```

You may install and updates its content and related packages via:

```
$ conda update -c conda-forge metview
```

Once installed, the platform is launched using the **`metview`** command:

```
$ metview
```

After a few seconds, the application will start and a window will appear on the screen as shown in *Figure* 7.2. There are many interesting examples using it that are presented in a series of Jupyter Notebooks on the following page:

https://confluence.ecmwf.int/display/METV/Python+Jupyter+Notebooks

Oceanography

Oceanography uses similar models to assess oceanic volumes and all the factors and processes that describe their evolution over time. Here too, the use of complex models on high-performance computers is envisaged to obtain valid simulations through the use of parallel computing.

On the basis of these studies, the data is collected and distributed to researchers and analysts through databases. Most of this data comes from satellite observations that are collected by government agencies such as **European Organization for the Exploitation of Meteorological Satellites** (**EUMETSAT**) or **National Centers for Environmental Information** (**NOAA**). These databases provide data regarding the parameters observable from space such as surface temperature, water color, wave height, and ice thickness, while other databases provide oceanographic data related to the seabed and other parameters about intermediate levels.

CTD data, that stands for **conductivity**, **temperature**, and **depth,** is the most commonly referred to type of data in oceanography. These values allow us to determine the physical properties of various water layers in oceans and are useful for obtaining TS *profiles (temperature-salinity)*.

All the data is then used for simulations, which allow us to predict the future state of the oceans. The models used for predictions are extremely complex and require the support of supercomputers.

As for Python, you can browse the whole series of Python libraries related to the various operational aspects of oceanography through:

SEA-PY (https://pyoceans.github.io/sea-py/)

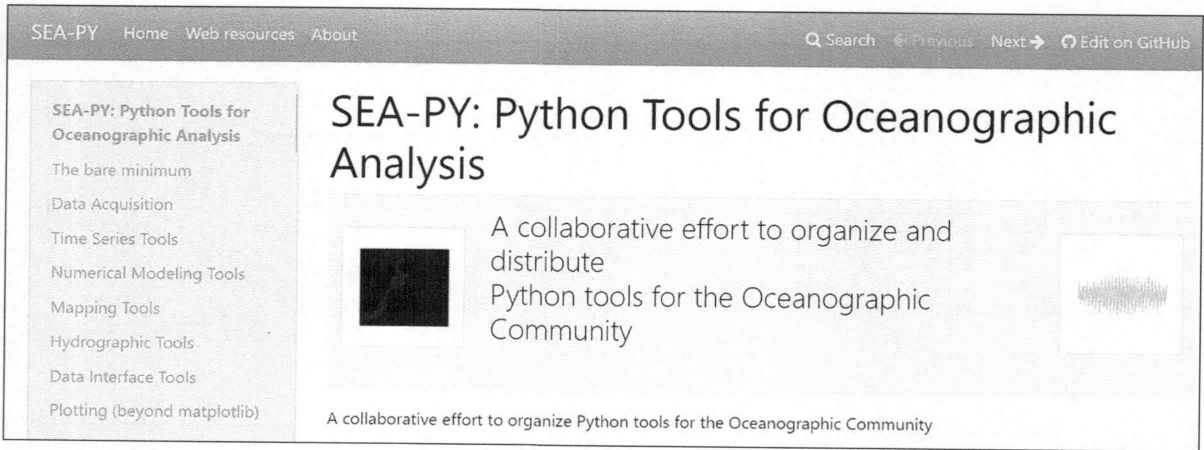

***Figure* 7.3**: *SEA-PY Official Website*

Seismology

We have seen how models are used to study the atmosphere of large oceanic masses. Similarly, they can be used to study the movements of tectonic plates under the earth's surface and predict earthquakes.

Seismology research is based on the use of complex models that cannot be easily calculated except through data acquired from numerous sources. Making predictions in this field is even more difficult than in meteorology and oceanography. It is because the nature of the underlying terrain is not easily detectable.

In this regard, seismic exploration is based on the reflection of seismic waves as they cross the earth's crust. When a seismic wave travels through the crust, it meets an interface that separates two different layers of soil and reflects part of it. In the end, a whole series of reflected waves of various shapes and intensities is obtained to be detected, recorded in the form of data, and then used to extrapolate a model that can reconstruct the underlying layers of the soil.

The calculations here are based on parallel computing, and are demonstrated in the following figure:

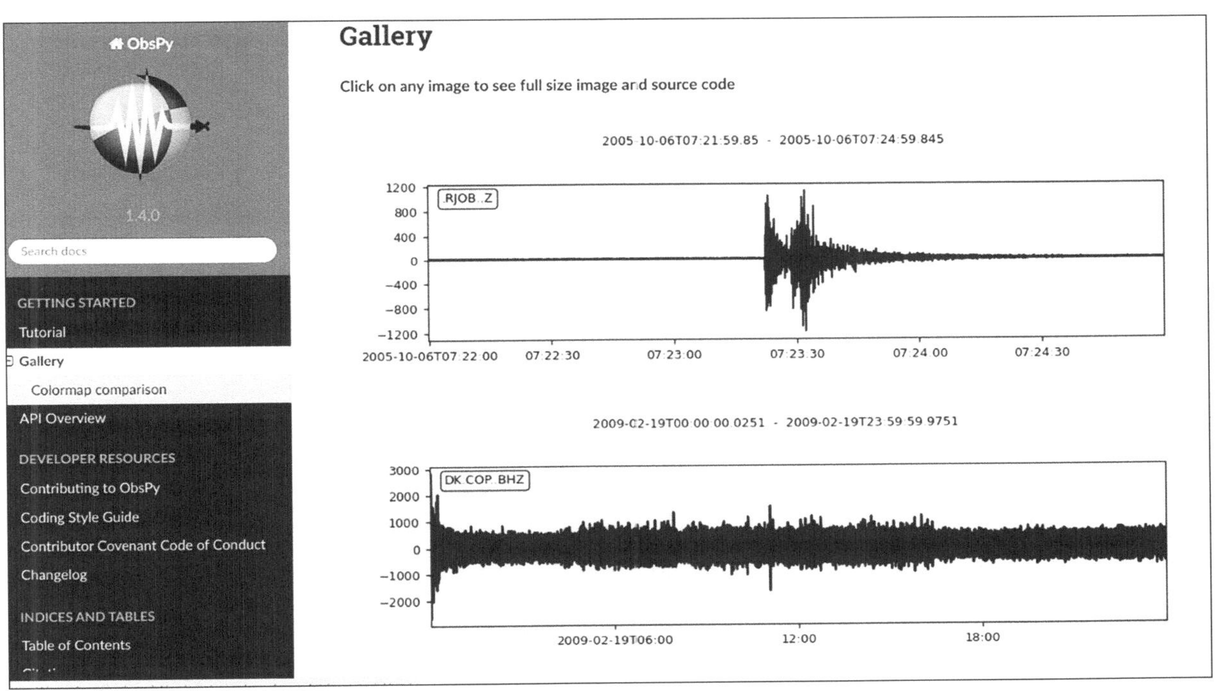

Figure 7.4: *Official Page of the Obs-Py Library*

Python has a specific library for seismic predictions, which is called **Obs-Py** (https://docs.obspy.org/). This is an *open-source library* that provides researchers with a useful framework for processing seismological data and provides a whole series of tools dedicated to these specific techniques, such as the signal processing of seismic wave records, as shown in *Figure 7.4*.

Astrophysics

Another branch of science that uses parallel programming to make simulations is astrophysics.

The behavior and evolution of a star is in the concern of astrophysics and is based on simulations that use complex physical laws which consider *hydrodynamics* and *magneto hydrodynamics*. The reference system has spherical geometry and the model uses spectral codes to subdivide physical quantities on the basis of spherical harmonics in orthogonal directions and *Chebyshev polynomials* along the radial direction. It is clear that these calculations are complex and can be processed only via high-performance computing systems like massively parallel architectures (supercomputers).

The results obtained from this type of simulation have proved to be very accurate and have allowed enormous progress in *astrophysics*.

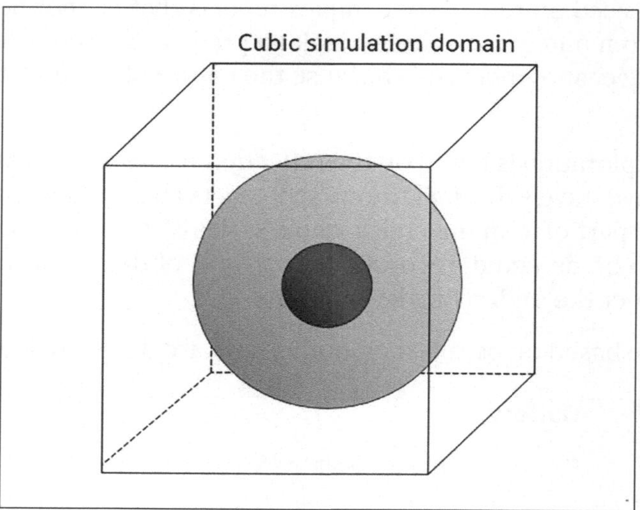

Figure 7.5: *Star-in-a-Box Model*

In Python, simulations of stellar behavior and evolution that follow a more recent approach are called *star-in-a-box*. These simulations are based on a different model, which is in turn based on Cartesian geometry. Here, a star is enclosed inside a cubic box (see *Figure* 7.5). One can obtain accurate results via the scientific libraries provided by Python such as **SciPy**, **NumPy**, and **Matplotlib**. Historically, libraries like **PyPar** were used to facilitate parallel implementations in Python, but since PyPar is no longer maintained, the modern standard for distributed-memory parallelism in Python is **mpi4py**, which provides full bindings to the MPI (Message Passing Interface) standard.

In addition to this, astrophysics has been tackling problems that, until recently, were considered impossible to counter. The explosion of a **supernova**, the movement of galaxies with their probable collision and merger, and the behavior of a black hole are complex problems and need models with enormous computing power to create simulations based on them.

To understand how these scientific disciplines and their progress are closely linked to the technological advance of parallel processing, we can provide an example. In 2019, a problem concerning black holes, that had been tormenting astrophysicists for over forty years, was solved. Researchers at the *Northwestern University*, the *University of Amsterdam*, and the *University of Oxford* showed in their simulations that the innermost matter that orbits and then collapses into black holes lines up with the latter. This demonstration was only possible with the permission to simulate a powerful supercomputer. It is therefore clear that with the growth of computing power, many other problems that have been insurmountable up to now will be solved.

With regards to the study and simulation of explosion and convective movements of stars such as **supernovae** and **novae**, Python provides a series of algorithms implemented in different modules, such as those distributed by *Michael Zingale, for this purpose*:

https://zingale. github.io/index.html

On his site, there are some interesting projects in this domain, with their code being downloadable from GitHub, as shown in *Figure* 7.6:

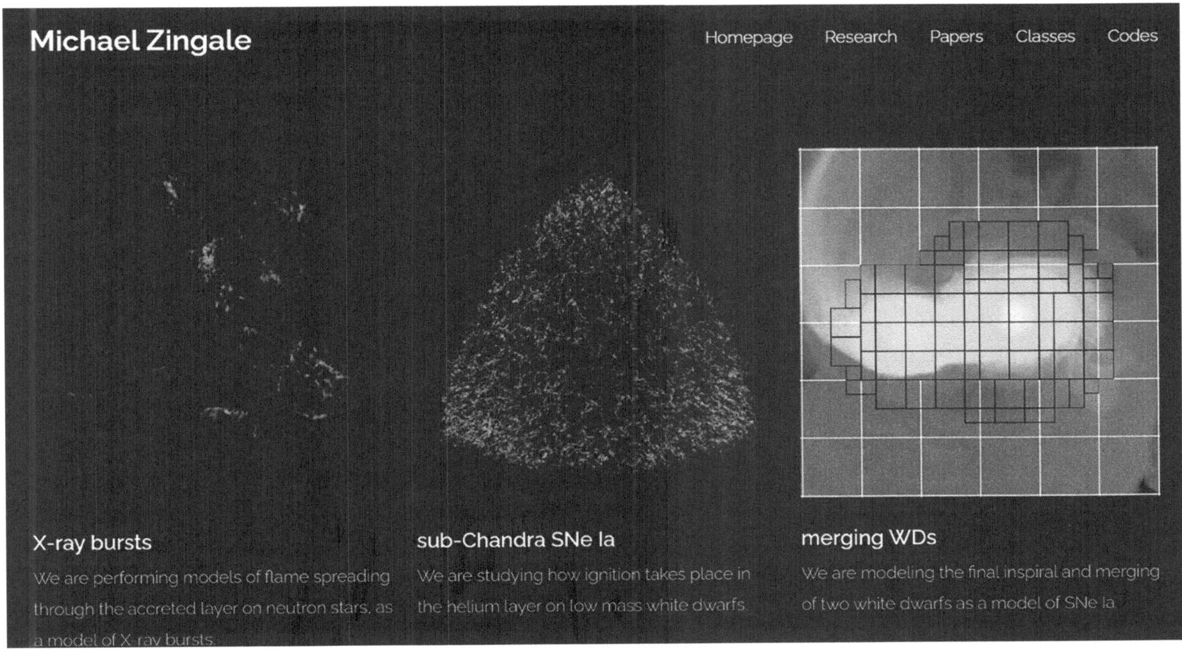

***Figure 7.6**: Michael Zingale Page*

A toolkit used by the astrophysics community is `yt`, which is designed for *volumetric data analysis* and *visualization*, particularly its `yt_astro_analysis` extension. This allows us to analyze and visualize the data generated by simulations of astrophysical phenomena on **high-performance computing** (**HPC**) systems. The data generated on different platforms is often *incompatible*; such a tool is able to integrate them to create visual representations and perform accurate analyses via parallel computing. This package is also present on *Anaconda* and can be installed with the following command:

```
conda install -c conda-forge yt_astro_analysis
```

There is an excellent site full of documentation and examples (https://yt-project.org/doc/cookbook/index.html), many of which are listed as **Jupyter Notebooks**, as shown in *Figure 7.7*:

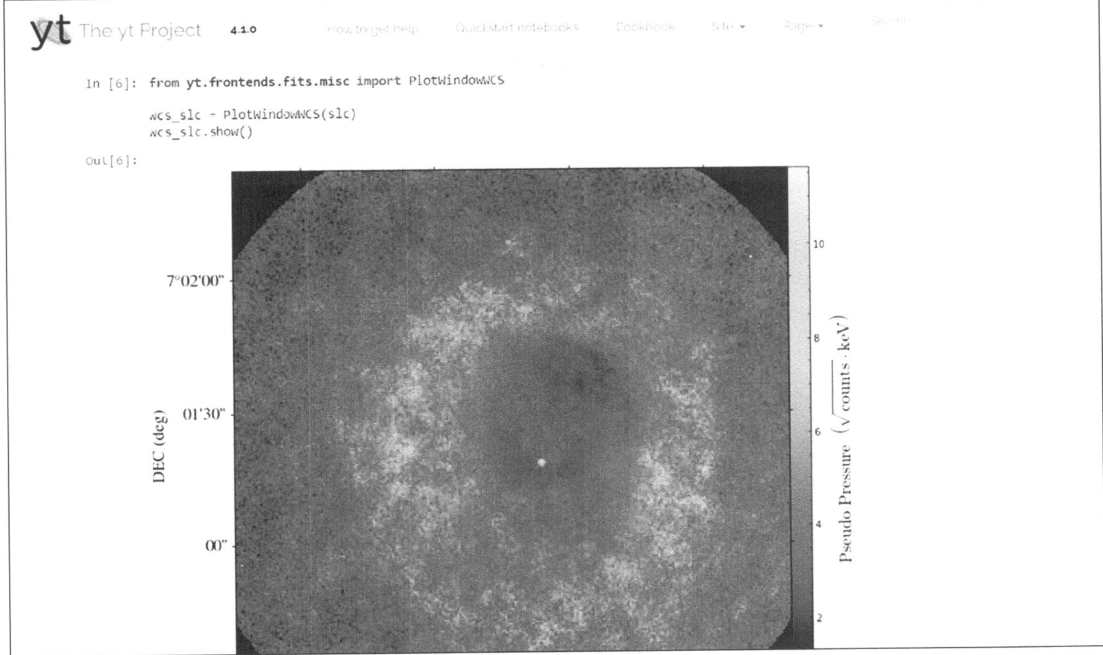

***Figure 7.7**: A Jupyter Notebook Showing yt_astro_analysis Usage in the yt Project Web Page*

Oil and Energy Industry

Resource exploration is a method of collecting and managing information about energy resources such as *oil*, *natural gas*, and so on. Computers help discover and manage such resources. Oil and gas companies are exploring every possible method to increase the probability of finding hydrocarbons under the ground.

The data collected by *Well Logging* consists of several gigabytes of information reported by *probes* and *sensors*. These data will have to be analyzed to reconstruct the *presence, extent and depth of layers of rock*, *oil*, *gas*, and *water*. To process this large amount of data, HPC systems and methodologies are necessary. They are the only ones able to process this data and extract the necessary information.

For example, in *Houston*, USA, the Bubba supercomputer (which is among the fastest on the planet) is built with thousands of *Intel Xeon Phi* multiprocessors that are cooled in refrigerated oil baths. The Xeon Phi line has since been discontinued (2020), but it represents the past architectures that were designed to push parallel performance. Modern supercomputers typically rely on combinations of AMD EPYC CPUs, NVIDIA GPUs, or similar high-performance components.

This particular technique boosts the performance and calculation speed of such a processor. Bubba belongs to the geo-processing company *DownUnder GeoSolutions* and is used to perform these calculations. From this, we can understand how every research sector interested in the business is very sensitive to the importance of simulations and the parallel computing on the basis of which they are processed.

As far as Python is concerned, we will be able to find several publications and examples of analyzes and simulations, besides its pros and cons.

Finance

In addition to academic and governmental research institutes, financial institutions are also using parallel computing-based processing systems.

Almost all the main aspects of today's banking are now based on operations carried out on parallel computing systems. **Cryptocurrencies** also require support on advanced computing systems that jointly exploit parallel computing due to the complexity of the underlying blockchain.

Among the most attractive approaches is **quantitative finance**, which is also called **Quantitative analysis**. This discipline is based on the use of mathematics and statistical methods applied to finance. The underlying processes consist of searching vast quantities of market data for patterns or correlations that suggest trends and thus apply strategies. Other purposes may be price trends, risk management, and investment management.

Today's technologies make it possible to access enormous data flows, through Big Data, and extract from them the data that can be used for quantitative finance. There are therefore many algorithms and methods that tend to exploit both BigData technologies, as well as data analysis and processing on parallel computing systems.

In Python, there are numerous examples that describe studies and applications of algorithms and methods which use parallel computing. Many of these applications use **Machine Learning (ML)**, which in Python finds ample space in the numerous libraries provided. However there is a whole series of specialized libraries for the financial activity that is fundamental for the creation and study of financial models. We describe some of them that could be useful for those interested.

Quandl is a library that allows you to access a vast collection of economic, financial, and market data collected from *central banks*, *governments*, *multinational organizations*, and many other sources. Most of the datasets are free to access upon registration, while others are paid.

Zipline and **Pyfolio** are two other libraries that allow you to perform the initial processing of financial data, for example, collected by Quandl, whose interfacing is well implemented. Both provide tremendous support for specialized algorithms for trading. Furthermore, **Pyfolio** allows you to easily obtain a *tear sheet* containing performance statistics that include important parameters such as *annual/monthly returns*, *return quantiles*, *rolling beta/Sharpe ratios*, and *portfolio turnover* (see Figure 7.8).

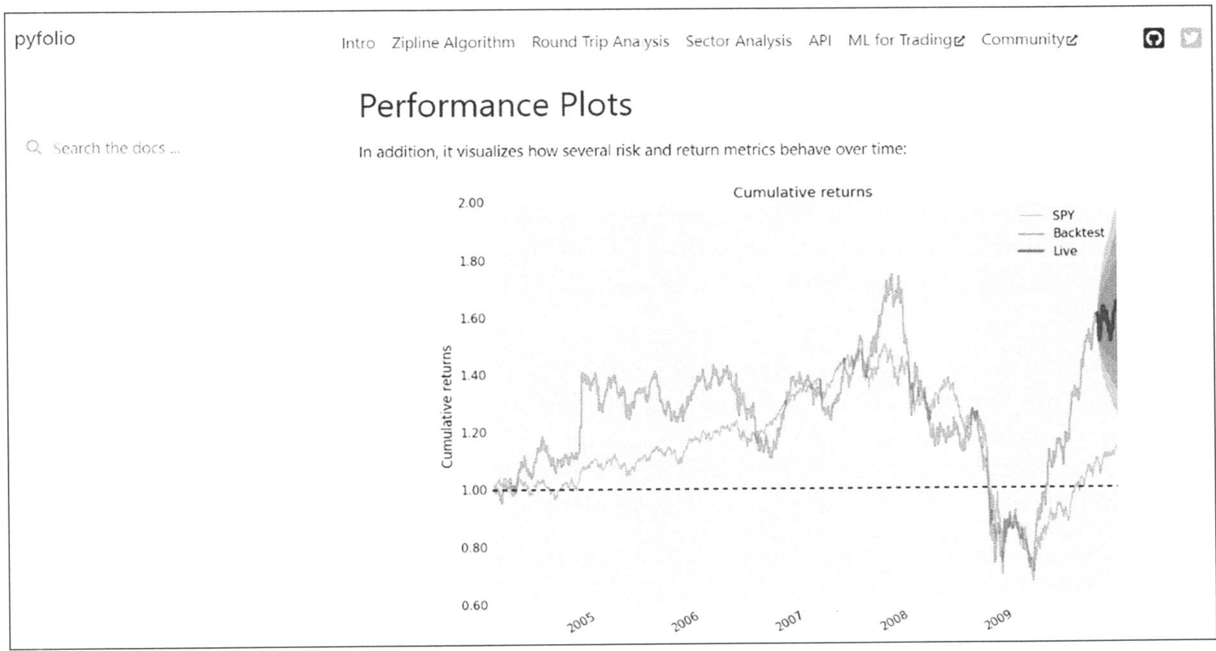

***Figure 7.8**: The Pyfolio Official Site*

In addition to these, there are libraries such as **QuantLib** and **Technical Analysis Library** (**TA-Lib**) that have been developed in C++ but are made available in Python, which provide even more advanced and specialized tools for the financial world. **QuantLib** allows you to develop models for trading and risk management, while offering a set of tools to design advanced algorithms including *market conventions*, *yield curve models*, *solvers*, PDEs, and Monte Carlo. **TA-Lib** provides additional financial tools that can be integrated with the previous library such as *overlap studies*, *momentum indicators*, *volume indicators*, *volatility indicators*, *price transformations*, *cycle indicators*, *pattern recognition*, and *financial statistics functions*.

All these libraries are available on the *Anaconda* platform, and can be installed via the following commands:

```
conda install -c anaconda quandl
conda install -c conda-forge zipline
conda install -c conda-forge quantlib
conda install -c conda-forge pyfolio
conda install -c conda-forge ta-lib
```

Engineering

Finite Element Analysis (**FEA**) is the simulation of any given physical phenomenon using a numerical technique called the **Finite Element Method** (**FEM**).

Engineers use FEA simulations to reproduce the behavior of virtual prototypes under various conditions without physically building them. From the data collected from these simulations, it is possible to optimize the choice of *components*, their *material*, and *shape*, without having to physically create and test them each time and wasting resources. To do this, however, it is necessary to use mathematical models that simulate reality as closely as possible. The models should also be able to quantify the effects of physical and structural phenomena like *heat transfer*, *wave propagation*, *resistance to pressure*, and so on. Most of these models are described by **Partial Differential Equations (PDEs)**.

The **Finite Element Analysis** method is the technique that has been successful at managing calculations and has provided excellent results. Therefore, it is clear that to carry out an increasingly accurate and efficient FEA, high-performance computers that use parallel computing are required. In an FEA, an extremely large number of partial differential equations are solved concurrently and then processed in parallel.

To perform simulations, a mesh consisting of millions of small elements that form the shape of the structure needs to be created.

Calculations are then made on each individual element. After combining the individual results, you get the final one that describes the whole structure. This means that an approximation of the interpolation is introduced in the space between the values obtained from the points (nodes) that describe the elements.

In other words, you know the value of some points, but not all. **Interpolation** can be improved by using increasingly complex systems, or by increasing the number of finite elements in the analysis. This is done at the expense of computing power, with a request for more complex calculations and memory. It is therefore clear that to improve the performance and accuracy of these simulations, it is necessary to enhance the calculation tool on which it is performed.

The advances obtained in parallel computing are in fact leading to improvements in FEA, as well as the results obtained from simulations.

As far as FEM methods in Python are concerned, we have many projects and libraries available, which are:

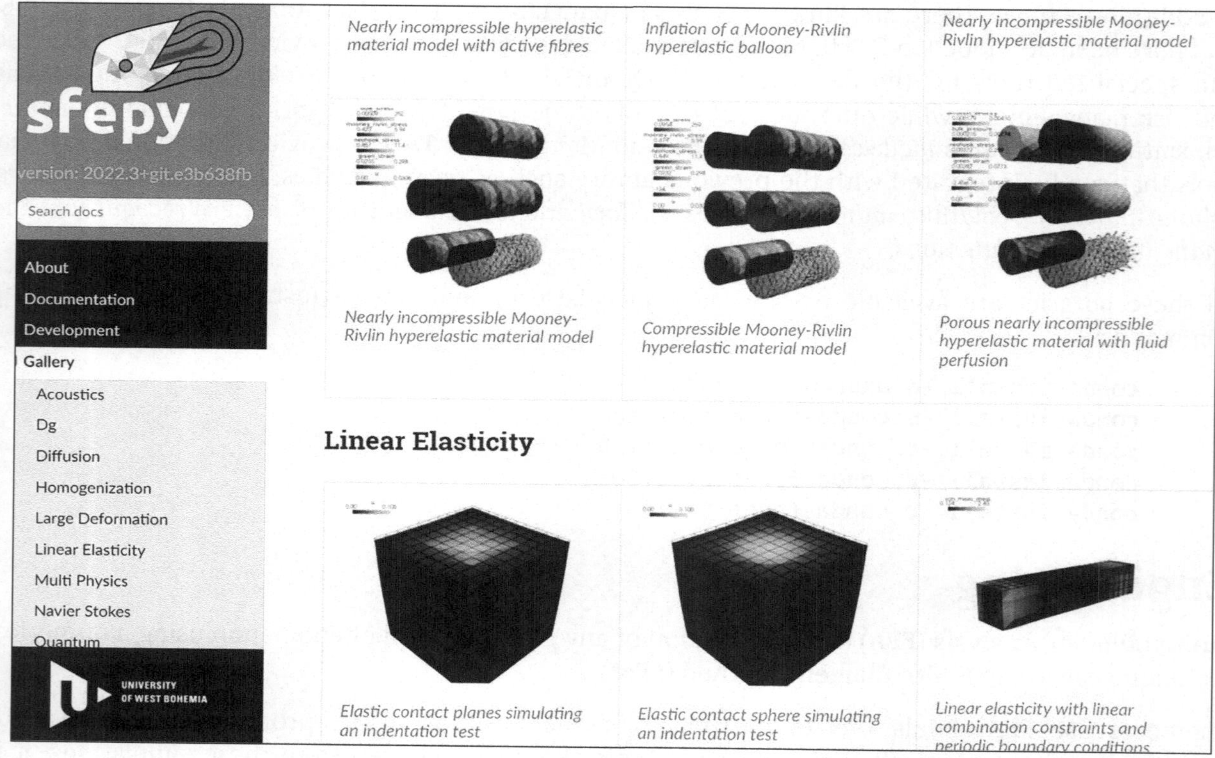

***Figure 7.9**: SfePy Official Website with Some Examples*

PolyFem is a library developed in C++ but also released in Python, which provides calculation methods for different PDEs such as:

- Laplace
- Helmholtz
- Linear Elasticity
- St. Venant–Kirchhoff Elasticity
- Neo-Hookean Elasticity
- Stokes
- Navier–Stokes

Here, the problems to be submitted to the calculation are easily set via a JSON *interface* or programmatically by defining a class.

This library is also available on the *Anaconda* platform. To install it, you can enter the following command:

```
conda install -c conda-forge polyfempy
```

An alternative is **SfePy**, which is another library designed to resolve systems of coupled PDEs via the finite element method in **1D**, **2D**, and **3D** (see *Figure* 7.9). For its installation, downloading the source code on GitHub and the compilation is recommended, but a pre-built version is available on the *Anaconda* platform and can be installed via:

```
conda install -c conda-forge sfepy
```

Medicine and Drug Discovery

Parallel computing is also used in medicine, especially in *image processing*. Diagnostic devices that scan the human body and brain use advanced technologies to produce images. One of the most widely used techniques in this field is **Magnetic Resonance Imaging** (**MRI**) reconstruction, which is used to reconstruct magnetic resonance images and for tasks such as brain fiber tracking. Similarly, Computed Tomography (CT) uses parallel reconstruction algorithms for X-ray images.

Python, as a scientific programming language, offers several widely used tools for this area. Libraries such as **`nilabel`** (for reading and writing medical image formats), **DiPy** (for diffusion imaging and tractography), and **SigPy** (for advanced reconstruction algorithms) provide a rich ecosystem for MRI research and analysis.

In particular, **SigPy** fully exploits the potential of parallel computing on both CPUs and GPUs. It offers a comprehensive set of tools for signal processing tasks and includes a dedicated module for MRI applications, **`sigpy.mri`**, which is specifically designed for magnetic resonance image reconstruction.

To install the latter you can use the *Anaconda* platform and the following code:

```
conda install -c frankong sigpy
# (optional for plot support) conda install matplotlib
# (optional for CUDA support) conda install cupy
# (optional for MPI support) conda install mpi4py
```

However, parallel signal processing techniques are also being adopted in other diagnostic sectors. Patients with *neuromuscular* or *cardiorespiratory* disease need constant monitoring. This constant monitoring produces a large amount of data in the form of signals which contain useful information of different types and have to be processed as soon as possible. So, we must use signal processing algorithms adapted for this type of application. A peculiar feature is that the data needs to be processed in real-time, which means that the window of time provided is rather brief. The data produced by monitoring consist of bio signals of different types (generally *electrocardiogram*, *respiration*, *electroencephalogram*, and *electromyogram*), that are acquired simultaneously. Their processing to extract useful information is not trivial and requires considerable time. It is clear that the classical approach generates delays and inefficiencies which could be critical, given that we are talking about human health.

Therefore the transition to parallel processing is an indispensable step to make these current monitoring systems more efficient and capable of giving answers in *real-time* for prompt intervention. Detecting sudden changes in the patient's vital signs must be accurate and fast enough to prevent serious complications.

In Python, one of the earlier libraries designed for biosignal processing was **BioSPPy,** a toolbox that provided various signal processing and pattern recognition methods for analyzing common biosignals such as PPG, ECG, EDA, EEG, EMG, and respiration. However, BioSPPy is no longer actively maintained. A more modern and actively developed alternative is NeuroKit2, which offers a wide range of tools for biosignal processing and analysis. NeuroKit2 can be easily installed from PyPI using the pip command:

```
pip install neurokit2
```

Even the research sector makes intensive use of complex algorithms in their activity in applications like drug discovery and genomics. It is clear that the conversion of these algorithms from serial to parallel and the use of calculation systems (supercomputers) is undergoing a phase of development.

Drug Discovery

Drug discovery is one of the most expensive, time-demanding, and challenging tasks pharmaceutical companies face. Identification and optimization of molecules or peptides are done on huge scales of available compounds. The molecules must meet particular requirements such as having high binding affinity and specificity with an associated target, which is generally an enzyme (**molecular docking technique**). The latter is linked to a disease and its activation-deactivation gives the molecule its efficacy as a drug. However, the molecule must also have favorable **pharmacodynamics** and **pharmacokinetic** properties, otherwise, it can be unassimilated or metabolized too quickly and not reach the target enzyme. The simulation of such an analysis requires a copious amount of computational resources and time that the introduction of parallel computing becomes very necessary.

Therefore, the pharmaceutical industry is giving a strong impetus to the development and innovation of the current analysis techniques and the calculators on which they are processed.

Drug discovery is a huge market and requires huge economic efforts. Despite this, it has been calculated that only one compound out of 10,000 proposed by *Research and Development* will prove to be a successful drug. So, it is clear that speeding up and lightening the simulation and analysis phases of a potential drug will reduce expenses.

Molecular docking consists of sampling the possible spatial configurations that the molecule can assume and calculating the scoring functions for each of these configurations when it is binding to the enzyme.

This activity is computationally very expensive, but it can be easily parallelized. Also, many algorithms used in the evaluation of a drug can be parallelized, thus increasing the performance of the whole process.

When these techniques are applied to supercomputers, there is an increase in the calculation speed and therefore the time needed for the extraction of potential drugs reduces.

However, research also opens the landscape for many other innovations.

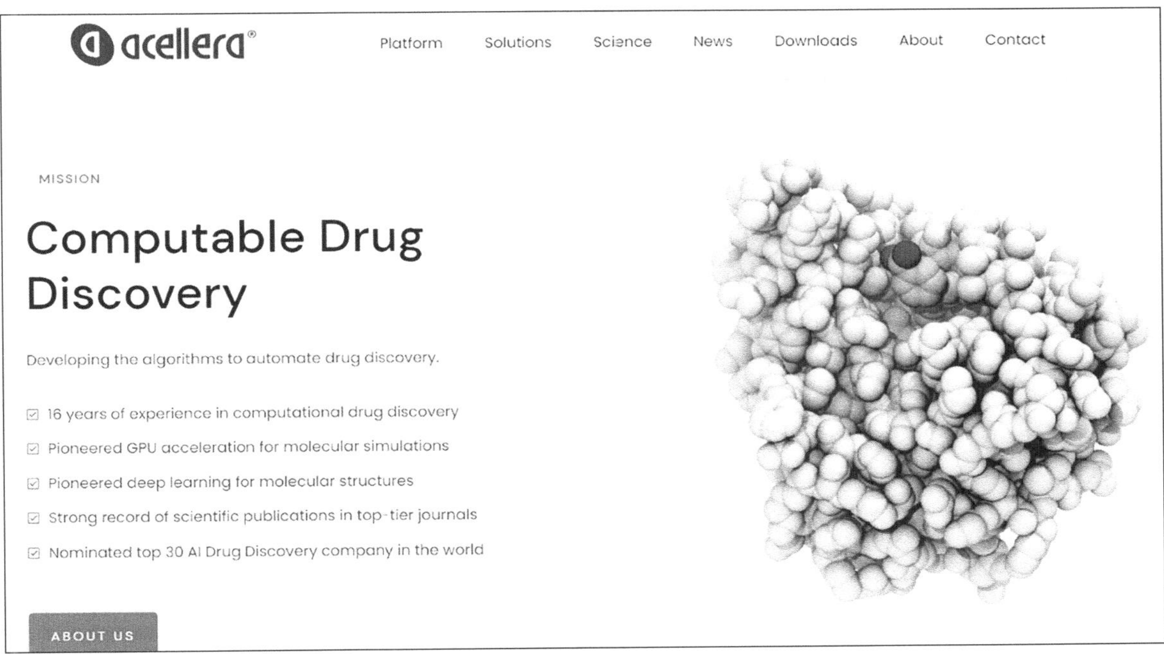

Figure 7.10: *Acellera Web Page for Computable Drug Discovery*

There are many software packages for **Molecular Docking**, including **Autodock**, which is made in C/C++ and has recently upgraded into a new version, called **Autodock-GPU**. The new version greatly exploits the potential of graphics cards. In fact, it has been found from many scientific research studies that the speed of operations of this latest version is hundreds times faster than the original version.

AutoDockFR (Flexible Receptor) is a Python-based suite that extends AutoDock for flexible docking studies. It introduces support for receptor flexibility and provides both a graphical interface and Python scripting tools. The suite can be downloaded from: **https://ccsb.scripps.edu/adfr/downloads/**.

However, there are other libraries for Molecular Docking. One of these is **`pyscreener`**, which has an internal tasking system that can efficiently adapt to the number of available cores, while scaling the calculations performed between the cores and the available CPUs in parallel.

Among the paid solutions, it is worth mentioning the libraries provided by **Acellera** (see *Figure* 7.10), which are available for free use (EULA *contract*) and are limited to a single GPU. Among these is HTMD, a programmable environment that allows you to *simulate*, *analyze*, and *visualize* molecular systems.

Genomics

As far as *genomics* is concerned, here too the massive use of supercomputers based on parallel computing is necessary. The study of an organism's genome requires manipulating and processing very large amount of data and information, which is difficult to manage if there are no algorithms that work in parallel.

Genomics is the most representative of bioinformatics disciplines as it compares structures such as DNA *sequences*, *genes*, and RNA between different organisms. However, the data runs in enormous dimensions (Terabytes) so much so that it can be defined as *Biological Big Data*. Without parallel computing, a single experiment could stretch over several weeks, if not months. It is therefore essential that parallelization and HPC techniques are applied in order to reduce these *processing times* and make it possible to manage, process and analyze this type of data.

However, the integration of algorithms used in bioinformatics with parallel computing is not a simple matter and is still being studied. There are two main approaches to address this challenge. Historically, software such as **FASTA**, **BLAST**, **HMMER**, **ClustalW**, and **RaxML** have been redesigned to leverage parallel computing, for example with MPI (see *Figure 7.11*). In modern genomics pipelines, however, the standard tools include **Bowtie2, BWA, STAR, GATK, and minimap2**, which are designed to efficiently handle the massive scale of next-generation sequencing data.

An alternative is to use distributed systems, or clouds, in which pipelines are developed for bioinformatics calculations and can be represented as workflows.

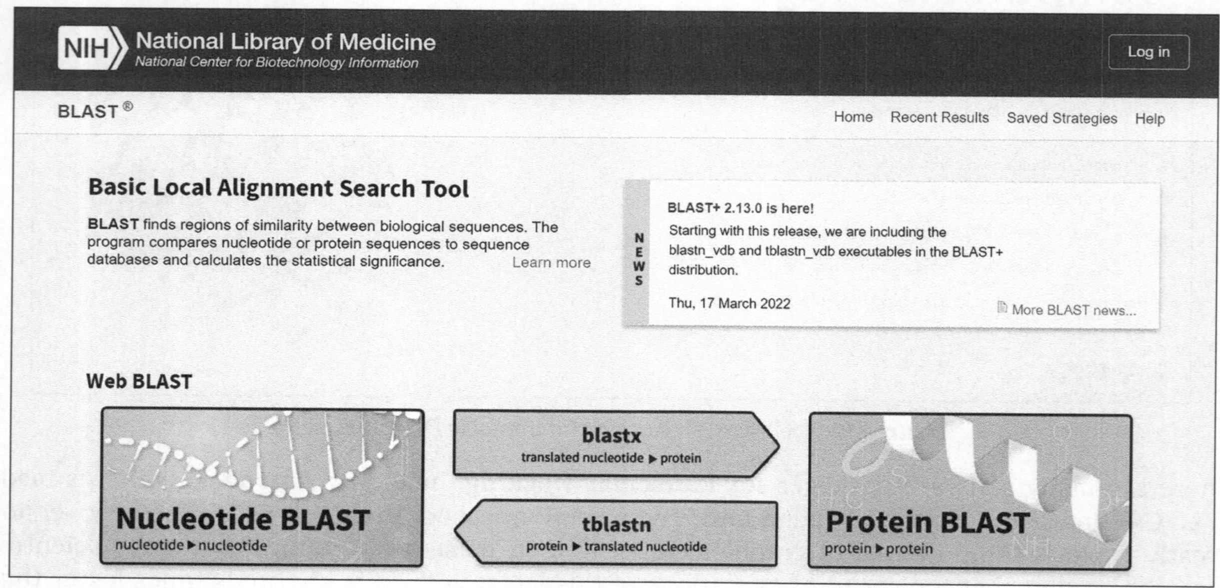

***Figure 7.11**: BLAST Official Page*

There are workflow systems such as **Tavaxy**, **Pegasus**, **Swift/T**, and **SciCumulus** that can manage bioinformatics processing in distributed infrastructures.

As for Python, there is the **pyrpipe** library, which is designed to process **RNA-Seq** data by developing computational pipelines entirely in Python. This library can be used both on local computers and in HPC environments and can be easily integrated into workflow management systems such as **Snakemake** and **Nextflow**.

This library can be easily installed on the *Anaconda* platform:

```
conda install -c bioconda pyrpipe
```

Along with **pyrpipe**, the *Anaconda* distribution includes a huge amount of bioinformatics-specific libraries, all gathered in a dedicated repository called **bioconda** (**https://anaconda.org/bioconda/repo**).

Furthermore, always on *Anaconda*, there is another library called **BioPython** which contains a series of useful tools for molecular biology. It can be downloaded using the command:

```
conda install -c conda-forge biopython
```

Entertainment – Games and Movies

After so many applications in various scientific and industrial sectors, it will be surprising to discover that parallel computing also has its roots in the world of entertainment. This really should not come as a surprise, given that GPUs were initially designed for the heavy graphics loads that are used in video games. It is in fact the video game market that has strongly pushed for the development of particular processors that enhance games and 3D environments. Games are constantly evolving and have now reached enormous levels in which the images flow smoothly, are rich in interactive features (often guided by AI), and are a part of increasingly realistic scenarios. It is in fact here that we discover the potential of the highly parallel structure of graphics cards.

Game Engines

At the heart of most games lies a complex structure called a **game engine**.

There are several game-engine models that are distributed in the market to make video games. Among the most important are:

- **The Unreal Engine**
- **Unity**
- **Godot**

These powerful game engines are easy to use and have intelligent features that can be used to create beautiful applications and ensure realistic gaming experiences (see *Figure* 7.12).

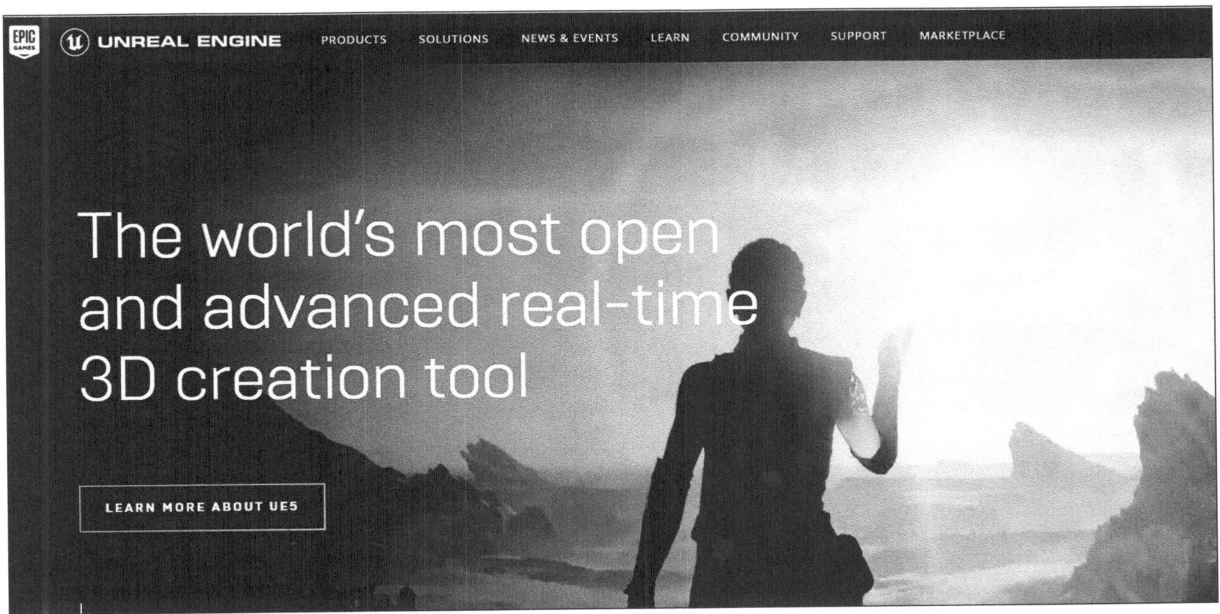

Figure 7.12: *Unreal Engine Official Web Page*

For developers, the provided user interfaces allow them to develop games in a simple way, while leveraging the strengths of powerful technologies in both **graphics** (supported by GPUs) and **learning** (AI). This yields the possibility of obtaining fluid movements of subjects in three-dimensional settings. These game engines are constantly evolving and incorporate within them all possible innovations in the field of parallel programming. Often, these technologies are then reused in other areas, as seen previously.

The power of game engines is also based on **3D rendering**. It allows players to have realistic gaming experience and creates images starting from three-dimensional modeling.

The *three-dimensional models of objects* that make up the virtual environment created by the game engine undergo a texturing phase. Two-dimensional images are applied to cover the surface of these objects, while giving them a material appearance, with a calculated sheen based on the orientation of the lighting. Other effects such as shadows are added and in the end; the 2D image is created, which as a photograph, converts virtual reality into a realistic image.

Using more powerful calculators generates better results and creates more realistic images. Furthermore, these images will have to be generated for each frame of the video game, which, like the frames of a movie, will have to flow smoothly. Therefore, it is easy to understand the demands this technology exerts on computing power. In addition to this, there are the necessary calculations for the management of sound, AI, network, and memory.

Parallel computing is a powerful tool for optimizing the underlying processes in a game engine. The most powerful game engines currently use CPU cores and GPUs through *multithreading*. In our book, we have seen that Python does not handle multithreading on CPUs well, and in fact, these game engines are based on programming languages such as C# and C++ that allow you to apply multithreading on CPUs.

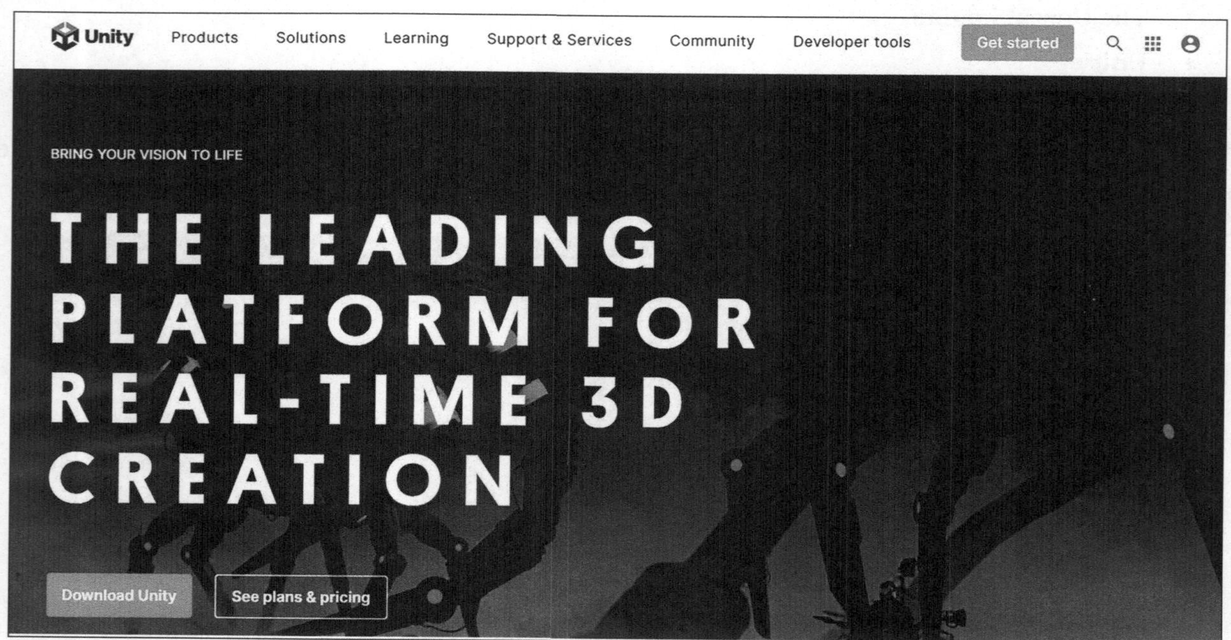

***Figure 7.13**: Unity Official Web Page*

In the **Unity** game engine (see *Figure 7.13*), *multithreading* is applied to execute rendering processes in parallel across threads. Parallel execution of multiple threads greatly reduces the *execution time of processes* within a frame. Therefore, more frames can be generated per second and the games will be *smoother*. This is where GPUs come into play, as their architecture is designed to resolve the calculation of pixel textures more efficiently than a CPU would. Furthermore, the enormously parallel internal structure allows this computation to be assigned to a large number of threads simultaneously, thereby lightening the workload and reducing execution times.

Furthermore, the CPU is free to carry out further tasks in the meantime. Since CPUs are powerful in mathematical calculations, they are used in parallel to perform calculations that make the 3D environment even more realistic. The behavior of objects, the effects of shocks, and the waves transmitted in the water, the responses to user interactions, and even the intelligence of Non-Player Characters (**NPCs**) are processed by algorithms destined for the CPU, whose cores allocate many threads for parallel computing.

As mentioned for Python, there are no full-fledged game engines comparable to Unreal Engine or Unity. Instead, most options are available as libraries. **PyGame** remains the most widely used, but it has limitations, especially regarding true multithreading due to Python's Global Interpreter Lock (GIL). Nevertheless, parallelism can still be achieved using multiprocessing or extensions such as Cython and Numba.

In addition to PyGame, there are other Python-native frameworks such as **Pyglet**, **Panda3D**, and **Ursina**, which go further in terms of 3D support and abstraction. While they are not as advanced as the major engines built in C++ or C#, they are viable options for Python-based game development.

Designing a Parallel Game Engine

There is a wonderful article on the Intel website, which is titled *Designing the Framework of a Parallel Game Engine*. You can access it via:

https://www.intel.com/content/dam/develop/external/us/en/documents/designing-a-parallel-game-engine-593584.pdf

The article illustrates the steps involved in designing a possible game engine. It can be a good stimulus to develop a new game engine in Python.

A good design for a game engine makes the most of all available processors. We have seen that other game engines leverage multithreading on CPUs to achieve this purpose. In Python, since we do not have this possibility, we can use *multiprocessing*. As far as GPU is concerned, we have seen that Python is not affected by major limitations compared to other programming languages.

A game engine works on a processing loop aimed at creating one frame after another. Each *frame* is the result of a series of processes that include the movement of objects in *three-dimensional space* and includes *texturing*, *rendering*, and *user interactions*. It is clear that the generation of the frame leads to a serial execution of the game. Serial execution refers to when the *frames* are generated in an ordered sequence consecutively. However, between the generation of one frame and another, the potential of parallel computing can be leveraged to the maximum possible degree. Between the two frames, *threads* and *processes* spawn and work in parallel to perform all necessary tasks, thereby reducing processing time. Then the generation of the frame will occur when all the threads or processes have finished executing to give a result. The exchange of information between them at this moment reduces the synchronization load significantly and prompts the system to react more quickly from one frame to another.

The article shows *two* execution modes:

1. The **Lock Step Mode** shown in *Figure 7.14*:

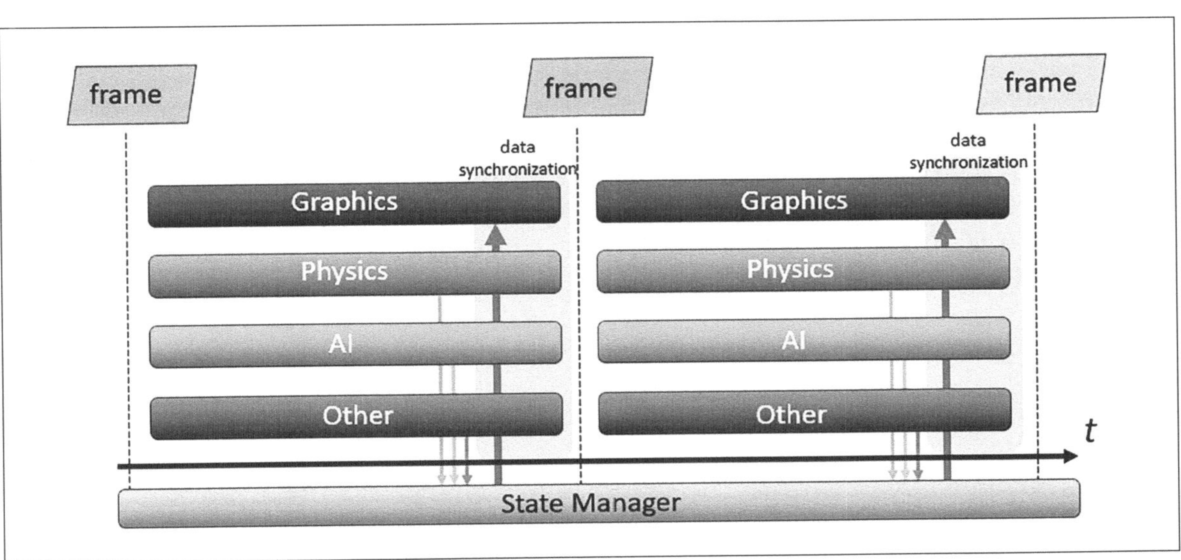

Figure 7.14: Lock Step Mode

2. The **Free Step Mode**, where not all the components must necessarily synchronize at each frame step, but can extend over several cycles (see *Figure 7.15*).

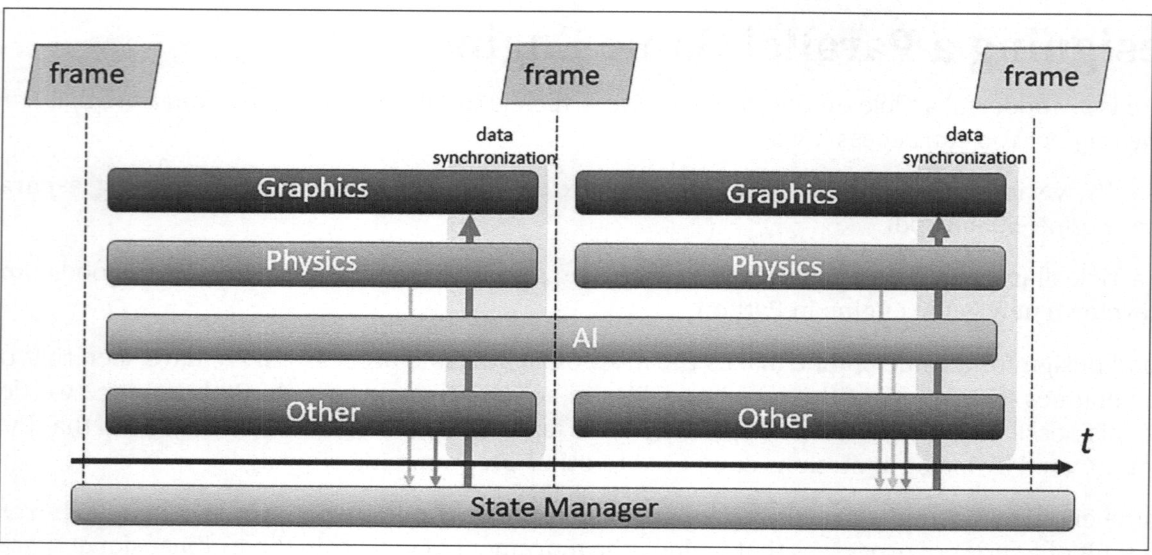

***Figure 7.15**: Free Step Mode*

Movies and 3D Animations

The power of game engines to create *three-dimensional environments* has generated results that often surpass reality itself. Some of the technologies used in creating images for video games have also been used in making movies. In the post-production phase of many recent films, the use of effects is frequent (and is often borrowed from video games). This allows animators to improve images acquired from reality or produce new surreal or expensive settings in which actors can move.

Techniques such as color correction and ray tracing harness the power of GPUs to enhance the images shot for a movie. All these visual effects are commonly referred to as VFX (*Visual Effects*) and are the result of processing processes of photorealistic images that are digitally generated or are derived from manipulating other images.

Special effects experts use distinct software that allows them to perform these functions. *DaVinci Resolve Studio*, for instance, is a special effects processing platform that makes heavy use of GPUs (see *Figure 7.16*). Films such as *Thor: Love and Thunder* (2022) and *Bullet Train* (2022) have used this software to color-correct the images shot via high-quality renderings based on *ray-tracing techniques*. These techniques are used to accentuate reflections, contrasts, and lighting effects using GPUs in parallel. This is demonstrated in the image here:

Figure 7.16: *DaVinci Resolve Studio Web Page*

Ray Tracing is a type of rendering algorithm that produces realistic light effects in computer graphics through a series of vector-based calculations and requires a huge amount of resources. So, if we imagine the costs of processing parts of images in a film, we can imagine that the scale of resources required for animated films will be like the ones from Pixar. These long movies use images that are made after rendering environments built on artificial three-dimensional models.

A freelance programmer from *Pixar Animation Studios*, *Peter Collingridge*, has revealed that *Pixar* has one of the 25 *most powerful supercomputers* in the world, consisting of 2,000 *machines* and 24,000 *cores to make its* animation films. Despite the availability of massive computing power, movies like *Monster Inc.* (2001) took about two years to render the footage alone.

It is clear that in the recent years, *Pixar* has increased the power of its supercomputer, but these films with highly realistic rendering effects require enormous computation, which is tough even for the best supercomputers available.

Since the release of *Monster Inc.*, *Pixar has continued to* produce increasingly fluid and realistic animated films, where the richness of detail and the complexity of the movements captivates the attention of the audience.

This is a clear sign that there have been many advances in the underlying technologies, including innovations in parallel computing. While not much information is available to the public about these techniques, but it is clear that those interested in working in this sector have to take parallel programming in consideration.

Conclusion

With this chapter, we have concluded the overview of the disciplines and application sectors that use parallel computing as a valid tool for innovation and research. We have excluded data analysis and artificial intelligence for now, as they will be addressed in detail in the further chapters of the book.

References

- https://www.intel.it/content/www/it/it/high-performance-computing/what-is-hpc.html
- https://www.hp.com/us-en/shop/tech-takes/parallel-computing-and-its-modern-uses
- https://builtin.com/hardware/parallel-processing-example
- https://www.eoas.ubc.ca/books/Practical_Meteorology/prmet102/Ch20-nwp-v102.pdf
- https://pyoceans.github.io/sea-py/
- https://biostats.w.uib.no/ctd/
- https://metview.readthedocs.io/en/5.23.1/tutorials/90_min_intro/part_1_intro.html
- https://confluence.ecmwf.int/display/METV/Metview
- https://prappleizer.github.io/textbook.pdf
- https://www.lupm.in2p3.fr/users/jmorin/pres/euroscipy2011-jmorin-pencil.pdf
- https://arxiv.org/pdf/1807.06128.pdf
- https://yt-astro-analysis.readthedocs.io/en/latest/
- https://github.com/yt-project
- https://www.researchgate.net/publication/346249862_DEVELOPING_PARALLEL_COMPUTING_ALGORITHMS_USING_GPU'S_TO_DETERMINE_OIL_AND_GAS_RESERVES_PRESENTED_IN_THE_UPSTREAM_EXPLORATION_SECTOR
- https://abhyankar-ameya.medium.com/parallel-computing-for-finance-ec053d8fb20f
- https://www.activestate.com/blog/top-10-python-packages-for-finance-and-financial-modeling/
- https://www.simscale.com/docs/simwiki/fea-finite-element-analysis/what-is-fea-finite-element-analysis/
- https://getfem-examples.readthedocs.io/en/latest/demo_unit_disk.html
- https://sfepy.org/doc-devel/index.html
- https://www.unrealengine.com/en-US
- https://unity.com/
- https://godotengine.org/
- https://www.intel.com/content/dam/develop/external/us/en/documents/codesample-unity-r1.pdf
- https://www.gamedeveloper.com/blogs/advantages-of-parallel-computing-in-unity
- https://www.dcp.dev/projects/distributed-ray-tracing
- https://sigpy.readthedocs.io/en/latest/mri.html
- https://run.unl.pt/bitstream/10362/8249/1/Chorao_2012.pdf
- https://www.mdpi.com/1424-8247/15/1/63/htm
- https://ccsb.scripps.edu/adfr/
- https://www.ncbi.nlm.nih.gov/pmc/articles/PMC4655901/

CHAPTER 8
Parallel Computing for Data Science

Introduction

In the previous chapter, we went through the possible applications of parallel computing in various scientific and industrial disciplines, especially in context of Python. We also suggested some available tools and libraries related to this language. However, we have deliberately left out *data science*, as we have dedicated an entire chapter to it. In this chapter, we will deal with a possible application of data science in the field of *parallel computing*, in particular, the **Dask** library. Dask is a powerful tool that allows us to extend our knowledge of the most commonly used data science libraries like **Pandas** and **NumPy**, and apply them to distributed systems in simple and rapid manner.

Structure

This chapter will address the following topics:

- Dask Library
- Pandas and Dask DataFrames
- Distributed Parallel Computing
- Dask Collections
- Task Graphs and Computing
- Kaggle
- Saturn.io Cluster

Data Science, Pandas Library, and Parallel Computing

Python has proved to be a suitable language for *data science* and *data analysis*, and has rivalled the popularity of languages like **R**. This is mainly due to the potential of the currently available Python libraries which in recent years have been some of the most premium tools for data science. One of these libraries is **Pandas**, which thanks to the **DataFrame** (see *Figure* 8.1) allows you to manipulate and manage huge amounts of data in an efficient and rapid way. Furthermore, this library, along with others like **NumPy**, **Scikit-Learn**, and **Matplotlib** acts as a fundamental tool kit for data science. This is because they create a robust environment for study and analysis that caters to all needs, while remaining within the scope of Python.

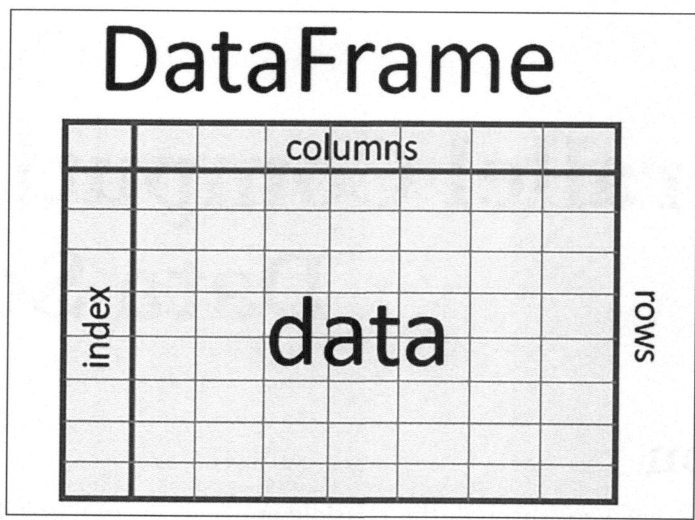

Figure 8.1: A DataFrame

A data scientist can build a development and analysis environment by gradually installing all these libraries, such as a series of specific virtual environments like the ones we created with the *Anaconda* distribution. You import the data (in form of CSVs available on the web) onto your computer, convert it into DataFrames *via* the **Pandas** library, clean and manipulate it according to your needs, and analyze it to extract useful information. **Pandas** is very efficient and is capable of manipulating several lines of data in a few seconds or even less, depending on the computing power of your system. But however powerful and efficient your system may be, sooner or later you will need to import CSV files or data in other formats, that might be larger than your computer's RAM. Therefore, while trying to import such data, you would get an error message. Furthermore, with the increase in the size of DataFrames the rise in complex procedures for data processing, execution times will lengthen considerably. This might be due to the underlying algorithms, but it also depends on computer resources which will gradually become more scarce as incoming data increases in volume.

You must wonder how to proceed in this case as you arrive at a crisis point. The good news is that the situation can be improved by *measuring the scale of* the problem. The best solution, therefore, will include distributing data across distant systems and not stay limited only to leveraging parallel computing. Among the systems that we have already seen in the book, distributed systems can meet these needs in the best way. Systems composed of multiple computing systems with their respective clusters work best for a data scientist who wants to scale from his *limited, albeit powerful system*, as shown in *Figure 8.2*:

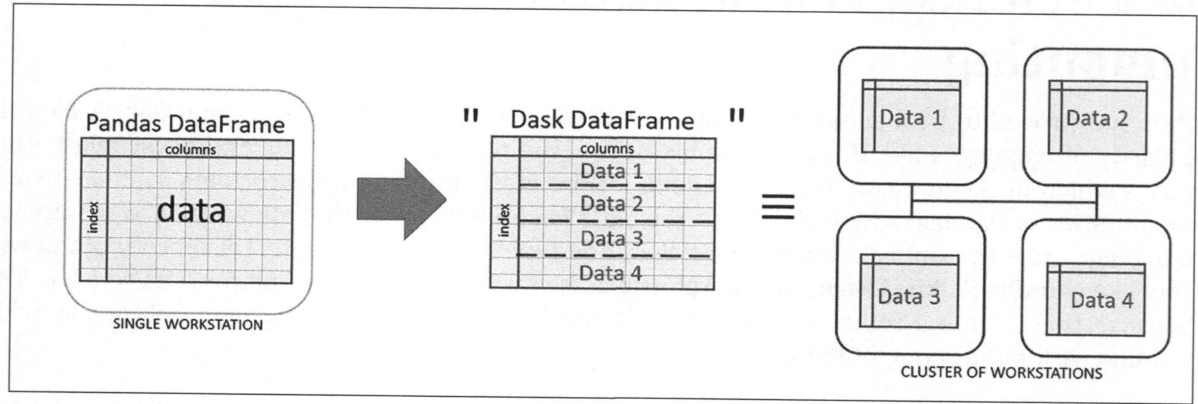

Figure 8.2: Scaling Out DataFrames

Pandas is designed to work on single machines, but in a distributed system, you can use a corresponding library similar to Pandas. It is called **Dask**.

Dask Library

Dask is a flexible library that allows you to extend many libraries such as **Pandas**, **NumPy**, **Scikit-learn**, and many others, on distributed systems for parallel computing in Python. These libraries are the staple for anyone working with data analysis in Python. Dask uses the *same syntax*, *methods*, and *operating modes* as these libraries. In this way, users of these libraries will be able to use their codes by extending them with Dask with minimal changes. Hence, scaling the code from a *single-machine system* to *distributed systems* becomes more rapid with Dask.

Thus, Dask allows us to build distributed applications to *scale up* in just a few steps, that is, it facilitates transition from a purely serial system to one with multiple processing systems in parallel. This can also be referred to as *scaling out*, which means that execution can be transferred to external distributed systems like the cloud.

Dask is conceptually split into *two* distinct parts:

- Dynamic Task Scheduling
- Big Data Collections

Dynamic task scheduling is used to optimize the calculations in a distributed system. It converts the Python code containing functions, methods, and definitions of objects into equivalent operations for parallel computing just like Pandas, but much more efficiently.

Big Data collections, on the other hand, are all series of objects containing data. These are very similar to NumPy arrays and DataFrames, which are instead designed to be distributed on clusters. These collections also preserve the interfaces of original data structures, as well as the names of the methods used, the parameters passed, and the syntax of the operations used on these objects.

In summary, Dask provides an extension to distributed systems with highly parallelized DataFrames and arrays. It does so while maintaining the same syntax of the original libraries to reuse the existing code and extend it to parallel computing in a simple and rapid way. Furthermore, once the code is integrated with Dask, it can work on clusters with over 1,000 *cores*, as well as on a single processor system. In this case, Dask will optimize the execution of the code as per the processing environment.

The operation of Dask can be summarized in *Figure 8.3 as follows*:

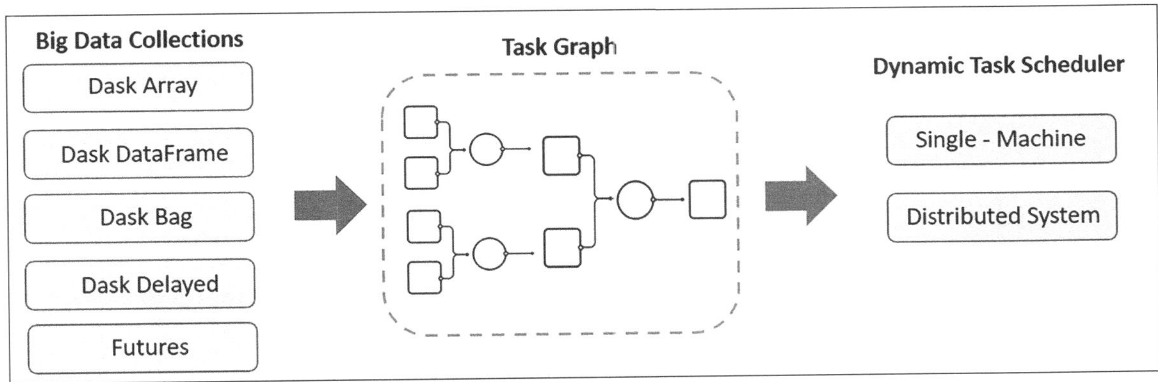

Figure 8.3: *Operation Diagram of the Dask Library*

Dask provides *three* different components:

- **Big Data Collections**: At a *high level*, this data structure is very similar to the corresponding objects present in other libraries, such as the DataFrame in Pandas. At a *low level*, they are designed to manage parallel computing in distributed systems.
- **Task Graphs**: They are generated by Dask from Big Data collections, as well as from the operations to be performed on them. They divide these operations into smaller parts called

tasks, which will then be distributed to the various processors of the system called the workers, who will have the task to run in parallel.

- **Dynamic Task Scheduler**: This component distributes tasks to available workers.

Getting Started on a Single Machine

To familiarize yourself with Dask and its features, there is no better way than to use your own computer. It will always be possible to pass the code developed on distributed systems like clusters (for a fee) if you experiment on your own system.

Dask works on multiple operating systems, including *Linux*, *macOS*, and *Windows*. Again, it is recommended to use **Anaconda Navigator to use it**. We will create a new specific virtual environment to work on our projects with Dask through the **Environments** panel in *Anaconda Navigator* and install **`dask`** and **`dask-core`**, as shown in *Figure 8.4*:

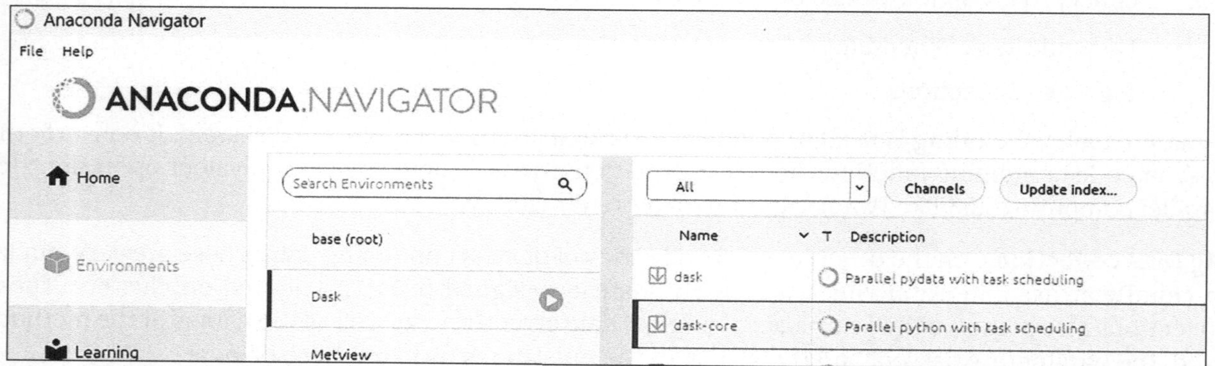

***Figure 8.4**: Installing Dask Packages in a New Virtual Environment in Anaconda Navigator*

Since we are working on data analytics, we will be using two core Python libraries: **NumPy** and **Pandas**. These *two* libraries need to be installed in the virtual environment via the following commands:

```
conda install numpy
conda install pandas
```

We can also install them via *Anaconda Navigator*, as we did for **Dask** (see *Figure* 8.5). This is shown in the following image:

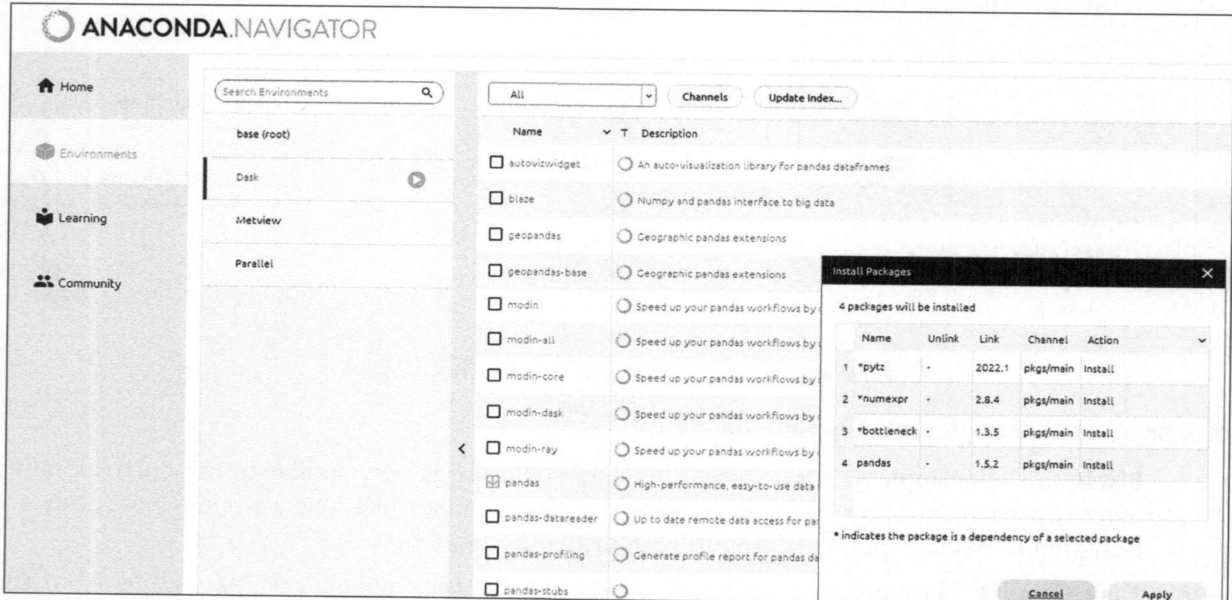

***Figure 8.5**: Installing NumPy and Pandas in Anaconda*

Another library that will later come in handy for displaying execution flow and memory distribution patterns through Dask is **graphviz**. We can also install this library using the command shell of the virtual environment via:

```
conda install graphviz
conda install python-graphviz
```

We can also install it by selecting it from the packages available in Anaconda Navigator.

If you work outside of Anaconda, it is advisable to create a virtual environment dedicated exclusively to Dask. Then, you will have to install your packages manually via PyPI with the **pip** command:

```
pip install dask numpy pandas graphviz python-graphviz
pip install dask[dataframe]
```

Once installed, we will import all the necessary packages into our code to test the correct installation, as follows:

```
import numpy as np
import pandas as pd

import dask.dataframe as dd
import dask.array as da
import dask.bag as db
```

You can use the command shell to launch these programs, but for data analysis, we will use **Jupyter Notebook**, where you can work with Python code in an *interactive* way, along with *textual* and *graphical* results. Jupyter Notebook will prove to be a fundamental choice to test the code and also study the analyzed data.

To activate Jupyter Notebook from the *Anaconda Home Screen*, press the **Launch** button directly above the quadrant that corresponds to the **Jupyter** application shown in *Figure 8.6*:

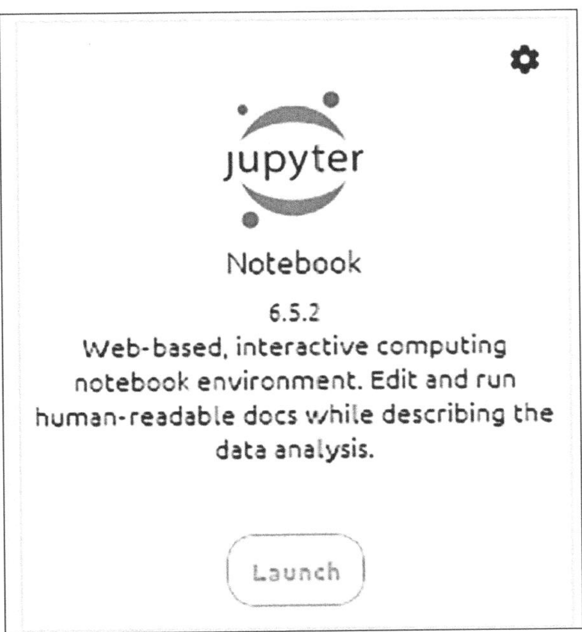

Figure 8.6: *Panel for Launching Jupyter Notebook*

In a few seconds after pressing the button, the application will automatically open on the default browser which will show the folders in which you will be able to **open**, **create**, and **save** the **Notebook** pages, as shown in *Figure 8.7*:

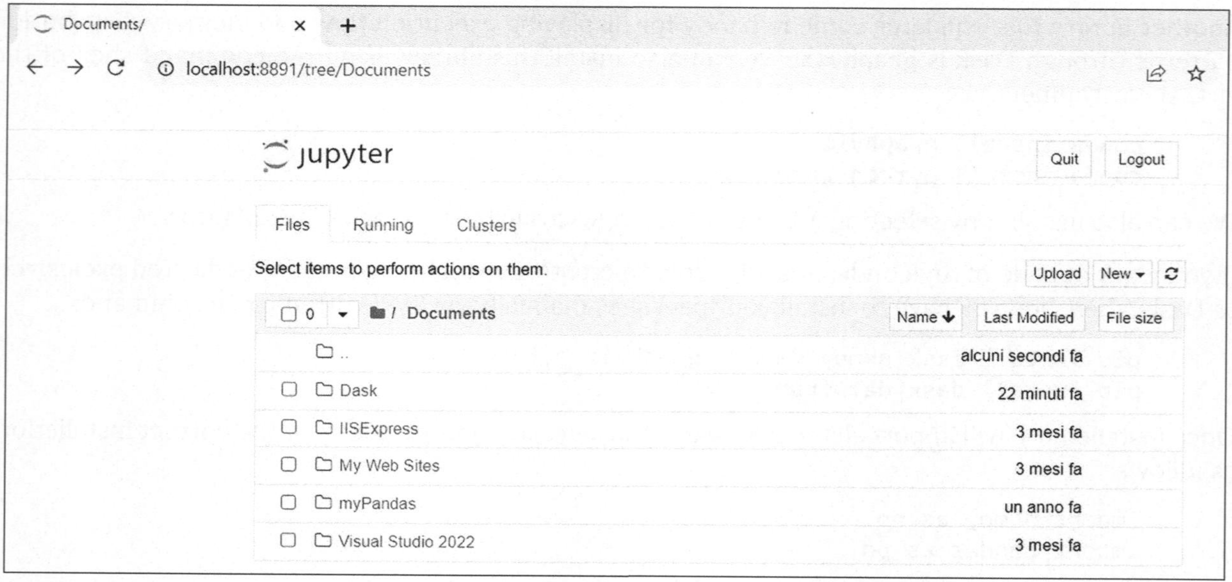

***Figure 8.7**: Jupyter Notebook*

So, let us create a new notebook and write the modules corresponding to the libraries to be imported in the first cell. If after running the first cell, we do not get any error message, then we can assume that the installation has passed correctly. See *Figure 8.8*:

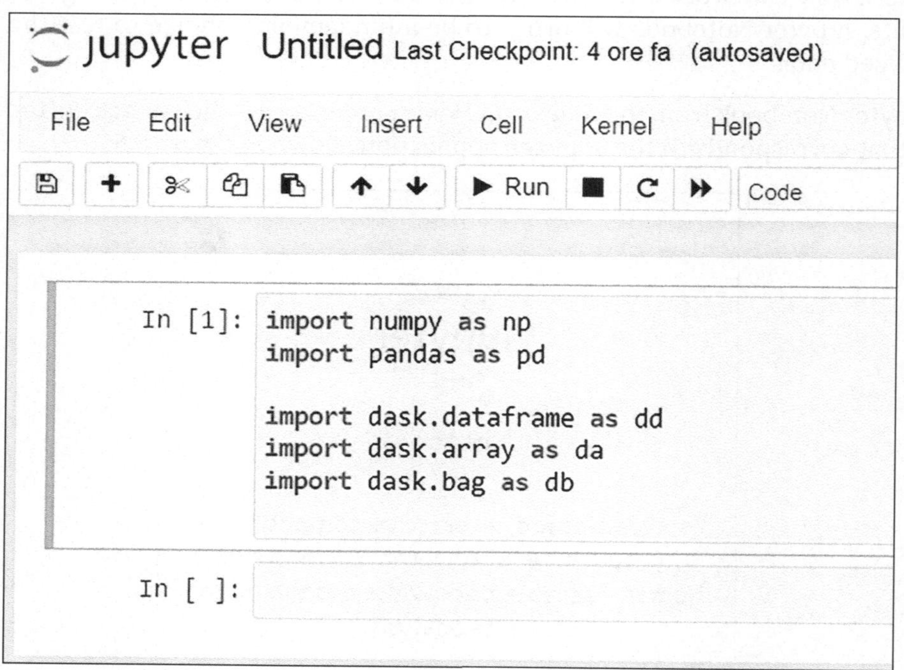

***Figure 8.8**: Importing the Modules Needed to Work with Dask*

Dask Collections

One of the peculiar characteristics of Dask is to *extend* data structures like the DataFrame of the **pandas** library and enable NumPy arrays to work efficiently in distributed systems. Dask offers a set of deployable objects called Collections, which include:

- Dask Array
- Dask DataFrame

Dask DataFrame is represented by many small DataFrame pandas that live in a *cluster*. When you interact with Dask DataFrame, the *functions* and *methods* you call are converted into smaller functions that run in parallel on multiple smaller Pandas DataFrames.

Dask Array is represented by smaller NumPy arrays that live in your cluster. When you interact with the Dask Array, the functions and methods you call are converted into smaller functions that run in parallel on smaller NumPy arrays.

Now, let us look at these concepts in more detail. We will create a new *Python 3 Notebook on Jupyter* and in the first cell, we will import the libraries and modules we will need. This is shown through the following code:

```
import numpy as np
import pandas as pd

import dask.dataframe as dd
import dask.array as da
```

We will execute the cell and then insert the code in the next one. First, let us see how we can create a simple pandas DataFrame which will be compared to the Dask DataFrame. This is indicated as:

```
df = pd.DataFrame(np.random.rand(60).reshape(10,6))
df
```

Running the cell will generate the result shown in *Figure* 8.9 (the values change because they are random):

	0	1	2	3	4	5
0	0.149034	0.604988	0.070560	0.298244	0.455134	0.896560
1	0.854942	0.291555	0.686519	0.856187	0.559002	0.737303
2	0.333051	0.779722	0.075977	0.891700	0.577997	0.544064
3	0.032463	0.374616	0.252517	0.291193	0.669397	0.687053
4	0.607324	0.337583	0.270796	0.799909	0.810546	0.530320
5	0.683711	0.048430	0.268431	0.286249	0.526409	0.981537
6	0.903745	0.823235	0.883192	0.379180	0.031492	0.094687
7	0.893327	0.700813	0.876160	0.313225	0.318481	0.726146
8	0.939292	0.308199	0.041690	0.667480	0.076510	0.504596
9	0.153619	0.025283	0.544786	0.339783	0.459579	0.020543

***Figure* 8.9**: A Pandas DataFrame

As we can see, the DataFrame contains 60 *random values* collected in *six different columns* and *ten records*. This is an example, but in reality, DataFrames are generally valued using a CSV file containing the data to be imported. There are many data sources on the web that provide CSV files full of precious data to be imported and analyzed.

For practice, let us now export the newly generated data to a CSV file. This can be done easily via the **`to_csv()`** method invoked on the DataFrame to be exported through the following command:

```
df.to_csv("myDataFrame.csv", index=False)
```

We will execute the command in a cell of the Notebook and then, we will check the directory we are working on. We will find a new **myDataFrame.csv** file containing the 60 *random data* generated earlier. We have used the **index=False** parameter to prevent the row numbering indexes of the DataFrame from being reported in the CSV file.

So, if we want to import data into a pandas DataFrame in our notebook, we just need to use the **from_csv()** function to invoke it from the library in the following manner:

```
df = pd.read_csv("myDataFrame.csv")
df
```

If we execute the cell, we will obtain a DataFrame identical to the previous one shown in *Figure* 8.9.

We can do the same thing to create a Dask DataFrame. The syntax to use is practically the same and is demonstrated here:

```
ddf = dd.read_csv("myDataFrame.csv")
ddf
```

After doing so, we will get the result shown in the following figure (*Figure* 8.10):

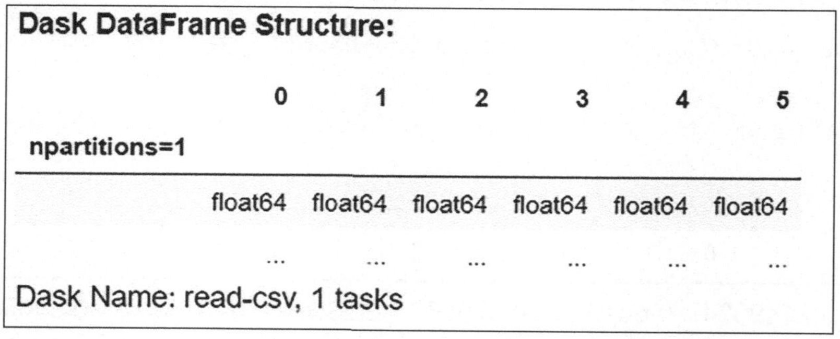

Dask DataFrame Structure:

	0	1	2	3	4	5
npartitions=1						
	float64	float64	float64	float64	float64	float64
	...	...	...	...	...	...

Dask Name: read-csv, 1 tasks

***Figure* 8.10**: *Structure of a Dask DataFrame with No Data*

As we can see, the data is not present inside the DataFrame. Here, only the internal structure of the DataFrame is displayed with the name of the columns and the relative types of data. But you might wonder where did the data go.

Although the syntax between Pandas and Dask is very similar, as is the structure of their DataFrames, their behavior is different. Dask does not perform the operations while invoking a method or defining an object like a DataFrame. To do this, it must wait for a specific command called **compute()**.

So, we will run the following command in the Jupyter Notebook to obtain the population of DataFrame with the same data as the one created with **pandas**:

```
ddf.compute()
```

Another way to import data into a Dask DataFrame is to get it directly from another Pandas DataFrame. This operation occurs more frequently, especially when you want to scale an already existing code. Therefore, the **from_pandas()** method allows us to perform this operation. In this case, we can choose the number of parts the original DataFrame will be divided into, while defining it using the **npartitions** option which is passed as an argument to the function. This is demonstrated here:

```
ddf = dd.from_pandas(df, npartitions=4)
ddf
```

By executing the previous code, we will obtain the result in *Figure* 8.11:

	0	1	2	3	4	5
npartitions=3						
0	float64	float64	float64	float64	float64	float64
3	...	...	...	...	...	...
6	...	...	...	...	...	...
9	...	...	...	...	...	...

Dask DataFrame Structure:

Dask Name: from_pandas, 3 tasks

***Figure 8.11**: Structure of a Dask DataFrame Divided into Four Parts*

Here, it can be seen that the four row indexes corresponding to the first rows of each partition of the Dask DataFrame are also reported. If we want this to be more explicit, we can run the following command:

```
ddf.divisions
```

This will give us a tuple of the indexes corresponding to the first rows of each partition of the DataFrame. It will further look like:

```
(0, 3, 6, 9)
```

As we can see, the result corresponds to the one shown in *Figure* 8.11.

We just have to enhance the DataFrame as *we did* through the **`compute()`** function and have shown it here:

```
ddf.compute()
```

We will get the same DataFrame that we obtained in the previous cases.

As for the Dask Arrays, the process is similar. However, in this case we use NumPy arrays instead of the pandas DataFrame. We then define a NumPy array of 100 *integer random values between* 0 *and* 9, collected in a 10x10 *matrix*, as shown here:

```
narr = np.random.randint(0,10,100).reshape(10,10)
narr
```

By executing the above, we will get the result here:

```
array([[5, 2, 5, 7, 2, 3, 9, 8, 2, 6],
       [9, 6, 3, 5, 0, 8, 5, 5, 1, 9],
       [6, 0, 3, 4, 3, 8, 1, 1, 7, 5],
       [3, 5, 5, 5, 3, 8, 3, 9, 3, 9],
       [3, 8, 5, 6, 0, 6, 0, 9, 7, 2],
       [7, 9, 4, 0, 4, 4, 3, 0, 6, 9],
       [9, 1, 7, 2, 4, 8, 9, 2, 6, 6],
       [5, 5, 3, 8, 1, 5, 7, 6, 4, 2],
       [8, 4, 8, 7, 0, 7, 6, 6, 9, 0],
       [1, 2, 8, 6, 8, 8, 0, 3, 0, 8]])
```

You can directly import the values of this NumPy array into a Dask Array via the **`from_array()`** function of the Dask library. The **`chunks`** option requires a tuple containing the size of the **`chunks`** that the Dask Array is split into, as shown here:

```
darr = da.from_array(narr, chunks=(5, 5))
darr
```

Executing the previous code generates the result shown in *Figure 8.12*:

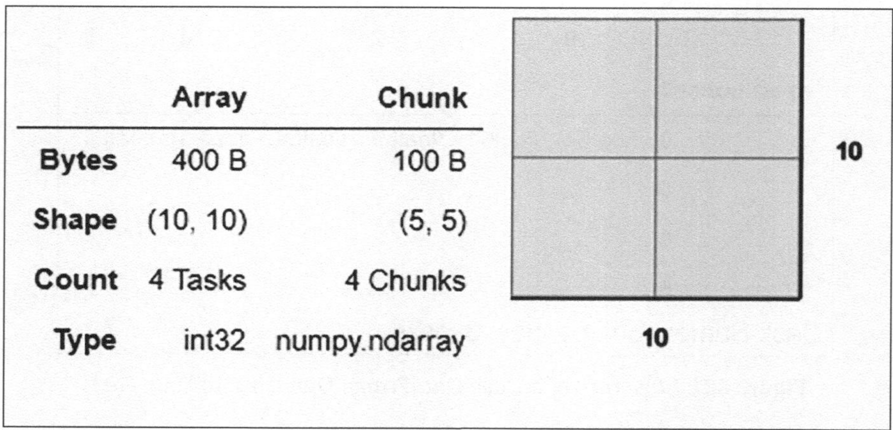

***Figure 8.12**: Structure of a Dask Array*

As we can see here, we obtained only the structure of the Dask Array, since it is not yet valued. In the indications, we can see the dimensions of each *portion* or *chunk*, which are the divided segments of the Dask Array. A task will be assigned to each chunk and the Dask Array will be populated in parallel.

If we want to obtain textual information about the partition of the Dask Array, we will use the **chunks** attribute as shown here:

```
darr.chunks
((5, 5), (5, 5))
```

To evaluate the Dask Array, the **compute()** function is launched once again:

```
darr.compute()
```

As a result, we will have the following output:

```
array([[2, 7, 3, 1, 3, 8, 1, 9, 0, 0],
       [0, 8, 0, 6, 3, 7, 7, 3, 4, 5],
       [0, 1, 2, 8, 6, 4, 3, 8, 5, 6],
       [1, 8, 4, 7, 8, 2, 4, 5, 1, 8],
       [4, 6, 4, 5, 5, 7, 4, 3, 8, 2],
       [8, 5, 3, 3, 9, 4, 5, 4, 2, 5],
       [9, 3, 1, 4, 0, 9, 5, 6, 7, 3],
       [5, 7, 1, 4, 8, 2, 2, 9, 3, 2],
       [1, 7, 9, 4, 7, 8, 9, 7, 2, 0],
       [6, 4, 3, 0, 6, 6, 6, 6, 4, 3]])
```

Methods on Collections

Now that we know how to define the most common collections like DataFrame and Array, let us see how to apply methods to them. The nomenclature and syntax of the methods should be the same (or almost) as the corresponding methods of the original libraries.

For example, if we want to calculate the average of the first column of the pandas DataFrame, we would write:

```
df[1].mean()
```

As a result, the average will be:

```
0.42944239885994107
```

Therefore, as far as the Dask DataFrame is concerned, things should not change much and should look like:

```
m = ddf[1].mean()
```

In this case, the function is assigned to a variable. As we have seen, the same rule also applies to the methods in DataFrame. The methods are not executed until the **compute()** function is called on the *invoked* method. To execute the method, we have to write:

```
m.compute()
```

The same result was obtained with the pandas DataFrame, which was:

```
0.42944239885994107
```

If you want to calculate the average of the values contained within the array, just write:

```
mm = np.mean(darr)
```

This calculation will be performed only when the **compute()** method is invoked through:

```
mm.compute()
```

This will give the following result:

```
4.52
```

Now, let us analyze the reason for this strange behavior of Dask and what actually takes place behind it.

Computing and Task Graphs

As seen before, the difference between the Dask library and traditional libraries like Pandas and NumPy is their behavior. Dask is a *lazy* library and we have seen that Dask enhances a data structure later and not while defining the concerned collection. It builds a *data structure* while defining it, which will be populated later. The same goes for the invocation of methods, which is never followed by the calculation but remains pending through its assignment to a variable.

The population of a collection and the execution of a method occurs only when the **compute()** method is invoked in the code on the relative object defined previously. This operation is called **computing** and it occurs differently than in Pandas or NumPy. As you must have noticed, the object is partitioned/divided into different parts while it is being defined. Each portion will then be assigned a task which in turn will be assigned to a different worker. The calculations within a collection will then be valued and executed in parallel. For instance, the different portions of a DataFrame will be *populated* and processed in *parallel*, which reduces the overall processing time. With small CSV files smaller than 1 GB, we will not face this problem. However, larger CSV files in data enhancement consume resources more heavily and take more time for, population. Therefore, the valorization times of these huge objects are significantly reduced in Dask, which also arranges its data structures in a distributed manner, so that the divided portions can be processed in parallel.

A related concept is that of the **task graph**. These graphs are generated before computing and describe how it will be done within a system or a single machine. Graphs represent the kind of execution path that the *task scheduler* will have to follow. Task graphs are dynamic and change according to the system used. They optimize parallel computing as much as possible.

You can view these graphs while computing in the Jupyter Notebook. For example, if we want to see the task graph of averaging on the Dask Array considered previously, we can write:

```
mm.dask
```

The list of layers into which the task graph is divided is shown in the following figure (*Figure* 8.13):

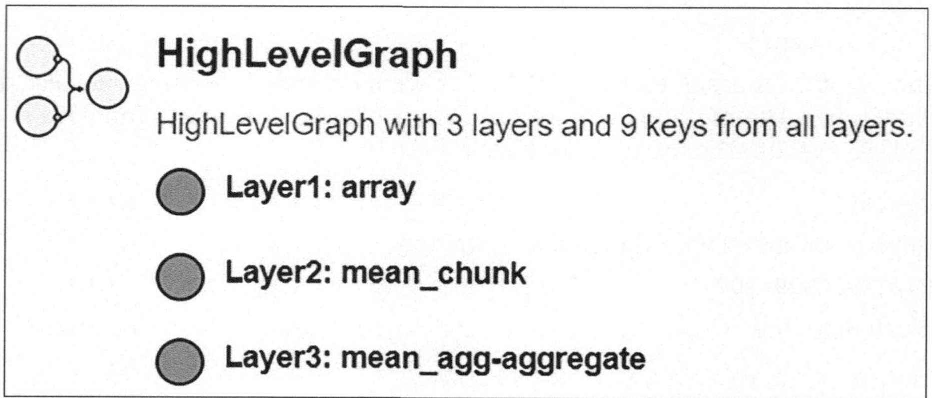

Figure 8.13: *Layers in the Task Graph*

Meanwhile, if we want to see the task graph, we write:

```
mm.visualize()
```

The resultant graph is shown in the following figure (*Figure* 8.14):

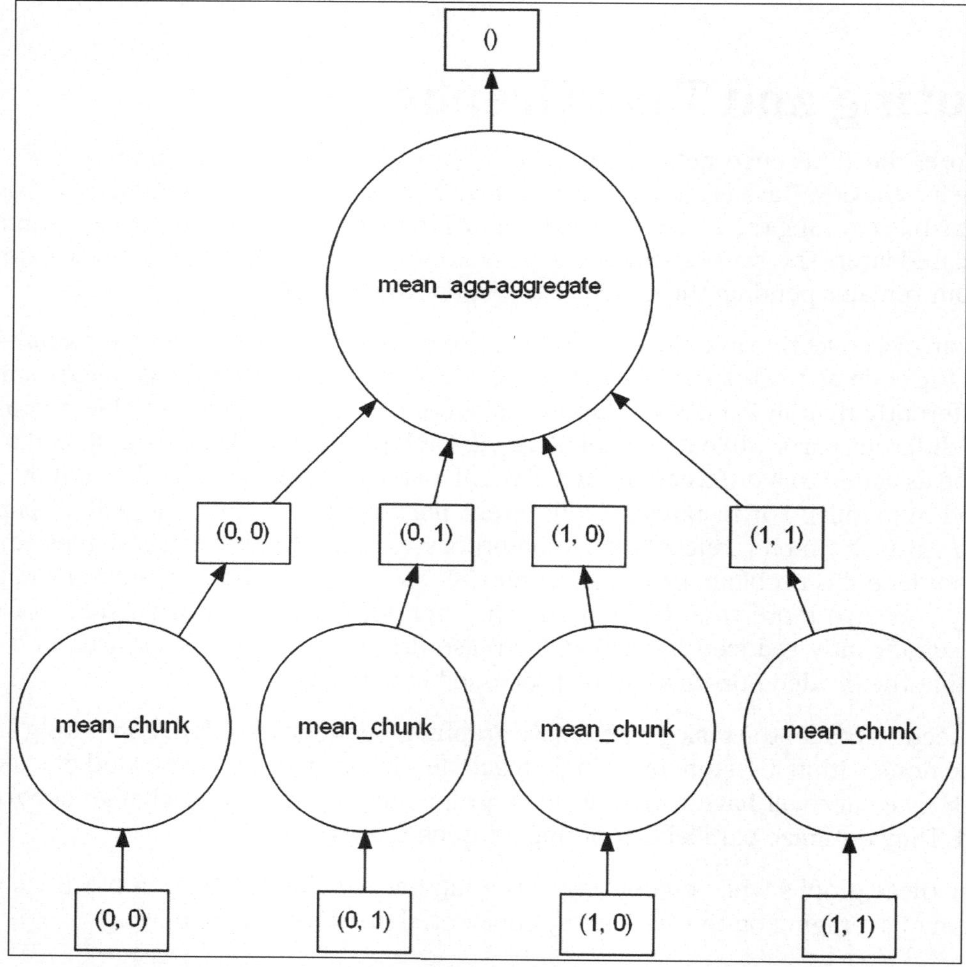

Figure 8.14: *Task Graph for Calculating the Average on the Dask Array*

As we can see, the average is calculated in parallel between the *four* portions (chunks) of the matrix. The four results from the individual tasks are then aggregated to obtain the final result.

Low-Level Interfacing with Dask Delayed

The methods provided by the Pandas and NumPy libraries which were then reproduced in the corresponding collections in Dask, can also be observed in the new methods applied to the code. But *how can we extend these new methods to parallel computing with Dask, if they have not been implemented within it?*

In this regard, Dask has a tool called **Dask Delayed**, which allows you to wrap individual functions by assigning them a task graph. These functions will be incorporated into the *low-level lazily construction mechanism* and will enter the same behavior as the methods and collections of Dask.

Practically speaking, the functions will be defined by a **`@dask.delayed`** decorator. For example, when defining a function that acts on the Dask Array and doubling all its elements, we will anticipate the following from the decorator:

```
import dask
@dask.delayed
def doubled(x):
   return 2*x
```

Therefore, if we now invoke this function, we will obtain a Dask **`Delayed`** object:

```
doubled(darr)
Delayed('doubled-5f08d4cc-aaeb-43bb-9577-7c8f055af1fd')
```

So, to perform the calculation of the function in parallel, we first invoke it by assigning the Dask Delayed to a variable and then launching the **`compute()`** method on it:

```
d = doubled(darr)
d.compute()
```

A matrix with doubled elements executed in parallel by four different tasks is thus obtained:

```
array([[ 4, 14,  6,  2,  6, 16,  2, 18,  0,  0],
       [ 0, 16,  0, 12,  6, 14, 14,  6,  8, 10],
       [ 0,  2,  4, 16, 12,  8,  6, 16, 10, 12],
       [ 2, 16,  8, 14, 16,  4,  8, 10,  2, 16],
       [ 8, 12,  8, 10, 10, 14,  8,  6, 16,  4],
       [16, 10,  6,  6, 18,  8, 10,  8,  4, 10],
       [18,  6,  2,  8,  0, 18, 10, 12, 14,  6],
       [10, 14,  2,  8, 16,  4,  4, 18,  6,  4],
       [ 2, 14, 18,  8, 14, 16, 18, 14,  4,  0],
       [12,  8,  6,  0, 12, 12, 12, 12,  8,  6]])
```

Getting Started on a Cluster of Machines

So far, we have been working with Dask on a single machine and have understood how it works, as well as its unique characteristics. Now, it is time to work on more realistic cases where you have to deal with huge datasets and run them in an environment composed of a cluster of different machines.

Kaggle Community

First, let us think about the data. As previously mentioned, there are many sites on the web that make datasets available to consult and analyze. A very interesting site to suggest is Kaggle (kaggle.com). **Kaggle** is a *web-based community* of data scientists, who primarily specialize in Machine Learning (ML). In addition to running many competitions and training courses on data analysis and the study of predictive models, Kaggle provides its visitors with many datasets spanning different topics.

Let us choose a dataset after browsing through the ones available on Kaggle. This example is based on the Russell 3000 *stock history dataset, which can be downloaded from:*

https://www.kaggle.com/datasets/williecosta/russell-3000-stock-history

It is also shown in the following figure (*Figure* 8.15):

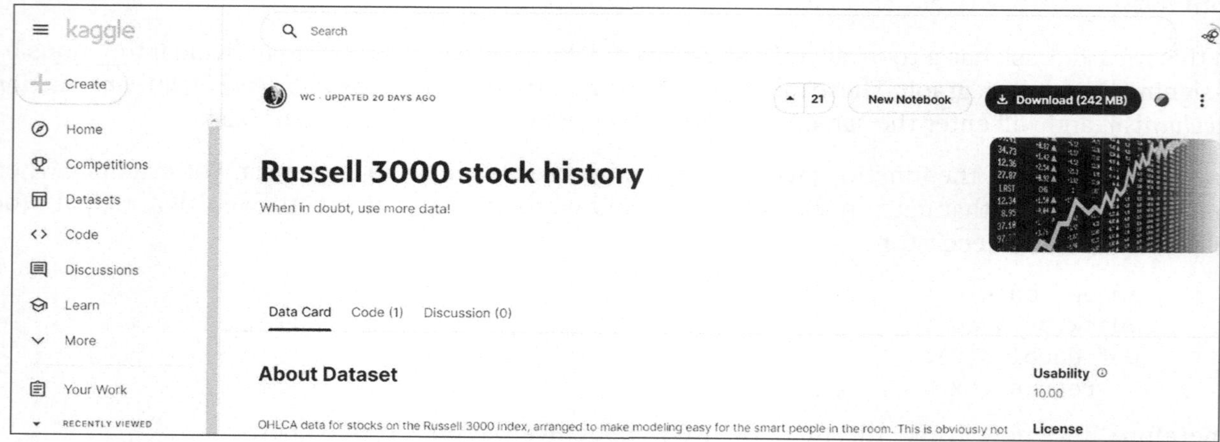

***Figure* 8.15**: *Russell 3000 Stock History Dataset in Kaggle*

From the dataset page, you can download a 242 MB **`archive.zip`** file by pressing the *black* button on the top right. Once the ZIP archive file has been downloaded, it must be decompressed. Inside, you will find a **`prices.csv`** file which occupies over 800 MB of memory, after it is extracted.

Saturn.io Cluster

There are various paid services on the web with available clusters for users to perform calculations on them. Among them is Saturn.io , which supports Dask library and offers a comfortable environment to work from. This service offers a series of data science applications that allow you to carry out distributed programming with Python and Dask, as well as specific languages like **R**, as shown in *Figure* 8.16. Furthermore, **Saturn.io** also offers online support via chat and features a series of interesting articles on Dask and other data science applications.

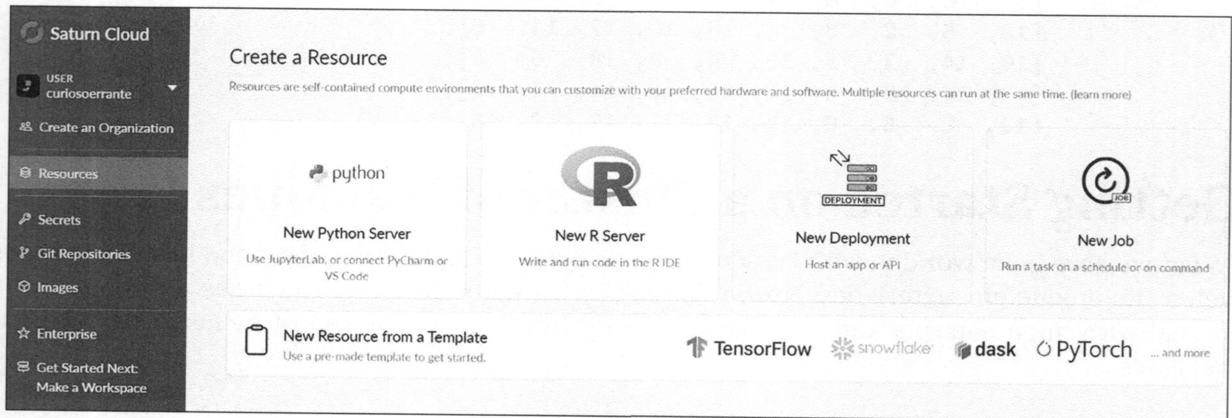

***Figure* 8.16**: *Saturn.io*

The interesting thing is that after user registration, Saturn.io offers the visitor an opportunity to configure and use a simple cluster of four machines for *free* for 30 *hours*. In this case, we have configured a system formed by a *Jupyter server*, which is directly connected to a Dask cluster composed of a *task scheduler* and *three workers*. You may select the characteristics of each machine through the options on the web page (see *Figure* 8.17).

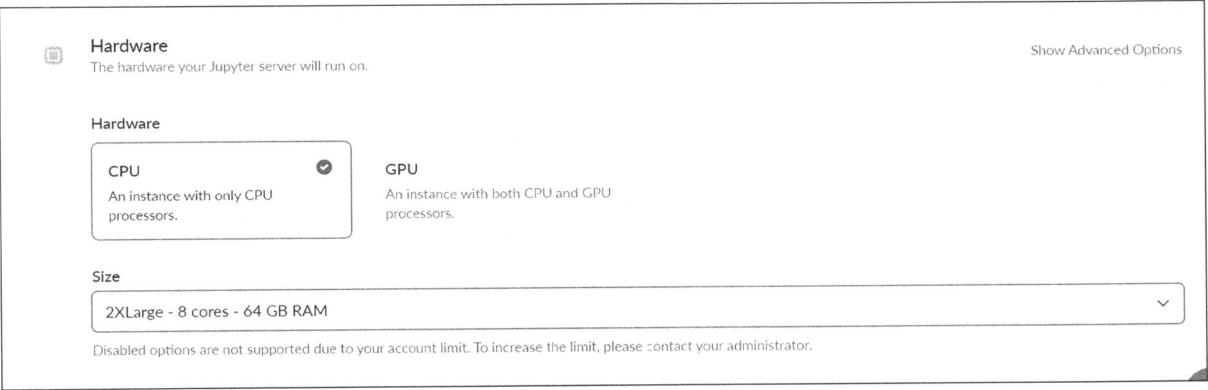

Figure 8.17: *Guided Configuration of Single Machines of the Cluster on Saturn.io*

Start all the machines after you have configured them. Press the **Start** button for the Jupyter Server and the Dask cluster. You will immediately see the startup steps for the individual machines appear in boxes that show the number of machines present in each stage, (see *Figure* 8.18). The entire *boot process* takes a few minutes.

Figure 8.18: *Startup Steps of the Machines of the Dask Cluster*

Finally, when all machines are operational, the boot steps disappear, as shown in *Figure* 8.19:

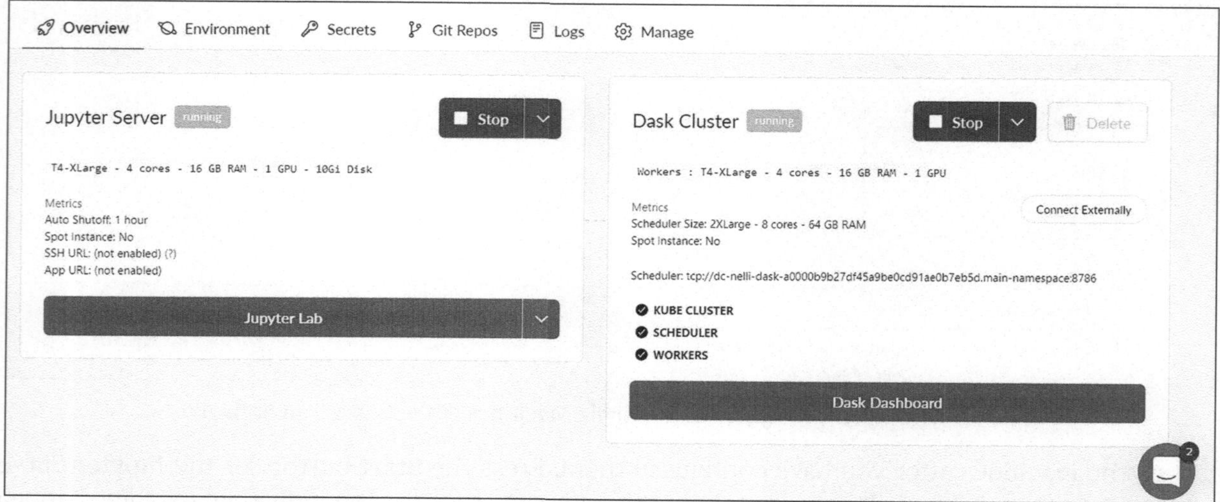

***Figure 8.19**: The Operational Dask Cluster with all Machines Started*

Uploading Data to the Cluster

Before you begin programming, you will need to upload the **`prices.csv`** data file on your system. To do this, you need to use **Jupyter Lab**. Open the application on the Jupyter server by pressing the *blue* button at the bottom and go to the Jupyter file system. Create a folder under *workspace* and then start uploading the file. Given the *size* of the file, the operation will take a few minutes. At the end of the operation, you will find an icon of the **`prices.csv`** file in the newly created directory (see *Figure* 8.20).

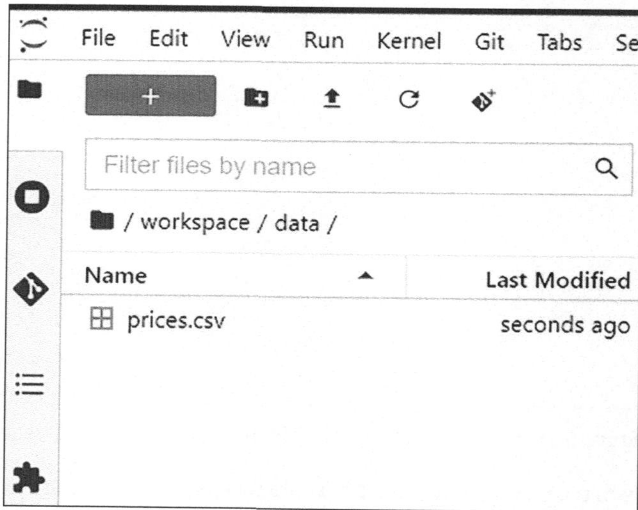

***Figure 8.20**: Uploading Dataset CSV File to Jupyter Lab*

Begin Programming the Cluster

Everything should be ready and configured to start programming. Open a new Jupyter Notebook on the Jupyter server and import the following modules:

```
from dask_saturn import SaturnCluster
from distributed import Client

cluster = SaturnCluster()
client = Client(cluster)
client
```

As we can see, these were not present in our *single-machine system*. To work in a cluster, it is necessary to import specific modules of the cluster environment on which you are working. However, they are provided by the host system already. Then, import the **SaturnCluster** class from the **dask_saturn** module and launch a cluster instance. To make Dask understand that you are not working on a single machine (default situation), you must also instantiate a client provided by the distributed module.

We are finally ready to import the libraries for data analysis. They are practically the same that are used in single-machine systems and look like as follows:

```
import dask.dataframe as dd
import pandas as pd
```

In the previous section, we uploaded the **prices.csv** file to the Jupyter Server. But the work is not yet complete. Our system includes five different machines, each with its own memory. It is therefore necessary to add the data synchronization code between the Jupyter Server and the workers to make data accessible for all machines. You can do this through the following:

```
from dask_saturn import RegisterFiles, sync_files

client.register_worker_plugin(RegisterFiles())
sync_files(client, 'data')
```

This way, all datasets imported into the Jupyter Server data folder will be accessible to all the machines in the cluster. While running this cell in Jupyter Notebook, you will notice that the operation will take several minutes to complete. At the end of the execution, you will get the situation of the file system after it is synchronized between all the machines in the cluster. The following command shows this:

```
./
./prices.csv
```

Now, we can finally import the data contained in the **prices.csv** file into a Dask DataFrame. To do this, we will write the same line of code used previously:

```
ddf = dd.read_csv('data/prices.csv')
```

The execution here will be rapid because no data has been loaded. If we look at the newly created Dask DataFrame, we will see that only the structure without data inside will have been loaded, as follows:

```
ddf
```

The obtained data structure is shown in *Figure 8.21*:

Dask DataFrame Structure:

	Unnamed: 0	symbol	date	open	high	low	close	volume	adjusted
npartitions=13									
	int64	object	object	float64	float64	float64	float64	int64	float64
	...	...	...	...	...	...	...	...	...
...	...	...	...	...	...	...	...	...	...
	...	...	...	...	...	...	...	...	...
	...	...	...	...	...	...	...	...	...

Dask Name: read-csv, 13 tasks

Figure 8.21: *Structure of the Dask DataFrame on the Cluster*

In order to load it, we have to use:

```
ddf.compute()
```

Only by invoking the **`compute()`** method will we be able to parse the data in the CSV file. In this case, however, we will get the following error message informing us of a problem with the data types:

```
ValueError: Mismatched dtypes found in `pd.read_csv`/`pd.read_table`.
```

Although Pandas and Dask use the same syntax, Dask is more demanding on the **`read_csv()`** method than its counterpart in **`pandas`**. If you try to load the CSV file with the latter, you will not get any error messages. However, in the following output text (*Figure* 8.22), the error suggests how to solve the problem:

```
+--------+---------+----------+
| Column | Found   | Expected |
+--------+---------+----------+
| volume | float64 | int64    |
+--------+---------+----------+

Usually this is due to dask's dtype inference failing, and
*may* be fixed by specifying dtypes manually by adding:

dtype={'volume': 'float64'}

to the call to `read_csv`/`read_table`.

Alternatively, provide `assume_missing=True` to interpret
all unspecified integer columns as floats.
```

Figure 8.22: *Error Message while Importing the CSV File*

We will then rewrite the **`read_csv()`** method after adding the suggested changes as follows:

```
ddf = dd.read_csv('data/prices.csv', dtype={'volume': 'float64'})
ddf.compute()
```

This time, we will get the following Dask DataFrame as shown in *Figure* 8.23:

	Unnamed: 0	symbol	date	open	high	low	close	volume	adjusted
0	1	FLWS	1999-08-03	21.7500	22.2500	17.875	18.1875	9543400.0	18.1875
1	2	FLWS	1999-08-04	18.9375	20.5000	16.875	17.0000	4731800.0	17.0000
2	3	FLWS	1999-08-05	17.0625	17.1250	13.500	16.0000	2851900.0	16.0000
3	4	FLWS	1999-08-06	16.0000	17.7500	16.000	17.0000	1411800.0	17.0000
4	5	FLWS	1999-08-09	17.9375	17.9375	15.875	16.0000	583000.0	16.0000
...	...	...	...	...	...	...	...	...	...
991985	12995441	ZUMZ	2022-11-07	22.4100	22.8800	22.020	22.6700	172900.0	22.6700
991986	12995442	ZUMZ	2022-11-08	22.8700	23.3600	22.220	22.4700	311800.0	22.4700
991987	12995443	ZUMZ	2022-11-09	22.3600	22.4300	20.640	20.7800	239800.0	20.7800
991988	12995444	ZUMZ	2022-11-10	21.8300	23.6900	21.780	23.5100	327600.0	23.5100
991989	12995445	ZUMZ	2022-11-11	23.7700	24.6200	23.670	24.2800	205000.0	24.2800

12995445 rows × 9 columns

Figure 8.23: *DataFrame Obtained from prices.csv*

Let us now see the characteristics of this DataFrame, which are mentioned here:

```
ddf.info(memory_usage="deep")
<class 'dask.dataframe.core.DataFrame'>
Columns: 9 entries, Unnamed: 0 to adjusted
dtypes: object(2), float64(6), int64(1)
memory usage: 892.3 MB
```

As we can see, the data type of the **Date** column is not **DateTime**, but an object. Also, the first column contains the indexes of the rows in the CSV file can be deleted. Then, we will rewrite:

```
ddf = dd.read_csv('data/prices.csv', dtype={'volume': 'float64'}, parse_dates =
['date'])
del ddf['Unnamed: 0']
ddf
```

At this point, the structure and data types will appear as (*Figure 8.24*):

Dask DataFrame Structure:

	symbol	date	open	high	low	close	volume	adjusted
npartitions=13								
	object	datetime64[ns]	float64	float64	float64	float64	float64	float64
	...	...	...	...	...	...	...	...
...	...	...	...	...	...	...	...	...
	...	...	...	...	...	...	...	...
	...	...	...	...	...	...	...	...

Dask Name: drop_by_shallow_copy, 26 tasks

Figure 8.24: *Data Structure of the Correct DataFrame*

It is also interesting to see how our Dask DataFrame has been automatically divided into *thirteen* partitions.

We just have to value it by using:

```
ddf.compute()
```

The desired results are shown in *Figure 8.25*:

	symbol	date	open	high	low	close	volume	adjusted
0	FLWS	1999-08-03	21.7500	22.2500	17.875	18.1875	9543400.0	18.1875
1	FLWS	1999-08-04	18.9375	20.5000	16.875	17.0000	4731800.0	17.0000
2	FLWS	1999-08-05	17.0625	17.1250	13.500	16.0000	2851900.0	16.0000
3	FLWS	1999-08-06	16.0000	17.7500	16.000	17.0000	1411800.0	17.0000
4	FLWS	1999-08-09	17.9375	17.9375	15.875	16.0000	583000.0	16.0000
...	...	...	...	...	...	...	...	...
991985	ZUMZ	2022-11-07	22.4100	22.8800	22.020	22.6700	172900.0	22.6700
991986	ZUMZ	2022-11-08	22.8700	23.3600	22.220	22.4700	311800.0	22.4700
991987	ZUMZ	2022-11-09	22.3600	22.4300	20.640	20.7800	239800.0	20.7800
991988	ZUMZ	2022-11-10	21.8300	23.6900	21.780	23.5100	327600.0	23.5100
991989	ZUMZ	2022-11-11	23.7700	24.6200	23.670	24.2800	205000.0	24.2800

12995445 rows × 8 columns

Figure 8.25: *Computed DataFrame Task*

At this point, we can apply an operation on the DataFrame. We will choose a medium complex operation that allows us to aggregate the result by grouping values on certain columns, as shown here:

```
mean = ddf.groupby(['symbol',ddf['date'].dt.year])
[['open','high','low','close','volume']].mean()
```

Since we are also interested in the performance aspect, we will introduce the word, **%%time**, which allows us to measure the time elapsed during the execution of the instructions in the cell. We will then perform the grouping operation on the Dask DataFrame:

```
%%time
mean.compute()
```

The following calculation times are obtained:

```
CPU times: user 6.23 ms, sys: 12.3 ms, total: 18.5 ms
Wall time: 2.04 s
```

We will obtain the following Dask DataFrame (see *Figure 8.26*):

		open	high	low	close	volume
symbol	**date**					
A	**1999**	33.984561	35.447962	33.226037	34.580651	5.739997e+06
	2000	49.966151	51.826004	48.017594	49.877136	4.238259e+06
	2001	23.837856	24.570816	23.174646	23.912350	3.311148e+06
	2002	16.433482	16.814270	16.050480	16.414407	3.700359e+06
	2003	14.447368	14.686315	14.223693	14.478762	3.244672e+06
...	**...**	...	...	...	...	...
ZUMZ	**2018**	23.494422	23.925498	22.961633	23.433625	4.686191e+05
	2019	26.504286	26.986825	26.019841	26.532857	4.514512e+05
	2020	27.748182	28.426561	26.997787	27.699881	3.554577e+05
	2021	44.467183	45.372540	43.545119	44.431587	2.604456e+05
	2022	32.647477	33.432982	31.858028	32.622982	3.536784e+05

53124 rows × 5 columns

Figure 8.26*: Result of Grouping on the Task DataFrame*

Now, we will perform the same operations but work locally with a **Pandas** DataFrame:

```
df = pd.read_csv('data/prices.csv', dtype={'volume': 'float64'}, parse_dates =
['date'])
del df['Unnamed: 0']
df
```

We will type this in the following cell of the notebook:

```
%%time
df.groupby(['symbol',df['date'].dt.year])[['open','high','low','close',
'volume']].mean()
```

This time, we will get the following processing times:

```
CPU times: user 1.96 s, sys: 396 ms, total: 2.35 s
Wall time: 2.35 s
```

As we can see, the execution times are much higher than in the previous case. Here we are on the order of seconds, while before with Dask, we were on the order of *milliseconds*. Things will change more as the size of the DataFrame and the complexity of the operations to be performed on it increase.

Now, let us quadruple the size of the DataFrame in question, while concatenating four copies of it together:

```
mddf = dd.concat([ddf, ddf, ddf, ddf])
mddf.info(memory_usage="deep")
mddf
```

In this way, we will get a considerably larger Dask DataFrame, as we can see from the result of the previous code and in *Figure 8.27*:

```
<class 'dask.dataframe.core.DataFrame'>
Columns: 8 entries, symbol to adjusted
dtypes: datetime64[ns](1), object(1), float64(6)
memory usage: 3.1 GB
```

Dask DataFrame Structure:

	symbol	date	open	high	low	close	volume	adjusted
npartitions=52								
	object	datetime64[ns]	float64	float64	float64	float64	float64	float64
	...	...	...	...	...	...	...	...
...	...	...	...	...	...	...	...	...
	...	...	...	...	...	...	...	...
	...	...	...	...	...	...	...	...

Dask Name: concat, 78 tasks

***Figure 8.27**: Structure of the Quadrupled DataFrame*

We will repeat the same operations performed previously:

```
mddf.compute()
mean = mddf.groupby(['symbol',mddf['date'].dt.year])
[['open','high','low','close','volume']].mean()
%%time
mean.compute()
```

This time, we will get the following result:

```
CPU times: user 15.9 ms, sys: 5.77 ms, total: 21.7 ms
Wall time: 2.92 s
```

As we can see, things have not changed much since the previous case. Now, let us pick the quadrupled DataFrame, but on **pandas**:

```
mdf = pd.concat([df, df, df, df])
mdf.info(memory_usage="deep")
mdf
%%time
mdf.groupby(['symbol',mdf['date'].dt.year])[['open','high','low','close',
'volume']].mean()
```

Here, we will get the quadrupled output without parallelization:

```
CPU times: user 7.98 s, sys: 1.39 s, total: 9.37 s
Wall time: 9.36 s
```

Performance Monitoring and Profiling

Dask provides **Dask Dashboard**, which is an effective tool to visualize CPU load, memory and worker usage in real-time. The dashboard allows you to easily identify tasks that are causing overloads or slowdowns. To use this tool, you need to have the bokeh module installed. To install it, use the following command on Anaconda:

```
conda install bokeh
```

You can also do it via:

```
pip install bokeh
```

The following will be displayed after activation:

```
from dask.distributed import Client

client = Client()
```

Once the preceding snippet is executed, the Dashboard will be activated and can be accessed from http://localhost:8787/status (see *Figure* 8.28).

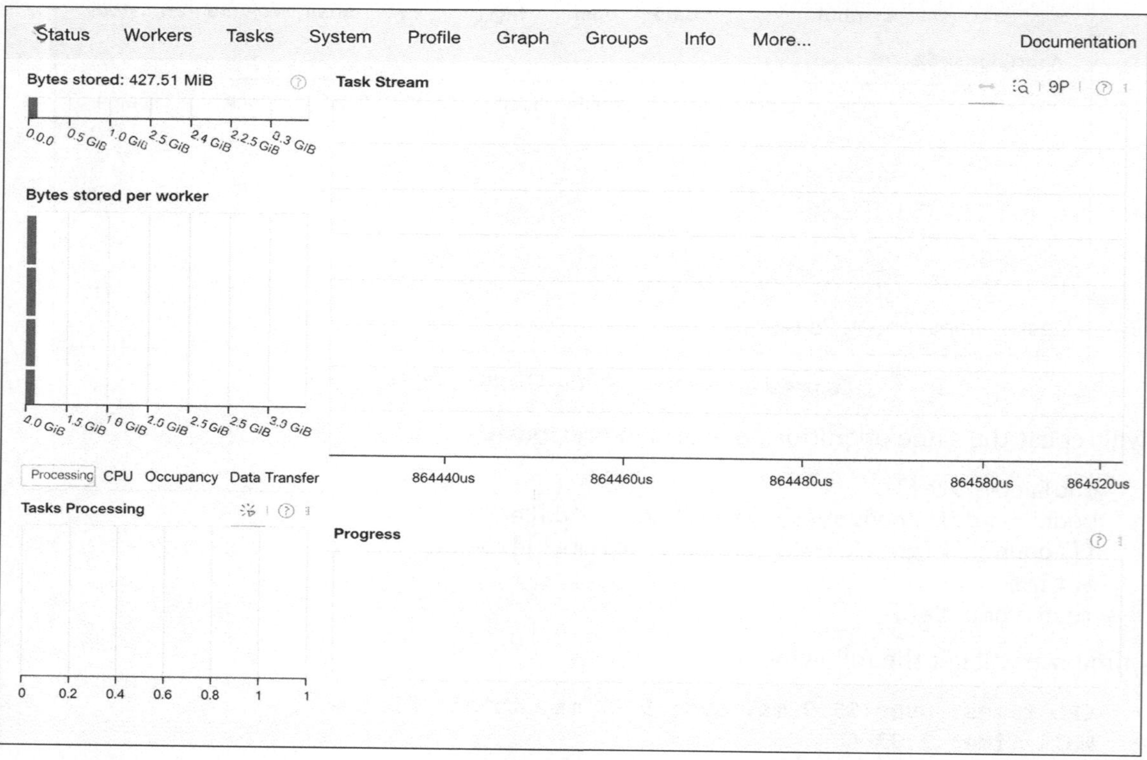

Figure 8.28: *Dask Dashboard*

To close or stop the service, you can execute:

```
client.close()
```

However, for proper use of this tool, it is suggested to visit the official page (`https://docs.dask.org/en/latest/dashboard.html`) As for profiling, the system generates performance reports that offer a detailed overview of the use of resources, memory and time spent in each task. Also, in this case, the generation of these reports occurs programmatically. Let us see a practical example:

```
import dask.dataframe as dd
import pandas as pd
import numpy as np
```

```
from dask.distributed import Client, performance_report
client = Client()
print(client)

np.random.seed(42)
data = pd.DataFrame({
    "user_id": np.random.randint(1, 1000, size=10_000_000),
    "category": np.random.choice(["Groceries","Electronics","Clothing",
"Books"], size=10_000_000),
    "amount": np.random.uniform(1.0, 500.0, size=10_000_000),
    "timestamp": pd.date_range("2023-01-01", periods=10_000_000, freq="s"),
})

future = client.scatter(data)
dask_df = dd.from_delayed(future)

with performance_report(filename="dask-performance-report.html"):
    summary = dask_df["amount"].describe().compute()
    category_distribution = dask_df.groupby("category")["amount"].sum().
compute()
    top_users = (
        dask_df.groupby("user_id")["amount"]
        .sum()
        .nlargest(5)
        .compute()
    )

print("Global statistics")
print(summary)
print("\nTransaction Distribution by category:")
print(category_distribution)
print("\nTop 5 users for transaction volume:")
print(top_users)
```

By running the program, we will get the following output:

```
<Client: 'tcp://127.0.0.1:50542' processes=4 threads=12, memory=15.69 GiB>
Global statistics
count 1.000000e+07
mean 2.505660e+02
std 1.440138e+02
min 1.000099e+00
25% 1.258837e+02
50% 2.506361e+02
75% 3.752849e+02
max 4.999999e+02
Name: amount, dtype: float64

Transaction Distribution by category:
category
Books          6.261710e+08
Clothing       6.263339e+08
Electronics    6.262630e+08
Groceries      6.268920e+08
Name: amount, dtype: float64

Top 5 users for transaction volume:
user_id
```

```
222    2.630110e+06
601    2.602268e+06
2      2.588972e+06
917    2.588517e+06
379    2.588414e+06
Name: amount, dtype: float64
```

Additionally, **performance_report** will generate an HTML file in the working directory called **dask-performance-report.html**, which will contain information about the scheduler and tasks, and the execution time (see *Figure* 8.29).

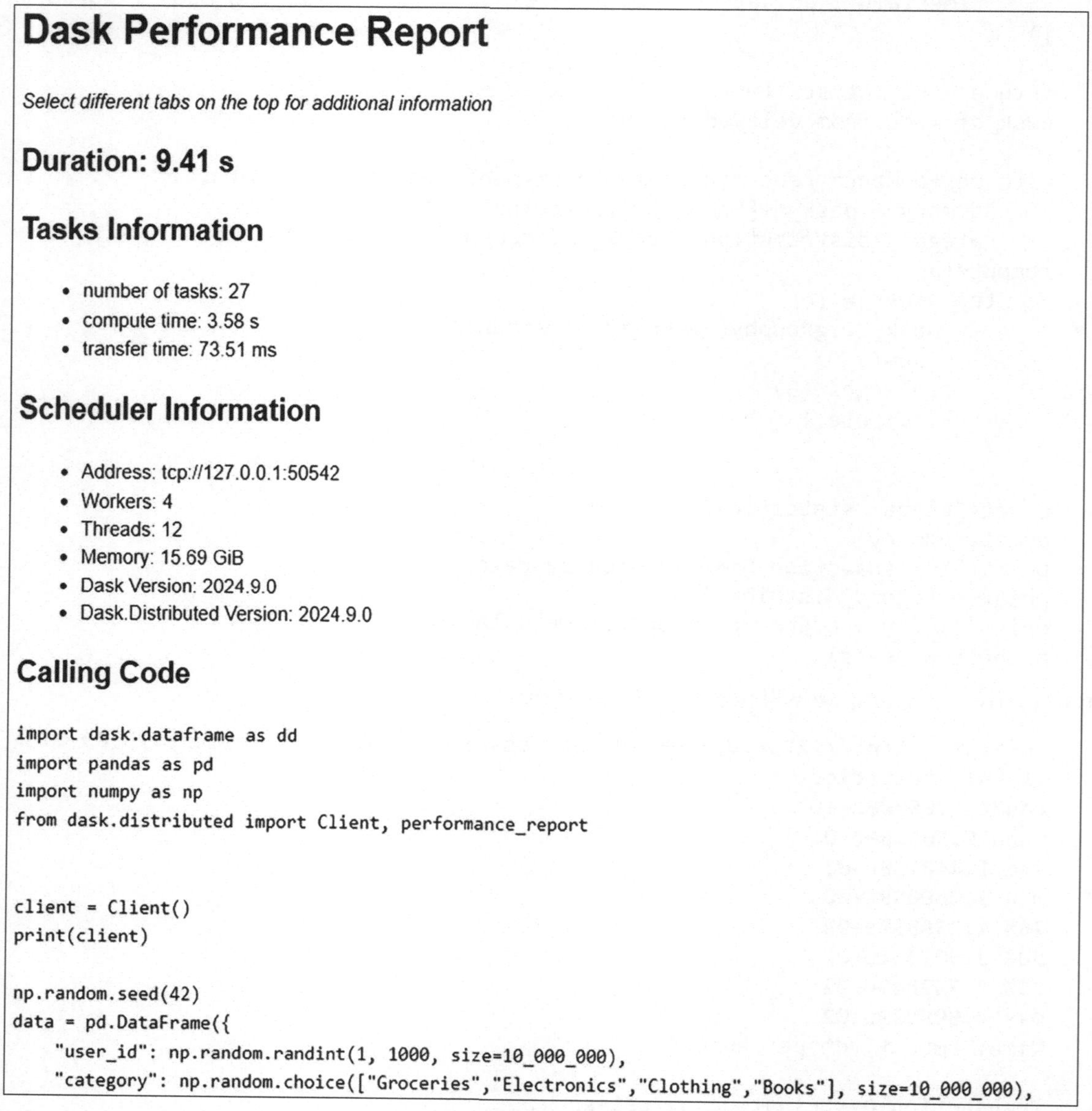

Dask Performance Report

Select different tabs on the top for additional information

Duration: 9.41 s

Tasks Information

- number of tasks: 27
- compute time: 3.58 s
- transfer time: 73.51 ms

Scheduler Information

- Address: tcp://127.0.0.1:50542
- Workers: 4
- Threads: 12
- Memory: 15.69 GiB
- Dask Version: 2024.9.0
- Dask.Distributed Version: 2024.9.0

Calling Code

```
import dask.dataframe as dd
import pandas as pd
import numpy as np
from dask.distributed import Client, performance_report


client = Client()
print(client)

np.random.seed(42)
data = pd.DataFrame({
    "user_id": np.random.randint(1, 1000, size=10_000_000),
    "category": np.random.choice(["Groceries","Electronics","Clothing","Books"], size=10_000_000),
```

Figure 8.29: *Dask Performance Report*

Advanced Performance Optimization Strategies with Dask

Now that we have seen how to monitor in detail the performance of individual Dask components through the dashboard and a reporting system, we can formulate a series of strategies to optimize them. Dask offers many features for parallel computing on clusters and multi-core systems, but obtaining maximum performance requires targeted optimization, especially for large datasets and complex tasks. This section will explore some advanced strategies to optimize the efficiency of Dask in production environments, while paying attention to each level of operability and focusing on the configuration of the various components involved. Some of these strategies are:

- Memory Optimization
- Data Persistence and Cache
- Data Chunk Size
- Task Merging
- Configuring Workers and Their Threads
- Configuring the Task Queue

Memory optimization is essential to keep Dask performing, especially while processing large data. Efficient memory management reduces the risk of overload and makes task completion faster. For example, by applying filter and data reduction operations in advance, and eliminating data that is not necessary for calculation, you can reduce the memory footprint. In this sense, it will be sufficient to apply the classic operations that are performed with the Pandas library like column selections (`df[['col1', 'col2']]`) and data filter applications (for example, `df[df['col'] > value]`) to limit the size of the dataset. Another technique to reduce memory consumption is with data typing, which reduces the size of variables by appropriately typing columns (for example, converting `float64` to `float32`). This can significantly reduce memory usage.

```
import dask
import dask.dataframe as dd
import pandas as pd
import numpy as np

n_rows = 10_000_000
data = {
    'int_column': np.random.randint(0,100, size=n_rows),
    'float_column': np.random.random(size=n_rows)* 100,
    'category_column': np.random.choice(['A','B','C','D'], size=n_rows),
    'string_column': np.random.choice(['lorem','ipsum','dolor','sit','amet'],
size=n_rows)
}
pandas_df = pd.DataFrame(data)
dask_df = dd.from_pandas(pandas_df, npartitions=10)
print("Original memory usage (Pandas):")
print(pandas_df.memory_usage(deep=True).sum() / 1e6, "MB")

#Memory optimization with typification
dask_df['int_column' ] = dask_df['int_column'].astype('int8')
dask_df['float_column'] = dask_df['float_column'].astype('float32')
dask_df['category_column'] = dask_df['category_column'].astype('category')

optimized_df = dask_df.compute()
print("Optimized memory usage (Pandas):")
print(optimized_df.memory_usage(deep=True).sum() / 1e6, "MB")

#Filtering optimization
filtered_df = dask_df[dask_df['float_column'] > 50].compute()
print("First 5 rows of filtered DataFrame:")
print(filtered_df.head())
```

To perform this test, we will first generate a DataFrame with 10 million rows and columns of various data types (int, float, string, and category). When converting to a Dask system, the Pandas DataFrame is divided into 10 parts. This will allow us to process the data in parallel, while improving performance with a distributed system. With the **memory_usage** method, we can evaluate the memory consumption of both the original and the optimized Dask DataFrame. To include memory usage for objects such as strings, we will add the **deep=True** option. Now, we will apply the two types of optimization. For typing, we can convert the integers from int64 (the default type) and convert it to int8, which will reduce memory consumption by 8 times. The same approach can be applied to **float64**, which we can convert to **float32**. This will also reduce the necessary memory by half. Also, since we have exploited the possibility of converting strings into category types that store numeric values internally, we will be able to significantly reduce the memory requirement. To make these codes effective, we will call the compute function. Finally, we will see the two different memory values as outputs.

By running this code, we will optimize the memory with a significant decrease in usage, as shown here:

```
Original memory usage (Pandas):
1153.99782 MB
Optimized memory usage (Pandas):
183.998029 MB
First 5 rows of filtered DataFrame:
  int_column  float_column category_column string_column
0          55     97.613930               D          amet
1          48     88.902390               C          amet
8          44     63.017277               C         lorem
9          14     60.553314               B         lorem
11         28     80.695457               B          amet
```

Another important approach in the optimization process is the manual use of Garbage Collection. Dask does not automatically initiate garbage collection between tasks. You can force garbage collection manually with **gc.collect()** between intensive tasks, which will free up unused memory.

Data persistence and cache is another strategy that can be applied to increase the performance of distributed computing in systems like Dask. This allows us to avoid data recalculation and improve the responsiveness of the pipeline. In this regard, the persist() function allows you to keep the results of a task in memory, while avoiding recalculation when these are reused in subsequent tasks. This practice is instrumental for frequently used intermediate data. To understand this strategy, let us see another example:

```
import dask
import dask.dataframe as dd
import pandas as pd
import numpy as np
import time

n_rows = 10_000_000
data = {
    'id': np.arange(n_rows),
    'value': np.random.random(n_rows)* 100,
    'category_column': np.random.choice(['A','B','C','D'], n_rows)
}
pandas_df = pd.DataFrame(data)
dask_df = dd.from_pandas(pandas_df, npartitions=10)

# Without persist()
start_time = time.time()
filtered_df = dask_df[dask_df['value']>50]
mean_without_persist = filtered_df['value'].mean().compute()
```

```
count_without_persist = filtered_df['value'].count().compute()
end_time = time.time()
time_without_persist = end_time - start_time
print(f"Mean without persist(): {mean_without_persist}")
print(f"Count without persist(): {count_without_persist}")
print(f"Time without persist(): {time_without_persist}")
# With persist()
start_time = time.time()
persisted_df = filtered_df.persist()
mean_with_persist = persisted_df['value'].mean().compute()
count_with_persist = persisted_df['value'].count().compute()
end_time = time.time()
time_with_persist = end_time - start_time
print(f"Mean with persist(): {mean_with_persist}")
print(f"Count with persist(): {count_with_persist}")
print(f"Time with persist(): {time_with_persist}")

print(f"Number of partitions after persist(): {persisted_df.npartitions}")
```

In this example, we will generate a synthetic dataset with 10 million rows. The columns will include a numeric ID (**int**), a random value (**float**), and a category (**string**). When switching from Pandas to Dask, the DataFrame will be divided into 10 partitions to take leverage parallelism of the distributed system. First, we apply a complex operation without using persist: we filter the rows where the **value** exceeds 50 and calculate their average. With this type of processing, at each calculation, we will reload the data and construct the partitions again. Then, we will perform the same operations, this time via the persist method. In this case, the subsequent operations (**mean** and **count**) are performed directly on the dataset that are already loaded into memory. Doing so helps us avoid recalculations and improves performance. By running this code, we will obtain a result that meets expectations and is faster at performing the operations on the dataset where **persist** is used.

```
Mean without persist(): 74.9972018740045
Count without persist(): 5001671
Time without persist(): 1.0948090553283691
Mean with persist(): 74.9972018740045
Count with persist(): 5001671
Time with persist(): 0.6098389625549316
Number of partitions after persist(): 10
```

Here, we see that Dask demonstrates lazy behavior while executing. Therefore, we will use the **compute()** function only when it is absolutely necessary. If used too frequently, the task optimization features are lost. Dask performs the computation in a lazy way and builds a task graph to optimize the execution order. By calling **compute()** too early, not only will we lose the optimization aspect, but might also risk overloading the system since this process consumes resources in its own way. Another strategy can be enacted at the level of data subdivision and distribution. Determining the **optimal size data chunk** balances memory use and computation efficiency. Chunks that are too small can increase the system overhead, while chunks that are too large could slow down tasks. As a rule, chunks of around 100 MB represent a good balance, but it is important to alter their size based on the specific workload.

```
import dask
import dask.dataframe as dd
import pandas as pd
import numpy as np
import time

n_rows = 10_000_000
data = {
    'id': np.arange(n_rows),
```

```
    'value': np.random.random(n_rows)* 100,
    'category_column': np.random.choice(['A','B','C','D'], n_rows)
}
pandas_df = pd.DataFrame(data)
dask_df_small_chunks = dd.from_pandas(pandas_df, npartitions=1000)
dask_df_large_chunks = dd.from_pandas(pandas_df, npartitions=1)
chunk_size_mb = 100
rows_per_partition = int((chunk_size_mb * 1e6) / pandas_df.memory_usage(deep-
=True).sum() * len(pandas_df))
n_partitions = max(1, len(pandas_df) // rows_per_partition)
dask_df_optimal_chunks = dd.from_pandas(pandas_df, npartitions=n_partitions)

# Time measuring for each configuration
def measure_performance(dask_df, label):
    start_time = time.time()
    mean = dask_df['value'].mean().compute()
    end_time = time.time()
    elapsed_time = end_time - start_time
    print(f"{label}: Media = {mean:.2f}, Time =  {elapsed_time:.2f} sec. Par-
titions = {dask_df.npartitions}")

print("\n=== Performance ===")
measure_performance(dask_df_small_chunks, "Too small chunks")
measure_performance(dask_df_large_chunks, "Too large chunks")
measure_performance(dask_df_optimal_chunks, "Optimal chunks")
```

By running the code here, we can verify the previous results and choose large chunks instead of smaller ones.

```
=== Performance ===
Too small chunks: Media = 49.99, Time =  2.22 sec. Partitions = 1000
Too large chunks: Media = 49.99, Time =  0.54 sec. Partitions = 1
Optimal chunks: Media = 49.99, Time =  0.52 sec. Partitions = 6
```

Tasks are another level where you can increase performance. **Task merging** can be considered as a strategy when tasks are too granular. Dask offers the ability to "**merge**" redundant tasks, while reducing the task management overhead. Functions like **map_partitions** on DataFrame and rechunk on `Array` can consolidate tasks. Again, we will walk through an example that demonstrates both cases, while showing the performance gains in Dask when we use them:

```
import dask
import dask.dataframe as dd
import dask.array as da
import pandas as pd
import numpy as np
import time

n_rows = 10_000_000
data = {
    'id': np.arange(n_rows),
    'value': np.random.random(n_rows)* 100,
    'category_column': np.random.choice(['A','B','C','D'], n_rows)
}
pandas_df = pd.DataFrame(data)
dask_df = dd.from_pandas(pandas_df, npartitions=10)

def add_squared_column(df):
    df['value_squared'] = df['value'] ** 2
    return df
```

```
# without map_partitions
dask_df_no_optimization = dask_df.assign(value_squared=dask_df['value'] ** 2)
start_time = time.time()
mean_no_optimization = dask_df_no_optimization['value_squared'].mean().compute()
end_time = time.time()
print(f"Squared mean without map_partitions: {mean_no_optimization:.2f}")
print(f"Time without map_partitions: {end_time - start_time:.2f} sec")

# with map_partitions
optimized_df = dask_df.map_partitions(add_squared_column)
persisted_df = optimized_df.persist()
start_time = time.time()
mean_squared = persisted_df['value_squared'].mean().compute()
end_time = time.time()
print(f"Squared mean with map_partitions: {mean_squared:.2f}")
print(f"Time with map_partitions: {end_time - start_time:.2f} sec")

dask_array = da.random.random((10_000, 10_000), chunks=(100,100))
print(f"Number of initial chunks: {dask_array.numblocks}")
# without rechunk
start_time = time.time()
sum_no_rechunk = dask_array.sum().compute()
end_time = time.time()
print(f"Sum of values without rechunk: {sum_no_rechunk:.2f}")
print(f"Time without rechunk: {end_time - start_time:.2f} sec")

# with rechunk
rechunked_array = dask_array.rechunk((1000,1000))
print(f"Number of chunks after rechunk: {rechunked_array.numblocks}")
start_time = time.time()
array_sum = rechunked_array.sum().compute()
end_time = time.time()
print(f"Sum of values: {array_sum:.2f}")
print(f"Time with rechunk: {end_time - start_time:.2f} sec")
```

After creating the classic synthetic dataset (same as the previous examples), we will analyze the efficiency contributions separately by merging tasks with both **map_partitions** and rechunk. We will define a function called **add_squared_column** to calculate the square of the values in a column of the DataFrame, while adding the results in a new column called **value_squared**. In this case, we will directly apply the **map_partitions** function to each partition without fragmenting the tasks any further. This operation should reduce the computational overhead instead of using more granular operations. In the second part, we will define an array with chunks that are too small to create more tasks. This is where rechunk comes in. It resizes the chunks to 1000×1000 and reduces the tasks that need to be managed. This should improve efficiency when applying operations such as sum. By running the code, we will also obtain a result that highlights the increase in efficiency in both cases (**map_partitions** and **rechunk**).

```
Squared mean without map_partitions: 3332.15
Time without map_partitions: 0.56 sec
Squared mean with map_partitions: 3332.15
Time with map_partitions: 0.02 sec
Number of initial chunks: (100, 100)
Sum of values without rechunk: 50002269.76
Time without rechunk: 3.79 sec
Number of chunks after rechunk: (10, 10)
Sum of values: 50002269.76
Time with rechunk: 2.79 sec
```

Workers can also be configured and managed optimally. A proper **configuration of workers** based on system resources reduces execution times and improves the overall efficiency of the cluster. The same goes for the **number of threads per worker**. When optimizing, a good strategy will be to configure **nthreads** per worker and balance the number of CPUs and the memory available for each worker. For example, on a system with 32 cores, it is possible to configure 8 workers with 4 threads each to maximize parallelism without overloading the CPU. This is shown as follows:

```
from dask.distributed import Client
client = Client(n_workers=8, threads_per_worker=4)
```

A particular attention in the optimization phase will be to study the **configuration of the task queue**. Several bottlenecks can emerge here, which, despite the optimizations made previously, would not have evident effects. A solution could be to increase the maximum length of the queue to ensure that workers do not remain inactive.

So far, we have illustrated the most evident and essential strategies that act on the different components of the distributed system by modifying their configuration through code. However, other unrelated factors can come into play, as they are often connected to other technologies. In distributed clusters, the latency of communication between nodes can become a significant bottleneck and necessitates acting in a circumstantial and defined manner in the cases and architectures used. In such cases, we can try limiting communication between workers as much as possible with technologies that compress the exchanged data and optimize the network. It is clear that these paths require knowledge and access to systems that often go beyond that of the programmer or the data scientist responsible for the calculation.

GPU Parallelization in Dask: Dask-CUDA and RAPIDS Ecosystem (Only Linux)

We have already seen that GPUs play a key role in intensive computation, thanks to their highly scalable parallel architecture. Dask, as an extremely powerful and versatile distributed system, supports GPU parallelization, which allows you to leverage the power of GPUs and accelerate data science operations on large datasets. This can be a great choice for computationally intensive applications such as ML training, large matrix computation, and extremely complex data processing. Dask's ability to integrate GPU processing allows you to scale your applications across multi-GPU infrastructures and distributed GPU clusters with supported libraries such as:

- **CuPy**: A library for numerical computation on GPUs that replicates the NumPy API and allows operations to be performed on large arrays
- **RAPIDS** and **cuDF**: A DataFrame management library that replicates the Pandas API and is optimized for GPU processing
- **PyTorch** and **TensorFlow**: Dask allows you to distribute ML tasks on GPUs using libraries like PyTorch and TensorFlow for distributed training and inference.

To integrate GPUs in the Dask distributed computing system, the Dask-CUDA has been implemented. This is an extension of Dask designed to integrate GPUs in local or distributed clusters by providing specific tools to configure clusters that automatically balance the load between multiple GPUs on one or more nodes. More specifically, the GPU load is managed automatically by distributing resources to balance tasks between the available cards. It also uses CUDA Unified Memory to manage datasets that exceed the available GPU memory. Another important feature is its ability to use GPU-specific libraries such as cuDF, cuML and cuGraph to speed up operations similar to those performed by Pandas and Scikit-learn on non-distributed systems. Furthermore, thanks to Dask being a distributed computing system, Dask-CUDA can facilitate the configuration, and use of GPU clusters on multiple machines.

RAPIDS is an ecosystem of GPU-accelerated libraries that offer tools similar to Pandas (cuDF), NumPy (cuPy), Scikit-learn (cuML), and more. Dask can integrate seamlessly with these libraries, while allowing you to leverage distributed computing directly on GPUs.

If you want to work with this extension on an Anaconda system (recommended), you may access a ready virtual environment. First, visit the RAPIDS installation guide page (**`https://docs.rapids.ai/install/`**). Here, you will find a selector tool to select the system configuration you wish to install (see *Figure* 8.30). This ecosystem has been implemented for Linux systems. As far as Windows is concerned, you might encounter numerous problems while loading the modules.

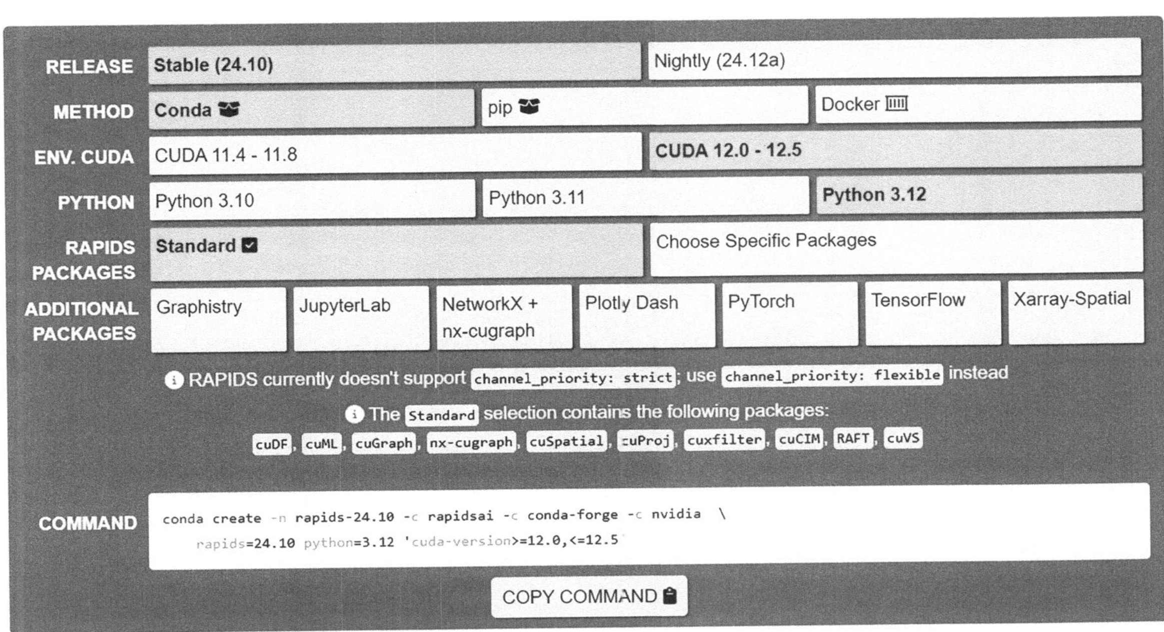

***Figure 8.30**: Interactive Window for Installing the Right RAPIDS Configuration on Anaconda*

Depending on your choices, a command for **conda** will be displayed below with a series of options that are compatible with your choice of the RAPIDS ecosystem. This is shown as follows:

```
conda create -n rapids-env -c rapidsai -c conda-forge \
  -c nvidia rapids=23-10 python=3.9 dask-cuda dask \
   numba jupyterlab -y
```

Once the installation of the virtual environment is complete, you can always activate it within conda through:

```
conda activate rapids-env
```

In Saturn Cloud, it is possible to use GPU for calculation in the Jupyter Lab server (for at least 30 working hours), all for free.

This installation will allow you to work independently on an isolated virtual system and autonomously manage the update of individual modules. It will not interfere in any way with the pre-selected Python module system. Dask-CUDA, **Numba** (for NVIDIA GPUs), and many essential packages of the RAPIDS ecosystem will already be loaded and will be available for use (**`cuDF`**, **`cuML`**, **`cuGraph`**).

An easier way is to create a single Jupiter Lab machine with Dask on Saturn Cloud (as shown in *Figure* 8.31) by installing other necessary packages, besides the basic configuration. These are shown here:

```
conda install conda-forge::dask-cuda
conda install rapidsai::dask-cudf
conda install rapidsai::cuml
conda install rapidsai::cugraph
```

```
* For CUDA 11, run:     conda install cudatoolkit cuda-version=11

* For CUDA 12, run:     conda install cuda-cudart cuda-version=12
```

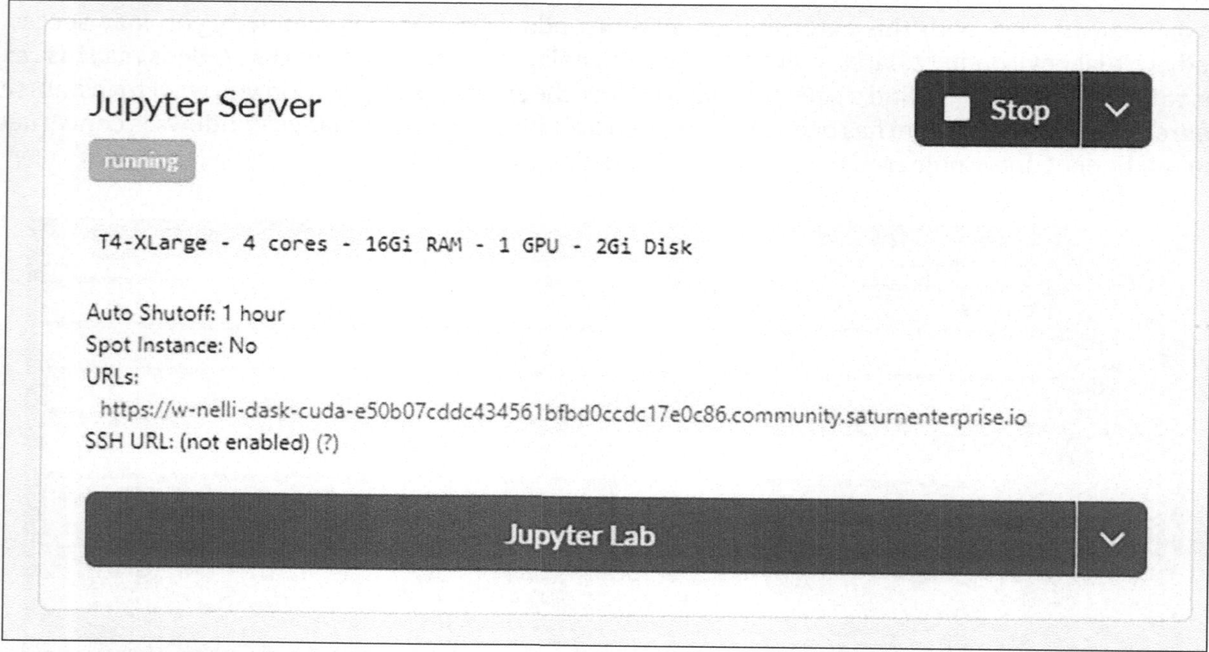

Figure 8.31: *Creating a Machine on Saturn Cloud with Necessary CPU and GPU Features*

To begin testing how Dask-CUDA and the RAPIDS ecosystem function, it is good to start working on a single machine with a GPU. This is an easily available system. If the reader wants to move on to real cases, they can extend what has been written here to get real access to the computing power of these systems (you can use paid cluster systems such as Saturncloud.io as seen previously. However, this is not available in the free version).

For example, cuDF with Dask-DataFrames allows you to work on large datasets in a parallel as well as distributed manner via GPUs. This is shown as follows:

```
import dask_cudf
import cudf
import numpy as np

n_rows = 1_000_000
data = {
    'value': np.random.random(n_rows) * 200,
    'category': np.random.choice(['A','B','C','D'], size=n_rows)
}
cudf_df = cudf.DataFrame(data)
df = dask_cudf.from_cudf(cudf_df, npartitions=10)
result = df[df['value'] > 100].groupby('category').mean()
print(result.compute())
```

Running the code gives the following result:

```
               value
category
A         149.885822
C         149.934240
B         149.881685
D         150.036930
```

This program first creates a dataset with a value column containing random numbers between 0 and 200, and a second category column that contains 4 random categories (A, B, C, D). The data is converted into a cuDF DataFrame, which is managed directly on a GPU. Then the DataFrame is split into 10 partitions and becomes a Dask-cudf Dataframe which allows for possible distributed processing between different GPUs. A filter is applied for rows with a value greater than 100. Finally, the computation is made effective by calling compute (lazy behavior).

Let us now talk about cuPy which is the equivalent of NumPy and extends its functionality directly to the GPUs. Here is a case where we can extend a Dask-Array to parallel GPU computation:

```
import dask.array as da
import cupy

x = da.random.random((10000,10000), chunks=(10000,10000)).map_blocks(cupy.
asarray)
y = x.dot(x.T)
result = y.compute()
print(result)
```

Looking at the code, we can see that we first generated a Dask-Array partitioned with **da.random.random** and mapped it into a CuPy array using **map_blocks(cupy.asarray)**. For computation, we will perform a scalar product of the newly generated array using **x.dot(x.T)** with GPU power. Executing the code will fetch you the following output:

```
[[3325.77865061 2534.40894497 2512.08573368 ... 2467.14293341
  2494.17758074 2529.18841799]
 [2534.40894497 3400.02678094 2543.33501092 ... 2507.91058194
  2520.25192682 2554.50193896]
 [2512.08573368 2543.33501092 3376.16001999 ... 2487.8169569
  2502.64706085 2530.56134704]
 ...
 [2467.14293341 2507.91058194 2487.8169569  ... 3266.98698995
  2446.93950787 2480.77823313]
 [2494.17758074 2520.25192682 2502.64706085 ... 2446.93950787
  3318.12449719 2512.52872237]
 [2529.18841799 2554.50193896 2530.56134704 ... 2480.77823313
  2512.52872237 3375.29084078]]
```

Even though we have only touched upon the features and potential of using Dask-CUDA and the RAPIDS ecosystem, it is clear that this is a powerful solution for distributed and GPU-accelerated computing. The ability to scale across multiple GPUs, both locally and in a distributed cluster, allows for tackling compute-intensive problems with unprecedented performance. Applications such as neural network-based ML, Big Data analytics, and scientific simulations gain a significant advantage this way. We invite the reader to explore this technology and explore the potential of using GPUs in a distributed system managed by Dask.

```
from dask_cuda import LocalCUDACluster
from dask.distributed import Client
import dask_cudf
import cudf
import cuml
import cugraph

# Dask-CUDA configuration
cluster = LocalCUDACluster()
client = Client(cluster)
print(client)
```

```
# Synthetic Dataset with loading in GPU
import numpy as np
data = {
    'customer_id': np.arange(1000),
    'transaction_value': np.random.uniform(10, 1000, size=1000),
    'transaction_count': np.random.randint(1, 100, size=1000),
}
# cuDf Dataframe
df = dask_cudf.from_cudf(cudf.DataFrame(data), npartitions=2)
filtered_df = df[df['transaction_value'] > 500]
print("Filtered Dataframe:")
print(filtered_df.compute())

#Clustering with cuML
from cuml.cluster import KMeans
kmeans = KMeans(n_clusters=3)
features = filtered_df[['transaction_value', 'transaction_count']].compute()
clusters = kmeans.fit_predict(features)
print("Assigned Clusters:")
print(clusters)

# Graph Analysis with cuGrph
edges = cudf.DataFrame({
    'src': np.random.randint(0, 1000, size=500),
    'dst': np.random.randint(0, 1000, size=500)
})
G = cugraph.Graph()
G.from_cudf_edgelist(edges, source='src', destination='dst')
pagerank = cugraph.pagerank(G)
print("Top 5 customers: ")
print(pagerank.sort_values('pagerank', ascending=False).head(5))
```

Running the code will give you the following result:

```
<Client: 'tcp://127.0.0.1:33195' processes=1 threads=1, memory=15.32 GiB>
Filtered Dataframe:
     customer_id  transaction_value  transaction_count
4              4         552.245006                 19
5              5         681.313781                 58
6              6         787.907235                 72
10            10         595.738462                 45
11            11         712.454780                 23
..           ...                ...                ...
993          993         663.097328                  8
994          994         841.045325                 88
995          995         885.501882                 26
996          996         938.861271                 45
999          999         903.206444                 64

[503 rows x 3 columns]
Assigned Clusters:
0      2
1      0
2      0
3      2
4      0
      ..
498    0
```

```
499    1
500    1
501    1
502    1
Length: 503, dtype: int32
Top 5 customers:
    vertex  pagerank
0       56  0.004496
2      694  0.003671
1      560  0.003587
14     415  0.003482
8      192  0.003472
```

Conclusion

In this chapter, we have seen how you can extend the computing capabilities of data science via systems distributed as clusters using the Dask library. It is possible to scale our code built with Pandas from a single-machine system to distributed systems. You have also seen how clusters on the web offer specific services that allow you to work through Jupyter Notebook on codes which use the Dask library. Through some practical examples, you have become familiar with these environments and how they perform better than a single machine, further allowing us to approach Big Data. In the next chapter, we will extend these concepts to **Artificial Intelligence** (**AI**), especially branches like ML and *Deep Learning* (DL) with *neural networks* that are gaining ground due to parallel computing on distributed systems.

References

- https://saturncloud.io/blog/what-is-dask/
- https://saturncloud.io/blog/should-i-use-dask/

CHAPTER 9
Parallel Computing for Artificial Intelligence

Introduction

With this chapter, we will conclude our journey of learning about parallel computing applications by closing with the last topic, which is **Artificial Intelligence (AI)**. This discipline deals with the development of applications that can simulate human intelligence. It is a complex objective that requires enormous studies and powerful technologies. However, in recent years, it has been making great strides. Among all the possible applications of AI is **Machine Learning (ML)**, which focuses on the simulation of human learning. ML has found its most representative programming language in Python, which has a series of well-stocked libraries of algorithms and pre-set models, such as **sci-kit-learn**. Even more advanced is **Deep Learning (DL)**, which is a subgroup of ML characterized by the use of artificial neural networks that can help in creating applications capable of recognizing information and analyzing data like images, sounds and texts. All these disciplines require a huge computational effort to process complex algorithms and data that is necessary for their learning phase. The use of parallel computing is therefore necessary with the integration of GPUs, as it significantly reduces processing times. Furthermore, it is proposed that these strategies should be used for processing on distributed systems, like clusters of computers equipped with GPUs, through the **Dask framework**. We will therefore see a series of examples that will address these cases, while providing basic ideas about how to approach these systems. For those wishing to learn more, it will offer a basis on which you can start working.

Structure

This chapter addresses the following topics:

- AI and Parallel Computing
- Parallel and Distributed Machine Learning
- Parallel and Distributed Deep Learning
- PyTorch and TensorFlow
- Dask e SaturnCloud Clusters

Artificial Intelligence (AI)

A recent field of development involving computers and data analysis is **Artificial Intelligence (AI)**. Through this term, we generally refer to *systems/machines*, which somehow manage to imitate human intelligence. These systems, often composed of various very complex algorithms, are able to continuously improve themselves while carrying out a given activity, thanks to the learning processes that *gain experience* on the basis of the information collected. The more information they collect, the better their performance will be.

Although AI is always associated with images of *robots* similar to human beings, it is a different reality. Today, AI systems are quite widespread and operate in different forms in our daily lives. They are incorporeal, abstract entities that manifest themselves in different ways from the common image of humanoids. More commonly, they manage search engines or operate behind social networks and other service distributors to study our habits, our tastes, and our needs. These systems study our past choices and reconstruct what our future needs could be on the basis of the information collected. For instance, it might be projecting recommendations of a series, films on *YouTube*, or topics in which we might be interested. Their purpose is to operate on the basis of the user's choice, without wasting time assessing thousands of possible choices.

Another recent application of AI are **chatbots**. These chats, often present on websites of service providers, collect requests for information or ask the customers about the problems encountered. After collecting information, they suggest the shortest way to obtain a solution such as suggesting the completion of a form, a phone number of a specific employee, or some steps to solve the problem without having to visit a service centre. These chatbots aim to replace a human operator by offering customer services 24 X7.

On the other hand, the more profound use of AI is less evident than that of learning through parameterizable model systems. This happens when AI uses large amounts of incoming data to become accurate, which enables it to predict complex phenomena. This approach has given rise to disciplines such as **Machine Learning (ML)** and **Deep Learning (DL)**.

AI, Machine Learning, and Deep Learning

AI is often used interchangeably with the terms ML and DL. However, there are clear differences between these concepts. ML is a *computational technique* focused on developing systems capable of learning and performing specific activities, based on the data provided. Therefore, it can be said that ML is a phenomenon of AI, but the opposite cannot be claimed. A scheme that can help us understand the differences between these concepts is shown in *Figure 9.1*:

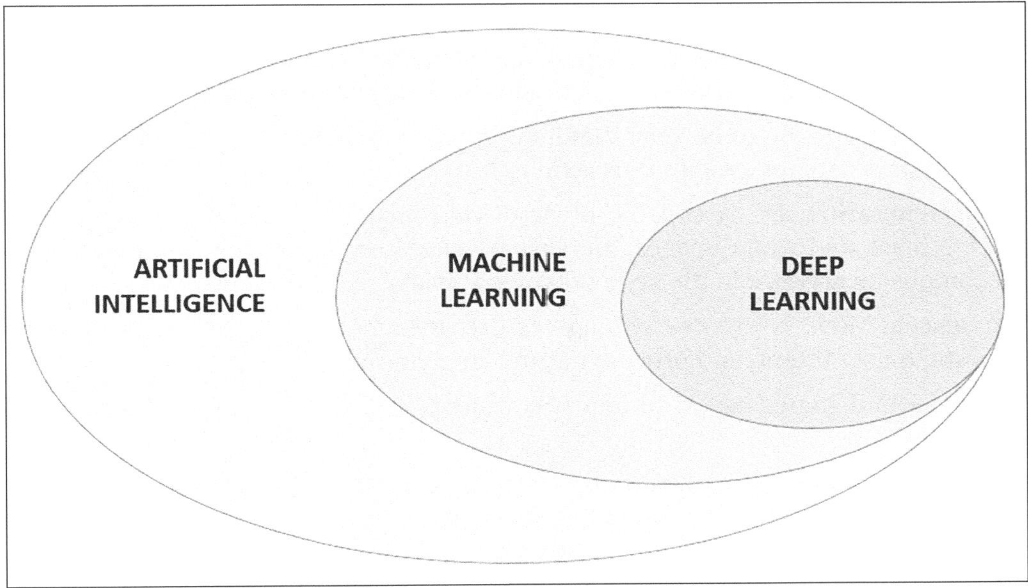

***Figure 9.1**: Differences between AI, Machine Learning, and Deep Learning*

DL is more complex. It is focused on developing systems that can learn, but are more similar to humans. These systems are based on *artificial neural networks* distributed in multiple layers similar to neurons in the human brain, as shown in *Figure 9.2*:

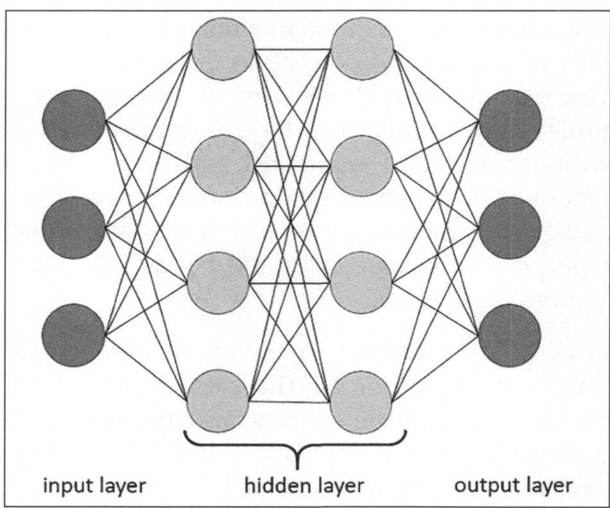

***Figure 9.2**: An Example of an Artificial Neural Network*

They are complex systems that can extract information and transform complex data such as human voices or images. They are therefore able to learn and *recognize* any objects or words in a complex context. Also, in this case, artificial neural networks must undergo a series of learning phases to fulfill their duties in an efficient way. Therefore, DL can be defined as a particular technique of ML, which is a form of AI (see *Figure* 9.1).

DL can be applied in many fields like:

- **Natural Language Processing (NLP)**: DL systems can recognize spoken words (*speech recognition*) and are particularly effective at processing written documentation. They can search for names, concepts and data within thousands of articles and various documents.
- **Computer Vision**: DL has laid the foundations for image interpretation, particularly in *facial recognition*, and for solving problems such as locating vehicles and pedestrians from webcam images.
- **Pharmacology**: DL can analyze diagnostic images and recognize any anomalies. It can also learn from physiological characteristics and the discovery of pathologies.
- **Biology**: DL is proving to be very useful in *protein classification*, genomics, *cell classification*, and *analysis of protein-protein interactions.*
- **Image Generation**: DL is capable of modifying images with complex operations such as coloring black and white images, increasing image resolution, removing noise from images, and composing artwork in the style of famous artists.
- **Web Search:** Modern web search engines use deep learning models to rank search results, understand user intent, and process natural language queries.
- **Games**: Several games use AI to improve strategy and simulate human behavior in artificial opponents.
- **Robotics**: DL is finding applications in the calculation of the trajectories and dynamics of complex robotic s**ystems for** object manipulation.

AI, whether it is ML or DL, will soon become the fundamental pillar of corporate *decision-making processes* in the future.

Supervised and Unsupervised Learning

Once the areas of learning within AI have been defined, it is important to introduce another fundamental concept before talking about their application in parallel computing.

All learning techniques, both ML and DL can follow *two* different approaches in the learning phase:

- Supervised Learning
- Unsupervised Learning

These *two* approaches differ on whether the data used is labeled or not. By *labeled*, we mean that the data is tagged with the correct answer or *not*.

Supervised learning uses data labeled with the correct answers to train models. Knowing the correct answer will be used to refine the model's capabilities in its predictions. This approach is used in *two* particular techniques:

- Classification
- Regression

Classification uses algorithms to classify the data under study. Some of the most used algorithms are:

- Logistic Regression
- K-Nearest Neighbors
- Random Forest
- Naïve Bayes
- Stochastic Gradient Descent
- Decision Trees

Regression instead uses algorithms that measure the relationship between a *dependent variable* and one or more *independent variables*. Some of the more famous ones include:

- Ridge Regression
- Lasso
- Neural Network Regression
- Logistic Regression

In **unsupervised learning**, the data comes without explicit labels. Therefore, such algorithms can work without human supervision. While this approach is valuable, most state-of-the-art DL applications such as image classification and NLP rely on supervised or self-supervised learning, rather than purely unsupervised methods.

There are *three* different techniques that follow this approach:

- Clustering
- Association
- Dimensionality Reduction

Clustering is based on the similarities or differences of the data under study by grouping them according to certain characteristics. The best-known algorithm that follows this technique is **K-means clustering**.

Association can identify the relationship between the variables within a dataset. Relationships are not yet defined before studying the dataset.

Dimensionality reduction reduces the number of features to be studied within a dataset that can sometimes be too large. Algorithms that follow this technique must be able to reduce the number of features that distinguish the data, without compromising their integrity.

Artificial Intelligence and Parallel Computing

As we can certainly guess, the creation of complex computer systems capable of carrying out forms of AI requires enormous computing resources. As their capabilities grow, more powerful computers will be required. This is why these AI systems have become widespread only in the recent years. It is therefore clear that in order to be able to operate in this sector and develop AI systems that are capable of carrying out their tasks, we will have to leverage systems based on parallel computing, as they are the only ones that can provide the necessary computing resources.

Clouds, for example, have abundant computational power that allow operators and developers to obtain high-performance computational power at affordable prices. Prior to this development, the only computing environments available for AI had to work on a small set of cost-prohibitive supercomputers. If you would have worked on single computers, you could have only create simple models with long processing times, which in any case would require the additional support of different GPU cards to operate. It is therefore clear that the latter case can be a choice for a study or development environment.

Parallel and Distributed Machine Learning

As far as ML is concerned, Python offers ample opportunities as it is a popular reference language for this discipline. There are many libraries available that provide ML algorithms, such as:

- scikit-learn
- XGBoost
- LightGBM
- TensorFlow

Furthermore, many of these libraries are designed to operate on parallel systems (*parallel computing*). They can also be extended in environments formed by multiple machines (*distributed computing*). This is precisely due to the fact that ML requires a lot of computing resources and therefore it is *natural* to use it on powerful systems capable of parallel computing.

For ML, we need to carry out operations for which the parallel computing approach is fundamental. The most important of these is *matrix multiplication*. We have already seen in the first few chapters of the book that it can greatly benefit from correct parallel implementation, especially if GPUs are used to perform this calculation. Multiplication between matrices is the basis of linear regression algorithms that are widely used in ML. Reducing the time taken in this type of calculation clearly affects the general performance of the learning phases and the calculation of the predictions made by ML models.

Another common operation in ML is calculating the *distance between two points*. This operation is common in many algorithms (such as **k-means clustering**) and is performed many times within the same algorithm. Since they take advantage of the fact that the individual distance calculation of subsequent iterations does not depend on other calculations in the same iteration, these calculations can be performed in parallel to reduce processing times.

Also, in the context of operations that could be onerous in terms of ML execution, there exists **k-fold cross-validation**, which is based on the intense processing of different segments of the dataset. This method is used to validate a model and is based on excluding one of the *k segments (fold)* from the calculation. All other *k-1 segments* are trained and then the *k-th* element is used as a test dataset. Since we are dealing with k segments, this operation is performed *k times*, each of which excludes a different segment from training. Once *k results* are obtained, their average is calculated. As can be understood, the *k-fold cross-validation* algorithm, if performed sequentially, takes a large amount of time as it has to repeat the same operations k times. If it is brought in parallel form, where each calculation performed on one of the *k folds* is performed simultaneously, we can observe significant gains in performance.

All these operations, if processed in a parallel computing system, can ML much more efficient and capable of tackling more complex problems. ML can then also process larger datasets and increase the forecasting capacity of the models, while also reducing processing times. These features can otherwise become prohibitive in a single machine system.

Machine Learning with Scikit-Learn

Scikit-learn is currently the most used Python library in Machine Learning and provides users with main algorithms such as:

- Classification
- Clustering
- Regression
- Dimensionality Reduction

Scikit-learn is a well-documented library with several available examples. To know how ML works with **scikit-learn**, let us look at a simple example of *linear regression*. Among the various examples, this one is simple to understand and is the perfect illustrative case even for people who are not familiar with ML. This technique is based on the construction of a very simple model of a system that is supposed to behave linearly, in order to predict the result from a given value of a variable in this system.

For simplicity, we will use data points generated around a straight line that distances them by a random value from the correct linear trend. In this way, we can simulate the data coming from a phenomenon that responds to a linear behavior from which we will have to obtain the linear trend (intercept and coefficient of the slope of the straight line). To do this, we generate a dataset of 30 *values* from the equation of a straight line with slope **`0.3`** and coefficient **`1.0`,** to which we add a random noise that simulates the deviation of the values from the correct trend.

```
import numpy as np
x = 50 * np.random.random((30, 1))
y = 0.3 * x + 1.0 + np.random.normal(size=x.shape)
```

Once the **`dataset(x,y)`** has been generated, in which **`x`** will be the variables and **`y`** will represent the labels with the results, we can divide it into *two* parts. We will use one of these as a *training set* and the other as a *testing set*. We can do this via a convenient function provided by **scikit-learn** called **`train_test_split()`,** which allows us to split a dataset based on a percentage defined by the **`test_size`** parameter. So, if we want 20% *of the dataset* for testing, we will write the following code:

```
from sklearn.model_selection import train_test_split
x_train, x_test, y_train, y_test = train_test_split(x, y, test_size=0.2)
```

Now that we have all the data necessary for learning and validating the model, we need to create one as well. Since this is a Linear Regression, it is possible to instantiate a specific model by defining the **`LinearRegression()`** constructor. Once the model has been generated, we will move on to the learning phase, using the **`fit()`** method and passing it to the training set as an argument.

```
from sklearn.linear_model import LinearRegression
model = LinearRegression()
model.fit(x_train, y_train)
```

As we can see, **scikit-learn** makes the implementation of ML very simple for us, as it condenses everything into just *two lines of code*. Once it is executed, we will have a model that can predict the corresponding values of **`y`** by passing it values of the variable **`x`**. We have said that this model is very simple and is based on parameterizing the equation of a straight line where the two parameters (intercept and slope coefficient) are gradually evaluated based on the learning phase. If we want to see the values of these two parameters, we will write the following code:

```
print(model.intercept_)
print(model.coef_)
```

The following result is obtained:

```
[1.41274643]
[[0.29301879]]
```

These values differ slightly from the real ones: **1** and **3**. Let us now move on to the evaluation of this model by testing its forecasting capabilities. To submit the model to an evaluation test, the **predict()** method is used, to which the testing set is passed as an argument.

```
y_new = model.predict(x_test)
```

The result will be a list of y values corresponding to the **x** passed in the testing set. By checking the difference between the expected values **y_new** and the real ones **y_test,** it is possible to evaluate the goodness of the model just created. Since these are numerical values that describe points around a straight line in a *Cartesian graph*, the best way to evaluate this model will be to represent them graphically. To do this we can use the **matplotlib** library, which is very useful for creating graphs to be displayed in the Jupyter Notebook, with the following lines of code:

```
import matplotlib.pyplot as plt
plt.figure()
plt.scatter(x,y)
plt.scatter(x_test,y_new, c='red')
```

By executing the cell of the notebook containing the previous code, we will obtain a graph which is shown in *Figure 9.3*:

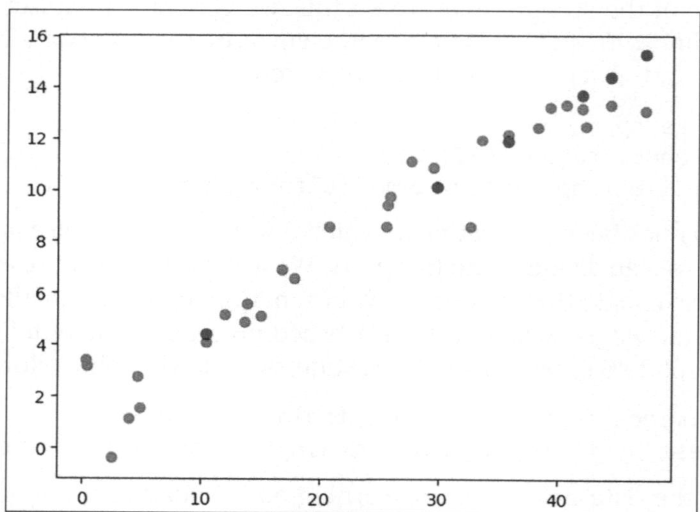

Figure 9.3*: Linear Regression Results (Training Set Points are in Blue, and the Testing Set Points are in Red)*

To evaluate the goodness of the model we have used, the **score()** method can be employed. It allows us to calculate the coefficient of determination, known as $\mathbf{R^2}$, for both *training* and *test* data. The maximum value is **1** and the minimum value is **0**. The closer this value is to 1, the better the model will fit. So, this value is a great parameter to judge the forecasting abilities of a trained model.

```
model.score(x_train, y_train)
0.920774873832153

model.score(x_test, y_test)
0.9011230374736323
```

Scaling Scikit-learn with Dask-ML

Just like what we saw in the previous *chapter*, Dask can be an excellent solution for scaling ML applications in distributed environments. Like **Dask DataFrames** for **Pandas** and **Dask Arrays** for **NumPy**, the **Dask-ML module** extends the **scikit-learn** library on distributed environments such as clusters.

This module takes advantage of one of scikit-learn's parallel computing features: **joblib**. Many scikit-learn algorithms have been implemented to run in parallel when using **joblib**, which provides *thread-based* and *process-based* parallelism natively. Dask-ML will use this capability to distribute these computations across a cluster. This same mechanism is also used to implement machine learning models of other libraries like **XGboost**.

To install **Dask-ML** in a virtual environment specifically created for ML, follow the given steps:

1. Open a command shell and enter the following command:

   ```
   conda install dask-ml -c conda-forge
   conda install joblib
   conda install matplotlib -c conda-forge
   ```

2. Once the installation is complete, we will open a notebook on Jupyter via:

   ```
   from dask.distributed import Client
   client = Client()
   ```

3. **Dask-ML**, similar to Dask, provides a set of methods and functions corresponding to the original libraries. However, they can work only on distributed environments. In this case, the **train_test_split()** function of scikit-learn will be replaced with the same function of the Dask-ML library, which is shown here:

   ```
   from dask_ml.model_selection import train_test_split
   x_train, x_test, y_train, y_test = train_test_split(x, y, test_size=0.2)
   ```

4. Like the scikit-learn functions, the models are also provided in their own version distributed by Dask-ML. Let us replace the **LinearRegression** class of scikit-learn with that of Dask-ML. At this point, the learning methods **fit()** and evaluation **predict()** will be \provided by Dask-ML for distributed environments.

   ```
   from dask_ml.linear_model import LinearRegression
   model = LinearRegression()
   ```

   Before moving on to the learning phase, we need to add the **joblib** library. This particular library allows Python libraries like scikit-learn to work in parallel on a single machine. With **parallel_backend** provided by this library, it is possible to do it by taking into account the features of Dask. In this way, we can execute the code in parallel computing mode even in a *distributed environment*, which enhance the library's performance even more.

   ```
   import joblib
   from joblib import parallel_backend

   with parallel_backend('dask'):
    model.fit(x_train,y_train)
    y_new = model.predict(x_test)
   ```

5. Now that we have trained and evaluated the model in parallel, we can check the results graphical via:

   ```
   import matplotlib.pyplot as plt

   plt.figure()
   ```

```
plt.scatter(x_train,y_train)
plt.scatter(x_test,y_new, c='red')
```

6. After running the code, you will get a graph like the one shown in *Figure* 9.4:

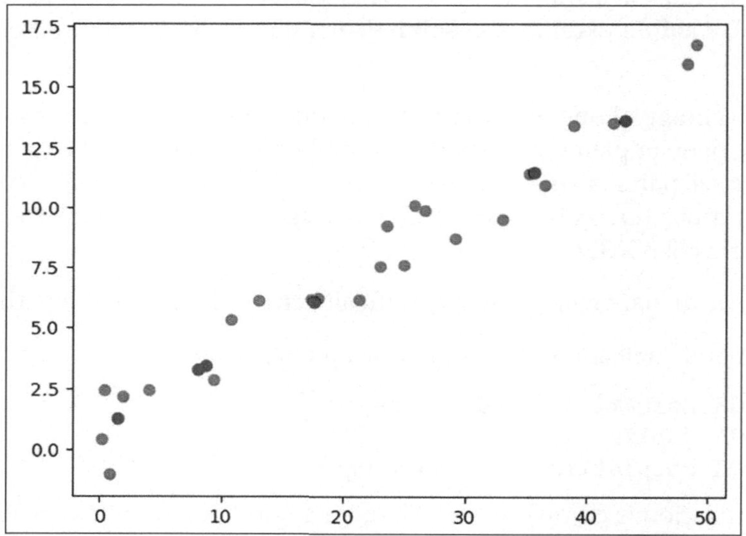

***Figure* 9.4**: *Results Obtained by the Model with Dask and Parallel Computing*

Parallel and Distributed Deep Learning

At the base of DL are neural networks, which are excellent for discovering the relationships and structures that are hidden behind unsupervised data. Their ability to *learn* and *analyze*, which in emulates the human way of learning, makes them suitable for working on data that is not strictly numerical in nature, such as images and sounds. This is why DL is particularly focused on *Natural Language Processing* and *Computer Vision*.

Artificial neural networks are complex structures that require huge computing resources to operate efficiently. The typical neural networks used in DL use millions of parameters that make up a model. These systems also take the advantage of a large amount of data for their learning. Therefore, this process is computationally intensive and will take an enormous amount of time in *single-machine systems*. Furthermore, many datasets are too large to be contained within the memory of a single machine. Fortunately, the particular layered structure of neurons in a neural network is perfectly suited to distributed systems and allows you to make the most of parallel computing. The models used for DL can be distributed over the different layers of the neural network, and its parameters (weights) are in turn distributed among the different neurons present in each layer. So, it is clear that we can use these features to distribute the load and information of the models used, as well as their relative calculation on different machines in a distributed system.

There are several methods to distribute and thereby parallelize computation when training on clusters of machines. These methods can be used singularly or in combination.

- **Parallel Processing**
  - Multi-Core Processing
  - GPU Processing
- **Distributed Training**
  - Data Parallelism
  - Model Parallelism

Through these methods, it will be possible to convert DL algorithms into parallel algorithms, where single tasks will be assigned to the different cores (multi-core processing), or to the different GPUs present on the machines (GPUs processing). As for datasets, since they tend to be enormous in size, they can be divided and distributed on different machines (*data parallelism) to reduce* memory overloads. Even DL models can be divided into smaller parts, while assigning a set of parameters for each machine (*model parallelism*). Both of these methods can reduce learning time significantly. However, **data parallelism** is often preferred over **model parallelism**. In fact, in the latter case, there are synchronization operations that require more processing time. Therefore, data parallelism is the fastest approach between the *two*. On the other hand, model parallelism produces better predictive results.

PyTorch and TensorFlow

Among the various possibilities offered by Python to work with DL, there are *two open-source frameworks* that have been very popular lately:

- PyTorch
- TensorFlow

PyTorch is a relatively new DL framework. This library was developed by the *Facebook AI Lab* and was released as open-source on *GitHub* in 2017. Its main purpose was to implement applications for **Natural Language Processing** (**NLP**). PyTorch soon gained success for its simplicity, efficient use of memory, and being largely native as it produced code with higher processing speed.

TensorFlow is also an *open-source framework* built specifically for DL. This library was developed by *Google* and first released in 2015. Compared to PyTorch, **TensorFlow** is more *popular*. This is because it has been present for longer and has a large amount of documentation available. It also has abundant support from other technologies that facilitate scalability on distributed systems and on different platforms like *Android*. Furthermore, since 2017, TensorFlow has integrated **Keras**, which is another DL framework that has existed for several years. TensorFlow is currently the *preferred tool* for many professionals and researchers and is used to train several models.

Deep Learning Example with PyTorch

Moving on to the practical part, we will choose PyTorch to implement a DL illustration. We will use a neural network to analyze a dataset of images and recognize their content.

PyTorch Installation

To install PyTorch on *Anaconda*, go to **Anaconda Navigator** and select the virtual environment dedicated to DL in the **Environments** panel. If you have not done so yet, create a new one by pressing the **Create** button as shown in *Figure* 9.5:

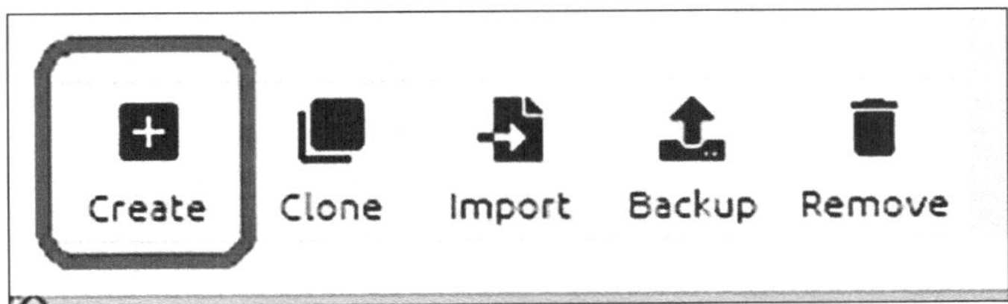

***Figure* 9.5**: *Create Button*

At this point, a dialog box will appear. Here, you can enter the name of the virtual environment and select the Python version. Choose version `3.10.9` as shown in *Figure* 9.6:

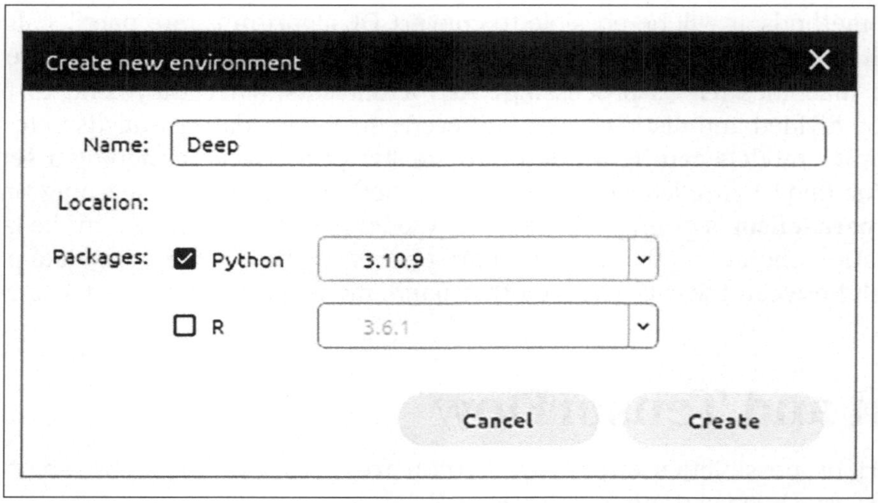

***Figure 9.6**: Dialog Box for Creating a New Virtual Environment*

Once the virtual environment has been generated and activated, we can install the packages needed to work with PyTorch. To do this, visit the PyTorch website (https://pytorch.org/get-started/locally/) and make the appropriate selections based on your work platform on the table of system features displayed in the center, as shown in *Figure* 9.7:

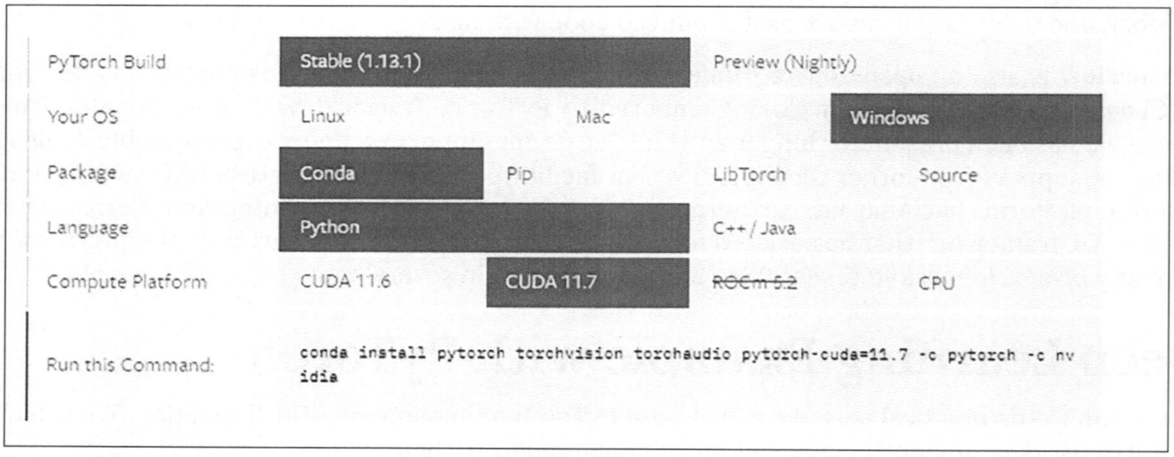

***Figure 9.7**: Panel for Selecting Packages*

Once you have selected the current configuration of the platform you use, the following **conda** command will show you a list of all the necessary packages:

```
conda install pytorch torchvision torchaudio pytorch-cuda=11.7 -c pytorch
-c nvidia
```

Open the virtual environment command shell and run the preceding **conda** command. At the package installation request, enter Y to confirm, and wait to download and complete the installation. At this point, we will open a new notebook on Jupyter and test the installation with the following lines:

```
import torch
torch.__version__
```

Hopefully, you will get the PyTorch version as a result:

```
'1.13.1'
```

Then we test interfacing with CUDA through the following code:

```
torch.cuda.is_available()
True

torch.version.cuda
'11.7'
```

If you get the results without any error messages, the installation has been successful. These packages can integrate seamlessly with CUDA and NVIDIA drives to use GPUs as well as process data in parallel.

Deep Learning Example with the Fashion-MNIST Dataset

To approach a DL problem, it is advisable to start from already implemented models and then continue while making some changes. You can look up an example on **Kaggle**, we have considered the study of the **Fashion MNIST dataset** with PyTorch, which can be downloaded from: https://www.kaggle.com/code/pankajj/fashion-mnist-with-pytorch-93-accuracy.

PyTorch comes with some *pre-loaded datasets* that can be used to test models. Inside the library you can find the following:

- Image Datasets
- Text Datasets
- Audio Datasets

For our example, that is, recognition of objects within images, we can use the **Fashion-MNIST dataset**. This dataset consists of around 60,000 small-sized (28x28 *pixels*) black and white (grayscale) garment images taken from **Zalando**.

As for the model used, we can find the convolutional Neural Network **`FashionCNN()`** to use with our example. So, once we open a new notebook on Jupyter, we can import all the necessary modules into the first cell, as shown here:

```
import torch
import torch.nn as nn
from torch.autograd import Variable

import torchvision
from torchvision import datasets
from torchvision.transforms import ToTensor
from torch.utils.data import DataLoader

import datetime
```

At this point, we start by extracting the data from the dataset and distributing them in a *training* set and a *testing* set, which is necessary for the *learning* and *testing* phase.

```
training_data = datasets.FashionMNIST(
    root="data",
    train=True,
    download=True,
    transform=ToTensor()
)
```

```
test_data = datasets.FashionMNIST(
    root="data",
    train=False,
    download=True,
    transform=ToTensor()
)
```

To understand the type of images used for both the training set and the testing set, let us visualize the first nine images of the *training* set via the following code:

```
import matplotlib.pyplot as plt
labels_map = {
    0: "T-Shirt",
    1: "Trouser",
    2: "Pullover",
    3: "Dress",
    4: "Coat",
    5: "Sandal",
    6: "Shirt",
    7: "Sneaker",
    8: "Bag",
    9: "Ankle Boot",
}
figure = plt.figure(figsize=(8, 8))
cols, rows = 3, 3
for i in range(1, cols * rows + 1):
    sample_idx = torch.randint(len(training_data), size=(1,)).item()
    img, label = training_data[sample_idx]
    figure.add_subplot(rows, cols, i)
    plt.title(labels_map[label])
    plt.axis("off")
    plt.imshow(img.squeeze(), cmap="gray")
plt.show()
```

If we execute the previous code, we will obtain a table of *nine black and white images* of different garments, each of which is labeled with one of the *ten garments* described in the **labels_map**. This is shown in *Figure 9.8*:

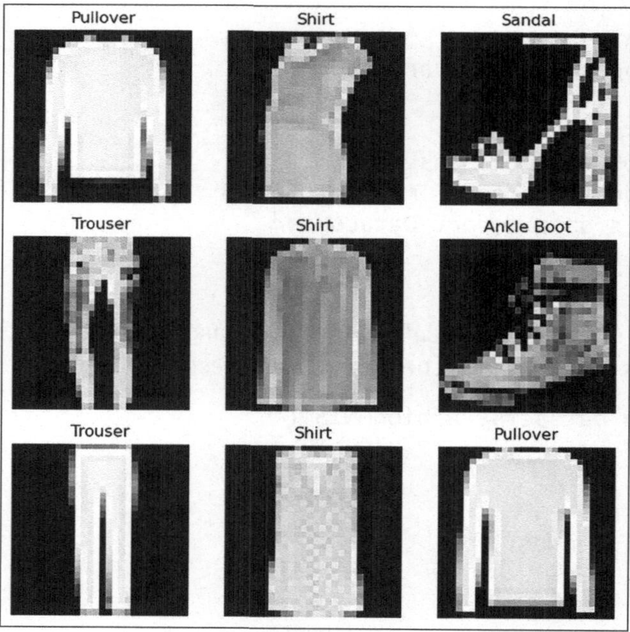

Figure 9.8: *Some Images of Clothing in the Training Set*

Now in the next cell of the Jupyter Notebook, we can write the following code related to the **Convolutionary Neural Network FashionCNN**:

```
class FashionCNN(nn.Module):

    def __init__(self):
        super(FashionCNN, self).__init__()

        self.layer1 = nn.Sequential(
            nn.Conv2d(in_channels=1, out_channels=32, kernel_size=3, padding=1),
            nn.BatchNorm2d(32),
            nn.ReLU(),
            nn.MaxPool2d(kernel_size=2, stride=2)
        )

        self.layer2 = nn.Sequential(
            nn.Conv2d(in_channels=32, out_channels=64, kernel_size=3),
            nn.BatchNorm2d(64),
            nn.ReLU(),
            nn.MaxPool2d(2)
        )

        self.fc1 = nn.Linear(in_features=64*6*6, out_features=600)
        self.drop = nn.Dropout2d(0.25)
        self.fc2 = nn.Linear(in_features=600, out_features=120)
        self.fc3 = nn.Linear(in_features=120, out_features=10)

    def forward(self, x):
        out = self.layer1(x)
        out = self.layer2(out)
        out = out.view(out.size(0), -1)
        out = self.fc1(out)
        out = self.drop(out)
        out = self.fc2(out)
        out = self.fc3(out)
        return out
```

Once both the datasets and the neural network model are ready, we can move on to implementing the model learning phases, and simultaneously calculating the model's *accuracy* and *loss* during the *learning* phase. These values will be useful later to evaluate the goodness of the model obtained.

```
def train(bs, lr):

    batch_size = bs
    learning_rate = lr
    train_loader = torch.utils.data.DataLoader(training_data,batch_size)
    test_loader = torch.utils.data.DataLoader(test_data,batch_size)

    #device = torch.device('cuda:0')
    device = torch.device('cpu')
    num_epochs = 5
    count = 0
    model = FashionCNN()
    model.to(device)
    error = nn.CrossEntropyLoss()
    learning_rate = 0.001
    optimizer = torch.optim.Adam(model.parameters(), lr=learning_rate)
```

```
        training_start_time = datetime.datetime.now()
        results = []

        for epoch in range(num_epochs):
            for images, labels in train_loader:
                images, labels = images.to(device), labels.to(device)
                train = Variable(images.view(100, 1, 28, 28))
                outputs = model(train)
                loss = error(outputs, labels)
                optimizer.zero_grad()
                loss.backward()
                optimizer.step()
                count += 1

            # Testing the model
                if not (count % 50):    # It's same as "if count % 50 == 0"
                    total = 0
                    correct = 0
                    for images, labels in test_loader:
                        images, labels = images.to(device), labels.to(device)
                        test = Variable(images.view(100, 1, 28, 28))
                        outputs = model(test)
                        predictions = torch.max(outputs, 1)[1].to(device)
                        correct += (predictions == labels).sum()
                        total += len(labels)

                    accuracy = correct * 100 / total
                    new_results = {
                       "batch_size": batch_size,
                       "loss": loss.data.item(),
                       "iteration": count,
                       "accuracy": accuracy.item(),
                       "elapsed_time_sec": (datetime.datetime.now() - training_
start_time).total_seconds(),
                    }
                    results.append(new_results)
        return results
```

Now, we will carry out the *training* process of the neural network by invoking the function just defined and passing the **batch_size** and the **learning_rate** as arguments.

```
# batch_size = 100, learning_rate = 0.001
results = train(100, 0.001)
```

The preceding code will take a while to run. After nearly a minute, the model will complete the *learning* phase. During this phase, we calculated and collected some parameters that take into account the quality of the learning phase such as *loss* and *accuracy*. These values are collected in the results variable and then passed in a Pandas **DataFrame**, so that they can be consulted more easily.

```
import pandas as pd

results_df = pd.DataFrame.from_dict(results)
results_df.head(10)
```

By executing the previous code, we will display the *first ten rows* of the DataFrame using the **head()** method, as shown in *Figure 9.9*:

	batch_size	loss	iteration	accuracy	elapsed_time_sec
0	100	0.503404	50	79.540001	10.698972
1	100	0.563143	100	81.220001	20.112245
2	100	0.452134	150	84.059998	29.749219
3	100	0.395133	200	85.709999	39.393635
4	100	0.441687	250	85.050003	48.891572
5	100	0.422865	300	84.529999	58.477025
6	100	0.347971	350	86.680000	68.099902
7	100	0.439388	400	86.589996	77.511428
8	100	0.620000	450	84.849998	87.049638
9	100	0.501260	500	87.669998	96.446948

Figure 9.9: *The First 10 Rows of the DataFrame Containing the Results*

As we can see from the DataFrame, we have collected the value of the *loss*, the *accuracy*, and the *time taken* in the execution of *every* 50 *iterations*, which in the present case is about 10 *seconds*. To see the time taken for the whole learning (3,000 *iterations*), we can see the last rows of the DataFrame through the **`tail()`** method as enacted here:

```
results_df.tail()
```

By executing the method, we obtain a table containing the last five results collected, which correspond to the last five steps of the *learning* phase, as shown in *Figure* 9.10:

	batch_size	loss	iteration	accuracy	elapsed_time_sec
55	100	0.250286	2800	90.449997	533.636908
56	100	0.484450	2850	89.900002	543.004209
57	100	0.292580	2900	90.570000	552.542618
58	100	0.195649	2950	90.129997	562.113212
59	100	0.211632	3000	89.910004	571.689600

Figure 9.10: *The Last Five Rows of the DataFrame Containing the Results*

Having put all the data collected from the results into a Pandas DataFrame, we have also taken advantage of the simplicity with which the data in these objects can be plotted with **`matplotlib`**. Let us see the trend of the loss throughout the learning phase by writing the following code in the following cell of the notebook:

```
import matplotlib.pyplot as plt

plt.plot(results_df['iteration'], results_df['loss'])
plt.show()
```

By executing the code, we obtain the following *linear graph* in which loss is represented throughout the learning phase (3,000 *iterations*) in *Figure* 9.11:

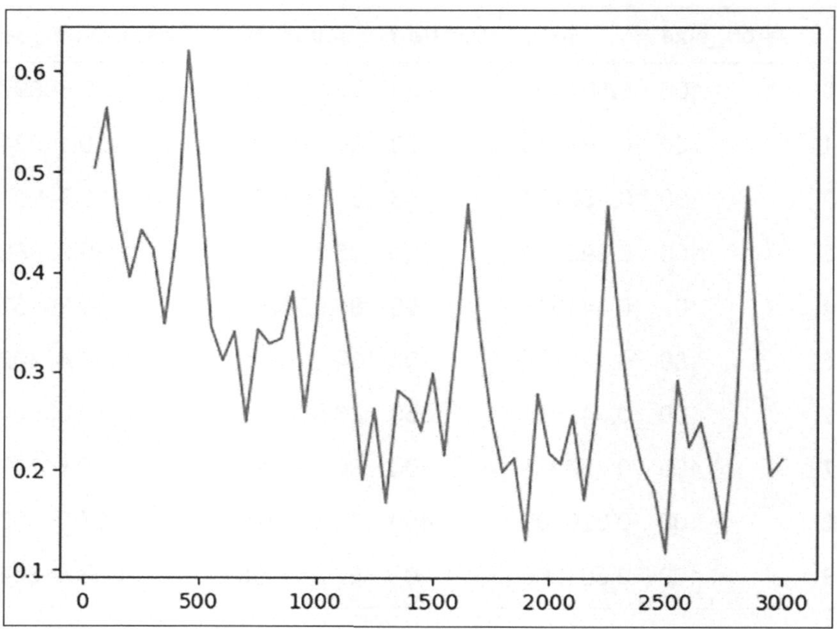

Figure 9.11: Loss Recorded During the Learning Phase

As can be seen from the figure, the *loss trend* is *highly variable*. *For every epoch*, there is a similar trend with *high and low values*. However, we can also observe a gradual improvement in loss, which changes from the initial **0.5** to a more stable value of **0.2** after five *learning* epochs.

The same can be done with accuracy. In order to plot the accuracy trend on the, we can write the following code:

```
plt.plot(results_df['iteration'], results_df['accuracy'])
plt.show()
```

By executing the previous code, we will obtain the graph in *Figure* 9.12:

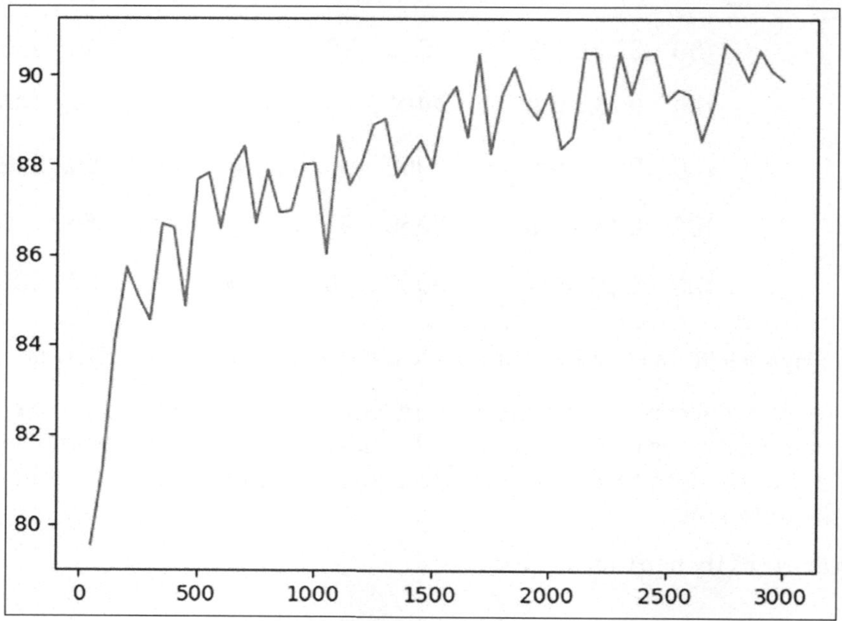

Figure 9.12: Neural Network Learning Accuracy Trend

In this graph, the accuracy fluctuates significantly across successive training iterations, resulting in alternating high and low peaks. These variations are typical of stochastic training processes;

nevertheless, the overall accuracy steadily improves from about 80% to 90% by the end of the learning phase.

Another interesting graph could record the time taken to execute the iterations during the entire learning process, which can be plotted via:

```
plt.plot(results_df['iteration'], results_df['elapsed_time_sec'])
plt.show()
```

Running the code will give us the output observed in *Figure 9.13*:

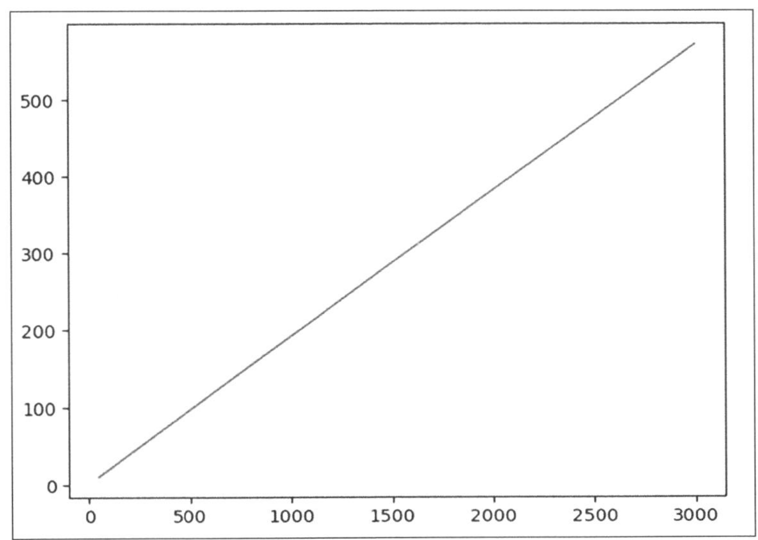

Figure 9.13: *Time Spent Learning the Neural Network*

In the graph, we can see that the execution times are homogeneous and remain unchanged throughout the learning process.

Deep Learning Example with PyTorch and GPU

Now that we have considered the example of learning a neural network model on a set of images performed on a single machine, it will be interesting to exploit the parallel computing technologies we have learned about. For instance, we can integrate the calculations via PyTorch with the GPU graphics card on our system. We can modify the used code and record the differences obtained in its execution.

In the training function of the neural network **train()**, we are going to modify the calculation device and replace **cpu** with **cuda:0**. We will run the code again to obtain parallelism through the NVIDIA graphics card *due to the* integration of CUDA.

```
def train(bs, lr):

    batch_size = bs
    learning_rate = lr
    train_loader = torch.utils.data.DataLoader(training_data,
                          batch_size=batch_size, shuffle=True)
    test_loader = torch.utils.data.DataLoader(test_data,
                          batch_size=batch_size, shuffle=False)

    device = torch.device('cuda:0')
```

```
num_epochs = 5
count = 0
model = MyCNN()
. . .
```

We reset the Jupyter Notebook by restarting the *kernel* and cleaning all the outputs obtained. To do this, select **`Kernel`** > **`Restart & Clear Output`** on the menu as shown in *Figure* 9.14 and wait for the Jupyter system to reset:

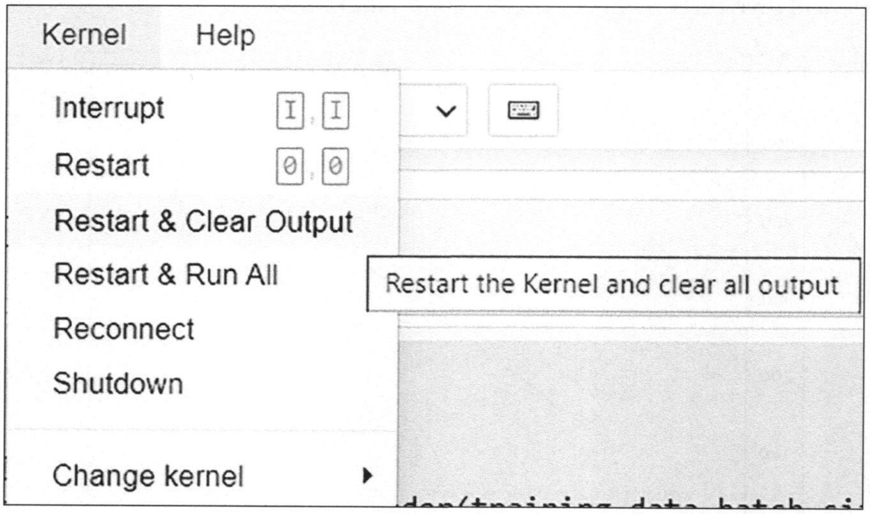

Kernel Help
Interrupt I, I
Restart 0, 0
Restart & Clear Output
Restart & Run All
Reconnect
Shutdown
Change kernel
Restart the Kernel and clear all output

***Figure* 9.14**: *Jupyter Notebook Resetting*

Once the Notebook has been reset and the device is modified in the code, we will re-execute all the cells from *start* to *finish* and observe the difference in the results obtained. Let us check the execution times from the DataFrame containing the calculation parameters of each iteration, as shown in *Figure* 9.15:

	batch_size	loss	iteration	accuracy	elapsed_time_sec
0	100	0.549456	50	78.680000	4.770011
1	100	0.449008	100	81.519997	7.666718
2	100	0.513790	150	84.449997	10.254896
3	100	0.434090	200	85.599998	12.682994
4	100	0.424354	250	86.070000	15.455611
5	100	0.348596	300	86.839996	17.886880
6	100	0.338119	350	87.209999	20.646353
7	100	0.411364	400	84.680000	23.106270
8	100	0.621500	450	86.419998	25.801914
9	100	0.430898	500	87.680000	28.419534

***Figure* 9.15**: *DataFrame of the Results Obtained by Adding the GPU*

As we can see in the previous figure (*Figure* 9.15) and the following one (*Figure* 9.16), the time has been reduced by *more than half*. The *duration of* 10 *seconds* to carry out about 50 *iterations* has been reduced to less than 4, while using GPU.

	batch_size	loss	iteration	accuracy	elapsed_time_sec
55	100	0.259191	2800	89.930000	147.375217
56	100	0.433528	2850	89.629997	150.086596
57	100	0.217143	2900	90.930000	152.501081
58	100	0.207694	2950	89.529999	155.274581
59	100	0.198218	3000	90.290001	157.656414

***Figure 9.16**: Last Rows of the DataFrame of the Results Obtained by Adding the GPU*

Let us also see the *loss* and the *accuracy* in the *two* graphs shown in *Figure* 9.17:

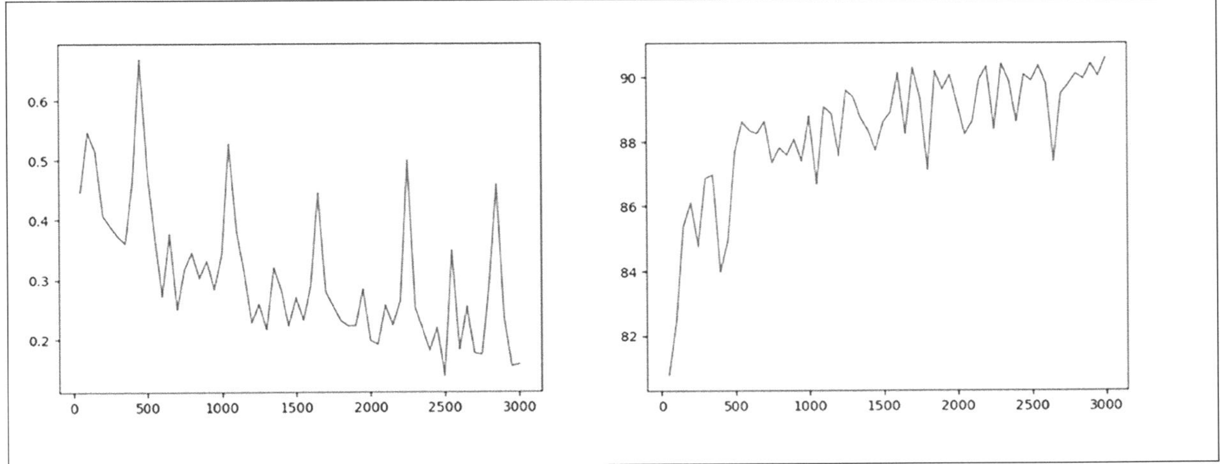

***Figure 9.17**: Loss and Accuracy Trends during GPU Learning*

In this case, the addition of parallel computing by the GPU graphics card does not make any difference (neither *improvement* nor *deterioration*) in the learning capabilities of the neural network. However, learning becomes faster.

Visualizing Neural Network Models Graphically with Pytorch

To visualize the graphic scheme of the neural network defined with PyTorch, or to get detailed information on the structure we are using, you can use the following tools:

- `torchviz`
- `torchsummary`
- `torchinfo`
- `Netron`

`torchviz` is a library that allows you to graphically visualize the PyTorch computational graph. First, you have to install it and check if the library is already present in your system with the following command:

```
pip install torchviz
```

If not, the installation will begin with all the related dependencies. To generate a graph that represents our neural network, we can define a function that we can reuse in other examples. Then, we will apply it to our FashionCNN model used previously via:

```
from torchviz import make_dot

def visualize_with_torchviz(model, input_size):
    example_input = torch.randn(input_size)
    output = model(example_input)
    dot = make_dot(output, params=dict(model.named_parameters()))
    dot.render("FashionCNN", format="png")
    print("Saved Graph as FashionCNN.png")
model = FashionCNN()
visualize_with_torchviz(model, input_size=(1,1,28,28))
```

By running the code, we will generate a PNG image file in the working directory and the following message will be printed as output:

```
Saved Graph as FashionCNN.png
```

Opening the PNG file named **FashionCNN.png** will give in the result shown in *Figure 9.18*:

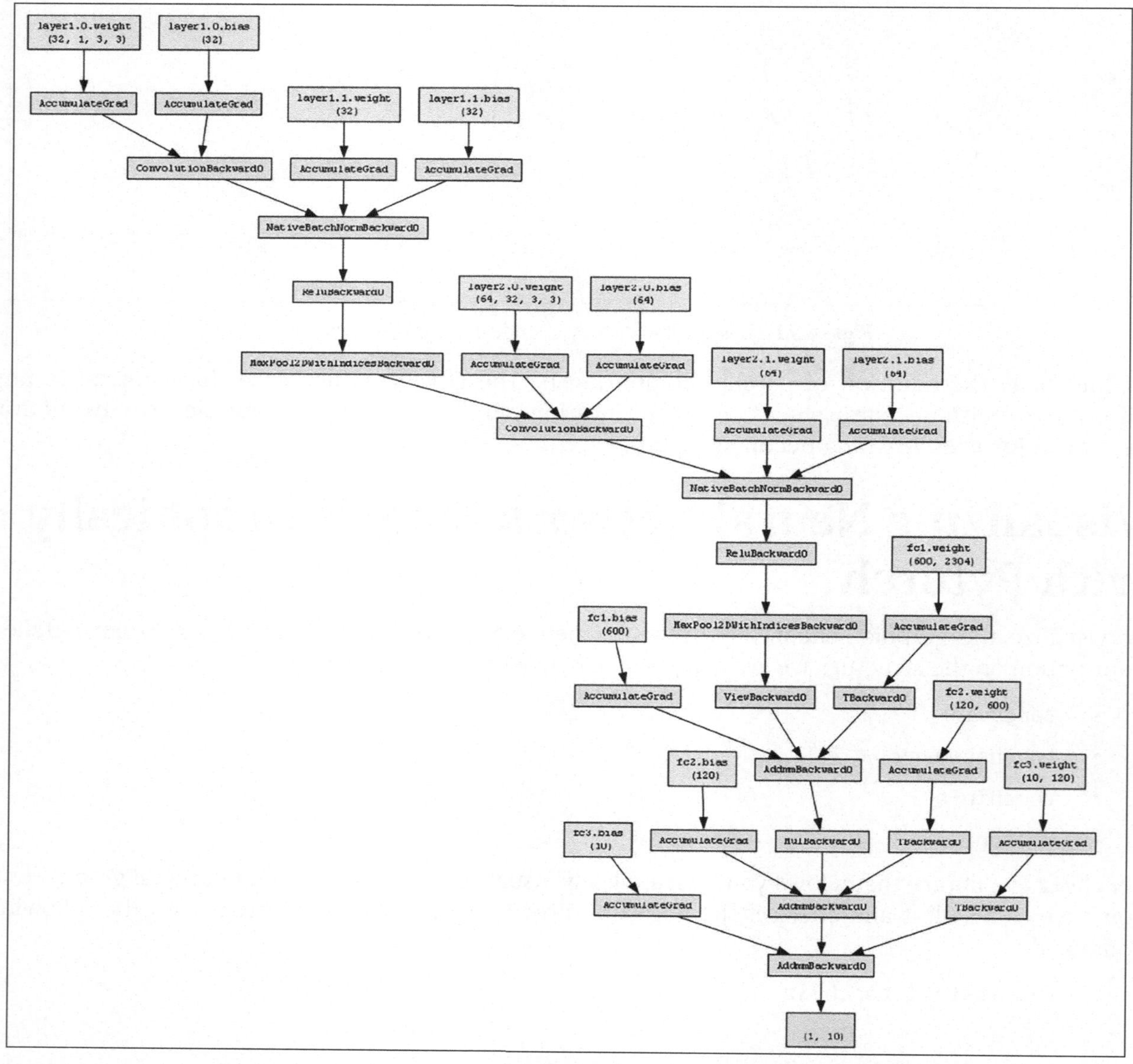

Figure 9.18: *Structure of the FashionCNN Model Used in Our Examples*

The graph generated with torchviz represents the dynamic computational graph of the FashionCNN neural network, which describes how tensors are transformed and passed through the various layers of the model to produce the output. The nodes represent an operation (for example, Convolution, ReLU, pooling, linear operations) or a transformation applied to the tensors. Each node is depicted as a rectangle labeled with the name of the related operation. The edges of the graph instead represent the flow of tensors in the model, showing how one operation feeds the next. Each connection represents an intermediate tensor. As for the nodes, these are represented with two colors. The main nodes are colored blue or purple and represent the operations explicitly defined in the model, while the gray ones are the intermediate nodes, and represent the intermediate tensors created during the forward pass.

Torchviz is therefore a useful tool to understand the functioning of complex models and to diagnose problems in the construction of the graph.

A different functionality is offered by **torchsummary** and **torchinfo**. These tools display information tables instead of graphs. In this case, there is no need to define an ad hoc function, but it is sufficient to call the summary method provided by both modules. Let us install the two modules, if it has not already been done:

```
pip install torchinfo torchsummary
```

We will then apply them to our model as follows:

```
from torchsummary import summary
summary(model, input_size=(1,28,28))
```

In this case, using **torchsummary** will give the following table:

```
----------------------------------------------------------------
        Layer (type)               Output Shape         Param #
================================================================
            Conv2d-1           [-1, 32, 28, 28]             320
       BatchNorm2d-2           [-1, 32, 28, 28]              64
              ReLU-3           [-1, 32, 28, 28]               0
         MaxPool2d-4           [-1, 32, 14, 14]               0
            Conv2d-5           [-1, 64, 12, 12]          18,496
       BatchNorm2d-6           [-1, 64, 12, 12]             128
              ReLU-7           [-1, 64, 12, 12]               0
         MaxPool2d-8             [-1, 64, 6, 6]               0
            Linear-9                  [-1, 600]       1,383,000
          Dropout-10                  [-1, 600]               0
           Linear-11                  [-1, 120]          72,120
           Linear-12                   [-1, 10]           1,210
================================================================
Total params: 1,475,338
Trainable params: 1,475,338
Non-trainable params: 0
----------------------------------------------------------------
Input size (MB): 0.00
Forward/backward pass size (MB): 0.86
Params size (MB): 5.63
Estimated Total Size (MB): 6.49
----------------------------------------------------------------
```

In the case of **torchinfo**, we will use:

```
from torchinfo import summary
summary(model, input_size=(1,1,28,28))
```

The following table will be obtained as a result:

```
==========================================================================================
Layer (type:depth-idx)                   Output Shape              Param #
==========================================================================================
FashionCNN                               [1, 10]                   --
├─Sequential: 1-1                        [1, 32, 14, 14]           --
│    └─Conv2d: 2-1                       [1, 32, 28, 28]           320
│    └─BatchNorm2d: 2-2                  [1, 32, 28, 28]           64
│    └─ReLU: 2-3                         [1, 32, 28, 28]           --
│    └─MaxPool2d: 2-4                    [1, 32, 14, 14]           --
├─Sequential: 1-2                        [1, 64, 6, 6]             --
│    └─Conv2d: 2-5                       [1, 64, 12, 12]           18,496
│    └─BatchNorm2d: 2-6                  [1, 64, 12, 12]           128
│    └─ReLU: 2-7                         [1, 64, 12, 12]           --
│    └─MaxPool2d: 2-8                    [1, 64, 6, 6]             --
├─Linear: 1-3                            [1, 600]                  1,383,000
├─Dropout: 1-4                           [1, 600]                  --
├─Linear: 1-5                            [1, 120]                  72,120
├─Linear: 1-6                            [1, 10]                   1,210
==========================================================================================
Total params: 1,475,338
Trainable params: 1,475,338
Non-trainable params: 0
Total mult-adds (M): 4.37
==========================================================================================
Input size (MB): 0.00
Forward/backward pass size (MB): 0.55
Params size (MB): 5.90
Estimated Total Size (MB): 6.46
==========================================================================================
```

In both cases, you will get very similar results: a detailed summary of the neural network architecture. This summary helps you understand the structure of the network, the size of the tensors in each layer, and the total number of parameters.

Finally, another tool available online is **Netron**, which accepts different model formats, including **torchScript**. Just like **torchviz**, **Netron** is a graphical tool for visualizing and analyzing neural network models. However, **Netron** offers a greater amount of information: in addition to the block diagram. Thanks to its interactive nature, it allows you to obtain detailed information for each element of the network (nodes and connections) by clicking on them, as well as zooming in to focus the study on particular sections of the model.

To convert our model into this format, we can use the following code:

```
def save_model_for_netron(model):
    model.eval()
    example_input = torch.randn(1, 1, 28, 28)
    traced_model = torch.jit.trace(model, example_input)
    traced_model.save("FashionCNN.pt")
    print("Saved model as FashionCNN.pt")

model = FashionCNN()
save_model_for_netron(model)
```

Go to the Netron web page (https://netron.app/) and upload the file you just generated. You will see a diagram like the one shown in *Figure 9.19*:

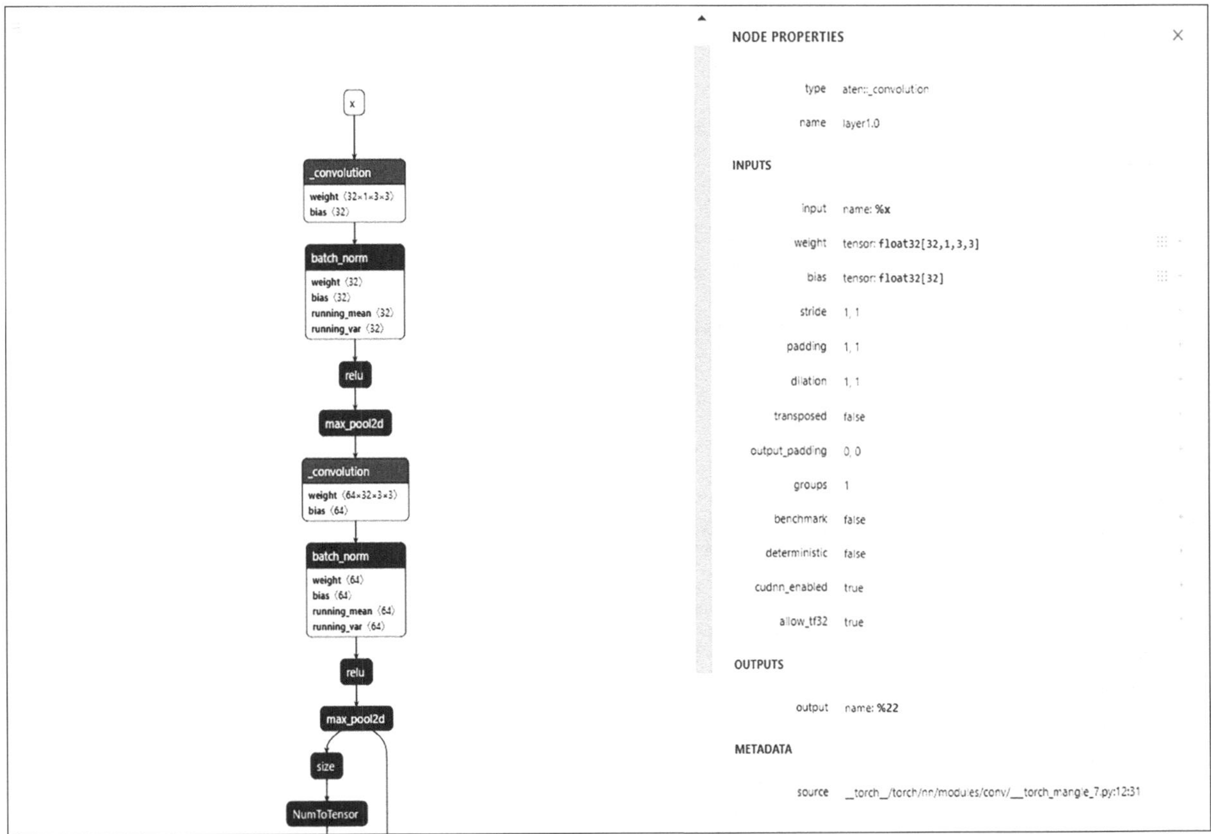

Figure 9.19: *An Interactive Structure of the FashionCNN Model with Netron*

As previously stated, Netron allows for a deep and detailed study of the model. It is also a tool that accepts many other formats from other development environments and implementations of neural network models.

Scaling PyTorch with Dask

So far we have seen an example of DL and the behavior of a neural network in a single machine system, with and without a GPU. Now, let us scale the same example into a distributed system through the use of a cluster of computers. As done in the previous chapter, we will use the service provided by **SaturnCloud.io** to access a cluster of machines for a 30-*hour trial period* for *free*.

In order to scale our PyTorch-based code in a distributed system, we will again use Dask and other related technologies. As we have seen in the previous chapters, it will be very simple to carry out this step, while making very small changes to the code we have just used. Dask will then take care of making the appropriate conversions at the time of execution.

We go to **SaturnCloud.io** and once logged in with an account, we *activate* a cluster of machines using a prepared template, which is created specifically for PyTorch. Go to **Resources** and click on the **New Resource from a Template** button, as shown in *Figure 9.20*:

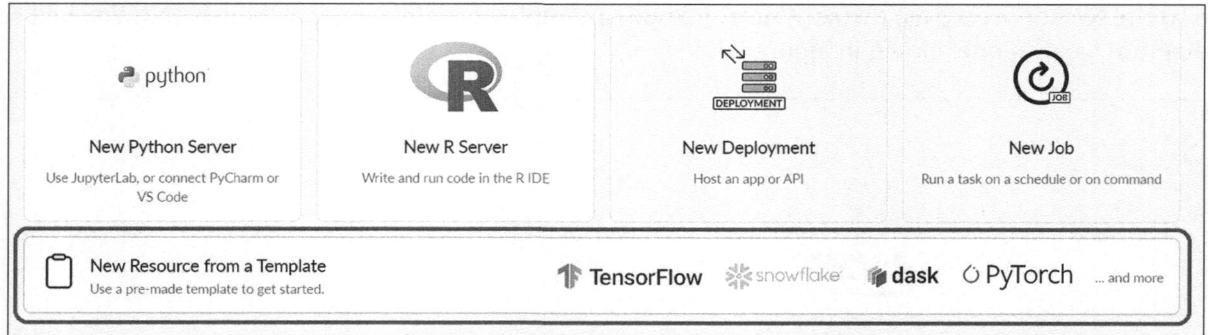

***Figure 9.20**: Resources Available on SaturnCloud.io*

After pressing the button, a series of possible options will appear demonstrating many templates, with each being specialized for a particular application, including PyTorch. Click on the *corresponding button* to activate a cluster already prepared for PyTorch with all the necessary libraries already installed (see *Figure* 9.21).

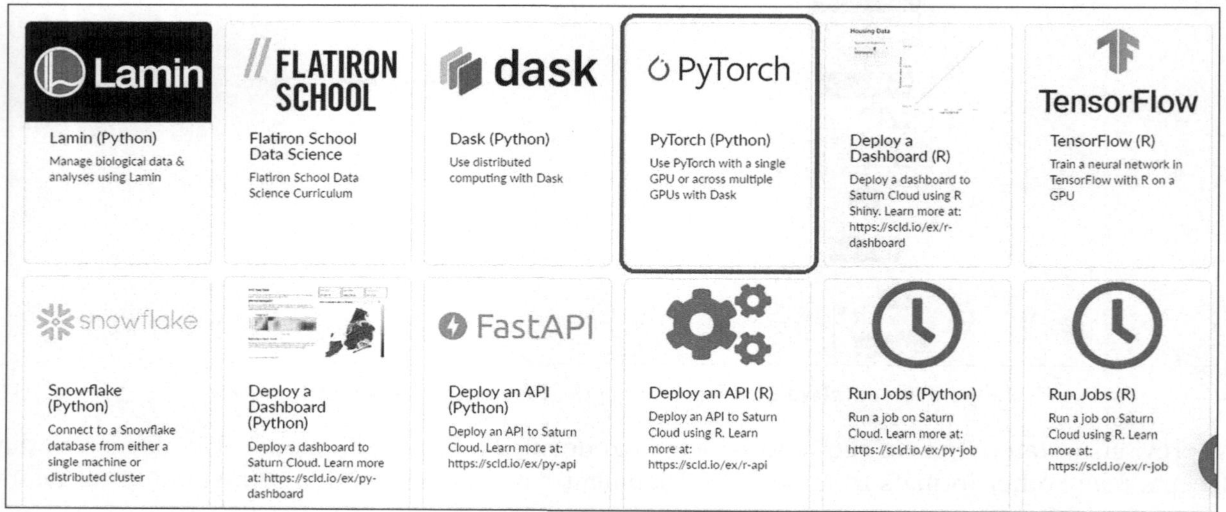

***Figure 9.21**: Pre-Installed Cluster Templates Available on SaturnCloud.io*

Immediately afterwards, a dialog box will appear. You will have to enter the name of the resource to be created. Feel free to leave the default name **`example-pytorch`** or enter a new one as you like, as shown in *Figure* 9.22:

Create Resource

Create a jupyter workspace with settings from **example-pytorch**.

Owner / Name

meccanismocomplesso / example-pytorch

Create Cancel

***Figure 9.22:** Naming the Resource on SaturnCloud.io*

Once you have created the resource, all constituent machines will activate, including a Jupyter server on which you will insert the *code, as well as four other machines* that include *three workers* (*Dask cluster*), and a *scheduler*. If everything goes correctly, you will end up with a newly created resource with the *green* indicators showing the **running** status as in *Figure* 9.23:

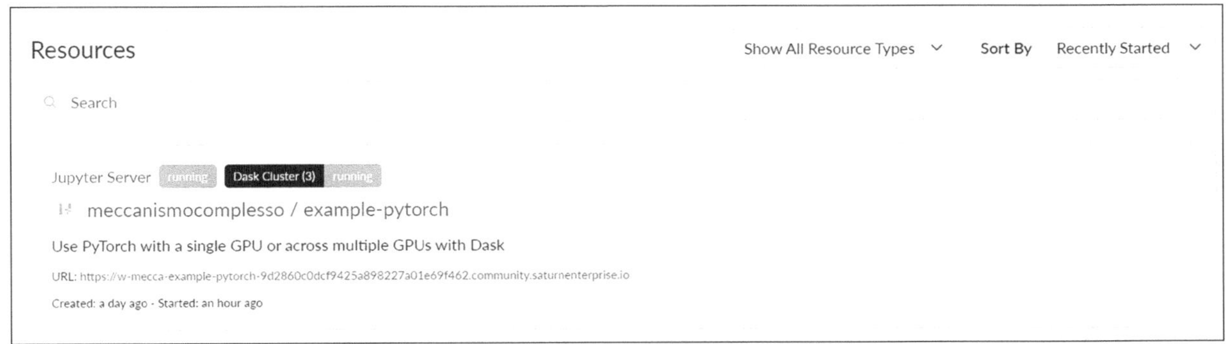

***Figure 9.23**: A Newly Created Dask Cluster Resource on SaturnCloud.io*

Select it to access the resource. You will find *two* different panels on the page, one dedicated to the **Jupyter Server** and the other for the **Dask Cluster**. At the bottom of the **Jupyter Server** panel, select the **Jupyter Notebook** button as shown in *Figure* 9.24, and click to access the application.

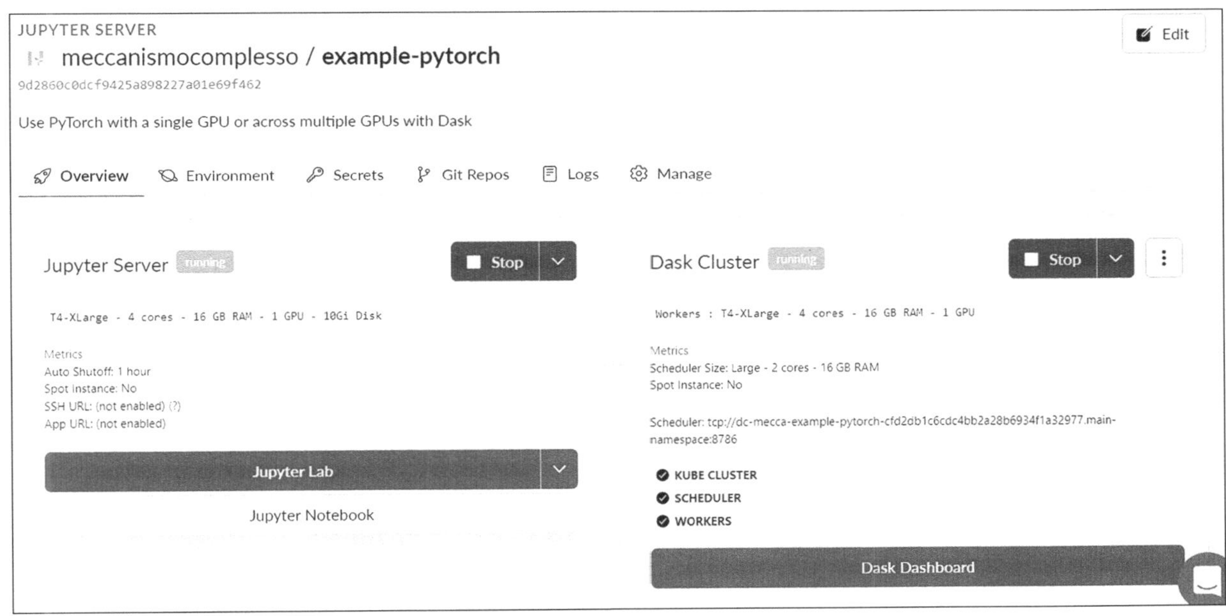

***Figure 9.24**: Dashboard of the Newly Created Resource on SaturnCloud.io*

Once Jupyter is open, create a new notebook and start entering the code we used earlier, but with some differences. As for the imports of the various *modules* and *libraries* needed, everything remains unchanged.

```
import torch
import torch.nn as nn
from torch.autograd import Variable

import torchvision
from torchvision import datasets
from torchvision.transforms import ToTensor
from torch.utils.data import DataLoader

import datetime
```

To add new libraries and import Dask, use this code in a distributed system like **SaturnCloud**. We will then import some proprietary libraries to integrate Dask into a SaturnCloud cluster.

```
import dask
from dask_saturn import SaturnCluster
from dask.distributed import Client
from distributed.worker import logger
```

In the following cell of the notebook, we signal to Dask the presence of the cluster and indicate the number of workers:

```
n_workers = 3
cluster = SaturnCluster(n_workers=n_workers)
client = Client(cluster)
client.wait_for_workers(n_workers)
```

By running the previous cell, you will get the following output which will indicate that the cluster is *ready* to run the code distributed via Dask:

```
INFO:dask-saturn:Cluster is ready
INFO:dask-saturn:Registering default plugins
INFO:dask-saturn:Success!
```

Once this is done, the code that relates to the import of data for *training* and *testing* the neural network is inserted. This piece of code has practically remained unchanged.

```
training_data = datasets.FashionMNIST(
    root="data",
    train=True,
    download=True,
    transform=ToTensor()
)

test_data = datasets.FashionMNIST(
    root="data",
    train=False,
    download=True,
    transform=ToTensor()
)
```

By executing this part of the code, you will see the data download start in the output as shown in *Figure 9.25*:

```
Downloading http://fashion-mnist.s3-website.eu-central-1.amazonaws.com/train-images-idx3-ubyte.gz
Downloading http://fashion-mnist.s3-website.eu-central-1.amazonaws.com/train-images-idx3-ubyte.gz to data/FashionMNIST/raw/trai
n-images-idx3-ubyte.gz

26422272/? [00:01<00:00, 26241060.82it/s]

Extracting data/FashionMNIST/raw/train-images-idx3-ubyte.gz to data/FashionMNIST/raw

Downloading http://fashion-mnist.s3-website.eu-central-1.amazonaws.com/train-labels-idx1-ubyte.gz
Downloading http://fashion-mnist.s3-website.eu-central-1.amazonaws.com/train-labels-idx1-ubyte.gz to data/FashionMNIST/raw/trai
n-labels-idx1-ubyte.gz

29696/? [00:00<00:00, 132190.39it/s]

Extracting data/FashionMNIST/raw/train-labels-idx1-ubyte.gz to data/FashionMNIST/raw
```

Figure 9.25: *Downloading Data to Jupyter Server in SaturnCloud.io*

The class describing the CNN neural network also remains unchanged.

```
class FashionCNN(nn.Module):

    def __init__(self):
```

```
        super(FashionCNN, self).__init__()

        self.layer1 = nn.Sequential(
            nn.Conv2d(in_channels=1, out_channels=32, kernel_size=3, pad-
ding=1),
            nn.BatchNorm2d(32),
            nn.ReLU(),
            nn.MaxPool2d(kernel_size=2, stride=2)
        )

        self.layer2 = nn.Sequential(
            nn.Conv2d(in_channels=32, out_channels=64, kernel_size=3),
            nn.BatchNorm2d(64),
            nn.ReLU(),
            nn.MaxPool2d(2)
        )

        self.fc1 = nn.Linear(in_features=64*6*6, out_features=600)
        self.drop = nn.Dropout2d(0.25)
        self.fc2 = nn.Linear(in_features=600, out_features=120)
        self.fc3 = nn.Linear(in_features=120, out_features=10)

    def forward(self, x):
        out = self.layer1(x)
        out = self.layer2(out)
        out = out.view(out.size(0), -1)
        out = self.fc1(out)
        out = self.drop(out)
        out = self.fc2(out)
        out = self.fc3(out)
        return out
```

Now, we need to insert the neural network training code that we enclosed in a **train()** function. Doing this facilitates the integration of this code with Dask. The Dask library provides a **@dask.delayed** decorator that allows you to distribute the code enclosed within the function to which it is related in different tasks. These will be then assigned to many workers who will execute them in parallel. The only concern for the developer is to add the decorator, which they can do via:

```
@dask.delayed
def train(bs, lr):

    batch_size = bs
    learning_rate = lr
    train_loader = torch.utils.data.DataLoader(training_data,batch_size)
    test_loader = torch.utils.data.DataLoader(test_data,batch_size)

    device = torch.device('cuda:0')
    num_epochs = 5
    count = 0
    model = FashionCNN()
    model.to(device)
    error = nn.CrossEntropyLoss()

    optimizer = torch.optim.Adam(model.parameters(), lr=learning_rate)

    training_start_time = datetime.datetime.now()
    results = []
```

```
    for epoch in range(num_epochs):
        for images, labels in train_loader:
            images, labels = images.to(device), labels.to(device)
            train = Variable(images.view(100, 1, 28, 28))
            labels = Variable(labels)
            outputs = model(train)
            loss = error(outputs, labels)
            optimizer.zero_grad()
            loss.backward()
            optimizer.step()
            count += 1

        # Testing the model
            if not (count % 50):
                total = 0
                correct = 0
                for images, labels in test_loader:
                    images, labels = images.to(device), labels.to(device)
                    test = Variable(images.view(100, 1, 28, 28))
                    outputs = model(test)
                    predictions = torch.max(outputs, 1)[1].to(device)
                    correct += (predictions == labels).sum()
                    total += len(labels)

                accuracy = correct * 100 / total
                new_results = {
                   "batch_size": batch_size,
                   "loss": loss.data.item(),
                   "iteration": count,
                   "accuracy": accuracy.item(),
                   "elapsed_time_sec": (datetime.datetime.now() - training_
start_time).total_seconds(),
                }
                results.append(new_results)

    return results
```

Until now, the code used was almost the same as the one used in the case of the single machine, except for some additions. Now, we will initiate is the part inherent to the particular behavior of Dask. In the following cell, we will launch the training execution using the **client.map()** mapping function:

```
experiment = [(100, 0.001)]
train_future = client.map(train, experiment)
```

In executing the previous cell, we will see that there is no actual execution and the output will be immediate. This happens because Dask is lazy; the invocation of the function does not trigger execution. Parallel code execution will only happen when we explicitly request the results by calling **client.gather(), like we have done here:**

```
results = client.gather(train_future)
```

This time, by executing the previous cell, we will have a longer execution time as the computations are really carried out. The results obtained for each iteration will be collected within results in a slightly different way, but in the same format as in the previous examples. Once the execution is finished, we can see the following results:

```
import pandas as pd

results_concatenated = [item for sublist in results for item in sublist]
```

```
results_df = pd.DataFrame.from_dict(results_concatenated)
results_df.head(10)
```

You will get a result similar to the one shown in *Figure* 9.26:

	batch_size	loss	iteration	accuracy	elapsed_time_sec
0	100	1.008428	50	61.660000	2.228519
1	100	1.139894	100	61.430000	3.704949
2	100	0.940989	150	65.250000	5.168618
3	100	0.805514	200	66.369995	6.641557
4	100	0.796870	250	65.830002	8.113434
5	100	0.962739	300	66.309998	9.618787
6	100	0.915788	350	64.669998	11.094542
7	100	1.013723	400	66.220001	12.570212
8	100	1.099278	450	65.309998	14.060075
9	100	0.881033	500	65.409996	15.532078

Figure 9.26: *DataFrame with Learning Outcomes*

We will do the same thing for the last five DataFrame values:

```
results_df.tail()
```

You will get the final part of the DataFrame as shown here(see *Figure* 9.27):

	batch_size	loss	iteration	accuracy	elapsed_time_sec
55	100	0.721782	2800	69.250000	83.680797
56	100	0.987083	2850	69.549995	85.286323
57	100	0.778295	2900	70.400002	86.749804
58	100	0.662645	2950	68.739998	88.234482
59	100	0.748363	3000	70.479996	89.732871

Figure 9.27: *Last Five Rows of the DataFrame with the Learning Outcomes*

As we can see from the previous figures (see *Figures* 9.24 and 9.25), the execution of 3,000 *iterations* was even faster than the case of parallel execution via GPU on single machines. The times are halved, with an average of 1.5 *seconds* spent every 50 *iterations*. This is about half the time taken in the preceding single GPU machine case (*about* 3 *seconds*).

```
import matplotlib.pyplot as plt

plt.plot(results_df['iteration'], results_df['loss'])
plt.show()
```

Let us now see the loss and accuracy values during the iterations using the graphs shown in *Figure* 9.28:

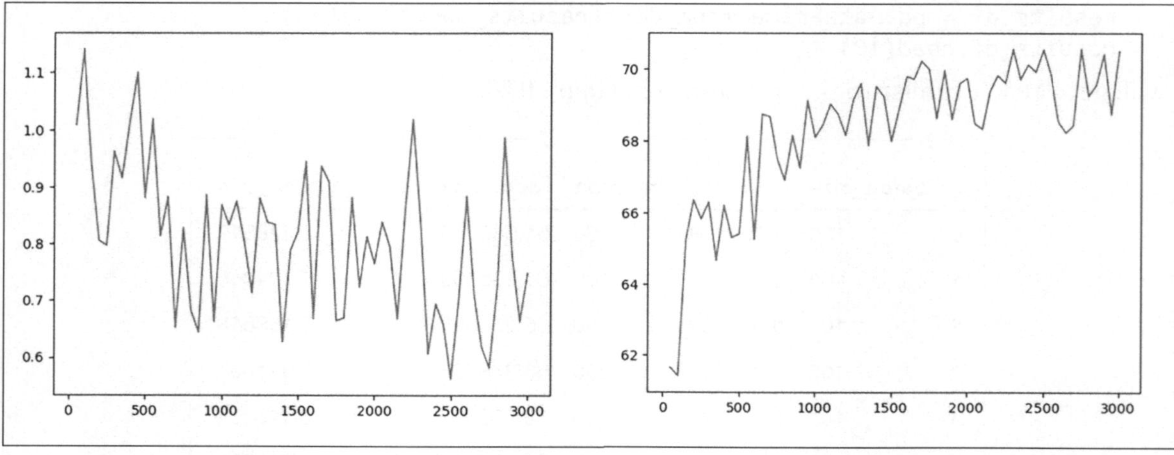

***Figure 9.28**: Loss and Accuracy Trends Obtained with Dask on SaturnCloud.io*

As we can see, this time the system has suffered and both loss and accuracy are no longer as good as the single machine case. This means that despite the increased performance of DL code execution in a distributed system, the quality of learning of the neural network here has not been preserved. This is due to the fact that we most likely have integrated the existing code in Dask on a distributed system while making too few changes and neglecting some scaling mechanisms that led to the loss in the learning quality of the neural network.

To better understand what might be the origin of the problems just mentioned. Consider analyzing the code you just used on a single machine. Dask, among its many features, allows you to execute its distributed code even in *single-machine architectures*.

To do this, simply change the **Dask Client** settings. On your PC, open a Jupyter Notebook in the *Anaconda* virtual environment dedicated to PyTorch and copy the preceding code into it. Then modify the cell relating to the Dask Client as follows:

```
import dask
#from dask_saturn import SaturnCluster
from dask.distributed import Client
#from distributed.worker import logger
#n_workers = 3
#cluster = SaturnCluster(n_workers=n_workers)
#client = Client(cluster)
#client.wait_for_workers(n_workers)

client = Client()
```

Running all the cells will give you the result shown in *Figure* 9.29:

	batch_size	loss	iteration	accuracy	elapsed_time_sec
0	100	0.446040	50	80.779999	4.762428
1	100	0.545907	100	82.389999	8.147475
2	100	0.513924	150	85.379997	11.207155
3	100	0.406646	200	86.110001	14.164868
4	100	0.388509	250	84.759995	16.760471
5	100	0.372058	300	86.860001	19.718247
6	100	0.360087	350	86.970001	22.391748
7	100	0.461946	400	83.979996	25.316237
8	100	0.668416	450	84.930000	28.051320
9	100	0.486805	500	87.669998	30.677633
55	100	0.294967	2800	90.099998	158.686704
56	100	0.458460	2850	89.939995	161.465027
57	100	0.235022	2900	90.409996	164.436711
58	100	0.153714	2950	90.029999	167.063556
59	100	0.156465	3000	90.570000	169.751957

***Figure 9.29**: DataFrame with the Results of the Integration with Dask on a Single Machine*

Similarly, the *loss* and *accuracy* trends will be represented in the graphs generated by **`matplotlib,`** as shown in *Figure 9.30*:

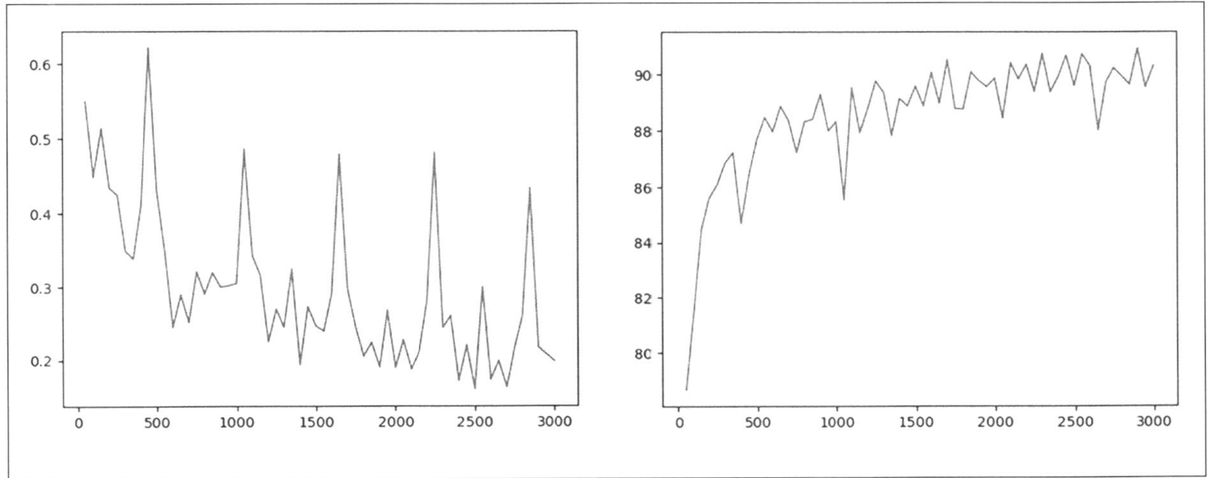

***Figure 9.30**: Graphs of Loss and Learning Accuracy with Dask on a Single Machine*

As we can see in this case, the *loss* and *accuracy* have returned to values similar to the previous examples on a single machine. So, the problem is not due to the integration of Dask into the code, but the distribution of tasks or data will affect the learning mechanisms of the neural network.

We therefore require a more accurate analysis of the code used and need to modify it wherever necessary. It is clear that scaling complex code like DL on distributed systems is not a simple operation like Pandas or Scikit-learn could be with their ML models. However, there are other approaches to integrate PyTorch models with Dask in a distributed system, for example, by wrapping with models that are more integrated with the Dask framework to guarantee better scaling efficiency. However, these analyses go beyond the simple context of this book. Those interested in discovering more are invited to seek innovative solutions to this problem.

On the other hand, despite the underlying mechanisms of the code used which have produced less efficient learning, it is evident how using a distributed system can lead to a considerable increase in calculation speed. This makes the learning phases of the networks neural much faster.

Conclusion

AI has developed rapidly in the world of information technology in the last decade, especially in the development and study of systems capable of learning. It is from this objective that ML has emerged and is so deeply rooted in AI that it has almost become synonymous to it. ML has found its best representation in the Python language, which has provided researchers and operators with powerful libraries containing all the necessary tools for this discipline. The models used, the data sizes, and the learning algorithms are becoming more complex and the transition to parallel computing has become necessary.

As far as DL is concerned, it is the last frontier of application of distributed systems. Artificial neural networks and their learning systems represent a complex phenomenon that requires more computing resources. The matter is so complex that the results are often unpredictable, and require further study. However, DL is a fascinating discipline, to which much can be added.

In the next chapter, we will wrap up the topic of parallel computing by discussing the future trends and technological innovations that will help you develop the concepts in this book. ML and DL are the indication of what awaits us. New technologies will bring new disciplines and the contribution of parallel programming developers will be increasingly required as they will have to keep up with times.

References

- https://www.oracle.com/it/artificial-intelligence/what-is-ai/
- https://www.meccanismocomplesso.org/deep-learning/
- https://medium.com/@gaurav2proud/what-is-the-need-of-parallel-processing-for-machine-learning-in-real-time-7bfc9b66e40c
- https://web.stanford.edu/~rezab/classes/cme323/S16/projects_reports/hedge_usmani.pdf
- https://www.alteryx.com/glossary/supervised-vs-unsupervised-learning
- https://analyticsindiamag.com/a-guide-to-parallel-and-distributed-deep-learning-for-beginners/
- https://www.e2enetworks.com/blog/demystifying-parallel-and-distributed-deep-learning
- https://www.simplilearn.com/keras-vs-tensorflow-vs-pytorch-article
- https://www.simplilearn.com/tutorials/deep-learning-tutorial/deep-learning-frameworks
- https://www.simplilearn.com/tutorials/deep-learning-tutorial/deep-learning-algorithm
- https://pytorch.org/docs/stable/notes/multiprocessing.html#asynchronous-multiprocess-training-e-g-hogwild
- https://pytorch.org/tutorials/intermediate/ddp_tutorial.html
- https://www.tensorflow.org/guide/distributed_training

Chapter 10
Future of Parallel Programming

Introduction

In the previous chapter, we saw how Artificial Intelligence (AI) is gaining ground among the disciplines that make more use of parallel computing. The success of this approach and the fascination associated with it has always inspired people to create an intelligent entity to work with. This has in turn pushed the sector towards greater progress. It runs in tandem with the technological potential on which these systems work.

In this chapter, we will see the next technological steps that involve parallel computing and AI in their development. These technological innovations lead to an evolution in the procedures and concepts discussed in this book, as well as foster creation of new concepts and paradigms that can keep pace with technological progress. Such progress is not confined to strictly scientific and professional environments, but has the potential to be more integrated into our social life, our customs, and habits. In all of this, parallel computing will eventually become the processing standard. Those who work in this area will be futuristic professionals as several interesting and stimulating job opportunities open up.

Structure

This chapter addresses the following topics:

- Massively Parallel Artificial Intelligence
- Edge Computing
- Cyber-Physical Systems
- Cybersecurity
- Exascale Computing
- Quantum Computing
- New Professional Opportunities
- Advances in Python Libraries

Massively Parallel Artificial Intelligence

Among the innovations in AI, the most imminent one is the development of **Massively Parallel Artificial Intelligence**, which is based on the increasing availability of massively parallel systems (see *Figure 10.1*).

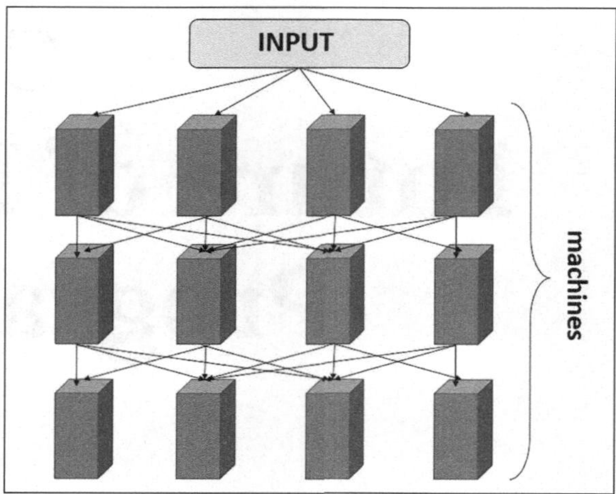

Figure 10.1: *Massively Parallel System Model*

The term, Massively Parallel System refers to a set of many processing units structured to carry out a certain operation by working in parallel.

These systems have existed before the 1970s and have evolved through technological innovations. Generally, we can identify these systems as linked to a particular type of supercomputer, where the processing units such as CPUs, GPUs, or separate machines (massively parallel machines) are arranged in parallel and perform a specific portion of a task.

Today, massively parallel systems are growing to be increasingly powerful. Facebook and Google are among the major users of these systems, as the latter are capable of managing immense amounts of data that arrives from search engines and social networks.

The particular parallel structure, made up of homogeneous and independent units, also allows these systems to be scaled according to calculation needs.

For example, if one of these systems requires more resources to keep up with applications, extra processing units can easily be added to the system, wherever necessary. If, on the other hand, the computing resources are excessive, they could be deactivated or allocated to other tasks, which prevents wastage of resources.

The nature of these particular systems, as well as their increasing power and flexibility, makes them suitable for the use of AI. The same AI is then used for to tune its own performance. This allows these systems to adapt dynamically in an autonomous and efficient way to cater to various calculation needs.

This new area of AI research possesses unimaginable computing power which will result into better and large scale computing performance. However, this is not the goal of such systems. As we have seen before, with the transition from Machine Learning (ML) to Deep Learning (DL), this computing power will certainly lead to the emergence of a new approach towards the creation of intelligent systems. For example, new methods are being developed to introduce forms of **memory-based reasoning** into applications. Another technique that has been in vogue is **parallel marker passing**, with which new highly parallel algorithms are being developed. These are able to reformulate the use of neural networks. These innovations, encouraged by the use of massively parallel machines, offer an opportunity for AI to tackle new and vast challenges and irregularities present in real-world data. Other new technologies introduced in the field data include **Very Large Knowledge Bases (VLKB)**.

Edge Computing

In the two preceding chapters (*Chapters* 8 and 9: *Parallel Computing for Data Science* and *Parallel Computing for Artificial Intelligence*, respectively), we have seen how the clusters of machines and cloud services are powerful tools that allow us to have distributed systems and therefore scale our parallel computing applications from a single machine to clusters of cars. This is currently the default approach for those who want to develop and study applications for ML and DL. However, that is not all as other disciplines that rely on parallel computing might switch to this form of calculation as these systems become more available.

In the future, we also foresee significant progress for these distributed systems. Recently, **edge computing** has been proposed as a new computing paradigm that will complement the ones covered in the book. In this type of system, the computing and memory resources are located near the data and near all information sources. With the introduction of edge computing, new paradigms and implementations will be added to the current distributed computing (or cloud computing). These paradigms will then take into account the latency and bandwidth of the information between the various components of the system. These characteristics will increasingly intertwine with the integration of security and policy systems and will gradually have to be integrated into data processing with the consequent diffusion of distributed systems in daily activities.

Therefore, the data processing will be divided into two levels: on the edge and the cloud, which are shown in *Figure 10.2*:

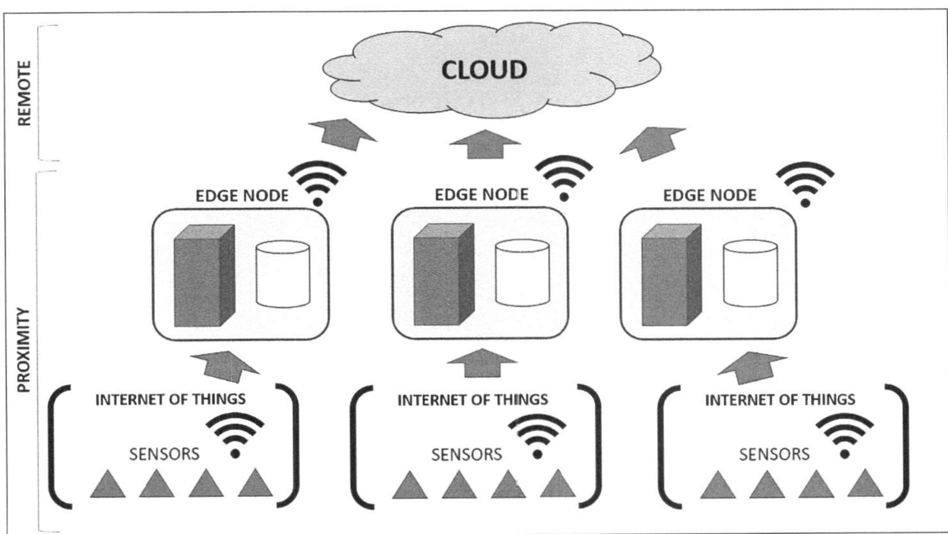

Figure 10.2: *Edge Computing in an IOT System*

The types of input data that will be processed by these techniques will comes from varied sources and objects. Even the data which is processed from the source to the edge, will end up with information that is extrapolated from appropriate models and evolve with the ever-increasing integration of intelligent systems. These systems will convert numerical data, images, sounds, and all current and familiar forms into abstract and summary information. These forms that are more suited to AI will be used by these systems to generate knowledge and build a solid foundation of reasoning.

However, this is an imprecise image of what the future will look like. There are still many steps for us to take, along with technological problems that need to be solved. Nevertheless, this illustration indicates the future trends for parallel computing applications.

For example, Google has created the Edge-TPU service (**https://cloud.google.com/edge-tpu**) which is available online at indicated costs. This service uses ML inference and provides a number of layered technologies like TensorFlow for you to choose as your framework (see *Table 10.1*).

	Edge	**Cloud**
Task	ML inference	ML training and inference

Service	Linux, Windows	AI platform, Kubernetes Engine, Computer Engine, Cloud IoT Core
ML Frameworks	TensorFlow Lite, NN API	TensorFlow, scikit-learn, XGBoost, Keras
HARDWARE ACCELERATORS	Edge CPU, GPU, CPU	Cloud TPU, GPU, CPU

Table 10.1: *Services Available on the Google Edge-TPU*

Distributed Computing Infrastructure with Cyber-Physical Systems

The previous section immediately brings to mind other disciplines and related technologies that are involved with the innovation of AI and the integration of increasingly intelligent systems in our society.

We talked about data sources, future edge computing, and the growing use of sensors and other forms of real-world data capture. Technological advances in communication technologies and the possibility of coverage by Wi-Fi systems have led to the birth and development of the **Internet of Things** (**IoT**). **Cyber-Physical Systems** (**CPS**) play a decisive role in this new "*distributed*" data acquisition system.

These are computer systems whose purpose is to interact continuously with the real environment in which they operate. CPS systems therefore must meet three fundamental requirements to be considered as such:

- Computing
- Communication
- Control

Systems equipped with these three properties collect data through a network of sensors or other human interfaces, process them in an increasingly intelligent way, and communicate the processed information with other computer systems connected to them (edge computing). *Figure* 10.3 shows the evolution of the scheme represented in *Figure* 10.2 with the introduction of Cyber-Physical Systems in edge computing. CPS are capable of processing input data, extrapolating abstract information, and interacting with the external environment via actuators or **Human-Machine interfaces** (**HMI**).

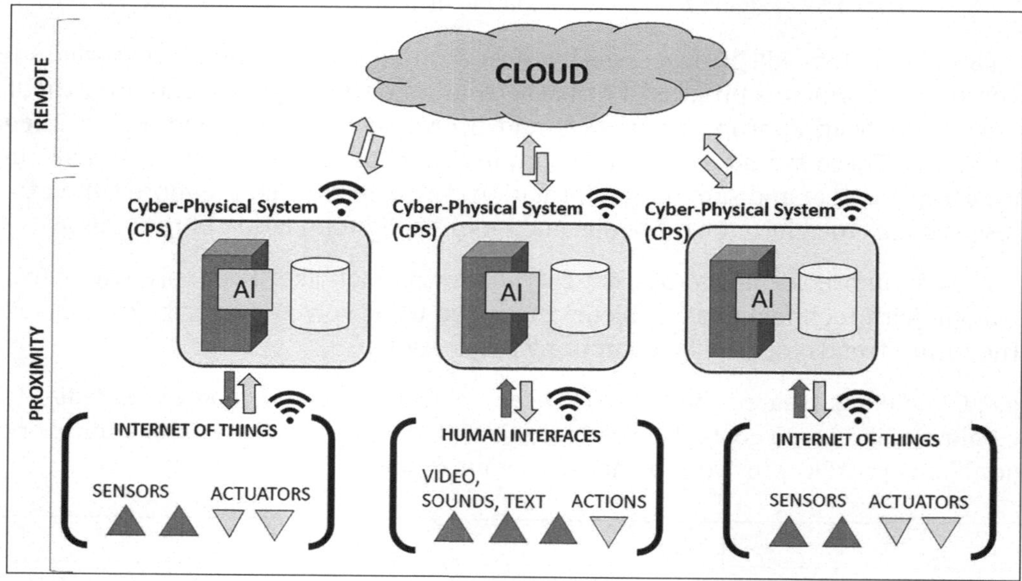

Figure 10.3: *The Evolution of Edge Computing through Intelligent Systems (Cyber-Physical Systems)*

Furthermore, this Cyber-Physical System will also be able to *control* the physical environment in which it operates through actuators or other physical interaction systems, based on the information processed or received. The future goal is to make these systems increasingly intelligent, while integrating them with applications capable of learning, reasoning, and actuating in a similar way to humans. Therefore, we can witness the development of new technologies, approaches, and methods to implement these new intelligent systems that utilize parallel computing.

Artificial Intelligence in Cybersecurity

The adoption of CPS therefore increases the integration of intelligent systems in all human activities. Entrusting all these operations and visibility to controlled intelligent systems requires a corresponding development of new security systems.

This reality is not that distant. Recent studies show that AI has already taken over many fields, some of which are sensitive enough to impact integral matters such as privacy and security. Sectors such as finance, military, transportation, and hospitals already use AI, with more applications yet to come in the next few years. Their intrusion of anti-social and criminal elements that misuse AI can wreck devastating damage on the society. It therefore necessitates the development of security systems capable of exerting control immediately and appropriately to avoid the misuse of AI.

Currently, **cybersecurity** deals with today's computers that are equipped with functional and dumb operating systems and is already operating on principles such as intrusion detection, privacy protection and social engineering. The extension of these problems to AI systems and their increased integration into daily life is a new challenge for those approaching the future.

Even in this case, AI can be used to address these security issues. The interconnection between AI and cybersecurity is a key factor for the right use of information systems that impacts the future of society.

In this regard, the **European Union Agency for Cybersecurity** (ENISA) has released an interesting report which can be downloaded for free online (**https://www.enisa.europa.eu/publications/artificial-intelligence-cybersecurity-challenges**). The document highlights the challenges cybersecurity will have to face in the imminent future. This is illustrated in *Figure 10.4*:

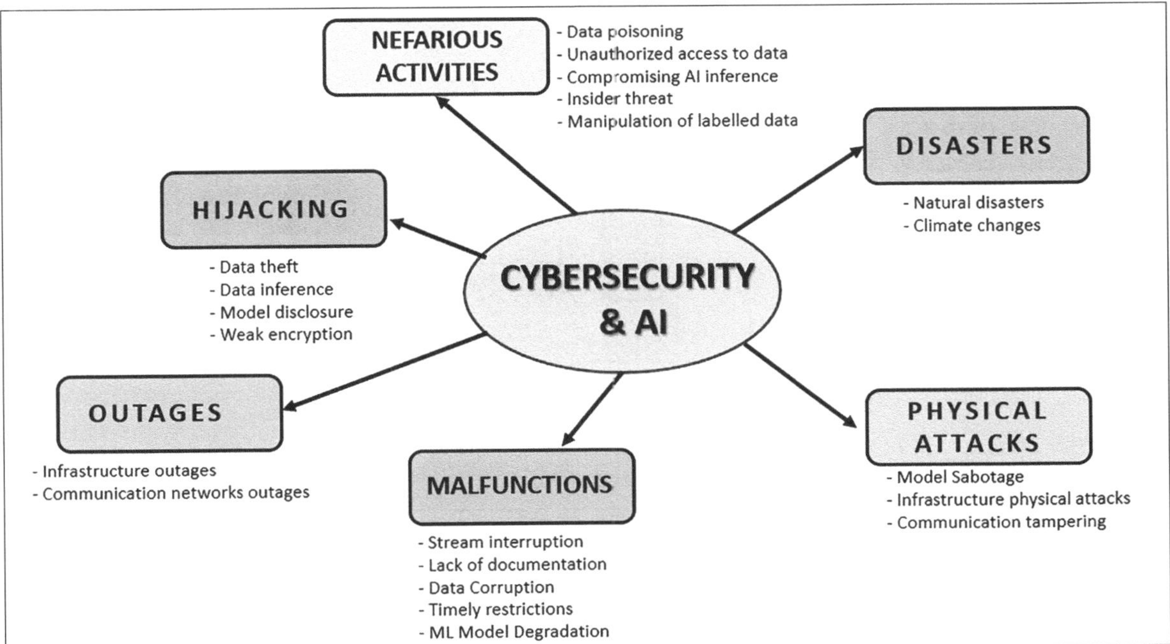

Figure 10.4: *Imminent Threats to Cybersecurity*

Advent of Web 5.0

The introduction of Web 5.0, which is also called *emotional web*, *telepathic web*, or *symbiotic web*, is expected to revolutionize the way users interact. This new paradigm aims to add emotions and sensoriality to the flow of data exchange, thereby facilitating more natural interactions between humans and machines.

Such an innovative system requires a new set of new technologies that produce data in new forms that are not considered by current information systems. This data will take on more complex and abstract forms of data, beyond simple numbers and text.

As data science in particular is based exclusively the on data produced by the web, it should be poised to adapt to these changes. Furthermore, if we consider the number of current daily requests for services (for example, Google processes around 3.5 billion requests per day) that require extremely powerful AI-powered computing systems, it is clear that new innovations should be able to deliver enhanced performance in order to be relevant.

These new forms of data will specific algorithms and corresponding AI systems that are capable of understanding them. Thereafter, all innovations should be integrated with concepts like intelligent Edge Computing as they will process the input data "*close*" to the source. This will reduce the costs of the central processing unit and the flow of data.

Therefore, Web 5.0 utilizes **Decentralized Web Nodes** (**DWNs**) that store data and allow people and organizations to send and store encrypted or public data messages. This allows the creation of various decentralized apps and protocols (as shown in *Figure* 10.5).

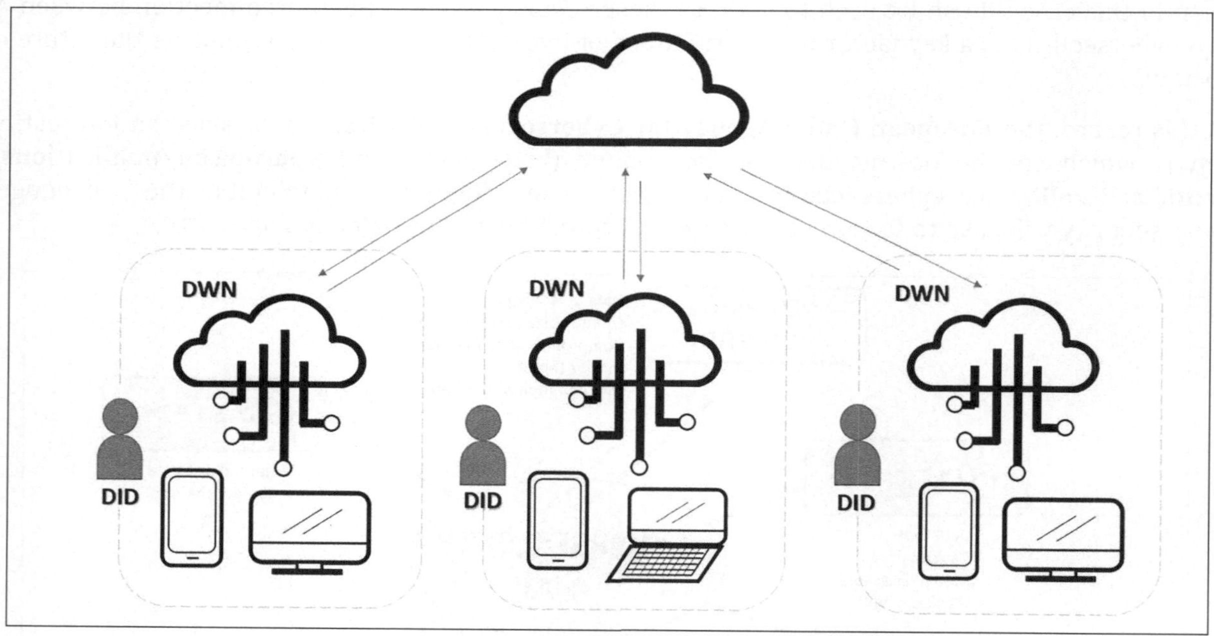

***Figure* 10.5**: Decentralized Web Nodes in Web 5.0

Another goal of Web 5.0 is to decentralize the identity of users, and how their data is stored. Account management can also be decentralized via **Decentralized Identifiers** (**DID**), which are self-owned identifiers used for decentralized authentication and routing. The applications developed in this area keep the identity data locally instead of sending it to the central unit. Even if this seems trivial, DID responds to many cybersecurity and data privacy needs. It will also revolutionize data processing and will require new processing systems for it.

Exascale Computing

Another emerging trend in technological innovations is **Exascale computing**. The term indicates a new level of supercomputing that is capable of performing at least 1,000,000,000,000,000,000 floating point operations per second (Exaflops). Such computing power can increase the performance of applications that use parallel computing.

The creation of supercomputers based on these systems will bring enormous benefits to the use of simulations, the development of AI and data analysis, thanks to the possibility of solving incredibly complex problems.

In the United States, the Californian company HPE has built the first exascale supercomputer called Frontier, which will be assembled at the Oak Ridge National Lab (2023), an interdisciplinary science and technology laboratory managed by the United States Department of Energy. This supercomputer recorded a performance of 1.1 exaflops breaking a hitherto unattainable limit and has thus positioned itself as the most powerful supercomputer in the world.

Frontier, like other exascale supercomputers, was built using combinations of CPUs and GPUs, multi-socket nodes, and other purpose-built devices based solely on parallel computing. It is clear that with the diffusion of such systems, there is a strong incentive for to formulate new approaches and methods in parallel programming.

Quantum Computing

Parallel computing is destined to evolve with the birth of new computing technologies that are completely different from the earlier versions. One of these is **Quantum Computing**. This computing system bases its operation on the quantum properties of matter, such as the superposition of states and entanglement. Thanks to these properties, these systems are able to perform operations on data on quantum bits instead of transistors that operate in binary state (0 or 1). Quantum bits are also called qubits and are capable of processing multiple values simultaneously, which completely distorts the basics of the binary code.

Computers based on quantum computing are already intrinsically parallel at a very low level. These characteristics promise upheavals in computing performance. It is clear that these technologies require an upheaval of parallel computing basics, which gives birth to new concepts and approaches.

The potential of quantum computers has led to a real race among various nations of the world to create such systems. Although the technology is fresh, these computers already exist and new versions are being created. The first quantum computer was marketed by IBM in 2019 and is called **IBM Q System One**. Subsequently, the US created a series of quantum computers called **Eagle** (127 qubits) in the form of chips that can be adapted to the new system: **IBM System Two** and its corresponding software.

In Canada, Xanadu has joined the superpowers with the creation of a quantum computer based on photon entanglement, which is called **Borealis** (216 qubits). This system was used to calculate the Gaussian boson sampling of 216 photons in just 36 microseconds. Such a problem would have required over 9,000 years of computation on today's fastest supercomputers.

As far as Europe is concerned, two quantum computers are already active (Paris in France, and Jülich in Germany) out of the 6 that are under construction (one of which is in Italy) which will form the first quantum computer network in the world. These machines will be used for research but will also be made accessible to European start-ups and companies in order to stimulate subsequent technological progress. Even more recent (2022) is the news from China that has created its first quantum computer, **Wuyan**, which is equipped with 24 qubits and is built by Origin Quantum Computing.

Quantum technology, when integrated with the existing HPC systems, will pave way for significant advances in all sectors of the industry.

New Professional Opportunities

A good note for future professionals in this field concerns a few comments made at the recent **World Economic Forums** (**WEF**). Among the new emerging professions that will define the work of the future are AI and data specialists, whose digital skills will intersect with human ones. Professions like data scientists, cloud engineers, cybersecurity experts, and AI experts are included in the list of 96 professions for the future and were listed in the WEF study *Jobs of Tomorrow: Mapping Opportunity in the New Economy*.

However, the WEF study projects that while the demand for AI specialists will increase, the available and open positions will be limited. This makes AI a niche profession for industry experts. On the other hand, the number of positions for data scientists will grow considerably, making it the third most popular emerging job by the number of open positions.

Regarding requisite skills in data science and AI, the study proposes the term tech disruptive skills to refer to more advanced digital skills that can be used to develop business model and impact the job market in a meaningful and lasting way. We will find the following competencies under the term:

- Data Science
- Natural Language Processing (NLP)
- Robotics and Automation
- Cybersecurity

The skills we have come across in the book are linked to AI and implicitly to parallel computing.

Required Advances in Parallel Computing for Python

As all computing hardware is multi-core these days, therefore it is imperative for Python to provide high-performance parallelism.

This is what was said at EuroPython 2019. Thus, it was projected as the imminent goal for all Python developers who would confront the push to innovate their libraries to adapt to current demands.

However, there is a long way to go. Despite everything we have seen in the book, a lot of changes will be needed to adapt their APIs more and more to these parallel systems, which will soon become the norm.

Given the nature of Python, this task will also involve the users of these libraries, who will have to signal their major professional needs of their professional activity for evolving libraries to cater to them.

Therefore, a new generation of developers will come into play. Parallel programming will be the dominant form of reasoning that the new professionals will use to devise efficient and intuitive constructs and patterns. For example, new developers will be able to create libraries by integrating the most modern technologies for parallel computing into them. Python can also be used to wrap native implementations that are often developed in C (for example, BLAS).

This feature allows Python to take advantage of innovations developed in other languages. An example is the recent **MPIRE** library, proposed as an evolution of the standard multiprocessing module. Sebastiaan Jansen, the author of MPIRE, conducted a series of benchmarking experiments in his article *[title of the article]* to evaluate the performance of common Python parallel computing libraries. *Figure* 10.6 reports Jansen's results, showing how execution time varies as the number of threads increases.

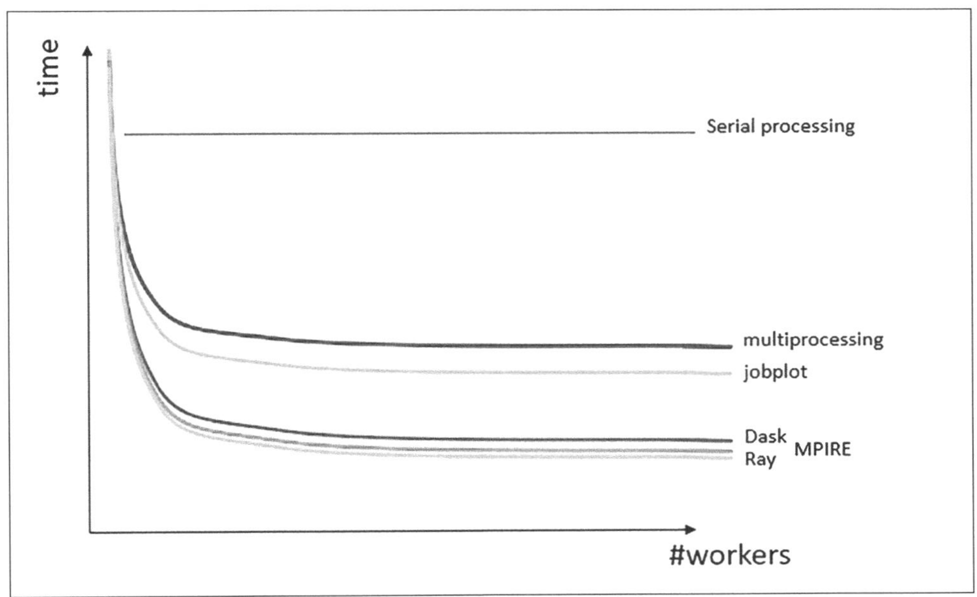

Figure 10.6: *Performance Graph for Parallel Computing Libraries*

As reported by Jansen, this library manages to achieve the same performance as distributed systems with libraries such as Dask and Ray, while remaining within the scope of the single machine. In this case, a user can observe improvement in performance without having to scale the calculation execution on clusters of machines. This reduces costs, and makes the implementation of the code easier.

MPIRE is only the beginning. Other libraries can take advantage of other mechanisms for parallel computing by wrapping other native libraries (such as CUDA with GPUs).

As far as ML and DL libraries are concerned, improvements and innovations will certainly occur with the introduction of new libraries and improving existing ones like PyTorch and TensorFlow.

Future of PyTorch and TensorFlow

As far as PyTorch and TensorFlow are concerned, their ability to incorporate modern technologies and provide services and models users is a unique feature.

In an interesting article by AssemblyAI, *PyTorch vs TensorFlow in 2023*, one can observe interesting dynamics between the possible futures of these libraries, despite them being in competition with each other. For example, it is stated that at present, building new models from scratch may be too expensive for small companies. Therefore, they will have to use pre-trained models. As a result, the future of PyTorch and TensorFlow shall be decided on the basis of the number and quality of pre-trained models offered by them.

To demonstrate this hypothesis, the article illustrates the success trend of these two frameworks by measuring the number of papers about them over time. An indicative reconstruction of this graph is shown in *Figure 10.7*:

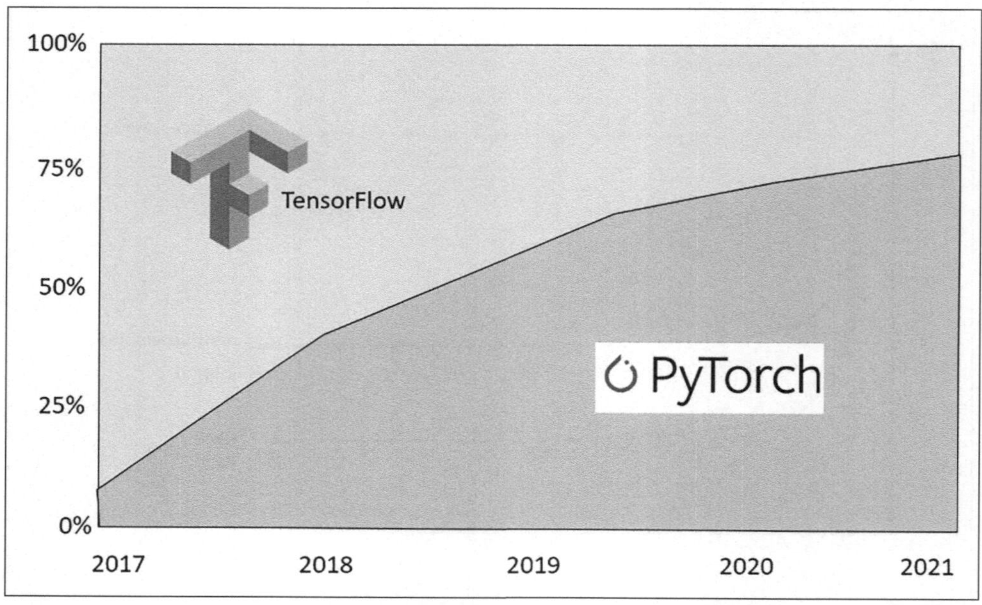

Figure 10.7: *Fractions of Papers about Pytorch or TensorFlow*

As we can easily see, PyTorch has been gaining ground in academic and research environments and has taken over TensorFlow. This happens despite the excellent performance of the latter. We can thus infer that a library (such as a programming language), despite being more resource intensive, can be more preferable than others due to the ease and availability of facilities like better pre-trained models.

The article also proposed another parameter to corroborate Jansen's theory; it asked the users to consider the number of repositories that use various DL frameworks, including PyTorch and TensorFlow. An indicative representation of the same is shown in *Figure 10.8*:

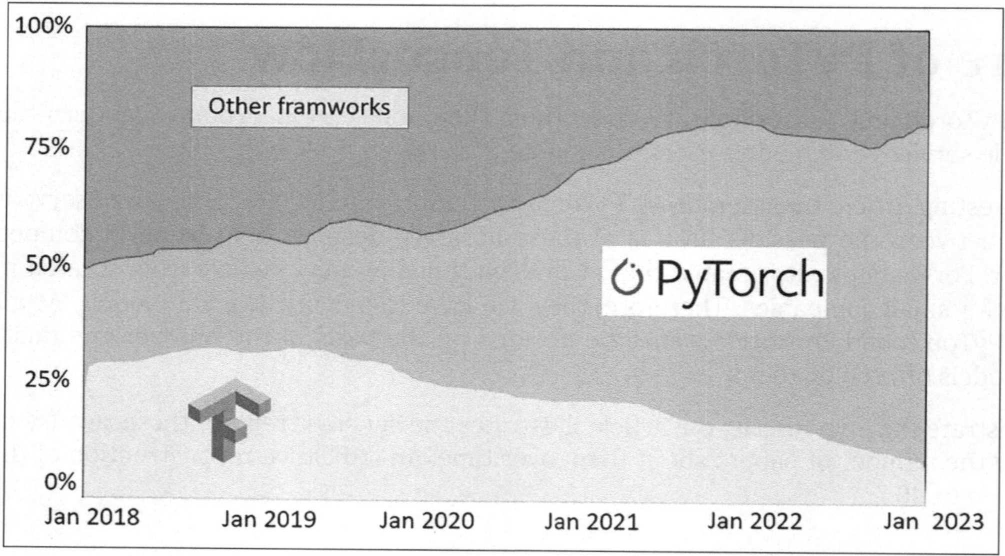

Figure 10.8: *Percentage of Repositories by Deep Learning Frameworks*

In the graph, we can see a greater diffusion of PyTorch compared to TensorFlow during the last three years. It is clear that these trends only capture the period from 2018 to 2023, and cannot guarantee that PyTorch will be the default reference library for DL in the near future. Innovations in TensorFlow, a mutation in user needs and the introduction of a new library can tilt the illustrated balance in a completely different direction.

Conclusion

This chapter provides an overview of the modern technologies and innovations that impact the world of parallel computing. Having read all the chapters of the book, you must now be clear about the parallel programming and computing, as well as evolutionary trends in the imminent future. You have now grasped the futuristic significance of these topics and their continuing relevance in various scientific, professional, and social fields. Those who master these systems will hold the keys to access more possibilities and will be able to comprehend changing demands that evolve constantly.

References

- https://ai.googleblog.com/2021/03/massively-parallel-graph-computation.html
- https://www.ijcai.org/Proceedings/91-1/Papers/087.pdf
- https://ieeeaccess.ieee.org/closed-special-sections/artificial-intelligence-in-parallel-and-distributed-computing/
- https://ieeeaccess.ieee.org/closed-special-sections/distributed-computing-infrastructure-for-cyber-physical-systems/
- https://ieeeaccess.ieee.org/closed-special-sections/artificial-intelligence-in-cybersecurity/
- https://www.hpe.com/it/it/what-is/exascale.html
- https://www.enisa.europa.eu/publications/artificial-intelligence-cybersecurity-challenges
- https://insidehpc.com/2019/10/parallel-computing-in-python-current-state-and-recent-advances/
- https://towardsdatascience.com/mpire-for-python-multiprocessing-is-really-easy-d2ae7999a3e9
- https://ethz.ch/en/news-and-events/eth-news/news/2020/06/the-first-intuitive-programming-language-for-quantum-computers.html

CHAPTER 11
Modern Frameworks for Parallelism and Distribution: Ray and Modin

Introduction

In this chapter, we further extend the world of distributed computing by introducing another framework called **Ray**, while adding it to Celery and Dask as an additional tool to handle complex computations. We take the Monte Carlo method as an example to show how some computations can be extended from local systems to distributed systems, while increasing performance and the ability to handle large, structured data. We also cover extensive modules such as **Ray Train**, **Ray Tune** and **Ray Serve** that are specifically designed to extend Machine Learning (ML) developed with TensorFlow, PyTorch and other frameworks in distributed environments. Finally, we introduce **Modin**, a library that provides methods for computing and manipulating DataFrame objects in distributed environments, preserving the Pandas syntax.

Structure

This chapter addresses the following topics:

- The Ray Framework
- Ray's Core Abstractions: Tasks and Actors
- Monte Carlo π with Ray
- Distributing ML with Ray
- Ray Train, Ray Tune, Ray Serve
- Modin
- Frameworks in Context: Ray vs. Dask vs. Celery

The Ray Framework

Ray is an open-source framework designed to simplify parallel and distributed computing in Python, while allowing developers to scale their applications across CPU and GPU clusters without making significant code changes. With its flexible architecture, Ray is used for a wide range of applications, including distributed machine learning, hyperparameter tuning, real-time inference, and reinforcement learning. With an intuitive API and advanced modules such as **Ray Tune** and **Ray**

Serve, Ray has become a must-have tool for those looking to leverage parallel computing at scale. Ray can be installed with a simple pip command. In a production environment, it can be deployed on clusters, Kubernetes, or cloud providers such as AWS. GCP, and Azure via:

```
pip install ray
```

Once installed, Ray can be initialized with **`ray.init()`** to use a local or distributed environment.

```
import ray

# Ray initialization
ray.init()
```

When you call **`ray.init()`** in a Python program, Ray performs a series of operations to set up and initialize the distributed computing environment. When Ray starts, it starts with some components such as the Ray Head Node, which is the local instance of the Ray runtime on your machine. This is when you would want to consider creating or using a local cluster, but you can also specify the address of a remote cluster that is already running, without having to start a new instance locally. If the cluster is local and has already started, you can use:

```
ray.init(address="auto")
```

If the cluster you are running is remote, you need to specify the address and port as:

```
ray.init(address="ray://123.45.67.89:10001")
```

When you start a Ray instance, a dashboard also appears on the default port 8265 in localhost (127.0.0.1) reachable via browser. If you are working on Jupyter Notebook, you will be shown a window (see *Figure 11.1*), which shows the versions of Python and Ray in use and the URL of the Ray Dashboard.

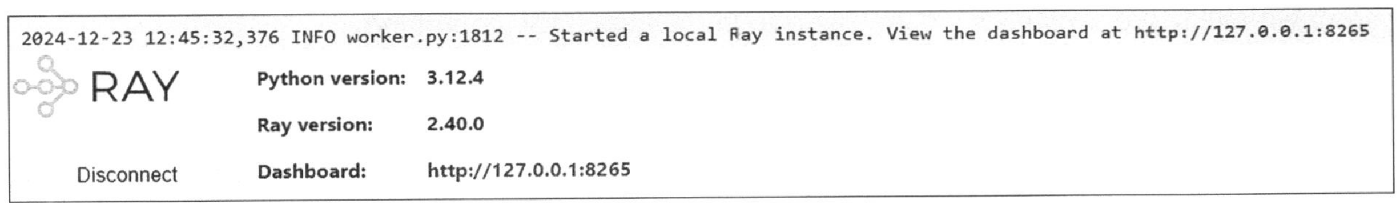

Figure 11.1: *Notice of a Ray Instance on a Jupyter Notebook*

Once Ray is instantiated, various processes are started in sequence to manage distributed computing and resources. Each node (including the local one) runs a process called Raylet (Resource Manager), which is responsible for managing the available resources (memory, CPU and GPU). These processes will be responsible for scheduling the execution of tasks and actors based on the available resources. Another process that will be started is Redis (which we have already seen in a previous chapter for distributed systems). Ray uses Redis as a Metadata Store to store system information and state data of the cluster in use. Then an Object Store (Plasma Store) will be started to manage distributed data. The objects that will be returned by the tasks will be stored here and will be accessible to all the workers of the cluster. Finally, Ray starts one or more worker processes that execute the remote tasks. A general scheme of the Ray architecture and how the components are distributed is shown in *Figure 11.2*.

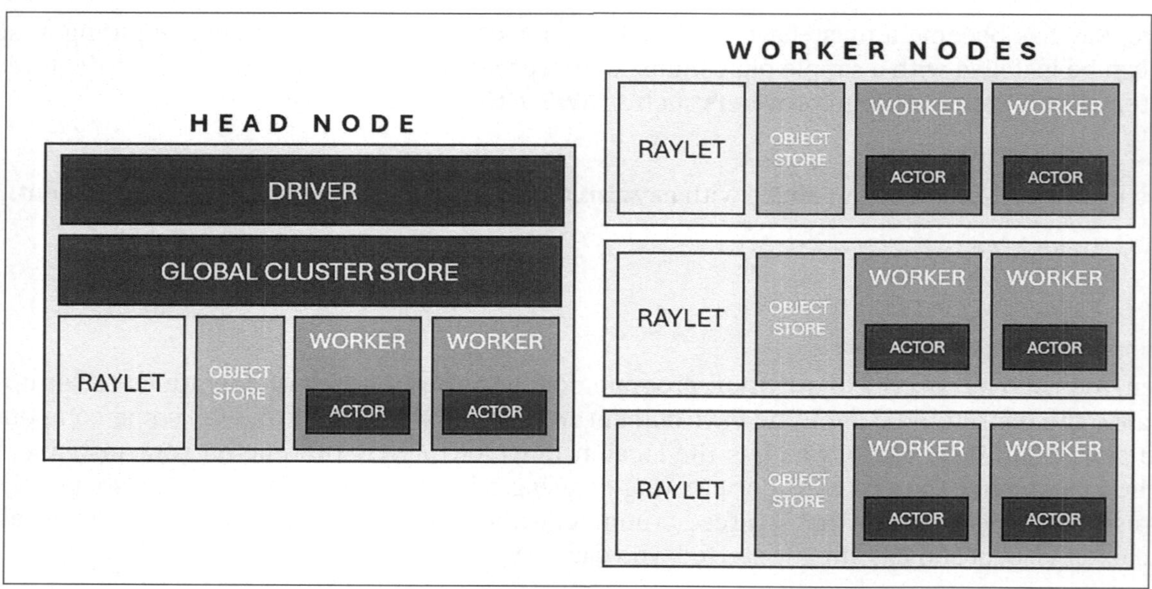

Figure 11.2: *Ray Architecture*

Also, when **ray.init()** is launched, the system will use the maximum of the available resources. If you want to use only a part of the resources, it will be better to specify it by passing the number of resources to dedicate to distribute computing as parameters explicitly.

```
ray.init(num_cpus=4, num_gpus=1)
```

Once all the necessary calculations have been performed, it is necessary to close the started Ray system with all its components. To do this, you must launch the command:

```
ray.shutdown()
```

This command is also useful to reset the system in development and start anew in case of an error. To know the number of workers available with Ray, that is the number of available computing resources (if we used **ray.init()** without parameters), the simplest way is to use **ray.available_resources()**, as demonstrated here:

```
resources = ray.available_resources()
print(f"Num of CPUs: {resources.get('CPU', 0)}")
print(f"Num of GPUs: {resources.get('GPU', 0)}")
```

By running these lines, you will get the following information about the resources available in the system:

```
Num of CPUs: 12.0
Num of GPUs: 0
```

The Basic Components of Ray: Task and Actor

A main feature of Ray is its ability to distribute computations easily and efficiently in an environment. Ray is able to distribute computations across multiple CPU and GPU cores both on a single machine and in a cluster, without the need to manually manage the complexity of networking or synchronization. It also allows you to manage almost automatically independent tasks and more complex applications with interdependent tasks.

The characteristics and operation of Ray can be described more quickly and comprehensively through its architecture. The framework is based on two main components:

- Task
- Actor

A **task** is a function that is executed in parallel and in a distributed way. Tasks can be executed on multiple cores or nodes in parallel: when you call a remote function, it is executed on a remote worker (which can be on the same machine or a cluster), and the result is returned as a future reference (`ObjectRef`). This also introduces asynchrony since this reference can be used after the task call to retrieve the result. Ray also has a system, called Directed Acyclic Graph (DAG) that tracks the dependencies between the various tasks and thus optimizes their execution in a completely automatic way.

Actors distribute Python objects that maintain their own state and provide remote methods. Actors are useful when you need to maintain a shared state or perform successive operations on the same distributed object. Their state is guaranteed to persist during the sequential execution of calls and their entire lifecycle develops within a single worker. Ray will then take care of creating multiple actor instances in cases where it will be necessary to distribute the work, by automatically scaling applications on CPU and GPU clusters, and adapting the number of workers based on the complexity of the workload. Actors will be particularly useful for scenarios such as:

- Data Caching
- Resource Pool Management
- Coordinating between Distributed Tasks

We will approach this library for the first time by directly seeing the operation of these two components through some example codes. In Ray, you can define both the functions and the classes defined within the code respectively as Ray Task and Ray Actor using the `@ray.remote` decorator. Once defined, they can be used inside the code with the suffix **.remote()** that tells Ray to execute on one of the workers in a distributed manner. However, to be able to use a distributed system efficiently we must ensure that the calculation occurs in parallel on multiple workers at the same time. Let us see an example in which we will perform a calculation on 10 values at the same time:

```
# Define a distributed and parallel function
@ray.remote
def compute_square(x):
    return x * x

# Parallel execution of tasks
futures = [compute_square.remote(i) for i in range(10)]
results = ray.get(futures)
print("Results: ", results)
```

Running the code generates the following result:

```
Results:  [0, 1, 4, 9, 16, 25, 36, 49, 64, 81]
```

Here, we are running the **compute_square()** task that calculates the square of a value on 10 values (from 0 to 9) generated by the **range()** function. The **square.remote(i)** call occurs 10 times, so 10 independent tasks will be started. The calculation does not return the result directly, but via an **ObjectRef**, which is a reference to an object that will be calculated in the future. In fact, the results are retrieved later, through the **ray.get()** function that takes futures references as an argument and returns the results calculated by the remote workers. If we run the code, we get the expected result, that is, a list of the squares of the numbers from 0 to 9.

It is also possible to combine multiple remote tasks, while creating calculation pipelines, as we see in the following example:

```
@ray.remote
def add(x,y):
    return x + y

@ray.remote
```

```
def multiply(x, y):
    return x * y

result = multiply.remote(add.remote(1, 2), 3)
print("Results: ", ray.get(result))
```

Executing the code fetches you the result shown here:

```
Results:  9
```

As for actors, we will explore the defined classes that have the decorator **@ray.remote**. Here is a simple example that uses a counter:

```
@ray.remote
class Counter:
    def __init__(self):
        self.count = 0

    def increment(self):
        self.count += 1
        return self.count

counter = Counter.remote()

print(ray.get(counter.increment.remote()))
print(ray.get(counter.increment.remote()))
```

Executing the code fetches you the result shown here:

```
1
2
```

The use of a counter shows the maintenance of the internal state of an actor, which in this case is **self.count**. To create a remote instance of this counter, the **remote()** suffix is also used in this case. In this way, the instance is executed directly on one of the available workers. Each actor will be assigned to a separate worker and its state will be local. The increment method is a remote method and will be executed on the worker where the relative actor persists. At each call, the value of the counter will be incremented by one unit, regardless of all the other operations performed (not present in the example code). Here too, **ray.get()** is used to recall the value returned by the remote method.

The behavior of the actors and the permanence of their states become more evident, if we instantiate two different counters:

```
counter1 = Counter.remote()
counter2 = Counter.remote()
counter1.increment.remote()
counter1.increment.remote()
futures = [counter2.increment.remote(), counter1.increment.remote()]
results = ray.get(futures)
print("Results:", results)
```

Running the code will fetch us this result:

```
Results: [1, 3]
```

As we can see in the code, counter 1 is incremented 3 times, while the second counter is incremented only once. We can capture the results only for the final increments and display the count values in the output.

An Example of Parallel Calculation with the Monte Carlo Method

Let us move on to a more complex computational case such as calculating the estimate of the value of π with the Monte Carlo method. This is a classic case already used in the book and is perfect for demonstrating parallelism because each point generated is independent of the others. This makes it ideal for distributed computing.

In this example, we generate random points (x, y) in a square of side 2 centered on the origin. We then count how many of these points fall inside a circle of radius 1, which is also centered on the origin. The fraction of points that fall inside the circle is approximately equal to the area of the circle divided by the area of the square, or π/4, from which we can estimate the value of π.

```
import ray
import random

@ray.remote
def monte_carlo_simulation(num_samples):
    inside_circle = 0
    for _ in range(num_samples):
        x = random.uniform(-1, 1)
        y = random.uniform(-1, 1)
        if x**2 + y**2 <= 1:
            inside_circle += 1
    return inside_circle

def estimate_pi(total_samples, num_workers):
    samples_per_worker = total_samples // num_workers
    futures = [monte_carlo_simulation.remote(samples_per_worker) for _ in
range(num_workers)]
    total_inside_circle = sum(ray.get(futures))
    pi_estimate = 4 * (total_inside_circle / total_samples)
    return pi_estimate

if __name__ == "__main__":
    ray.init()
    total_samples = 10_000_000
    num_workers = 8
    pi_estimate = estimate_pi(total_samples, num_workers)
    print(f"Estimate of π with {total_samples} samples distributed in
{num_workers} workers: {pi_estimate}")
    ray.shutdown()
```

The **`monte_carlo_simulation`** function calculates the number of points falling inside the circle for a given number of samples. This function is decorated with **`@ray.remote`**, which means that each call to this function will be executed on a separate worker. To distribute the Monte Carlo computation load, the **`estimate_pi`** function is defined, which divides the total number of samples among the number of workers. Each worker will run the Monte Carlo simulation on a fraction of the total. Inside it, the parallel computation will be performed through a list of futures by issuing as many **`.remote()`** calls to the **`monte_carlo_simulation`** function as there are workers available in Ray. The result is then retrieved by collecting the results from all the individual workers via **`ray.get(futures)`** and adding them together. Running this gives the following result:

```
Estimate of π with 10 000 000 samples distributed in 8 workers: 3.1416712
```

As we can see, we have obtained an estimated value of π that differs from the original (3.14159) in the fourth decimal place.

We can also compare the results in terms of the efficiency of the distributed computation with the classical sequential one. We will introduce the measure of the time taken to perform the Monte Carlo computation. Let us insert the appropriate measurements in the previous code:

```
import time

if __name__ == "__main__":
    total_samples = 10_000_000
    num_workers = 8
    start_time = time.time()
    pi_estimate = estimate_pi(total_samples, num_workers)
    end_time = time.time()
    print(f"Estimate of π with {total_samples} samples distributed in
{num_workers} workers: {pi_estimate}")
    print(f"Calculated in {end_time - start_time} sec")
```

Running the code will fetch us this result (it can vary from system to system and from the number of available workers):

```
Estimate of π with 10000000 samples distributed in 8 workers: 3.1419852
Calculated in 1.084900140762329 sec
```

Now let us write the code equivalent to the previous one for the classical sequential computation of the estimate of π:

```
import random
import time

def monte_carlo_pi_sequential(num_samples):
    inside_circle = 0
    for _ in range(num_samples):
        x = random.uniform(-1, 1)
        y = random.uniform(-1, 1)
        if x**2 + y**2 <= 1:
            inside_circle += 1
    return 4 * (inside_circle / num_samples)

total_samples = 10_000_000
start_time = time.time()
pi_estimate = monte_carlo_pi_sequential(total_samples)
end_time = time.time()
print(f"Estimate of π with {total_samples} samples: {pi_estimate}")
print(f"Calculated in {end_time - start_time} sec")
```

By executing in this case, we obtain a time approximately 4 times greater:

```
Estimate of π with 10000000 samples: 3.141688
Calculated in 4.491239547729492 sec
```

You can increase the number of samples in the two systems. You should have a greater efficiency gap for the distributed systems as this value increases.

	Ray (4 worker)	**Ray (8 worker)**	**Ray (12 worker)**	**Sequential**
10000000	1.76	1.08	0.92	4.49
50000000	7.71	4.95	4.09	21.92
100000000	14.91	9.87	8.59	47.41
200000000	30.79	20.91	17.73	86.45

400000000	64.37	41.05	37.81	169.16
800000000	127.93	86.46	76.04	368.01

Table 11.1: *Performance Comparison With and Without Ray Execution*

Using Ray to Distribute AI Applications and Machine Learning Tasks

Ray is a versatile tool for distributing AI and ML applications across CPU and GPU clusters, as it allows you to run complex and intensive tasks in parallel. Ray's ability to handle asynchronous tasks and support distributed pipelines makes it particularly useful for processing resource-intensive ML processes such as model training, hyperparameter tuning, and distributed inference. This section explores how to use Ray to distribute AI applications and ML tasks, while analyzing best practices and some practical examples. Ray is an excellent tool for distributing ML model training, thanks to the integration of advanced modules that extend its functionality. These are listed as follows:

- **Ray Train** for distributed learning
- **Ray Tune** for hyperparameter optimization
- **Ray Serve** for distributed model serving
- **Ray Rllib,** which is a reinforcement learning toolkit

This set of libraries are specifically created to integrate with popular ML libraries such as PyTorch, TensorFlow, XGBoost, and scikit-learn, while providing scalability in distributed systems and running experiments on multiple cores, GPUs or nodes in a cluster.

Note: *These modules have been used in this book with PyTorch, but they can be used in many other contexts. They have been implemented to work in Linux environments and present a series of problems that require ad hoc corrections if you are working on Windows environments (such as path names that are too long and exceed the maximum number of characters allowed, and so on.). It is advisable to work in a Linux context for this kind of study.*

Ray Train is designed to simplify distributed training of ML models across multiple machines, CPUs, GPUs, and nodes in a cluster. Distributed training takes advantage of the parallelism between multiple machines and GPUs in a cluster, while allowing you to use large datasets for learning in a scalable way. It can dynamically add resources during the learning process, if necessary. It also implements special techniques, such as **`AllReduce`**, which synchronize gradients during distributed training. Finally, it is also able to save and restore checkpoints to ensure resilience in case of errors. To integrate this library into the Ray framework, run the following command:

```
pip install -U ray[train]
```

This integration allows the use of trainers from existing Deep Learning systems such as **`TorchTrainer`** or **`TensorFlowTrainer`**, while running them in a distributed manner. Distributed datasets are also supported in this integration, which allow developers to manage large amounts of data during the learning phase. In addition, a monitoring system is provided with the **`train.report()`** method that records metrics during training.

Ray Tune is a library built into Ray and is designed to simplify and streamline the process of optimizing hyperparameters for ML models. It offers advanced capabilities to explore the hyperparameter space in an efficient and scalable way, while leveraging the power of distributed computing. To install this module, run the following command:

```
pip install -U ray[tune]
```

It also provides advanced logging capabilities by tracking results and supporting tools such as TensorBoard, Weight & Biases, and MLFlow.

The optimization process with Ray Tune involves the following steps:

- Defining the training function that accepts a dictionary of hyperparameters
- Specifying the space of hyperparameters to explore
- Choosing a search strategy
- Running the tuning process

In *Chapter* 9, we discussed Deep Learning (DL) while referring to PyTorch as a framework to perform ML calculations. Now, in this context, we will integrate Ray to use all the benefits of distributed (and parallel) computing in Machine Learning. Let us therefore examine the same FashionCNN model used previously and subject it to a series of operations performed by the advanced modules Ray Train, Ray Tune and Ray Serve.

First of all, since it is a neural network model, its efficiency in learning and the accuracy of its predictions will be linked to a series of hyperparameters. We will use the power of distributed computing to test a whole series of values of these parameters to see which of them will be the most efficient. To do so, we will use both Ray Train and Ray Tune at the same time.

In many versions, Ray Tune (but not only, also the other modules) often has problems when you are logging it with TensorBoardX. To eliminate the problem, uninstall the module via:

```
pip uninstall tensorboardX
```

Now, let us implement the code for tuning hyperparameters during training. We will start with the FashionCNN model and adapt it to this context:

```
# Tuning code
import torch
import torch.nn as nn
import torch.optim as optim
from torch.utils.data import DataLoader
from torchvision import datasets, transforms
import ray
from ray import tune, train
from ray.tune.schedulers import ASHAScheduler
from ray.tune import CLIReporter

# Definition of the FashionCNN model with Ray Tune
class FashionCNN(nn.Module):
    def __init__(self, hidden_units=600):
        super(FashionCNN, self).__init__()
        self.layer1 = nn.Sequential(
            nn.Conv2d(in_channels=1, out_channels=32, kernel_size=3,
padding=1),
            nn.BatchNorm2d(32),
            nn.ReLU(),
            nn.MaxPool2d(kernel_size=2, stride=2)
        )
        self.layer2 = nn.Sequential(
            nn.Conv2d(in_channels=32, out_channels=64, kernel_size=3),
            nn.BatchNorm2d(64),
            nn.ReLU(),
            nn.MaxPool2d(2)
        )
        self.fc1 = nn.Linear(in_features=64*6*6, out_features=hidden_units)
        self.dropout = nn.Dropout(0.25)
```

```
        self.fc2 = nn.Linear(in_features=hidden_units, out_features=120)
        self.fc3 = nn.Linear(in_features=120, out_features=10)
    def forward(self, x):
        x = self.layer1(x)
        x = self.layer2(x)
        x = x.view(x.size(0), -1)
        x = self.fc1(x)
        x = self.dropout(x)
        x = self.fc2(x)
        x = self.fc3(x)
        return x
```

In *Chapter 8*, we performed a simple training with a fixed set of hyperparameters chosen from other similar models or taken from literature. Now, we will apply both Ray Train and Ray Tune to this model and elaborate an estimate of the best hyperparameters, while activating a form of training in a distributed (and parallel) system to make this operation highly efficient.

First, let us take care of training the model and specify a **train_fashion_mnist** function with the functions made available by Ray Train:

```
def train_fashion_mnist(config):
    # Dataset and transforms
    transform = transforms.Compose([
        transforms.ToTensor(),
        transforms.Normalize((0.5,), (0.5,))
    ])
    train_dataset = datasets.FashionMNIST(
        root=".data",
        train=True,
        download=True,
        transform=transform
    )
    train_loader = DataLoader(
        dataset=train_dataset,
        batch_size=int(config["batch_size"]),
        shuffle=True
    )
    # Model initialization
    model = FashionCNN(hidden_units=int(config["hidden_units"]))
    criterion = nn.CrossEntropyLoss()
    optimizer = optim.Adam(model.parameters(), lr=config["lr"])
    # Training loop
    for epoch in range(5):
        model.train()
        running_loss = 0.0
        for images, labels in train_loader:
            optimizer.zero_grad()
            outputs = model(images)
            loss = criterion(outputs, labels)
            loss.backward()
            optimizer.step()
            running_loss += loss.item()
        # Record loss per epoch
        train.report({"loss": running_loss / len(train_loader)})
```

This function accepts as a parameter (**config**) the configuration to test sent by Ray Tune, which contains one of the possible combinations of hyperparameters. These combinations are chosen based on the values defined by the hyperparameter space that have to be added to the previous code.

```
# Hyperparameter Space
search_space = {
    "lr": tune.loguniform(1e-4, 1e-1),
    "batch_size": tune.choice([32, 64, 128]),
    "hidden_units": tune.choice([400, 600, 800])
}
```

As we can see, we have given Ray Tune three possible choices (via **tune.choice**) of configuration of the hidden layer units and the batch size to use in the learning phase. Furthermore, we have also defined a learning rate range between 0.1 and 0.0001.

While analyzing the code of the function inside it, we can see that the images of the FashionMNIST dataset (28x28) are preprocessed using **transforms.Compose**. This first converts them into a PyTorch tensor via the **transforms.ToTensor()** method and then normalizes the pixel values with a mean of 0.5 and a standard deviation of 0.5 with **transform.Normalize()**.

DataLoader takes care of loading the dataset, setting the batch size based on the configuration to be passed to the function. Furthermore, thanks to shuffle=True, the data is mixed to avoid recurring patterns.

At this point, the FashionCNN model is ready to be initialized with a hidden layer with different units, depending on the configuration to be tested. This parameter is very important because it modifies the neural network itself and its ability to learn. Then the loss and optimization functions are defined: **CrossEntropyLoss** suitable for multi-class classification problems and Adam, an optimizer with a learning rate that also varies with the past configuration. Training occurs in five epochs with a repeated cycle for each batch.

- A forward pass is performed to calculate the predictions.
- The loss is calculated by comparing the predictions with the real labels.
- A backward pass is performed to calculate the gradients.
- The weights of the model are updated with the optimizer.

Finally, at the end of each epoch, the average loss is calculated (on the training dataset) and recorded via **train.report()**. This value is sent to Ray Tune which uses it to establish which are the best hyperparameters.

Another function to define is the one that regulates the tuning, which we will call **tune_fashion_mnist**. Here, we will set its configuration through a series of parameters shown as follows:

```
# Ray Tune configuration
def tune_fashion_mnist():
    scheduler = ASHAScheduler(
        max_t=5,
        grace_period=1,
        reduction_factor=2
    )
    reporter = CLIReporter(
        metric_columns=["loss", "training_iteration"]
    )
    result = tune.run(
        train_fashion_mnist,
        resources_per_trial={"cpu": 1, "gpu": 0},
        config=search_space,
        metric="loss",
        mode="min",
```

```
            num_samples=10,
            scheduler=scheduler,
            progress_reporter=reporter,
            storage_path="/home/myname/ray_results"
        )
        # Return the best hyperparameters
        best_trial = result.get_best_trial("loss", "min", "last")
        print(f"Best trial config: {best_trial.config}")
        print(f"Best trial final loss: {best_trial.last_result['loss']}")
```

In the function code, the ASHAScheduler (Asynchronous Successive Halving Algorithm) is defined, which is used to manage the tuning process through a series of parameters such as **max_t=5,** which defines the maximum number of epochs for training; **grace_period=1** in which at least 1 epoch is guaranteed before interrupting the test; and **reduction_factor=2** in which the least promising tests are eliminated. This halves the number of tests at each stage. The purpose of this scheduler is therefore to reduce computational costs by performing and filtering the most promising tests.

Another object defined within the function is the **CLIReporter** which is used to monitor the progress of the tuning in the terminal through the **metric_columns** parameter. This parameter displays the variables on the terminal during tuning, which in our case is loss and **training_iteration**.

Finally, the tuning is started via **tune.run**, where the Ray Train training function (**train_fashion_mnist**) is along with the resources available for each trial, the search space of the hyperparameters to be considered, the metrics to be minimized, the total number of combinations to be considered (**num_samples=10**), and the scheduler to be used. The results will finally be displayed in output on the console.

You can start the tuning directly via the following lines of code:

```
# Starting Ray Tune
if __name__ == "__main__":
    ray.init(_temp_dir="/home/myname/ray_temp")
    tune_fashion_mnist()
    ray.shutdown()
```

By writing all the previous code inside a file, such as **tune_model.py**, and running it in a virtual environment specifically created to work with Ray and PyTorch, it will be sufficient to launch it to start training and tuning in a distributed manner via Ray.

```
$ python tune_model.py
```

Once the startup is launched, you will have a whole series of tables and messages of saves and reports on the progress and results obtained during the training phases of the various tests performed. The execution of all these operations will be carried out in parallel with a completely automated distribution of tasks using all the available resources (for example, in this case the GPUs were not used, but only 12 CPUs). A tuning operation such as the one in our example should take about 5 minutes, at the end of which you will obtain a table with the combination of all the tested parameters and the corresponding loss values (see *Figure 11.3*).

```
Trial status: 10 TERMINATED
Current time: 2024-12-30 14:11:52. Total running time: 42s
Logical resource usage: 1.0/12 CPUs, 0/0 GPUs
Current best trial: 892ec_00007 with loss=0.002492996421195805 and params={'lr': 0.0004811398463638836, 'batch_size': 64, 'hidden_units': 400}
```

Trial name	status	lr	batch_size	hidden_units	iter	total time (s)	loss
train_fashion_mnist_892ec_00000	TERMINATED	0.0306092	32	800	2	23.1054	0.0617035
train_fashion_mnist_892ec_00001	TERMINATED	0.00261341	32	400	5	21.7457	0.0125195
train_fashion_mnist_892ec_00002	TERMINATED	0.00135599	128	600	2	23.8809	0.0104909
train_fashion_mnist_892ec_00003	TERMINATED	0.0365056	128	800	1	24.7254	0.00488195
train_fashion_mnist_892ec_00004	TERMINATED	0.0186206	64	400	2	21.9678	0.0273328
train_fashion_mnist_892ec_00005	TERMINATED	0.000266366	32	400	5	21.5672	0.00556872
train_fashion_mnist_892ec_00006	TERMINATED	0.00168688	128	600	1	18.4229	0.00509244
train_fashion_mnist_892ec_00007	TERMINATED	0.00048114	64	400	1	21.7315	0.002493
train_fashion_mnist_892ec_00008	TERMINATED	0.00243027	64	400	4	21.0412	0.0205711
train_fashion_mnist_892ec_00009	TERMINATED	0.00155905	128	400	1	23.5016	0.00488608

```
Best trial config: {'lr': 0.0004811398463638836, 'batch_size': 64, 'hidden_units': 400}
Best trial final loss: 0.002492996421195805
```

Figure 11.3: *Ray Tuning Returns the Optimal Hyperparameters of the Model Under Study*

Now that we have the best hyperparameters for the FashionCNN model, we can use it to:

- Train a final model with these hyperparameters
- Save the final model for future inferences
- Deploy the optimized model using Ray Serve

Let us train the final model with the best hyperparameters, using the best hyperparameters found by Ray Tune and save it locally as a **`model.pth`** file.

```
import torch
import torch.nn as nn
import torch.optim as optim
from torch.utils.data import DataLoader
from torchvision import datasets, transforms

# PyTorch Model Optimized
class FashionCNN(nn.Module):

    def __init__(self, hidden_units=400):
        super(FashionCNN, self).__init__()

        self.layer1 = nn.Sequential(
            nn.Conv2d(1, 32, kernel_size=3, padding=1),
            nn.BatchNorm2d(32),
            nn.ReLU(),
            nn.MaxPool2d(2)
        )

        self.layer2 = nn.Sequential(
            nn.Conv2d(32, 64, kernel_size=3),
            nn.BatchNorm2d(64),
            nn.ReLU(),
            nn.MaxPool2d(2)
        )

        self.fc1 = nn.Linear(64*6*6, hidden_units)
        self.fc2 = nn.Linear(hidden_units, 120)
        self.fc3 = nn.Linear(120, 10)

    def forward(self, x):
        x = self.layer1(x)
        x = self.layer2(x)
```

```
        x = x.view(x.size(0), -1)
        x = self.fc1(x)
        x = self.fc2(x)
        x = self.fc3(x)
        return x

def train_final_model():
    #Hyperparameter optimized
    best_lr = 0.00048113984
    best_batch_size = 64
    best_hidden_units = 400

    #Dataset and transforms
    transform = transforms.Compose([
        transforms.ToTensor(),
        transforms.Normalize((0.5,), (0.5,))
    ])
    # Loading of the FashionMNIST dataset
    train_dataset = datasets.FashionMNIST(
        root='./data',
        train=True,
        transform=transform,
        download=True
    )
    train_loader = DataLoader(dataset=train_dataset, batch_size=best_batch_
size, shuffle=True)
    # Model initialization and Optimization
    model = FashionCNN(hidden_units=best_hidden_units)
    criterion = nn.CrossEntropyLoss()
    optimizer = optim.Adam(model.parameters(), lr=best_lr)
    # Training Loop
    for epoch in range(10):  # Numero di epoche
        running_loss = 0.0
        for images, labels in train_loader:
            optimizer.zero_grad()  # Resetta i gradienti
            outputs = model(images)  # Predizione
            loss = criterion(outputs, labels)  # Calcola la perdita
            loss.backward()  # Backpropagation
            optimizer.step()  # Aggiorna i pesi
            running_loss += loss.item()
        # Loss Log
        print(f"Epoch {epoch + 1}, Loss: {running_loss / len(train_loader)}")
    # Save trained model
    torch.save(model.state_dict(), "fashion_cnn.pth")
    print("Model saved as 'fashion_cnn.pth'")
# Start Training
if __name__ == "__main__":
    train_final_model()
```

Write the preceding code in a file and save it as **final_model.py**. Run the file from Python using:

```
$ python final_model.py
```

We will get the following results:

```
Epoch 1, Loss: 0.39343519438939817
Epoch 2, Loss: 0.27951515193528204
Epoch 3, Loss: 0.24434951206704955
Epoch 4, Loss: 0.22308132382058132
```

```
Epoch 5, Loss: 0.20513936407220706
Epoch 6, Loss: 0.1896869861352037
Epoch 7, Loss: 0.17724832037150035
Epoch 8, Loss: 0.16653012170363019
Epoch 9, Loss: 0.15879877303232517
Epoch 10, Loss: 0.1450476723133342
Model saved as 'fashion_cnn.pth'
```

Now that we have trained the final model with the best hyperparameters, we can save it as a **fashion_cnn.pth** file. Now we will deploy it using Ray Serve.

Ray Serve is a Ray library designed for scalable serving of ML models. This tool allows you to serve ML models and pipelines as HTTP endpoints or gRPC-type APIs. This module integrates with the Ray framework using workers to serve models, while other components of this system are added to those already part of Ray, such as **ingress,** which is an HTTP or gRPC interface to receive requests; a **router** that dispatches requests to the appropriate endpoints; and d**eployment,** which is an instance of a model that can be scaled in the distributed system. To install this module in the Ray system, run the following command:

```
pip install ray[serve]
```

Now let us go back to the previous example, serving the previous model over the network so that clients can send images to it remotely and get predictions from it.

Going back to the FashionCNN model example, we now need to create the **serve_model.py** file. We can do so via the following code:

```
from ray import serve
import torch
import torch.nn as nn
import requests
import numpy as np
from starlette.requests import Request
from typing import Dict
from PIL import Image
from io import BytesIO
from torchvision import transforms
import base64
from final_model import FashionCNN

# Deployment for the model
@serve.deployment
class ModelDeployment:
    def __init__(self):
        self.model = FashionCNN()
        self.model.load_state_dict(torch.load("fashion_cnn.pth")) # Load the
weights of the model
        self.model.eval()

    async def __call__(self, starlette_request: Request) -> Dict:

        # Get data from request
        #data = await starlette_request.json()
        #image_data = data["image"]
        image_payload_bytes = await starlette_request.body()
        pil_image = Image.open(BytesIO(image_payload_bytes))
        print("[1/3] Parsed image data: {}".format(pil_image))
```

```
        # decode image (base64) and pre-processing
        #image_bytes = base64.b64decode(image_data)
        #image = Image.open(BytesIO(image_bytes)).convert("L")
        #input_tensor = self.transform(image).unsqueeze(0)
        pil_images = [pil_image]  # Our current batch size is one
        input_tensor = torch.cat(
            [self.preprocessor(i).unsqueeze(0) for i in pil_images]
        )
        print("[2/3] Images transformed, tensor shape {}".format(input_tensor.
shape))

        # Execute inference
        with torch.no_grad():
            output = self.model(input_tensor)
            predicted_class = output.argmax(dim=1).item()
        print("[3/3] Inference done!")
        return {"predicted_class": predicted_class}

modelD = ModelDeployment.bind()
```

This time, the code written in the **serve_model.py** file will have to be launched through the Ray server with the following command:

```
$ serve run serve_model:modelD
```

In this way, the model optimized through Ray Tune and Ray Train will be available for clients to make predictions. We need to create a PNG file with an image taken from the MNIST dataset to submit via **GET** or **POST** request.

```
from torchvision import datasets
from torchvision.utils import save_image
from torchvision.transforms import ToTensor

dataset = datasets.FashionMNIST(
    root="./fashion_data", train=False, download=True, transform=ToTensor()
)
save_image(dataset[0][0], "mnist_image.png")
```

We extracted the image of a garment represented in *Figure* 11.4, which corresponds to an ankle boot, a category corresponding to class 9.

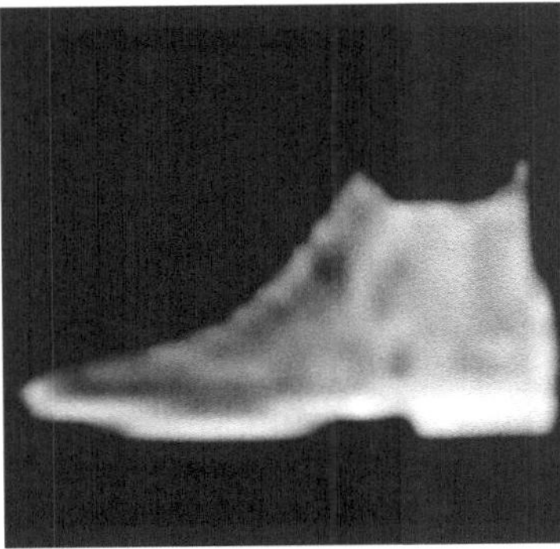

Figure.11.4: *Ankle Boot*

Now that we have an image for our model to classify, we can open a Python session from a terminal and send the image via an HTTP request mentioned as follows:

```
import requests
import base64
from PIL import Image
```

```
import io

with open("mnist_image.png", "rb") as image_file:
    #image_data = base64.b64encode(image_file.read()).decode("utf-8")
    image_bytes = image_file.read()

response = requests.post(
    "http://localhost:8000/",
    data=image_bytes,
    headers={"Content-Type": "application/octed-stream"}
)

print(response.json())
```

After sending the image to the model, we will get the prediction of the class it belongs to as the result.

```
{'predicted_class': 9}
```

This prediction is correct as it perfectly matches the garment present in the image.

Modin as a Parallel Alternative to Pandas

Modin is an open-source library designed to streamline and parallelize data analysis operations in Python and is a high-performance alternative to Pandas. Maintaining the same API as Pandas, Modin allows you to scale operations on large datasets by leveraging multiple cores and distributed resources such as CPU clusters, GPUs, and clouds. Thanks to its compatibility with Pandas syntax, Modin allows users to improve performance without changing the existing code, which makes this transition particularly easy for those who already use Pandas.

Data analysis libraries such as Pandas are essential for data manipulation in Python. However, Pandas is primarily optimized for single-core computation, which can be limiting for large datasets. Modin addresses this limitation by introducing multi-core parallelism and support for distributed infrastructure such as CPU and GPU clusters by using backends such as Ray and Dask to distribute tasks across multiple resources. Also, Modin is uniquely designed to manipulate tabular data in a scalable manner. It takes advantage of parallelism in distributed environments. The transition from Pandas to Modin is almost natural and can be done very easily.

Modin installation is simple and can be done with the following pip. Since this library also requires you to install distributed computing engine, you can choose which backend to use (Ray or Dask) at the time of installation.

```
pip install modin[ray]
```

or

```
pip install modin[dask]
```

If you install Modin without specifying a backend, recent versions will default to Ray as the execution engine.

After installing it, you can start using it by importing Modin instead of Pandas.

```
import modin.pandas as pd  # Replacing Pandas with Modin
```

Once configured, Modin automatically distributes operations across multiple cores, while accelerating processing without the need to modify the original code. Let us look at a very simple example where we load a CSV file via Pandas.

```
import pandas as pd

df = pd.read_csv("employees.csv")
df
```

By running the code, you will get the DataFrame that contains the values present in the CSV file, as shown in *Figure 11.5*:

	ID	Name	Surname	Salary	Level
0	104	John	Smith	45000	B
1	133	Paul	Norris	35000	C
2	214	William	Moore	57000	A
3	223	Natalie	Moretti	67000	A
4	443	Rose	Hoover	43000	B
5	444	Richard	Black	33000	C

Figure 11.5: *The DataFrame from employees.csv*

Let us run a grouping and aggregation operation with Pandas on the DataFrame loaded previously:

```
df[["Level","Salary"]].groupby("Level").mean().round()
```

We will get the result shown in *Figure 11.6*:

	Salary
Level	
A	62000.0
B	44000.0
C	33667.0

Figure 11.6: *Result of Pandas Operation*

We can now bring all these operations to work in a distributed system simply by replacing Pandas with Modin in the import line via:

```
import modin.pandas as pd

df = pd.read_csv("employees.csv")
df[["Level","Salary"]].groupby("Level").mean().round()
```

As we have seen, the code and syntax remain the same and only the module import is changed. The results are identical, but in the second case, the active distribution service begins, which in this example is the Ray instance. For such a small and simple CSV file, enabling distribution does not provide any meaningful benefit. However, this approach becomes useful when dealing with large CSV files.

Let us write another example code, in which we will generate a large CSV file and use it to compare the two different approaches between them. We will do this while highlighting the differences in performance. We therefore expect Modin to optimize many of Pandas' operations, which will make them faster and more scalable, especially for datasets that exceed the memory capacity of a single machine. In fact, it can read and write large files (such as CSV and Parquet) in parallel, while automatically dividing the files into blocks and processing them simultaneously.

```
import pandas as pd
import modin.pandas as mpd
import time
import numpy as np

# Generation of a big CSV file
def generate_large_csv(filename, rows=10**6):
    start = time.time()
    np.random.seed(42)
    data = {
        "id": np.arange(1, rows + 1),
        "name": np.random.choice(["Alice", "Bob", "Charlie", "Diana"], 
size=rows),
        "surname": np.random.choice(["Black", "Woods", "Smith", "Stewards"], 
size=rows),
        "salary": np.random.randint(30000, 120000, size=rows),
        "level": np.random.choice(["A","B","C"], size=rows)
    }
    df = pd.DataFrame(data)
    df.to_csv(filename, index=False)
    pandas_time = time.time() - start
    print(f"File CSV {filename} generated with {rows} rows.")
    print(f"Elapsed time with Pandas: {pandas_time:.2f} seconds")

# Testing performance function
def benchmark_pandas(filename):
    #Test with Pandas
    start = time.time()
    df_pandas = pd.read_csv(filename)
    result_pandas = df_pandas.groupby("level")["salary"].mean()
    pandas_time = time.time() - start
    print(f"Elapsed time with Pandas: {pandas_time:.2f} seconds")
    print("Pandas results sample:\n", result_pandas.head())

def benchmark_modin(filename):
    #Test with Modin
    start = time.time()
    df_modin = mpd.read_csv(filename)
    result_modin = df_modin.groupby("level")["salary"].mean()
    modin_time = time.time() - start
    print(f"Elapsed time with Modin: {modin_time:.2f} seconds")
    print("Modin results sample:\n", result_modin.head())
```

Now that we have all the necessary functions, let us generate the large dataset contained in a CSV file:

```
filename = "large_dataset.csv"
generate_large_csv(filename, rows=10**8)
```

This operation may take a few minutes to complete. At the end, a new CSV file of just under ~3 GB should be present in the current directory. The console output should be similar to:

```
File CSV large_dataset.csv generated with 100000000 rows.
Elapsed time with Pandas: 405.93 seconds
```

Now before you start benchmarking and are using Ray as your Modin backend, activate an instance while dedicating a good percentage of your system resources to it. This can be done through:

```
import ray
ray.init(num_cpus=8)
```

Note: *As Modin is configured to use the Ray backend, Ray will start automatically. Explicit calls to* **ray.init()** *are not required unless you want to customize resource allocation or runtime parameters.*

Remember, once you have finished your work, terminate the ray instance with:

```
ray.shutdown()
```

If you have both the backends available in your Python environment, you can always choose which one to activate. For example, to activate Ray as a backend, you can add the following code:

```
import modin.config as cfg
cfg.Engine.set("Ray")
```

Once the backend is started, we will start the benchmark by measuring the time taken by Pandas through:

```
benchmark_pandas(filename)
```

After a few minutes, you will get the following result:

```
Elapsed time with Pandas: 68.61 seconds
Pandas results sample:
 level
A    74998.656080
B    74999.558685
C    74996.492414
Name: salary, dtype: float64
```

Now, let us perform the same calculation with Modin through:

```
Elapsed time with Modin: 62.75 seconds
Modin results sample:
 level
A    74998.656080
B    74999.558685
C    74996.492414
Name: salary, dtype: float64
```

Although the CSV file in this example is nearly 3 GB in size, the performance difference is not particularly pronounced. This is mainly because the benchmark was executed locally: although the machine had 12 CPUs available, only 8 were allocated to Ray to avoid saturating system resources. Pandas, being optimized for single-node execution, was able to exploit local performance efficiently. In a cluster environment where Pandas cannot operate, the number of workers available to Ray would have been higher, which would reduce execution times. Furthermore, the packages must be distributed. This would requires time and resources that would have to be subtracted from the general performance. Here, Pandas does not have to compensate locally, and thus gains efficiency. By increasing the size of the CSV file, loading it into memory as a DataFrame will be impossible locally due to memory issues. Therefore, the choice to operate in a distributed manner will be a preferential and not the default. In the previous example, we used aggregation operations (such as **mean**) and grouping operations using **GroupBy** on the DataFrame, where distributed calculations offered by Modin are more efficient. Another type of operation on DataFrames that can be optimized with Modin is Join and Merge. This time we will create an example where we will generate two large datasets on which we will then perform these operations under benchmark. We will measure the difference in performance here as well.

```
import pandas as pd
import modin.pandas as mpd
import time
import numpy as np
import ray
import modin.config as cfg
```

```
def generate_large_datasets(rows=10**6):
    np.random.seed(42)
    data1 = {
        "key": np.random.randint(1, rows // 10, size=rows),
        "value1": np.random.rand(rows),
    }
    df1 = pd.DataFrame(data1)

    data2 = {
        "key": np.random.randint(1, rows // 10, size=rows),
        "value2": np.random.rand(rows),
    }
    df2 = pd.DataFrame(data2)
    return df1, df2

def benchmark_pandas_merge(df1, df2):
    print("\n------- Pandas -----------")
    start = time.time()
    df_pandas1 = df1.copy()
    df_pandas2 = df2.copy()
    merged_pandas = df_pandas1.merge(df_pandas2, on="key", how="inner")
    pandas_time = time.time() - start
    print(f"Elapsed time with Pandas for Merge: {pandas_time:.2f} sec.")
    print(merged_pandas.head())

def benchmark_modin_merge(df1, df2):
    print("\n------- Modin -----------")
    start = time.time()
    df_modin1 = df1.copy()
    df_modin2 = df2.copy()
    merged_modin = df_modin1.merge(df_modin2, on="key", how="inner")
    modin_time = time.time() - start
    print(f"Elapsed time with Modin for Merge: {modin_time:.2f} sec.")
    print(merged_modin.head())
```

Once the code is inserted, we will create the two datasets and measure the performances.

```
df1, df2 = generate_large_datasets(rows=10**7)
benchmark_pandas_merge(df1, df2)
benchmark_modin_merge(df1, df2)
```

In this case, two datasets with 10 million rows were generated, since creating larger datasets was not feasible on a local system due to limited memory resources.

```
------- Modin -----------
Elapsed time with Modin for Merge: 8.78 sec.
      key    value1    value2
0  121959  0.392188  0.748413
1  121959  0.392188  0.561301
2  121959  0.392188  0.842688
3  121959  0.392188  0.008650
4  121959  0.392188  0.519996


------- Pandas -----------
Elapsed time with Pandas for Merge: 7.92 sec.
      key    value1    value2
0  121959  0.392188  0.748413
```

```
1  121959  0.392188  0.561301
2  121959  0.392188  0.842688
3  121959  0.392188  0.008650
4  121959  0.392188  0.519996
```

As you can see, the time taken by Modin is slightly higher than Pandas. Therefore, it is clear that using this library efficiently is only valuable for large datasets (over 10^8 rows) and on distributed systems involving clusters of machines.

Modin as a Ray-Integrated Tool

We have seen that Modin uses Ray as a backend to distribute the computation on tabular datasets. Now, let us reverse the main concerns of this chapter. We started by talking about the Ray framework and its specific use in ML with Ray Tune and Ray Serve that extend it to distributed systems. We will also consider Modin as a tool to integrate into the Ray ecosystem and will use it to manage larger tabular datasets or simulate parallel preprocessing operations before passing the data to the model. An example for explanatory purposes can be the following one. Here, the dataset that is to be subjected to the ML model is present in a large CSV file of that a single machine will not able to manage.

```
import modin.pandas as pd

def preprocess_data(file_path):
    print("Loading dataset with Modin..")
    # Parallel loading
    data = pd.read_csv(file_path)

    data["label_normalized"] = data["label"] / data["label"].max()
    print("Pre-processing completed!")
    return data

metadata = preprocess_data("fashion_metadata.csv")
```

The content of the CSV file is loaded in a distributed manner in a cluster of machines, where each of them is assigned a portion of the content to work on. Even the pre-processing (here represented by a simple normalization) is carried out in parallel between the various machines present in the cluster.

Comparison of Ray, Dask, and Celery: Architecture and Performance

We have now arrived at the end of this chapter. Let us look at the entire distributed computing environment through the following frameworks and compare them:

- **Ray**
- **Dask**
- **Celery**

All three of them are designed to solve parallelization and resource distribution problems. They also share the goal of distributing tasks across multiple cores or nodes. So, which one should you choose?

First, these three frameworks have different architectures and performance. Furthermore, despite their common goals, each framework is optimized for specific types of workloads like managing asynchronous tasks and scaling machine learning applications. Therefore, you should choose which framework to use based on the specific area in which you want to use distributed computing.

- **Ray**: Distributed Computing and ML
- **Dask**: DAG and Cluster for Big Data and Data Science
- **Celery**: Asynchronous Task Queues for Job Background

As we have seen in this chapter, Ray is particularly suited for distributed machine learning, reinforcement learning, and hyperparameter tuning applications. Advanced modules such as Ray Tune and Ray Serve are ideal for large-scale distributed AI pipelines. Dask is designed for distributed computing on CPU and GPU clusters as it has a Directed Acyclic Graph (DAG)-based architecture.

This approach makes Dask ideal for tasks with many dependencies, such as data analysis pipelines and Big Data processing. Dask is also compatible with Pandas and NumPy, which makes it easy to migrate data science operations to a larger scale.

Celery is an asynchronous task framework that uses message queues like Redis or RabbitMQ to handle the execution of background tasks. It is particularly useful for repetitive or non-real-time critical tasks such as sending emails, file processing, and ETL pipelines.

Additionally, it may be interesting to take a look at the differences between these frameworks from a comparative point of view. Here is a table that compares their features:

Feature	Ray	Dask	Celery
Type of Tasks Supported	Asynchronous tasks, stateful actors	Task with dependencies (DAG)	Asynchronous background tasks
Hardware Optimization	CPU, GPU, TPU	CPU, GPU	CPU
Scalability	High (multi-core, multi-GPU, cluster)	High (distributed clusters)	Limited to asynchronous tasks
Fault Tolerance	Moderate	High	High
Task Latency	Low (latency optimized)	Media (throughput optimized)	Medium-High (Batch Optimized)
State Management	Actor support for persistent state	Not supported	Not supported
Optimization	For low latencies and scalability across GPU and TPU clusters, ideal for high-performance tasks such as training machine learning models	For throughput on large amounts of data, supporting tasks with complex dependencies and batch data processing pipelines	For asynchronous execution of independent tasks, with good fault tolerance and support for automatic rescheduling of failed tasks

Table 11.2: *Comparison of Ray, Dask, and Celery*

Conclusion

In this chapter, we added another important framework for parallel and distributed computing with Python called **Ray**. It can be used similarly to Dask and Celery to implement complex calculations in a distributed manner through active workers both locally and on clusters. Thus, using Ray makes parallel and easily scalable computing feasible. Today, Ray has found utility, thanks to a series of extensive modules such as **Ray Train**, **Ray Tune** and **Ray Serve**, in ML and DL, while integrating with specialized frameworks such as **PyTorch** and **TensorFlow**. Now you can scale model training in distributed environments, while increasing performance and efficiency in the learning phase by facilitating tuning on the model. Finally, you learned about **Modin**, which is made for manipulating DataFrame objects in a distributed manner. This allows you to work on large datasets that are not treatable locally by libraries like Pandas.

In the next chapter, we will learn about the world of distributed computing again and introduce you to **PySpark**, which is a powerful ecosystem of frameworks and tools that has been enjoying enormous success. We will see all its aspects and analyze its main components such as **MLlib**, **Spark Streaming**, **Kafka** and **GraphFrame** through a series of application examples on their use and functioning.

Chapter 12
PySpark

Introduction

PySpark is the Python API which works with Apache Spark, an open-source framework for distributed computing and processing of large volumes of data. PySpark allows you to harness the power of Spark using a more accessible language such as Python, without having to necessarily write code in Java or Scala.

In this chapter, we will introduce the core concepts of PySpark and illustrate its execution model for distributed data processing. You will learn how to create and manipulate distributed datasets, apply transformations and actions, and understand how Spark executes operations across a cluster. By the end of the chapter, you will be able to identify appropriate use cases for PySpark, and build simple, scalable data processing pipelines.

Structure

This chapter will address the following topics:

- Apache Spark
- PySpark
- Machine Learning with PySpark: MLlib
- Distributed Computing Optimization
- Spark UI
- Spark Streaming and Real-Time Data Processing
- Kafka
- Writing Data to HDFS or Amazon S3
- GraphFrame

Apache Spark

Apache Spark is one of the most popular and powerful platforms for distributed processing of large volumes of data. Designed to be fast, flexible and easy to use, Spark has revolutionized the way data is managed and analyzed at scale. Born as an open-source project at UC Berkeley in 2009, Spark has quickly become a reference tool in the Big Data ecosystem.

From a more technical point of view, Apache Spark is a distributed computing framework that allows you to process data on clusters of computers in a scalable and resilient way. Unlike other distributed computing frameworks, Spark stands out for its speed, flexibility and ease of use.

Thanks to the in-memory computation engine, Spark is able to process data much faster than other systems. It also supports a wide range of workloads like batch processing, real-time analytics, Machine Learning (ML) and graph processing, which make it one of the most flexible distributed systems in its field of use. It is also very simple due to its intuitive API and is available in different languages such as Python, Java, Scala and R.

Spark offers an integrated ecosystem of the following modules that allow you to tackle different types of processing:

- **SparkSQL** for working with structured data using SQL and DataFrames
- **Spark Streaming** to process data streams in real-time
- **MLlib,** a scalable ML library
- **GraphX** to process and analyze graphs (not supported in Python)
- **Spark Core,** the main engine for managing distributed computing and resources

Furthermore, Spark can operate in many cluster platforms that range from a simple standalone cluster to Apache Hadoop and Apache Mesos systems, and containerized systems such as Kubernetes.

Thanks to all these features, Apache Spark has become an essential tool for those who want to extract value from data.

PySpark

PySpark is the Apache Spark API designed to enable Python developers to harness the power of Spark's distributed computing. Due to its ease of use and the flexibility of Python, PySpark represents an ideal bridge between the world of Big data and the community of developers, data scientists, and analysts who work with Python on a daily basis.

You can install PySpark directly via this pip:

```
pip install pyspark
```

PySpark is structured to provide Python developers with an interface to interact with Apache Spark functionality. Its structure is composed of several core modules, each designed for a specific task.

SparkContext is the heart of every Spark application. It takes connects to the Spark cluster and coordinates the distribution of operations among the cluster nodes. When a working session (**`SparkSession`**) is created, PySpark automatically starts a **`SparkContext`** instance. The **Resilient Distributed Dataset (RDD)** is the basic element for Spark and represents a distributed collection of immutable objects that can be processed in parallel. Once created, these objects cannot be modified and in case of error, RDDs are regenerated by Spark. Two different types of operations are performed on these objects, which are:

- Transformations (Lazy)
- Actions (Eager)

Transformations are "**`lazy`**" operations (executed only when requested) such as **`map`**, **`filter`**, and **`groupBy`**. On the other hand, actions are "**`eager`**" operations (executed when declared) that produce a result and start data processing such as **`collect`**, **`count`**, and **`take`**. **DataFrames** are an evolved form of RDDs, and are very similar to those used in Pandas, but are optimized to be instantiated and processed in a distributed manner. On these structured or semi-structured octets, PySpark offers a large set of intuitive methods for manipulating the data contained within them. Furthermore, by exploiting the Catalyst engine, PySpark allows you to use SQL-like query methods to apply to DataFrames. In fact, **SparkSQL** is a module that can be integrated into the framework that allows you to work on data using SQL syntax: DataFrames are recorded as temporary tables on which to execute SQL queries. Another very important tool in the Spark ecosystem is the **Machine Learning Library (MLlib), which can also be used with PySpark**. It is a real library that provides a large set of algorithms for regression, classification, clustering, dimensionality reduction and model evaluation. Spark is a suitable tool for processing Big Data. However, there are others for streaming data. For instance, Spark Streaming, which is based on micro batches, allows processing data streams in real-time. Structured Streaming is a more recent approach to streaming and is based on the use of DataFrame for real-time data analysis.

Finally, **GraphFrame** is a support tool for graph processing for Python (as GraphX is for Scala) of the Spark ecosystem.

Once you install PySpark on your system, you can create a session called **SparkSession**, which will be the main access point for all Spark resources, contexts and modules. PySpark can run both in local mode (standalone) and connected to a remote Spark cluster (distributed mode). In local mode, PySpark uses your computer as a Spark environment and emulates the behavior of a cluster without connecting to an external Spark server. This mode is useful in the development or testing phase and allows you to work on small datasets. This configuration is simple to use since it does not require any additional installation. It is set automatically or explicitly specified in the **SparkSession** through the **master("local[*]")** method. In particular, the asterisk inside the square brackets indicates that the **SparkSession** will have to use all available resources (all CPUs).

```
from pyspark.sql import SparkSession

spark = SparkSession.builder \
                        .appName("PySpark in local mode") \
                        .master("local[*]") \
                        .getOrCreate()
```

However, the configuration you should work with is connected to a remote Spark server. It allows you to take advantage of the benefits of parallel computing and distributed processing across multiple available resources. To do this, Spark uses one of the following cluster managers:

- YARN (on Hadoop systems)
- Mesos (on generic clusters)
- Kubernetes (on containerized clusters)

In this case, we will specify in the master method the IP address of the server with the port related to the service.

```
spark = SparkSession.builder \
                        .appName("PySpark in cluster mode") \
                        .master("spark://10.0.0.27:7077") \ # example of URL address
                        .getOrCreate()
```

To check the active configuration in the code you can use:

```
print(spark.sparkContext.master)
```

This will return the operating mode: **local[*]** or the URL of the Spark server.

Once all the calculations are completed, you will have to close the session and we can do this by adding the following at the end of the code:

```
spark.stop()
```

This ensures proper cleanup of resources at the end of a Spark application or script.

Also, it may be necessary to configure some environment variables in the system depending on the features used, the operating system, and the applications installed. On Ubuntu, for example, you only need a Java JDK installed for Spark to run. PySpark itself must be installed separately via:

```
pip install pyspark,
```

This can be done unless you are running Spark from the official distribution, where PySpark is already bundled.

The only necessary step is to install Java JDK on Ubuntu, which is necessary to run the Spark ecosystem that runs on Java. This looks like the following:

```
sudo apt install openjdk-21-jdk
```

After the installation is complete, set the global variable **JAVA_HOME** in the **etc/environment** file through:

```
JAVA_HOME="/usr/lib/jvm/java-21-openjdk-amd64"
```

Finally, activate the changes made with the following command:

```
$ source /etc/environment
```

Before starting, it would be good to dedicate a virtual environment to work with PySpark through:

```
$ python3 -m venv myspark
$ source myspark/bin/activate
$ (pyspark) pip3 install pyspark
```

Note: *With PySpark, it is preferable to work with Linux systems to minimize the possibility of problems related to incompatibility and dependencies between the different versions present. It is also easier to manage any visibility between them.*

First, let us start a Spark session in local mode through:

```
from pyspark.sql import SparkSession

spark = SparkSession.builder \
                    .appName("PySpark in local mode") \
                    .master("local[*]") \
                    .getOrCreate()
```

Once a session has been created, we can approach PySpark and create a simple example that reads, manipulates and analyzes a structured dataset. To perform this test, we will use the local configuration. Let us imagine we have a dataset that represents a list of people with name, age and city:

```
data = [("Alice", 29, "Rome"),
        ("Bob", 35, "Milan"),
        ("Cathy", 23,  "Naples"),
         ("David", 40, "Venice")]
columns = ["Name", "Age", "City"]
df = spark.createDataFrame(data, schema=columns)
df
```

Running the code gives you a reference to the object. but not its contents.

```
DataFrame[Name: string, Age: bigint, City: string]
```

Actually, no operation has been performed, given the "**lazy**" nature of PySpark. To activate the previous operations, it is necessary to launch an action command such as **show()**, which displays the content of the DataFrame.

```
df.show()
```

You get the following result when you use the previous command:

```
+-----+---+------+
| Name|Age|  City|
+-----+---+------+
|Alice| 29|  Rome|
|  Bob| 35| Milan|
|Cathy| 23|Naples|
|David| 40|Venice|
+-----+---+------+
```

Let us now see some operations that can be performed on this DataFrame such as filtering, grouping and sorting. These are all transformations and therefore lazy: they will be implemented only when an action command is used in the code, such as **show()**.

To filter the DataFrame we will use the **filter()** function to select people older than 30 years.

```
df_filtered = df.filter(df["Age"] > 30)
df_filtered.show()
```

You will get the following result:

```
+-----+---+------+
| Name|Age|  City|
+-----+---+------+
|  Bob| 35| Milan|
|David| 40|Venice|
+-----+---+------+
```

For grouping, we can use **groupBy()**to joining all the rows by city and calculate their average age.

```
df_grouped = df.groupBy("city").avg("Age")
df_grouped.show()
```

You will get the following result:

```
+------+--------+
|  city|avg(Age)|
+------+--------+
| Milan|    35.0|
|  Rome|    29.0|
|Venice|    40.0|
|Naples|    23.0|
+------+--------+
```

Finally, for sorting, we will use **orderBy()**. We can sort the people in the DataFrame from oldest to youngest.

```
df_sorted = df.orderBy(df["Age"].desc())
df_sorted.show()
```

You will get the following result:

```
+-----+---+------+
| Name|Age|  City|
+-----+---+------+
|David| 40|Venice|
|  Bob| 35| Milan|
|Alice| 29|  Rome|
|Cathy| 23|Naples|
+-----+---+------+
```

These are very common operations that are applied to Spark DataFrame and have the same syntax as a Pandas DataFrame. However, it is possible to perform similar operations using a completely different approach. For those who are used to working and manipulating data in database tables, they will be more comfortable using SQL queries. We have already established that it is possible to use SQL-like queries on Spark DataFrame thanks to SparkSQL. Let us see how to apply SQL queries to the previous DataFrame.

The first step will be to register the DataFrame as a temporary table to execute SQL queries, regardless of the type of search or selection that we want to apply to the data.

```
df.createOrReplaceTempView("citizens")
```

With this command, we have created a temporary view from the contents of the DataFrame.

Now, we will perform operations like the previous transformations **filter, groupBy** and **orderBy**), but using an SQL-like language. To do this, there is a specific function **spark.sql(,** in which the SQL query is passed as a string argument. For example, if we want to filter people over 30 years of age, we will insert the following code:

```
spark.sql("SELECT Name, Age, City FROM citizens WHERE Age > 30").show()
```

By executing, we will get the same result that we got with the **filter()** action:

```
+-----+---+------+
| Name|Age|  City|
+-----+---+------+
|  Bob| 35| Milan|
|David| 40|Venice|
+-----+---+------+
```

We can operate the following command for grouping and sorting:

```
spark.sql("SELECT City, AVG(Age) AS Age FROM citizens GROUP BY City").show()
```

You will get the following result by running the previous command:

```
+------+----+
|  City| Age|
+------+----+
| Milan|35.0|
|  Rome|29.0|
|Venice|40.0|
|Naples|23.0|
+------+----+
```

```
spark.sql("SELECT * FROM citizens ORDER BY Age DESC").show()
```

This will give you the following result:

```
+-----+---+------+
| Name|Age|  City|
+-----+---+------+
|David| 40|Venice|
|  Bob| 35| Milan|
|Alice| 29|  Rome|
|Cathy| 23|Naples|
+-----+---+------+
```

As we can see, the results are identical to the transformations. Therefore, there is an interoperability between DataFrame API and SQL. The choice lays with the person who wants to use it and depends on the context, but both approaches are interchangeable.

Let us close the session with the command:

```
spark.stop()
```

A More Complex Example Introducing a Parallel Calculation

The previous example was simple, but a great explainer of the features offered by PySpark to operate and manipulate a DataFrame and the data contained within it. Now let us move on to another example which is slightly more complex and highlights the advantages of parallel computing offered by the distributed environments on which PySpark works. Here, we use the concept of **Resilient Distributed Dataset (RDD)** to perform a parallel mapping and reduction operation, while simulating a distributed analysis.

Imagine that we have a large text dataset, and we want to calculate the frequency of words in a parallel way. Let us reopen a new Spark session locally, and define a list of strings as follows:

```
from pyspark.sql import SparkSession

spark = SparkSession.builder \
                    .appName("PySpark in local mode") \
                    .master("local[*]") \
                    .getOrCreate()

lines = ["PySpark is powerful and fast",
         "Distributed computing is useful for large datasets",
         "PySpark supports parallel computing",
         "with Spark we can process large volumes of data",]
rdd = spark.sparkContext.parallelize(lines)
```

The input is transformed into an RDD distributed across the available cores. PySpark divides the work into multiple partitions to process the data in parallel. Now, let us perform a parallel word count through the following code:

```
words = rdd.flatMap(lambda line: line.split(" "))
word_pairs = words.map(lambda word: (word.lower(), 1))
word_counts = word_pairs.reduceByKey(lambda a, b: a + b)
df_word_counts = word_counts.toDF(["Word", "Count"]).orderBy("Count",
ascending=False)
df_word_counts.show()
```

In this code, we have introduced some transformations that operate in parallel. These are explained as follows:

- `flatMap` splits each line into words creating a larger RDD distributed in parallel.
- `map` associate each word with the value 1.
- `reduceyByKey` combines the values associated with each key (word) by adding the counts.

Since PySpark operates in lazy mode, the reduceByKey operation is optimized to reduce the data locally on each node before combining the results. Finally, the final results are converted to a DataFrame for a clearer representation. Running the code will give the following result:

```
+-----------+-----+
|       Word|Count|
+-----------+-----+
|    pyspark|    2|
|         is|    2|
|  computing|    2|
|      large|    2|
|   powerful|    1|
|     useful|    1|
|        and|    1|
|   datasets|    1|
|       fast|    1|
|   supports|    1|
|distributed|    1|
|   parallel|    1|
|        for|    1|
|         we|    1|
|       with|    1|
|    process|    1|
|      spark|    1|
|    volumes|    1|
|        can|    1|
|         of|    1|
+-----------+-----+
only showing top 20 rows
```

RDDs offer more low-level control, while DataFrames are more user-friendly. Let us close the session again via:

```
spark.stop()
```

Machine Learning with PySpark: MLlib

Now, we will see how to use MLlib to exploit the benefits of parallel and distributed computing in ML via the tools made available by the Spark ecosystem. Before starting from Ubuntu, let us install the OpenBLAS library that we will need during the training phase of ML. This can be done via:

```
sudo apt-get install libopenblas-base
```

Let us see an example by building a logistic regression model for a binary classification. As a scenario, we have to predict whether a customer will buy a product or not. In this regard, let us imagine we have a dataset of customers with the following information:

- Age
- Income
- Subscribed (0 = No, 1 = Yes)
- Bought (0 = No, 1 = Yes)

We want to train a machine learning model to predict whether a customer will buy a product based on the features provided. You can observe it as follows:

```
from pyspark.sql import SparkSession

spark = SparkSession.builder \
                    .appName("PySpark in local mode") \
                    .master("local[*]") \
```

```
                    .getOrCreate()

    data = [
          (25, 30000, 1, 0),
          (35, 50000, 0, 1),
          (45, 100000, 1, 1),
          (22, 35000, 0, 0),
          (44, 60000, 1, 1),
          (33, 35000, 1, 1),
          (50, 22000, 0, 0),
          (30, 47000, 0, 1),
          (48, 50000, 1, 1),
    ]
    columns = ["Age", "Salary", "Subscriber", "Purchased"]
    df = spark.createDataFrame(data, schema=columns)
```

After opening a Spark Session, we will define a fictitious dataset with characteristics that distinguish a set of customers (**features**) and the target variable (**purchased**). This is demonstrated as follows:

```
from pyspark.ml.feature import VectorAssembler
# Pre-process data
feature_columns = ["Age", "Salary", "Subscriber"]
vector_assembler = VectorAssembler(inputCols=feature_columns,
outputCol="features")
df_transformed = vector_assembler.transform(df)

# Training and testing set
train_data, test_data = df_transformed.randomSplit([0.8, 0.2], seed=42)
```

Before training the model, some fundamental steps are necessary. The columns with the features are combined into a single "**features**" column with **VectorAssembler**. Then, to divide the dataset into a training set and testing set, **randomSplit()** is used, which randomly assigns 80% of the elements of the dataset to the training set, and the remaining 20% to the testing set. Now, everything is ready for the training phase of a model.

```
from pyspark.ml.classification import LogisticRegression
# Training model
lr = LogisticRegression(featuresCol="features", labelCol="Purchased")
lr_model = lr.fit(train_data)
```

Since we are talking about a binary classification problem, we will choose one of the simplest and most common models suitable for solving it: **LogisticRegression**. Once the model has been trained, we can evaluate it through:

```
from pyspark.ml.evaluation import BinaryClassificationEvaluator
# Evaluate model
predictions = lr_model.transform(test_data)
evaluator = BinaryClassificationEvaluator(labelCol="Purchased",
rawPredictionCol="rawPrediction")
accuracy = evaluator.evaluate(predictions)

# Showing results
predictions.select("features", "purchased", "prediction").show()
print(f"Model accuracy: {accuracy:,2f}")

spark.stop()
```

For the evaluation, we choose **BinaryClassificationEvaluator**, which was created specifically to evaluate the accuracy of binary classification problems. Running it will get us the following results:

```
+-----------------+---------+----------+
|         features|purchased|prediction|
+-----------------+---------+----------+
|[35.0,50000.0,0.0]|        1|       0.0|
|[30.0,47000.0,0.0]|        1|       0.0|
+-----------------+---------+----------+

Model accuracy: 1.00
```

As we can see, the model performs a check between the predictions and the target. The accuracy in this case is equal to 1.00, that is, it is 100% able to predict the cases (we are talking about an evaluation carried out only on two clients). It is just an example but it is useful to understand how to use MLlib for ML with Spark.

Distributed Computing Optimization

Distributed computing optimization is essential to make the most of a cluster's resources and improve the performance of PySpark applications. There are several key aspects that can be useful in this regard. A simple but effective example to explain and get familiar with these aspects could be to choose a dataset containing a series of data such as financial transactions, and then process it.

Let us start by setting up a simple-to-use dataset, which we will call **transactions.csv**:

```
user_id,amount
1,100
2,200
1,300
2,400
3,500
```

First, let us implement some basic code to read the file, process the data, and calculate the total sum and average transactions per user. Write the following code to a file and save it, for example, as **optimized.py**:

```
from pyspark.sql import SparkSession

spark = SparkSession.builder \
    .appName("Distributed Optimization") \
    .master("local[*]") \
    .getOrCreate()

# Read CSV file as RDD
rdd = spark.sparkContext.textFile("file:///transactions.csv")

# Transform data into (user_id, amount)
header = rdd.first()  # Salta l'header
data = rdd.filter(lambda row: row != header) \
          .map(lambda row: row.split(",")) \
          .map(lambda cols: (int(cols[0]), float(cols[1])))

# Calculate the sum and average of transactions per user
user_totals = data.mapValues(lambda amount: (amount, 1)) \
                  .reduceByKey(lambda a, b: (a[0] + b[0], a[1] + b[1])) \
                  .mapValues(lambda x: (x[0], x[0] / x[1]))
print(user_totals.collect())
spark.stop()
```

Running it will get us the following results:

```
[(2, (600.0, 300.0)), (1, ((400.0, 200.0)), (3, (500.0, 500.0))]
```

Although we have used a very small dataset for convenience, it is sufficient to explain the optimization aspects. The first optimization we will talk about is **efficient partitioning**. Partitioning is how Spark divides data into smaller chunks, called partitions, that are distributed and processed across the cluster nodes. Each partition is processed by a single task. This is important because it introduces parallelism, which means that more partitions/nodes can work at the same time. Spark does this automatically, but there are situations where this may not be optimal. In fact, while automatic partitioning works in most cases, there are situations where **manual partitioning** is useful. This is possible in Spark using the **`repartition()`** method, which takes as a parameter the number of partitions to use. In fact, the automatic process could use too many partitions for the necessary calculations, which can create an overhead and make the calculation inefficient. In a large cluster, automatic partitioning might not be able to make the most of all the available resources.

Starting from the previous code, we will divide the data into 4 partitions, while inserting the following line immediately after defining the **`data`**:

```
data = data.repartition(4)
```

Another approach to optimization is **persistence and caching**. If the data will be reused in multiple operations, we can store it in memory to avoid recalculations. For this purpose, we will use the **`cache()`** function. Replace the previously updated line with this command:

```
data.cache()
```

This instruction activates caching, which means that the data will be stored in memory for quick access. This operation reduces the processing time for repeated passes. In addition, with **`persist()`** it is possible to choose the specific level of storage of data, as shown here:

```
data.persist(StorageLevel.MEMORY_AND_DISK)
```

Another optimization approach that can be applied to the example code is filtering via **broadcast variables**. These allow you to share small datasets or reference values among all the nodes in a cluster without replicating them. Without broadcast, Spark ships a copy of the variable with every task, which leads to significant network overhead. Suppose we have a list of VIP users that we want to use as a reference to filter the data:

```
# VIP User List
vip_users = [1, 2]
# Filter VIP users only
vip_data = data.filter(lambda x: x[0] in vip_users)
```

With this code, we will have a separate copy of **`vip_users`** for each task. When you use this list in the code without broadcast variables, each task gets a separate copy of the vip_users list. This means that if you have 1,000 tasks, the list will be replicated 1,000 times. Each node will get a separate copy of the list from the driver creating network overhead. Also, there will be a waste of memory, since each task stores a separate copy that consumes memory.

Let us introduce a broadcast variable in the code by passing the list of VIP users as an argument to `broadcast()`:

```
# VIP User List
vip_users = [1, 2]
# List broadcast
broadcast_vip = spark.sparkContext.broadcast(vip_users)
# Filter VIP users only
vip_data = data.filter(lambda x: x[0] in broadcast_vip.value)
```

In this case, the driver will send a single copy of the **vip_user** list to each node. Each node stores this copy in memory and shares it with all tasks running on that node. Tasks access the broadcast list as a global reference without creating separate copies. This way, the VIP user list is shared efficiently across all nodes, while reducing network traffic and ensuring quick processing.

Another optimization is to carefully choose between **reduceByKey** and **combineByKey**. Both operations can trigger shuffles when data needs to be grouped by key, which is costly in terms of time and resources due to data transfers and (de)serialization overhead.

The key difference is that reduceByKey applies the same function both within and across partitions, while combineByKey allows you to define separate functions for creating while merging within and across partitions. This makes combineByKey more flexible, though not necessarily efficient in every case. Minimizing unnecessary shuffles in either case significantly improves performance. For our example, we can replace **user_totals** in the code with the following definition:

```
user_totals_optimized = data.combineByKey(
    lambda value: (value, 1),  # Initialization
    lambda acc, value: (acc[0] + value, acc[1] + 1),  # within the partition
    lambda acc1, acc2: (acc1[0] + acc2[0], acc1[1] + acc2[1])  # between
partitions
).mapValues(lambda x: (x[0], x[0] / x[1]))
```

The **combineByKey** function combines data locally before transferring it between partitions. This reduces the number of shuffles, while improving performance.

Another optimization is the switch to DataFrame. This operation will allow us to take advantage of more efficient components within PySpark such as Catalyst Optimizer and Tungsten Execution Engine. **Catalyst Optimizer** is the optimization engine for queries on DataFrame and SQL in Spark. This component performs logical and physical transformations to improve execution. **Tungsten Execution Engine** optimizes the use of CPU and memory through binary data formats and low-level operations. Therefore, switching data to Spark DataFrame automatically improves queries on that data and makes them faster. It also reduces the number of operations needed and optimizes the use of resources. Furthermore, it can also be said that the code becomes simpler and more readable. To do this, you can convert an RDD to a DataFrame through the **toDF()** method that accepts as an argument a list with the names of the columns of the DataFrame. This is shown as follows:

```
from pyspark.sql import Row
df = rdd.toDF(["user_id", "amount"])
```

In this case, you can modify the initial code of **optimized.py** as follows:

```
from pyspark.sql import SparkSession
from pyspark.sql import functions as F
import os

# Set the PYSPARK_PYTHON environment variable to the default python3
os.environ["PYSPARK_PYTHON"] = "/usr/bin/python3"

spark = SparkSession.builder \
    .appName("Distributed Optimization") \
    .master("local[*]") \
    .getOrCreate()

# Read CSV file as RDD
rdd = spark.sparkContext.textFile("transactions.csv")
```

```
# Transform data into (user_id, amount)
header = rdd.first()  # salta l'header
data = (rdd.filter(lambda row: row != header)
          .map(lambda row: row.split(","))
          .map(lambda cols: (int(cols[0]), float(cols[1]))))

df = data.toDF(["user_id", "amount"])

user_totals_df = df.groupBy("user_id").agg(
    F.sum("amount").alias("total_amount"),
    F.avg("amount").alias("avg_amount")
)

user_totals_df.show()
```

We will obtain the following output:

```
+-------+------------+----------+
|user_id|total_amount|avg_amount|
+-------+------------+----------+
|      1|       400.0|     200.0|
|      2|       600.0|     300.0|
|      3|       500.0|     500.0|
+-------+------------+----------+
```

Using **toDF()** to convert an RDD to a Spark Dataframe increases performance, but in cases where it is possible, like our example, further performance optimization is required to read the data source directly as a DataFrame. In our case, since it is a CSV file, a particular construct is used:

```
df = spark.read.format("csv") \
    .option("header", "true") \  # Indicates that the file has a header
    .option("inferSchema", "true") \  # Automatically infers data types
    .load("transactions.csv")
```

When reading a file directly as a DataFrame, Spark takes full advantage of the Catalyst Optimizer which uses techniques such as column pruning (reading only the necessary columns) and filter pushdown (by applying filters as soon as possible to avoid loading unnecessary data). Additionally, an RDD stores data as Python objects, which are less memory efficient. A DataFrame, on the other hand, uses an optimized binary format (Tungsten Execution Engine) which allows for more efficient memory and CPU management. Spark offers optimized native readers for many file formats such as CSV, Parquet, and JSON.

The initial code of **optimized.py** then becomes very simple and readable. It looks something like this:

```
from pyspark.sql import SparkSession
spark = SparkSession.builder \
    .appName("Read CSV as DataFrame") \
    .master("local[*]") \
    .getOrCreate()
df = spark.read.format("csv") \
    .option("header", "true") \  # Indicates that the file has a header
    .option("inferSchema", "true") \  # Automatically infers data types
    .load("file:///path/to/transactions.csv")
df.printSchema()
df.show()
```

Spark UI

While running a Spark Session, you can visit the Spark UI by opening a browser and connecting to http://localhost:4040. You will see a screen like the one in *Figure 12.1*:

***Figure 12.1:** Spark Web Tools Accessed via Port 4040*

This web interface provides a detailed view of Spark applications with useful information for many operations such as:

- Monitoring job progress
- Performance analysis
- Identifying bottlenecks
- Diagnosing errors and various problems

The interface is divided into several sections, each of which provides detailed information as follows:

- **Jobs** shows a list of all jobs executed or running with related information (status, number of tasks, execution time).
- **Stages** shows the details of the stages in each job. A stage is a set of parallel tasks that follow the same type of operation (for example, map or reduce). The related information (number of tasks, execution time, operations performed, shuffle details) is shown here as well.
- **Tasks** displays detailed information about individual tasks executed within a stage, along with related information (status, execution time, CPU and memory usage, amount of data read and written).
- **Storage** displays information about datasets stored in memory or on disk, which includes both RDD and DataFrame.
- **Environment** shows Spark environment information (component and dependency versions, environment variables, and configurations).
- **Executors** shows information about running executors. These are the processes that run tasks distributed across the cluster nodes.

Spark UI can become an essential tool for monitoring and optimizing Spark applications.

Spark Streaming and Real-Time Data Processing

At the beginning of the chapter we talked about PySpark allowing real-time data processing with two different approaches:

- Spark Streaming
- Structured Streaming

Spark Streaming is an Apache Spark module designed for real-time data stream processing and is based on the concept of micro-batches. It collects data in small time windows (batches) and processes them sequentially. Each time interval produces a new RDD, which represents the data in the micro-batch. At the end, you get a continuous sequence of RDDs. This concept is called **Dstream** (Discretized Stream).

Structured Streaming is based on the DataFrame extension for structured stream processing.

However, the most modern and recommended approach for processing streaming data with PySpark is Structured Streaming. In fact, Dstream has been "deprecated" since version 3.4, and it is therefore advisable to abandon this approach in favor of Structured Streaming, which is based on the use of DataFrames.

Let us simulate a Spark Streaming application that reads incoming data from a TCP socket (for example a local server) and calculates the word rate in real-time:

Write the following code in a file and then save it as **sstream.py**.

```
from pyspark.sql import SparkSession
from pyspark.sql.functions import explode, split

spark = SparkSession.builder \
    .appName("Spark Streaming") \
    .master("local[*]") \
    .getOrCreate()

print("Start of acquisition time")
# Reading data stream from a socket
lines = spark.readStream \
    .format("socket") \
    .option("host", "localhost") \
    .option("port", 9999) \
    .load()

# Splitting lines into words
words = lines.select(
    explode(
        split(lines.value, " ")
    ).alias("word")
)

# Counting word occurrences
word_counts = words.groupBy("word").count()

# Writing the result to the console
query = word_counts.writeStream \
    .outputMode("complete") \
    .format("console") \
    .start()

# Waiting for manual stop
query.awaitTermination(60)
print("End of acquisition time")
spark.stop()
print("Spark Session Closed")
```

To simulate a real-time data source, we will use NetCat, which is a very versatile network tool and is capable of simulating a simple and configurable TCP server. This tool is generally always present by default on Linux Ubuntu systems.

At this point, you must open a console and launch the server with the following command:

```
$ nc -lk 9999
```

This command launches the TCP server with two options: (-l) which indicates that the server must work in "listener" mode, that is, it must remain listening for incoming connections; the option (-k) makes NetCat accept multiple consecutive connections. Without this option, the listener would close after accepting a single connection. As for the port, the number 9,999 is a number chosen at random so that it does not overlap with active services.

As soon as the server starts, you can launch the program in another console in Python via:

```
$ python sstream.py
```

When you see the message "Start of acquisition time" in the console, the system will start receiving data from the TCP server. From this point on, you have 60 seconds to enter the following lines of text in the console where NetCat is running:

```
hello world
spark is powerful
hello spark
```

Write the first line and press the Return key. Wait a few seconds before inserting the second line of text. Wait a few more seconds to insert the third.

NetCat will send each input line as data to the client (in this case PySpark). This system simply simulates a data source such as a log server, an IoT sensor or another, while generating data packets at indeterminate intervals (waiting times between each one are always different).

While you insert the text strings, check the output on the other console. You will find that the output shows the DataFrame containing the count of words read via TCP by PySpark. These will be reprinted every certain period of time (Batch 0, batch 1 and batch 2). If you have inserted the three lines of text at the right interval of time, you will be able to see the time taken before the counting results are updated in the table.

The tables represented are updated in the output gradually, while showing the word counts of the lines added.

At the end, you will get the total count after 60 seconds of acquisition. For example, after batch 0, you get an empty table (rightly so). This is shown here:

```
-------------------------------------------
Batch: 0
-------------------------------------------
+---------+-----+
| word    |count|
+---------+-----+
+---------+-----+
```

In the second batch (batch 1), you will get the previous results. The counts correspond to the words of the first two lines of text:

```
-------------------------------------------
Batch: 1
-------------------------------------------
+---------+-----+
| word    |count|
+---------+-----+
| powerful|    1|
|    hello|    1|
|       is|    1|
|    spark|    1|
|    world|    1|
+---------+-----+
```

Finally, at the end of 60 seconds, the set acquisition time is over and the Spark Session will close.

In the third batch (batch 2) we will have the final counts of all the words sent, which looks like as follows:

```
-------------------------------------------
Batch: 2
-------------------------------------------
+---------+-----+
| word    |count|
+---------+-----+
| powerful|    1|
|    hello|    2|
|       is|    1|
|    spark|    2|
|    world|    1|
+---------+-----+
```

Collecting Results on Storage Systems

In the previous case, we saw all that all the results were reported on the console. This is a very simple case, which is apt for educational or debugging purposes. In the real world, the results obtained from the streaming computation will have to be stored on some form of storage or an additional processing and analysis platform (HDFS files, S3, Kafka or an SQL database). In the example code for writing to the console, we have used "**complete**" as the output mode, but Spark Streaming offers three different output modes, which are:

- **Complete** writes all the resulting data to each batch (the one we used in the output).
- **Append** writes only the new lines added in the current batch.
- **Update** writes only updated rows from the previous batch (not always supported).

Instead of displaying our results on the console, we will write them to a **Parquet** file, which is a columnar format and is highly efficient and compatible with Spark (and many other systems), without the need for extra manipulation.

However, since it is written to a file, we need to make some changes to the previous code. First, we set the output mode to "append". We also need to add a watermark. This is a mechanism that allows Spark to handle late data and determine when older data can be removed from the state inside the aggregation. So, the watermark specifies a time limit for the data that can be considered for aggregation. This requires that the data has a timestamp.

When finished, the code will look like the following example. Write it to a text file and save it as **stream2.py**.

```
from pyspark.sql import SparkSession
from pyspark.sql.functions import explode, split, current_timestamp, window

spark = SparkSession.builder \
     .appName("Structured Streaming") \
     .master("local[*]") \
     .getOrCreate()

# Reading data stream from a socket
lines = spark.readStream \
    .format("socket") \
    .option("host", "localhost") \
    .option("port", 9999) \
    .load()

# Adding timestamp
```

```
lines_with_timestamp = lines.withColumn("timestamp", current_timestamp())
print("Start of acquisition time")

# Splitting lines into words
words = lines_with_timestamp.select(
    explode(
        split(lines_with_timestamp.value, " ")
    ).alias("word"),
    "timestamp"
)

# Word count with watermark and windowing
word_counts = words \
    .withWatermark("timestamp", "10 seconds") \
    .groupBy(
        window("timestamp", "1 minute"),
        "word"
    ).count()

# Writing results in Parquet format
query = word_counts.writeStream \
    .outputMode("append") \    # Please, read the note below the code!
    .format("parquet") \
    .option("path", "output") \
    .option("checkpointLocation", "checkpoint") \
    .start()

# Waiting and terminating the job
query.awaitTermination(300)
print("Stop of acquisition time")

# Spark session closure
spark.stop()
print("Spark Session closed. Check results in output directory.")
```

Note: *Using outputMode("append") with aggregations requires event-time processing with a watermark. Without a watermark, Spark cannot determine when a window is complete and will raise an error. In the example above, we will parse the event timestamp from the incoming data and set a 10-second watermark, which tells Spark when it is safe to finalize windows and emit results incrementally.*

The Parquet format is suitable for this operation as it supports complex structures and is optimized for analytical queries with Spark and other tools. This format is compatible with many frameworks like Pandas and Hadoop.

As part of the code changes, we have set the watermark to ignore data with timestamps delayed by more than 10 seconds compared to it. The 1-minute time window groups the data by time intervals.

A timestamp column is also added to the two existing columns (words and count). As in the previous case, the text is divided into words using split and explode creating a new row in the DataFrame for each of these words.

The results are written in Parquet format in the output directory, together with a checkpoint directory used to manage the streaming status. To avoid problems during the execution of Spark Streaming and to write files, the directories must already be present, but should be empty. To facilitate this task at each execution, it will be simple to launch the following commands in sequence:

```
$ rm -rf output checkpoint
$ mkdir output checkpoint
```

The **start()** method starts the streaming query while **awaitTermination()** takes the time the application runs for as a parameter. The **stop()** command finally closes the Spark session and frees up resources. Text strings warn in console output when streaming is started and when it is closed.

The "**append**" mode (the only one applicable to writing parquet files) writes the new batches of data without overwriting those already saved.

At this point, you must restart the NetCat server socket on port 9999:

```
nc -lk 9999
```

Then run the script **sstream2.py** via the command:

```
python stream2.py
```

Once all the services and Spark sessions are started, the message "**Start streaming**" will appear on the console. Now, enter some text in the console where you launched the socket server. The program will start receiving the text sent by NetCat. In this case, to have effective results, we will extend the acquisition times to 5 minutes. We will also use a slightly longer text as shown here:

```
This is a fantastic idea
Just thinking about
A wonderful idea
Spark is wonderful
A fantastic tool for distributed calculation
hello world
hello spark
After a lot of seconds
help me a lot
```

After 60 seconds, the Python program will stop running and will display the following message:

```
End of acquisition time
Spark Session closed. Check results in output directory.
```

When you see the contents of our working directory (where the Python file was launched) and you will see that an output directory and a checkpoint directory have been generated. In the output folder, you will find a series of **parquet** files.

There are many ways to read and analyze their content. If we prefer to work inside PySpark, we can write the following code in a text file, and save it, for example, as **read_parquets.py**. The code looks like this:

```
from pyspark.sql import SparkSession

spark = SparkSession.builder \
            .appName("Parquet Reader") \
            .master("local[*]") \
            .getOrCreate()

parquet_df = spark.read.parquet("output")
parquet_df.show()

parquet_df.printSchema()

spark.stop()
```

Running the code will give you the result shown in *Figure 12.2*:

```
+--------------------+-----------+-----+
|              window|       word|count|
+--------------------+-----------+-----+
|{2025-01-09 19:43...|calculation|    1|
|{2025-01-09 19:43...|distributed|    1|
|{2025-01-09 19:43...|  fantastic|    2|
|{2025-01-09 19:43...|  wonderful|    2|
|{2025-01-09 19:43...|   thinking|    1|
|{2025-01-09 19:44...|    seconds|    1|
|{2025-01-09 19:43...|      about|    1|
|{2025-01-09 19:43...|      world|    1|
|{2025-01-09 19:43...|      Spark|    1|
|{2025-01-09 19:43...|      hello|    1|
|{2025-01-09 19:44...|      spark|    1|
|{2025-01-09 19:44...|      hello|    1|
|{2025-01-09 19:44...|      After|    1|
|{2025-01-09 19:43...|       This|    1|
|{2025-01-09 19:43...|       Just|    1|
|{2025-01-09 19:43...|       tool|    1|
|{2025-01-09 19:44...|       help|    1|
|{2025-01-09 19:43...|       idea|    2|
|{2025-01-09 19:43...|        for|    1|
|{2025-01-09 19:44...|        lot|    2|
+--------------------+-----------+-----+
only showing top 20 rows

root
 |-- window: struct (nullable = false)
 |    |-- start: timestamp (nullable = true)
 |    |-- end: timestamp (nullable = true)
 |-- word: string (nullable = false)
 |-- count: long (nullable = false)
```

Figure 12.2: *Count of Words Entered via Streaming Stored inside .parquet Files*

The result is a DataFrame table with the received words and their count. Also, further down the DataFrame, the structure is reported with a STRUCT introduced in this example along with the start and end timestamp.

The parquet files produced can also be read during a Python session with the Pandas library. Let us first make sure we have the requisite apparatus to use them by installing PyArrow or other similar libraries (for example, **`fastparquet`**).

```
pip install pyarrow
```

Use the following code after you have enacted the command:

```
import pandas as pd
df = pd.read_parquet("output")
df.head()
```

Executing this will give you the result shown in *Figure 12.3*:

```
                                              window     word  count
0  {'start': 1736448240000000000, 'end': 17364483...  seconds      1
1  {'start': 1736448240000000000, 'end': 17364483...       me      1
2  {'start': 1736448180000000000, 'end': 17364482...      for      1
3  {'start': 1736448180000000000, 'end': 17364482...     This      1
4  {'start': 1736448180000000000, 'end': 17364482...        A      2
```

Figure 12.3: *The Head (First 6 Rows) of the Spark DataFrame with the Counting Words in Streaming*

In the case of huge datasets, Pandas does not allow you to manage and read this data. Therefore, Dask can be used as a library on distributed systems via:

```
import dask.dataframe as dd

df = dd.read_parquet("output")
df.head()
```

The result is the same as the one obtained previously in *Figure 12.3*.

Beyond that, PySpark allows you to follow a SQL-like approach to analyze the data collected in Parquet files. In fact, you can execute SQL queries directly on Spark DataFrames generated by such files through:

```
from pyspark.sql import SparkSession

spark = SparkSession.builder \
             .appName("Parquet Reader") \
             .master("local[*]") \
             .getOrCreate()

parquet_df = spark.read.parquet("output")
parquet_df.createOrReplaceTempView("words")
result = spark.sql("SELECT word, SUM(count) as total FROM words GROUP BY word
ORDER BY total DESC")
result.show()
spark.stop()
```

Running this code will give you a result similar to the one we previously got with the **read_parquets.py** file (see *Figure 12.4*):

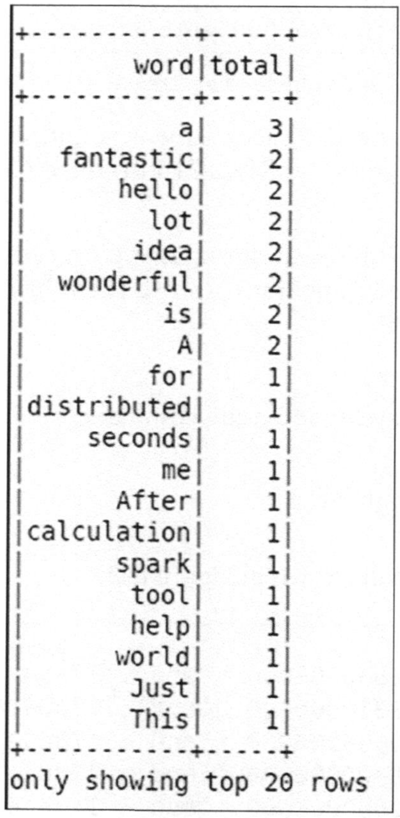

```
+-----------+-----+
|       word|total|
+-----------+-----+
|          a|    3|
|  fantastic|    2|
|      hello|    2|
|        lot|    2|
|       idea|    2|
|  wonderful|    2|
|         is|    2|
|          A|    2|
|        for|    1|
|distributed|    1|
|    seconds|    1|
|         me|    1|
|      After|    1|
|calculation|    1|
|      spark|    1|
|       tool|    1|
|       help|    1|
|      world|    1|
|       Just|    1|
|       This|    1|
+-----------+-----+
only showing top 20 rows
```

Figure 12.4: *Result of SQL-Like Query on Parquet Files*

Kafka

Kafka is an open-source platform for real-time messaging and data stream processing. It works as a pub-sub (publish/subscribe) messaging system and allows producers and consumers to communicate asynchronously.

Kafka is composed of:

- **Broker** servers that handle message traffic
- **Producer** that posts messages on a topic
- **Consumer that** reads messages from a topic
- **Topic**, which is a logical channel to organize messages and is divided into partitions to improve scalability

To install it on Linux Ubuntu 24, you need to download the files from the Apache website. The latest version at the time of writing this book was 3.9.0. Open a terminal and enter the following commands:

```
wget https://downloads.apache.org/kafka/3.9.0/kafka_2.13-3.9.0.tgz
tar -xzf kafka_2.13-3.9.0.tgz
mv kafka_2.13-3.9.0 kafka
```

Kafka requires Zookeeper to work. The latter is included with the package for development and testing purposes. For production environments, it should be replaced with a real Zookeeper cluster. For our purpose, just follow the mentioned instructions.

We will create a directory for Zookeeper and update the newly created directory in the configuration file through the following command:

```
mkdir -p kafka/data/zookeeper
nano kafka/config/zookeeper.properties
```

Update the following line using the path where you installed Kafka (adjust the path according to your system):

```
dataDir=/home/myname/kafka/data/zookeeper
```

Now, let us configure the Kafka Broker by creating a data folder for Kafka and updating the configuration file with the new directory:

```
mkdir -p kakfa/data/kafka
nano kafka/config/server.properties
```

Update the following line using the path where you installed Kafka (adjust the path according to your system):

```
log.dirs=/home/myname/kafka/data/kafka
```

Let us open two terminals and start Zookeeper first through:

```
./kafka/bin/zookeeper-server-start.sh ./kafka/config/zookeeper.properties
```

We can start Kafka through:

```
./kafka/bin/kafka-server-start.sh ./kafka/config/server.properties
```

Now, we need to install the Java Kafka-Spark connectors. To do this, we need to know about the versions of the components that we are going to connect. For these examples, the PySpark version is 3.5.4, while the Kafka version is 3.9. If you want to see the installed version of PySpark, you can use the following command:

```
pip list | grep spark
```

To know the Scala version, we have to launch the following command:

```
spark-submit --version
```

You will get the Spark header output with the version of the components involved, including Scala, as shown in the following figure. The Scala version used in this book is 2.12.18 (see *Figure 12.5*).

```
Welcome to
      ____              __
     / __/__  ___ _____/ /__
    _\ \/ _ \/ _ `/ __/  '_/
   /___/ .__/\_,_/_/ /_/\_\   version 3.5.4
      /_/

Using Scala version 2.12.18, OpenJDK 64-Bit Server VM, 21.0.5
Branch HEAD
Compiled by user yangjie01 on 2024-12-17T04:51:46Z
Revision a6f220d951742f4074b37772485ee0ec7a774e7d
Url https://github.com/apache/spark
Type --help for more information.
```

Figure 12.5: *The Spark Header with the Reported Versions of Various Components*

So now, you have all the information to download the right connectors. You can have a look at the following jar files here:

```
wget https://repo1.maven.org/maven2/org/apache/spark/spark-sql-kafka-0-10_2.12/3.5.4/spark-sql-kafka-0-10_2.12-3.5.4.jar
wget https://repo1.maven.org/maven2/org/apache/kafka/kafka-clients/3.9.0/kafka-clients-3.9.0.jar
```

These jar files will be available when you are running Python scripts, while specifying their path and version.

In Spark Structured Streaming, Kafka can be used as a source or destination. In our case, we will configure Kafka to read messages in real-time, perform a word count, and write the results to parquet files. Let us write the following code and save it as **kafka.py**:

```
from pyspark.sql import SparkSession
from pyspark.sql.functions import explode, split, current_timestamp, window


spark = SparkSession.builder \
    .appName("Kafka with Structured Streaming") \
    .config("spark.jars.packages", "org.apache.spark:spark-sql-kafka-0-10_2.12
:3.5.4") \
    .master("local[*]") \
    .getOrCreate()

spark.sparkContext.setLogLevel("WARN")
print("Start of acquisition time")

# Reading data from Kafka
kafka_df = spark.readStream \
    .format("kafka") \
    .option("kafka.bootstrap.servers", "localhost:9092") \
    .option("subscribe", "word_topic") \
    .load()
```

```
# Convert Kafka values to strings
lines = kafka_df.selectExpr("CAST(value AS STRING)")

# Split lines into words and add a timestamp
words = lines.withColumn("timestamp", current_timestamp()) \
             .select(explode(split(lines.value, " ")).alias("word"),
"timestamp")

# Word count with watermark
word_counts = words \
    .withWatermark("timestamp", "10 seconds") \
    .groupBy(
window("timestamp", "1 minute"),
"word"
    ).count()

# Writing results in Parquet
query = word_counts.writeStream \
    .outputMode("append") \
    .format("parquet") \
    .option("checkpointLocation", "checkpoint") \
    .option("path", "output") \
    .start()

query.awaitTermination(300)
print("Stop of acquisition time")

# Spark session closure
spark.stop()
print("Spark Session closed. Check results in output directory.")
```

Let us now see some new features inserted in the code. Since we are working with Kafka as a source, some behaviors have changed compared to what we observed while working with NetCat. Once the session begins, the console output can be extremely verbose, so we add **`setLogLevel("WARN")`** to reduce the level of logging. To specify Kafka as a data source there is the **`format("kafka"`**), while in **`option(),`** the address and port of the Kafka server are specified. The Kafka data is read as a value column of type binary **`CAST(value AS STRING), which`** converts the binary data into strings. For the rest of the steps, the code behaves exactly like the previous example, where the received text messages were divided into words and then counted. The word count is written inside the parquet files in the output directory here as well.

Now before using Spark Structured Streaming, we will perform a test to see if the entire Kafka system is perfectly configured or not.

Let us start with a topic on Kafka:

```
./kafka/bin/kafka-topics.sh --create --topic word_topic --bootstrap-server
localhost:9092
```

Now, let us start the Kafka producer that will allow us to send the lines of text to the topic:

```
./kakfa/bin/kafka-console-producer.sh --topic word_topic --bootstrap-server
localhost:9092
```

Enter the text as you did with the NetCat server socket. Enter a series of lines of text as you like. Then in another terminal, we will start a Kafka consumer to check if the text is received and then passed correctly:

```
./kafka/bin/kafka-console-consumer.sh --topic word_topic --from-beginning
--bootstrap-server localhost:9092
```

You should get all the lines of text you entered as output. If everything goes well, we stop both the Kafka consumer and producer and empty the output and checkpoint directories. We will start the Kafka producer again here.

```
./kafka/bin/kafka-console-consumer.sh --topic word_topic --from-beginning
--bootstrap-server localhost:9092
```

Now, let us proceed with the rest and start with the Python script: **kafka.py**.

```
spark-submit --packages org.apache.spark:spark-sql-kafka-0-10_2.12:3.5.4
kafka.py
```

A Spark session will start and will remain in acquisition for 5 minutes. During this time, insert some lines of text into the Kafka producer. For example, you can insert the following text:

```
hello world
this text is sent to kafka
hello spark
spark is a powerful tool
hello again
this is another text
I waited for one minute
hello spark again
```

After 5 minutes, the Spark session will end, interrupting the execution of the **kakfa.py** file and returning the prompt. At this point, we should have the output folder with Parquet files inside. To check its content, we will launch the **read_parquet.py** script created previously:

```
python read_parquet.py
```

As a result, we will get the table of word counts that was previously inserted into the Kafka producer. If you have entered the suggested text before, you will get a table like the one shown in *Figure 12.6*:

```
+--------------------+--------+-----+

|              window|    word|count|
+--------------------+--------+-----+
|{2025-01-10 11:47...|powerful|    1|
|{2025-01-10 11:47...|   kafka|    1|
|{2025-01-10 11:47...|   hello|    3|
|{2025-01-10 11:47...|   world|    1|
|{2025-01-10 11:47...|   again|    1|
|{2025-01-10 11:47...|   spark|    2|
|{2025-01-10 11:47...|    text|    1|
|{2025-01-10 11:47...|    tool|    1|
|{2025-01-10 11:47...|    this|    1|
|{2025-01-10 11:47...|    sent|    1|
|{2025-01-10 11:47...|      to|    1|
|{2025-01-10 11:47...|      is|    2|
|{2025-01-10 11:47...|       a|    1|
+--------------------+--------+-----+

root
 |-- window: struct (nullable = false)
 |    |-- start: timestamp (nullable = true)
 |    |-- end: timestamp (nullable = true)
 |-- word: string (nullable = false)
 |-- count: long (nullable = false)
```

Figure 12.6: *The Word Count in the Text Entered by the Kafka Consumer*

As we can see, we have also integrated Kafka into the PySpark Structured Streaming system successfully.

This integration is important because Kafka is a distributed streaming platform specifically designed to manage real-time data streams. This allows it to be processed, thanks to the distributed computing power of Spark Structured Streaming. This synergy is essential for scenarios such as monitoring and event processing (server logging, traffic analysis, IoT data, messaging, and so on).

Kafka also supports integration with multiple data sources to then send them to various destinations. So, its integration with PySpark allows you to extract and manipulate data from streams coming from multiple sources at the same time. The data is then sent to storage systems (HDFS, S3), real-time dashboards or database or data warehousing systems (Snowflake, Redshift).

Writing Data to HDFS or Amazon S3

Spark is an extremely flexible system; therefore, it is possible to switch the saving of extracted data from local to external storage easily, while making small changes to the codes created.

Among the most commonly used destinations in this type of distributed system such are HDFS and S3.

Hadoop Distributed File System (HDFS) is a distributed file system designed to manage large amounts of data on computer clusters. It is a fundamental part of the Hadoop ecosystem and allows you to store data in a distributed manner on multiple nodes. The files are divided into blocks (generally 128MB or 256MB) and then distributed on different nodes of the cluster. Each of these blocks is replicated on multiple nodes, ensuring that the data is available even in the event of a node failure.

Amazon S3 (Simple Storage Service) is a scalable cloud storage service offered by Amazon Web Services (AWS) and is designed to store and retrieve virtually unlimited amounts of data. Being a cloud service, data is accessible everywhere via the internet.

The choice between these two will depend on the needs of your project, the available infrastructure and the desired architecture.

HDFS is ideal for local environments (on-premises) and is useful for traditional ETL processes and long-term archiving on Hadoop clusters.

S3 instead is perfect for cloud scenarios, when data will need to be accessible globally or to AWS systems (Redshift, Athena, SageMaker).

Considering the previous example with Kafka, in order to write the result of our processing, it is sufficient to change the output and the checkpoint path within the **kafka.py** code.

If you want to save your data to an HDFS cluster, you can simply change the output path. Spark supports HDFS natively and can therefore specify an HDFS path as the destination. This is shown in the following code:

```
# Writing data to HDFS
query = word_counts.writeStream \
    .outputMode("append") \
    .format("parquet") \
    .option("checkpointLocation", "hdfs://<HDFS-NAME-NODE>:9000/checkpoint") \
# Directory per i checkpoint
    .option("path", "hdfs://<HDFS-NAME-NODE>:9000/output") \  # Directory di
output su HDFS
    .start()
```

Replace **<HDFS-NAME-NODE>** with the address of your HDFS NameNode (for example **hdfs//namenode-host:9000/output**). However, make sure that you have the permission to write to the destination directory.

For Amazon S3, things are not so straightforward. You need to configure Spark to access the S3 bucket using the **s3a://** protocol. First, you need to configure your AWS credentials as follows:

```
export AWS_ACCESS_KEY_ID=<your-access-key>
export AWS_SECRET_ACCESS_KEY=<your-secret-key>
```

You then need to install the AWS libraries using a jar file like **hadoop-aws** and an AWS connector compatible with your version of Hadoop and Spark. It is at this point that you can insert the output paths and checkpoints in the code, which is shown as follows:

```
query = word_counts.writeStream \
    .outputMode("append") \
    .format("parquet") \
    .option("checkpointLocation", "s3a://<your-bucket-name>/checkpoint") \  #
Directory for checkpoint on S3
    .option("path", "s3a://<your-bucket-name>/output") \  # Output Directory
on S3
    .start()
```

GraphFrame

GraphFrame is an Apache Spark-based library designed for graph processing and analysis. Unlike GraphX, which is only developed in Scala and Java, GraphFrame is natively available for PySpark, which makes it the ideal choice for those who work with Python and need to manage distributed graphs. Due to its integration with Spark SQL and DataFrame, GraphFrame provides a simple and powerful interface to represent, manipulate, and analyze graphs, while combining the processing capabilities of Spark with advanced graph analysis algorithms.

GraphFrame extends the GraphX data model, while relying on DataFrame to represent edges and nodes. The model is called GraphFrame and is made up of two DataFrames:

- **Vertices**, that represent the nodes of the graph, where each node identified by a unique ID and additional properties
- **Edges,** that represent the connections between nodes, with each edge identified by a source ID (**srv**), a destination ID (**dst**), and optional properties

Let us now implement an example to understand how to create a graph. This is an example shows a very simplified social network where people are associated with each other through a set of relationships that form a graph.

First of all, you will need to install the library in your virtual environment via:

```
pip install graphframes
```

You also need to download the GraphFrame JAR package. At the moment, the latest one can be downloaded via:

```
wget https://repos.spark-packages.org/graphframes/graph-
frames/0.8.4-spark3.5-s_2.12/graphframes-0.8.4-spark3.5-s_2.12.jar
```

Otherwise, you can consult the different packages available at **https://spark-packages.org/package/graphframes/graphframes**.

Once the library is installed and the JAR file is downloaded, we will import the necessary modules and create a SparkSession as follows:

```
from pyspark.sql import SparkSession
from graphframes import GraphFrame

spark = SparkSession.builder \
    .appName("GraphFrame Example") \
    .master("local[*]") \
    .getOrCreate()
spark.sparkContext.setLogLevel("ERROR")
```

We will also set the logging level to eliminate most of the messages and make the output more readable. At this point, we will define the social network using Edge and Vertices as follows:

```
vertices = spark.createDataFrame([
    ("1", "Robert"),
    ("2", "Jean"),
    ("3", "Joe"),
    ("4", "David")
], ["id", "name"])

edges = spark.createDataFrame([
    ("1", "2", "friends"),
    ("2", "3", "colleagues"),
    ("3", "4", "family"),
    ("4", "1", "friends")
], ["src", "dst", "relationship"])
```

In Vertices, we defined 4 people, each identified by their name and an ID. In the Edge DataFrame, we defined the type of relationship between the various people, identified by two IDs, source and destination.

At this point, we can define the graph as follows:

```
graph = GraphFrame(vertices, edges)
```

Once defined, it is possible to view the contents of the two DataFrames that make up the graph, as shown here:

```
print("Nodes:")
graph.vertices.show()
print("Edges:")
graph.edges.show()
```

Once we finish working with the Spark Session, we can close it via the following command:

```
spark.stop()
```

Write all the preceding code in a file and save it as **graphs.py**. Now, we can run it with the following command:

```
spark-submit --jars graphframes-0.8.4-spark3.5-s_2.12.jar graphs.py
```

The following results are obtained:

```
Nodes:
+---+------+
| id|  name|
+---+------+
|  1|Robert|
|  2|  Jean|
|  3|   Joe|
|  4| David|
+---+------+

Edges:
+---+---+------------+
|src|dst|relationship|
+---+---+------------+
|  1|  2|     friends|
|  2|  3|  colleagues|
|  3|  4|      family|
|  4|  1|     friends|
+---+---+------------+
```

Graphframe offers a large number of graph analysis algorithms that are designed to perform advanced analysis on large networks in a distributed manner. These algorithms range from calculating node centrality to detecting communities in graphs. Since they are integrated with Spark, they are scalable and can handle huge datasets. In our example, we can use **PageRank** for example. This is an algorithm that assigns a score to nodes in a graph based on connections. The main idea is that a node is considered important if many other nodes connect it and if these nodes are important themselves. In our code, we can insert the following lines:

```
pagerank = graph.pageRank(resetProbability=0.15, maxIter=10)
print("PageRank:")
pagerank.vertices.show()
```

Running the code on our social network model will give us the following result:

```
Pagerank:
+---+------+--------+
| id|  name|pagerank|
+---+------+--------+
|  3|   Joe|     1.0|
|  1|Robert|     1.0|
|  4| David|     1.0|
|  2|  Jean|     1.0|
+---+------+--------+
```

It is clear that we all have a pagerank equal to 1 as our model is very simple and each person has only one relationship with another. Let us replace it with a more complex one:

```
vertices = spark.createDataFrame([
    ("1", "Robert"),
    ("2", "Jean"),
    ("3", "Joe"),
    ("4", "David"),
    ("5", "Martin"),
    ("6", "Grace"),
    ("7", "Jessica"),
    ("8", "Mike")
```

```
], ["id", "name"])

edges = spark.createDataFrame([
    ("1", "2", "friends"),
    ("2", "3", "colleagues"),
    ("3", "4", "family"),
    ("4", "1", "friends"),
    ("5", "1", "friends"),
    ("5", "3", "colleagues"),
    ("6", "3", "family"),
    ("6", "7", "friends"),
    ("7", "5", "colleagues"),
    ("8", "6", "friends"),
    ("8", "7", "family"),
    ("2", "8", "colleagues")
], ["src", "dst", "relationship"])
```

Running the code again will give the following result:

```
Pagerank:
+---+-------+------------------+
| id|   name|          pagerank|
+---+-------+------------------+
|  7|Jessica| 0.6694823170948746|
|  3|    Joe| 1.2509854786758527|
|  8|   Mike| 0.7499087293049072|
|  5| Martin| 0.7112157549826926|
|  6|  Grace|0.47394068631988606|
|  1| Robert| 1.4828192827561528|
|  4|  David| 1.2316408241530263|
|  2|   Jean| 1.4300069267126065|
+---+-------+------------------+
```

This time we have different pagerank values which depend on the fact that people with Robert have the maximum value. This means that his node is at the center of the graph and receives more connections from people, who are in turn more connected than others (at the edges of the graph). In a social network context, Robert could be defined as an “influencer”.

In addition to PageRank, there are many other algorithms that can be consulted on the official page here: (**https://graphframes.github.io/graphframes/docs/_site/api/python/index.html**).

Conclusion

In this chapter, we have addressed all the components offered by **PySpark**, which is the perfect combination of the power of the Apache Spark framework and the simplicity of the Python language. PySpark is therefore a tool for distributed computing and is suitable for tackling the challenges of Big Data. In the first section, you understood the basic elements such as the **Spark Session**, the **DataFrame RDDs** and its characteristics. Then you had the opportunity to approach the world of distributed ML via **MLlib library,** which offers many models and techniques like other similar libraries such as scikit-learn. We discussed some performance optimization techniques through simple code examples. Finally, we delved into the study and analysis of data flows generated in real-time, thanks to **Spark Streaming**. We did so while gradually integrating other technologies related to the Spark ecosystem such as Kafka and the storage of processed data. We closed the chapter with **GraphFrame**, which is the Python equivalent of Java's GraphX and Scala for the computation and analysis of graphs in a distributed manner.

In the next chapter, we will conclude the overview of libraries that are used for high-performance computing and will learn about **Joblib**. Although it is not comparable in power to PySpark and other tools seen in previous chapters, you will discover how this small library has managed to carve out its niche due to its simplicity and ease of use. Through a series of examples, you will also become increasingly familiar with this calculation tool.

CHAPTER 13
Joblib

Introduction

With this chapter, we will conclude our exploration of high-performance and parallel programming tools in Python, while introducing **Joblib**. This library, although not as versatile as the tools already seen in the book like Dask, Ray or Spark, excels in targeted areas and rightfully deserves a place in this book. In fact, Joblib was designed to optimize specific operations in intensive computing contexts and to improve the scalability of computation pipelines and therefore finds its scope of work in simple parallelization, resulting in caching and efficiency in serialization. Joblib is therefore proposed as a minimalist solution for scenarios that do not require the full infrastructure of a distributed system. It can be seen as a "*lightweight*" tool to improve efficiency and productivity in projects that do not need the complexity of advanced task management.

Structure

This chapter will address the following topics:

- Joblib and Its Uses
- Process Parallelization
- Joblib with NumPy
- Data Persistence with Joblib
- Cache Management with Joblib
- Joblib in Machine Learning
- Joblib in Data Processing
- Limitations of Joblib

Joblib and Its Uses

Joblib is an open-source library written in Python and is designed to make heavy computing more efficient. It focuses on three main areas, which are:

- Process Parallelization
- Data Persistence
- Cache Management

Parallelization allows you to run independent operations in parallel, while leveraging the multicore capabilities of modern CPUs. It is particularly useful for accelerating intensive computations without having to write complex processes or thread management code. For persistence, Joblib offers tools to quickly and efficiently save and load complex Python objects such as NumPy arrays or machine learning models, thus avoiding the recomputation of expensive results or the retraining of existing models. Finally, cache management allows you to store the results of computationally heavy functions, further allowing them to be reused in future executions and optimizing repetitive pipelines and applications.

Joblib is a natural choice for improving computational efficiency in Python, thanks to its simplicity and optimized performance. While alternatives like multiprocessing, **`concurrent.futures`**, and pickle exist for parallelization and serialization respectively, Joblib stands out due to some key features. Its intuitive syntax makes it easy to adopt even for developers with little experience in parallel computing. Furthermore, it is highly optimized to handle large objects such as NumPy arrays or scikit-learn models, which also support data compression to improve I/O efficiency. Another distinctive aspect is the advanced parallelization management, with support for backends such as loky (default), threading and multiprocessing, each suited to specific types of workloads. Finally, Joblib is tightly integrated with scikit-learn, which makes it an indispensable tool for both serialization and parallelization of complex operations.

Process Parallelization

Parallelization is a key technique for accelerating intensive computational operations by distributing work across multiple CPU cores. **Joblib** is particularly appreciated for its ability to handle parallel tasks with a simple and readable syntax, while still offering high efficiency in contexts where it excels. Unlike more complex libraries such as multiprocessing, Joblib automatically manages the creation and management of processes without requiring detailed configuration. It also offers high optimization for numerical calculations. Joblib is particularly suited to working with numpy and pandas data structures as it leverages optimized serialization and efficient memory use.

Unlike more heavyweight tools such as Dask or Ray which shine in clustered distributed computing contexts, Joblib is designed for single-machine parallel operations, while maintaining an optimal balance between simplicity and performance.

Thanks to constructs such as **Parallel** and **delayed**, it is easy to transform an iterative loop into a parallel operation, which makes coding simple and intuitive. Parallel is the main object that coordinates the parallel execution of tasks. When called, it creates a pool of separate processes (or threads, depending on your configuration) to perform the work in parallel. The tasks will be then distributed among the processes, which will work on a portion of the total load. When finished, Parallel collects the results from all the processes and returns them as a sorted list, while corresponding to the original order of the tasks.

The **`delayed()`** function is used to "*delay*" the execution of an operation. In other words, instead of immediately executing a function, **`delayed()`** creates an object representing the task that will then be passed to **`Parallel()`** for execution.

The combined use of **`Parallel()`** and **`delayed()`** makes parallelization extremely simple, avoiding having to manually manage the creation of processes or threads. Let us see in detail how they work, starting from a simple example and then applying it to more complex scenarios.

Before starting to work, however, it is necessary to check whether joblib is already present on your system. If not, you can simply install it with the following command:

```
pip install joblib
```

Let us start with the parallelization of a simple calculation like the square of a number, while using multiple cores in parallel present in the local machine in the following example:

```
from joblib import Parallel, delayed

# Function to be parallelized
def process_number(number):
    return number ** 2
```

```
# Applying the function in parallel over a range of numbers
results = Parallel(n_jobs=4)(delayed(process_number)(i) for i in range(10))
print(results)
```

In this example, **n_jobs=4** specifies the number of cores that will be used. **Parallel** manages the execution of tasks across multiple cores, while **delayed** constructs the tasks that will be executed in parallel.

Running the code will result in the following:

```
[0, 1, 4, 9, 16, 25, 36, 49, 64, 81]
```

Let us now move on to a more complex function that simulates an expensive and time-consuming mathematical operation, through **time.sleep()**:

```
from joblib import Parallel, delayed
import time

def expensive_operation(number):
    time.sleep(1)  # Simulates a long computation
    return number ** 3

start_time = time.time()
results = Parallel(n_jobs=3)(delayed(expensive_operation)(i) for i in
range(6))
end_time = time.time()

print(f"Results: {results}")
print(f"Execution time: {end_time - start_time} seconds")
```

You will get the following result after you run the code:

```
Results: [0, 1, 8, 27, 64, 125]
Execution time: 2.011380910873413 seconds
```

We have launched 6 calculations that are executed in one second each. From the time taken of about two seconds, we can see how Joblib parallelizes this calculation efficiently. In fact, in a sequential execution of the code where Joblib is not used, we expect an execution time of at least 6 seconds. Replace the line with the call to **expensive_operation** in the code with the following:

```
results = [expensive_operation(i) for i in range(6)]
```

When you execute it, you get the expected result in about 6 seconds.

```
Results: [0, 1, 8, 27, 64, 125]
Execution time: 6.002941608428955 seconds
```

Joblib and NumPy

NumPy is one of the most used libraries when a user is dealing with numerical calculations and it seems almost obvious the intention is to increase the efficiency of such calculations by integrating Joblibs. Before doing this, however, it is good to look at their operation in detail to understand when and do Joblibs lead to improvements.

To illustrate this, let us consider the normalization of a large dataset and comparing between the calculations performed via Joblib versus without it.

```
from joblib import Parallel, delayed
import numpy as np
import time
```

```
# Creating a large array
large_array = np.random.rand(1000000)

def normalize(value):
    return (value - np.mean(large_array)) / np.std(large_array)

# Parallelizing the normalization operation
start_time = time.time()
results = Parallel(n_jobs=-1)(delayed(normalize)(value) for value in
large_array[:1000])
end_time = time.time()

print(results[:10])  # Displays the first 10 results
print(f"Execution time with joblib: {end_time - start_time} seconds")

start_time = time.time()
results = [normalize(value) for value in large_array[:1000]]
end_time = time.time()

print(f"Execution time without joblib: {end_time - start_time} seconds")
```

After running the calculations, you will get the following values:

```
[-1.125502589834455, 0.11072912500629643, -1.6438488989933995,
-0.6463887112818013, -0.7808273343766107, 0.8657708984693347,
1.023557520797839, -1.4455264352256898, 0.8948754162891444,
1.5255891289196097]
Execution time with joblib: 2.4436957836151123 seconds
Execution time without joblib: 6.39542031288147 seconds
```

In this case, greater efficiency is highlighted when we perform calculations using Joblib. However, we will have to clarify something while dealing with NumPy. This library has internal vectorization systems that, if used, will lead to greater efficiency compared to Joblib, since it also bypasses the operation of Python. In fact, NumPy is designed to exploit low-level optimizations, by using libraries such as:

- Basic Linear Algebra Subprograms (BLAS)
- LAPACK
- Single Instruction, Multiple Data (SIMD)

These libraries perform operations directly at the CPU level, while taking advantage of the instructions optimized for numerical calculations. When normalizing an array with NumPy, the entire operation occurs in memory and on blocks of data, without the overhead of Python loops. Let us see, for example, how to use vectorization in the previous case.

```
mean = np.mean(large_array)
std = np.std(large_array)

start_time = time.time()
results = (large_array[:1000] - mean) / std
end_time = time.time()

print(results[:10])
print(f"Execution time: {end_time - start_time} seconds")
```

After running the calculations, you will obtain the following values:

```
[-1.12550259  0.11072913 -1.6438489  -0.64638871 -0.78082733  0.8657709
  1.02355752 -1.44552644  0.89487542  1.52558913]
Execution time: 0.0 seconds
```

As we can see, the execution time is less than the tenth of a second. However, with Joblib, additional costs slow down the process and make it less efficient than the illustration where we have used vector calculation. Now, let us see how they operate in two different cases which are explained as follows:

The steps for executing the calculation with **Joblib (Parallelization)** are:

1. Split the array into blocks.
2. Each block is sent to a separate process.
3. The results must be combined at the end.
4. Introduce overhead for inter-process communication.

The steps of performing the calculation with **NumPy (Vectorization)** are:

1. The entire operation takes place in memory, in a single pass.
2. No overhead to create processes or transfer data.
3. The optimal use of low-level libraries (SIMD) makes the computation extremely efficient.

So, in general, Joblib is not the ideal choice for accelerating NumPy operations on large datasets when the operations can be performed vector-wise. This is because NumPy is already optimized to handle large arrays using vector computations without the overhead of parallelization. However, there are some specific scenarios where Joblib can also be useful along with NumPy and large datasets.

There are **operations that are not vectorizable**, that is, they cannot be transformed into a single vector operation. For instance, using custom functions that work on each element or complex calculations depend on conditions or branched logic. In these cases, Joblib can parallelize the work by splitting the dataset.

Let us implement a complex case where vectorization with NumPy is not directly possible because the **`complex_function`** used here includes a series of complex operations. The example looks something like the following:

```
from joblib import Parallel, delayed
import numpy as np
import time
import math

# Creating a large array
large_array = np.random.rand(1000000)

# Complex function to process each element
def complex_function(x):
    # Here we use math.sin and math.cos, which run in the Python interpreter
    # for each element. This makes it slower than vectorized NumPy functions
    # (np.sin, np.cos). However, this design simulates a CPU-bound workload
    # where joblib's parallelization can still help.
    result = sum(math.sin(x * i) ** 2 + math.cos(x / (i + 1)) ** 3 for i in
range(1, 1000))
    # Conditional logic
    if x > 0.5:
        return result ** 0.5
    else:
        return result ** 0.33
```

```
start_time = time.time()
results = Parallel(n_jobs=-1)(delayed(complex_function)(x) for x in
large_array)
end_time = time.time()

print(f"Results (first 10): {results[:10]}")
print(f"Execution time with joblib: {end_time - start_time} seconds")

# Sequential processing
start_time = time.time()
results = [complex_function(x) for x in large_array]
end_time = time.time()

print(f"Results (first 10): {results[:10]}")
print(f"Execution time without joblib: {end_time - start_time:.2f} seconds")
```

In this code, we have defined a function as the **`complex_function`**, in which occurs a series of operations that does not allow direct vectorization. It also includes the following elements:

1. **Iterative Operations (for loop)**: The sum of over 1000 terms inside the function depends on iterative calculations for each input value. NumPy excels when it can apply bulk operations on entire arrays, but in this case, it is not immediately possible to "*vectorize*" the sum of the trigonometric terms for each element of the array.

2. **Using Python functions like `math.sin` and `math.cos`**: NumPy functions such as np.sin and np.cos can replace the math versions, but they still have to be restructured in order to leverage vectorization.

3. **Conditional Logic (`if` statement)**: The conditional operation, if x > 0.5, introduces a non-linear path into the calculation. This further complicates the ability to apply vector operations directly.

After running the code, we will get the following results that how we can achieve greater efficiency through Joblib:

```
Results (first 10): [11.165207843137143, 11.165520086314524, 38.70445033343853,
11.164008288486713, 38.71422223821382, 11.169357434803986, 11.166704276170297,
11.166146477981385, 38.70460093976833, 38.70540447973965]
Execution time with joblib: 193.57406902313232 seconds
Results (first 10): [11.165207843137143, 11.165520086314524, 38.70445033343853,
11.164008288486713, 38.71422223821382, 11.169357434803986, 11.166704276170297,
11.166146477981385, 38.70460093976833, 38.70540447973965]
Execution time without joblib: 878.53 seconds
```

This approach highlights a scenario where Joblib can be advantageous as the computational cost of each task is high enough to compensate for the overhead of parallelization.

Data Persistence with Joblib

Data persistence is an essential component in developing Python applications, especially when dealing with large or complex objects such as machine learning models, NumPy arrays, or data processing pipelines. Joblib simplifies this process by providing fast and scalable functions for saving and loading Python objects.

Joblib uses an optimized serialization, designed to be faster and less memory-intensive than the standard pickle module, especially for objects containing numeric arrays such as those from NumPy.

An example of this case is when **saving large arrays.** While older versions of Pickle can be slow, modern Pickle (protocol 5 and above) is already efficient when dealing with NumPy arrays. The main advantage of Joblib lies in its support for chunked storage and transparent compression, which makes it particularly convenient for handling very large datasets. Let us implement the following code to compare Pickle with Joblib while saving a large array created with NumPy:

```
import numpy as np
import pickle
from joblib import dump, load
import gzip
import time
import os

# Creating a large dataset
large_array = np.random.rand(100000000)  # 100 million of elements

# Joblib without compression
start_time = time.time()
dump(large_array, 'large_array_joblib.joblib')
end_time = time.time()
joblib_save_time = end_time - start_time

start_time = time.time()
loaded_array_joblib = load('large_array_joblib.joblib')
end_time = time.time()
joblib_load_time = end_time - start_time

# Joblib with compression
start_time = time.time()
dump(large_array, 'large_array_compressed.joblib', compress=3)
end_time = time.time()
joblib_compressed_save_time = end_time - start_time

start_time = time.time()
loaded_array_compressed = load('large_array_compressed.joblib')
end_time = time.time()
joblib_compressed_load_time = end_time - start_time

# Pickle without compression
start_time = time.time()
with open('large_array_pickle.pkl', 'wb') as f:
    pickle.dump(large_array, f)
end_time = time.time()
pickle_save_time = end_time - start_time

start_time = time.time()
with open('large_array_pickle.pkl', 'rb') as f:
    loaded_array_pickle = pickle.load(f)
end_time = time.time()
pickle_load_time = end_time - start_time

# Pickle with compression (gzip)
start_time = time.time()
with gzip.open('large_array_pickle_compressed.pkl.gz', 'wb') as f:
    pickle.dump(large_array, f)
end_time = time.time()
```

```
pickle_compressed_save_time = end_time - start_time

start_time = time.time()
with gzip.open('large_array_pickle_compressed.pkl.gz', 'rb') as f:
    loaded_array_pickle_compressed = pickle.load(f)
end_time = time.time()
pickle_compressed_load_time = end_time - start_time

# Check file sizes
joblib_file_size = os.path.getsize('large_array_joblib.joblib')
joblib_compressed_file_size = os.path.getsize('large_array_compressed.joblib')
pickle_file_size = os.path.getsize('large_array_pickle.pkl')
pickle_compressed_file_size = os.path.getsize('large_array_pickle_compressed.
pkl.gz')

# Results
print("=== Save and Load Time ===")
print(f"Joblib (uncompressed):")
print(f"  Save time: {joblib_save_time:.2f} seconds")
print(f"  Load time: {joblib_load_time:.2f} seconds")
print(f"Joblib (compressed):")
print(f"  Save time: {joblib_compressed_save_time:.2f} seconds")
print(f"  Load time: {joblib_compressed_load_time:.2f} seconds")
print(f"Pickle (uncompressed):")
print(f"  Save time: {pickle_save_time:.2f} seconds")
print(f"  Load time: {pickle_load_time:.2f} seconds")
print(f"Pickle (compressed - gzip):")
print(f"  Save time: {pickle_compressed_save_time:.2f} seconds")
print(f"  Load time: {pickle_compressed_load_time:.2f} seconds")

print("\n=== File Sizes ===")
print(f"Joblib (uncompressed): {joblib_file_size / 1e6:.2f} MB")
print(f"Joblib (compressed): {joblib_compressed_file_size / 1e6:.2f} MB")
print(f"Pickle (uncompressed): {pickle_file_size / 1e6:.2f} MB")
print(f"Pickle (compressed - gzip): {pickle_compressed_file_size / 1e6:.2f}
MB")
```

Running the code gives the following results.

```
=== Save and Load Time ===
Joblib (uncompressed):
  Save time: 0.67 seconds
  Load time: 0.57 seconds
Joblib (compressed):
  Save time: 40.82 seconds
  Load time: 7.24 seconds
Pickle (uncompressed):
  Save time: 1.74 seconds
  Load time: 0.50 seconds
Pickle (compressed - gzip):
  Save time: 46.57 seconds
  Load time: 6.89 seconds

=== File Sizes ===
Joblib (uncompressed): 800.00 MB
Joblib (compressed): 758.69 MB
Pickle (uncompressed): 800.00 MB
Pickle (compressed - gzip): 754.41 MB
```

The code explores the comparison between Joblib and Pickle for managing data persistence in compressed and uncompressed versions. The goal is to evaluate which tool performs better in terms of saving and loading time as well as the size of the generated files.

The results show that Joblib, in the uncompressed version, is faster than Pickle due to its internal optimizations that are specifically designed to work with NumPy arrays. Loading times are similar between Joblib and Pickle, which further highlights that both tools can handle uncompressed data efficiently. However, the sizes of uncompressed files are identical for both, which confirms that there are no significant differences in data representation in this scenario.

The situation changes after compression is introduced. Joblib with compression stands out for its ability to slightly reduce the file size compared to the uncompressed version, but it significantly increases saving and loading time. This happens because the compression process involves an additional computational load. In particular, the saving time with compressed Joblib is much higher than that of the uncompressed version, while the loading time is also increased, albeit slightly.

In its uncompressed form, Pickle is slightly slower than Joblib while saving, but loads faster. This makes it a good option for simple operations that do not require compression. However, when gzip compression is added, Pickle exhibits similar behavior to the compressed Joblib, both in terms of save and load times and the file size. Again, compression introduces a significant time cost but results in slightly smaller files than those compressed with Joblib.

After assessing at these results, we can conclude that Joblib is particularly useful when working with complex objects, such as machine learning models or data pipelines, which cannot be serialized easily with Pickle. Joblib is also good at handling large datasets as it can automatically split files into multiple parts to improve manageability. Moreover, Joblib's built-in compression provides additional flexibility, which makes it a suitable choice for scenarios with limited disk space.

On the other hand, Pickle is confirmed as a fast and effective solution for managing simple and uncompressed data, which proves that it is particularly useful for quick operations or prototyping. Even while using gzip compression, Pickle performs well, but requires more complex code than Joblib.

Ultimately, the choice between Joblib and Pickle is highly context-dependent. Joblib is best suited for more complex and scalable applications, especially in ML projects, while Pickle is preferable for simpler scenarios or as a fast tool for serializing objects. When considering whether to use compression, it is important to consider the priorities of the project like saving disk space or prioritizing the speed of operations. In either case, both Joblib and Pickle are versatile and powerful tools for managing data persistence in Python.

Cache Management with Joblib

Cache management is one of the most powerful features of Joblib, and is especially useful for storing and reusing the results of expensive computations. This approach can significantly reduce execution time in situations where the same function is called multiple times with the same arguments. Compared to standard approaches like using manual data structures (for example, dictionaries to store intermediate results), Joblib's caching system is simpler to implement. It does not require manual management of the storage logic. The cache can be saved to disk, which allows it to handle very large objects without consuming RAM. Therefore, the stored results are available even after the program is restarted.

Joblib is designed to work with objects such as NumPy arrays, datasets or MLmodels, while serializing them efficiently. With traditional approaches, implementing a cache system can require manual management of the stored data, often using structures such as dictionaries or databases. This introduces limitations in scalability since the stored data remains in memory and does not persist between different executions of the program. It also introduces more complexity in code, especially for large or complex objects.

Joblib simplifies this. Decorating a function with **@memory.cache** is enough to enable persistent caching, leaving the library to handle the technical details. It is illustrated in the following example:

```
from joblib import Memory
import time

# Creating the cache system
memory = Memory(location='cache_dir', verbose=0)

@memory.cache
def expensive_function(x):
    print(f"Calculating {x}...")
    return x ** 2

# Measure the time for the first execution (actual computation)
start_time = time.time()
print(expensive_function(10))  # Computed
first_execution_time = time.time() - start_time
print(f"Execution time (first call): {first_execution_time:.4f} seconds")

# Measure the time for the second execution (retrieved from cache)
start_time = time.time()
print(expensive_function(10))  # Retrieved from cache
second_execution_time = time.time() - start_time
print(f"Execution time (second call): {second_execution_time:.4f} seconds")

# Comparison between the two times
print(f"Speed improvement due to caching: {first_execution_time /
second_execution_time:.2f} times faster")
```

Assuming that the computation of the function is not particularly expensive (for example, squaring a number), the result should show a significant improvement in the time of the second run, which would be almost instantaneous. The improvement is expressed as the ratio of the time of the first run to the time of the second run. Running the code generates the following result:

```
100
Execution time (first call): 0.0120 seconds
100
Execution time (second call): 0.0020 seconds
Speed improvement due to caching: 6.00 times faster
```

When you run the program again, you will see that the time will remain low even during the first run. **Joblib caching** persists between different runs of the program if the cache system is configured correctly. This means that, once a result is calculated and saved in the directory specified in **Memory(location='cache_dir')**, the stored results can be reused even if the program is restarted.

Note, however, that Joblib's **@memory.cache** mechanism hashes both the function's arguments and its source code. If you change the inputs or the function body, the cache will be invalidated and the computation will be re-executed.

Joblib in Machine Learning

Joblib is mainly applied in Machine Learning, thanks to its native integration with libraries such as Scikit-learn. The library is particularly useful for handling computationally intensive tasks like saving and loading trained models or preprocessing pipelines, which optimizes both execution times and memory usage.

When working with machine learning models, it is often necessary to save the model object after training in order to reuse it later. This approach is useful for model deployment, where the model can be saved and loaded on different environments like production servers or local devices. This avoids unnecessary recalculations, thereby saving the time required to retrain it.

Saved models can be easily reloaded to make predictions or continue training.

Here is an example of how to save and load a trained model using Joblib:

```
from sklearn.ensemble import RandomForestClassifier
from sklearn.datasets import load_iris
from joblib import dump, load

# Load dataset
iris = load_iris()
X, y = iris.data, iris.target

# Train the model
model = RandomForestClassifier(n_estimators=100)
model.fit(X, y)

# Save the model
dump(model, 'random_forest_model.joblib')

# Load the model
loaded_model = load('random_forest_model.joblib')

# Make predictions with the loaded model
print(loaded_model.predict(X[:5]))
```

The Iris dataset is loaded using Scikit-learn. This dataset is often used to demonstrate classification techniques as it is small and easily manageable. A **Random Forest** model is trained using the loaded data. The parameter **`n_estimators=100`** specifies that the model uses 100 decision trees. The Joblib dump function is used to save the trained model to a .joblib file. This file can be shared or archived for future use. The saved model is reloaded with the load function. After being loaded, the model can be used to make predictions without having to be retrained. The reloaded model is used to make predictions on the first five samples of the dataset. This demonstrates that the saved model retains all the information needed to continue working as before.

Running this gives the following result:

```
[0 0 0 0 0]
```

The Iris dataset contains 150 samples divided into three classes: 0, 1, and 2, representing three different flower species. The data is sorted by class, so the first five samples (**`X[:5]`**) belong to class 0. The model, therefore, predicts correctly.

The next step is to parallelize the **Hyperparameter Search** with Joblib. Hyperparameter search is a critical step in machine learning, where we try to find the best combination of parameters for a model. This process can be computationally intensive, especially with complex models or large datasets.

Joblib is used in this context to enable parallelization, while allowing the use of multiple CPU cores to speed up the evaluation process. In particular, Scikit-learn leverages Joblib to run the evaluation of different hyperparameter combinations in parallel during Grid Search.

We will continue working with the previous model, as we load and run it through hyperparameter search:

```
from sklearn.model_selection import GridSearchCV
from sklearn.ensemble import RandomForestClassifier
from sklearn.datasets import load_iris
from joblib import dump, load

# Load the dataset
iris = load_iris()
X, y = iris.data, iris.target

# Load the previously trained model
try:
    # Attempt to load a previously saved model
    model = load('random_forest_model.joblib')
    print("Model loaded successfully!")
except FileNotFoundError:
    # If no model is found, train a new one
    print("No pre-trained model found. Training a new model...")
    model = RandomForestClassifier(n_estimators=100)
    model.fit(X, y)
    dump(model, 'random_forest_model.joblib')

# Define the parameter grid for hyperparameter tuning
parameters = {
    'n_estimators': [10, 50, 100, 200],
    'max_depth': [None, 10, 20, 30],
}

# Perform hyperparameter tuning
grid_search = GridSearchCV(model, parameters, n_jobs=-1, cv=5)
grid_search.fit(X, y)

# Save the best model found by GridSearchCV
best_model = grid_search.best_estimator_
dump(best_model, 'best_random_forest_model.joblib')

# Output the best parameters
print("Best parameters:", grid_search.best_params_)

# Use the best model for predictions
loaded_best_model = load('best_random_forest_model.joblib')
predictions = loaded_best_model.predict(X[:5])
print("Predictions for the first 5 samples:", predictions)
```

Let us look at the code together. First, it loads the previous model. If a saved model (**random_forest_model.joblib**) already exists, it is loaded to be used directly in the hyperparameter search. If it is not found, the model is trained from scratch and saved. At this point, we move on to the hyperparameter search. The loaded or trained model is used as a basis for the hyperparameter search by performing a Grid Search on an extended parameter grid to find the optimal configuration. After the search, the best model found is saved in a new file (**best_random_forest_model.joblib**), so it can be easily reused in the future. The optimized model is used to make predictions on the first 5 samples of the dataset. Running the code gives the following result:

```
Model loaded successfully!
Best parameters: {'max_depth': None, 'n_estimators': 100}
Predictions for the first 5 samples: [0 0 0 0 0]
```

This approach combines efficiency and scalability, allowing you to work with pre-trained models or dynamically create new ones.

During machine learning pipelines, it is common to perform transformations like normalization, dimensionality reduction, or other forms of preprocessing on datasets. These operations, if applied repeatedly, can become time-consuming, especially on large datasets. Using Joblib, we can save the transformed datasets, as well as the objects used for the transformation (for example, scaler or PCA), while avoiding unnecessary repetition of expensive calculations. Once the dataset is transformed, the results can be saved and loaded later and can be shared between different environments.

The following code links to the saved and optimized model in the previous example. After loading the model, we add a data preprocessing step and save both the transformed dataset and the scaler.

```
from sklearn.preprocessing import StandardScaler
from joblib import dump, load
from sklearn.datasets import load_iris
import numpy as np

# Load the Iris dataset (original dataset)
iris = load_iris()
X, y = iris.data, iris.target

# Try to load the transformed dataset and scaler
try:
    X_scaled = load('dataset_transformed.joblib')
    scaler = load('scaler.joblib')
    print("Transformed dataset and scaler loaded successfully!")
except FileNotFoundError:
    print("No transformed dataset found. Transforming the original data-
set...")
    # Apply the same preprocessing (scaling)
    scaler = StandardScaler()
    X_scaled = scaler.fit_transform(X)

    # Save the transformed dataset and scaler
    dump(X_scaled, 'dataset_transformed.joblib')
    dump(scaler, 'scaler.joblib')
    print("Transformed dataset and scaler saved successfully!")

# Load the optimized model from the previous step
try:
    best_model = load('best_random_forest_model.joblib')
    print("Best model loaded successfully!")
except FileNotFoundError:
    raise RuntimeError("Best model not found. Ensure the previous step has
been completed.")

# Use the transformed dataset for predictions
predictions = best_model.predict(X_scaled[:5])
print("Predictions on the transformed dataset:", predictions)
```

Let us look at the code together. First, we try to load the transformed dataset. If a transformed dataset exists (**`dataset_transformed.joblib`**), it is loaded directly to save time. Otherwise, a new random dataset is generated, transformed, and saved for future use. Next, we use the **`StandardScaler`** to standardize the data (bring it to mean 0 and variance 1), a common practice in data preprocessing. Both the transformed data (**`X_scaled`**) and the scaler itself are saved with Joblib. The optimized model from the previous step (**`best_random_forest_model.joblib`**) is loaded to make predictions. Finally, the model uses the first five samples of the transformed dataset to make predictions. Running the code gives the following result:

```
No transformed dataset found. Transforming the original dataset...
Transformed dataset and scaler saved successfully!
Best model loaded successfully!
Predictions on the transformed dataset: [0 0 0 0 0]
```

This code shows how to integrate the persistence of transformed datasets into an ML pipeline, while ensuring efficiency and reproducibility. The combination of Joblib to save both the transformed data and the model, and Scikit-learn for preprocessing and training represents a complete and scalable solution for working with complex pipelines.

Joblib in Data Processing

Joblib is an extremely useful tool for handling large datasets and computationally intensive operations. Its ability to parallelize custom transformations and save transformed datasets makes it ideal for pre-processing pipelines, especially in Extract, Transform, Load (ETL) flows.

In this section, we will explore two main use cases:

- Parallelization of transformations
- Persistence of pre-processed datasets

A common use case is to apply a transformation function to each row or element of a large dataset. With Joblib, we can parallelize the operation to significantly improve performance. Let us look at an example of this:

```
import numpy as np
import pandas as pd
from joblib import Parallel, delayed

n_rows = 1_000_000
data = pd.DataFrame({
    'column1': np.random.rand(n_rows),
    'column2': np.random.rand(n_rows)
})

def transformation_tuple(row):
    return row.column1 * 2 + row.column2**2

# Parallel application of the transformation
results = Parallel(n_jobs=-1)(
    delayed(transformation_tuple)(row)
    for row in data.itertuples(index=False)
)
data['result'] = results
print(data.head())
```

The program generates a synthetic dataset containing 1 million rows with two columns, column1 and column2. The values are random numbers generated with NumPy and distributed uniformly between 0 and 1. The transformation function is defined to calculate a value derived from each row of the dataset. In this case, the transformation multiplies the value of **column1** by 2 and adds the square of the value of **column2**. The transformation is applied to each row of the dataset using Joblib to perform the operations in parallel. **Parallel(n_jobs=-1)** specifies that Joblib should use all available CPU cores to perform the operation, maximizing efficiency, while **delayed(transformation)(row)** converts the transformation function to a delayed operation, which is only executed when assigned to a core. The **data.iterrows()** method is used to iterate over each row of the dataset, supplying a row to the transformation function. The results of the parallel transformation are saved in a new column in the dataset, which is called the result.

When executed, the program prints the first 5 rows of the transformed dataset, showing the result of the transformation for each row:

```
   column1   column2    result
0  0.246092  0.534664  0.778050
1  0.459580  0.314444  1.018035
2  0.978096  0.138893  1.975483
3  0.084165  0.161032  0.194262
4  0.499338  0.618522  1.381245
```

Note: *The* ***iterrows()*** *approach works well for small and medium-sized datasets, but it may not be the most efficient option for very large datasets, since* ***iterrows()*** *introduces a significant overhead. A faster alternative could be to apply the transformations directly to the DataFrame columns (if the transformation is vectorizable). However, this approach may not be able to take advantage of Joblib's parallelization.*

After applying complex transformations to a dataset, it is often useful to save the result for future use. This approach is particularly useful in data processing pipelines that need to be run multiple times or distributed across different environments.

With Joblib, we can save transformed datasets quickly and optimize them. Saved files are persistent and can be loaded into other work sessions, allowing for:

- **Efficiency**: There is no need to reprocess the dataset each time.
- **Scalability**: Transformed datasets can be distributed across different work environments.
- **Reproducibility**: Saving the result ensures that pipelines produce consistent results.

The following code extends the previous example and shows how to save and load the transformed dataset:

```
from joblib import dump, load

# Saving the transformed dataset
dump(data, 'preprocessed_dataset.joblib')
print("Dataset saved successfully!")

# Loading the dataset
loaded_data = load('preprocessed_dataset.joblib')
print("Loaded dataset:")
print(loaded_data.head())
```

The transformed dataset (which includes the new result **column**) is saved to disk using the dump command. The resulting file, **preprocessed_dataset.joblib**, can be used in future sessions without having to recalculate the transformations. The saved dataset is loaded with the load command, returning the same pandas DataFrame that was saved previously. The code prints the first few rows of the loaded dataset to verify that it was saved and retrieved correctly.

```
Dataset saved successfully!
Loaded dataset:
   column1   column2    result
0  0.246092  0.534664  0.778050
1  0.459580  0.314444  1.018035
2  0.978096  0.138893  1.975483
3  0.084165  0.161032  0.194262
4  0.499338  0.618522  1.381245
```

This approach is particularly useful in complex data pipelines, where elaborate transformations can take significant time. Saving the transformed dataset ensures that the results can be reused without additional costs, thus improving efficiency and reproducibility. Additionally, the saved file can be distributed across multiple systems, thereby facilitating its integration into larger business processes.

Joblib Limitations

While Joblib is an extremely useful tool for parallelization, data persistence, and optimization of machine learning pipelines, it has limitations that are important to consider. These limitations arise mainly due to its architecture, underlying dependencies, and specific application contexts.

As for parallelization, Joblib works very well for CPU-bound operations, that is, those that require intensive use of the CPU. However, for very simple and fast tasks, the overhead associated with creating parallel processes can cancel out the benefits of parallelism, thus making sequential processing more efficient. Furthermore, while Joblib uses the multiprocessing library to avoid Global Interpreter Lock (GIL) constraints, some pure Python operations that do not release the GIL may limit the effectiveness of parallelism. Even for I/O-bound operations such as frequent file reads and writes or access to network resources, Joblib is not the ideal option; libraries such as **asyncio** or **Dask** might be more suitable in these cases.

Another issue is memory management. When parallelizing tasks on large datasets, Joblib can generate multiple copies of the data in memory, which increases RAM consumption. Modern Joblib (≥0.12) mitigates this for large NumPy arrays by using memory mapping and reduces duplication across workers. However, plain Python objects and pandas DataFrames may still be pickled and duplicated in memory. Although Joblib's cache system allows saving results to disk, working with very large files can slow down reads and writes.

Handling complex objects is another limitation. Joblib uses Pickle-based serialization, which has some inherent limitations. Non-serializable objects, such as open files or network connections, cannot be saved. Additionally, Pickle can be inefficient when working with nested objects or very complex data structures. Compatibility can also become an issue: files saved with Joblib may not be compatible with future versions of Python or the libraries used, causing difficulties in project portability.

When dealing with large datasets, Joblib offers good performance as long as the data can be handled in memory. However, using methods such as pandas' iterrows(), which are often used to apply row-by-row transformations, introduces significant overhead. This approach is less efficient than fully vectorized solutions with NumPy or pandas. However, it can offer superior performance for very large datasets with other libraries such as Dask due to their ability to handle distributed data.

Joblib is also limited to single-machine operations and does not directly support distributed parallelization across clusters. In scenarios that require distributed processing across multiple machines, tools such as Dask, Apache Spark, or Ray are more suitable alternatives. The lack of native support for distributed processing can be a significant limitation in large-scale applications or in the context of big data.

Finally, maintenance and debugging can become cumbersome when working with parallel processes. Errors in child processes are not always clearly reported to the parent process, which makes it more difficult to identify and resolve issues. Additionally, verbosity or logging must be explicitly configured to obtain detailed information about parallel execution and increase development complexity.

Ultimately, Joblib is an excellent tool for CPU-bound operations on memory-sized datasets, for independent parallel tasks, and for machine learning or data processing pipelines in non-distributed contexts. However, if you have I/O-bound tasks, extremely large datasets, or a need for distributed infrastructure, you should consider other libraries such as Dask, Ray, or Spark, which are designed to handle these scenarios more effectively. Understanding these limitations is essential to leveraging Joblib efficiently and making an informed choice about the tool that best fits your needs.

Conclusion

In this chapter, we explored the main aspects of Joblib and highlighted its usefulness, applications, and limitations. We started with an overview of Joblib's parallelization capabilities, showing how to use Parallel and delayed distributing work across multiple CPU cores.

If we put it conclusively, Joblib is an indispensable tool for those working with Python, especially in areas such as ML, data processing and parallelization of intensive operations. However, like any tool, its efficacy depends on the context and a deep understanding of its strengths and limitations. Thanks to its ease of use and the ability to integrate with other libraries, Joblib remains an excellent choice for those looking for efficiency and scalability in their applications.

In the next chapter, we will learn about **Parallelization on Cloud and Serverless Systems**, while introducing a whole new set of environments and solutions. We will also cover fundamental concepts and notions to navigate the ever-changing world of the cloud.

CHAPTER 14

Parallelization on Cloud and Serverless Systems

Introduction

In today's technology landscape, parallel processing has reached new heights, thanks to **cloud computing and serverless systems**. These two technologies that have transformed the way computational resources are used and managed. The growing need to manage large volumes of data and computationally intensive tasks has driven developers, data scientists, and companies to leverage these platforms to achieve scalability, high performance, and optimized costs.

In this chapter, we will explore how **Python** can be used to implement parallelization solutions on cloud and serverless platforms. Through practical examples and real-world use cases, we will illustrate tools and technologies such as **AWS Lambda, Google Cloud Functions, Azure Functions,** and **Kubernetes**, while highlighting their distinctive features and their utility for parallel and distributed tasks.

We will also delve into strategies to optimize costs and performance, while providing practical guidelines on how to reduce spending without compromising performance by using spot instances, strategic caching, and the adoption of automatic scaling systems. Finally, we will show how these tools can be integrated into data processing pipelines, Machine Learning (ML) inferences, and other modern applications. By the end of this chapter, the reader will be able to navigate the world of serverless systems and choose an apt option for their tasks and goals.

Structure

This chapter will address the following topics:

- Cloud Computing
- AWS Lambda
- Google Cloud Functions
- Azure Functions
- Serverless vs. Traditional Parallelization
- Auto Scaling and Load Balancing on Cloud
- Kubernetes
- Real-World Use Cases of Cloud Data Processing

Cloud Computing and Parallelization Models

In recent years, **cloud computing** has transformed the technology landscape and has revolutionized the way computing resources are provisioned and used. With this technology, one can access virtually unlimited computing power on the web, without having to physically manage expensive servers or hardware. The cloud's **on-demand scalability** model allows resources to be quickly adjusted as needed, while significantly reducing operating costs and improving efficiency.

A distinctive feature of cloud computing is its ability to support **large-scale parallelization**, or the simultaneous execution of multiple computational tasks broken down into smaller subtasks. This practice is essential for managing large amounts of data or performing complex calculations that would otherwise take a lot of processing time on a single machine. In a cloud context, parallelization leverages distributed infrastructures, where multiple virtual machines or serverless functions work together to complete a task.

The **parallelization models** offered by the cloud are divided into two main categories: the traditional model, which is based on manually orchestrated virtual machines or containers; and the serverless model, where code execution is completely abstracted from the underlying infrastructure. **Traditional parallelization** offers greater control over hardware and configuration, which makes it ideal for long-running applications and predictable workloads. In contrast, **serverless parallelization** allows you to run lightweight and short-run functions, which is ideal for on-demand tasks, without worrying about resource management.

Python is one of the most versatile and popular languages used to implement parallel solutions on cloud platforms. There are many tools offered by the main cloud computing providers, such as AWS Lambda and Google Cloud Functions.

Cloud computing is not just a technology; it is a paradigm that has changed the way companies and researchers tackle complex computational problems. The combination of **elasticity**, **distributed computational power**, and advanced management tools makes the cloud the ideal platform to fully leverage the potential of parallelization. This chapter is an invitation to understand and master these tools to develop robust, scalable, and efficient applications.

Cloud Parallelization Tools

Cloud platforms provide a wide range of tools to deploy and manage parallel workloads. These tools allow you to leverage distributed computing to accelerate the processing of large amounts of data or perform computationally intensive tasks efficiently. Among the leading serverless computing services are:

- **AWS Lambda**
- **Google Cloud Functions**
- **Azure Functions**

Each of them offers unique features and distinctive advantages for using Python in high-performance computing.

AWS Lambda

AWS Lambda is one of the most popular solutions for running code in a serverless environment. It provides developers with a fully managed model for executing functions in response to events, where they do not have to manage servers or worry about scalability. This paradigm, known as *Function-as-a-Service (FaaS)*, has transformed the way applications are designed and has made them more modular and easily scalable.

Introduced by Amazon Web Services in 2014, Lambda has quickly established itself as a key technology for real-time data processing, workflow automation, and backend management for web and mobile applications. Its key strength is its ability to automatically scale based on demand: whenever a Lambda function is triggered, AWS allocates the necessary resources and transparently manages the workload, which allows thousands of instances to run simultaneously. This aspect makes it particularly suitable for scenarios where it is necessary to process large volumes of data in parallel, such as file processing, event management from message queues, or distributed processing of data coming from real-time streams.

From a cost perspective, AWS Lambda follows a pay-per-use pricing model, where you only pay for the actual execution time and the amount of memory used. This allows you to optimize your spending compared to traditional solutions based on virtual servers or persistent containers, especially in those cases where the workload is variable or unpredictable. Additionally, support for different programming languages like Python, Node.js, Java and Go makes it accessible to a wide range of developers, who can write and deploy code in a few minutes without worrying about the configuration of the underlying infrastructure.

From a technical point of view, the execution of tasks is implemented through a **Lambda function**. When it is invoked, AWS runs the code in an isolated environment, inside a managed container, ensuring optimal security and performance. Each invocation can be triggered by events from different AWS services, such as changes in an S3 bucket, new messages in an SQS queue, or HTTP requests received through API Gateway. This event-driven approach allows you to build reactive and scalable applications with a completely serverless architecture.

For parallel processing, AWS Lambda offers significant advantages. Functions can be executed simultaneously on different datasets, while distributing the computational load efficiently. For example, to process a large log file stored on S3, you can split it into multiple parts and process them simultaneously through Lambda functions that work in parallel. This significantly reducing the processing time compared to a sequential execution. However, there are some limitations to consider, such as the maximum timeout of 15 minutes for the execution of a single function and the fact that the resources allocated are limited to a maximum of 10 GB of memory and proportional CPU.

One aspect to keep in mind is that of the so-called cold starts, or the time required to start a Lambda instance when it has not been recently used. This can introduce an initial latency, especially for functions written in languages that require longer startup times. To mitigate this problem, AWS offers some strategies, such as keeping functions "*hot*" through periodic invocations, or using provisioned concurrency which pre-allocates ready-to-use instances.

Using AWS Lambda for parallel computing can be particularly effective when integrated with other AWS services like Step Functions to orchestrate complex workflows or DynamoDB for managing highly scalable structured data. Furthermore, by combining Lambda with services such as Kinesis or Apache Kafka, it is possible to build highly performant streaming processing pipelines that are capable of handling real-time events with minimal latency.

In conclusion, AWS Lambda is a powerful solution for running serverless code and parallel computing in the cloud. Thanks to its automatic scalability, consumption-based pricing model, and tight integration with the AWS ecosystem, it is an excellent choice for those who need to manage highly distributed workloads without having to worry about the underlying infrastructure. However, it is important to carefully evaluate the limitations of the service and adopt the right strategies to maximize its performance. This ensures efficient use of resources and cost optimization.

Python and AWS Lambda

Python plays a central role in using AWS Lambda for parallel computing and serverless computing. Thanks to its simplicity, the wide range of available libraries, and the native support in Lambda, Python is a natural choice for developers and data scientists who want to harness the power of the cloud without managing the infrastructure directly.

From a practical point of view, writing Lambda functions in Python is immediate; you only need to define a function that takes the following two parameters:

- The **event**, which contains the input data
- The **context**, which provides information about the execution of the function

Launch AWS Lambda Functions with the AWS Console

If you want to experiment with **AWS Lambda** and test the codes provided here, follow these steps. These step by step instructions will guide you through creating and deploying a Lambda function using the **AWS Console** and **AWS CLI** with Python.

Before you begin, make sure you have an AWS account. Then, visit the page `https:\\aws.amazon.it` and create a personal one to use for your examples. Once you have registered and confirmed the registration you will be able to access the **AWS Console**, the dashboard from which you can access all the available services (see *Figure 14.1*).

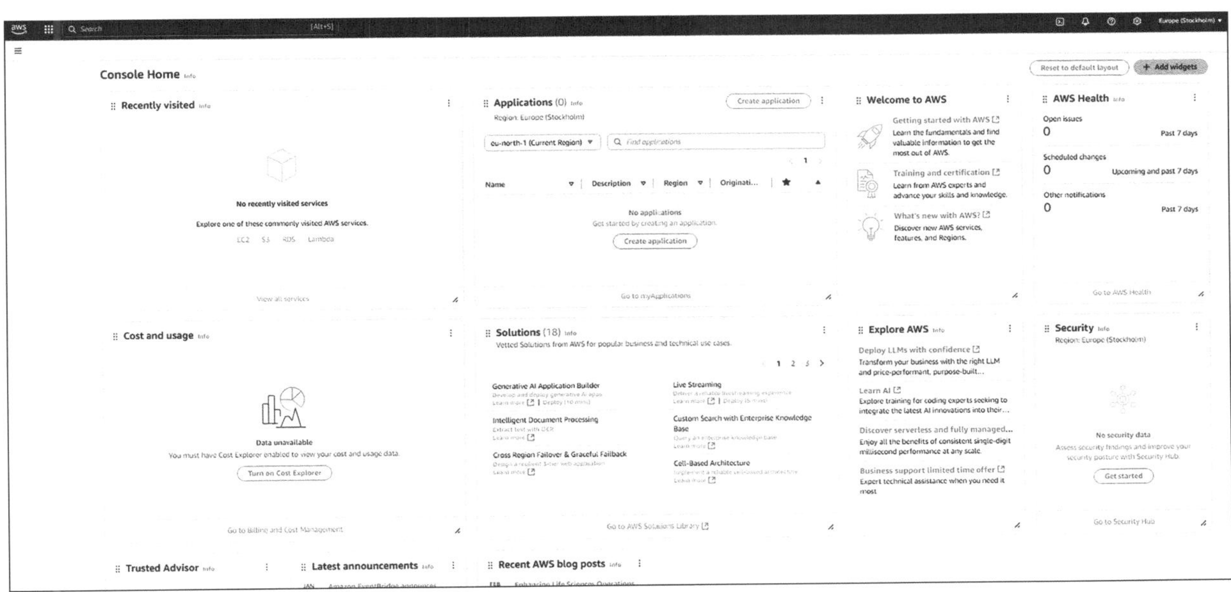

Figure 14.1: AWS Console

The next step is to install and configure the AWS CLI. If you have not already installed it, visit `https://docs.aws.amazon.com/cli/latest/userguide/getting-started-install.html` and follow the instructions for your operating system. Once finished, you can run the following command to see if the installation was successful:

```
aws --version
```

Running this command displays the installed AWS CLI version along with information about the Python runtime and the platform:

```
aws-cli/2.24.5 Python/3.12.6 Windows/11 exe/AMD64
```

We need to generate a secret access key in the AWS Console. To create it for your root account, use the Security Credentials page by selecting **IAM > Security Credentials** from the Console Menu. Expand the Access Keys section, and then click **Create Access Key**. Here you should get two codes:

- Access Key ID
- Secret Access Key

Copy these values to some file and keep it safe, as this code will come in handy. Now, you need to configure it by running the following command:

```
aws configure
```

You will be asked for:

- AWS Access Key ID (code obtained previously)
- AWS Secret Access Key (code obtained previously)
- AWS Region (You can find it in the top right of the console, just before your account name. By clicking on it, all the region names will appear, such as **`eu-north-1`**, **`ap-south-1`**...)
- Default output format (write json)

Now, since we are working with the Python language, we need to install the Boto3 package in the virtual environment that we will dedicate to AWS Lambda projects. Use the pip:

```
pip install boto3
```

Now, we are ready to start working with AWS Lambda. To test the code from the previous section, log in to the AWS Console and go to AWS Lambda (`https://eu-north-1.console.aws.amazon.com/lambda/`) as shown in *Figure* 14.2:

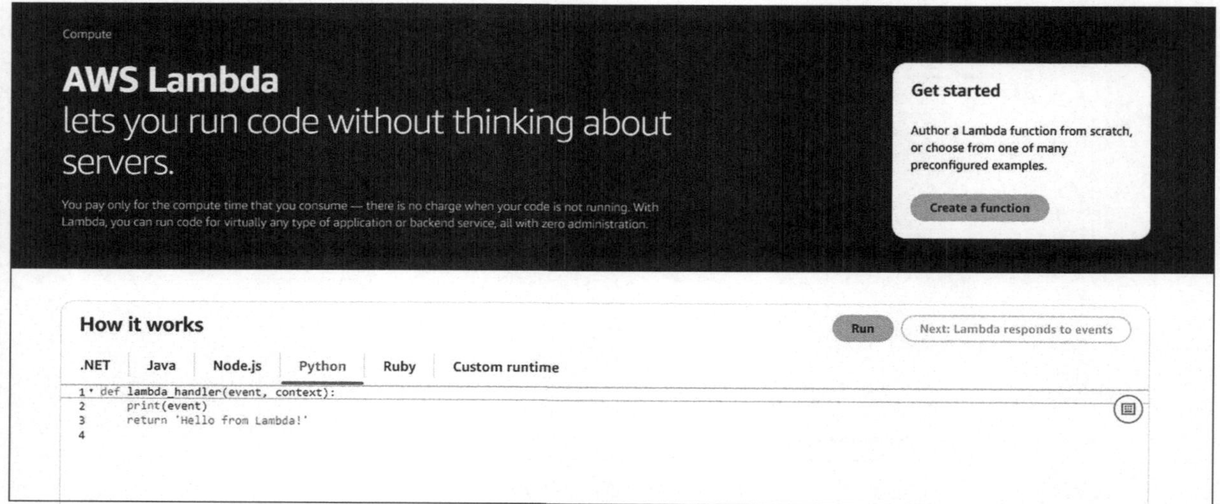

***Figure* 14.2:** *AWS Lambda*

Click on the Create a Function button and select Author from scratch. Set it to:

- **Function Name**: `myLambdaFunction`
- **Runtime**: Python 3.x
- **Architecture**
- **Execution Role**: Select "**`Create a new role with basic Lambda permissions`**".

Click on "**`Create function`**". After creation, you will find an inline code editor as shown in *Figure* 14.3:

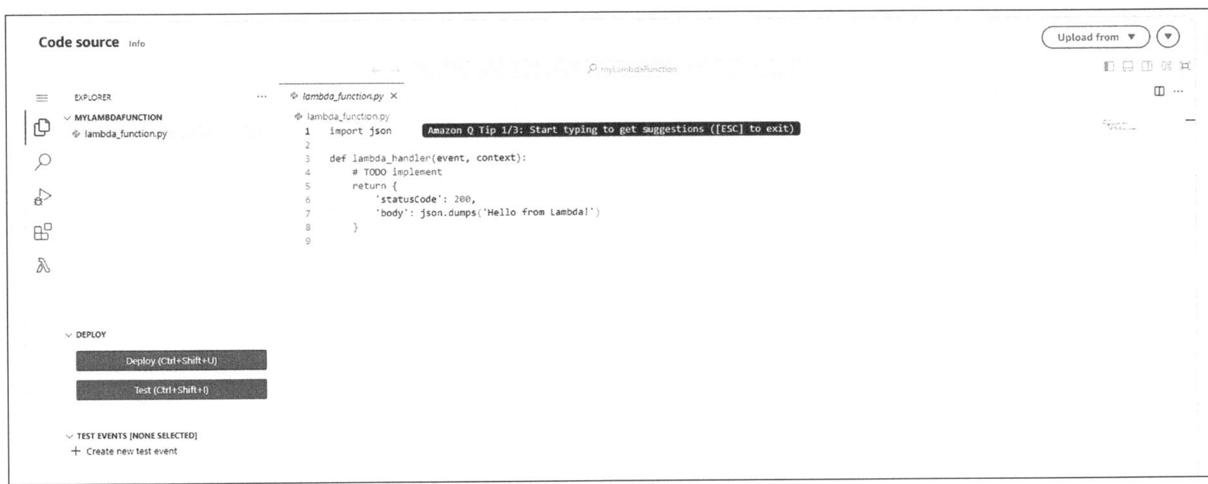

Figure 14.3: AWS Lambda

Here, you can paste the sample Python code via:

```
import json

def lambda_handler(event, context):
    return {
        'statusCode': 200,
        'body': json.dumps('Hello from AWS Lambda!')
    }
```

Click on "**`Deploy`**" and then on "**`Test`**". At the bottom left, click on "**`create new test event`**" and save it as **`MyEventName`** and click on the **`Invoke`** button (the triangle to the right of the event, as shown in *Figure* 14.4).

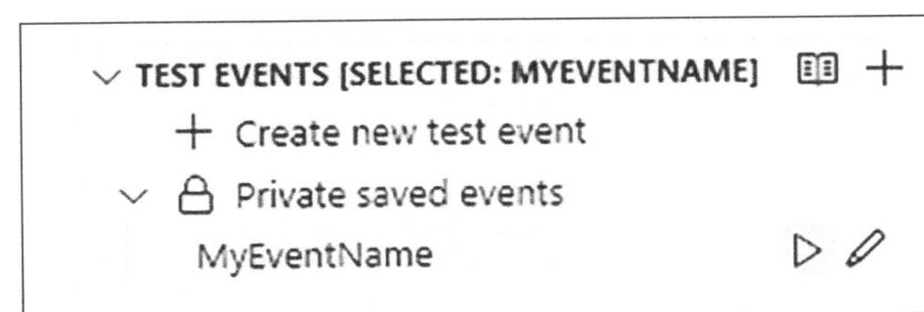

Figure 14.4: *Create and Invoke the Test Event in the Context Menu*

You will find the following JSON response in the output panel at the bottom:

```
Status: Succeeded
Test Event Name: MyEventName

Response:
{
  "statusCode": 200,
  "body": "\"Hello from AWS Lambda!\""
}
```

Launch AWS Lambda Functions from Terminal

If you prefer to work from the terminal instead of the AWS Console on the web, you can create and deploy a Lambda function with the **AWS CLI**. Open the terminal in your operating system and create a folder for your project through the following command:

```
mkdir myLambda && cd myLambda
```

Inside this directory, create a **lambda_function.py** file and copy the code we used previously from the Lambda function into it. In order to load the Lambda function, you need to compress the Python file into a ZIP archive through:

```
zip my_lambda_function.zip lambda_function.py
```

Now, if we want to use AWS Lambda, we will need to use an IAM role with basic permissions for execution. First, open a text editor, copy the following code and save it as **trust-policy.json** inside the **myLambda** folder:

```
{
  "Version": "2012-10-17",
  "Statement": [
    {
      "Effect": "Allow",
      "Principal": {
        "Service": "lambda.amazonaws.com"
      },
      "Action": "sts:AssumeRole"
    }
  ]
}
```

Then, we will run the following command to create the IAM role for Lambda:

```
aws iam create-role --role-name LambdaExecutionRole --assume-role-policy-
document file://trust-policy.json
```

As a response, you should get the role **ARN**. Copy it and save it for the next step. Now, you can upload the function to AWS. In our case we have already uploaded it to AWS console in the previous example. Replace the role ARN with the one you received in the output of the previous command:

```
aws lambda create-function --function-name myLambdaFunction \
  --runtime python3.12 \
  --role arn:aws:iam::YOUR_ACCOUNT_ID:role/lambda-execution-role \
  --handler lambda_function.lambda_handler \
  --zip-file fileb://my_lambda_function.zip
```

After creating it, you can test the function directly from the terminal via:

```
aws lambda invoke --function-name myLambdaFunction output.json
```

Open **output.json** to see the following result:

```
{"statusCode": 200, "body": "\"Hello from AWS Lambda!\""}
```

Launch an AWS Lambda function with API Gateway

If you want to call your Lambda function via an HTTP URL, you can connect it to AWS API Gateway. From the AWS Console, look up one of the services as shown in *Figure* 14.5.

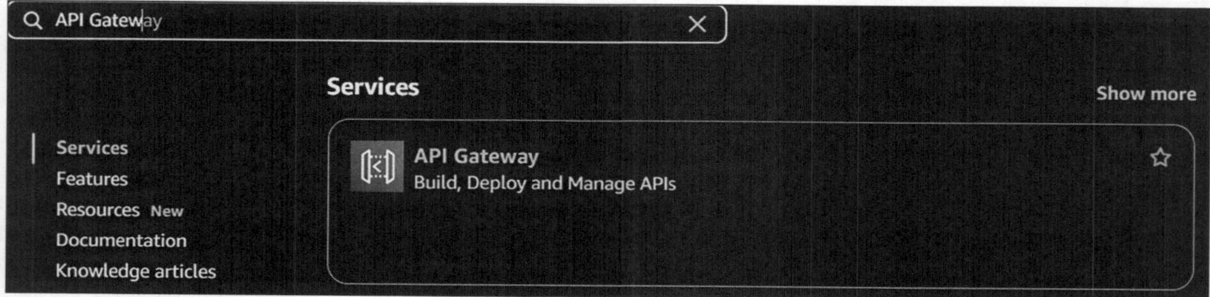

Figure 14.5: *Finding Services like API Gateway through the Search Field of the AWS Console*

After doing so, the Amazon Gateway API page will load. In the Choose an API Type section, press the **`Build`** button in HTTP API. Another page will open where we will set the configuration (see *Figure* 14.6), which will look like as follows:

- **`Integrations`**: **`Lambda`**
- **`AWS Region`**: <<your-region>>
- **`Lambda Function`**: Select your **`Lambda Function`**
- **`API Name`**: Enter a name, for example, "**`mylambda`**"

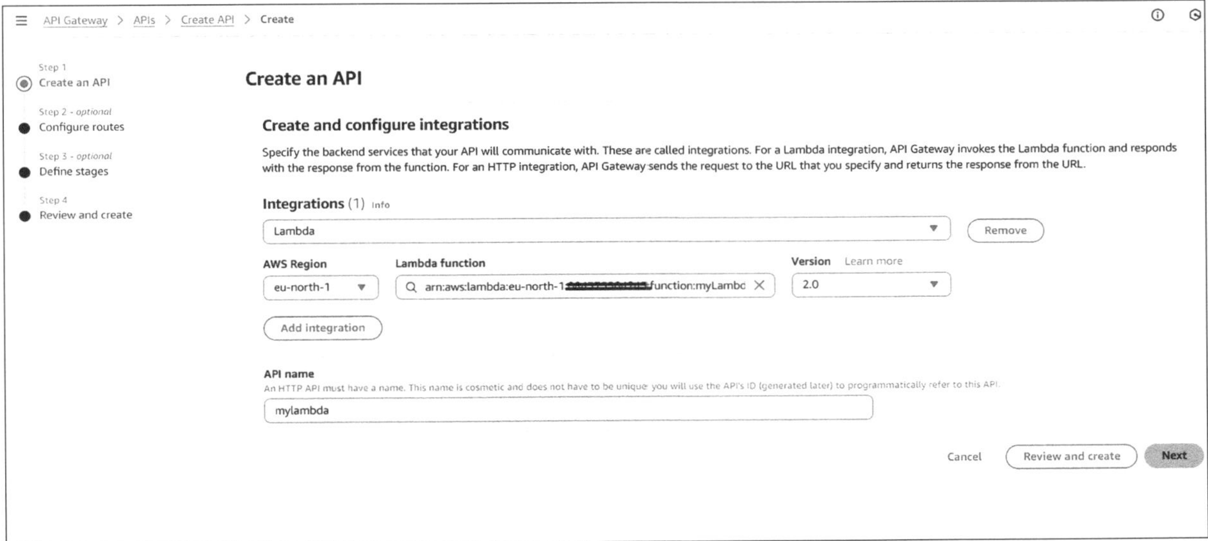

Figure 14.6: *Creating an API Panel in the AWS Console*

Press the "**`Review and Create`**" button, and then on the next page the "**`Create`**" button.

Go to **`Deploy`** > **`Stages`** and press the "**`Create`**" button next to "**`Stages for mylambda`**" (see *Figure* 14.7). Create a new stage named **`mystage`**.

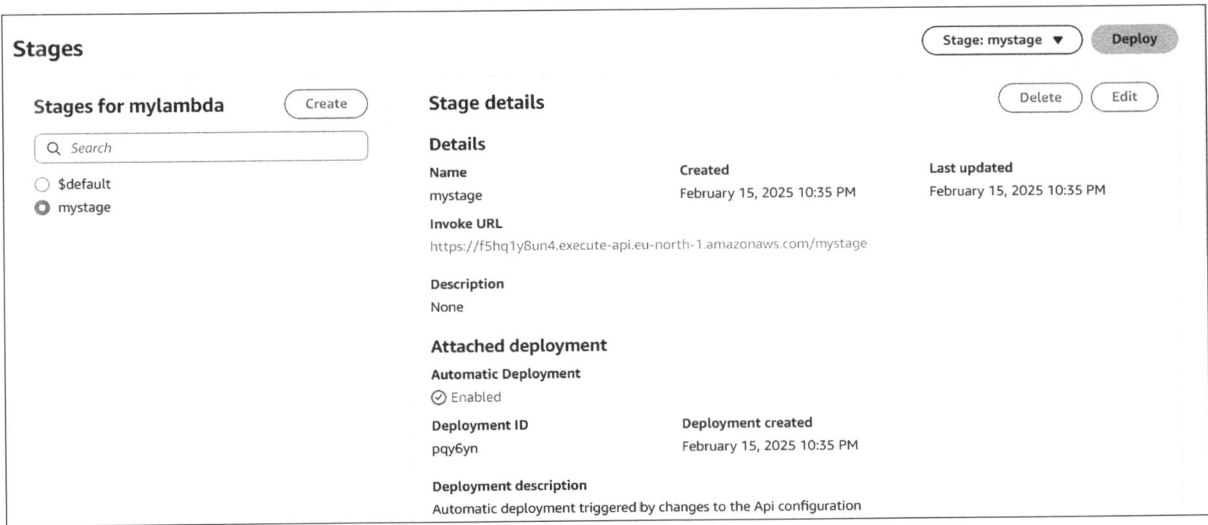

Figure 14.7: *Creating and Managing Stages in API Gateway*

After selecting the newly created stage with the drop-down menu at the top right, you will be able to view all the information, including the Invoke URL. Copy this value and add the route name connected to the AWS Lambda function to make an HTTP request on a browser or on a console using the `curl` command which is shown here:

```
curl -X GET https://f5hq1y8un4.execute-api.eu-north-1.amazonaws.com/mystage/
myLambdaFunction
```

As a result, you will get this output:

```
"Hello from AWS Lambda!"
```

Modify the Function to Process Data

If you want to try something more advanced, you can modify the function to accept the input data and return a result. For example, you can calculate the sum of numbers passed in the payload, which is indicated in this code:

```
import json

def lambda_handler(event, context):
    body = json.loads(event["body"])
    num1 = body.get("num1", 0)
    num2 = body.get("num2", 0)

    return {
        'statusCode': 200,
        'body': json.dumps({'sum': num1 + num2})
    }
```

Let us now test the new AWS Lambda function from the AWS Console. This time we fill the Test Event with a JSON payload in which the input values for the function calculation are passed (as shown in *Figure* 14.8):

```
{
  "body": "{\"num1\": 10, \"num2\": 5}"
}
```

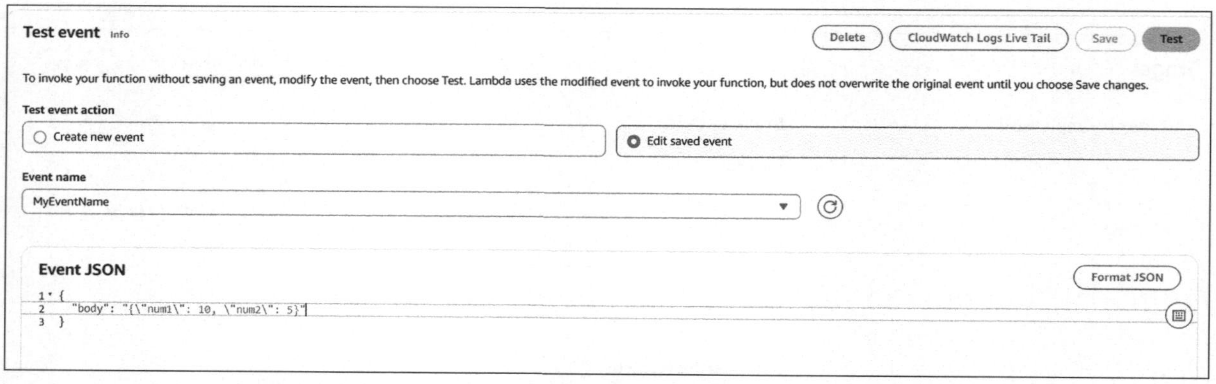

Figure 14.8: *AWS Lambda Function Test Event Panel in AWS Console*

Pressing the Test button will give you the following result:

```
Status: Succeeded
Test Event Name: MyEventName

Response:
{
  "statusCode": 200,
  "body": "{\"sum\": 15}"
}
```

We can run the AWS Lambda function via terminal, but first we need to write the JSON payload to a file. Copy the following code and save it in myLambda directory as `invoke-payload.json`:

```
{
  "body": "{\"num1\": 10, \"num2\": 5}"
}
```

At this point, we will launch the function invocation as follows:

```
aws lambda invoke --function-name myLambdaFunction output.json --payload
fileb://invoke-payload.json
```

In the **`output.json`** file, you will find the same result obtained in the AWS Console, that is the sum of the two numbers: 15.

Parallel S3 File Processing with AWS Lambda and DynamoDB

One of the most interesting scenarios in which Python fits is parallel and distributed data processing. When we run thousands of Lambda functions at the same time, it is possible to distribute the work in multiple processes without worrying about server management. A typical use case is data processing in S3; suppose we have a large dataset divided into multiple files and we want to process each file independently. An efficient solution is to create a Lambda function that is automatically triggered every time a file is uploaded to an **S3 bucket**.

This procedure will guide you through the configuration of a system in which every file uploaded to an S3 bucket automatically triggers a **Lambda function**, which processes the file and saves the results in **DynamoDB**.

The first thing to do for this example is to create an S3 Bucket which is the storage space where we will upload the files.

Open the AWS Console and search for the S3 service as shown in *Figure* 14.9.

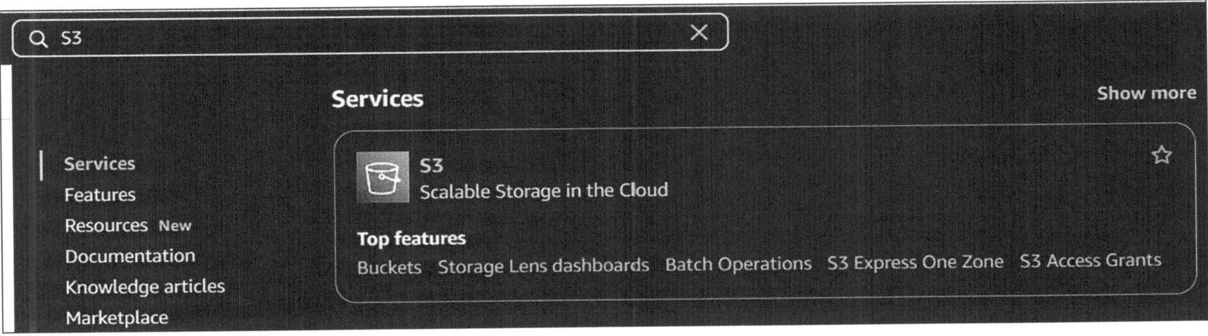

***Figure* 14.9:** *Searching for S3 Service on AWS Console*

Click S3 and load the S3 service page. Click on "**`Create Bucket`**" and the settings panel will load immediately. Choose "**`General Purpose`**" and give the bucket a name, such as **`mybucketforabookexample`** (see *Figure* 14.10).

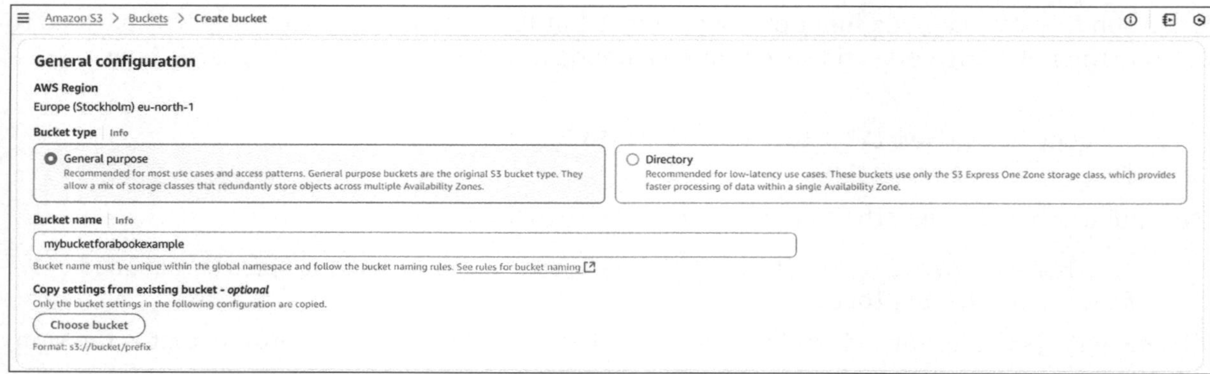

Figure 14.10: *Bucket Creation Panel on S3*

Once you have configured the settings, you will find another **`Create Bucket`** button at the bottom of the page. Click on it to start creating the bucket.

Now, let us create a table on DynamoDB to store the processing results. Search DynamoDB in the AWS console, as shown in *Figure* 14.11.

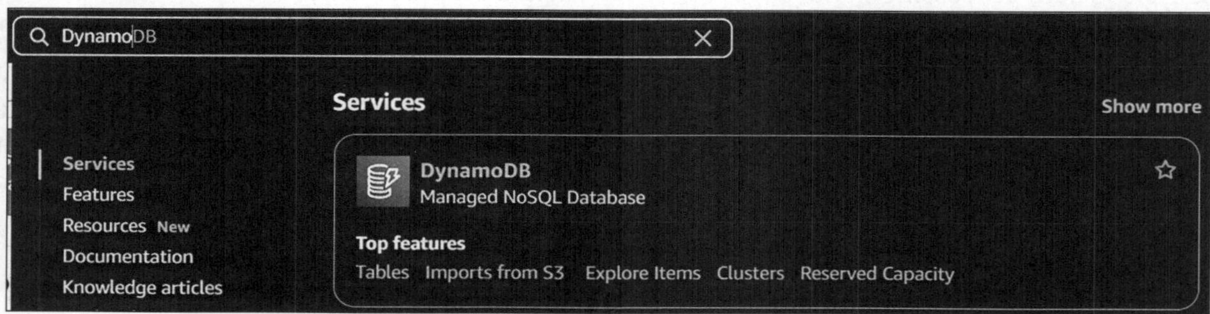

Figure 14.11: *Searching for the DynamoDB Database in the AWS Console*

Once the DynamoDB service page is loaded, press the "**`Create Table`**" button to open the table creation panel (see *Figure* 14.12).

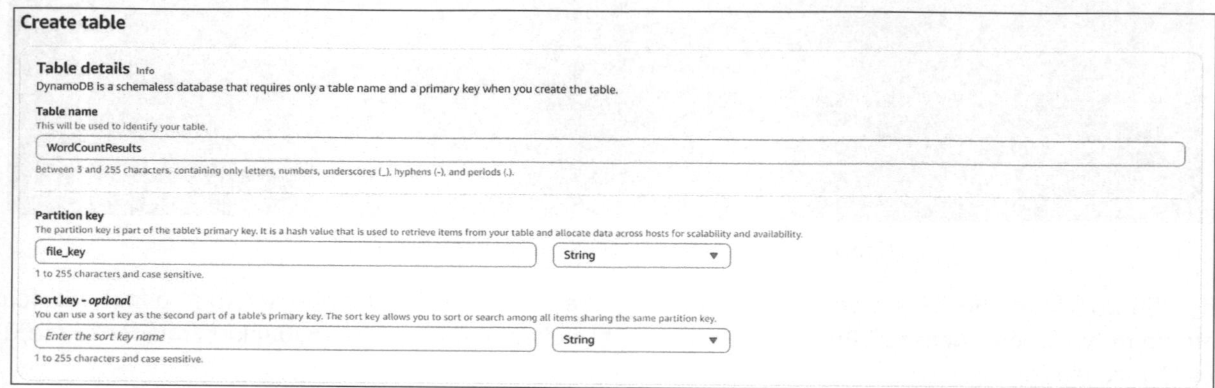

Figure 14.12: *Settings Panel for Table Creation on DynamoDB*

Set the table name to **`WordCountResults`**, name the partition key as **`file_key`**, and type **`String`**. Finally click the "**`Create Table`**" button to create the table. We now have all the tools we need to create the AWS Lambda function. This function will be triggered every time a file is uploaded to S3. Search for Lambda in the AWS console and click on "**`Create Function`**". The function configuration panel will appear, as shown in *Figure* 14.13.

Figure 14.13: Create Function Panel in AWS Console

Select "**`Author from scratch`**" and enter the name of the function as **`ProcessS3File`**. Select **`Python 3.13`** or another recent version as the runtime. Leave the other settings as default and press the "**`Create Function`**" button at the bottom of the page. Once the AWS Lambda function is created, we must give it permissions to access S3 and DynamoDB. Search in the AWS console for the IAM service as shown in *Figure 14.14*.

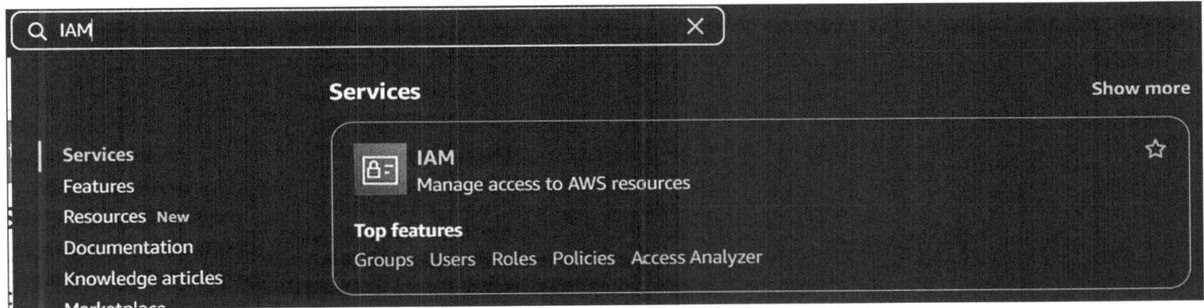

Figure 14.14: Finding IAM in the AWS Console

Click on *Roles* and find the one with the Lambda function name **`ProcessS3File-role-xxxxxx`**. Click on the role and then on **`Add Permissions`** > **`Attach policies`**. Search for the following policies and add them:

- **`AmazonS3ReadOnlyAccess`** (to read files from S3)
- **`AmazonDynamoDBFullAccess`** (to write to DynamoDB)

Once you have selected them, click on "**`Add Permissions`**". Now the AWS Lambda function has access to S3 and DynamoDB. Let us now add the code to the function we just created. Go to the Lambda service page and search for the `ProcessS3File` function. In the code panel enter the following code:

```
import boto3
import json
import os

# AWS Client Configuration
s3_client = boto3.client('s3')
dynamodb = boto3.resource('dynamodb')

# DynamoDB Table Name
table_name = "WordCountResults"
table = dynamodb.Table(table_name)
```

```
def lambda_handler(event, context):
    results = []

    for record in event['Records']:
        try:
            bucket_name = record['s3']['bucket']['name']
            file_key = record['s3']['object']['key']

            # Download file from S3
            response = s3_client.get_object(Bucket=bucket_name, Key=file_key)
            file_content = response['Body'].read().decode('utf-8')

            # Word count
            word_count = len(file_content.split())

            # Save results to DynamoDB
            table.put_item(
                Item={
                    'file_key': file_key,
                    'word_count': word_count
                }
            )

            results.append({'file': file_key, 'word_count': word_count})

        except Exception as e:
            print(f"Errore durante il processing di {file_key}: {str(e)}")
            results.append({'file': file_key, 'error': str(e)})

    return {
        'statusCode': 200,
        'body': json.dumps(results)
    }
```

Once you have entered the code, click on **`Deploy`**. Now, we need to connect S3 to a trigger on Lambda, which fires when a file is uploaded to S3. Go to S3 and open your bucket (**`mybucketforabookexample`**). Click on **`Properties > Event Notification > Create Event Notification`** panel. In the general configuration panel, set **`TriggerLambdaOnUpload`** as the event name and leave the other fields empty. In the event type panel, select "**`Put`**" in object creation. This is equivalent to the file upload event. Finally in the destination panel select Lambda Function as the destination and choose **`ProcessS3File`**. Once you have done this, click on **`Create Event`**.

At this point, the AWS Lambda function will be executed every time you upload a file to S3. To test the system, we can upload a file to S3. Go to the S3 bucket and click on **`Load`**. Select a **`.txt`** (text) file with some content. For instance, you can select an **`example.txt`** file with "**`This is my text`**" written inside, as shown in *Figure 14.15*.

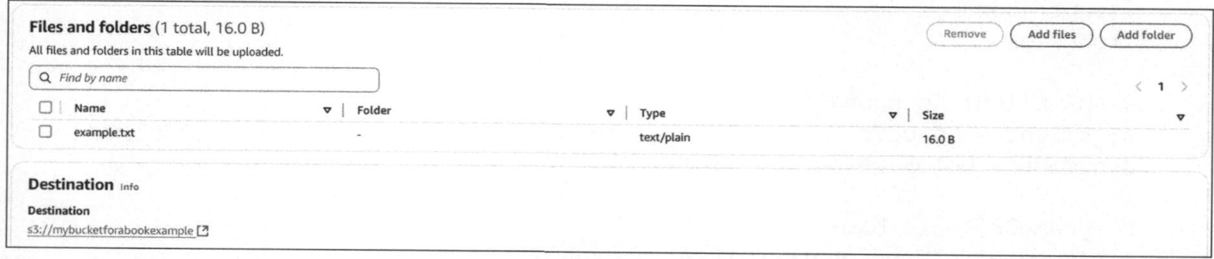

Figure 14.15: *Load a File TXT in the S3 Bucket*

Finally, click on **`Upload`** at the bottom of the page. This will automatically activate the AWS Lambda function. To check the results on DynamoDB, go to **`DynamoDB`** > **`Tables`** > **`WordCountResults`** and click **`onExplore Table Items`**. You should see a line in the items returned panel with the file name and the number of words in the file, as shown in *Figure 14.16*.

Figure 14.16: *Word Count of a File*

AWS Lambda is a serverless compute service that automatically runs code in response to events, while scaling dynamically based on demand. In the specific case of the function that processes files uploaded to S3 and counts the words in them, parallel computation emerges from the way Lambda manages function execution. Each time a file is uploaded to an S3 bucket, an event is generated and passed to Lambda. If multiple files are uploaded at the same time, AWS Lambda can launch multiple instances of the function in parallel, while distributing the work without requiring explicit management by the developer.

This ability to run multiple instances at once is what makes Lambda particularly powerful for high-concurrency scenarios. Instead of processing files sequentially and waiting for one process to finish before launching another, Lambda creates multiple independent executions, where each works on a different file. The system automatically scales to the number of incoming events and can run **`severl`** instances of the function at the same time, as per the need. This means that if a user uploads ten files to S3 at the same time, up to ten instances of the Lambda function can be launched, where each is dedicated to processing a single file. This speeds up the overall processing time dramatically.

However, there are some important considerations to factor in while leveraging such parallelism. AWS imposes a limit on the maximum number of concurrent Lambda executions. If this threshold is exceeded, the excess events are queued or can be rejected. Additionally, if multiple Lambda function instances are writing to DynamoDB at the same time, it is critical to ensure that no write conflicts occur by using unique primary keys or concurrency management strategies. Another aspect to consider is error handling; if one of the Lambda executions fails while processing a file, you can configure retry mechanisms or send the unprocessed events to an error handling queue like AWS SQS or a Dead Letter Queue.

Leveraging parallel computing with AWS Lambda means allowing the system to automatically manage scalability and load distribution without the need for complex infrastructure. By optimizing the memory and resources assigned to the function, you can further improve performance, making the entire file processing process faster and more efficient.

Advanced Approaches with AWS Lambda

Another area where Python is particularly useful on AWS Lambda is the integration with machine learning and data processing. Thanks to libraries such as NumPy, Pandas, SciPy and scikit-learn, it is possible to perform real-time data analysis directly within a Lambda function. Python is therefore an ideal tool for AWS Lambda for ease of writing code and exploiting a rich ecosystem of libraries for data processing, machine learning, and management of cloud services. Furthermore, AWS offers advanced tools such as AWS Lambda Layers, which allow you to load external libraries efficiently and avoid including them directly in the function package. This reduces execution times and resource consumption.

The only limitation is that some data science and machine learning libraries such as TensorFlow or PyTorch, can be too heavy for the standard AWS Lambda execution environment. To overcome this problem, AWS allows you to run Lambda inside Docker containers, while allowing you to create custom environments with all the necessary dependencies.

In short, Lambda and Python form a powerful and scalable combination which is can adapt to numerous distributed computing scenarios in the cloud.

Google Cloud Functions

Google Cloud Functions is Google's alternative to AWS Lambda's serverless model that offers a highly scalable environment to run code in response to events without having to directly manage servers or infrastructure. Based on an event-driven architecture, Cloud Functions lets you automatically react to changes in Google Cloud services like changes in a Cloud Storage bucket, new messages in a Pub/Sub queue, or HTTP requests via Cloud Run or API Gateway.

One of the key benefits of Google Cloud Functions is its tight integration with the Google Cloud ecosystem. While AWS Lambda is particularly powerful for automating workflows within AWS, Cloud Functions stands out for its ability to seamlessly interact with services such as BigQuery, Firestore, and Cloud Pub/Sub. This makes it an ideal solution for applications that require real-time data processing, workflow automation, or orchestration of ML pipelines.

From a development perspective, Google Cloud Functions supports Python as a native programming language and allows developers to write lightweight, modular functions that run automatically when a certain event occurs. Creating a function with Python is easy: just define a handler and specify a trigger, which can be HTTP, Pub/Sub or an event generated by Cloud Storage. This function, once deployed in the cloud, will be accessible via a public URL and can be invoked from any HTTP client.

An important aspect to consider when using Google Cloud Functions for parallel computing is managing runtime limitations. Currently, each function has a maximum execution time of 60 minutes and can use up to 16 GB of RAM, which makes it more suitable for fast processing tasks rather than intensive and long-running workloads. For more complex operations, it may be useful to combine Cloud Functions with other solutions such as Cloud Run or Kubernetes Engine to ensure greater flexibility.

In summary, Google Cloud Functions is a powerful platform for serverless computing and is particularly suitable for integration with the Google Cloud ecosystem and for real-time data processing. With support for Python and the ability to execute functions in response to events, it is an ideal solution for automation tasks, data pipelines, and parallel computing, especially when combined with Pub/Sub and other Google services. However, for more intensive workloads, you may need to consider alternatives such as Cloud Run or Dataflow to gain more control over your compute resources.

Example of How to Make a Google Cloud Function

If you want to try out your code with **`Google Cloud Functions`**, follow these detailed instructions to create, test, and deploy a function to **Google Cloud Platform (GCP)** with Python.

Before you begin, you need to have a Google Cloud account. If you do not have one yet, you can sign up on Google Cloud (`https://cloud.google.com/`) and create one. Go to the GCP console and search for Cloud Functions API in your project. You should see a panel to enable them. Press the *Enable* button (as shown in *Figure 14.17*).

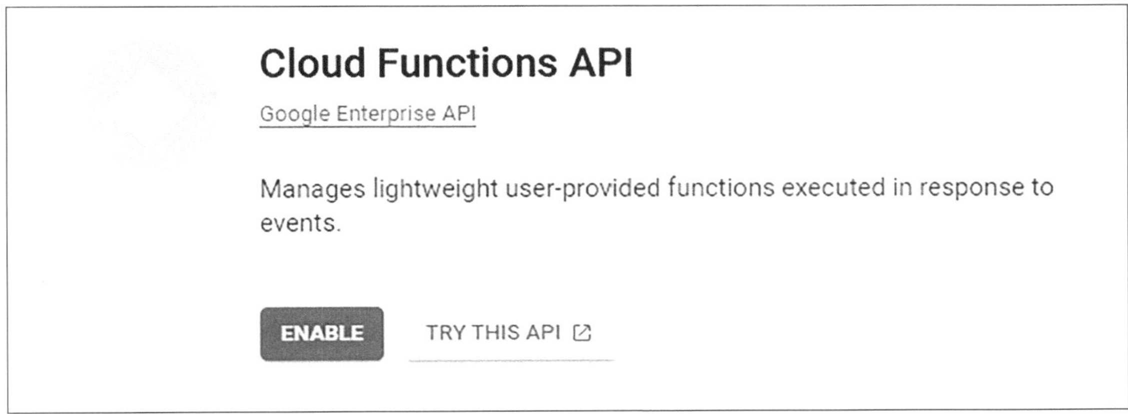

Figure 14.17: *Cloud Functions API Enablement Panel*

Then, you will need to download the Google Cloud SDK, where you will find the installation procedure on the official page (`https://cloud.google.com/sdk/docs/install`). The procedure will differ as per different operating systems. During installation, you will be asked to connect your Google account and choose the project to work on by ID. To know this value, click on *Settings and Utilities* (the three vertical dots in the top right). Select *Project settings* from the drop-down menu (see *Figure* 14.18) to view the information regarding the project, including its ID.

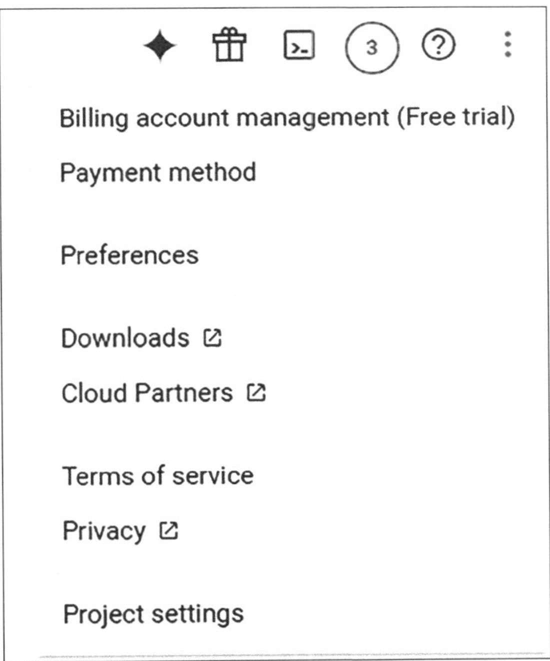

Figure 14.18: *Context Menu to Search for Information about the Current Project*

The same operation can be performed later through the terminal by entering the following commands:

```
gcloud auth login
gcloud config set project YOUR_PROJECT_ID
```

Replace **`YOUR_PROJECT_ID`** with your Google Cloud project ID.

Now, we are ready to create a function in Google Cloud Functions. There are two main ways to do this:

- Via GCP console
- Via terminal with Gcloud

Create a Google Cloud Function from GCP

Let us first see how to create the function via the GCP console. From there, search for Cloud Run Functions and click on the Create Function button, as shown in *Figure 14.19*:

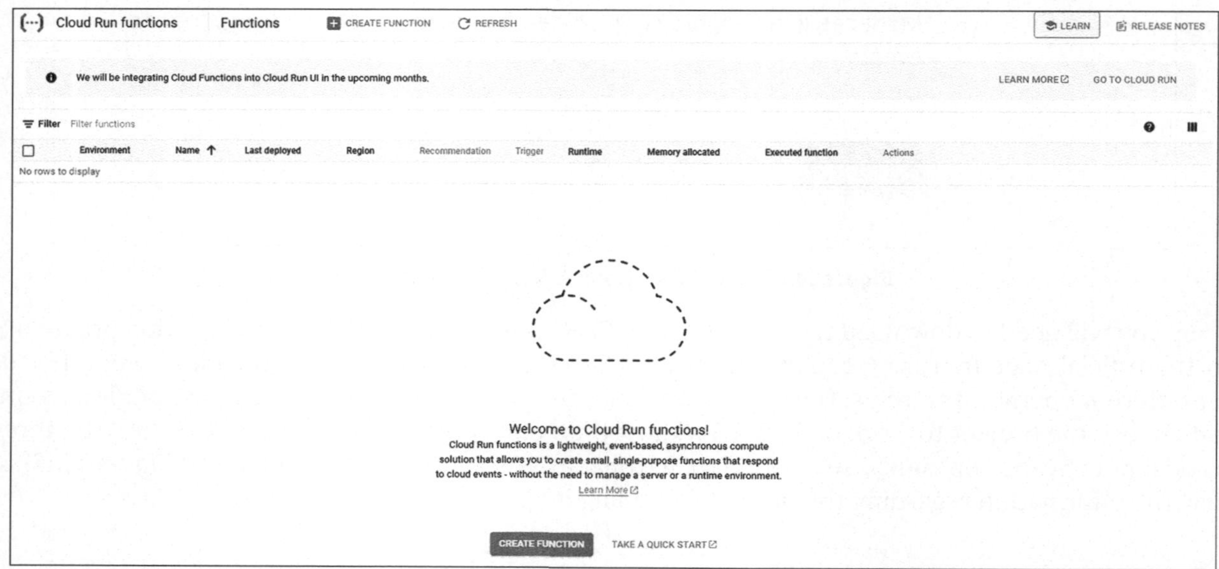

Figure 14.19: *The Cloud Run Functions Section in GCP*

Sometimes a window may appear that reports any services not enabled, press enable and go ahead. Give the function a name (for example, `my_function`) and select "`HTTPS`" as the trigger type, as shown in *Figure 14.20*:

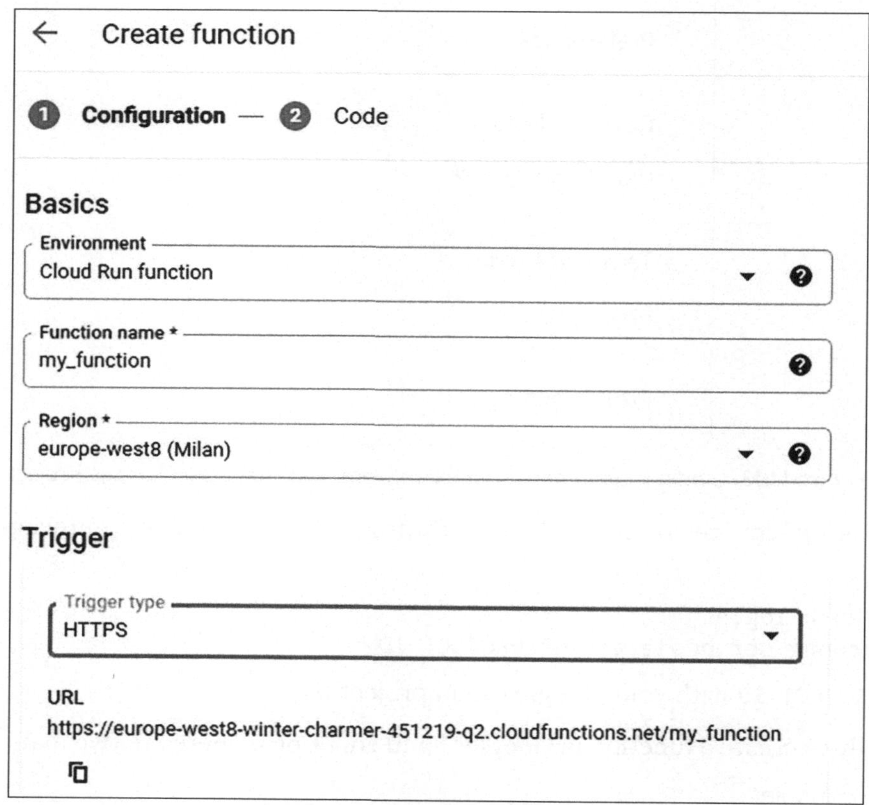

Figure 14.20: *Creating a Function on GCP*

Press *Next* and the function editor page will open (as shown in *Figure 14.21*). Select Python 3.12 in the Runtime field and enter the following function code in the editor:

```
def hello_http(request):
    return "Hello from Google Cloud Functions!"
```

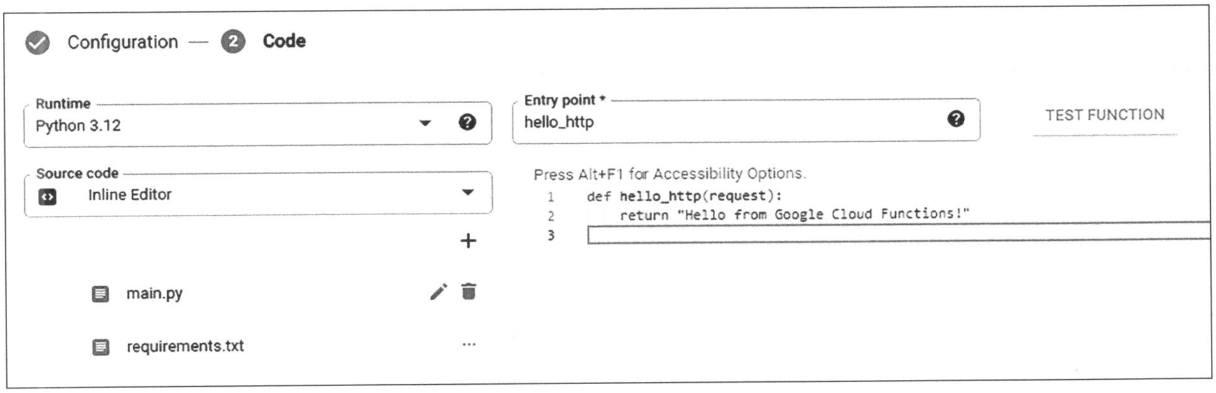

Figure 14.21: *Function Editor in GCP*

Click on *Deploy* and wait for it to complete. After deployment, you will find a public URL to test the feature. You can test it by running the following command from the terminal:

```
gcloud functions add-invoker-policy-binding my_function --region="REGION-
PROJECT_ID" --member="allUsers"
curl -X "GET https://REGION-PROJECT_ID.cloudfunctions.net/my_function"
```

Replace **REGION** and **PROJECT_ID** with your region (for example, **europe-west8**) and the project ID. You will get the following message as output:

```
Hello from Google Cloud Functions!
```

You can also launch the URL from a browser to get the same result.

Create Google Cloud Feature from Terminal with gcloud

An alternative to the previous method is to work entirely from the terminal without using the GCP console. After opening the terminal, let us create a folder for the project you are working on and save it as:

```
mkdir my_cloud_function && cd my_cloud_function
```

Inside the new folder, create a main.py file with the code of the function used in the previous example:

```
def hello_http(request):
    return "Hello from Google Cloud Functions!"
```

Now, create a dependency file **requirements.txt**. Google Cloud Functions uses this file to install dependencies. If your function uses external libraries (for example, Pandas, Boto3), then add them here. Then, create this file and add it even if it is empty:

```
touch requirements.txt
```

The next step will be to deploy the feature on Google Cloud via the following code:

```
gcloud functions deploy hello_http \
    --runtime python312 \
    --trigger-http \
    --allow-unauthenticated \
```

The operation will take some time. Once the deployment is completed, the system will provide you with the public URL to call it. At this point, you can finally test the function and replace the URL with the one obtained in the output here:

```
curl -X "GET https://REGION-PROJECT_ID.cloudfunctions.net/hello_http"
```

Again, you should get the same result as the previous example:

```
Hello from Google Cloud Functions!
```

As we can see, creating, configuring, and running functions on Google Cloud is very similar to that on AWS Amazon. Here too, more advanced approaches can be followed in the same way.

Azure Functions

Azure Functions is Microsoft's serverless offering which is designed to run code in response to events without having to directly manage servers or infrastructure. Like AWS Lambda and Google Cloud Functions, Azure Functions follows an event-driven model and allows you to automate workflows, process data in real time, and build scalable applications with ease. One of its strengths is its native integration with the Microsoft Azure ecosystem, which makes it particularly suitable for those who already use services such as Azure Blob Storage, Cosmos DB, Event Grid, Service Bus, and Kubernetes.

One of the distinctive aspects of Azure Functions is its flexibility in execution models. Functions can be run on a consumption-based model, where they are automatically scaled based on demand and you only pay for the actual execution time, or on a Premium or dedicated plan, which offers more resources and the ability to run functions without the typical limitations of the consumption model, such as cold starts.

From a development perspective, Azure Functions supports several programming languages, including Python, JavaScript, C#, Java, and PowerShell. Thanks to its flexible environment, you can develop and test functions locally using the Azure Functions Core Tools, a toolkit that allows you to simulate the behavior of the Azure runtime before deploying your code to the cloud.

However, like all serverless platforms, Azure Functions also has some limitations. In the consumption plan, each execution is limited to a maximum of 5 minutes, although in the Premium plan this limit can be extended up to 60 minutes. Additionally, the execution environment has a longer startup time than Lambda and Cloud Functions in some scenarios, especially for applications with many dependencies.

From a parallel computing perspective, Azure Functions integrates seamlessly with Durable Functions, which is an extension that allows you to orchestrate serverless functions in complex workflows, execute operations in parallel, and manage the state of the executions. For example, a map-and-reduce workflow (similar to the MapReduce pattern) can be implemented using Durable Functions to split a dataset into multiple parts, process them in parallel, and then combine the final results.

In conclusion, Azure Functions is a powerful solution for serverless computing, ideal for applications that need to scale automatically and interact with the Microsoft ecosystem. Thanks to the integration with Azure Storage, Event Grid, IoT Hub and Kubernetes, it is particularly suitable for real-time data processing tasks, automation and orchestration of distributed workflows. Python proves once again an effective tool for developing Azure Functions, thanks to its flexibility and the wide range of libraries available for data processing and machine learning. However, for more complex and computationally intensive workloads, it may be useful to evaluate hybrid solutions combining Azure Functions with Kubernetes or Azure Batch to gain greater control over resources and performance.

Creating Azure Function from Microsoft Azure

If you want to try Azure Functions with Python, follow these detailed steps to create, test and deploy a function on Microsoft Azure. We will work both through the Azure Portal and the Azure CLI in this section.

Creating an Azure function with Python is simple. Suppose we want to create an HTTP function that responds to user requests. After deployment, the function will be accessible through a public URL and can be invoked through HTTP requests.

Before starting, make sure that you have an Azure account; if you do not have one, you can create it on the official page (`https://azure.microsoft.com/`). Also, download the Azure CLI following the instructions on the page (`https://learn.microsoft.com/it-it/cli/azure/install-azure-cli`), depending on your operating system. Once installed, download the Azure Functions Core Tool package from the same page. You can then access the Microsoft Azure portal, as shown in *Figure 14.22*.

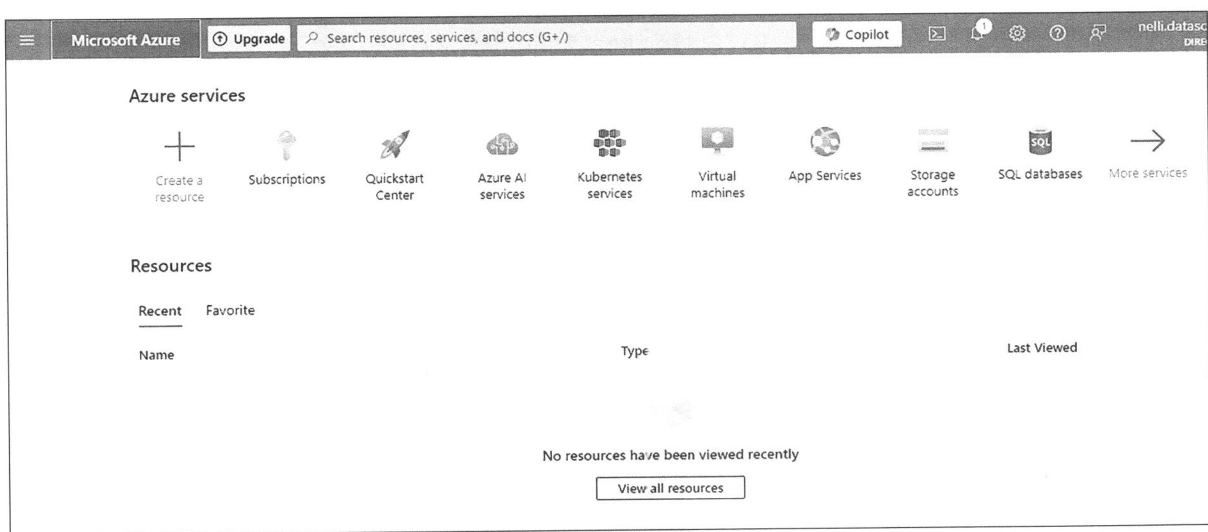

Figure 14.22: *Microsoft Azure*

Subscribe to Azure CLI with the following command:

```
az login
```

You will be asked for the account you registered with and your subscription ID to select from a list. Open the terminal and create a new folder for the project:

```
mkdir my_azure_function && cd my_azure_function
```

Then create a virtual environment inside the folder:

```
python -m venv venv
```

On Mac/Linux, activate the virtual environment with the following command:

```
source venv/bin/activate  # Mac/Linux
```

If you are working with Windows instead, use the following command:

```
venv\Scripts\activate     # Windows
```

At this point, install the appropriate module for Azure Functions via:

```
pip install azure-functions
```

Create the function project using:

```
func init my_azure_function --python
cd my_azure_function
```

Now, we can create an http function with the following command:

```
func new --name hello_function --template "HTTP trigger" --authlevel
"anonymous"
```

This will generate a file `my_azure_function/function_app.py` with some basic code that you will need to manually replace with the following:

```
import azure.functions as func
import logging

# Questa è l'istanza globale che Azure Functions cerca
app = func.FunctionApp()

@app.route(route="hello_function", auth_level=func.AuthLevel.ANONYMOUS)
def hello_function(req: func.HttpRequest) -> func.HttpResponse:
    logging.info('Python HTTP trigger function processed a request.')
    return func.HttpResponse("Hello, Azure!", status_code=200)
```

To test the newly defined function locally, use:

```
func start
```

You should see an output like this:

```
Found Python version 3.11.6 (py).

Azure Functions Core Tools
Core Tools Version:       4.0.6821 Commit hash: N/A +c09a2033faa7ecf-
51b3773308283af0ca9a99f83 (64-bit)
Function Runtime Version: 4.1036.1.23224

[2025-02-18T20:13:09.750Z] Worker process started and initialized.

Functions:

        hello_function:  http://localhost:7071/api/hello_function

For detailed output, run func with --verbose flag.
```

The system has provided us with the URL to run the Azure function in the browser. Copy the following URL and paste it into your system's browser:

```
http://localhost:7071/api/hello_function
```

You will get a response page that will display the following text:

Hello, Azure!

You can also call the function directly from the terminal with the following command:

```
curl -X GET http://localhost:7071/api/hello_function
```

The answer will be the same here and will show up as:

```
Hello, Azure!
```

Comparison and Choices

Each of these serverless services offers unique features for parallelization with Python. AWS Lambda is ideal for environments that already leverage the AWS ecosystem and need to scale quickly. Google Cloud Functions excels at applications integrated with Google services and data analysis workflows. Azure Functions is highly suitable for complex enterprise scenarios, thanks to its flexibility and hybrid execution options.

Feature	AWS Lambda	Google Cloud Functions	Azure Functions
Execution Model	Event-driven, serverless	Event-driven, serverless	Event-driven, serverless
Supported Runtime	Python, Node.js, Java, Go, .NET, Ruby, Custom Runtime (via container)	Python, Node.js, Go, Java, .NET, PHP, Custom Runtime	Python, Node.js, Java, .NET, PowerShell, Custom Runtime
Scalability	**Automatic,** up to thousands of concurrent instances	**Automatic**, Google Cloud event support (Pub/Sub, Storage, etc.)	**Automatic**, but with options for finer scaling (Durable Functions)
Execution limit	**15 minutes** per invocation	**60 minutes** per invocation	**5 minutes** (Consumption Plan), up to 60 minutes (Premium Plan)
Costs	Based on execution time and memory (free tier: 1M requests/month)	Based on execution time and memory (free tier: 2M requests/month)	Based on time and resource consumption (free tier: 1M requests/ month)
Supported triggers	S3, DynamoDB, SQS, Kinesis, API Gateway, SNS, CloudWatch, etc.	Pub/Sub, Cloud Storage, Firestore, HTTP, Scheduler, Firebase	Event Grid, Service Bus, Storage, Cosmos DB, HTTP
Cold Start	Faster than GCP and Azure, but still present	Higher cold start, especially on Java	Slow on Consumption Plan, faster on Premium Plan
Security & IAM	IAM + VPC + Secrets Manager	IAM + Cloud IAM Policies	IAM + Active Directory + Key Vault
Deployment	ZIP, container Docker, CloudFormation, Serverless Framework	ZIP, Cloud Build, Firebase Functions	ZIP, Serverless Framework, Kubernetes, Azure DevOps
Native integration	AWS S3, DynamoDB, Step Functions, EventBridge	BigQuery, Firestore, Firebase, Cloud Run	CosmosDB, Event Hub, IoT Hub, Kubernetes

***Table 14.1**: Comparing AWS Lambda, Google Cloud Functions, and Azure Functions*

AWS Lambda, Google Cloud Functions, and Azure Functions are the three main serverless solutions offered by their respective cloud providers. Each has specific characteristics that makes them more or less suitable for certain contexts. The choice between these platforms depends on a series of factors like scalability, costs, integration with other services, performance, and deployment models.

AWS Lambda is the most mature and widely adopted serverless solution, thanks to its deep integration with the AWS ecosystem and the ability to automatically scale up to thousands of concurrent instances. It supports several programming languages like Python, Node.js, Java, Go, and .NET, and offers a wide range of triggers that allow you to execute functions in response to events from S3, DynamoDB, SQS, Kinesis, and other AWS services. One of its main features is the efficient management of latency in executions compared to other solutions. It does so with an optimized cold start system. However, it has a fifteen-minute execution limit per function, which can be a constraint for longer and more computationally intensive operations. In terms of cost, AWS Lambda follows a pay-per-use pricing model with a free tier that includes one million requests per month and four hundred thousand GB-seconds of execution. Thus, it is a convenient choice for workloads with intermittent or on-demand executions.

Google Cloud Functions stands out for its native integration with Google Cloud services, which makes it the ideal choice for those who already use tools such as BigQuery, Firestore, Firebase and Cloud Pub/Sub. Its execution model is event-based, which supports triggers through changes in Cloud Storage buckets, notifications on Pub/Sub, or HTTP requests. One of its main strengths is the higher maximum execution time compared to AWS Lambda, which can reach up to sixty minutes. This makes it a more suitable solution for workloads that require longer operations. However, compared to AWS Lambda, it suffers from a more pronounced cold start, especially for applications developed in languages like Java. Google Cloud Functions also adopts a consumption-based pricing model which offers two million free requests per month and is double that of AWS. This is an advantage for applications that require a greater quantity of executions.

Azure Functions is a serverless solution offered by Microsoft and is particularly suitable for those who already operate within the Azure ecosystem. Its strength lies in the integration with services such as Cosmos DB, Event Hub, Service Bus and IoT Hub, which make it an excellent choice for business applications and enterprise automation scenarios. Compared to the alternatives, Azure Functions offers the possibility of scaling automatically. It also offers greater flexibility in resource management with the Premium plan option, which allows you to overcome some limitations present in the Consumption Plan, such as the maximum execution time of five minutes. To mitigate the cold start problem, which is particularly evident in the consumption plan, Azure allows the use of instance provisioning to maintain pre-loaded and ready-to-use functions. From a cost point of view, it follows the same model based on execution time and number of invocations, while offering one million free requests per month, in line with AWS Lambda.

From a performance perspective, AWS Lambda stands out for its lower startup latency compared to Google Cloud Functions and Azure Functions. This makes it more suitable for applications that require rapid responses. However, Google Cloud Functions offers longer execution and is better suited to workloads that require greater duration over time, such as batch data processing or analysis on large datasets. Azure Functions, thanks to the Durable Functions option, is particularly useful for complex workflows and distributed process orchestrations where multiple functions must collaborate with each other while maintaining a state between executions. Scalability management also varies between the three solutions. AWS Lambda is able to scale quickly and completely automatically, while supporting a large number of concurrent requests with efficient resource management. Google Cloud Functions, while offering a similar scaling system, has a slightly slower response in the cold start phase that penalizes applications that require high reactivity. Azure Functions, on the other hand, offers greater control over scalability thanks to flexible execution plans that can help you adapt resources based on workloads.

Finally, choosing the most suitable serverless platform depends on the specific context and the tools you are already using. AWS Lambda remains the best choice for those who work with AWS services and need a highly scalable infrastructure with low latency. Google Cloud Functions is more advantageous for applications that use BigQuery, Pub/Sub and Firebase and offers a greater execution time and efficient management of long-running workloads. Azure Functions, on the other hand, adapts perfectly to enterprise environments and complex architectures due to its tight integration with Active Directory, IoT Hub, and enterprise automation tools. Regardless of the platform chosen, each of these solutions offers significant advantages for serverless computing, which allows you to develop scalable, efficient and cost-optimized applications in the cloud.

Serverless vs. Traditional Parallelization

The trade-off between serverless computing and traditional parallelization is one of the most important choices in modern application architecture. While both models aim to optimize processing and management of computational resources, their approaches and implementations differ significantly with advantages and limitations that make one or the other better suited for certain scenarios.

Serverless computing has introduced a new execution paradigm in which the code runs on infrastructure managed by the cloud provider, without the need to directly allocate or administer servers. In this model, developers can write functions that run in response to events without worrying about resource provisioning or scalability. Services such as AWS Lambda, Google Cloud Functions, and Azure Functions enable code to be executed reactively, while automatically scaling the number of instances based on demand. This approach is particularly beneficial for applications with variable or unpredictable workloads where dynamic resource allocation reduces waste and operational costs. Serverless is ideal for short, modular tasks such as real-time event processing, webhook management, file processing, and integration with other cloud services.

On the other hand, traditional parallelization is a more structured and manual approach, where applications are designed to exploit parallelism through server clusters, containers, or distributed architectures. Technologies such as Apache Spark, Kubernetes, MPI (Message Passing Interface), and OpenMP allow computationally intensive tasks to be split across multiple nodes, thus providing greater control over performance and resources used. This model is often preferred for applications that require massive data processing, scientific simulations, deep learning, and high-performance computing (HPC). Traditional parallelization offers significant advantages when fine-grained resource management is needed, such as in applications that run on-premises infrastructure or in cloud environments with advanced optimization requirements.

The most important aspects in choosing between serverless and traditional parallelization are scalability and resource management. Serverless is designed to automatically scale based on demand, while activating function instances only when needed. This eliminates the problem of underutilization of resources, but introduces limitations on the computational capabilities of each function. This makes it less suitable for intensive workloads or with long execution times. In contrast, traditional parallelization allows you to allocate specific resources and maintain persistent processes, while offering greater flexibility in controlling performance and long-term costs. However, this scalability is not always immediate and requires careful infrastructure planning. Another determining factor is the operational cost. The serverless model is based on a consumption approach where you only pay for the actual execution time of the functions. This eliminates the need to maintain active instances when they are not in use. This makes it very advantageous for applications with irregular or sporadic workloads. On the other hand, traditional parallelization architectures often allocate fixed costs for the resources regardless of their usage, which makes them more suitable for scenarios where the workload is constant and predictable. In environments such as AWS, Google Cloud, and Azure, it is possible to combine both approaches using compute clusters for the heaviest tasks and serverless functions to handle light and reactive operations.

From a performance perspective, serverless parallelization has some limitations, especially when it comes to the latency of starting functions (cold start). When a function has not been executed recently, it can suffer an initial delay due to the provisioning of the execution environment, which is less of an issue in traditional architectures where server instances remain up and running at all times. This makes traditional parallelization more suitable for tasks that require consistently low response times or long-running computations.

Another aspect to consider is the complexity of management and deployment. With the serverless model, the developer can focus exclusively on the application logic, while the cloud provider automatically manages the infrastructure, load balancing, and security. This approach greatly simplifies the development and deployment of distributed applications, especially in multi-cloud or hybrid environments. Traditional parallelization, on the other hand, requires more careful management of computational resources, networking, and communication between processes. Tools such as Kubernetes and Apache Spark offer solutions to orchestrate distributed workloads more efficiently, but require advanced skills for configuration and optimization.

In summary, the choice between serverless computing and traditional parallelization depends on the specific needs of the project and the type of workload. Serverless is ideal for modular, reactive applications with variable workloads, while traditional parallelization is better suited for high-performance scenarios, large-scale distributed processing, and advanced resource management. In many cases, a hybrid approach that combines both models can offer the best balance of scalability, efficiency, and cost, while leveraging the flexibility of serverless for dynamic tasks and the reliability of traditional parallelization for long-running operations.

Auto Scaling and Load Balancing on Cloud

In the context of distributed computing and parallelization, one of the key aspects that ensures high performance and reliability is the ability to dynamically adapt to changes. This is achieved through two key mechanisms: automatic scaling and load balancing. These elements work together to keep applications and services up and running efficiently, regardless of the workload.

Automatic scaling allows a cloud system to dynamically add or remove resources without the need for manual intervention. This process is especially important for applications with variable or unpredictable workloads, which optimizes resources based on actual demand. There are two main ways to scale: horizontally and vertically. Horizontal scaling (scale-out) involves adding new instances, containers, or compute nodes, while distributing the load across multiple resources and improving the overall reliability of the system. This approach is widely used in cloud-native and containerized systems such as Kubernetes where pods are created and destroyed as needed. Vertical scaling (scale-up), on the other hand, involves enhancing a single instance, while increasing its CPU, memory, or storage capabilities. While it can be useful in specific scenarios, it is generally less flexible and more expensive than horizontal scaling.

Major cloud platforms provide tools to automate scaling. AWS Auto Scaling, Google Cloud Autoscaler, and Azure Autoscale monitor metrics such as CPU utilization, latency, and throughput. They automatically scale the system to meet load requirements. For example, an application that processes data in parallel on AWS EC2 can use Auto Scaling to increase the number of instances during peak times and reduce them during idle periods, thereby optimizing performance for cost. Similarly, in a Kubernetes cluster, the Horizontal Pod Autoscaler (HPA) can dynamically increase the number of pods based on resource usage, while ensuring that each instance receives an appropriate amount of traffic.

Another key element to maintaining an efficient system is load balancing, which allows you to distribute traffic across multiple resources to avoid overloading individual nodes. Modern load balancers, such as AWS Elastic Load Balancer (ELB), Google Cloud Load Balancer, and Azure Load Balancer offer advanced capabilities to handle different types of traffic. HTTP/HTTPS-based load balancing distributes web requests based on HTTP headers, content, or routes, which is essential for large-scale scalable applications. Network-level load balancing, on the other hand, focuses on distributing TCP/UDP traffic and is useful for non-web services such as distributed databases or microservice communications. In containerized and Kubernetes-orchestrated systems, load balancing is natively integrated through the Kubernetes Service, which automatically assigns traffic to available pods to optimize resources.

These mechanisms are especially effective in scalable cloud architectures, where automatic scaling and load balancing work together. When the workload increases, the automatic scaling system launches new instances or containers to meet the demand. The load balancer automatically detects these new resources and redistributes traffic fairly, while avoiding overloading specific nodes. During periods of low activity, unnecessary instances are eliminated, thereby optimizing resource consumption and reducing costs. This process ensures not only optimal performance, but also resilience and high availability, which reduces the risk of downtime due to sudden overloads.

One of the main advantages of this combination is the ability to build highly available applications that can handle variable loads without degrading performance. Resources are dynamically allocated based on demand to avoid waste and optimize the cost-benefit ratio. However, implementing these systems correctly requires careful configuration of monitoring metrics, scaling thresholds, and load balancer rules. These aspects may require advanced skills. Another challenge is the cold start of new instances; if the system takes too long to start new resources in response to a traffic spike, there is a risk of temporary performance degradation. In the landscape of parallel computing and distributed load management, automatic scaling and load balancing are two essential elements for building modern and resilient cloud systems. Their implementation allows you to manage complex workloads with a flexible approach, while ensuring that resources are used efficiently and are not wasted.

In contexts with varying workloads such as in data processing, distributed machine learning, and microservice orchestration systems, combining these two approaches becomes essential. Thanks to the tools provided by the main cloud providers, companies can design scalable, efficient and resilient architectures, while adapting to business needs with maximum agility.

Kubernetes

Kubernetes is an open-source container orchestration platform designed to automate the deployment, scaling, and management of containerized applications. Originally developed by Google and now maintained by the Cloud Native Computing Foundation, Kubernetes has revolutionized the way distributed workloads are managed in the cloud and has become the de facto standard for container orchestration. Its architecture allows you to distribute and coordinate containers on a cluster of machines, while automatically balancing the load and ensuring that services remain available and operational even in the event of failures. Thanks to these features, Kubernetes has established itself as a powerful and flexible solution for managing scalable applications, both on public clouds and in on-premises environments. In the context of parallelization and distributed computing, Kubernetes offers a structured alternative to the serverless model and allows to user to gain greater control over resources and advanced management of parallelism. Unlike serverless platforms such as AWS Lambda or Google Cloud Functions which rely on fully managed, pay-per-use execution, Kubernetes lets you deploy intensive workloads across custom clusters with dynamic scalability that can be configured and optimized based on the specific needs of the application. This makes it an ideal solution for distributed computing scenarios, large data processing, and ML workflows where autonomous management of computational resources is key to optimizing performance.

One of the strengths of Kubernetes is its ability to manage clusters of distributed nodes, while automatically assigning workloads across different pods which represent the operational units of Kubernetes. Thanks to the Horizontal Pod Autoscaler (HPA), the platform constantly monitors resources and dynamically scales the number of pods based on demand, thus ensuring efficient use of resources and a reduction in operating costs. This makes it particularly effective for ETL pipelines, batch processing, and real-time data flows, where the workload can vary significantly over time.

To facilitate development and testing, Kubernetes offers tools such as Minikube, which allows you to run a Kubernetes cluster on a single local machine. This is particularly useful for simulating data processing pipelines or distributed applications before deploying them on cloud infrastructures. The concept of Deployment in Kubernetes plays a key role in managing the lifecycle of applications; through a YAML file, you can define the desired state of an application, while specifying the number of replicas, the container image to use, and update strategies to minimize downtime.

Kubernetes' integration with data processing and machine learning tools further amplifies its potential. Frameworks such as Apache Spark on Kubernetes and Dask enable computationally intensive workloads to be deployed at scale, while leveraging the power of the cluster to execute parallel tasks more efficiently. For example, in an architecture for processing large datasets, Kubernetes can orchestrate a system in which the dataset is split into multiple independent jobs, each processed by a pod. Intermediate results can be saved to shared storage systems such as Amazon S3, Google Cloud Storage, or Azure Blob Storage before they are aggregated into a final result.

From an operational perspective, Kubernetes simplifies the management of distributed applications thanks to its automation of operations, which reduces the workload of developers. The platform is also resilient by nature and automatically detects any failures in the pods. It also restarts them without manual intervention. Its portability makes it particularly advantageous for multi-cloud architectures like AWS, Google Cloud, Microsoft Azure, and other on-premises environments, while ensuring that configurations are consistent across different infrastructures.

Compared to the serverless model, Kubernetes offers greater control over resources and advanced scalability optimization, but also requires more careful management of the infrastructure. While a serverless model is ideal for reactive, modular, and consumption-based tasks, Kubernetes is a better solution for complex and high-performance applications with advanced customization requirements. However, in many scenarios, the hybrid approach is ideal. Here, Kubernetes is used to orchestrate distributed tasks at scale, while serverless platforms manage lighter and asynchronous operations, thus maximizing efficiency and resource optimization.

Real-World Use Cases of Cloud Data Processing

In the modern cloud computing world, data processing has become more scalable, efficient, and cost-effective, thanks to the combination of elasticity, distributed computational power, and advanced tools. The cloud approach allows you to tackle computationally intensive tasks in a fully managed manner, while leveraging both serverless architectures and orchestrated platforms such as Kubernetes. Real-world applications of these tools span across multiple domains, from analyzing large amounts of data to inferencing machine learning models in real time. This demonstrate how cloud-native parallelization can be effectively applied to meet diverse needs.

One of the most popular use cases is large-scale log analytics, which is crucial for monitoring modern applications. Using services such as AWS Lambda with Amazon S3 allows you to build fully scalable pipelines, where log files are analyzed immediately after being uploaded to a storage bucket. This approach allows you to extract actionable information in real time, such as errors, warnings, and operational statistics, while optimizing the management of distributed applications. The results can be saved in NoSQL databases like Amazon DynamoDB or accessed through visualization tools like Amazon QuickSight, which provides an efficient and automated way to monitor performance. Another common application of cloud computing is image processing, which is essential in industries like e-commerce and social media. Services like Google Cloud Functions and Google Cloud Storage allow you to create serverless pipelines that process images uploaded by users in real time while applying changes like resizing, compression, or filtering. Each image uploaded to a storage bucket automatically triggers a function that performs the requested operation and saves the processed file in a dedicated area. This reduces the load on servers and ensures highly scalable processing.

The cloud is also extremely effective for real-time ML applications, thanks to its ability to distribute inference models on serverless infrastructures. A practical example is the use of AWS Lambda for image recognition. AWS Lambda is a pre-trained model saved on Amazon S3 and is loaded every time a new image is loaded. It runs the inference and stores the result in a database. This approach allows to reduce operational costs, since the computation resources are used only when needed, thus avoiding waste.

For more complex tasks, such as the transformation of large datasets, containerized platforms offer a more suitable solution than the serverless model. Using Kubernetes with frameworks such as Apache Spark or Dask distributes the workload on multiple nodes, while orchestrating the processing efficiently. A dataset can be divided into blocks and can be assigned to different Kubernetes pods, each of which processes a part of the data in parallel. The intermediate results are then aggregated and saved on shared storage such as Google Cloud Storage or Amazon S3, thereby ensuring optimal scalability for the entire process.

Integration with Big Data and advanced analytics services represents a further advantage of cloud data processing. Tools such as Google BigQuery, AWS Redshift, and Azure Synapse Analytics allow you to manage huge volumes of data and perform complex analyses while maintaining excellent performance. A widespread use case is IoT data monitoring, where logs generated by millions of sensors are collected and analyzed in real time to identify anomalies or generate predictions based on AI models.

All these scenarios demonstrate how cloud data processing can tackle a wide range of computational problems in a scalable and efficient way, while ensuring high performance and without complex infrastructure management. Integration with serverless computing and containerized orchestration tools offers an unprecedented level of flexibility, which allows developers and companies of all sizes to optimize their workloads. Due to Python's wide availability of libraries for data science, ML, and automation, these solutions are becoming more accessible and powerful. As a result, they have opened up new possibilities in the field of distributed processing and cloud-native parallelization.

Conclusion

In this chapter, we have examined the main parallelization models available in the cloud, while comparing serverless solutions, characterized by automatic scalability and completely abstract management with traditional models that offer greater control and flexibility for intensive and long-running tasks. Through practical examples such as the use of AWS Lambda, Google Cloud Functions, Azure Functions, and orchestration on Kubernetes, we have demonstrated how these technologies can be integrated into Python applications to address real-world challenges like dataset transformation and ML model inference. In the next chapter, we will discover the world of **FPGAs** and their use in new high-performance technologies.

CHAPTER 15
Parallel Programming with FPGAs

Introduction

In the era of high-performance computing, the demand for hardware solutions that offer energy efficiency, low latency, and extreme parallelism is constantly growing. **Field-Programmable Gate Arrays (FPGAs)** have emerged as a key solution to address these needs, thanks to their unique ability to combine flexibility and customized performance. Unlike CPUs and GPUs, which offer fixed architectures designed for general-purpose applications, FPGAs can be programmed to implement specific hardware circuits and are optimized for particular applications.

This chapter delves into the world of FPGAs, and examines their architecture as well as advanced use cases. We will further learn how these technologies excel in areas such as **Artificial Intelligence (AI)**, **cryptography**, and **physics simulations**, while being advantageous in terms of performance and energy consumption. Through a comparison with CPUs and GPUs, we will understand when and why can FPGAs be the best choice for certain applications. Furthermore, the most modern tools for programming FPGAs will be introduced, with a special focus on high-level languages such as Python, which has made this technology accessible even to novice software developers.

The chapter is full of practical and detailed examples which show how to exploit FPGAs to solve complex problems like parallel computing and real-time data processing. Through these examples, the reader will be able to understand the promising potential of FPGAs and how to integrate them into workflows that combine specialized hardware with existing technologies.

Structure

This chapter will address the following topics:

- Introduction to FPGAs (Field-Programmable Gate Arrays)
- FPGA Architecture
- PyOpenCL and PyCUDA
- AMD Vitis
- FPGA Simulation Libraries: MyHDL
- FPGA vs. GPU: Advantages and Limitations of Using FPGAs
- Advanced Applications in Artificial Intelligence, Cryptography, and Physical Simulations

Introduction to FPGAs (Field-Programmable Gate Arrays)

Field-Programmable Gate Arrays, also known as FPGAs, are semiconductor devices that can be configured by the end user to perform specific tasks. Unlike general-purpose chips, such as CPUs and GPUs, FPGAs offer extraordinary flexibility as they allow you to define custom digital circuits without having to build a dedicated chip. This ability is made possible by their architecture, which is based on a combination of programmable logic blocks and configurable interconnects. This structure allows the device to be adapted for a wide range of applications like scientific computing to cryptography and AI.

A basic FPGA architecture diagram is shown in *Figure* 15.1:

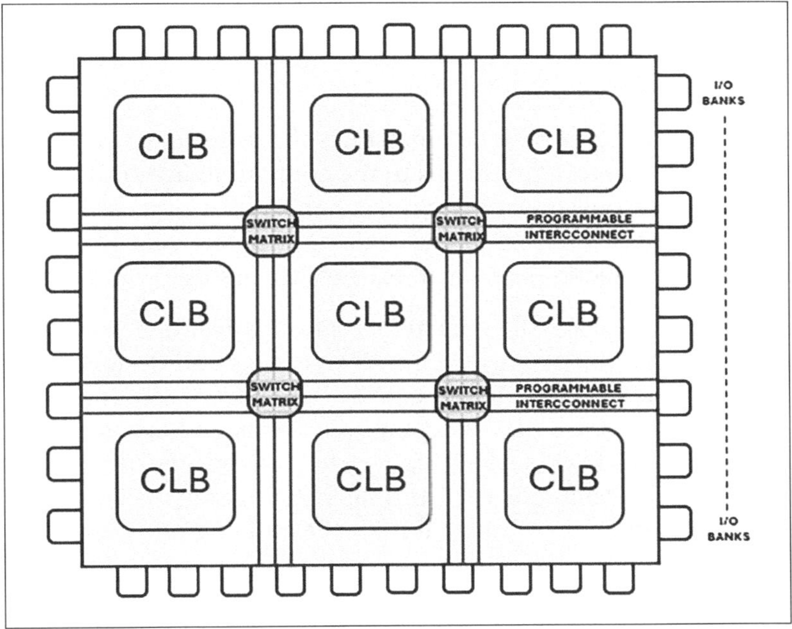

***Figure* 15.1**: *Basic Schema of an FPGA*

The architecture of an FPGA is organized as a grid, where the main components, called the **Configurable Logic Blocks (CLB)**, are regularly distributed and connected to each other via a network. At the corners and edges are the I/O blocks that offer access to the outside world. CLBs are the basic building blocks of FPGAs. Each CLB usually contains multiple configurable logic elements like lookup tables (LUTs), flip-flops, and multiplexers. These blocks perform the fundamental logic operations of the digital circuit configured by the user.

CLBs can communicate with each other via programmable interconnections. The user, through specific configuration software, can program how these lines connect the CLBs to each other and create paths for the required operations. This is done via Programmable Interconnect Points (PIPs) enclosed within matrix switches. The I/O Blocks at the edges of the FPGA facilitate the connection between the FPGA chip and the outside world. These elements are configurable and allow the management of input and output signals with different voltage and speed standards.

Inside the device, several types of memory like distributed RAM and dedicated Block RAM (BRAM) are available for storing temporary data or lookup tables.

A crucial aspect for many advanced applications is represented by **DSP (Digital Signal Processing) blocks**. These are separate from CLBs and are specifically designed for complex mathematical operations like multiplications and accumulations. DSP blocks are important for signal processing and artificial intelligence applications, where both speedy and precise calculations are essential.

Thanks to their peculiar architecture, FPGAs have some distinctive characteristics compared to GPUs and CPUs, among which the most important is reconfigurability. The term refers to the ability to be programmed and reprogrammed multiple times after production. This aspect allows developers to adapt the hardware design to requirements that may evolve over time, while avoiding the high costs associated with the production of custom chips like **ASICs (Application-Specific Integrated Circuit)**. However, apart from offering flexibility, reconfigurability also comes with the possibility of optimizing the device for specific tasks, while eliminating bottlenecks and improving overall efficiency.

Another element that makes FPGAs particularly interesting is their ability to exploit massively parallel processing. Unlike CPUs, which execute instructions sequentially, and GPUs, which process large amounts of data in parallel, FPGAs can implement thousands of logical operations simultaneously. This is possible due to the dedicated logic executed by every logical block, which brings about a degree of parallelism that is difficult to achieve with other architectures.

FPGAs also excel at optimal resource scheduling, which allows users to customize computation and efficiently manage data flow and storage. Thanks to the configurability of their interconnections, they can be optimized to minimize power consumption or maximize processing speed, while adapting to the needs of the application. This level of customization is particularly useful in scenarios where power consumption is a critical factor, such as in IoT devices or edge computing applications.

The flexibility offered by FPGAs makes them ideal for many applications. For example, they are widely used in rapid prototyping as they allow developers to test ideas and designs before moving to large-scale production. Their ability to adapt to ever-changing hardware requirements also makes them a favored option in dynamic industries like telecommunications and automotive. In scenarios where real-time processing is critical, FPGAs offer highly customized performance that overcomes the limitations of general-purpose architectures. The ability to upgrade device design over time extends the device's longevity, while reducing overall maintenance and upgrade costs.

However, despite their many advantages, FPGAs present some significant challenges. One of the main ones is the complexity of the design, which requires specific skills and a good knowledge of hardware architectures. Additionally, the initial cost of an FPGA-based design can be high for high-volume applications. Although highly customizable, FPGAs cannot achieve the same performance as an ASIC, which is specifically designed for an application. This limitation can be particularly relevant in contexts where computational density is a top priority.

Programming FPGAs with Python

Traditionally, programming FPGAs required the use of hardware description languages such as Verilog or VHDL. These languages are designed to describe the low-level behavior of the circuit and require a deep understanding of hardware architectures. This approach, although very powerful, is complex and often unsuitable for developers with a background in software rather than hardware.

In recent years, thanks to the evolution of programming tools, it has become possible to configure and use FPGAs through high-level languages such as Python, which has greatly simplified the process. In fact, there are a number of libraries that allow you to interface with FPGAs and configure them with this language. It should be immediately clarified that a general approach for all FPGAs with Python is very premature, but each of the libraries currently available is specific to a particular set of FPGA models used. It is therefore good practice to document the FPGA model to be used and the Python libraries available (if any).

Despite this, the choice of using Python to program FPGAs offers the following advantages over other traditional approaches:

- **Ease of use:** Python is known for its simplicity and readability, which reduces the learning curve compared to traditional HDLs.
- **Rapid Prototyping:** Developers can test ideas quickly without having to implement complex circuits.

- **Integration with existing workflows:** Python integrates seamlessly with data analytics, machine learning, and automation tools. This makes FPGAs more accessible to software developers.
- **Reduced time to market:** Using predefined libraries and high-level tools allows you to accelerate the development cycle.

PyOpenCL and PyCUDA

PyOpenCL and **PyCUDA** are Python libraries that we have already learned about in the chapter dedicated to GPUs. In fact, they are interfaces for OpenCL and CUDA, which are two frameworks for parallel programming on heterogeneous hardware, including CPUs, GPUs, and in some cases FPGAs.

PyOpenCL allows you to write OpenCL kernels in C language and manage them directly from Python. Through this library it is possible to perform operations like allocating shared memory between the device (for example an FPGA) and the host. As with GPUs, we can define kernels for custom processing, compile them, and run them directly on the hardware. PyOpenCL also manages the interaction between the host and the various connected devices with a focus on heterogeneous platforms (FPGAs, CPUs, and GPUs). However OpenCL, support on FPGAs is not universal; only certain vendors such as Intel (Altera) and Xilinx/AMD provide OpenCL toolchains for specific FPGA families. Therefore, it is necessary to verify whether the target FPGA supports the required OpenCL version or vendor-specific extensions.

PyCUDA is a specific interface for CUDA-enabled devices like NVIDIA GPUs. Although not all FPGAs support CUDA, some advanced architectures offer compatibility for CUDA-like kernels, making PyCUDA a possible option.

PYNQ: Python Productivity for Zynq

PYNQ is a framework developed by Xilinx that simplifies the use of FPGAs through Python. It is designed specifically for Xilinx Zynq family of FPGA boards, which combine an FPGA with an embedded ARM processor.

PYNQ allows you to interact with the FPGA using Jupyter Notebook, providing an interactive and easy-to-use environment. It provides pre-built libraries for common applications such as machine learning, image processing, and signal processing. It supports importing and using pre-compiled bit streams, which can be loaded into the FPGA to perform specific operations without having to write HDL code. It integrates Python APIs for data management and communication between the ARM and the FPGA.

AMD Vitis

Vitis is Xilinx's unified software/hardware development platform, designed by AMD to simplify FPGA programming, including the use of Python. One of the most interesting components is Vitis AI, which integrates machine learning tools and supports acceleration on FPGAs.

Vitis AI allows you to optimize and convert pre-trained machine learning models (such as TensorFlow or PyTorch) to run on FPGAs. Use Python APIs to manage AI models on accelerated hardware. Easily integrate deep learning applications into your software workflow. A typical use case would be to accelerate an image classification model on an FPGA using Python.

For those interested in learning more about the topic, visit the official page (`https://www.amd.com/en/products/software/adaptive-socs-and-fpgas/vitis.html`) to learn more.

FPGA Simulation Libraries: MyHDL

Python libraries like **MyHDL** allow you to simulate and verify FPGA designs directly in Python, while making it simple to test hardware designs.

Through MyHDL, you can design reconfigurable digital circuits based on hardware description languages (HDL). You can also use this library to write hardware logic in Python and then simulate it directly, without requiring a physical FPGA. After testing your design, you can convert it to VHDL or Verilog for implementation on real FPGAs.

As a practical example, we can simulate a simple 4-bit counter. Counters are essential components in digital systems, used to count events, generate timing signals, and implement control states. Our goal is to write a synchronous counter with synchronous reset, which increments at each rising edge of the clock and resets when it reaches the maximum value (15 in this case).

You can create a dedicated virtual environment to work with **`myhdl`** and then install the library using **`pip`**:

```
pip install myhdl
```

Let us now implement a code that simulates a 4-bit counter:

```
from myhdl import block, always_seq, always, Signal, ResetSignal, intbv,
delay, instance, Simulation, StopSimulation

@block
def counter(clk, reset, count):
    """ 4-bit counter with synchronous reset """

    @always_seq(clk.posedge, reset=reset)
    def logic():
        if reset:
            count.next = 0
        else:
            count.next = (count + 1) % 16  # Ensures that the value remains 4
bits
    return logic

@block
def testbench():
    """ Testbench to simulate the counter """

    # Signal Definition
    clk = Signal(0)
    reset = ResetSignal(0, active=1, isasync=False)
    count = Signal(intbv(0, min=0, max=16))  # Range corretto (0-15)

    # Instantiate the counter
    dut = counter(clk, reset, count)

    @always(delay(5))  # Clock with period of 10 time units
    def clk_gen():
        clk.next = not clk

    @instance
    def stim():
        print("Start simulation")
```

```
            # Apply reset
            reset.next = 1
            yield clk.posedge
            reset.next = 0

            # Simulation for 20 clock cycles
            for i in range(20):
                yield clk.posedge
                print(f"Clock cycle {i+1}, Count: {int(count)}")

            raise StopSimulation

        return dut, clk_gen, stim

    # Creating and starting the simulation
    tb = testbench()
    tb.run_sim()
```

In this implementation, the code is divided into two blocks, which can be recognized by the **@block** decorator. The first block defines the counter via the counter function where clk is the clock signal that marks the time and reset is a **ResetSignal**, which forces count to zero when active. **count** is a variable **intbv(0)[4:]** that represents a 4-bit binary value. The **always_seq** function is activated at each rising edge of clk and updates count accordingly.

The second block is defined in the testbench function that defines the signals and simulates the activation of the clock, while observing the behavior of the counter. The clock is generated with a separate function **clk_gen**, which alternates the signal every 5 time units. The reset is applied at the beginning to initialize the counter. With this implementation, the behavior of the circuit is simulated for 20 clock cycles, where the value of count is printed at each cycle.

If we run the code, we get the following output:

```
Start simulation
Clock cycle 1, Count: 0
Clock cycle 2, Count: 1
Clock cycle 3, Count: 2
Clock cycle 4, Count: 3
Clock cycle 5, Count: 4
Clock cycle 6, Count: 5
Clock cycle 7, Count: 6
Clock cycle 8, Count: 7
Clock cycle 9, Count: 8
Clock cycle 10, Count: 9
Clock cycle 11, Count: 10
Clock cycle 12, Count: 11
Clock cycle 13, Count: 12
Clock cycle 14, Count: 13
Clock cycle 15, Count: 14
Clock cycle 16, Count: 15
Clock cycle 17, Count: 0
Clock cycle 18, Count: 1
Clock cycle 19, Count: 2
Clock cycle 20, Count: 3
```

You can see that the counter increments at each clock cycle and returns to 0 after clock cycle 16 (4-bit behavior). The initial reset forces the count to zero at startup.

Parallel Vector Adder with MyHDL

An interesting idea is to implement parallel vector adders, a multiplier array or a digital filter (FIR), which exploit the intrinsic parallelism of FPGAs. The code implements and simulates a parallel adder that calculates the sum of two vectors of numbers simultaneously in an FPGA. Parallel operations are essential in embedded and digital systems to improve efficiency in numerical calculations. In this example, we have implemented a hardware module that takes two vectors of numbers as input and calculates their sum in parallel. Each element of the two vectors is processed simultaneously on multiple hardware units, thereby exploiting the parallelism of the FPGA.

The goal will be to take two vectors of 4 8-bit numbers, add each pair of numbers in parallel, and return the result in an output vector.

```
from myhdl import block, always, always_seq, Signal, ResetSignal, intbv,
delay, instance, Simulation, StopSimulation, concat

@block
def vector_adder(clk, reset, a, b, result):
    """
    4-element parallel adder (8 bits each).
    Performs calculations at each clock cycle.
    """

    @always_seq(clk.posedge, reset=reset)
    def logic():
        for i in range(len(a)):
            result[i].next = a[i] + b[i]  # Parallel sum of elements

    return logic


@block
def testbench():
    """ Testbench for parallel adder """

    # Signal Definition
    clk = Signal(0)
    reset = ResetSignal(0, active=1, isasync=False)

    N = 4  # Number of elements in the vector
    bit_width = 8  # Width in bits of each element

    a = [Signal(intbv(0)[bit_width:]) for _ in range(N)]
    b = [Signal(intbv(0)[bit_width:]) for _ in range(N)]
    result = [Signal(intbv(0)[bit_width+1:]) for _ in range(N)]  # +1 bit per
overflow

    # Instantiate the module
    dut = vector_adder(clk, reset, a, b, result)

    @always(delay(5))  # Clock with period of 10 time units
    def clk_gen():
        clk.next = not clk

    @instance
    def stim():
        print("Start simulation")
```

```
        # Initial reset
        reset.next = 1
        yield clk.posedge
        reset.next = 0

        # Assign values to vectors and simulate
        test_vectors = [
            ([10, 20, 30, 40], [1, 2, 3, 4]),
            ([5, 15, 25, 35], [10, 20, 30, 40]),
            ([255, 128, 64, 32], [1, 2, 3, 4])  # Test di overflow
        ]

        for cycle, (vec_a, vec_b) in enumerate(test_vectors):
            for i in range(N):
                a[i].next = vec_a[i]
                b[i].next = vec_b[i]

            yield clk.posedge
            print(f"Cycle {cycle+1}: A={vec_a}, B={vec_b}, Result={[int(r) for
r in result]}")

        raise StopSimulation

    return dut, clk_gen, stim

# Creating and starting the simulation
tb = testbench()
tb.run_sim()
```

Again, to implement this system, we need two main components: the hardware module (**vector_adder**), which performs the parallel addition, and the testbench (**testbench**), which generates the clock signal, assigns values to the vectors, and verifies the circuit's operation.

The heart of the implementation is the adder module, which performs the parallel addition of the elements of the two vectors. Each operation occurs in a single clock cycle, thus allowing for simultaneous and fast processing. The module receives a clock signal (**clk**) and a reset signal (**reset**). The inputs are two vectors a and b, containing 8-bit numbers. The result is stored in the output vector result. As the addition operation is performed in parallel, each element of a is added to the corresponding element of b in the same clock cycle.

The second block is the testbench, which is necessary to verify the correct operation of the circuit, that is, a test environment that generates the input signals and checks the circuit's behavior. In the testbench, we have three fundamental components: a clock generator, which alternates the value of **clk** at regular intervals; an input stimulus, which assigns different values to the vectors during the simulation; and a monitoring process, which prints the results of the sum to verify the correctness of the circuit. After three test cycles, the simulation ends with **StopSimulation**.

Running the code gives the following result:

```
Start simulation
Cycle 1: A=[10, 20, 30, 40], B=[1, 2, 3, 4], Result=[0, 0, 0, 0]
Cycle 2: A=[5, 15, 25, 35], B=[10, 20, 30, 40], Result=[11, 22, 33, 44]
Cycle 3: A=[255, 128, 64, 32], B=[1, 2, 3, 4], Result=[15, 35, 55, 75]
```

The circuit correctly performs the parallel addition of the elements of the vectors. The third test shows an overflow: the first value 255 + 1 becomes 0, since the numbers are limited to 8 bits.

This example demonstrates the power of parallel computing on FPGAs, which is essential for high-performance applications such as signal processing and artificial intelligence.

PyOpenCL Code Example

This example shows how to use PyOpenCL to run an OpenCL kernel. Even if you do not have an FPGA, you can run the code on a CPU or GPU to understand how the programming paradigm works.

First install the PyOpenCL library through the pip:

```
pip install pyopencl
```

Then write the following code:

```
import pyopencl as cl
import numpy as np

# Create an OpenCL context and command queue for the FPGA
platform = cl.get_platforms()[0]  # Select the OpenCL platform
device = platform.get_devices()[0]  # Select the FPGA or CPU device
context = cl.Context([device])
queue = cl.CommandQueue(context)

# Create memory buffers
data = np.array([1, 2, 3, 4, 5], dtype=np.float32)
data_buffer = cl.Buffer(context, cl.mem_flags.READ_ONLY | cl.mem_flags.COPY_HOST_
PTR, hostbuf=data)
result_buffer = cl.Buffer(context, cl.mem_flags.WRITE_ONLY, data.nbytes)
# Output buffer

# Define an OpenCL kernel
kernel_code = """
__kernel void square(__global float* input, __global float* output) {
    int i = get_global_id(0);
    output[i] = input[i] * input[i];  // Write the result to the output buffer
}
"""
program = cl.Program(context, kernel_code).build()

# Execute the kernel on the FPGA
kernel = program.square  # Get the kernel
kernel.set_args(data_buffer, result_buffer)  # Set kernel arguments

# Run the kernel with a workgroup size equal to the length of the data
cl.enqueue_nd_range_kernel(queue, kernel, data.shape, None)

# Synchronize the queue to avoid concurrency issues
queue.finish()

# Read the result
result = np.empty_like(data)
cl.enqueue_copy(queue, result, result_buffer)

print("Result:", result)
```

Eseguendo si ottiene il seguente risultato:

```
Result: [ 1.  4.  9. 16. 25.]
```

This code uses PyOpenCL to write a simple kernel that calculates the square of an array of numbers.

In our case, this is a simulation that runs on our computer. Currently, the code selects the first available device, which could be a CPU or GPU. To use an FPGA, you must explicitly select the correct device. The code we wrote uses PyOpenCL to run an OpenCL kernel on a compatible device. However, it will only work on an FPGA if the hardware and FPGA-specific OpenCL drivers are properly configured. Also, for the code to work on an FPGA, you must verify:

- **Supported Hardware:** Your FPGA must support OpenCL. Some manufacturers such as Intel (Altera), Xilinx, and AMD (Xilinx Vitis) provide OpenCL support for specific FPGAs.
- **OpenCL Driver for FPGA:** You need to install the specific OpenCL runtime for your FPGA. Intel FPGA requires the Intel FPGA SDK for OpenCL, while Xilinx FPGA requires the Xilinx Vitis OpenCL.
- **Compiling OpenCL kernel for FPGAs:** Unlike GPUs and CPUs, FPGAs do not support JIT (just-in-time) compilation. The OpenCL kernel must be compiled in advance for the target FPGA. Intel devices generate **`.aocx`** binaries, while Xilinx/AMD devices use **`.xclbin`** files.

When running on CPU or GPU, you can call **`.build()`** directly in PyOpenCL to compile the kernel at runtime. On FPGAs, instead, you need to load the precompiled binary, such as the following:

```
program = cl.Program(context, open("kernel.aocx",
             "rb").read()).create_program_with_binary( context, [device])
```

This ensures that the FPGA uses the vendor-compiled binary, rather than attempting JIT compilation.

A Practical Example on Using FPGAs with PyOpenCL

A practical example that illustrates a typical application of FPGAs: the acceleration of the matrix-vector product calculation, a fundamental operation in many applications such as artificial intelligence (neural networks) or physical simulation. The matrix-vector product example is not just an academic exercise, but represents a fundamental use case in applications that require high computational performance. FPGAs (Field Programmable Gate Arrays) excel in this type of operations thanks to their parallel architecture and the ability to optimize the data flow for repetitive calculations.

This example uses PyOpenCL, which can be run on FPGA or emulated on a GPU/CPU. It is demonstrated as follows:

```
import pyopencl as cl
import numpy as np

# Step 1: Create OpenCL context and command queue for FPGA
platform = cl.get_platforms()[0]
device = platform.get_devices()[0]
context = cl.Context([device])
queue = cl.CommandQueue(context)

# Step 2: Define matrix and vector
matrix = np.array([[1, 2, 3], [4, 5, 6], [7, 8, 9]], dtype=np.float32)
vector = np.array([1, 2, 3], dtype=np.float32)

# Step 3: Create memory buffers
matrix_buffer = cl.Buffer(context, cl.mem_flags.READ_ONLY | cl.mem_flags.COPY_
HOST_PTR, hostbuf=matrix)
vector_buffer = cl.Buffer(context, cl.mem_flags.READ_ONLY | cl.mem_flags.COPY_
HOST_PTR, hostbuf=vector)
```

```
result_buffer = cl.Buffer(context, cl.mem_flags.WRITE_ONLY, vector.nbytes)

# Step 4: Define optimized OpenCL kernel
kernel_code = """
__kernel void mat_vec_mult(__global const float* matrix,
                           __global const float* vector,
                           __global float* result,
                           const int N) {
    int row = get_global_id(0);
    float sum = 0;

// Note: #pragma unroll is supported by Intel FPGA SDK for OpenCL,
// but it is not guaranteed to be portable across all compilers.
// For example, Xilinx Vitis may require #pragma unroll N
// or vendor-specific directives.
    #pragma unroll  // Optimize loop unrolling for FPGA
    for (int col = 0; col < N; col++) {
        sum += matrix[row * N + col] * vector[col];
    }

    result[row] = sum;
}
"""

# Step 5: Compile OpenCL kernel
program = cl.Program(context, kernel_code).build()

# Step 6: Execute the kernel
matrix_size = np.int32(matrix.shape[0])
program.mat_vec_mult(queue, (matrix_size,), None, matrix_buffer, vector_buffer,
result_buffer, matrix_size)

# Ensure completion before reading results
queue.finish()

# Step 7: Read and print results
result = np.empty_like(vector)
cl.enqueue_copy(queue, result, result_buffer)
queue.finish()  # Ensure all operations are done

print("Optimized Matrix-Vector Multiplication Result:", result)
```

The code is composed of two fundamental parts: managing the OpenCL environment in Python and defining the OpenCL kernel, which is the program executed directly on the FPGA. The first part deals with the configuration of the computing environment, data transfer and memory management; the second implements the actual calculation, while exploiting the parallelism offered by the FPGA architecture.

At the beginning of the code, the OpenCL environment is initialized, which is necessary to execute the kernel on the FPGA. We begin by identifying the OpenCL platform available in the system and selecting the first compatible device, which can be a CPU, a GPU or, as it is in our case, an FPGA. Once the device has been identified, an OpenCL context is created, which represents the environment in which the calculations will be executed, and a command queue, which will manage the flow of operations between the processor and the FPGA.

Next, the code defines the input data, which is a 3x3 matrix and a vector of size 3. Both are represented as NumPy arrays of type float32. This data is transferred to the FPGA through the allocation of memory buffers, which allow data to be sent from the processor to the FPGA and vice versa. In particular, the matrix and the vector are stored in read-only buffers (**cl.mem_flags.READ_ONLY**), while the result will be written to a write-only buffer (**cl.mem_flags.WRITE_ONLY**).

At this point, the OpenCL kernel is defined, which is the program that will be executed directly on the FPGA. The kernel is written in C with OpenCL extensions and implements the calculation of the matrix-vector product in a highly parallel manner. Inside the kernel, the index of the current row of the matrix to be processed is determined and an accumulator is initialized (**sum = 0**). Next, a for loop iterates through the columns of the matrix, multiplying the corresponding element of the row by the element of the vector and adding the result. Once the sum is complete for that row, the value is stored in the output buffer.

The kernel is then compiled and loaded onto the FPGA using **cl.Program(context, kernel_code).build(),** thus allowing the device to perform the computation. To launch the kernel, the **program.mat_vec_mult()** function is called to specify the number of work-items or the number of parallel operations that need to be performed. In this case, the number of work-items is equal to the number of rows in the matrix, which allows the FPGA to process each row at the same time.

After the kernel is executed, **queue.finish()** is used to ensure that all operations are completed before reading the results. The output buffer containing the result is copied from the FPGA memory to the processor memory using **cl.enqueue_copy(queue, result, result_buffer)**. Finally, the code prints the result vector, which is the product of the matrix and the input vector.

Running the preceding code will thus give the following result:

```
Optimized Matrix-Vector Multiplication Result: [14. 32. 50.]
```

The example of matrix-vector product on FPGAs is a concrete example of hardware acceleration for intensive mathematical operations. This type of computation is essential in many advanced applications, including AI, physics simulations, digital signal processing, and computational finance. The reason why FPGAs are particularly effective for this operation is their parallel architecture, which allows multiple elements of the vector to be processed simultaneously, optimize the data flow, and significantly reducing computation times compared to traditional CPUs.

In AI, matrix-vector product is the basis of the operation of artificial neural networks, used in deep learning for image processing, speech recognition, and many other applications. In these models, matrix and vector multiplications are performed on millions of parameters during the training and inference process. FPGAs, due to their hardware pipeline capacity, perform these calculations with much lower latency than CPUs. They also are less power-intensive than GPUs and are therefore ideal for real-time inference and edge computing systems.

Matrix and vector multiplication are key operations in physics simulations and computational engineering. Complex mathematical models, such as those used in computational fluid dynamics or finite element analysis, rely on systems of linear equations that must be solved repeatedly. FPGAs can accelerate these calculations by distributing the computational load across multiple hardware units, thereby improving the scalability of simulations without the typical CPU overhead.

Another area where this operation has a significant impact is Digital Signal Processing (DSP). In radar systems, communications devices, and audio processors, digital filtering and Fourier transforms require matrix and vector multiplication to process large amounts of data in real time. Here, the ability to configure the FPGA architecture to handle high-speed data streams in parallel enables superior performance compared to software solutions.

Even in the world of computational finance, the matrix-vector product finds application in risk modeling and financial option valuation, where numerous matrix calculations are performed on real-time data. In high-frequency trading systems, processing speed is essential, and FPGAs are used precisely to perform these operations in extremely short times, which gives it a competitive advantage over CPUs and GPUs.

What makes this example really interesting is how it demonstrates the advantage of FPGAs in parallel computing. Unlike CPUs, which must process data sequentially, and GPUs, which require batch processing, FPGAs execute each row of the matrix in parallel, thereby reducing execution times and improving efficiency. Furthermore, thanks to direct memory management and the absence of an operating system that introduces latency, FPGAs guarantee optimal performance in critical contexts where latency must be minimized.

In conclusion, this example is not just a simple programming exercise with OpenCL, but an illustration of how a common operation can be radically optimized via the FPGA architecture. It clearly shows how FPGAs are able to accelerate fundamental operations in computationally intensive fields and thus are ideal for applications that require high performance, low power consumption, and reduced processing times..

FPGA vs. GPU: Advantages and Limitations of Using FPGAs

In recent years, the debate between FPGAs and GPUs has intensified, especially in the context of high-performance computing and real-time data processing. Both technologies have peculiar characteristics that make them more or less suitable for specific usage scenarios. Let us analyze the main advantages and limitations of FPGAs, while comparing them with GPUs:

- Extremely Low Latency
- Energy Efficiency
- Adaptability

One of the main strengths of FPGAs is their extremely low latency. Due to the possibility of implementing custom circuits, these solutions enable real-time processing with minimal delay. Unlike GPUs and CPUs, which execute operations via software on a predefined architecture, FPGAs allow you to configure the hardware specifically for a given application. This eliminates software-related bottlenecks and significantly improves system responsiveness.

Another key aspect is energy efficiency. When used for specific workloads like matrix-vector product calculations, FPGAs offer a higher performance-per-watt ratio than GPUs. This is due to the fact that, in FPGAs, the processing flow is optimized directly at the hardware level and does not require the user to execute software instructions that introduce energy overhead. This characteristic makes them particularly suitable for embedded applications, IoT devices and data centers that require high performance without compromising on energy consumption.

Finally, FPGAs stand out for their adaptability. While a GPU is designed with a fixed architecture and must be programmed to perform specific tasks, an FPGA can be reconfigured to accommodate different computational needs. This means that the hardware design can be optimized to maximize the efficiency of each task, thus managing data accuracy and available resources more efficiently. This makes them ideal for applications in areas such as AI, computer vision, and cryptography, where processing needs can vary over time.

Despite their many advantages, FPGAs also have some limitations that make their adoption more difficult than GPUs.

- Longer Development Time
- Performance for Variable Loads
- Initial Cost

The first disadvantage is the **longer development time**. Designing an optimized FPGA architecture requires specific skills in using hardware languages like VHDL or Verilog, as well as a synthesis and implementation process that can be long and complex. In contrast, GPUs are programmable with higher-level languages like CUDA or OpenCL, which makes them more accessible for more developers.

Another limitation is performance for variable workloads. FPGAs are excellent at handling specific tasks like parallel processing of structured data, but they are not always the ideal solution for more general or highly dynamic workloads. GPUs, with their flexible architecture optimized for massively parallel computing, are better suited to scenarios where the data types and operations to be performed change frequently, like in deep learning and computational graphics.

Finally, we also need to consider the initial cost. High-end FPGAs tend to be more expensive than GPUs, especially when factoring in development and optimization costs. However, this cost can be offset in the long run by energy efficiency and optimized performance, especially in applications where reducing energy consumption is a priority.

Let us look at *Table* 15.1 together, which compares the performance of GPUs with FPGAs:

Feature	**GPU**	**FPGA**
Parallelism	High, SIMD optimized	High, fully customizable parallelism
Latency	High	Very Low
Energy efficiency	Moderate	Very High
Personalization	Limited to what the hardware supports	Complete, with dedicated hardware design
Software flexibility	High	Low (hardware-specific)
Cost	Relatively low	High

Table 15.1: *FPGA vs. GPU Performance Comparison*

So, when should you prefer GPUs and when FPGAs?

GPUs are particularly preferable for large datasets or general-purpose computations, in applications where throughput is more important than latency, as well as for rapid development or prototyping, due to mature libraries such as CUDA/cuBLAS.

FPGAs are more preferable for latency-sensitive applications like high-frequency trading or signal processing in embedded or edge computing contexts where power consumption is critical and when high hardware customization is required.

In conclusion, FPGAs and GPUs offer distinct advantages and are suitable for different use cases. FPGAs excel in applications with low latency, high energy efficiency, and hardware customization requirements, while GPUs are more suitable for general-purpose computations, variable workloads, and rapid development of parallel applications. The choice between FPGAs and GPUs depends on the specific needs of the application, cost constraints, and the level of expertise available in the development team.

Advanced Applications in Artificial Intelligence, Cryptography, and Physical Simulations

FPGAs find advanced applications in many industries due to their flexibility and ability to perform customized processing in real time. In AI, FPGAs are mainly used to optimize neural network inference. This process, which consists of applying a pre-trained model to new data, greatly benefits from the ability of FPGAs to process parallel operations with low latency. Compared to GPUs, FPGAs offer similar performance with significantly lower power consumption, which makes them particularly suitable for edge devices such as IoT systems or smart cameras. Thanks to their configurability, FPGAs can be optimized to support specific neural network architectures such as convolutional (CNN) or recurrent (RNN), while implementing fundamental operations like convolution, pooling and activation directly in hardware. This hardware customization also allows the use of reduced precision levels such as INT8 or INT4 to increase performance without compromising model accuracy. Common applications include facial recognition, autonomous driving systems, and wearable healthcare devices, where real-time data processing is essential.

In cryptography, FPGAs are used to implement real-time encryption and decryption algorithms. This is due to their ability to execute complex mathematical operations in parallel. Compared to other hardware solutions, FPGAs combine processing speed with flexibility, which allows them to support a wide range of cryptographic algorithms such as AES, RSA, SHA, and Elliptic Curve Cryptography (ECC). Unlike ASICs, which are designed to implement a specific algorithm, FPGAs can be reprogrammed to adapt to new standards or emerging algorithms. This flexibility makes them indispensable in security applications like protecting government or military communications, where it is necessary to implement advanced and continuously upgradeable cryptographic algorithms. FPGAs are also widely used in the blockchain sector, where they accelerate operations like mining and transaction validation, while improving energy efficiency compared to CPU- or GPU-based solutions. In digital payment systems and bank backend terminals, FPGAs ensure secure and fast transactions, which ends us strengthening the cybersecurity infrastructure.

Physics simulations are another area where FPGAs excel, thanks to their ability to perform complex calculations with high precision and speed. Applications such as computational fluid dynamics (CFD) require simultaneous processing of numerous differential equations to simulate the behavior of gases, liquids, or aerodynamic flows. FPGAs, due to their parallel architecture, can perform these calculations significantly faster than CPUs or GPUs. This makes them ideal for aeronautical, automotive and naval design. FPGAs are also widely used in particle simulation, where they accelerate the calculation of complex interactions between particles in physical or chemical systems, such as in high-energy physics applications or in materials research. In the meteorology sector, FPGAs are used to process huge amounts of environmental data in real time, which improves the accuracy and timeliness of climate forecasts.

FPGAs, due to their combination of computing power, energy efficiency, and flexibility, are proving to be indispensable tools in these advanced technological areas. Their ability to rapidly adapt to ever-changing scenarios and requirements makes them a key choice for driving technological innovation in areas such as AI, security, and scientific simulations.

Conclusion

In this chapter, we explored the key concepts behind FPGA and analyzed their unique architecture and differences from general-purpose architectures. We saw how these technologies do not just compete with CPUs and GPUs, but also integrate with them to create hybrid systems that are capable of maximizing performance. Thanks to modern tools such as **PyOpenCL**, **MyHDL**, FPGA programming has become more accessible, which allows Python developers to prototype and implement applications without necessarily having any deep hardware experience. In the next and final chapter, we will explore the fascinating topic of quantum computing, and illustrate the basics of quantum computers as well as how they work.

CHAPTER 16

Introduction to Quantum Computing and Quantum Architectures

Introduction

In this last chapter, we will explore the world of quantum computing by illustrating its basics and how it works. As for Python, tools like **Qiskit allow its implementation. Qiskit** is a library made available by IBM that allows simulations to be carried out on classical computers. We will cover some fundamental topics of quantum programming such as gates and the Bloch sphere. We will then implement algorithms such as Deutsch-Jozsa and Grover, which highlight the superiority of quantum computing compared to classical computing in relevant fields. Finally, we will explore application fields such as **Quantum Machine Learning** (QML) and **Quantum Neural Networks** (QNN).

Structure

This chapter will address the following topics:

- Quantum Computing
- Quantum Gates
- Qiskit
- Visual Diagrams and Bloch Sphere
- Quantum Superposition
- Quantum Parallelism
- Deutsch-Jozsa and Grover Algorithm
- Quantum Machine Learning
- Quantum Neural Networks

Quantum Computing

Quantum computing is a computational paradigm that uses the principles of quantum mechanics to process information in fundamentally different ways than classical computers. While a classical computer uses bits (which can take the value 0 or 1) to represent and manipulate data, a quantum computer uses **qubits** (quantum bits). Qubits offer potential advantages in terms of speed and capacity to solve some specific problems.

Qubits exploit quantum properties such as:

- Superposition

- Entanglement
- Interference
- Measurement

A classical bit can exist in a well-defined state: 0 and 1. A qubit, on the other hand, can be in a superposition state, which is a linear combination of the states |0⟩ and |1⟩. In mathematical notation, a quantum state of a qubit is represented as:

$$|\psi = \alpha|0 + \beta|1$$

Where α and β are complex numbers called **probability amplitudes.** The probability of measuring the state |0 is $|\alpha|^2$ and that of measuring the state |1 is $|\beta|^2$. The sum of the probabilities is always 1, as is shown here:

$$|\alpha|^2 + |\beta|^2 = 1$$

A qubit can exist in a superposition of 0 and 1. This means that it carries probability amplitudes for both states until measurement, which allows a quantum computer to explore many possibilities simultaneously.

Entanglement is when two or more qubits can be entangled in such a way that the state of one depends on the state of the other, even if they are separated by large distances. This property allows for a high level of parallelism.

The probability amplitudes α and β can interfere constructively or destructively, while displaying the **interference** property and optimizing calculations towards the desired solutions.

Another important property is with **measurement**. When a qubit is measured, it "*collapses*" into a classical state (0 or 1). The probability of the outcome depends on its probability amplitude.

The Advantage of Quantum Computing

Quantum computers are not always more powerful than classical computers, but they offer significant advantages in some areas. One of the best-known examples is the factorization of large numbers, which is made possible by Shor's algorithm that has important implications for cryptography. Another example is searching unstructured databases, where Grover's algorithm reduces search time from O(N) to O(√N) and offers a significant speedup compared to classical methods. Quantum computers are also particularly effective at simulating complex physical systems such as molecules and materials, which is a task that classical computers cannot handle efficiently.

Although they are still in an early stage of development, accessible platforms for experimenting with quantum computing already exist. Among these, IBM Quantum Experience offers the possibility of running quantum algorithms on real quantum computers or simulators. Google Quantum AI has demonstrated so-called "*quantum supremacy*" with its Sycamore processor, which is an achievement that marks a great leap in research. Others like D-Wave specialize in quantum annealing, which is a technique useful for solving optimization problems. Companies like Rigetti, IonQ, and others are developing both the hardware and software needed to make quantum computing increasingly accessible.

Although we are still in the early stages of development, the progress in this field promises to revolutionize several sectors like cryptography to artificial intelligence (AI) through the simulation of innovative materials.

Quantum Gates

The basis of the functioning of a quantum computer are quantum circuits, which are composed of fundamental elements such as qubits, that represent the unit of quantum information. The behavior of these qubits is manipulated through quantum gates, which perform specific operations on their state.

These gates are represented by unit matrices that act on the state vectors, while modifying their evolution. Among the most common gates are:

- **Pauli-X Gate**
- **CNOT Gate**
- **Hadamard (H) Gate**

The **Hadamard (H) gate** allows the user to create a superposition of states, while the **CNOT gate** introduces entanglement between two qubits, which is essential for quantum computing. The **Pauli-X gate**, on the other hand, inverts the state of a qubit, and is similar to the NOT operation in classical computers.

The measurement process is closely linked to the use of quantum gates, as it converts the quantum state into an observable classical value. Measurement is a fundamental step because it allows for an interpretable result. However, it can collapse the qubit into a well-defined state, which destroys the superposition and entanglement already present.

Python Development Tools for Quantum Computing: Qiskit

The interest in quantum computing is constantly growing. Thanks to software tools such as Qiskit, it is possible to write and run quantum algorithms using the Python language. Qiskit is developed by IBM and is an open-source library that provides a complete framework for quantum programming. This makes the field more accessible to researchers, developers and enthusiasts.

Qiskit is designed to work on both quantum simulators and real quantum hardware and allows users to run experiments on IBM quantum computers through the IBM Quantum Experience. The library is based on a modular architecture and is composed of several core packages like:

- **Qiskit Terra**: Enables the construction and optimization of quantum circuits, while providing tools for simulation and execution on quantum hardware
- **Qiskit Aer**: Offers high-performance quantum simulators to test algorithms without the need for a real quantum computer
- **Qiskit Ignis:** (now deprecated) Included tools for error mitigation and characterization of quantum devices
- **Qiskit Aqua:** (now fully integrated into Qiskit and split into domain-specific packages) Was used to develop applications in fields such as optimization, finance, and quantum chemistry

To start using Qiskit and the entire suit of tools, you need to install it through this pip:

```
pip install qiskit[all] --upgrade
```

To use high-performance quantum simulators, it is recommended to install the Qiskit Aer package, which uses the power of the GPU (if available) to improve simulation performance. You can do it through:

```
pip install -U qiskit-aer
```

Visual Diagrams

Visual diagrams of quantum circuits are a fundamental tool to understand the concepts of quantum computing. Qiskit allows you to generate graphical representations of circuits using the **`QuantumCircuit.draw()`** method, which helps you to clearly visualize the operations that are applied to qubits during the computation.

Let us start from the initial state of a qubit. A qubit always starts in the basic state $|0\rangle$, which represents the classical value 0 in a quantum computation. A quantum circuit containing only one qubit and no operations and can be implemented with Qiskit as follows:

```
from qiskit import QuantumCircuit

circuit = QuantumCircuit(1)
circuit.draw(output='mpl')
```

By running it, you will get a graphical representation of the initial state of a qubit, as shown in *Figure 16.1*. You can see an empty circuit, which represents the qubit that is initially in the state $|0\rangle$.

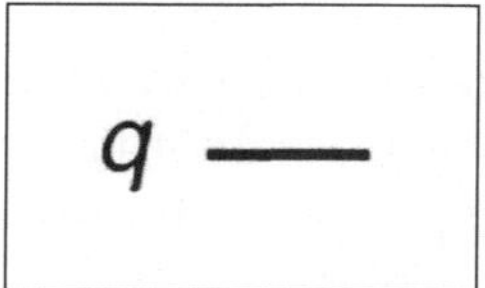

Figure 16.1: *Initial State of a Qubit*

The **Hadamard gate (H)** is one of the fundamental operations in quantum computing. It transforms a qubit from the basic state $|0\rangle$ or $|1\rangle$ into a quantum superposition state, where the qubit simultaneously assumes both states with a certain probability. Mathematically, the Hadamard gate acts as follows:

$$H|0\rangle = \frac{|0\rangle + |1\rangle}{\sqrt{2}}, \quad H|1\rangle = \frac{|0\rangle - |1\rangle}{\sqrt{2}}$$

If we apply the Hadamard gate to a qubit which is initially in the state $|0\rangle$, we will obtain a balanced superposition between $|0\rangle$ and $|1\rangle$ with equal probability of measuring both states.

Here is the code to create and display the circuit with Hadamard gate in Qiskit:

```
from qiskit import QuantumCircuit

circuit = QuantumCircuit(1)
circuit.h(0)
circuit.draw(output="mpl")
```

Running the code will yield a graphical representation of the door, as shown in *Figure 16.2*.

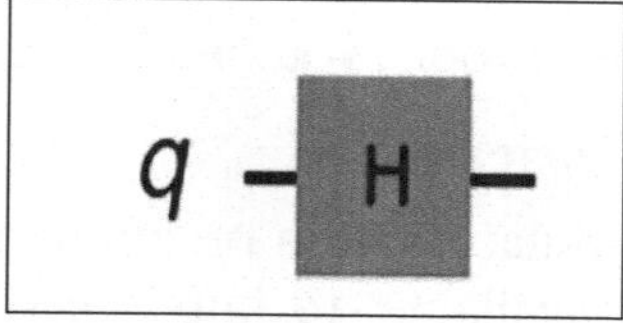

Figure 16.2: *Hadamard Gate*

The output will show the symbol "H" above the qubit, which indicates that the Hadamard transformation has been applied.

Thanks to this operation, the qubit is no longer in a defined state, but in quantum superposition, which is a fundamental concept that allows quantum computers to perform multiple calculations simultaneously.

Now, let us move on to **Entanglement with the CNOT Gate**. Quantum entanglement is one of the most fascinating properties of quantum mechanics and is essential for quantum computing. When two qubits are entangled, measuring one of them affects the other instantaneously, regardless of the distance that separates them.

To create entanglement between two qubits, a combination of a Hadamard (H) gate and a CNOT (Controlled-NOT) gate is used. The Hadamard gate is applied to the first qubit to put it in quantum superposition. After this operation, qubit 0 will be in the following state:

$$H|0\rangle = \frac{|0\rangle + |1\rangle}{\sqrt{2}}$$

The CNOT (Controlled-NOT) gate is then applied between the two qubits; qubit 0 acts as the control, while qubit 1 is the target. If the control qubit is in the $|0\rangle$ state, the target qubit remains unchanged; if it is in the $|1\rangle$ state, the target qubit is inverted ($|0\rangle \rightarrow |1\rangle$ and $|1\rangle \rightarrow |0\rangle$). After the CNOT gate is applied, the state of the two qubits will be as follows:

$$\frac{|00\rangle + |11\rangle}{\sqrt{2}}$$

This is an entangled state, in which the two qubits are correlated; measuring one will instantly influence the result of the other.

Here is the code to create this circuit with Qiskit and display it graphically:

```
from qiskit import QuantumCircuit

circuit = QuantumCircuit(2)
circuit.h(0)
circuit.cx(0, 1)
circuit.draw(output='mpl')
```

Running the code will yield a graphical representation of the entanglement with the CNOT gate, as shown in *Figure 16.3*.

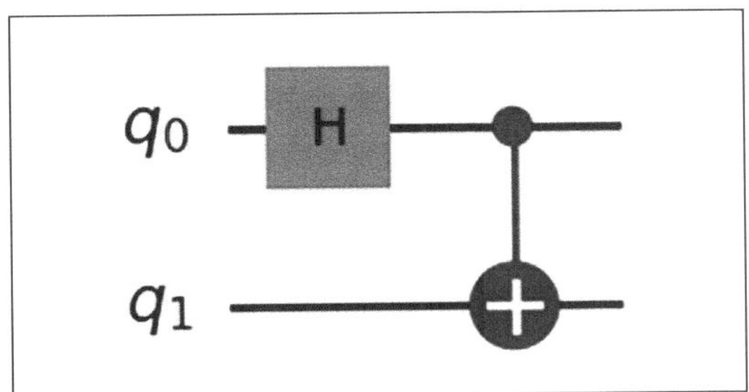

***Figure 16.3**: Entanglement Diagram with CNOT Gate*

The diagram will show:

- A Hadamard gate (H) on qubit 0, to create the superposition
- A CNOT gate (• → ⊕) that connects qubit 0 (control) with qubit 1 (target)

After this operation, the two qubits are entangled; measuring the first qubit instantly gives the same value for the second, regardless of the distance between them. This phenomenon is the basis of many applications of quantum computing, such as secure quantum communication and advanced quantum algorithms.

After creating entanglement between two qubits using the Hadamard gate and the CNOT gate, the next step is measurement. Measurement is a fundamental operation in quantum computing, as it converts a superposed or entangled quantum state into a classical result.

In this example, we build a quantum circuit that:

- Applies the Hadamard gate to qubit 0, putting it in superposition
- Applies the CNOT gate between qubit 0 (control) and qubit 1 (target) to create entanglement
- Measures both qubits, while recording the result in the associated classical bits

```
from qiskit import QuantumCircuit

circuit = QuantumCircuit(2, 2)
circuit.h(0)
circuit.cx(0, 1)
circuit.measure([0, 1], [0, 1])
circuit.draw(output='mpl')
```

Running the code will yield a visual diagram of the measurement, as shown in *Figure 16.4*.

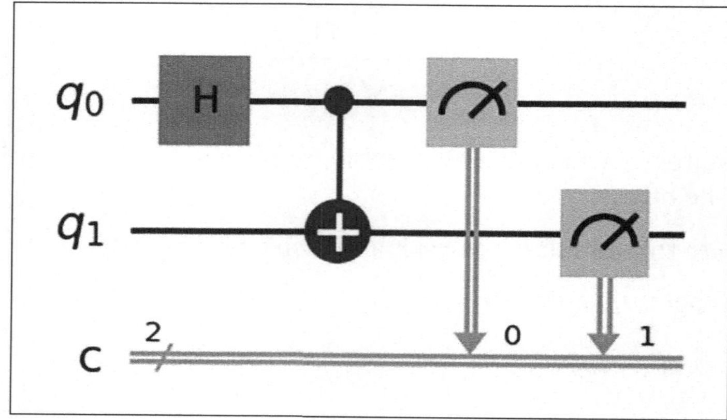

***Figure 16.4**: Visual Measurement Diagram*

The resulting diagram will show:

- A Hadamard gate (H) on qubit 0 to create superposition
- A CNOT gate that connects qubit 0 (control) with qubit 1 (target) to generate entanglement
- Measurement operations on both qubits, represented by the symbol gauge to record the results in the associated classical bits

To analyze the circuit results, we can run the simulation using the Qiskit **AerSimulator**, which allows us to collect the results of many runs (shots) and visualize the distribution of measurements with a histogram. You can use the following code:

```
from qiskit_aer import AerSimulator
from qiskit import transpile
import matplotlib.pyplot as plt

simulator = AerSimulator()
compiled_circuit = transpile(circuit, simulator)
result = simulator.run(compiled_circuit, shots=1000).result()
counts = result.get_counts()

plt.bar(counts.keys(), counts.values())
plt.xlabel('Measured States')
```

```
    plt.ylabel('Occurrences')
    plt.title('Measuring results')
    plt.show()
```

Running the code will yield a histogram display with the measurement results (see *Figure* 16.5).

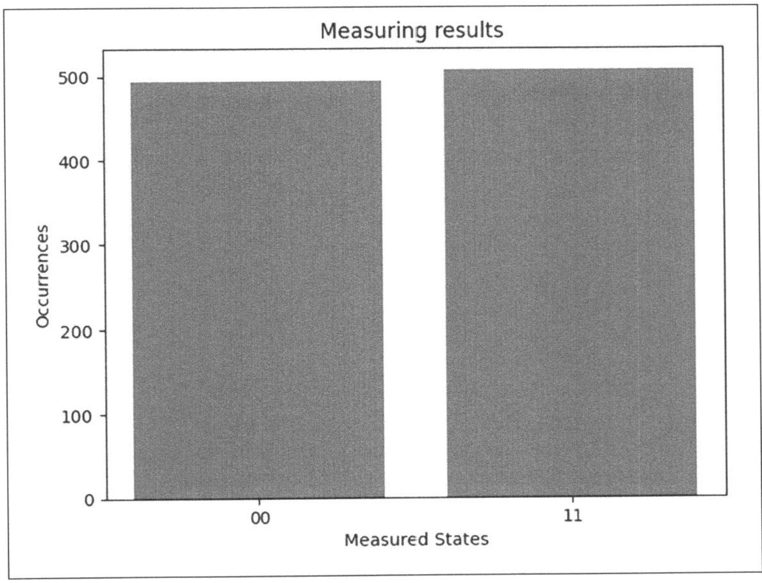

***Figure* 16.5**: *Histogram of Measurements*

The resulting histogram shows the frequencies of the measured states. We will see two main states: "00" and "11", each with a probability of about 50%.

This confirms that the two qubits are entangled; once the first qubit is measured, the second is always in the same state, while maintaining the correlation created by the entanglement. If the first qubit is measured as "0", the second will also be "0"; if the first is "1", the second will also be "1".

Visualizing a Qubit: Bloch's Sphere

A qubit can be represented geometrically as a point on the surface of a sphere, known as the Bloch Sphere. This model provides an intuitive visual representation of the quantum state and the operations that transform it.

In the Bloch Sphere:

- State $|0\rangle$ is found at the north pole.
- State $|1\rangle$ is located at the south pole.
- Superposition states are found elsewhere on the surface of the sphere.

The general mathematical representation of a quantum state on the Bloch Sphere is:

$$|\psi\rangle = \cos\frac{\theta}{2}|0\rangle + e^{i\phi}\sin\frac{\theta}{2}|1\rangle$$

Where:

- θ is the angle with respect to the Z-axis, which determines the probability of measuring the state $|0\rangle$ and $|1\rangle$.
- ϕ is the angle with respect to the X-axis in the XY-plane, which represents the relative phase of the quantum state.

Using Qiskit, we can create a qubit in superposition and visualize its state on the Bloch Sphere before measurement. This will look like:

```
# qubit in the state |0⟩
circuit = QuantumCircuit(1)
circuit.h(0)
# Simulation of measurements
circuit_with_measure = circuit.copy()
circuit_with_measure.measure_all()
simulator = AerSimulator()
compiled_circuit = transpile(circuit_with_measure, simulator)
result = simulator.run(compiled_circuit, shots=1000).result()
counts = result.get_counts()
print("Results of the measurements:", counts)

state = Statevector.from_instruction(circuit)
plot_bloch_multivector(state)
```

After applying the Hadamard gate to the qubit initially in the $|0\rangle$ state, it is transformed into a quantum superposition of the $|0\rangle$ and $|1\rangle$ states, which is represented as:

$$\frac{|0\rangle+|1\rangle}{\sqrt{2}}$$

Running the code will yield a measurement result like:

```
Results of the measurements: {'0': 489, '1': 511}
```

Since the qubit is in a balanced superposition, the probability of measuring 0 or 1 is about 50% for either state.

Before measurement, the state of the qubit is plotted on the Bloch Sphere (see Figure 16.6), which shows the qubit positioned on the positive X-axis while reflecting the uniform superposition created by the Hadamard gate.

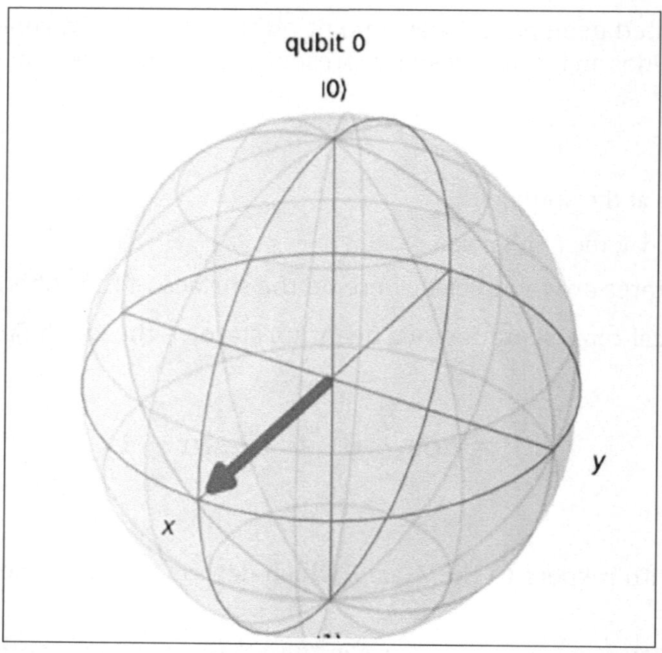

Figure 16.6: *Bloch Sphere*

The Bloch Sphere is an essential tool for understanding the quantum state of a qubit and the transformations induced by quantum gates. Measurement is a critical step, as it collapses the quantum state into one of the two possible classical values, thus eliminating quantum superposition.

Advanced Bloch Sphere Operations

The Bloch Sphere is a geometric representation of the quantum states of a qubit. It allows us to intuitively visualize the transformations that occur when quantum gates are applied. This particularly refers to the rotations around the X, Y and Z axes, which change the position of the state vector on the sphere.

We can visualize these transformations in the Bloch Sphere:

- **RX(θ)** moves the qubit back and forth along the YZ plane, which can be done with the **`circuit.rx()`** function.
- **RY(θ)** rotates the qubit around the Y-axis while changing the measurement probability, which can be done with the **`circuit.ry()`** function.
- **RZ(θ)** only changes the phase of the qubit, without changing its measurement probability, which can be done with the **`circuit.rz()`** function.

If a qubit starts in the $|0\rangle$ state, applying sequences of rotations allows it to be moved to any point on the Bloch Sphere, which helps us determine any possible quantum state.

To experiment with these transformations, we can use Qiskit to apply rotation gates and visualize the result on the Bloch Sphere. For example, let us apply a rotation of $\pi/4$ around the X-axis through the following code:

```
from qiskit import QuantumCircuit
from qiskit.quantum_info import Statevector
from qiskit.visualization import plot_bloch_multivector
import matplotlib.pyplot as plt
import numpy as np

# Create a circuit with 1 qubit
circuit = QuantumCircuit(1)

# Apply the Rx(pi/4) rotation
circuit.rx(np.pi/4, 0)

# Get the state of the qubit
state = Statevector.from_instruction(circuit)

# Visualize it on the Bloch Sphere
plot_bloch_multivector(state)
plt.show()
```

Running this code gives the Bloch sphere with the vector rotated shown in *Figure* 16.7.

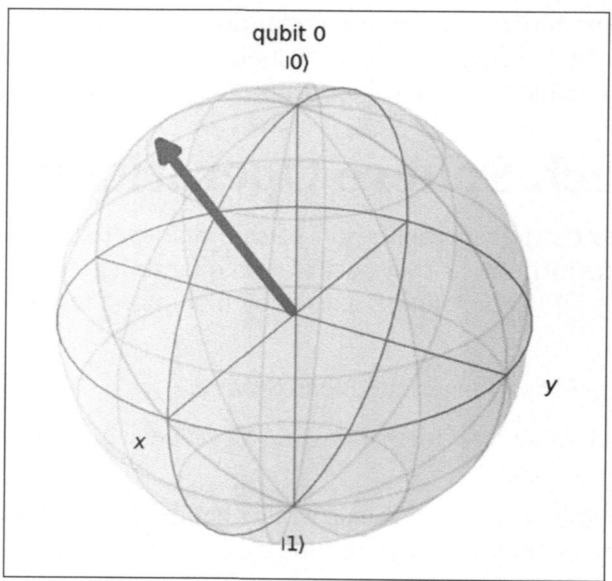

***Figure 16.7**: Rotation of π/4 around the X-Axis*

Quantum rotations are fundamental to controlling the state of a qubit. Since each state can be obtained with a combination of RX, RY and RZ rotations, these operations are the basis of all quantum algorithms, while implementing quantum error correction, preparing custom states, and optimizing the performance of a quantum computer.

The ability to exploit such rotation gates allows us to have precise control over quantum states. RX, RY and RZ allow us to move the state of a qubit to any point on the Bloch Sphere. If we reach any point on the sphere, we can realize any desired quantum state. This is crucial to program a quantum computer flexibly.

Quantum algorithms like Grover's algorithm for search or Shor's algorithm for factorization use these transformations. Quantum algorithms are based on quantum interference: rotations determine the probability amplitudes, while adjusting the constructive and destructive interference that make the algorithm effective. Additionally, rotation gates optimize the phases of a qubit, which maximizes the chances of getting the correct answer.

In current quantum computers, qubits are subject to errors due to decoherence and noise. Quantum rotations are used to mitigate errors and correct fluctuations in qubits. Custom rotations are used in Quantum Error Correction (QEC) protocols to correct errors introduced by environmental fluctuations.

Quantum teleportation allows quantum information to be transmitted between two entangled qubits without physically sending the qubit itself. To reconstruct the original information, the recipient must apply specific rotations RX, RY, and RZ based on the sender's measurement result. Without the correct rotations, the received qubit would not be identical to the one sent.

In Quantum Machine Learning (QML), quantum neural networks (QNNs) use quantum states to represent and manipulate data. To map classical data to quantum states, custom transformations that combine RX, RY, and RZ rotations are needed. This allows information to be encoded within a quantum state so that it can be processed more quickly than with classical methods.

Mathematical Verification of Qubit Operations

When we manipulate qubits with quantum gates, we can mathematically verify the effect of these operations using linear algebra. In quantum mechanics:

- Every quantum state is a column vector in a Hilbert space.

- Each quantum gate is a unitary matrix acting on these vectors.

We can use Python and NumPy to perform calculations and verify the results.

Let us first look at the Hadamard gate (H). This creates a quantum superposition by transforming the state $|0\rangle$ in the following way:

$$H|0\rangle = \frac{|0\rangle + |1\rangle}{\sqrt{2}}$$

Let us see the verification code:

```
import numpy as np

# Definition of the |0⟩ state and the Hadamard matrix
state_0 = np.array([[1], [0]])
H = (1 / np.sqrt(2)) * np.array([[1, 1], [1, -1]])

# Application of the Hadamard gate
state_superposition = np.dot(H, state_0)
print("State after Hadamard:\n", state_superposition)
```

Running the code will yield the following result:

```
State after Hadamard:
 [[0.70710678]
 [0.70710678]]
```

This result confirms that the qubit is now in a superposition with equal probability of being measured as $|0\rangle$ or $|1\rangle$.

Mathematically, the Hadamard matrix is defined as:

$$H = \frac{1}{\sqrt{2}}\begin{bmatrix} 1 & 1 \\ 1 & -1 \end{bmatrix}$$

If we start from the initial state $|0\rangle$:

$$|0\rangle = \begin{bmatrix} 1 \\ 0 \end{bmatrix}$$

The action of the Hadamard gate is given by the matrix-vector product:

$$H|0\rangle = \frac{1}{\sqrt{2}}\begin{bmatrix} 1 & 1 \\ 1 & -1 \end{bmatrix}\begin{bmatrix} 1 \\ 0 \end{bmatrix}$$

We calculate each element of the new resulting vector:

$$\begin{bmatrix} \frac{1}{\sqrt{2}}(1 \cdot 1 + 1 \cdot 0) \\ \frac{1}{\sqrt{2}}(1 \cdot 1 + (-1) \cdot 0) \end{bmatrix} = \begin{bmatrix} \frac{1}{\sqrt{2}}(1) \\ \frac{1}{\sqrt{2}}(1) \end{bmatrix} = \begin{bmatrix} 0.70710678 \\ 0.70710678 \end{bmatrix}$$

So, the result obtained with the code confirms the new state:

$$\frac{|0\rangle + |1\rangle}{\sqrt{2}}$$

Superposition: The Heart of Quantum Computing

Superposition is the fundamental property that distinguishes quantum computing from classical computing. A qubit can exist in a linear combination of states $|0\rangle$ and $|1\rangle$ and is characterized by complex probability amplitudes. This allows quantum computers to explore multiple solutions simultaneously, while dramatically improving the computation speed of certain problems.

Mathematically, a qubit in superposition can be written as:

$$|\psi = \alpha|0 + \beta|1$$

Where α and β are complex numbers called probability amplitudes, and satisfy the normalization condition:

$$|\alpha|^2 + |\beta|^2 = 1$$

This condition guarantees that when we measure the qubit, we always get a valid state with probability:

$$P(0) = |\alpha|^2 \qquad P(1) = |\beta|^2$$

For example, the state

$$\frac{|0\rangle + |1\rangle}{\sqrt{2}}$$

represents a perfectly balanced superposition, where the qubit has a 50% chance of being measured in $|0\rangle$ and a 50% chance of being measured in $|1\rangle$.

The default way to create a superposition is to use a Hadamard gate (H). This transforms $|0\rangle$ and $|1\rangle$ into an equal combination of both states, as shown here:

$$H = \frac{1}{\sqrt{2}}\begin{bmatrix}1 & 1\\ 1 & -1\end{bmatrix}$$

When applied to $|0\rangle$:

$$H|0\rangle = \frac{1}{\sqrt{2}}\begin{bmatrix}1 & 1\\ 1 & -1\end{bmatrix}\begin{bmatrix}1\\ 0\end{bmatrix} = \frac{1}{\sqrt{2}}\begin{bmatrix}1\\ 1\end{bmatrix} = \frac{|0\rangle + |1\rangle}{\sqrt{2}}$$

When applied to $|1\rangle$:

$$H|1\rangle = \frac{1}{\sqrt{2}}\begin{bmatrix}1 & 1\\ 1 & -1\end{bmatrix}\begin{bmatrix}0\\ 1\end{bmatrix} = \frac{1}{\sqrt{2}}\begin{bmatrix}1\\ -1\end{bmatrix} = \frac{|0\rangle - |1\rangle}{\sqrt{2}}$$

Let us perform a practical implementation with Qiskit here:

```
from qiskit import QuantumCircuit
from qiskit_aer import AerSimulator
from qiskit import transpile

# Create a qubit in the |0⟩ state
circuit = QuantumCircuit(1, 1)
circuit.h(0)
circuit.measure(0, 0)

# Measurement simulation
simulator = AerSimulator()
compiled_circuit = transpile(circuit, simulator)
result = simulator.run(compiled_circuit, shots=1000).result()
counts = result.get_counts()

# Print the measurement results
print("Measurement results:", counts)

# Draw the circuit
circuit.draw(output='mpl')
```

Running the code will yield the following result with an attached quantum circuit (*Figure* 16.8):

Measuring results: {'0': 514, '1': 486}

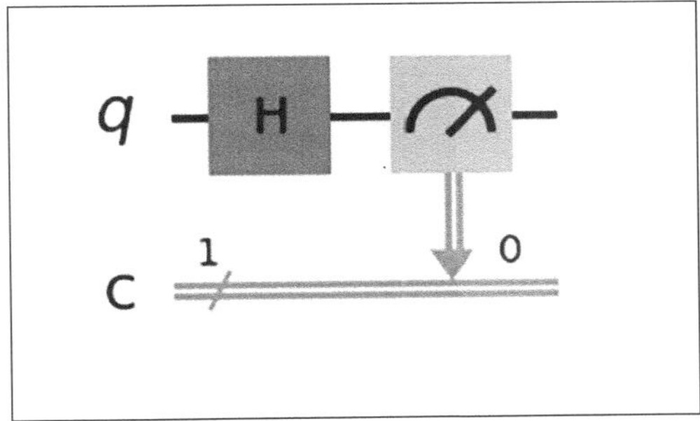

***Figure* 16.8**: *Overlap Circuit Using Hadamard Gate*

The expected result is a 50%-50% distribution with small deviations due to quantum randomness and the finite number of shots (1000).

Applying the Hadamard gate to a qubit and measuring it might seem trivial, but it is one of the key concepts of quantum computing. Superposition, when combined with other quantum operations, allows us to explore many solutions at the same time and is the basis of the superior speed of quantum algorithms compared to classical ones.

We have seen that the Hadamard gate creates a balanced superposition, with a 50%-50% probability of obtaining $|0\rangle$ or $|1\rangle$. But what if we want to have a different probability distribution? We can create non-uniform superpositions by applying other operations, such as a Ry rotation such as in the following code:

```
from qiskit.circuit.library import RYGate

circuit = QuantumCircuit(1,1)
circuit.append(RYGate(theta=1.57), [0])
circuit.measure(0,0)

circuit_with_measure = circuit.copy()
```

```
simulator = AerSimulator()
result = simulator.run(circuit_with_measure, shots=1000).result()
counts = result.get_counts()
print("Measuring results:", counts)
circuit.draw(output='mpl')
```

The code applies an RY rotation with θ=1.57 radians (about π/2 or 90°) on a qubit which is initially in the |0⟩ state and then measures it. Running the code will yield the following result with the corresponding quantum circuit (*see Figure* 16.9):

Measuring results: {'0': 530, '1': 470}

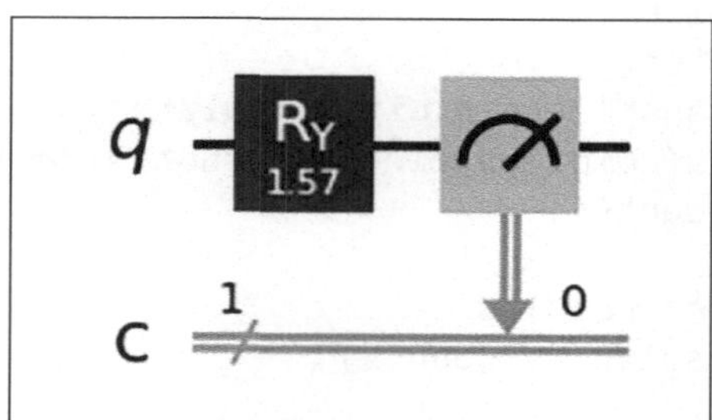

Figure 16.9: *Non-Uniform Superposition Circuit with Rotation*

When the RY(θ) gate rotates the qubit around the Y-axis of the Bloch Sphere by 1.57 radians, we get:

$$R_Y(1.57)|0\rangle \approx 0.707|0\rangle + 0.707|1\rangle$$

This is very similar to the superposition generated by Hadamard, which is:

$$H|0\rangle = \frac{|0\rangle + |1\rangle}{\sqrt{2}}$$

This comes with the following expected probabilities:

$$P(0) = \cos^2(1.57/2) \approx 0.50 \text{ (50\%)}$$

$$P(1) = \sin^2(1.57/2) \approx 0.50 \text{ (50\%)}$$

Therefore, it is normal for the results to be close to 50%-50% because the chosen rotation produces a state very similar to the Hadamard one. If you want a more evident non-uniform superposition, you should choose a different angle, say θ. If you want to increase the probability of getting |0⟩, you can use θ=π/4 (about 0.78 rad). Let us replace the line in the code with:

```
circuit.append(RYGate(theta=0.78), [0])
```

We will get the following result:

```
Measuring results: {'0': 849, '1': 151}
```

If you want to increase the probability of obtaining |1⟩, you can use θ=3π\4 (about 2.35 rad) as follows:

```
circuit.append(RYGate(theta=2.35), [0])
```

The following result is obtained:

```
Measuring results: {'1': 852, '0': 148}
```

We have seen how superposition allows qubits to exist in multiple states at once. This property radically differentiates quantum computers from classical ones. But why is it so important? When we put a qubit in superposition, we are effectively computing multiple states simultaneously.

With n qubits in superposition, a quantum computer can explore 2n combinations in a single step. This principle is the basis of faster quantum algorithms such as Grover's search and Shor's factorization.

Quantum Parallelism

Quantum parallelism is one of the most powerful features of quantum computers and is directly related to quantum superposition. Thanks to this property, a quantum computer can process multiple states simultaneously, while dramatically accelerating computation compared to classical computers.

In classical computers, a bit can only assume one state at a time, that is, 0 or 1.

In quantum computers, however, a qubit can exist in a superposition of both states at the same time, which is shown as follows:

$$|\psi\rangle = \alpha|0\rangle + \beta|1\rangle$$

If we have multiple qubits, the superposition extends to all possible states at once. Here is an example with two qubits:

$$H|00\rangle = \frac{|00\rangle + |01\rangle + |10\rangle + |11\rangle}{2}$$

This means that instead of processing one state at a time, the quantum computer can process all of them at once! With n qubits, we can represent 2n states at once (see Table 16.1).

Number of Qubits	Number of States Processable in Parallel
1 qubit	2 states
2 qubits	4 states
3 qubits	8 states
10 qubits	1024 states
50 qubits	2^{50} (~10^{15}) states

Table 16.1: *Number of States Processable in Parallel, Depending on the Number of Qubits*

With just 50 qubits, we can represent more states than there are atoms on Earth! This is what makes quantum computers potentially more powerful than classical ones.

We can demonstrate quantum parallelism by applying Hadamard on multiple qubits with the following code:

```
from qiskit import QuantumCircuit
from qiskit_aer import AerSimulator

# Create a circuit with 2 qubits and 2 classical bits
circuit = QuantumCircuit(2, 2)

# Apply Hadamard gate to both qubits
circuit.h(0)
circuit.h(1)

# Measure both qubits
circuit.measure([0, 1], [0, 1])
```

```
# Simulate the measurements
simulator = AerSimulator()
result = simulator.run(circuit, shots=1000).result()
counts = result.get_counts()

# Print the results
print("Measuring results:", counts)

# Draw the circuit
circuit.draw(output='mpl')
```

Running the code gives the following result along with the related quantum circuit (see *Figure 16.10*):

```
Measuring results: {'10': 240, '11': 260, '00': 248, '01': 252}
```

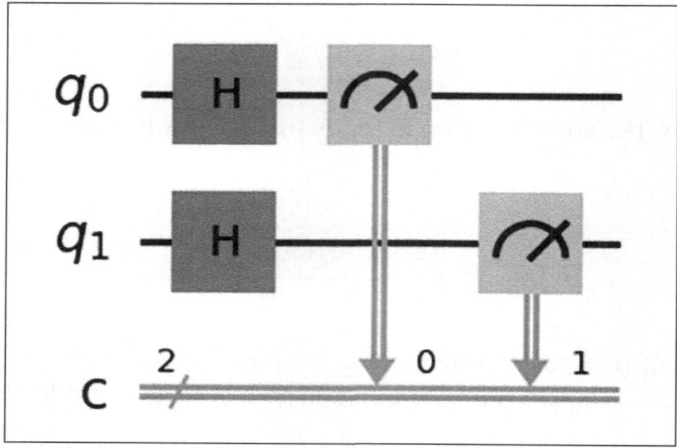

***Figure 16.10**: Applying Hadamard on Multiple Qubits*

We have generated 4 states with equal probability. This is an example of quantum parallelism as all states exist simultaneously before the measurement.

Although quantum parallelism is a revolutionary concept, it alone does not guarantee an advantage over classical computers. In fact, we will encounter a measurement problem; if we directly measure a qubit in superposition, we will obtain only one random state and lose all the information about the other states. Furthermore, quantum interference is needed. To select the right solution, algorithms must manipulate quantum phases to amplify the probability of obtaining the correct result. Not all problems benefit from Quantum Parallelism. In fact, some problems remain difficult even for a quantum computer.

Deutsch-Jozsa Algorithm (Quantum Superspeed)

Quantum Parallelism is useful, but it is not enough on its own; a mechanism is needed to select and amplify the right answer. This is done through quantum interference in algorithms. The Deutsch-Jozsa algorithm is a perfect example of applied quantum parallelism.

- In classical computers, you need to check all the states one by one.
- In quantum computers, we create a superposition with Hadamard and use interference to find the answer in one step.

The problem is solved in constant O(1) time instead of exponential $O(2^n)$ time.

The Deutsch-Jozsa algorithm is one of the first examples of how a quantum computer can solve a problem exponentially faster than a classical computer.

This is achieved by combining quantum parallelism and quantum interference, which are two fundamental concepts in quantum computing. The algorithm is used to determine whether a binary function:

$$f(x) : \{0,1\}^n \rightarrow \{0,1\}$$

is constant or balanced, where:

- A function is constant if it always returns 0 or always 1 for every input.
- A function is balanced if it returns 0 for half of the inputs and 1 for the other half.

In classical computers, we need to check 2n–1 inputs to determine the nature of the function with certainty in the worst case. This makes the problem exponentially difficult as n increases. The quantum Deutsch-Jozsa algorithm, on the other hand, solves the problem in a single step.

The Deutsch-Jozsa algorithm consists of five steps that are:

1. **State Initialization**
    a. n input qubits initialized to |0⟩.
    b. 1 auxiliary qubit initialized to |1⟩, then transformed to |–⟩ with Hadamard
2. **Application of Hadamard Transformation**
    a. This operation creates a uniform overlay of all inputs.
3. **Application of the U_f Oracle**
    a. The function is evaluated in parallel.
4. **Second Hadamard Transformation**
    a. This operation amplifies the interference between the states.
5. **Measuring the input qubits**
    a. If the function is constant, the qubits collapse into |00...0⟩.
    b. If the function is balanced, a different state is obtained.

Let us now see the code in Qiskit to run the algorithm with 2 input qubits and 1 auxiliary qubit:

```
from qiskit import QuantumCircuit, transpile, assemble
from qiskit.visualization import plot_histogram
from qiskit_aer import Aer
from qiskit import transpile

# Number of input qubits
n = 2

# Create the circuit
circuit = QuantumCircuit(n + 1, n)

# Initialize the auxiliary qubit in the |1> state and apply Hadamard
circuit.x(n)
circuit.h(n)

# Apply Hadamard to the input qubits
for qubit in range(n):
    circuit.h(qubit)
```

```
# Oracle for a balanced function (Example: XOR between the two qubits)
circuit.cx(0, n)
circuit.cx(1, n)

# Apply Hadamard again to the input qubits
for qubit in range(n):
    circuit.h(qubit)

# Measure the input qubits
circuit.measure(range(n), range(n))

# Simulate the circuit
simulator = Aer.get_backend('qasm_simulator')
compiled_circuit = transpile(circuit, simulator)
job = simulator.run(compiled_circuit, shots=1000)
result = job.result()

counts = result.get_counts()

# Print the results
print("Measurement Results:", counts)

# Display the histogram
plot_histogram(counts)
```

Running the code gives the the following result:

```
Measurement Results: {'11': 1000}
```

The result indicates that the Deutsch-Jozsa algorithm has correctly identified the function as balanced. The circuit performed the test on a function f(x). In this case, we used an oracle that implements the XOR function between the two qubits shown here:

$$f(x_1, x_2) = x_1 \oplus x_2$$

If the function is balanced, quantum interference will lead to a result other than $|00\rangle$. In our case, the output is always $|11\rangle$. The fact that you always get 1000 measurements in state 11 alone indicates that the circuit is correct and has identified the function as balanced.

Grover's Algorithm: Quantum Research Accelerates

Grover's algorithm is one of the most important developments in quantum computing, as it demonstrates a quadratic advantage over classical methods in searching for elements in an unordered database.

Imagine that we need to find a specific element in a set of NNN possibilities. In a classical computer, the only way to do this in an unordered database is to check the elements one by one until the correct one is found and requires O(N) operations on average. This means that if the database contains a million elements, it will need to examine five hundred thousand elements on average before arriving at the solution. Grover's algorithm exploits the properties of quantum mechanics like superposition and quantum interference to reduce the number of operations required to $O(\sqrt{N})$. This means that instead of examining half a million elements, a quantum computer will only need to check about a thousand, resulting in a significant speedup in the search.

The algorithm follows three fundamental steps. First, the system is trained in a uniform superposition state, which allows all possible states of the database to be represented simultaneously. To achieve this, we use the Hadamard gate, which transforms each qubit from the initial state |0⟩ into a combination of |0⟩ and |1⟩. Applying this transformation to a set of n qubits results in a uniform distribution of all 2^n possible states, which ensures that the quantum system explores all possible solutions in parallel.

The second phase of the algorithm is where the solution is amplified through two essential operations: the quantum oracle and the diffusion operator. The oracle identifies the correct solution by inverting its phase. This means that the state corresponding to the solution becomes negative with respect to the others. However, the oracle alone is not enough to increase the probability of finding the solution and this is where the diffusion operator comes into play. This transformation performs an operation similar to a "*reflection*" with respect to the average of the states, while amplifying the probability of observing the correct state and reducing the probability of all the other states. By repeating this process for an optimal number of times, the probability of the correct solution progressively increases until it becomes dominant. In the last phase of the algorithm, the system is measured and the result obtained corresponds with a very high probability to the correct solution. Since the number of iterations required is proportional to the square root of the number of elements in the database, Grover's algorithm represents a significant improvement over classical methods.

To understand how the algorithm works in practice, it can be implemented using Qiskit. Suppose we want to find an element in a database of four elements and consider the case where the solution is the state |11⟩. To begin, the quantum circuit is initialized with two input qubits and two classical bits for the final measurement. Next, Hadamard gates are applied to create the uniform superposition. The oracle is implemented using a CZ gate, which inverts the phase of the |11⟩ state only. After that, the diffusion operator is applied, which consists of a sequence of Hadamard transforms, X gates, and a CX gate to reflect the state with respect to the mean. Finally, the qubits are measured, and the circuit is run on a quantum simulator. The following code shows this:

```
from qiskit import QuantumCircuit, Aer, transpile
from qiskit.visualization import plot_histogram

# Create a circuit with 2 input qubits and 2 classical bits for measurement
n = 2
circuit = QuantumCircuit(n, n)

# Create initial superposition using Hadamard gates
circuit.h([0, 1])

# ORACLE: Flip the phase of the target state (|11⟩)
circuit.cz(0, 1)

# DIFFUSION OPERATOR
circuit.h([0, 1])
circuit.x([0, 1])
circuit.h(1)
circuit.cx(0, 1)
circuit.h(1)
circuit.x([0, 1])
circuit.h([0, 1])

# Measure the qubits
circuit.measure([0, 1], [0, 1])

# Simulate the circuit using the QASM simulator
simulator = Aer.get_backend('qasm_simulator')
compiled_circuit = transpile(circuit, simulator)
job = simulator.run(compiled_circuit, shots=1000)
result = job.result()
```

```
counts = result.get_counts()

# Print the results
print("Measurement Results:", counts)

# Display the histogram
plot_histogram(counts)
```

Running the code gives the following result:

```
Measurement Results: {'11': 1000}
```

The expected result of this execution is that the solution, that is, the state |11⟩, is measured with a probability close to 100% in the 2-qubit case. More generally, Grover's algorithm does not guarantee certainty, but yields a high probability (typically greater than 0.9 after the optimal number of iterations) of finding the correct element without performing a sequential search through all the states.

The effectiveness of Grover's algorithm is especially evident when considering a comparison with classical methods. If you have a database with a large number of elements, the time needed to find a solution with a classical computer increases linearly with the size of the database. In the case of a database of a billion elements, a classical system would require on average five hundred million operations to find the solution, while the quantum algorithm would only require about thirty thousand. This advantage becomes even more evident with larger databases.

In addition to database search, Grover's algorithm has numerous applications in various sectors. In cryptography, it can be used to attack symmetric cipher systems such as AES, while drastically reducing the time needed to find a secret key. This has prompted security experts to consider cryptographic systems that are resistant to quantum computers. Another area of application is combinatorial optimization, where Grover's algorithm is used to find optimal solutions to difficult problems, such as planning logistics routes or solving scheduling problems.

Thanks to its efficiency and versatility, Grover's algorithm is one of the most concrete demonstrations of the superiority of quantum computers over classical ones for specific problems. Although the advantage is quadratic and not exponential as in other quantum algorithms, its practical applications are vast and could revolutionize several sectors like information search, computer security, optimization, and AI.

Quantum Machine Learning (QML)

Quantum machine learning (QML) is one of the most promising areas of quantum computing. By combining the capabilities of quantum computers with the concepts of AI and machine learning (ML), it gains an exponential advantage in model training and optimization.

QML uses the principles of quantum mechanics to improve ML techniques. The main idea is that qubits and quantum operations can provide greater computational power than classical bits, which can accelerate key operations of ML algorithms:

Quantum technologies can improve ML in two main ways:

- **Quantum-Enhanced Machine Learning (QEML),** in which quantum computers are used to improve classical models
- **Quantum Native Machine Learning (QNML),** where fully quantum models are developed and data and processing are entirely based on quantum states

One of the main advantages of QML is its ability to exploit quantum **`superparallelism`**. Unlike classical computers, which process information sequentially or in parallel on multiple processors, quantum computers can simultaneously process a huge number of data combinations thanks to quantum superposition. This means that while a classical ML model analyzes data one at a time or in small batches, a quantum model can explore multiple configurations at the same time, thereby significantly accelerating learning.

Another key aspect is the increased modeling capacity. Quantum states allow information to be encoded in spaces of exponential size compared to the number of qubits used. This means that a small number of qubits can represent and manipulate copious amounts of data that would be otherwise impossible to manage with a classical computer. This offers enormous potential in solving complex problems such as image recognition or analyzing high-dimensional data.

Finally, QML shows high efficiency in high-dimensional problems, thanks to techniques such as Quantum Kernel Methods (QKM). These methods map data into highly complex quantum spaces, while identifying hidden patterns. This is particularly advantageous in classification and clustering problems, where quantum models could outperform traditional approaches, while providing more accurate and computationally efficient solutions.

There are several strategies to combine ML and quantum computing. Some of the most studied algorithms are:

- **Quantum Support Vector Machines (QSVM)**: Support Vector Machines (SVMs) are ML models used for classification. QSVMs exploit Quantum Kernel Estimation, which allows us to represent and separate data in high-dimensional spaces more efficiently than classical approaches.
- **Variational Quantum Circuits (VQC).** VQCs are quantum neural networks in which weights are learned through parameterized quantum circuits. These models can be optimized using quantum gradients.
- **Quantum Boltzmann Machines (QBM).** Boltzmann Machines are probabilistic models used for unsupervised learning. Quantum Boltzmann Machines (QBMs) use quantum computing to sample probability distributions more efficiently.
- **Quantum Approximate Optimization Algorithm (QAOA)**. QAOA is a quantum algorithm used to solve combinatorial optimization problems such as the traveling salesman problem or data clustering.

Quantum Neural Networks with `EstimatorQNN` in Qiskit

Quantum Neural Networks (QNN) are an innovative approach to machine learning that exploit the properties of quantum computing to improve information processing. In this implementation, we will use **Qiskit Machine Learning** to build a QNN based on a variational quantum circuit and a quantum estimator, which calculates the expected value of observables.

In earlier tutorials, the class **`QNNCircuit`** was sometimes used as a predefined quantum neural network circuit. However, in recent versions of Qiskit, **`QNNCircuit` is experimental and subject to deprecation**. At the same time, in version **0.8.3** of Qiskit Machine Learning, the helper class **`TwoLayerQNN`** is not yet available.

For this reason, the most robust and future-proof approach is to **build the QNN manually**, while combining:

- A **feature map** (for example, **`ZZFeatureMap`**) to encode classical input data into quantum states
- An **ansatz** (for example, **`RealAmplitudes`**) to introduce trainable parameters
- The **`EstimatorQNN`** class to tie everything together with the **`StatevectorEstimator`**

The first step is to define the number of qubits and the estimator. Here we will use the **StatevectorEstimator**, which works with the **statevector** representation and avoids noise from real hardware. Use the following code:

```
import numpy as np
from qiskit.circuit.library import ZZFeatureMap, RealAmplitudes
from qiskit_machine_learning.neural_networks import EstimatorQNN
from qiskit.primitives import StatevectorEstimator

# Number of qubits
num_qubits = 2

# Initialize the Estimator (statevector simulator)
estimator = StatevectorEstimator()

# Define feature map and ansatz
feature_map = ZZFeatureMap(feature_dimension=num_qubits, reps=2)
ansatz = RealAmplitudes(num_qubits, reps=2)

# Compose the full variational circuit
circuit = feature_map.compose(ansatz)

# Build the EstimatorQNN
qnn = EstimatorQNN(
    circuit=circuit,
    input_params=feature_map.parameters,
    weight_params=ansatz.parameters,
    estimator=estimator
)
```

Once the QNN is defined, we can feed input data and a set of weights to compute the **forward pass**, which corresponds to the prediction of the model. This is shown as:

```
# Example input and weights
input_data = np.array([0.5, 1.5])
weights = np.random.RandomState(42).rand(len(ansatz.parameters))

# Compute the output
output = qnn.forward(input_data=input_data, weights=weights)
print("Raw output ([-1,1]):", output)

# Normalize to [0,1] if desired
def normalize_output(x):
    return (x + 1) / 2.0

print("Normalized output:", normalize_output(output))
```

Running the code gives the following result:

```
No gradient function provided, creating a gradient function. If your Estimator
requires transpilation, please provide a pass manager.
Raw output ([-1,1]): [[-0.48457969]]
Normalized output: [[0.25771016]]
```

Note: *The message, "No gradient function provided..." is purely informational.* `EstimatorQNN` *detects that no gradient function was passed and automatically creates an internal fallback. When* *using* **Statevectorestimator**, *no pass manager is required, so this message can be safely ignored. If you wish to silence it, you can lower the logging level as:*

```
import logging
logging.getLogger("qiskit_machine_learning").setLevel(logging.ERROR)
logging.getLogger("qiskit.primitives").setLevel(logging.ERROR)
```

The raw output lies in **[-1, 1]**, since it represents the expectation value of a Pauli observable. For classification purposes, it is often normalized to **[0, 1]**.

Training a neural network requires gradients. **EstimatorQNN** does not provide gradients automatically, so we approximate them using **finite differences**, as shown here:

```
def finite_difference_gradient(qnn, input_data, weights, epsilon=1e-3):
    gradients = np.zeros_like(weights, dtype=float)
    for i in range(len(weights)):
        w_plus = weights.copy();  w_plus[i] += epsilon
        w_minus = weights.copy(); w_minus[i] -= epsilon
        out_plus = qnn.forward(input_data=input_data, weights=w_plus).item()
        out_minus = qnn.forward(input_data=input_data, weights=w_minus).item()
        gradients[i] = (out_plus - out_minus) / (2 * epsilon)
    return gradients

grad = finite_difference_gradient(qnn, input_data, weights)
print("Gradient:", grad)
```

Running the code gives the following result:

```
Gradient: [ 28.83707651   0.98427757  -5.32154647 -15.76403864   3.20191176
  -6.62047988]
```

The finite-difference method perturbs each weight by a small amount ϵ. It measures the change in the output and approximates the derivative.

We can extend the idea to multiple input points and assign them to classes. Here, we will normalize the output and classify based on a threshold at 0.5, as shown:

```
# Multiple input samples
input_samples = np.array([
    [0.1, 0.2],
    [0.5, 1.5],
    [0.8, 0.9],
    [0.3, 0.7],
    [0.9, 1.0]
])

# Classification function
def classify(p):
    return 1 if p > 0.5 else 0

print("\n--- Classification Results ---")
for i, x in enumerate(input_samples):
    y = qnn.forward(input_data=x, weights=weights).item()
    y_norm = normalize_output(y)
    pred = classify(y_norm)
    print(f"Input {i+1}: {x} > Output: {y_norm:.4f} > Predicted Class: {pred}")
```

The sample output might look like:

```
--- Classification Results ---
Input 1: [0.1 0.2] > Output: 0.4483 > Predicted Class: 0
Input 2: [0.5 1.5] > Output: 0.2623 > Predicted Class: 0
```

```
Input 3: [0.8 0.9] > Output: 0.5365 > Predicted Class: 1
Input 4: [0.3 0.7] > Output: 0.4968 > Predicted Class: 0
Input 5: [0.9 1. ] > Output: 0.3940 > Predicted Class: 0
```

To better understand the separation, we can visualize the classified points via:

```
import matplotlib.pyplot as plt

# Compute classifications
outputs = [normalize_output(qnn.forward(input_data=x, weights=weights).item())
for x in input_samples]
classes = [classify(o) for o in outputs]

# Scatter plot
for x, c in zip(input_samples, classes):
    color = "blue" if c == 0 else "red"
    plt.scatter(x[0], x[1], color=color, label=f"Class {c}")

plt.xlabel("Feature 1")
plt.ylabel("Feature 2")
plt.title("QNN Classification Results")
plt.show()
```

Note: *The following are the problems of compatibilization during the preparation of the layout of the plot library:*

```
pip install --upgrade --force-reinstall --no-cache-dir matplotlib
```

Running the last code fragment gives you the visualization, as shown in *Figure 16.11*.

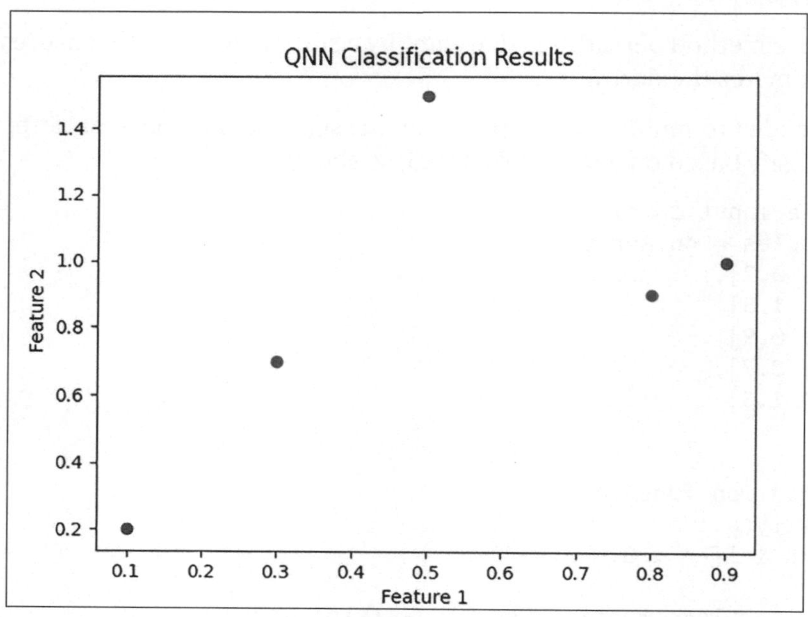

Figure 16.11: *Classification of Inputs by QNN*

The scatter plot shows how the QNN assigns inputs into two groups, despite the model being unsupervised (no explicit training labels).

The previous example, which is based on only five data points, is deliberately simple. Its purpose is purely didactic; it illustrates how a Quantum Neural Network can produce binary outputs (class 0 and class 1) from numerical inputs. However, such a small dataset is not statistically meaningful and cannot be considered a realistic classification task. In practice, many more observations are needed both to train the model and to evaluate its performance with appropriate accuracy metrics. For this reason, the five-point example should be seen as a visual introduction to the mechanics of a QNN, rather than a demonstration of its full potential.

It is also important to emphasize that there is no true labeling of the points in this example. The QNN divides the inputs into two groups according to its internal transformation and the threshold rule we defined, but there is no "*ground truth*" to compare against. In this sense, the model behaves in an unsupervised fashion as it separates the inputs according to the structure induced by the quantum circuit. The figure produced in this case is correct as an illustration of how the network partitions the data, but it does not prove that the classification matches any objective criterion.

To illustrate a more realistic case, we can extend the example by evaluating the QNN on a dense grid of feature values. Instead of only five inputs, we generate dozens of points across the input space and let the QNN assign them to classes. The result is a visualization of the decision surface, which shows that the quantum model partitions the feature space into two regions.

Here is a "*dense*" variant of the classification example with many points (40×40 grid). We use 2 qubits with **ZZFeatureMap** + **RealAmplitudes**, normalize the output to [0,1], and classify with a threshold of 0.5. This is shown as follows:

```
import numpy as np
import matplotlib.pyplot as plt
from qiskit.circuit.library import ZZFeatureMap, RealAmplitudes
from qiskit_machine_learning.neural_networks import EstimatorQNN
from qiskit.primitives import StatevectorEstimator

# ----- QNN (2 qubits) -----
num_qubits = 2
estimator = StatevectorEstimator()
feature_map = ZZFeatureMap(feature_dimension=num_qubits, reps=2)
ansatz = RealAmplitudes(num_qubits, reps=2)
circuit = feature_map.compose(ansatz)

qnn = EstimatorQNN(
    circuit=circuit,
    input_params=feature_map.parameters,
    weight_params=ansatz.parameters,
    estimator=estimator
)

rng = np.random.RandomState(7)
weights = rng.rand(len(ansatz.parameters))

def qnn_prob(x_vec):
    """Forward normalizzato in [0,1] per un vettore di 2 feature."""
    y = qnn.forward(input_data=x_vec, weights=weights).item()
    return (y + 1) / 2.0

n = 40
f1 = np.linspace(0.0, 1.0, n)
f2 = np.linspace(0.0, 1.5, n)   # range più ampio sul secondo asse
(come negli esempi)
F1, F2 = np.meshgrid(f1, f2)
grid = np.c_[F1.ravel(), F2.ravel()]

probs = np.array([qnn_prob(p.tolist()) for p in grid]).reshape(F1.shape)
classes = (probs > 0.5)
```

```
# ----- Plot: decision surface + punti -----
plt.figure(figsize=(7,5))
# sfondo: decision surface
plt.contourf(F1, F2, probs, levels=np.linspace(0,1,21), alpha=0.35)
# punti per le due classi
mask0 = ~classes
mask1 = classes
plt.scatter(F1[mask0], F2[mask0], s=12, label="Class 0")
plt.scatter(F1[mask1], F2[mask1], s=12, label="Class 1")

plt.xlabel("Feature 1")
plt.ylabel("Feature 2")
plt.title("QNN Classification on a Dense Grid (2 qubits)")
plt.legend()
plt.tight_layout()
plt.show()
```

Running the code will yield a graph that appears in the background (decision surface) and the grid points will be shown as follows (see *Figure 16.12*):

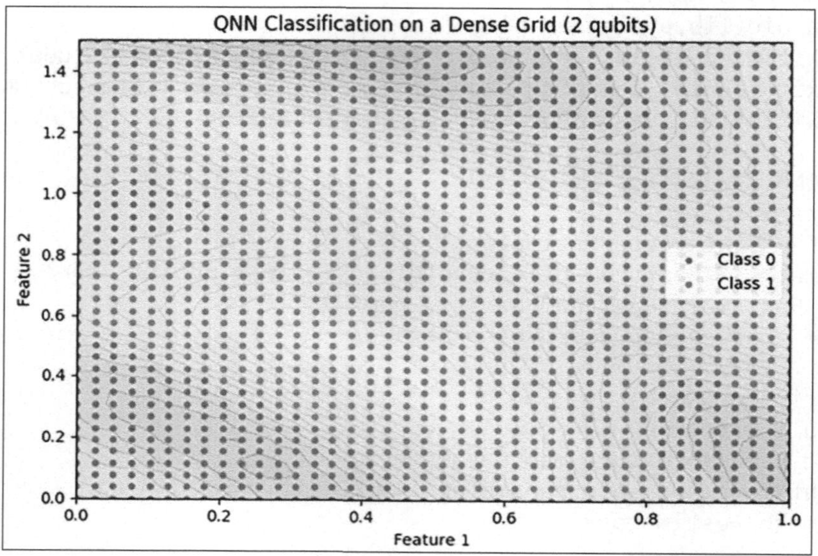

Figure 16.12: *QNN Classification on a Dense Input Grid*

Figure 16.12 shows this extended classification, where the background shading corresponds to the QNN output and the markers indicate the assigned classes. Compared to the previous example, the dense grid makes the nonlinear boundaries of the QNN much clearer and gives a better sense of how the network behaves across the entire feature domain.

This concludes our exploration of QNNs for classification. Even with relatively simple architectures, quantum neural networks can separate data into distinct regions of the feature space and suggest their potential as powerful models for more complex classification problems where hidden correlations may be difficult for classical methods to capture.

QNN for Regression

Unlike classification, where the output is discretized into classes, in regression, the QNN approximates a continuous mapping demonstrated by the following equation:

$$f : \mathbb{R}^n \to \mathbb{R}$$

Since the **EstimatorQNN** naturally outputs expectation values in the interval [−1,1][-1,1][−1,1], it becomes suitable for regression tasks once the output is scaled appropriately.

In this section, we will consider a simple yet illustrative example of **approximating the sine function**. Our goal is to train a QNN that can reproduce the curve **`y=sin(x)`** in the interval [0,π]. This setting is ideal because the sine function is smooth, bounded between [0,1] in the chosen range, and therefore compatible with the QNN output.

We start with a single qubit. For the input encoding we cannot use the **`ZZFeatureMap`**, which requires at least two qubits. Instead, we adopt a minimal feature map based on a single rotation gate RY(x) that maps the input variable into the state of the qubit. For the variational part of the model, we will choose a standard ansatz (**`RealAmplitudes`**). The two circuits are combined and are then passed to **`EstimatorQNN`**. The resulting network receives one real number as input and produces a continuous output value that we want to align with sin(x).

To train the model, we sample a small set of input points uniformly from [0,π] and compute the corresponding target values sin(x). (xi,sin(xi)) that will form our training dataset.

Since **`EstimatorQNN`** does not provide analytical gradients by default, we approximate them using **finite differences**: each weight parameter is perturbed slightly, and the effect on the output is measured. This numerical approximation is then used in a simple **gradient descent loop** that updates the weights step by step to reduce the **mean squared error (MSE)** between the QNN predictions and the true sine values.

Even with this basic approach, the weights gradually adapt so that the quantum model produces values closer and closer to the target curve. It looks like this:

```
import numpy as np
from qiskit.circuit import QuantumCircuit, Parameter
from qiskit.circuit.library import RealAmplitudes
from qiskit_machine_learning.neural_networks import EstimatorQNN
from qiskit.primitives import StatevectorEstimator
import matplotlib.pyplot as plt

# ----- Model -----
num_qubits = 1
estimator = StatevectorEstimator()

x = Parameter("x")
feature_map = QuantumCircuit(1)
feature_map.ry(x, 0)

ansatz = RealAmplitudes(num_qubits, reps=2)
circuit = feature_map.compose(ansatz)

qnn = EstimatorQNN(
    circuit=circuit,
    input_params=[x],
    weight_params=ansatz.parameters,
    estimator=estimator
)

# ----- Data (y=sin x on [0, pi]) -----
rng = np.random.RandomState(42)
x_train = np.linspace(0.0, np.pi, 12)
y_train = np.sin(x_train)                    # in [0,1] on [0, pi]
```

```
y_train_scaled = 2*y_train - 1            # scale to [-1,1] to match QNN output

# ----- Helpers -----
def preds_scaled(qnn, x_vals, w):
    return np.array([qnn.forward(input_data=[float(xv)], weights=w).item() for 
xv in x_vals])  # [-1,1]

def mse_loss(qnn, x_vals, y_scaled, w):
    p = preds_scaled(qnn, x_vals, w)
    return np.mean((p - y_scaled)**2)

def fd_grad_on_loss(qnn, x_vals, y_scaled, w, eps=1e-2):
    g = np.zeros_like(w, dtype=float)
    for i in range(len(w)):
        w_plus  = w.copy(); w_plus[i]  += eps
        w_minus = w.copy(); w_minus[i] -= eps
        l_plus  = mse_loss(qnn, x_vals, y_scaled, w_plus)
        l_minus = mse_loss(qnn, x_vals, y_scaled, w_minus)
        g[i] = (l_plus - l_minus) / (2*eps)
    return g

# ----- Training (finite-difference GD) -----
weights = rng.rand(len(ansatz.parameters))
lr = 0.2
for epoch in range(40):
    grad = fd_grad_on_loss(qnn, x_train, y_train_scaled, weights)
    weights -= lr * grad
    if (epoch+1) % 5 == 0:
        print(f"Epoch {epoch+1:02d}  Loss: {mse_loss(qnn, x_train, y_train_
scaled, weights):.4f}")
```

Running the code gives you a result similar to the following:

```
No gradient function provided, creating a gradient function. If your Estimator 
requires transpilation, please provide a pass manager.
Epoch 05  Loss: 1.4087
Epoch 10  Loss: 0.3314
Epoch 15  Loss: 0.3276
Epoch 20  Loss: 0.3044
Epoch 25  Loss: 0.3036
Epoch 30  Loss: 0.3037
Epoch 35  Loss: 0.2992
Epoch 40  Loss: 0.2960
```

After training, we can test the QNN on unseen points in [0,π]. The predictions are not exact as the circuit is small and the optimization is very rudimentary, but the overall trend of the sine function clearly emerges. The QNN outputs continuous values that oscillate in phase with the target curve, demonstrating its ability to approximate nonlinear functions. This looks like:

```
# ----- Evaluation & Plot -----
x_test = np.linspace(0.0, np.pi, 30)
y_true = np.sin(x_test)
y_pred_scaled = preds_scaled(qnn, x_test, weights)
y_pred = (y_pred_scaled + 1)/2
# Print a few sample points for inspection
print("\n--- QNN Regression Evaluation ---")
print("   x        sin(x)   pred_scaled   pred_rescaled")
```

```
for xv, yt, yp_s, yp in zip(x_test[:8], y_true[:8], y_pred_scaled[:8], y_
pred[:8]):
    print(f"{xv:5.2f}   {yt:6.3f}     {yp_s:7.3f}        {yp:7.3f}")
```

Running the model evaluation generates an output similar to the following:

```
--- QNN Regression Evaluation ---
   x       sin(x)   pred_scaled   pred_rescaled
 0.00    0.000       0.062           0.531
 0.11    0.108       0.153           0.577
 0.22    0.215       0.247           0.623
 0.32    0.319       0.372           0.686
 0.43    0.420       0.458           0.729
 0.54    0.516       0.565           0.783
 0.65    0.605       0.653           0.826
 0.76    0.688       0.735           0.868
```

Let us implement a graphical representation of the regression results:

```
import matplotlib.pyplot as plt

plt.plot(x_test, y_true, label="sin(x)")
plt.scatter(x_test, y_pred, label="QNN predictions")
plt.xlabel("x"); plt.ylabel("y")
plt.title("QNN Regression: Approximating sin(x)")
plt.legend(); plt.tight_layout(); plt.show()
```

Running this short code gives you a chart like the one shown in *Figure 16.13*.

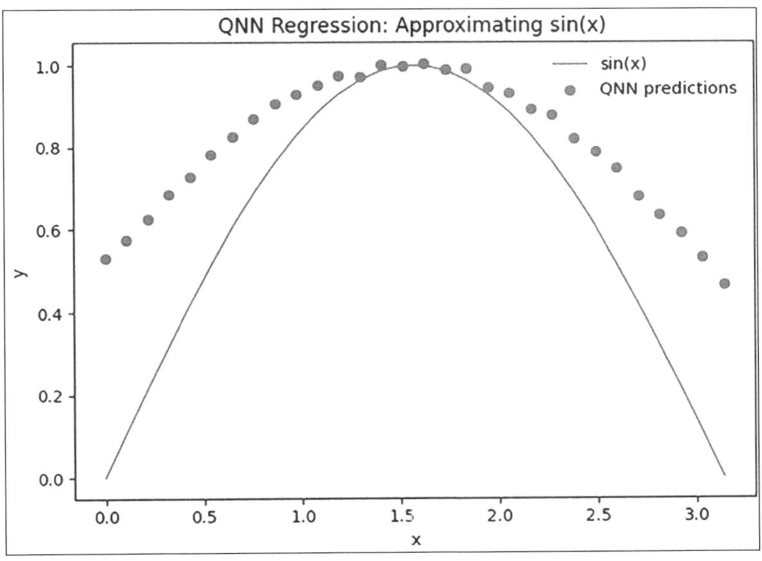

Figure 16.13: *Classification of Inputs by QNN*

Figure 16.13 shows the comparison between the true sine function and the predictions produced by the quantum neural network. The solid blue line corresponds to the analytical function **`y=sin(x)`**, while the blue dots represent the outputs generated by the QNN.

The results confirm that, although the 1-qubit model is too simple to perfectly reproduce the target function, it is still able to capture the overall sinusoidal trend. Achieving higher accuracy would require moving to multi-qubit architectures which introduce additional expressive power, but also demand more complex training strategies and longer optimization times. This example illustrates both the current limitations and the potential of quantum neural networks, while showing how they can be extended beyond classification tasks to tackle regression problems as well.

Conclusion

In the recent years, quantum computing has moved from being just a theoretical concept to becoming a reality in real experiments, advanced hardware, and emerging applications. In this chapter, we explored the foundations of quantum computers, how they work, and their possible applications, while focusing on QML. In this final chapter, we learned the principles of quantum computing, and learned how qubits differ from classical bits, while exploiting properties such as superposition, entanglement, and quantum interference to process information in new ways.

We also discussed the visualization of quantum circuits and introduced the basis of the operation of fundamental quantum algorithms.

By learning about quantum algorithms, we analyzed how quantum computers can overcome the limits of classical computation in certain problems. To conclude the chapter, we delved into QML, which offers new perspectives for ML.

I wished to conclude this book with a chapter dedicated to quantum computing as the opening of a new frontier for parallel and high-performance computing. The requirements exist, the developments are enormous, and the prospects are attractive. Let us foresee the development and diffusion of this technology with the expectation of revolutionizing the trends, and applications outlined in this book.

Index

E

F

G

H

J

K

L

M

N

O

P

Q

R

S